COCKTAILS & CAPERS

Cult Cinema, Cocktails, Crime, & Cool

Keith Allison

Teleport City Press, New York, NY

Copyright © 2018 by Keith Allison

All rights reserved. No part of this publication may be reproduced, distributed, or transmitted in any form or by any means, including photocopying, recording, or other electronic or mechanical methods, without the prior written permission of the publisher, except in the case of brief quotations embodied in critical reviews and certain other noncommercial uses permitted by copyright law.

ISBN 978-1724787873

Teleport City Press
New York, NY
www.cocktailsandcapers.com
Back cover author photo by Ellie Tam

Printed in the United States of America

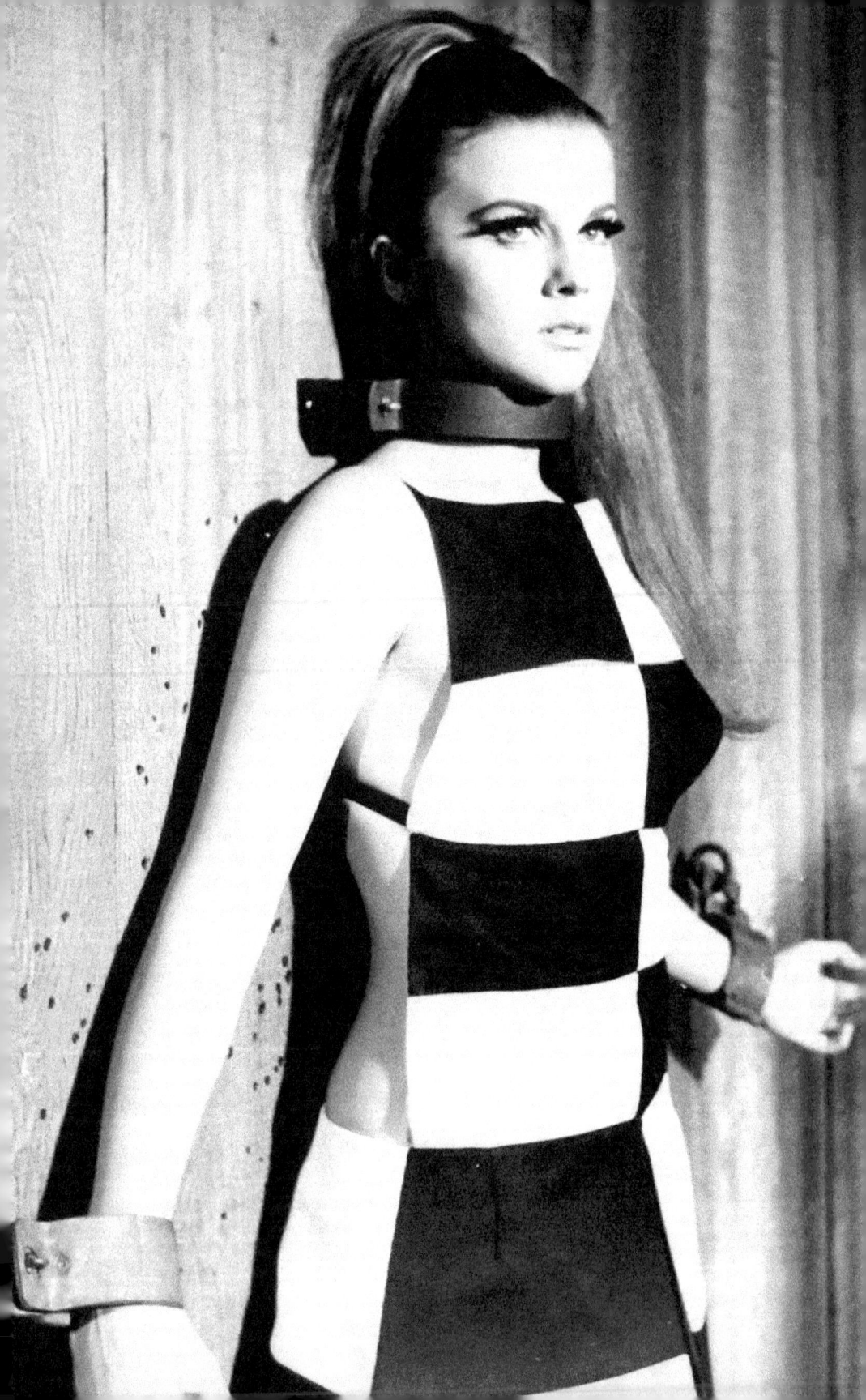

CONTENTS

- 6   INTRODUCTION
- 10   I LOVE THIS DIRTY TOWN
- 42   GENTLEMEN & PLAYERS
- 80   MYTHS OF THE MARTINI
- 96   IL FAIT PEUR!
- 148   DEEP DEEP DOWN
- 182   LEGEND OF THE MASK
- 246   HOTEL AMARO
- 302   THEIR PLACE IN THE SUN
- 358   BIBLIOGRAPHY

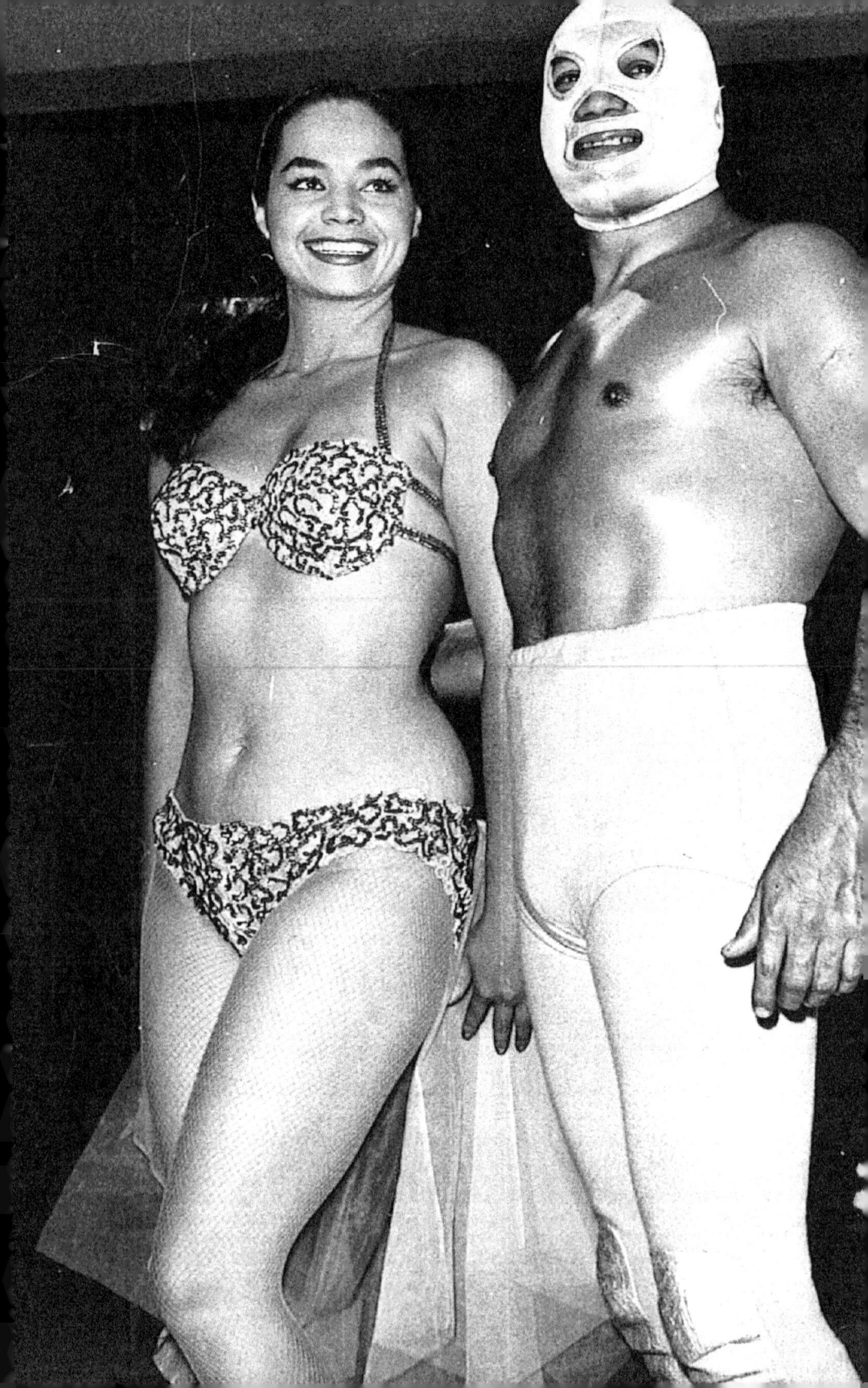

INTRODUCTION: THE OLD JUNK SHOP ON THE EDGE OF TOWN

You've just sat down next to an amiable drunk who has a lot of stories about a lot of strange things.

Like many weird people, I have an obsession with the mythical concept of the eclectic old curio shop, those place bursting with dusty shelves full of old pulp novels, dried homunculus heads, and wonderful old vinyl records with covers sporting elegant women in various states of undress, as befits moonlight serenades and pink champagne for dancing. Yes, yes, I know as well as you do, from first hand experience, that these stores, at least nowadays and in the United States, do not reflect the reality of our situation, that these stores as they exist today are far more mundane and disappointing. But that doesn't kill the dream of walking into one and instead of finding chrome clocks, Snuggies, and bootleg NASCAR gear, we might instead find ourselves having to choose between the hideous dried monkey paw that grants three wishes, the cursed ventriloquist doll, or the dusty grimoire containing unspeakable secrets.

Digging through the truly countless number of obscure cult and b-movies in the world is a lot like sifting through the piles in a wonderfully seedy and disorganized junk shop doubtlessly run by some old guy who stares at you a lot, keeps smacking his lips for no reason you'd want to contemplate, and occasionally interrupts your browsing to see if you'd be interested in a rumpled issue of *Oui* or a ring decorated with a witch's fingernails or some other such weird shit. In a town down south where I lived for many years and where I cut my teeth as a true obsessive regarding tracking down and watching strange movies, there was a shop just such as this. Ostensibly, it specialized in old sci-fi novels and magazines, but that stuff took up only a small corner of the completely chaotic mounds that were crammed from floor to ceiling, wall to wall. Most of the store was given over to dusty electronics, old records and 8-tracks, porno mags from the '70s and '80s, racist salt and pepper shakers, grungy looking mugs and souvenir glasses, military memorabilia, and other glorious, offensive treasure.

Rumor held that there was a special "back room" for VIPs, where the owner would let you peruse and purchase "the good stuff," which I assume meant dried human skins, Nazi stuff, and I don't know. Raffle tickets to win a night spent hunting a hobo or something. Credence was lent to the rumor by the fact that the shop hovered just past the city limits, and thus presumably, the reach of all human law, and shared a parking lot with the town's sleaziest strip club. But on the other hand, they also shared a parking lot with a hibachi grill restaurant.

Well, the place was weird, whatever the case, but I'm sure people say that about me, too. And who am I to judge, since me and plenty of friends were in there from time to time, digging through his wares in search of old cameras, 50 cent VHS tapes, and that issue of *Playboy* featuring Sherilyn Fenn. You never knew what kind of crazy shit you'd stumble across in that store. It was like an old museum, from back before they gave a damn about organization, and natural scientists and explorers and crackpots would just bring in any old thing, an interesting fungus or a big or a skeleton with two skulls, and they'd pile it all onto shelves using a system of categorization that was, at best, esoteric, and probably made no sense to anyone but the one mad old coot in charge of curating the sprawling menagerie.

When I set about writing this jumbled collection of film criticism, history, cocktail lore, and juicy gossip for people who still care what people from the 1930s got up to, I used that junk shop as my model. I didn't want to do an A-to-Z collection of reviews, and I didn't want to do something dry and academic. I wanted to do something strange and fun, something that gave you a good chance of stumbling across something interesting you weren't necessarily looking for. And so I present to you my junk shop, cluttered with thoughts, legends, and recollections that are, at least in my mind, bound together by a common, if at times tenuous, thread.

Initially, this was going to be a collection of essays and reviews culled from the twenty years worth of rambling I've logged on the cult film site Teleport City, which launched in 1998. But it didn't seem fair to simply harvest past work and ask you to pay for what had previously been free. Then it became a book about the history of booze and cocktails told through the lens of one of my personal obsessions: James Bond. But I found, as I was writing that version, it didn't quite satisfy the itch. Plus, other people were doing the same thing and doing it better, so I decided to rethink things. And then, as if at the junk shop, I decided to just stop thinking about things, plunge my hand into the pile, and see what I could extract. The results are what you now hold.

Starting with a chapter about silent-era serials, I followed what seemed an organic growth that encompassed gentleman thieves, Dean Martin spy films, crusading masked wrestlers, pop art cat burglars, and of course James Bond. Sometimes, the connections between seemingly disparate topics was surprising. And rather than lock the story into a rigid structure, I figured I might as well just go along for the ride. So if it seems at times convoluted, I hope it's made up for by being entertaining.

Some of what appears in *Cocktails and Capers* was previous published on Teleport City. Some of it was originally written for the website Alcohol Professor, for which I began writing about spirits and spirits history in 2013. Much of what's here, however, is new, and that which was previously published has been substantially rewritten. I want to thank Amanda Schuster, my editor at Alcohol Professor, for allowing me to rework some of my articles for this volume.

It is my work with her that led me to the idea of including cocktail recipes in some of the chapters. Usually, the cocktails included have at least some passing connection to where they appear, either because they are mentioned explicitly in the chapter, or because they conjure a certain mood or sense of time and place. The recipes come from a number of sources dated from between the 1890s and 1950s, including *The Savoy Cocktail Book*, Charles Baker's *Jigger, Beaker, and Glass*, Frank Caiafa's *Waldorf-Astoria Bar Book*, Ted Haigh's *Vintage Spirits and Forgotten Cocktails*, and various old issues of *Esquire*. Others I knew because, come on. It's a Negroni.

I also want to thank Todd Stadtman, the tireless creative force behind the website Die Danger Die Die Kill, author of Funky Bollywood, and a long-time partner in Teleport City. Without his work on that site and his contributions to this book's chapter on Blue Demon and El Santo, nothing would be quite as much fun.

Film and cocktail history both is fraught with hearsay masquerading as fact, or with things long accepted that turn out not to be true. I've done my best to be accurate, or when I can't be sure of something, note that we've wandered into the realm of "legend has it." Sometimes, however, the bullshit is just too entertaining not to tell, especially when it comes to tales of old Hollywood and the group of jokers known in the media as the Rat Pack. In the end, I'm comfortable claiming this book is, at least, moderately more accurate than *Hollywood Babylon*.

And there you have it. Maybe the "jumble it all up" approach will prove misguided. If so, I'm sure I'll hear about it. But hopefully, it'll lead you to some strange and unusual fun, which is the best kind of fun. So pull up a stool and join me at the bar. It's going to be a long night, and did I ever mention that I have a fascinating story about Ian Fleming, John Kennedy, and Fidel Castro's beard?

—Keith Allison, August 2018

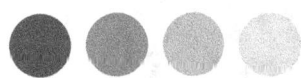

"Academia is the death of cinema. It is the very opposite of passion. Film is not the art of scholars, but of illiterates."
—Werner Herzog

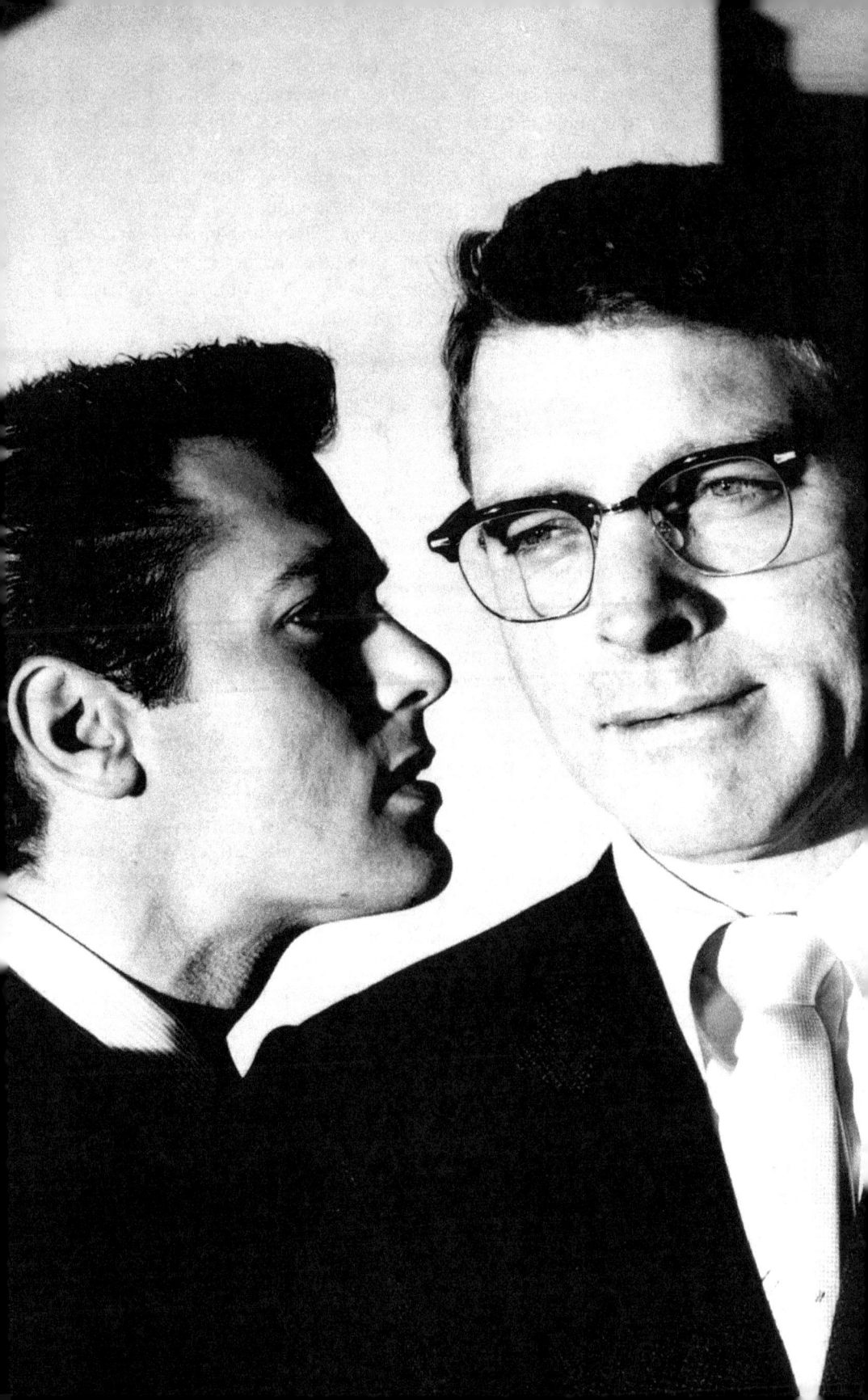

01 I LOVE THIS DIRTY TOWN

Sweet Smell of Success, Swing Street, and the voices and vices that made mid-century Manhattan

It's after dark, when the city is at its best. We drift through the desperate, glorious chaos of New York at night, to the brassy, aggressive strains of a jazz anthem composed by Elmer Bernstein. Men in suits and women in cocktail dresses stumble into and out of cabs, into and out of nightclubs. People who want to be seen, people who want to see. Movers, shakers, power players, hustlers, hyenas. The kings and queens, the wannabes, the has-beens, the never-will-be's. Our eye is the lens of James Wong Howe's camera, in moody, beautiful black and white and at a depth-of-focus that is overwhelming, like the city at night. Too many people. Too many cars. Too many blinking neon signs. There's too much too see. Too much. And never enough.

Through these dangerous waters that stink of booze and cigarettes and perfume swims J.J. Hunsecker, a merciless, emotionally-remote gossip columnist who can make or destroy a career with a single sentence—and who relishes that power of professional life and death. Around him swirls a cloud of sycophants looking to make themselves seem more impressive by association or looking to catch J.J.'s eye so that he might throw a kind word the way of their new play or new client. In the middle of the pack—and dreaming of leading the herd—is Sidney Falco, a hungry press agent with no morals, a man willing to pull any con, use anyone, hustle any way he can to claw his way out of mediocrity. Hunsecker is Sidney's ticket out of the bush leagues. Hunsecker knows that. And Hunsecker isn't the kind of man not to use it.

This is the world of *Sweet Smell of Success*, an acerbic showbiz noir from 1957 directed by Alexander Mackendrick and written by Clifford Odets and Ernest Lehman (who also wrote the novel on which the movie is based). It is one of the meanest films of the late noir era, full of cynical, misanthropic characters. It accomplishes this without gangsters, without shootouts, without murder or most of the *accoutrements* one usually associates with film noir. It is one of a handful of noir that focus on the cutthroat nature of the very business that created it: entertainment.

Burt Lancaster is the remorseless J.J. Hunsecker. Tony Curtis, in a role so slimy that his fans revolted against the besmirching of his good guy persona, stars as "anything to get ahead" press agent Sidney Falco. As J.J. says, "I'd hate to take a bite outta you. You're a cookie full of arsenic." They were both New York boys—Lancaster, from 209 East 106th Street in Manhattan; and Curtis, the son of a tailor from The Bronx—in one of the quintessential New York movies.

Much of the film's action takes place in two locations. The interiors were sets, but the exteriors and the locations were real. Sidney Falco throws himself into the sweaty, drunken crowd at the rowdy night spot Toots Shor's. J.J., impeccably dressed and observing the world like a bird of prey, holds court in the estimable 21 Club. One of these places is gone; the other still stands in a city that always moves forward, the last remaining bastion of an area that once boasted jazz clubs and night clubs. Where the action was. The street that played host to the likes of Frank Sinatra and Billie Holiday.

They called it Swing Street.

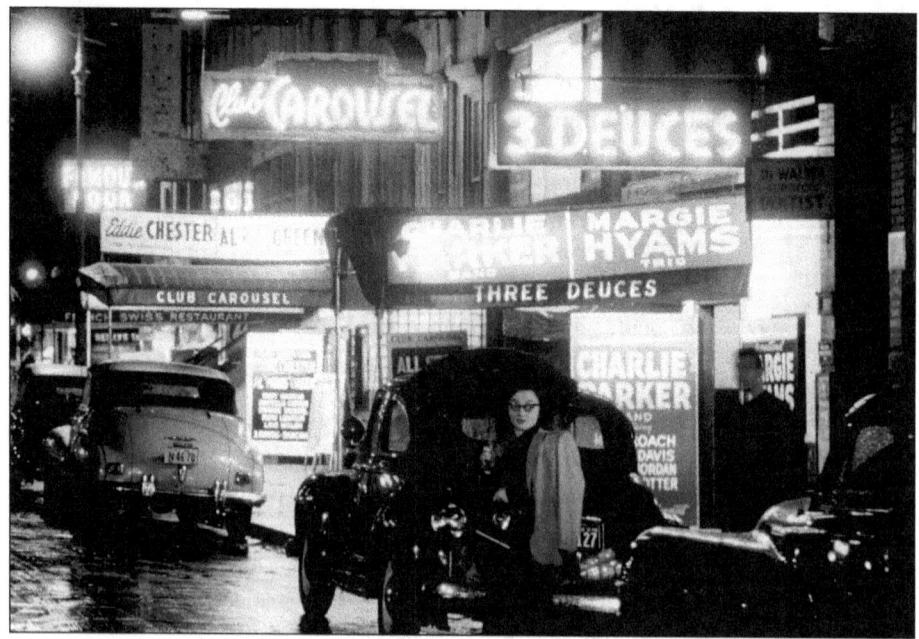

WHEN MIDTOWN USED TO SWING: 52nd in its Swing Street heyday. Photo by William P. Gottlieb.

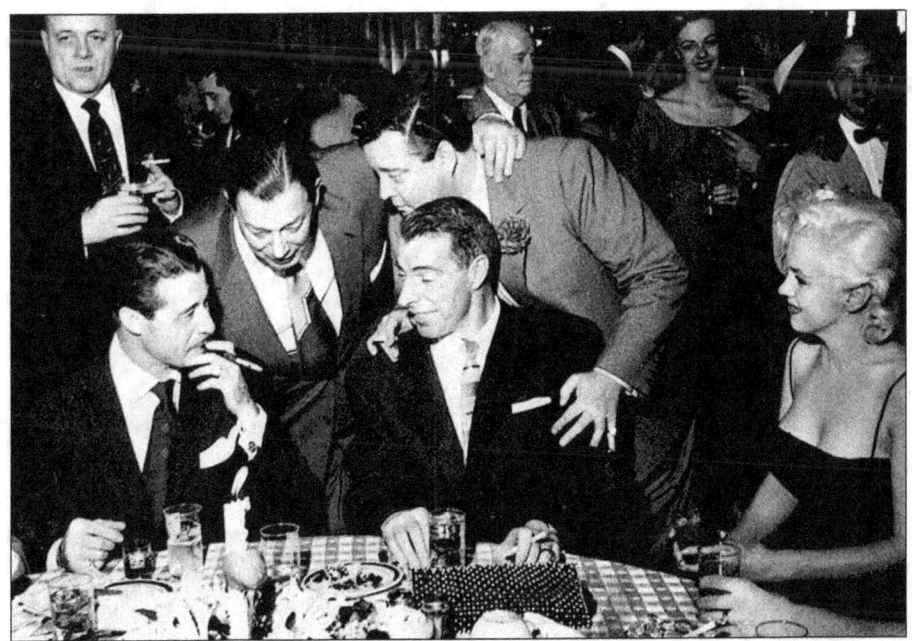

HOW SWEET IT IS: Toots and Jackie Gleason drop in on Errol Flynn, Joe DiMaggio, and Marilyn Monroe.

Nuttin' Fancy

Just over half a century ago, in a Manhattan defined by sharp suits and three-Martini lunches, there was a joint called Toots Shor's. It was the kind of place where Joe DiMaggio would go to enjoy a drink with Jackie Gleason; where Frank Sinatra would drop in to keep himself from brooding; where Marilyn Monroe could be found sitting at the famous round bar. Yet despite its place as one of the great celebrity watering holes of the Golden Age, it was no bastion of elegance. When they called it a joint, they meant it was a joint. Smoke and crowd and noise. Toots Shor, the man behind it, wasn't a polished member of the aristocracy looking to foster the rarefied airs of café society. If Toots Shor's was a cocktail, it would have been a whiskey sour. If it was food, it would have been "maybe you should eat somewhere else."

I mean, yeah, they had a kitchen. It served up standard fare for a time when "fine dining" wasn't very fine: shrimp cocktail, baked potatoes, Yankee pot roast. There's a reason mid-century America is remembered for drinking, style, design, and architecture—but not cuisine. You didn't go to Toots Shor's for the food. You went for the atmosphere and the booze. Sure, you wore your suit and tie or your cocktail dress (wives were discouraged, though mistresses and "broads" were welcome—mid-century America isn't celebrated for its cuisine, and it's sure as hell not celebrated for gender politics.). But this place was all back-slapping drunks with their arms around each other...and occasionally their fists in each other's faces. But only occasionally.

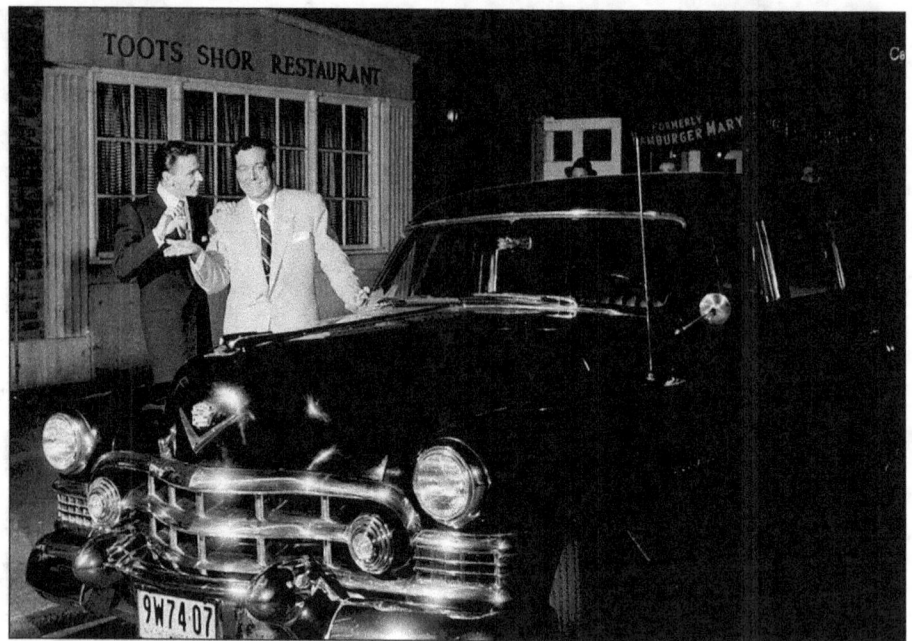
KEYS TO THE KINGDOM: Gleason and Frank Sinatra outside Toots Shor's.

    Toots was born in Philadelphia in 1903 to Orthodox Jewish parents who didn't call him "Toots." They called him Bernard. Both parents died tragically when Toots was young. When he was 15, his mother was killed in a traffic accident while she was sitting on the stoop of their apartment. His father went five years later. Suicide. Toots attended college, bounced into a job as a traveling salesman (shirts and underwear), and ended up in New York working the door at speakeasies. There, he met and befriended many of New York's celebrities, politicians, and gangsters, all of whom came together for an illegal drink or two at places like the Five O'Clock Club and Lahiff's Tavern. Gregarious, but capable of socking an unruly drunk when he needed to, Toots worked his way from the door to floor, then to manager, and finally to owner, when he opened his own place in the 1940s at 51 West 51st Street.

    The celebrities he'd befriended over the years were happy to come along, especially when it became obvious that Toots was never going to call in their tab. Or even keep one. Through the 1940s and '50s, Toots Shor's was the place. Toots himself described it as "nuttin' fancy." An after-watering-hole watering hole. Jackie Gleason was practically a resident, showing up to drink away the afternoon, heading home for a nap (rumor had it he took an apartment in the same building so he wouldn't have to walk far), then returning for the late-night scene. Sinatra name-dropped the place in "Me and My Shadow," a duet with Sammy Davis, Jr., placing it alongside his other favorite hangout, Jilly's Saloon. Judges, writers, stars, and mobsters flocked to Toots Shor's, forming an inebriated brotherhood Toots lovingly referred to as "crum-bums."

But above all others, Toots courted baseball players. Joe DiMaggio was a fixture, at least for a while. He stopped dropping by after Toots referred to Joe's wife using a vulgar term for a lady of the night. Joe's wife at the time being Marilyn Monroe. Joe and Marilyn split after less than a year of unhappy marriage. She wanted freedom. He wanted a housewife. Ugly though the split was, Joe never forgave Toots for insulting Marilyn. Not that he was any sort of dream husband for the blonde bombshell. His anger boiled over, left her bruised. After it all came unglued, DiMaggio sought companionship in Frank Sinatra—probably not the best drinking buddy at the time. Frank was a manic-depressive going through a serious depressive phase and a nasty break-up with Ava Gardner. It also probably wouldn't have soothed Joe much to know Sinatra's crew used Marilyn mercilessly.

Marilyn died in 1962. By 1962, Toots Shor's was also gone, or at least relocated. It turned out that no matter how packed your place is, if you're not making anyone pay their bill, it's hard to pay the bills. Toots had to sell the 51st Street location in 1961, but he landed on his feet. Toots Shor's reopened at a new location, 33 West 52nd Street. It was an address with a storied, perfectly sordid past as a place called Leon & Eddie's, opened by entertainers Eddie Davis and Leon Enkin. It was one of the most infamous places along what became Swing Street but was then known as Strip Street. Toots himself had even worked there in the 1930s. Leon & Eddie's catered to American servicemen looking for one last, memorable fling before shipping out to the War. Naked chorus girls, ribald stand-up comedians, and flirtatious dancers were happy to send the boys off with a smile that would last them to Berlin.

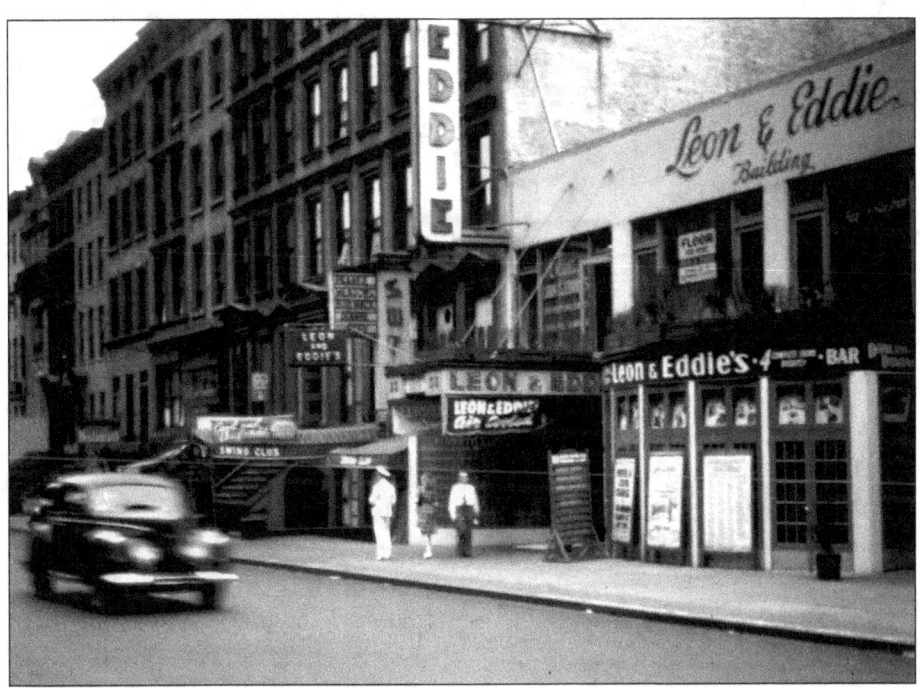

HEY, SAILOR: The infamous Leon & Eddie's, later the home of Toots Shor's mark II.

A TALE OF TWO TRILBYS

••••••••••••••••••••

George du Maurier's popular 1894 book *Trilby* spawned a stage play, a fantastic movie starring Marian Marsh as the ill-fated dancer and John Barrymore as her diabolical Svengali, and a cocktail named for the hapless heroine. As is often the case with long-lived and largely forgotten libations, there are variations. The two below are very different from one another. The first is from the *Waldorf-Astoria Bar Book*. The second, an adaptation from an old recipe in the *Savoy Cocktail Book*, was later renamed in honor of Toots Shor, who probably never had one in his life.

••••••••••••••••••••

TRILBY NO. 1
- 2 oz Old Tom Gin
- 1 oz Extra Dry Vermouth
- ¼ oz Creme Yvette
- 2 dashes Orange Bitters

Add all ingredients to a mixing glass. Add ice. Stir for 30 seconds. Strain into a chilled cocktail glass. Garnish with a lemon twist.

••••••••••••••••••••

TRILBY NO. 2/TOOTS SHOR
- 2 oz Blended Scotch Whisky
- 1 oz Sweet Vermouth
- ¼ oz Parfait d'Amour
- 1 dash Pernod Pastis
- 1 dash Orange Bitters

Add all ingredients to a mixing glass. Add ice. Stir for 30 seconds. Strain into a chilled cocktail glass. Garnish with a lemon peel.

After Prohibition, some speakeasies going legit sought to cultivate an elegant clientele of celebrities and "café society." Leon and Eddie's, however, was the place local businessmen, adventurous tourists, cheap hustlers, and soldiers went to collect a secret, "a place where they didn't have to worry about getting the high hat" as *Billboard* described it in 1946. Later, it became famous for regularly featuring two of America's most celebrated burlesque queens: Noel Toy, a legend in the Chinatown nightclubs of San Francisco; and Sherry Britton, who peeled off clothes to Tchaikovsky and was made an honorary Brigadier General by President Franklin D. Roosevelt.

Just when Toots found himself out at 51st Street, Leon and Eddie were looking to call it a day. Shor, who had been a bouncer at the place in its speakeasy days, moved in. The new Toots Shor's operated from 1961 until 1971, but the magic never returned. The late '60s and early '70s weren't the '50s or early '60s. A turned-on, tuned-in young crowd was now in charge of defining the city's sense of cool, and old cats like Toots weren't able to run with the glitter and love brigade. He tried to franchise, selling the name to a management company that went on to handle TGI Fridays, but there just wasn't much bank in a name like Toots Shor post-*Sgt. Pepper's*. The space existed for a while as the New York, New York disco, home of the world's first laser light show, until eventually the entire building was demolished. A massive glass and concrete high-rise looms there now.

Short of a whiskey and soda or Martini, about the only cocktail you'd order at Toots Shor's was shrimp. Still, while researching the latest edition of the *The Waldorf-Astoria Bar Book*, writer/bartender Frank Caiafa came across a cocktail named in honor of Toots, though perhaps not with the character of the man or his joint particularly well reflected. According to Caiafa's research, the "Toots Shor" as listed in the 1960 *Calvert Party Encyclopedia* was actually a Trilby No. 2 from the *Savoy Cocktail Book*, which already had a Trilby, even though the Trilby No. 2 probably predated the other Trilby, because it appeared in a 1900 manual by bartender Harry Johnson, where it was just called a Trilby. The history of cocktails is a nightmare. Whatever the case, the Toots Shor cocktails uses scotch, vermouth, Pernod, and Parfait d'Amour. The notion that Toots Shor would own a bottle of Parfait d'Amour, let alone drink it, is hilarious. But then again, who knows? Frank Sinatra painted himself up like a sad clown on one of his album covers. Those guys could cometimes contain untold depths.

The more suitable glass to raise in Toots' honor is the whiskey sour, though it's likely more than a few Rickeys and Gimlets got ordered at Toots Shor's iconic round bar. The gimlet in particular has a storied past and a place of honor in the halls of hardboiled cocktails thanks to Raymond Chandler's *The Long Goodbye*:

"We sat in a corner of the bar at Victor's and drank gimlets. 'They don't know how to make them here,' he said.

GIMLETS WITH MARLOWE AND BAKER

Unlike the Trilby, variations of the Gimlet are recognizably the same drink. The difference is the nature of the lime: juice or cordial. The old *Savoy Cocktail Book* insists that a Gimlet made with fresh lime juice is a Gimblet. The third recipe is from globetrotting *bon vivant* Charles Baker's *Jigger, Beaker, and Glass*. His variation transforms the drink into a bit more of a cooler, which the storied globetrotter claims was quite popular throughout the various colonial outposts of steamy South Asia.

GIMLET NO. 1
- 2 oz Dry Gin
- 1 oz Rose's Lime Juice Cordial

Add all ingredients to a mixing glass. Stir for 30 seconds. Strain into a chilled cocktail glass. Garnish with a lime wheel.

GIMLET NO. 2/GIMBLET
- 2 oz Dry Gin
- ¾ oz Simple Syrup
- ¾ oz Fresh Lime Juice

Add all ingredients to a shaker. Add ice. Shake well. Strain into a chilled cocktail glass. Garnish with lime wheel.

FAR EASTERN STYLE GIMLET
- 1 oz Dry or Old Tom Gin
- 1 tsp Gomme Syrup
- ½ tsp Lime Cordial

Add all ingredients to a champagne glass. Top off with plain, chilled water. Add ice. Garnish with a lime wheel.

'What they call a gimlet is just some lime or lemon juice with a dash of sugar and bitters. A real gimlet is half gin and half Rose's Lime Juice and nothing else. It beats martinis hollow'."

Rose's Lime Juice was invented in 1867 by Lauchlan Rose as a way to preserve limes for the British Navy. The gimlet was invented when British Naval officers started mixing their daily dose of Rose's Lime Juice with gin (non-officers mixed it with their rum and invented the first margarita). Why all the lime juice? The Merchant Shipping Act, also of 1867, required Navy vessels to provide a daily lime ration to sailors to prevent scurvy, a habit that earned British sailors the nickname "limeys." Carrying Rose's Lime Juice was much easier than hauling fresh limes around. Unfortunately, Rose's Lime Juice (and limes in general) was terribly ineffective protection from scurvy.

It was believed at the time that acidity was what kept you from getting scurvy, so any sufficiently acidic fruit would do. This belief came about because in the mid-1700s, sailors who dosed their ration of grog (rum and water) with juice from citrus fruit were substantially healthier than other soldiers. This phenomenon was eventually attributed to the acidity of the fruit. Because the British Navy had easier access to limes than they did oranges or lemons, limes became the go-to—and didn't do much of anything, especially once they had been processed into commercial lime juice. It wasn't the acidity that was staving scurvy outbreaks; it was the vitamin C, and limes have very little vitamin C. Rose's Lime had even less.

The Gimlet never really caught on in the United States, but Raymond Chandler's hardboiled private detective, Philip Marlowe, enjoyed them (at least until tragic deaths spoiled his taste for the drink). Just as James Bond's Vespers and shaken vodka Martinis cause debate, so too does Chandler's recipe for a gimlet. His half-and-half proportions were likely because they were drinking rot gut gin. A saner ratio scales back the 50/50 scenario and uses better-quality gin. Just about everyone will tell you it has to be Rose's, otherwise it is not a gimlet. As the 1954 *Esquire's Handbook for Hosts* wrote, "A true Gimlet must be made with Rose's bottled lime juice, which vanished like nylons during the war but is now seen around again." But of course, what's seen around now and what was seen around in then? It's probable that Rose's Lime today is not the same concoction it was.

So if you're looking to stave off scurvy, keep dosing your grog with lemon and orange. But if you are just looking to sit in a corner booth in an old bar and enjoy a drink while you puzzle out the strands of a particularly convoluted case, the gimlet is there for you. Drink it under the same circumstances Marlowe's doomed friend Terry Lennox prefers:

"I like bars just after they open for the evening. When the air inside is still cool and clean and everything is shiny and the barkeep is giving himself that last look in the mirror to see if his tie is straight and his hair is smooth. I like the neat bottles on the bar back and the lovely shining glasses and the anticipation. I like to watch the man mix the first one of the evening and put it down on a crisp mat and put the little folded napkin beside it. I like to taste it slowly. The first quiet drink of the evening in a quiet bar—that's wonderful."

The Playlist: Toots Shor's

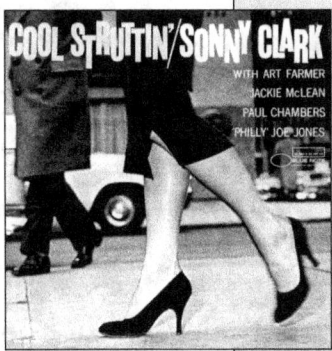

COOL STRUTTIN'
Sonny Clark, 1958

Blue Note was never the home of what became known as "cool jazz," but that didn't stop them from releasing one of the coolest jazz albums ever recorded. Like many groundbreaking albums of the time, piano player Sonny Clark's *Cool Struttin'* was met with critical indifference and lukewarm sales, leading to Blue Note letting it go out of print after a short run, which in turn resulted in it becoming one of the most sought-after jazz collectibles. But we're here for the music, and the music is perfect for the trip to, the evening at, and the night after a cool jazz club. Put most simply: it sounds like the cover.

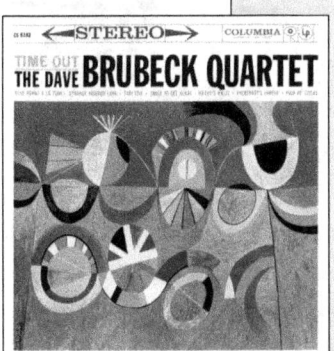

TIME OUT
The Dave Brubeck Quartet, 1959

"The soundtrack of New York City's bachelor pads in the 60's" wrote website *ManMade*, and one would be hard-pressed to find a more succinct summary of this mid-century jazz classic, one of the most acclaimed and influential jazz recordings of all time. The album's style was inspired by a trip Brubeck took to Turkey. Critics lambasted it when it was first released. They were wrong. "Blue Rondo a la Turk" pulsates with barely-contained urban energy, and nothing captures the mood of sophisticated high living quite like the album's titular track.

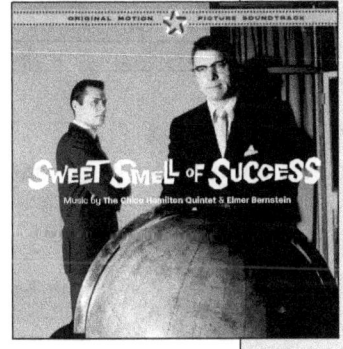

SWEET SMELL OF SUCCESS
Elmer Bernstein & Chico Hamilton, 1959

Well, obviously. The soundtrack to *Sweet Smell of Success* is a split deal between two composers. Part was composed by Elmer Bernstein and captures the frenetic, brassy, do-eat-dog world inhabited by Hunsecker and Falco. The other part was composed and performed by the Chico Hamilton Quintent, who capture some quieter, more contemplative moments. Together they make for a fantastic score. On your way to a business meeting? On your way to destroy some small fish? Just need something to keep you company while you wander the street during the dark hours? Whatever the case may be, Hamilton and Bernstein have you covered.

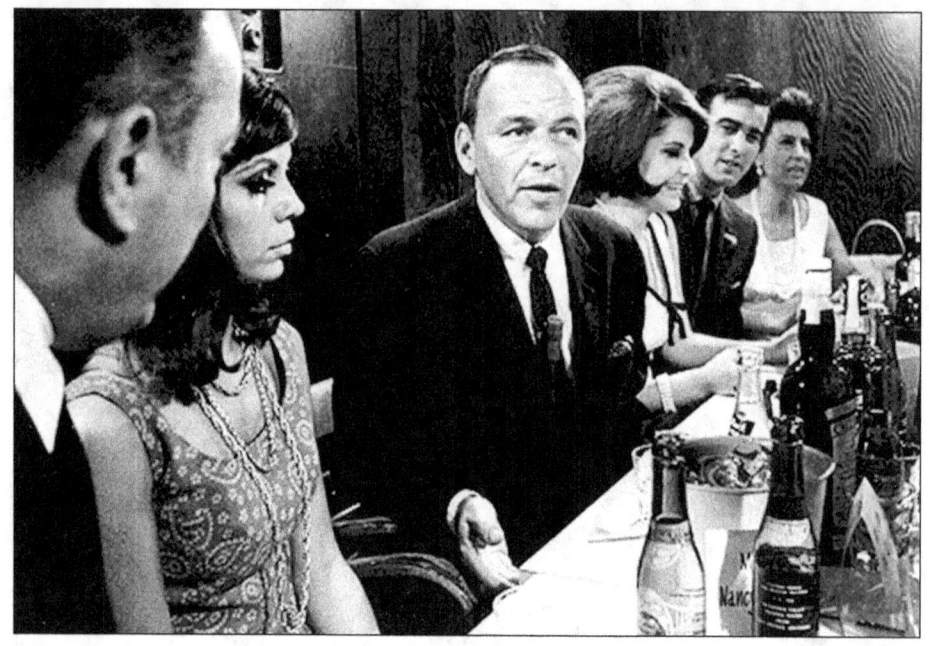

We'll Wind up at Jilly's Right After Toots Shor's

West 52nd Street between Broadway and 8th Ave. is, today, one of those anonymous New York blocks that seems, at first glance, to offer very little other than the entrances to the Neil Simon and August Wilson theaters. But tucked beneath a nondescript red awning next to the buzzing neon Neil Simon sign is a piano bar and restaurant called Russian Samovar. The entrance is plain. The awning promises a "House of Flavored Vodkas," which for some drinkers, is not an enticement, conjuring as it does chilling images of whipped cream or birthday cake-flavored shots of Smirnoff. The menu posted in the front window advertises traditional Russian fare: caviar and *blini*, salmon *kulebyaka*, *vareniki*, *tabaka*, beef stroganoff, and of course Chicken Kiev. Russia's climate doesn't inspire light, delicate victuals.

Russian Samovar opened in 1986, a partnership between three Russian expatriates: literature professor Roman Kaplan, famed poet Joseph Brodsky, and legendary ballet dancer Mikhail Baryshnikov. All three men considered themselves "fundamentally pro-Russian, yet vehemently anti-Soviet Union." They wanted a place where like-minded artists could gather, talk, listen to music, and eat. Though most of the world didn't realize it at the time, the Soviet Union was only a few years from dissolution, the Berlin Wall just a couple years from being overwhelmed and sledgehammered by jubilant Germans.

Before those momentous occasions, for many members of the Soviet diaspora who found themselves in New York, Russian Samovar became a home far away from home, where everything from politics to poetry was discussed over food and vodka.

The Soviet Union is gone now, but Russian Samovar is still there. Through the door, away from the crowd waiting to see *Jersey Boys* across the street, one is greeted by red boudoir lights, like something a saloon madam might have once hung in her cathouse. On the right is a long wooden bar behind which are arranged, among other liquors, some fifteen different house-infused vodkas. The vodka arrived in the 1980s, but the wooden bar has been there since the '60s, when the place was called Jilly's Saloon after its owner, Jilly Rizzo. Jilly's was famous for a number of reasons, but two stand out above all others. One, it's where someone once decided to murder Johnny Carson; and two, when Frank Sinatra was in New York, it's where he would hold court, dining there several nights a week flanked by friends and associates while three waiters and Jilly himself ran interference on anyone hoping to drop by Frank's booth without having been invited.

Despite being an icon of high living for generations, Sinatra was not a fan of *haute cuisine*. A high school drop-out from Hoboken, he was the only child of a lightweight boxer turned fireman and a political activist who ran an illegal abortion business that provided services for free. Even after he became famous, Sinatra preferred simpler fare and cozier surroundings than were found in the five-star restaurants of the world. There was P.J. Clarke's at 915 Third Ave., where Sinatra carefully scheduled his nights to avoid gossip columnist Dorothy Kilgallen, whose favorite topic was anything going wrong in Sinatra's life, especially if it concerned his tumultuous relationship with Ava Gardner. Then there was Patsy's at 236 W. 56th St., where Frank ordered the breaded veal and spaghetti with red sauce on the side.

There's a story about that place. As it goes, one Thanksgiving, Sinatra found himself on the skids, depressed, without company and without plans. So he made a reservation at Patsy's, which wasn't open that day. But owner Pasquale Scognamillo scrambled his staff and family so that when Frank rolled in at 3pm, the place was full. Rocky Lee Chu-Cho Bianco at 987 Second Ave was where Frank would go for pizza. And of course there was the spot on 52nd with the jockeys out front. But above and beyond them all was Sinatra's affection for Jilly's Saloon.

Jilly was born Ermenigildo Rizzo on May 6th, 1917. His career in food services started early. He worked for his father, delivering Italian ice. He eventually opened his first restaurant, Jilly's Saloon, on West 49th Street but later moved it to West 52nd, in the heart of Swing Street. It was this incarnation that attracted Sinatra's patronage. On any given night when he was in town, he could be found at his regular booth surrounded by his regular friends. They would have received the call earlier in the day telling them to be there. Having grown up an only child, Sinatra swore he would never dine alone.

Jilly's kitchen specialized not in Italian fare but in Cantonese food. Sinatra spent so much time there that Jilly became Sinatra's closest friend, his right-hand man, and his bodyguard. By 1962 he and Jilly Rizzo were so close that Sinatra was securing bit parts for the saloon owner in films such as *The Manchurian Candidate*.

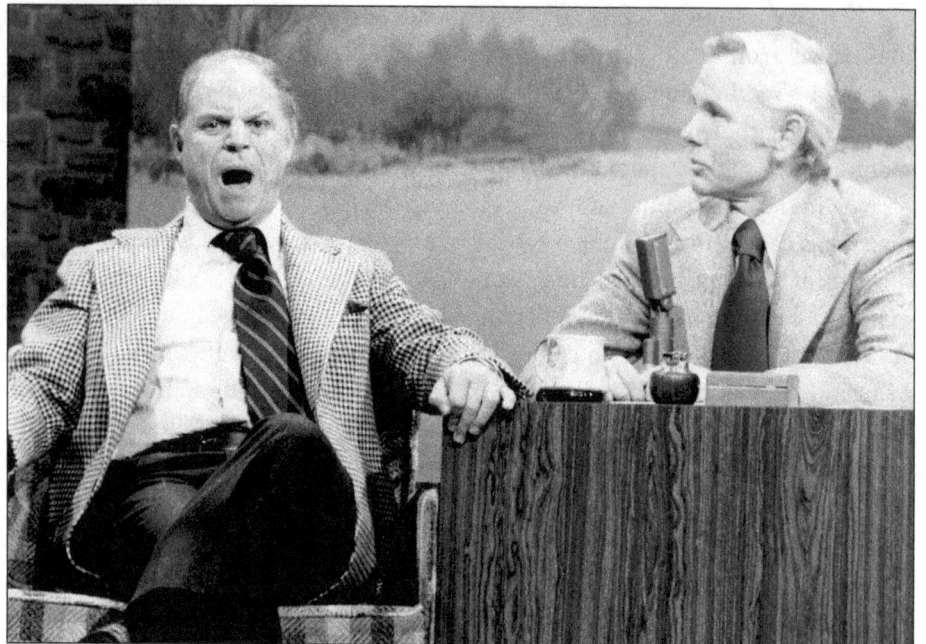
DEAD MAN TALKING: Comedian Johnny Carson narrowly avoided being murdered one night at Jilly's.

That same year, Sinatra and fellow Rat Packer Sammy Davis Jr. recorded the duet "Me and My Shadow," which twice mentions ending up at Jilly's. He also name-dropped it in the 1968 song "Star," in which he crooned "If they've got a drink with her name in Jilly's bar, the chances are the lady's a star." In Sinatra's 1968 detective movie *Lady in Cement*, he paid tribute to his long-time friend by naming a seedy Miami strip club after him.

Jilly's was also famous as the spot where a mobster decided to murder comedian Johnny Carson. Inebriation had gotten the better of the funnyman's judgment that night. He started flirting with a woman who'd caught his eye. According to Carson biographer Henry Bushkin, the popular funny man was doing his best to convince the young woman to leave with him. Unfortunately for Carson, that young woman was already spoken for by a jealous (and rather humorless) mobster. Enraged by Carson's amorous intent toward the lady, the unnamed mobster and his crew roughed Carson up, even throwing him down a flight of stairs. It would have gotten uglier had Jilly Rizzo himself not intervened and cooled the situation down. Level heads prevailed only briefly, long enough for Carson to limp away. But he soon discovered that all was not forgiven. The mobster, still fuming, decided that night the world would be better off without Carson. A hit was put out on Johnny, who spent the next three days hunkered down in his room at the UN Plaza hotel, canceling multiple appearances and hoping things might simmer down.

They did eventually, but only after Carson cut a deal with crime boss and "civil rights activist" Joseph Colombo. Under the terms of his agreement with Colombo, Carson brokered a deal with NBC to cover Colombo's Italian-American Civil

Rights League Italian Unity Day rally. Mafioso Colombo formed the League to protest the stereotyping of Italian-Americans as a bunch of Mafiosos. The hit was called off, and Carson was free to resume his life. Colombo, on the other hand, was less fortunate. He was gunned down in 1971 during the second (and final) Italian Unity Day rally in Columbus Circle. The trigger man was a street hustler named Jerome Johnson, working presumably on orders from Vincenzo Aloi, right hand man of Colombo's rival crime boss, "Crazy" Joe Gallo.

Colombo survived but was left completely paralyzed. He passed away in 1978 and was buried in Saint John Cemetery in Queens. Gallo was himself gunned down in 1972 while dining at Umberto's Clam House (129 Mulberry St.). Coincidentally, Gallo, his family, and his crew had just come from seeing Sinatra's favorite comedian, Don Rickles, at the Copacabana.

Jilly's wasn't the kind of place that was going to last forever, not with the way they made a habit—not always by choice—of letting wise guys run up huge tabs without ever paying them. The passing of time inevitably faded the glory of the Rat Pack. By the 1970s, Tony Delvecchio, who had bought the place from Rizzo with a partner and done his best to keep it afloat despite changing times and unpaid tabs, had to shut it down. His experience running Jilly's is detailed in a frequently-hilarious stream-of-conscious memoir titled *Sinatra, Gotti, and Me*. Jilly, who still served as the face of the bar, retired. The location ended up in the hands of Roman Kaplan, Joseph Brodsky, and Mikhail Baryshnikov.

WHISKEY SOUR NO. 1

- 2 oz Rye or Bourbon
- ¾ oz Fresh Lemon Juice
- ½ oz Simple Syrup
- ½ oz Egg White

Add all ingredients to a shaker. Add ice. Shake well. Strain into a rocks glass. Garnish with a lemon twist. There are two variations of the whiskey sour: one that uses egg white and one that doesn't.

WHISKEY SOUR NO. 2

- 2 oz Rye or Bourbon
- 1 oz Fresh Lemon Juice
- ¾ oz Simple Syrup
- Soda Water

Add all ingredients except soda water to a shaker. Shake well. Strain into a rocks glass. Top with soda water. Garnish with a cherry and a lemon twist.

RUSTY NAIL

- 2 oz Blended Scotch Whisky
- ½ oz Drambuie

Add all ingredients to a rocks glass with ice. Stir well. Garnish with a lemon twist.

DANIELS, SINATRA STYLE

- 2 fingers of Jack Daniels
- 4 Ice Cubes
- Splash of Water

Add all ingredients to a rocks glass. Thinking you'll get on Frank's good side by giving him a little extra? "Don't try to be his friend by mixing it heavy," a bodyguard of Sinatra's once said. "He don't like it like that."

MUDDLED HISTORY

The Old Fashioned is a foundational cocktail. Every bar should be able to make one, but not every bar makes them the same way. Once again, longevity resulted in variations. What started out as a very simple concoction got more fanciful, had more and different ingredients added, until finally bartenders had turned it into a circus and needed to pull back to something more like the original. Something more...old fashioned? There are two versions below: the stripped-down original and the slightly more fruit-featured version popular in the 1950s.

OLD FASHIONED OLD FASHIONED

- 2 oz Rye Whiskey
- 2 dashes Angostura Bitters
- ½ tsp Sugar

Add the sugar and bitters to a mixing glass to dissolve sugar. Add whiskey and ice. Stir well. Strain into a rocks glass filled with ice. Garnish with an orange peel.

MID-CENTURY OLD FASHIONED

- 2 ½ oz Bourbon
- 1 Orange Slice
- 1 Brandied Cherry
- 1 cube Demarera Sugar
- 1 dash Orange Bitters
- 2 dashes Angostura Bitters

Add orange slice and brandied cherry to a rocks glass. Add sugar cube and bitters. Muddle to dissolve sugar. Add whiskey. Stir well. Add large ice cubes and stir again. Garnish with an orange wheel and a cherry.

Brodsky was born in Leningrad in 1940. As a child, he endured antisemitism, poverty, and the brutal siege of Leningrad during World War II. He was a rebellious kid who disliked the omnipresent images of Lenin that peppered the USSR. After dropping out of school, he drifted through a series of jobs and, in 1955, started writing poetry for an underground journal, *Sintaksis*. His fame spread rapidly, and for several years he enjoyed a great deal of success.

As success was wont to do during those paranoid years, it got Brodsky on the bad side of the government. He was denounced as a poor contributor to society, a pornographer, anti-Communist, and most outlandishly, "a pseudo-poet in velveteen trousers." He was sentenced to five years of hard labor in the icy arctic north, only 18 months of which he served. Protests by prominent Soviet and foreign citizens secured his early release.

Contrary to the intentions of his rivals, Brodsky was fond of his time in the Arctic. He was invigorated by the labor and enjoyed the time for quiet contemplation, reading, and writing that the rustic isolation afforded him. After his return to Leningrad, he continued to write and continued to rub authorities the wrong way. In 1972, the Soviet government strongly suggested that Brodsky would be happier in Israel or, really, anywhere other than the USSR. Brodsky disagreed, stating flatly that he wanted to stay in Leningrad. Less than two weeks later, the government again suggested that he leave the country—this time by burglarizing his home, stealing all his papers, and forcibly placing him on a plane bound for Vienna. Having no interest in Israel or England, the exiled poet settled in the United States.

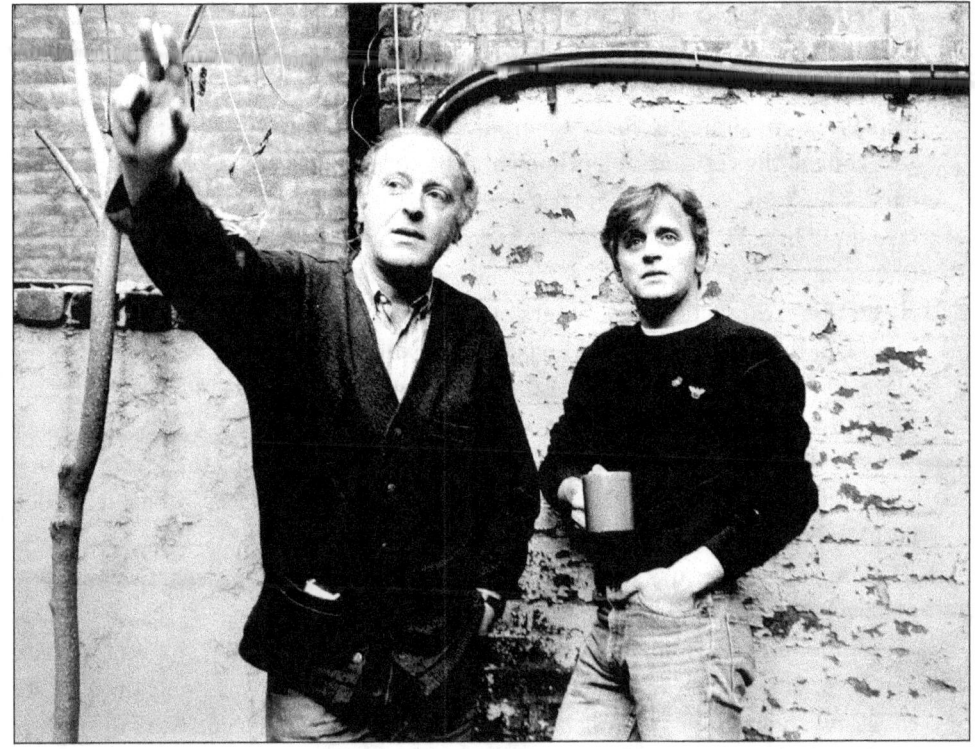

THE POET AND THE DANCER: Joseph Brodsky and Mikhail Baryshnikov. Photo by Leonid Lubianitsky.

As Brodsky was being hustled onto a plane by the KGB, his countryman Roman Kaplan was boarding a plane for Israel with no intention of coming back to the Soviet Union. Kaplan, like Brodsky, was born in Leningrad around the same time (1938) and endured many of the same hardships during the war. He moved to Moscow and became a professor of American English and literature. By the 1970s, he was ready to live somewhere less oppressive. Eventually, Kaplan found himself in New York, where his passion for Russian art led to a job in a gallery. At the gallery, he met many prominent people, including Russians who were, like him, exiled from their home, their culture, and their food. Inspired by this, Kaplan opened his first restaurant, Kalinka, in 1984. In 1986, he sold Kalinka and opened a new restaurant at 256 W 52nd St., moving into the former home of Jilly's. His contacts in the art world brought two business partners into Russian Samovar. One was Brodsky. The other was the most famous ballet dancer in the world. In 1974, Mikhail Baryshnikov, defected while in Toronto. In 1986, Baryshnikov became a naturalized citizen of the United States and agreed to get involved with Russian Samovar. In 1987, Brodsky won the Nobel Prize in Literature and invested the earnings into his friend's new restaurant, a friendly, open space that would encourage art and expression.

Kaplan read about the process of infusing vodka with flavors in old Russian texts and decided to introduce an infused vodka bar in the restaurant, a trend that would be copied by many bars and restaurants and that shouldn't be blamed for the proliferation of birthday cake vodka. Infused vodka may be easy to find these days, but in 1986 when Kaplan got the idea, it was still a new concept in the U.S. Originally fabled to be aphrodisiacs (isn't everything?), Kaplan and his bartenders encourage drinkers to consume the vodka the traditional way: with a compliment of pickles.

Though the restaurant has been around for decades now, Roman Kaplan still eats at Russian Samovar regularly. Enthusiastic and welcoming, with a wizened face lined by a fringe of well-groomed facial hair, he's no hands-off owner. He's there almost every night. There's still music at Russian Samovar, and Frank's table is still there, though few customers are aware of the role the spot once played in the life of the Chairman of the Board. If you want to talk about the history of the place, Kaplan will make time over the sounds of diners and live music. It might not be Sinatra, but the music is lively.

Jilly Rizzo, retired and moved to Palm Springs but still living the sort of life that led to things like a 1991 conviction for fraud (for which he was sentenced to 1000 hours of community service), was killed on May 6, 1992—his 75th birthday—when his car was struck by a drunk driver. Joseph Brodsky passed away in 1996 of a heart attack at the age of 55.

While vodka may be the star attraction at Russian Samovar, if you want to raise a glass to Sinatra, his "gasoline" of choice all those years was bourbon: four ice cubes, two fingers of Jack Daniels, and a splash of water. And if you were the type to "well, actually..." Sinatra about Daniels—he never called it "Jack"—being Tennessee whiskey and not bourbon, you'd soon get acquainted with the sidewalk out front of Jilly's Saloon with a gruff warning from Jilly that it'd be in your best interest not to come back. But don't worry. Swing Street had plenty more to offer than a chance to gawk at Frank Sinatra eating sweet and sour chicken.

The Playlist: Jilly's Saloon

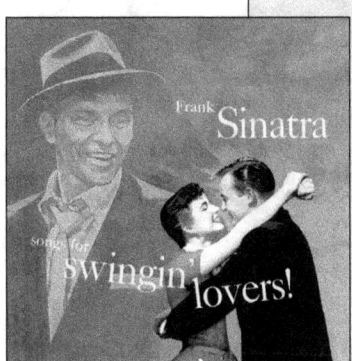

SONGS FOR SWINGIN' LOVERS!
Frank Sinatra, 1956

Kick the night off. *Songs for Swingin' Lovers!* is one of the best albums from one of the best periods in Sinatra's recording career. It's the first album arranged start to finish by Nelson Riddle, who would become a frequent Sinatra collaborator. It's an upbeat, energetic collection of tunes made for raising glass after glass at a place like Jilly's. Frank avoids the melancholy of his previous album, *In the Wee Small Hours*, and deals listeners a slice of pure swingin' joy. But don't worry. If you like sad clown of life Sinatra...

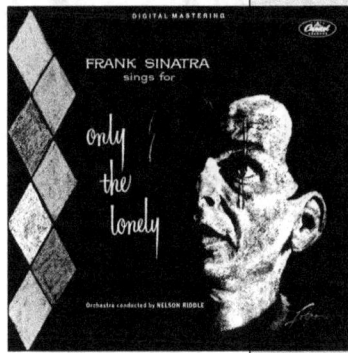

SINGS FOR ONLY THE LONELY
Frank Sinatra, 1958

Then end the night. Sinatra called it "suicide music." This album was recorded while he and Ava Gardner were divorcing, an event that did indeed lead to Frank attempting suicide. Arranger Nelson Riddle had recently lost his mother and daughter. Not surprisingly, it results in one of Sinatra's bleakest, most haunted albums. Nothing but lost love and regrets. It competed for an Album of the Year Grammy against another Sinatra album, the far cheerier *Come Fly With Me*. Neither won, but the sad clown nabbed him a Grammy for Best Album Cover.

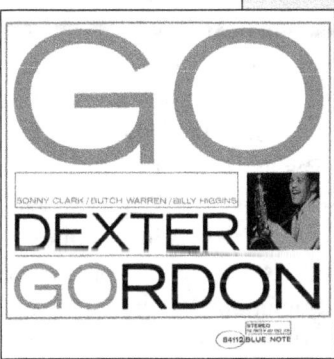

GO
Dexter Gordon, 1962

If you were hosting a cocktail party in 1962 and you didn't have this on in the background, well then chances are you weren't hosting much of a cocktail party. "Cheese Cake" for when the apartment's full; "I Guess I'll Hang My Tears Out to Dry" for when it's just the two of you and a bottle of champagne. If you need a pick-me-up to get you where you need to go in the wee small hours, "Three O'Clock In the Morning" is the juice you need to propel you those final few blocks. Gordon, Sonny Clark, Butch Warren, and Billy Higgins recorded the whole thing in a single session, aiming to capture the essence of a live show. There's not many better at bringing home a smoky nightclub.

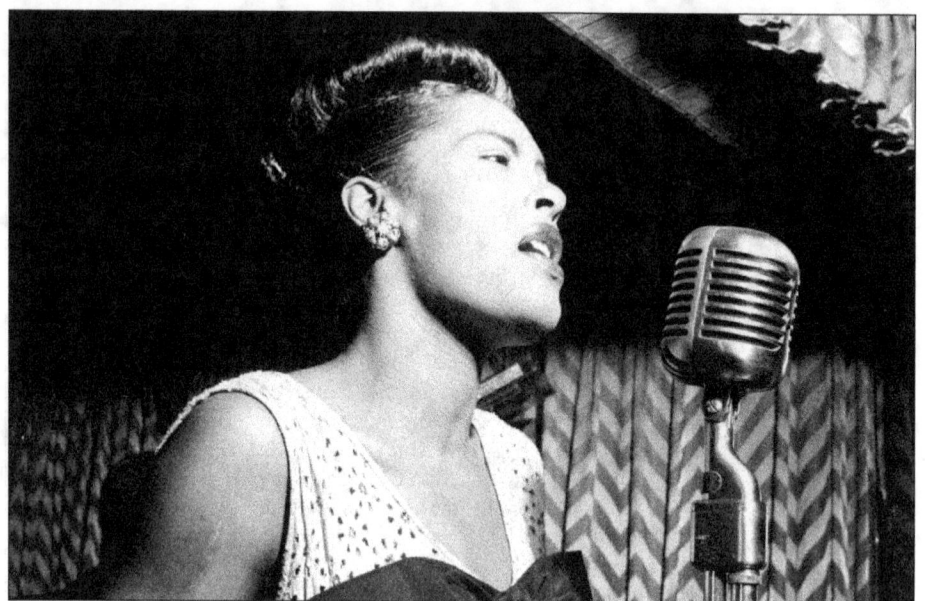
LADY DAY: Billie Holiday, the voice of America. Photo by William P. Gottlieb.

Lady Sings the Blues

There are few moments more perfect than walking into a dimly-lit bar late at night and hearing a Billie Holiday song. "These Foolish Things" is practically custom-made for sliding onto a stool and ordering an Old Fashioned as you prop your elbows up on the bar and think about lost loves and life's regrets. Her discography is not composed entirely of anthems for the lonely, but few American artists seem to have captured the melancholy of 2 a.m. quite like the woman who would become known as Lady Day. For much of her career, her unique voice could be heard in one of the many clubs that used to line Manhattan's 52nd Street, that stretch of the city once known as Swing Street.

Verifiable details about Holiday's life before her stardom are scant. Her own autobiography is vague and riddled with inconsistencies (it was, in fact, written by a man named William Dufty, and when questioned about some obvious errors in it, Holiday famously shrugged and said "I ain't never read that book."). She was born Eleanora Fagan in Philadelphia and raised in Baltimore. Her father split, and her mother worked such long hours that Eleanora was usually left in the care of her mother's half-sister, Eva Miller, who herself worked so much that she left young Eleanora in the care of her own mother-in-law. As a girl, she was in and out of a reform school called House of the Good Shepherd. The first time was after she was caught skipping school. The second time was after a neighbor attempted to rape her, and the police needed to keep her somewhere with more protection than her empty home.

She found work as an errand girl in a brothel, and it was there that she first heard the music of Louis Armstrong, the artist she credits as inspiring her to become a performer. In 1929, she moved with her mother to Harlem, where both of them found work in a brothel. Eleanora was thirteen at the time. When the house was raided by police, she was placed in the workhouse on Blackwell's Island (later renamed Roosevelt Island). When she was released, she decided she'd had enough of being Eleanora Fagan. She sought work as a singer, taking the stage name Billie from her favorite actress, Billie Dove, and the last name Holiday from musician Clarence Holiday, the most likely candidate for being her father. She teamed up with neighbor and aspiring saxophonist Kenneth Hollan and began knocking on club doors. It didn't take long for managers to realize there was something special about this tragic young kid. She soon had a new home, on the original Swing Street—133rd Street between Seventh and Lenox in Harlem. The Renaissance was in full swing, and Swing Street was its artistic heart.

Something as momentous as the Harlem Renaissance doesn't have a specific start date. Such large cultural awakenings grow organically over time, and sometimes it's only in hindsight that we can see a Movement. For the sake of having *some* starting point, many people cite 1917, the year in which white playwright Ridgely Torrence cast black actors in a series of performances that allowed them to actually *be* actors—no minstrelry, no blackface. In 1919, poet Claude McKay wrote the poem "If We Must Die," a piece that served as a clarion call for black Americans to stand up and defy the racism and subjugation that had been their lot in life for so long.

It all happened to the wild sound of a new piano style called Harlem Stride. Jazz, previously regarded as low-class and "Southern," not really the stuff for

COCKTAIL BOOTHBY'S HARLEM

This is one of two different cocktails bearing the name Harlem. This one, the rarer and less sweet, comes from William "Cocktail" Boothby's 1930 manual *Swallow*.

- 1 ½ oz Rye Whiskey
- 1 ½ oz Dry Gin
- ½ oz Fresh Lime Juice
- ½ oz Simple Syrup
- ½ Egg White

Add all ingredients to a shaker with ice. Shake well. Strain into a chilled cocktail glass.

OLD MISTER BOSTON HARLEM

This one is the more commonly published recipe, though its provenance as a specialty of the Cotton Club is undocumented. It's more fruit and sweetness forward. This recipe comes from 1935's *Old Mr. Boston Official Bartenders Guide*.

- 2 oz Dry Gin
- ¼ oz Maraschino Liqueur
- 2 oz Fresh Pineapple Juice

Add all ingredients to a shaker with ice. Shake well. Strain into a chilled cocktail glass. Garnish with a cherry or a pineapple wedge.

BEATNIK

- ½ oz Averna
- 1 oz Tawny Port
- 1 oz Bourbon

Add all ingredients to a mixing glass with ice. Stir well. Strain into a chilled cocktail glass. Garnish with an orange wheel.

more sophisticated urbanites, began to gain popular acceptance among Harlem's more progressive residents. New clubs opened to showcase the new sound. During Prohibition, many of the Harlem jazz clubs—Tillie's Chicken Shack, Pod's and Jerry's, the Rhythm Club, the LGBTQ-friendly Harry Hansberry's Clam House—continued on as speakeasies. White patrons who fancied themselves adventurous began making the trip up to Harlem to see this once-in-a-lifetime gathering of musicians that included artists such as Louis Armstrong, Duke Ellington, and Fats Waller. The influx of white patrons was a mixed blessing. It was good because it exposed whites to black culture—not just the music, but also to social and political thinking. It was good because it resulted in integrated streets. But it was bad because those streets sometimes integrated at the expense of black locals, who found themselves pushed out of their own neighborhood by newcomers. And it was bad because some of the clubs, including the famous Cotton Club, opened specifically to showcase black talent for white-only audiences.

It was in this dynamic, tumultuous time and place that Holiday took the stage. Her reputation grew quickly. In 1933 producer John Hammond heard her sing for the first time and, that same year, arranged for her first recording, backed by Benny Goodman. Her first recording resulted in her first hit, "Riffin' the Scotch."

Hammond had never heard anyone sing like Billie Holiday. There was something about Billie's voice, something unique. Something to do with smoke and shadow and sex. Something that seems melancholy even when the lyrics and melody are happy. Something a little slurred, a little muddled. Something that could stun you into silence. Exactly the voice you need late at night. Exactly the voice to define a new America. Hammond paired her with an impressive array of musicians, both black and white, including Teddy Wilson, Artie Shaw, and Count Basie, who was at the time in a musical duel with Chick Webb, whose lead vocalist was Ella Fitzgerald. Holiday's working relationship with Basie was tense. He said she was temperamental, unprofessional, difficult. She claimed he was cheap, and that he demanded artistic changes that undermined the very reason people were coming to see her. The differences between Basie and Billie proved irreconcilable. After a short time together, she left the band.

By the end of the 1930s, Harlem's Swing Street was gone. The Depression, the end of Prohibition, the rise of organized crime, and the brutal suppression of demonstrations that became the Harlem Riot of 1935 kept patrons away. By then, Billie Holiday was a star who transcended any neighborhood. Hammond booked her at a new place, downtown in New York's bohemian Greenwich Village, called Café Society. It was opened in 1938 by New Jersey shoe salesman Barney Josephson. From the get-go he intended it as a thumb to the nose of high-falutin' society. The name was chosen as a joke, a satirical reference to writer and socialite Clare Boothe Luce's praise of sophisticated "café society." Josephson referred to his club as "the wrong place for the Right people" — the word "Right" being specifically capitalized as a reference to the conservatives he thought throttled American culture.

Most notable, however, was that it was a racially-integrated nightclub, one of the first in the city. Nightclubs in New York, and indeed across America, had a long history of booking black talent but only allowing white clientele. Josephson's

The Playlist: Harlem Renaissance

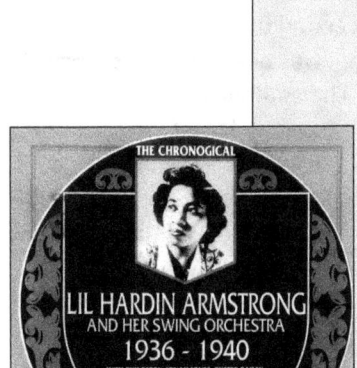

THE CHRONOLOGICAL CLASSICS
Teddy Wilson, 2002

The "Chronological Classics" collect recordings from artists who predated the concept of the LP. Wilson, one of the most influential and successful piano players of the era, has several discs dedicated to him, but the first three volumes, 1934-1935, 1935-1936, and 1936-1937 contain the earliest recordings of Billie Holiday, who sang with Wilson's various groups. The style is a mix of Harlem Stride piano, hot jazz, and swing. The span of years also includes Ella Fitzgerald, Helen Ward, Buck Clayton, and Benny Goodman. If you can't find these, Billie's work with Wilson is also compiled in *Lady Day: The Complete Billie Holiday on Columbia - 1933-1944*.

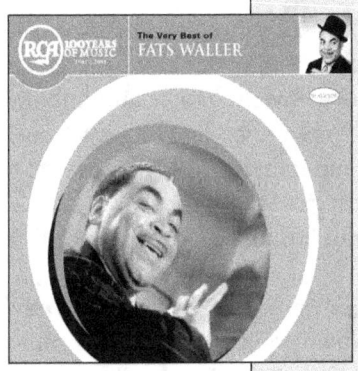

THE CHRONOLOGICAL CLASSICS
Lil Hardin Armstrong, 1996

Another hit from the Chronological Classics, this time compiling the music of vocalist Lil Hardin Armstrong, including what is perhaps her best-known song, "Oriental Swing." She was a true Renaissance Woman despite being based in Chicago rather than Harlem: a musical scholar, pianist, composer, arranger, singer, tailor, and band leader, not to mention being married to Louis Armstrong for a time, who she met while performing with King Oliver in Chicago's Dreamland Café during the '20s. She even taught Armstrong how to dress. Truly one of the great pioneering women in music history.

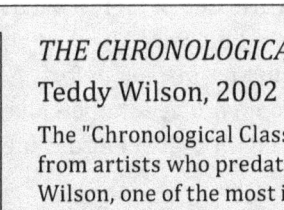

THE VERY BEST OF FATS WALLER
Fats Waller, 2000

Fats Waller was one of the biggest musicians of the Harlem Renaissance. A native New Yorker, the son of a preacher, and an international phenomenon, Waller's piano playing formed the foundation of jazz piano. His compositions are a mix of blues, Harlem swing, and hot jazz. While artists like Duke Ellington and Cab Calloway were developing the swanky jazz sound that would become big band, Waller was more intimate—less glitzy bandstand, more smoky nightclub. Many of the songs he wrote or co-wrote, including "Honeysuckle Rose," and "Ain't Misbehavin'" became timeless American standards.

club welcomed black as well as white patrons, treating both equally. The list of performers who worked the stage at Café Society is staggering. Billie was one of their star performers, and also one of their most daring. There was a night in 1939 when she took the stage and delivered her usual wonderful set...until she got to the last song, one she hadn't performed before. Audience members were thrown for a loop. Wait service stopped. They shut off all the lights but one, a spotlight on Billie's face, her eyes closed. In that silent darkness, Lady Day launched into the song, "Strange Fruit."

The song was originally written as a poem by teacher Abel Meeropol, who was moved to pen it after seeing a photo taken by Lawrence Beitler in 1930 depicting the lynching of two black men, Thomas Shipp and Abram Smith. Meeropol searched unsuccessfully for a partner who could set the poem to music. Eventually, he did it himself, performing "Strange Fruit" with vocalist Laura Duncan. Someone at Café Society, either Josephson or director Robert Gordon, heard it and convinced Holiday to perform the song at the club.

At first, she was wary. It is a chilling song, subverting the image of trees laden with fruit by likening it to hanged black men. Holiday was nervous about reprisals, but Josephson convinced her to go through with it. The audience was awestruck. It was so well received that it became a regular part of her Café Society shows. When it came to recording it, however, producers were as wary as Holiday had first been. After Columbia, the label to which Holiday was signed, refused to let her record the song, she turned to producer John Hammond, who also balked. Holiday then took the song to Milt Gabler's small, avant-garde Commodore label. It was there she was finally able to record "Strange Fruit."

Café Society continued challenging the establishment, breaking down barriers, and fostering incredible musical talent, until the club came under intense harassment from the House Un-American Activities Committee, that Congressional mob charged, in theory, with ferreting out Communist threats at the expense of any sense of free speech or Constitutional rights. After Barney Josephson's brother, Leon, was called to testify before the committee and refused, a propaganda campaign was waged against Café Society. In 1947, Barney had no alternative but to close it down, another victim of the Red Scare plaguing the country.

Social upheaval and the end of Prohibition may have shuttered many of the famous nightclubs on 133rd Street, but jazz proved it could adapt and survive. It found a new home in the cafés and nightclubs of Greenwich Village, and it found a new Swing Street on 52nd between Fifth and Seventh Avenue. Clubs such as 3 Deuces, The Onyx, and Club Carousel kept the Harlem Renaissance alive, even if it wasn't in Harlem anymore (the biggest club in Harlem at that time was Minton's, popular because the owner was more than happy to indulge musicians with free food and drink).

The pioneers of the '20s and '30s turned these new stages over to the new generation of jazz legends: Charlie Parker, Thelonious Monk, John Coltrane, Miles Davis. Big band and swing gave way to bebop, and bebop to cool jazz and hard bop. But Lady Day remained. In 1939, Frank Sinatra—born the same year as Holiday—saw her at the Uptown House. He was entranced (and probably smitten). "Standing

The Playlist: Café Society

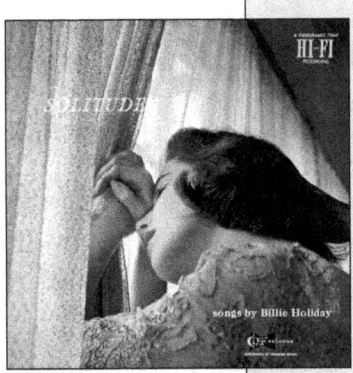

SOLITUDE
Billie Holiday, 1952/1956

By the time her first 10-inch solo recording, *Billie Holiday Sings*, was released in 1952, Lady Day had been performing for two decades. So it's no debut effort. It's Billie Holiday in full, glorious bloom and at the top of her game. *Billie Holiday Sings* was replaced in 1956 by the LP *Solitude*, which contains all the original tracks plus a few more. *Solitude* is packed with signature Holiday tunes and trends just a little bit blue with a dash of swing, as was her way. It is, quite simply, one of the greatest American records ever recorded.

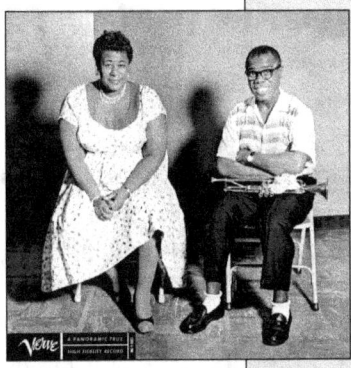

ELLA AND LOUIS
Ella Fitzgerald & Louis Armstrong, 1956

New Orleans trumpeter Louis Armstrong was one of the most important musicians in jazz, a New Orleans prodigy who helped define Chicago jazz. Ella Fitzgerald was one of the most important voices. Both were regulars on the stage at Café Society. In 1956, they recorded a fantastic album of duets. *Ella and Louis* is a collection of standards executed with perfection. There's not a weak track on the entire album, and while it may showcase both artists later in their careers, it packs as much energy as anything they recorded in their youth.

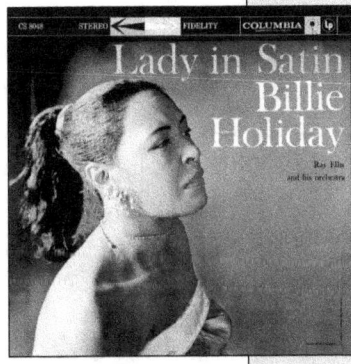

LADY IN SATIN
Billie Holiday, 1958

With critics and audiences alike having written her off as a casualty of changing times and hard living, Billie Holiday defied them all and released one of the greatest albums of her career. It's true that life had taken its toll on her voice, but in the context of these songs, that raspier, smokier quality is to her advantage. Billie earned her melancholy at an early age, and by 1958 that darkness had obtained additional *gravitas*. She makes you believe. *Lady in Satin* was the last album released in Holiday's lifetime. A posthumous release from MGM claims the somber honor of being her final album, but *Lady in Satin* is truly the capstone of her career.

JACK ROSE

- 1 ½ oz Applejack Brandy
- ¾ oz Fresh Lemon Juice
- ½ oz Grenadine

Add all ingredients to a shaker with ice. Shake well. Strain into a chilled coupe glass. Garnish with a lime or lemon twist.

••••••••••••••••••••••••••

BOULEVARDIER

- 1 oz Campari
- 1 oz Sweet Vermouth
- 1 ¼ oz Rye Whiskey

Add all ingredients to a rocks glass filled with ice. Stir well. Garnish with an orange twist. If you prefer, this one can also be served up (no ice) by straining into a chilled cocktail glass after stirring. Either way, garnish with an orange twist.

••••••••••••••••••••••••••

BRANDY CRUSTA

- 2 oz Cognac
- ¼ oz Triple Sec
- ½ oz Fresh Lemon Juice
- ½ oz Simple syrup
- 1 tsp Maraschino liqueur
- 1 dash Angostura bitters

Add all ingredients to a shaker. Fill with ice. Shake well. Strain into a Champagne Coupe with a sugared rim. Garnish with a lemon twist.

••••••••••••••••••••••••••

COMMUNIST

- 1 oz Dry Gin
- 1 oz Fresh Orange Juice
- ½ oz Cherry Heering
- ¾ oz Fresh Lemon Juice

Add all ingredients to a shaker filled with ice. Shake well. Strain into a chilled cocktail glass.

under a spotlight in a 52nd Street jazz spot," he recalled, "I was dazzled by her soft, breathtaking beauty."

Sinatra undoubtedly learned lessons from Holiday, like how to use emotion and how to turn a song into a story. He later said of Billie, "It is Billie Holiday who was, and still remains, the greatest single musical influence on me." Throughout the 1940s, her popularity continued to grow. Her best known and biggest hits, songs like "God Bless the Child" and "Lover Man," were from this era. She well and truly was the voice of America, and it seemed there was really no stopping her. Then, in 1947, it all started to fall apart.

Though an open secret among the people with whom she worked, Holiday's addiction to heroin became public knowledge when she was arrested in 1947. Many who owed their success to her abandoned Billie during this setback. When her lawyer no-showed the trial, she plead guilty and was sent to Alderson Federal Prison Camp, better known as Camp Cupcake (later the temporary residence of Martha Stewart). She was released less than a year later and, despite having no albums released in years, performed to a sold-out house at Carnegie Hall. A successful follow-up show on Broadway in 1948 seemed to signal that, despite addiction, legal setbacks, and the march of time, Lady Day was still a force to be reckoned with.

But in 1949, she was arrested once again on possession charges, this time in San Francisco. Although she recorded another of her most famous songs, "Crazy He Calls Me," in the wake of this second arrest, her popularity took a hit. She began to disappear from American radio. New York used her drug arrests to justify revoking her Cabaret Card. Implemented in 1940, the New York City Cabaret Card system required artists be licensed to perform in any establishment that served alcohol. The law was repealed in 1967, thanks largely to Frank Sinatra's threat to never perform in New York again, but for Holiday in 1949, it meant she was effectively banned from just about every club in the city. At least she was in good company—over the years, Charlie Parker, Chet Baker, Thelonious Monk, and Lenny Bruce had their cards revoked as well.

Loss of the card forced Billie into smaller venues for less pay. Critics said her voice was shot, that it was all over, but she soldiered on. In the 1950s, she toured Europe and began recording for the Verve label, releasing albums that proved audiences still wanted her music, and that reports of the demise of her voice were greatly exaggerated. In 1956, in support of the release of her suspect autobiography, she recorded "Lady Sings the Blues," the song that would become synonymous with Billie Holiday. She returned triumphantly to Carnegie Hall that same year. In 1957 she married a hustler named Louis McKay, a small-fry goon who, liked most of the men Billie ended up with, treated her poorly. But he was committed to getting her off heroin, even if it was not for altruistic reasons. He lived better when she was performing well, and he planned to franchise her name to open a chain of Billie Holiday recording studios.

In 1958, she once again proved the critics who were writing her off wrong, recording *Lady in Satin*, one of the greatest albums of her career. She toured Europe again in 1959 and began recording an album for MGM. It was released posthumously. Billie Holiday died on July 17, 1959, at the age of 44.

Swing Street didn't survive, either. The Cotton Club, 3 Deuces, Onyx—all gone. Most of the Greenwich Village clubs are gone as well. No plaque commemorates Café Society, though a block away is another historic joint, the Stonewall Inn. But despite the changes, despite all that has come and gone, despite the fact that New York has torn down and rebuilt itself a dozen times since she first set foot on a Swing Street stage, Billie's voice remains. You can still bow your head at the bar, feel the chills as you let Billie's voice wash over you, and take one last drink before you bid goodbye to the bartender and head out into the night.

You don't want to wish woe on anyone, but when tragedy forges a talent like Billie Holiday, you can tell yourself at least some of it was worth it. Like Sinatra said, "Lady Day is unquestionably the most important influence on American popular music in the last 20 years. With a few exceptions, every major pop singer in the United States during her generation has been touched in some way by her genius."

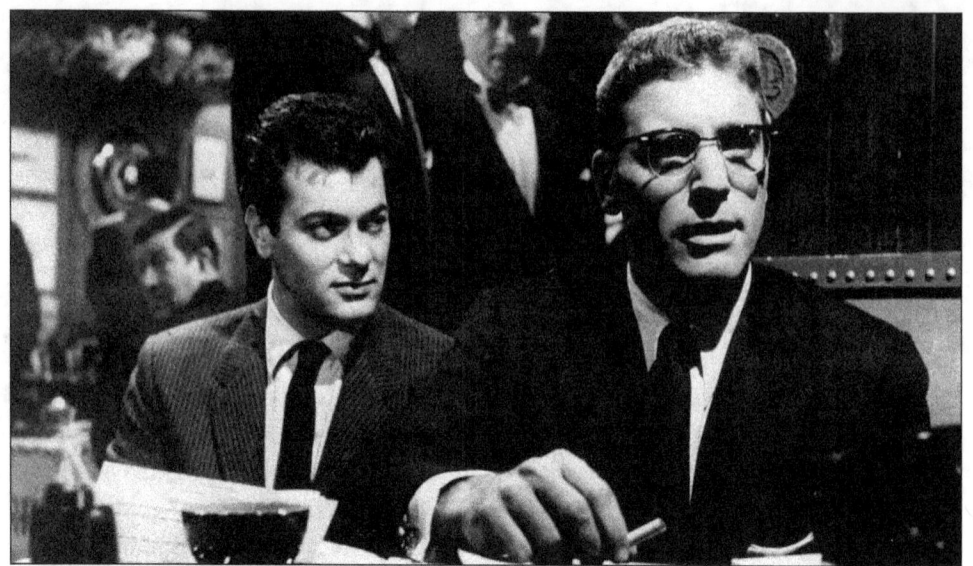

The Start of Something Big

While Sidney Falco was pushing through the drunks at Toots Shor's, J.J. Hunsecker was presiding over a more refined—but no less frenzied—scene a short distance away at the 21 Club, which, despite the changes in the city over the years, remains a stalwart presence on the block that used to swing but now mostly manages investments and whatever else it is bankers do in those austere, anonymous skyscrapers. Located at 21 West 52nd Street and opened (as a speakeasy, naturally) during a wild party on Dec. 31, 1929, it's one of the city's few remaining establishments that expects you to dress up. Jeans are forbidden, and a jacket is required (sadly, they relaxed the rule about ties in 2009).

Before settling in at the address that would stay theirs for decades, 21 bounced from location to location. In 1922, cousins Jack Kreindler and Charlie Berns opened the first incarnation, known as the Red Head, in Greenwich Village. They later moved to Washington Place and changed the name to Fronton, then moved again to 42nd St., where it was known as the Puncheon Club. It was at this location they introduced the more elegant atmosphere, which stayed in place when they moved to 52nd St. and christened the new location Jack and Charlie's '21'.

"A more elegant atmosphere" doesn't mean a reserved atmosphere. This was still Prohibition after all, and what went on at 21 was still illegal. Like many speakeasy proprietors, Jack, Charlie, and their staff devised a number of ingenious contraptions to help them avoid getting busted during raids. There was a lever near the bar which, when thrown, would tilt the shelves so the booze dropped down a chute into the city sewer. The bar itself could rotate into a hiding place behind the wall. There was also a secret door leading to the club's wine cellar.

When J.J. Hunsecker used it as his office away from the office in *Sweet Smell of Success*, 21 was a hive of activity. This was the age of two, three, four martini lunches and lots of business in the dining room. Each table had a phone jack nearby. Writers, advertising executives, and celebrities would stay for hours with assistants running in and out all day. It wasn't a quiet, romantic night out, but if you were making the scene, or like J.J., breaking someone's scene, 21 was where you staked your territory. "Still the snappiest restaurant in New York," wrote *Spy* magazine in 1960, in a description of the place that perfectly captures its appearance in *Sweet Smell of Success*. "A caste system operates in this plush spot, separating the big from the small and the biggest from them all."

Sidney Falco is one of the small, looking to sit at the biggest table. J.J.'s table. Ostensibly, it's because Falco wants his latest client to succeed, and a kind mention from J.J. would cement that. As the film progresses, it becomes less about client success and more about Sidney's obsessive drive to make it, for himself to succeed. J.J., recognizes that whiff of desperate fear, like any well-honed predator would. He is more than happy to dangle the bait in front of Sidney and offer him a deal. It might destroy a couple lives, and it would definitely blacken Sidney's soul, but hey...what's that compared to the sweet smell of success?

Toots Shor's was a place for a whiskey sour and a plate of indifferent grub. Jilly's slung cheap Chinese food. 21 was where you went for a good

SOUTHSIDE
- 2 oz Plymouth Gin
- 1 oz Fresh Lemon Juice
- 5 Mint Leaves
- 1 oz Simple Syrup

Add mint and lemon juice to a shaker. Muddle gently. Add remaining ingredients. Fill with ice. Shake well. Strain into a chilled Martini glass. Garnish with a mint sprig or a lemon twist.

FRENCH 75
- ½ oz Lemon Juice
- ½ oz Simple Syrup
- 1 oz Dry Gin
- 3 oz Champagne

Add all ingredients except the Champagne to a shaker. Fill with ice. Shake well. Strain into a Champagne flute. Top with the Champagne. Garnish with a lemon twist.

CLOVER CLUB
- 1 ½ oz Dry Gin
- ½ oz Dry Vermouth
- ½ oz Lemon Juice
- ½ oz Raspberry Syrup
- ¼ oz Egg White

Add ingredients to shaker. Shake well. Strain into mixing glass. Discard ice and pour back into shaker. Shake again. Strain into a chilled cocktail glass. Garnish with a couple of skewered raspberries.

SIDECAR
- 1 ½ oz VS or VSOP Cognac
- ¾ oz Cointreau
- ¾ oz Fresh Lemon Juice

Coat the rim of a cocktail glass with sugar. Add ingredients to a shaker and fill with ice. Shake well. Strain into sugar-rimmed glass. Garnish with an orange peel.

meal. They prided themselves on their food and have worked for some 85 years to maintain that reputation. Similarly, they've sought to keep pace with the changing face of cocktail culture, from the classics like Manhattans and Martinis that would have been the lifeblood of Hunsecker to the craft cocktails that define the landscape today. But people still expect a certain level of old-school tradition from 21, so they're not going to stray far from the classics. You won't find dry ice and mystery pearls in their cocktails. And if there's one cocktail, besides the Martini and Manhattan, that characterizes the 21 from the era of *Sweet Smell of Success*, it's the Southside.

Today, the atmosphere at 21 has calmed down a little, and alas, the table-side phone jacks are gone, but it's still a place to see and be seen, as well as the site of countless business deals. World leaders, artists and actors, and business moguls can still be seen there any day of the week. In its long history, the restaurant has played host to writers, movie stars, singers, average folks looking for a fancy experience to remember, and every American President since Franklin Roosevelt, except for George W. Bush. You will also find local New Yorkers and visitors who have come to experience the history. While people can wait months to get a reservation at whatever the new trendy restaurant might be, it's easier to secure a table at a classic like 21.

The Club was even dragged into a brouhaha when President-elect Donald Trump ditched the press corps and sneaked out for a private meal. His destination? 21 Club, where so many other presidents and dignitaries and dukes and duchesses have enjoyed a meal beneath the dining room's ceiling of knick knacks, including a model PT boat donated by John Kennedy.

"Prohibition raids, Hemingway escapades, Marilyn Monroe and Joe DiMaggio, a gift from JFK," says Avery Fletcher, current Director of Sales and Marketing for 21. "Jackie Gleason swapping a model train for the pool cue from *The Hustler*, Gordon Gecko (Michael Douglas) declaring 'Lunch is for wimps' in *Wall Street*, Nelson Mandela, Bette Midler, Jimmy Fallon crossing the room to offer Wes Anderson a taste of his Chicken Hash."

It's hard to think of a place where so many disparate temperaments, political alignments, and types of people have gathered peacefully, entering the street-side iron gates flanked by a retinue of ever-vigilant jockeys. As, one by one, the famous clubs of Swing Street began to die off, 21 weathered the storm, thanks perhaps to the fact that they proved a little more competent in managing their money than neighbors like Toots Shor and Jilly Rizzo, both of whom it seemed could never stay out of debt or off the IRS' radar. The food was also better. Even as skyscrapers sprouted up around them, replacing the old establishments, 21 remained, as Fletcher describes it, "the lone reminder of Swing Street's previous self; standing tall figuratively though dwarfed physically."

The Playlist: 21 Club

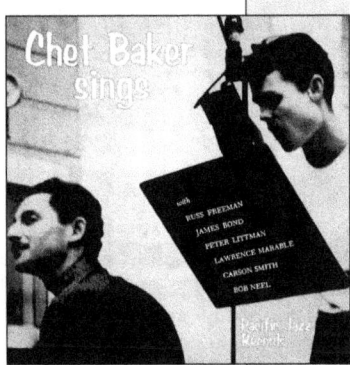

CHET BAKER SINGS
Chet Baker, 1954

Chet Baker was best known as a brilliant, troubled trumpet player, but he recorded this album of vocal standards back before heroin took its hold. It's a dreamy, romantic, sorrowful collection of songs that straddles the world of bohemian jazz clubs and Frank Sinatra when he's in one of his moods. Baker's voice is soft and flows like honey. He accomplished great things with more complex music, including stints in Paris and working on Italian movie soundtracks with composer Piero Umiliani, but *Chet Baker Sings* is one of his most charming, emotionally-moving albums.

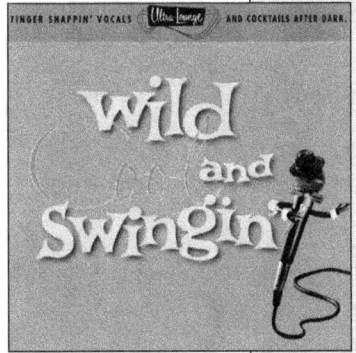

WILD, COOL, AND SWINGIN' VOLS. 1-3
Various Artists, 1996

The Ultra-Lounge compilation series, first on CD and later as digital downloads, is hands-down one of the greatest resources for fun, varied mid-century cocktail lounge and easy listening. Across three volumes, the *Wild, Cool, and Swinging* discs collect the greatest vocalists of that swingin' era. Dean Martin, Bobby Darin, Sam Butera, Peggy Lee, Julie London, Sammy Davis Jr., Vic Damone, Nat "King" Cole, Tony Bennett, Dinah Washington, Louis Prima...you name 'em, and chances are they're here. Put these three in rotation, and you won't have to worry about anything else the rest of the night.

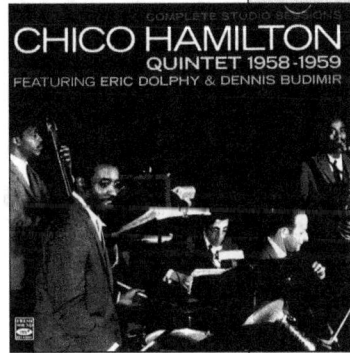

COMPLETE STUDIO RECORDINGS
Chico Hamilton Quintet, 2006

The Chico Hamilton Quintet gave us one-half of the stellar *Sweet Smell of Success* soundtrack. It seems only fair, then, that you get to know the rest of their body of work, which plays along the same lines. There's a tremendous amount of variation on display, including songs that use violins and others that bridge the gap between small-combo jazz, easy listening, and lush orchestral arrangements. Whether your in the club or out on the streets, whether you're solving a crime, committing a crime, or staying in for the evening, Chico Hamilton is essential.

The Playlist: The Long Trip Home

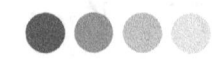

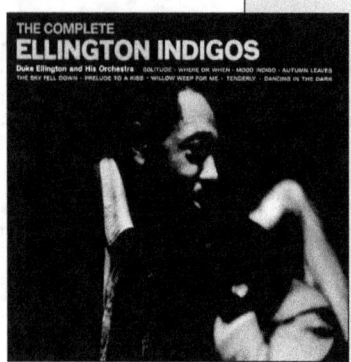

THE COMPLETE ELLINGTON INDIGOS
Duke Ellington, 1958

So the evening didn't go exactly how you planned? You're in the back of that cab alone, or walking down the rain-slicked, neon-stained street with no one to keep you company but the occasional distant barking dog? Don't worry. The Grand Duke is there, providing the ultimate soundtrack for that long trip home. This album features Ellington putting his most melancholy spin on timeless classics, the ultimate "Mood Indigo" for your mood indigo. It's all solemn mood music until the final track, "Commercial Time." The sun is rising by then. It's another day. Time to grab breakfast.

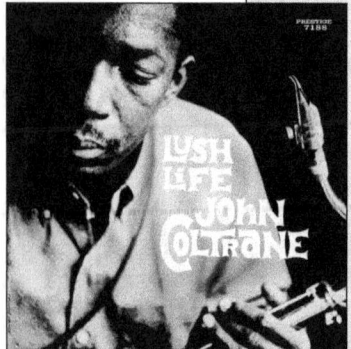

LUSH LIFE
John Coltrane, 1961

You had one too many, didn't you? About three drinks ago. One more for the road was a bad idea, but what could you do? The barman was wiping down the counter, the night manager was stacking chairs. It was just you and them and that sad-looking fool with his head in his hands. Oh. That's a mirror you say? Well, it's all good as long Coltrane is playing "Lush Life" for you, the signature song for last call. The rest of the album keeps that later-than-late-night groove. If "I Love You" sounds a little free-form for the hour, just think of it as musical accompaniment for your staggering gait.

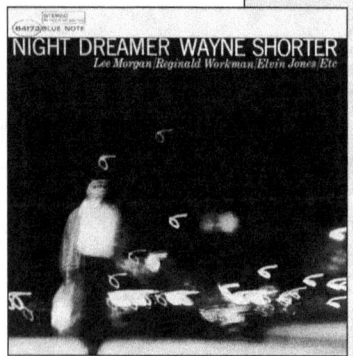

NIGHT DREAMER
Wayne Shorter, 1964

Shorter is one weird cat in a business populated by weird cats. He often explored esoteric, even occult ideas through music. As the name suggests, *Night Dreamer* is about the night, and about contemplation. Or in Shorter's words: "What I'm trying to express here is a sense of judgment approaching—judgment for everything alive from the smallest ant to man. I know that the accepted meaning of Armageddon is the last battle between good and evil—whatever it is. But my definition of the judgment to come is a period of total enlightenment in which we will discover what we are and why we're here."

Match Me, Sidney

By the time *Sweet Smell of Success* hits its closing shot, as the mournful menace of the Chico Hamilton Quintet's "Night Beat" signals a ceasefire to the evening's battles, the viewer, like the characters, has been through the ringer. No one emerges unscathed. Lives are ruined, perhaps more and different lives than J.J. Hunsecker hoped…including his own. There is a sense of exhaustion, carnage, defeat. Not everyone survives a night in New York. Not everyone returns in the morning.

But other lives go on. Other people have found the inspiration, however ugly the source, to be reborn, to pick themselves up and strike out in search of something new. As the sun rises on the streets of New York, littered with the casualties of another night of revelry, deal-making, and sin, the grime and filth seems somehow… admirable? Maybe. A red badge of courage? Perhaps.

And those who didn't survive the night? Maybe they'll be remembered. Maybe not. Maybe someone will eulogize on their behalf…if they can remember the names. If there's even time to bother. After all, it all starts again the next evening. Some will return for another go-round. Others will be taking the field for the first time. That's the game. That's the city. It's not going to pause for you to catch your breath and lick your wounds. This city doesn't have time to stand still, and why would anyone want to live in a New York that stands still?

Even if Toots Shor's is gone, even if Swing Street is gone, even if 21 Club is the lone guardian of that wild, damaged, enthralling Swing Street era, it's hard, if you really have the city in your blood, not to stand there surrounded by all the concrete and glass and human wreckage and say to yourself, like J.J. Hunsecker, "I love this dirty town." §

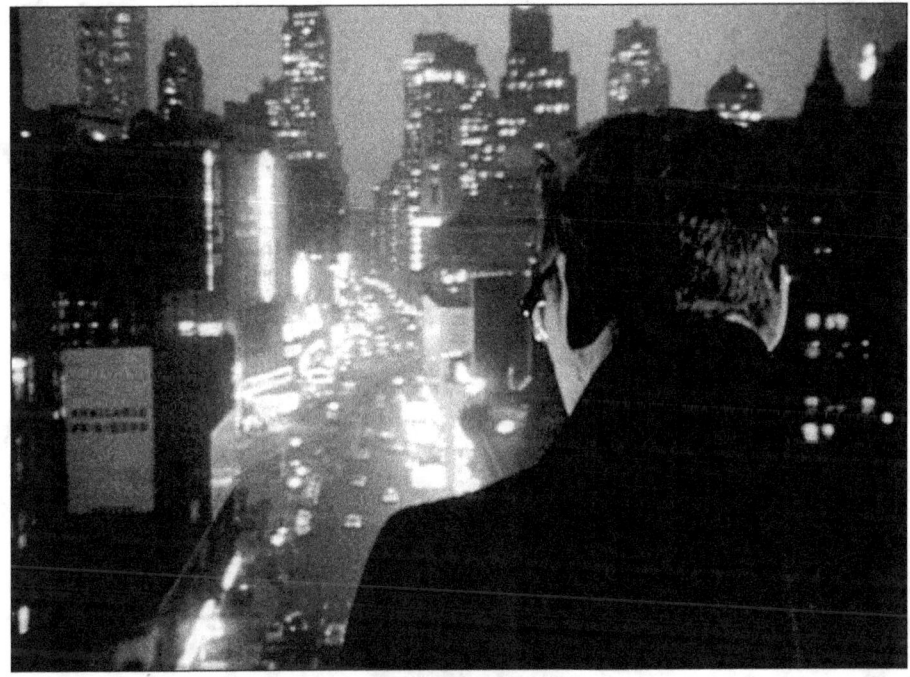

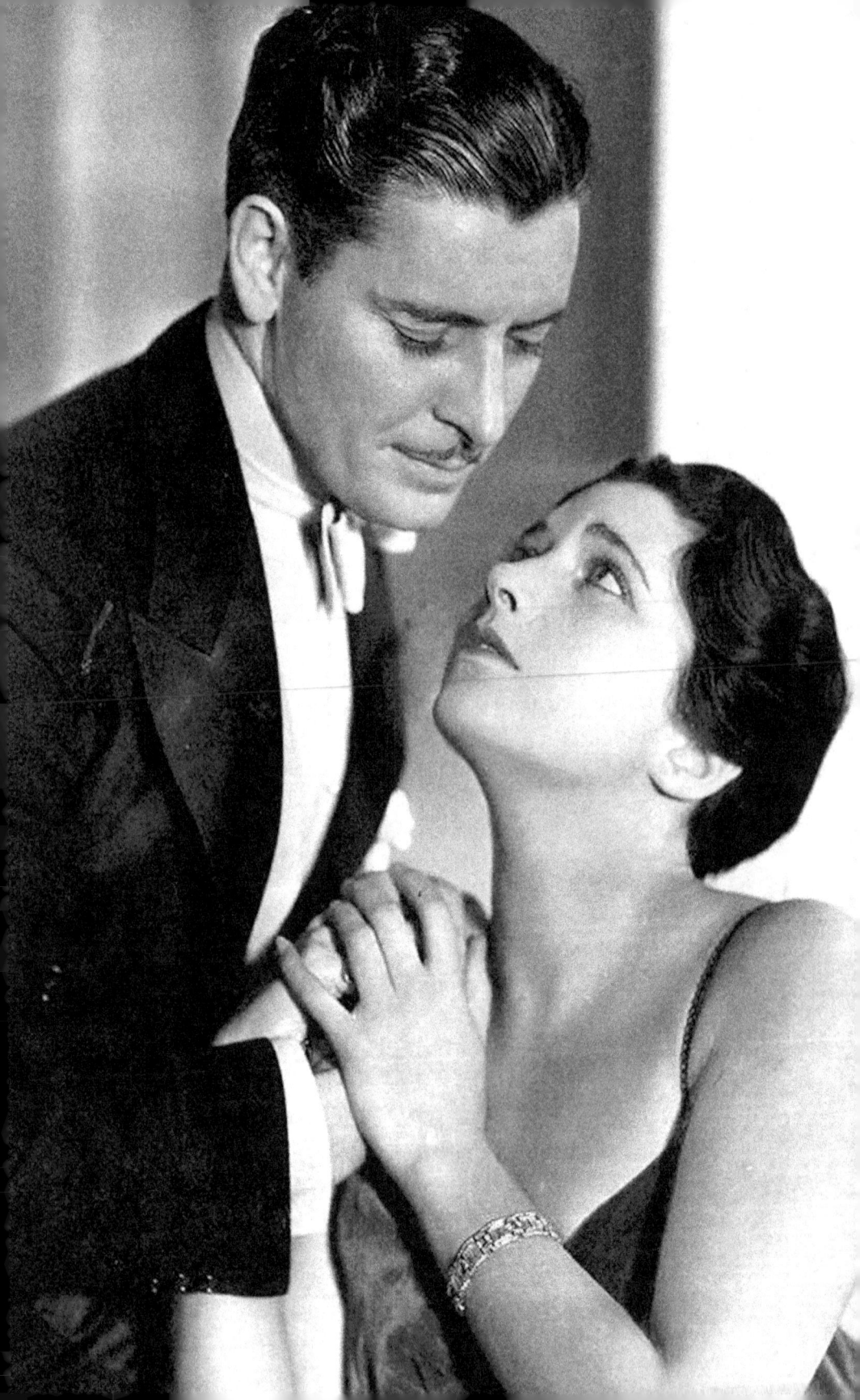

02 GENTLEMEN AND PLAYERS

A.J. Raffles, decadent dandies, and the birth of the gentleman thief

Ernest William Hornung had a large shadow with which to contend as part of his chosen profession as a writer of crime fiction. His brother-in-law was Arthur Conan Doyle, creator of Sherlock Holmes, a character that struck such a chord with society that it reverberates to this day. Hornung, known as Willie to his friends and family and as E.W. to the rest of the world, was an enthusiastic but untalented cricket player plagued by persistent ill health. His family sent him from England to Australia in hopes that the warmer, drier climate would fortify his dubious constitution. The health benefits of working in an isolated corner of the Outback remain up for debate, but what Hornung did discover out there was a talent for writing. There was precious little else to do. He began contributing articles to a weekly magazine and, upon his return to England in 1886, pursued a career as a journalist at a time when the top story was a series of murders in the Whitechapel district of London perpetrated by a shadowy killer known as Jack the Ripper. Cutting his journalistic teeth in this gruesome time instilled in young Hornung an interest in criminal psychology.

In 1890, his first novel, *A Bride from the Bush*, was serialized in *Cornhill* magazine and met with critical and popular success. In 1891, he joined a cricket club called the Idlers, among whose members was Arthur Conan Doyle, who had skyrocketed to international fame in 1887 with the publication of *A Study in Scarlet*, the first story to feature consulting detective Sherlock Holmes and his trusted assistant, Dr. John Watson. In Doyle, Hornung found a kindred spirit interested in the workings of the criminal mind. He also found Doyle's sister, Constance Aimée Monica Doyle.

Hornung wrote several more novels, each of them inspired by his time in Australia and one, 1896's *The Rogue's March*, which integrated his growing interest in crime. Unlike his soon-to-be brother-in-law, however, Hornung was more interested in criminals than detectives. In 1898, he wrote the first of the short stories that would become his legacy. It introduced a character that, if not quite as beloved as Sherlock Holmes, was nevertheless a much-admired contribution to the canon of crime fiction: A.J. Raffles, the wellspring from which the concept of the "gentleman thief" flows. Raffles and his slightly-dense sidekick, Harry "Bunny" Manders, debuted in the short story "The Chains of Crime," published in June of 1898 under the title "The Ides of March." If there was any suspicion that Hornung would follow in the footsteps of Arthur Conan Doyle, they were quickly put to rest. Raffles and Bunny were no Holmes and Watson. Raffles would have been more at home in the company of smirking society cads like P.J. Wodehouse's Bertie Wooster than he would have Sherlock Holmes.

Raffles was reportedly based on an number of Hornung's friends and associates: George Cecil Ives, a criminologist and avid cricketer who in real life shared the same address as Raffles; Oscar Wilde, with whom Hornung was friends; and Wilde's companion, Lord Alfred Douglas. Douglas lent an additional dynamic to the relationship between Raffles and Bunny, though initially there's not much in the way of homoerotic subtext. Well, unless you count the gushing praise Bunny heaps on Raffles' skill at handling bats and balls. It's notable that Raffles exists in a world almost totally devoid of women (except as marks). He resides in an all-male boarding house, is a member of all-male social clubs, plays on an all-male cricket team, and associates almost entirely with men. His only relationship of significance is Bunny, whose schoolboy nickname "feminizes" him and renders Bunny, in a way, the abused girlfriend of the duo. Homoerotic undertones mounted as the series progressed, however, culminating in a story set aboard a steamer and in which Bunny achieves an almost camp level of jealousy when Raffles entertains the attentions of a young woman.

Hornung wrote anther six Raffles story in quick succession. They were compiled into an omnibus called *The Amateur Cracksman*, released in 1899. "The Ides of March" wastes no time plunging the reader into the world of Raffles and Bunny, from whose point of view the stories are told. It begins with Bunny suffering an unlucky night of gambling that has left him with a debt he is unable to pay. Short of suicide, the only solution Bunny can think of is to throw himself at the mercy of A.J. Raffles, an old school chum Bunny has not seen for years. Bunny expects that showing up out of the blue, hat in hand, will not engender much help from Raffles, but to Bunny's surprise, Raffles is enthusiastic about helping. There is, however, one problem: Raffles is as broke as Bunny.

Before depression can set in, Raffles pitches Bunny a solution that will take care of their financial straits. All they need to do is visit a casual acquaintance, a jeweler who might not be home when they call upon him at 2 A.M., and who might not actually *know* Raffles, and who might have a series of security measures Raffles will have to crack. Bunny wavers between stupid obliviousness to the fact that they are committing a crime and suspicion, but is willing to go along.

Hornung's prose is direct and journalistic, but it's effective at drawing you, like Bunny, into the world of the enthusiastic, at times overbearing, cricketer and amateur burglar. There's a breezy collegiate atmosphere to the story, a spring in its step that makes "The Ides of March" a good deal of fun. The sequel, "A Costume Piece," picks up shortly thereafter, with Raffles and Bunny living a life of luxury off the ill-gotten proceeds of their burglary. Bunny is happy to chalk up their escapade as a one-time deal, but Raffles is anxious to get on with a new bit of rapscallionry—of course with only the *noblest* of intentions.

While attending a party, Raffles is subjected to the endless bragging of a coarse lout shoving his magnificent diamonds in everyone's face while waving around a gun. Offended as a gentleman and thief, Raffles thinks he and Bunny have a moral obligation to put this jack-ass in his place by stealing those magnificent diamonds. Bunny, less enthused about returning to a life of crime, goes along regardless. "A Costume Piece" introduces another aspect of Raffles illicit career: He is revealed, when casing diamond owner Rosenthal's mansion, to be a master of disguise with a secret hideout (granted, it's just a studio apartment he rents under the guise of being a struggling artist). Once again, the story is short and to the point, more of a comedy of errors this time than the last, as the well-armed Rosenthal and his brutish enforcer Purvis the Pugilist provide a substantially greater challenge to Raffles than an empty jewelry store. It reminds you, over the course of its action, that Raffles is, after all, an *amateur* cracksman.

In "Gentlemen and Players," the third in the series, Raffles leans on his renown as a cricketer to gain access to a high society party, and in doing so introduces yet another dimension to the stories. Raffles and Bunny are reluctant criminals (well, Bunny is; Raffles pays lip service to reluctance, but his first solution for any problem is, to paraphrase *Repo Man*, to "go do some crimes") because they've found themselves part of a society they can't afford to be part of. They must turn to brigandry to survive, as they've been educated in a way that means just stepping away to pursue more modest lives is unthinkable; in fact, it never even occurs to them.

Raffles' hold on high society is tenuous, dependent upon his fame as a sportsman. He's aware that he is a pretender, that this is just another one of his disguises. As Raffles says to Bunny, "We're *in* Society but not *of* it." Class struggle as motivation (or justification) for Raffles' mischief is nowhere more apparent in "Gentlemen and Players" then when Raffles states bluntly that it's OK to rob Lord and Lady Amersteth because the nobleman treats Raffles like a servant to perform for the betters in society, and because the Amersteths "can afford it." As it was with Rosenthal, Raffles feels honor bound to "punish" the bragging, condescending rich. Criticizing the class structure of England, not to mention making his leads criminals, didn't enamor Hornung to critics. Even Doyle expressed misgivings about glorifying antisocial behavior. "I think there are few finer examples of short-story writing in our language than these," he once wrote, "though I confess I think they are rather dangerous in their suggestion. I told him so before he put pen to paper, and the result has, I fear, borne me out. You must not make the criminal a hero."

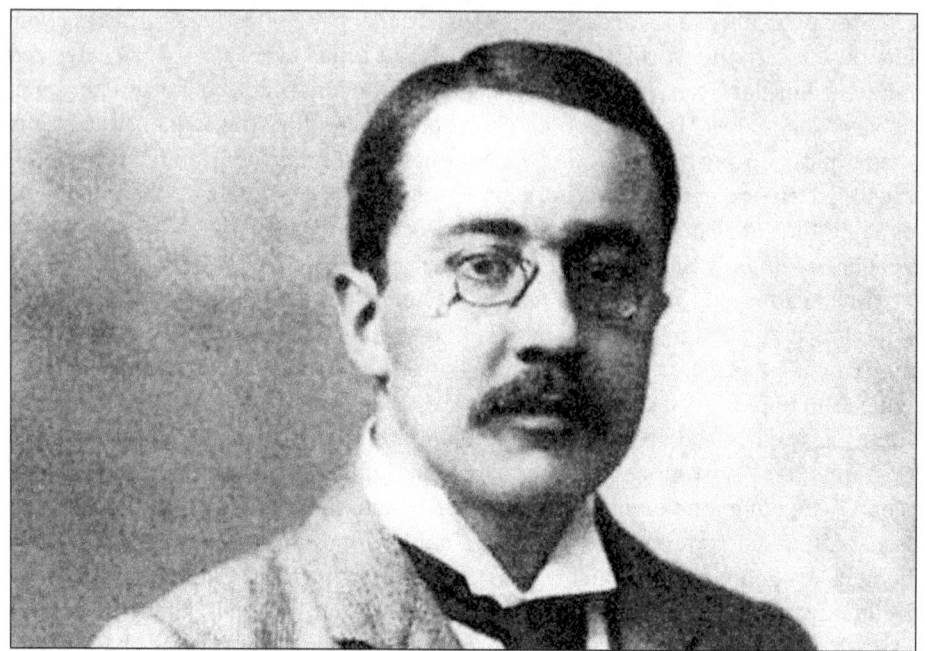

CRIMINAL MASTERMIND: *Raffles creator E.W. Hornung*

Ironically, one would be hard-pressed to find a series of stories as squeaky-clean as *Raffles*. George Orwell observed in his essay *Raffles and Miss Blanding*, "Though the stories are convincing in their physical detail, they contain very little sensationalism—very few corpses, hardly any blood, no sex crimes, no sadism, no perversions of any kind." Readers, like Orwell, disagreed in large numbers with Doyle and other critics, turning Raffles into the second-most popular character in British crime fiction—after Sherlock Holmes, of course. And like Holmes, Raffles inspired dozens of similar stories and characters, some of whom would take that criminal streak to greater extremes.

"Gentlemen and Players" also brings Raffles' narcissism into the forefront. The story marks the third time Raffles has pressured Bunny into a crime knowing full well the other man is uncomfortable with such things. It is the first and most notable crack in the cracksman's polished veneer. In the story's opening, Bunny marvels that Raffles is such an accomplished cricketer but has no interest in following the sport of cricket. He doesn't keep track of teams and doesn't show any interest in the game unless he's playing in it. A dark streak in Raffles begins to emerge. Even when Bunny takes a stand and calls burgling from people who have invited you over "vulgar," Raffles persists, knowing that in the end Bunny will follow his lead, no matter what nefarious scheme it entails.

In the case of this particular crime, Raffles and Bunny are once again put to a more difficult test than they expected. A couple of professional thieves from London show up with the same crime in mind and bring, in their wake, Scotland Yard inspector Mackenzie, who has been tailing them. With cops and professional crooks on the scene, and with Lord Amersteth alert to the danger his valuables are in, what chance do a couple of amateurs have?

The next two stories, "Le Premier Pas" and "Wilful Murder," paint an even darker portrait of the seemingly playful cracksman. In "Le Premier Pas," being something of an origin story, Raffles recounts to Bunny how he came to indulge in a secret life of crime. It's hardly flattering, with Raffles callously justifying a bank heist to cover a debt incurred as a result of his own irresponsibility. He even, upon discovering a possible distant relative, capitalizes upon the relative's apparent murder by highwaymen. At no point does Raffles feel remorse, the death of this man being nothing more than first an inconvenience, and then an opportunity. Nor does Raffles feel guilty for robbing the bank or for conning the men in charge, men who are friendly and accommodating to Raffles at every step.

In "Wilful Murder," Raffles, afraid that his identity has been discovered by the local fence who will blackmail him, casually but seriously tells Bunny it's time to graduate from burglary to murder. Bunny is aghast but, as always, goes along with the domineering Raffles, who sees no problem with murdering the fence since the guy is a jerk anyway. Although Raffles never descends into the realm of outright villainy *a la* later antiheroes such as Fantômas, it is nevertheless a jarring shift from playful fun perpetrated by a couple of lads to something more ominous. Each step further into the shadows is easy for Raffles to justify, and while Bunny is hesitant, he always acquiesces in the end. Raffles only regret in pressuring Bunny comes not from moral conflict, but simply because he's afraid Bunny might fold under pressure.

SCOFFLAW

- 1 ½ oz Rye Whiskey
- 1 oz Dry Vermouth
- ¾ oz Fresh Lemon Juice
- ¾ oz Grenadine

Add all ingredients to a shaker with ice. Shake well. Strain into a chilled cocktail glass. Garnish with a lemon twist. Note: with that much Grenadine, be sure to get a good one.

••••••••••••••••••••••••

SATAN'S WHISKERS

- ½ oz Dry Gin
- ½ oz Dry Vermouth
- ½ oz Sweet Vermouth
- ½ oz Fresh Orange Juice
- 2 tsp Orange Curaçao
- 1 tsp Orange Bitters

Add all ingredients to a shaker with ice. Shake well. Strain into a chilled cocktail glass. Garnish with an orange twist. If you prefer, use Grand Marnier in place of orange curaçao.

••••••••••••••••••••••••

PEGU CLUB

- 2 oz Dry Gin
- ¾ oz Orange Curaçao
- ½ oz Fresh lime juice
- 1 dash Orange bitters
- 1 dash Angostura bitters

Add all ingredients to a shaker. Fill with ice. Shake well. Strain into a chilled cocktail glass.

••••••••••••••••••••••••

MILLIONAIRE

- 1 ½ oz Dark Rum
- ¾ oz Sloe Gin
- ¾ oz Apricot Brandy
- Juice of One Fresh Lime

Add all ingredients to a shaker filled with ice. Shake well. Strain into a chilled cocktail glass. Garnish with a lime wedge.

RICKEY

- ½ oz Fresh Lime Juice
- 2 oz Dry Gin
- 4 oz Club Soda

Squeeze lime juice into a Collins glass. Add ice. Add gin. Fill with club soda. Garnish with a lime wedge. If you add 4 dashes of grenadine before adding the soda, you have a Savoy Hotel style Rickey.

AVIATION

- 2 oz Dry Gin
- ½ oz Maraschino Liqueur
- ¼ oz Crème de Violette
- ¾ oz Fresh Lemon Juice

Add all ingredients to a shaker. Fill with ice. Shake well. Strain into a chilled cocktail glass. Garnish with a brandied cherry.

CORPSE REVIVER NO. 1

- 1 oz Calvados
- 1 oz Cognac
- ½ oz Sweet Italian Vermouth

Add all ingredients to a shaker. Fill with ice. Shake well. Strain into a chilled cocktail glass. Garnish with an orange peel.

CORPSE REVIVER NO. 2

- 1 oz Dry Gin
- 1 oz Cointreau
- 1 oz Lillet Blanc
- 1 oz Fresh Lemon Juice
- 1-3 drops Pernod

Add all ingredients to a shaker. Fill with ice. Shake well. Strain into a chilled cocktail glass. Garnish with an orange peel.

Of course, Raffles always expresses this in a way that encourages and insults Bunny in one go. In "The Return Match," Bunny mentions Raffles' "little laugh of light-hearted mastery" and describes the cracksman's powers of influence by stating, "there was never anybody in the world so irresistible as Raffles when his mind was made up." Although never described in explicitly menacing terms, Raffles' powers of persuasion place him alongside some of the more threatening criminals that followed in his wake, most notably Fritz Lang's mad mastermind, Dr. Mabuse. Raffles may be charming and likable, but he wields those attributes as weapons. In this regard, he is less like his inspiration, Sherlock Holmes, and more like the sort of anti-hero one would find in the *fin-de-siecle* writing of the Decadence movement, which is probably no accident, given Hornung's friendship with Oscar Wilde.

The literary movement known as Decadence arose in Paris during the 1870s and came to fruition in the 1880s-'90s. The era preceding the turn of the century was one of great change that created a "petty *bourgeois*" the Decadents claimed represented the death of society, a sentiment expressed many times by Raffles. Direct descendants of the dandy Charles Baudelaire, who can be grouped among the men he inspired, the Decadents cultivated a sarcastic disdain for the vulgar commercialism and mundane mainstream which had consumed society. They stood in defiance of a wave of mass consumerism they thought drained the world of meaning and, in the world of art, sacrificed creativity in favor of "content."

In opposition to this shift toward the mass-produced and mass consumed, Decadents explored aspects of human appetite deemed taboo, immoral, and transgressive. Drugs, mysticism and the occult, madness, and a whole range of unwholesome sexual experiences were the obsessions of the Decadents, who often set their stories in disreputable locations such as brothels, drug dens, shabby hotels, and crumbling old estates.

Although he objected to Hornung's perceived glorification of crime, Doyle didn't entirely escape the influence of Decadence, however much a paragon of law and order he might have thought Sherlock Holmes to be. Holmes' cocaine habit, though less scandalous then than it is now, places the detective in the realm of a minor decadent dabbling in drugs. However, it's the *why* of Holmes' drug use that makes him more of a Decadent. He was too smart to find much to engage him in the mundane world. If he didn't have a masterful crime to solve, the only way he could salve his over-active mind was with "the needle."

Raffles might not have dabbled in the Occult, or with drugs, and his relationship with Bunny might only hint at homosexuality (and then, primarily, on the part of Bunny, who fawns over Raffles and seems a slave to the man's will), but in pursuing a life of crime, justified by disgust with *haute* society, Raffles fulfills the Decadent requirement of tweaking one's nose at the acceptable. In "The Return Match," Raffles professes his admiration for a criminal who escapes from prison. Devoid of any moral judgment regarding the criminal's misdeeds, Raffles perceives it as nothing more than a sporting flight and a middle finger in the direction of polite society. When the two meet, there's a spirit of comradeship between them that Raffles shares with no one else, not even Bunny, at least until Raffles starts talking down to the guy. Raffles may have it in for polite society, but he's not above declaring himself the better of the working-class man at the same time. Crawshay the criminal, the same thief with whom Raffles matched wits in "Gentlemen and Players", naturally appreciates Raffles' snobbery and is further endeared to the junior criminal. In at least one regard, Raffles is correct in his assaying of the other man. As a member of society, even if only because he's a sportsman, Raffles is afforded access, freedom of movement, and a lack of suspicion the rough-hewn Crawshay will never enjoy.

In the same story, Raffles reveals to Bunny that he plans most of his crimes while sitting in a church. So, perhaps Raffles doesn't swear his soul to the Occult, but surely plotting crimes in a church constitutes at least a *mild* desecration of a Christian institution.

Along with a rejection of the concept of taboo and a propensity for wallowing in the perversion polite society condemned (but often lusted for), the Decadents believed progress was an illusion, that man was as miserable as ever, and all progress had done was make everything more boring. They called it "the banalization of the sacred mysteries." Few things embodied this progress quite like Emile Zola's Naturalism, an artistic movement many Decadents considered *anathema*. They practiced experimental writing styles to contrast what they regarded as the soulless "reportage" style championed by Naturalism. Theirs was "literature of exhaustion," written by authors and populated by characters who were physically and mentally exhausted by popular culture; who were, quite simply, *bored* by what society deemed appropriate and so sought "*nouveau frissions*," thrills derived from the taboo.

Often suffering from some malady either real or imagined (hypochondria was practically *de rigueur* for the aspiring Decadent, and Raffles at the very least suffers from narcissism and a persecution complex), both authors and characters indulged cerebral and sensual thrills. The rise of these inward-looking men—and they were almost always men—corresponded to the ascension of Freud, psychoanalysis, and the psychological sciences. Given the preoccupation so often shown in the Decadent canon with madness, perversion, and grotesqueness, it's no wonder that Decadence would have substantial influence on horror during the era of German Expressionism (to say nothing of sleazy Eurocult films from the 1970s, which were often based on the works of Decadent writers, if only loosely). It's also no mystery how Edgar Allan Poe, who lived in a country where the Decadent movement never gained purchase, found himself admired by so many writers of the Decadent school. Roderick Usher in *The Fall of the House of Usher* is the very model of a Decadent dandy with his isolation, hatred of loud noises and crowds, mental instability, and fabulous dressing gowns.

Decadence found acolytes outside of Paris, primarily in Russia and Britain though in each case Decadence was tailored to the predilections of different national identities. Italy gave rise to one of the most acclaimed of Decadents, Gabriele D'Annunzio, who among other things assembled his own private army and seized a small Italian town which he then declared an independent nation.

In later Raffles stories, the cricketer-criminal is revealed, like D'Annunzio, to possess a patriotic streak when he enlists fight in the Boer War. One can question the purity of Raffles' patriotic action as something perhaps less inspired by allegiance to King and Country and having more to do with Raffles' sense that he should punish himself for his transgressions, that he deserves to suffer for his sins (or at least evade their consequences) even as he continues to indulge them. But before he could seek redemption, Raffles had to die.

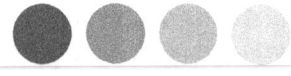

"Again I see him, leaning back in one of the luxurious chairs with which his room was furnished. I see his indolent, athletic figure; his pale, sharp, clean-shaven features; his curly black hair; his strong, unscrupulous mouth. And again I feel the clear beam of his wonderful eye, cold and luminous as a star, shining."

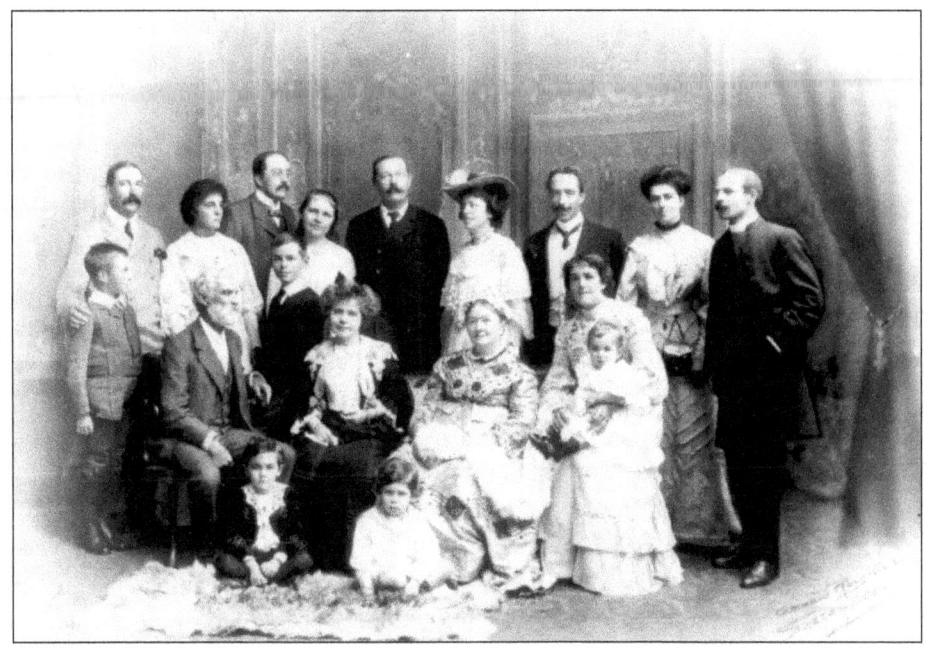

ALL IN THE FAMILY: E.W. Hornung, second from left in the back, with Arthur Conan Doyle and family.

Death and Rebirth

Hornung's first collection of short stories wraps with "Nine Points of the Law," "The Return Match," and "The Gift of the Emperor," the last one confronting Raffles with his own personal Reichenbach Falls. "Nine Points of the Law" is a return to the breezier, comedic capers that came before "Wilful Murder." Raffles and Bunny are hired to steal a priceless painting from a boorish lout who acquired it through suspicious means. True to form, the mark is an obnoxious member of high society for whom money can't buy taste. Raffles thinks it his duty to take the man down a peg or two. Alas, it's another comedy of errors proving once again that, for all their daring and their planning, Raffles and Bunny aren't actually a very good team. It's also another example of Raffles endlessly criticizing Bunny while seeming to compliment the faithful buffoon. Far from seeking to subtly undermine Bunny's self-confidence, however, Raffles considers his backhanded comments to be genuinely inspiring. If Raffles was a boyfriend, he would be the kind who doles out "compliments" like "You're attractive for someone of your weight."

The last story, "The Gift of the Emperor," was for A.J. Raffles what "The Final Problem" was for Sherlock Holmes. Doyle, famously tired of writing Holmes stories, decided to kill the detective. Locked in mortal combat with his nemesis Moriarty, both men plummet over a waterfall to their apparent deaths. For Doyle, it was a celebratory send-off for his creation, a blaze-of-glory duel to the death in which Holmes sacrifices himself while ridding the world of the most diabolical criminal mind it had ever produced. Readers, however, were not as enthusiastic about putting Holmes in a watery grave. Even Doyle's mother was against the idea. In

1891, Doyle wrote to her and confessed, "I think of slaying Holmes...and winding him up for good and all. He takes my mind from better things." His mother replied, "You won't! You can't! You mustn't!"

But he did, in December of 1893. The world sided with Doyle's mother. In 1901, Doyle caved to near-constant public pressure, writing one of the most famous Holmes adventures, *The Hound of the Baskervilles*, set before the events of "The Final Problem." In 1903, he published "The Adventure of the Empty House," a Sherlock Holmes story that bent to the will of the public even further, confirming that Holmes had narrowly avoided death and was back in action. Sherlock Holmes went on to another 56 short stories and four more novels, the final story being published in 1927. Doyle died in 1930, but even the death of his creator could not stop Sherlock Holmes, who continued to live on in film, television, stage plays, and stories written by others.

Death knell though "The Gift of the Emperor" appeared to be for Raffles, there was little of melancholy or world-weariness or the sense of impending apocalypse that infused Holmes' final act. Instead, the story has an air of camp absurdity as Raffles contrives to rob a cartoonish German military courier while Bunny jealously fumes over the fact that part of Raffles' hopelessly convoluted scheme involves flirting with a pretty young woman. This is the first story in which a woman other than a batty old society dowager has played a role in their lives, and Bunny is not the least bit happy about it. He pouts constantly about the fact that Raffles is spending all his time with *her* and not paying enough attention to *him*. He undercuts and insults her at every opportunity, commenting cattily on everything from her clothes to her intellect to her voice. It is the most overt evidence so far that Bunny harbors unrequited love for Raffles. Raffles, for his part, picks up on it and spends his time twisting the knife.

The situation also introduces one of the more dreadful traits common in writing of the Decadence period: misogyny. Though they did not create the *femme fatale*, the Decadents certainly perfected the modern version of it, which would manifest in cinema as the man-eating "vamp," the woman who through her sexual desires and allure brings a man to destruction, often knowingly and with considerable relish. In the *fin-de-siecle* writing of the Decadents, one finds the same fear of the "New Woman" as would surface in the vamps of the silent film era. The source of the vitriol aimed at women differs from author to author. For some, it came from bitter and disastrous romantic relationships and marriages (that old chestnut). For others, it was the age-old reaction to an oppressed group demanding the liberties and opportunities previously afforded only to an elite (that "elite" almost always being white men). Literature is replete with examples of men blaming their weakness and shortcomings on women. "She tempted me. She ridiculed me. She did not give me what I feel I am owed, and so she deserves abuse and hate." At no point does the man consider the fault may be his own or that the woman doesn't owe him anything. Perhaps ironically, the most memorable *femme fatale* of the silent cinema era, Louise Brooks' Lulu in *Pandora's Box*, is a subversion of the very thing she is superficially meant to be. That film examines the male tendency to demand things from a woman while blaming that woman every time something goes wrong. As Marlene Dietrich sings in "Falling In Love Again," the signature song in *The Blue Angel*, another subversive femme fatale classic: "Men cluster to me like moths around a flame; And if their wings burn, I know I'm not to blame."

Although by no means excusable, this portrayal of women in many of the key Decadent texts contains a complexity beyond the simple rejection of the female and enshrinement of male privilege. Just as there was a "male gaze," so too was there a "dandy gaze," and the dandy gaze tended to regard everything with a cold, detached contempt. Sometimes, the greater criticism isn't aimed at women so much as it is at the banality and hypocrisy of monogamous domestic life. Unfairly, women are identified as the source of this dreariness because they demand marriage and family. Which is why not all women in Decadent writing are treated with the same contempt as "bourgeois breeders." Women who have embraced the counter-culture, the same perversions and philosophies as the Decadents generally fare better. Women with "careers of vice: prostitutes, polymorphs, nymphomaniacs, androgynes, herma-phrodites..." are usually regarded more favorably. These types serve as practically a blueprint for the underground culture in the city that became the embodiment of Decadence, even more so than Paris: Weimar-era Berlin.

With women blamed for heartbreak and/or the tedium of marriage and children, it's hardly a shock that Decadence was, by and large, a boys' club, even if those boys were prone to clasp a lavender-scented handkerchief between pale, slender fingers trembling with frailty. The rare exception to this "no girls allowed" mentality was Marguerite Vallette-Eymery, known by the pen name Rachilde. Although she wrote Decadent more than lived it (she was, in reality, married to a publisher and lived a normal, quiet life), when she wrote she made waves. Novels like *Nono*, *La Marquise de Sade*, and *The Juggler* explore lesbianism, cross-dressing, dominance, and polyamory. Rachilde, sort of a proto-Colette or Anaïs Nin and dubbed "Mademoiselle Baudelaire" by Maurice Barres and "a distinguished pornographer" by Jules Barbey d'Aurevilly, affords one the opportunity to re-examine the feminine as presented in Decadent writing. Or, at the very least, she provides a break from male-dominated woman-bashing. Like Colette, Rachilde celebrates female "perversity" with the same gusto as her male counterparts. Prostitutes, cross-dressers, lesbians, and adulteresses were not, in her hands, tragic figures to be pitied or redeemed. They were to be celebrated, reclaiming female sexuality and wielding it for their own enjoyment rather than as something to satisfy (or alienate) a man.

Few people indulged the Decadent preference for the lurid and grotesque quite as boldly as Rachilde, but she was not at all alone in probing and embracing these dark avenues. Catulle Mendès' *Zo'har* was a tale of incest featuring a virile woman and an impotent man, and his *Mephistophela* indulges a wide range of taboos, including lesbian incest and drugs. Jean Lorrain was friends with Oscar Wilde and introduced the British writer to Decadence, challenged Marcel Proust to a duel (Lorraine was openly gay and accused Proust of being in the closet), and garnered personal infamy with works like *Sonyeuse*, *Buveurs d'ames*, and *Monsieur de Phocas*. French Decadence produced a number of writers who garnered acclaim and condemnation, but two works stand above all others as the pillars of French Decadence: Baudelaire's *Fleur du Mal* (*Flowers of Evil*), published in 1857, and Joris-Karl Huysmans' *À rebours* (*Against Nature*), published in 1884.

Bunny's attitude toward any woman seeking to catch Raffles' eye is pure, acidic jealousy as he cast his dandy gaze in their direction and finds them all wanting. As for Raffles, though later stories reveal some of his amorous pursuits, he remains the purest form of Decadent; the only true love in Raffles life is Raffles.

Hoping for better luck than Doyle, E.W. Hornung concluded *The Amateur Cracksman* by sending Raffles plunging to a watery death—though in the case of Raffles, ever the gentleman, it was a graceful swan dive off the deck of a cruise ship. Granted a glorious and thoroughly sportsmanlike exit from this mortal coil, Raffles leaves poor Bunny in the lurch. The duo have been exposed. They are at long last found out and branded criminals, never again to be entertained by the polite society upon which they had clandestinely preyed for so long. But where Raffles meets his doom with a wink and a leap, Bunny is hauled off in irons, a common thief bound for a stint in prison. Ironically, the book that began with Raffles saving Bunny by preventing his suicide ends with Raffles dooming Bunny by committing his own suicide. It's a perfectly inconsiderate and unfair turn of events, and perfectly in keeping with how Raffles has manipulated Bunny throughout the stories.

Unsurprisingly, readers weren't any more thrilled with Raffles bidding his mortal coil *adieu* than they had been with Holmes. Critics who lambasted Hornung for glamorizing crime must have extracted some satisfaction in seeing that, finally, crime does not pay. That is, they would have been if A.J. Raffles had stayed dead. In 1901, the same year Doyle wrote *The Hound of the Baskervilles*, Hornung also caved to popular demand and published *The Black Mask*, a second collection of Raffles stories that, to the surprise of no one but Bunny Manders, reveals Raffles to be alive if not exactly well.

The tone of the stories in *The Black Mask* is darker than those in *The Amateur Cracksman*. Even when Raffles was plotting a "wilful murder," there was a spirit of consequence-free adventure to the earlier stories. Not so for the second go-round. Bunny is a disgraced ex-con stitching together a hardscrabble life as a poet and essayist on the need for prison reform. He has little money, no friends, and leaps at the opportunity to better his station slightly when a relative takes pity on him and sets him up with a job. It's a position below the honor of a gentleman, but Bunny is no longer a gentleman. He agrees to become a nurse for a cantankerous old eccentric. Obviously, that eccentric turns out to be A.J. Raffles in disguise. Whatever happened to Raffles after his exit from the boat has left him partially broken, psychologically haunted, and physically diminished, including prematurely white hair. Although his "on death's door" act is partially an exaggeration, Raffles is not a healthy man.

No sooner are Bunny and Raffles reunited than they are up to their old tricks, with about the same rate of success. They can't call themselves *amateurs*; crime is their only profession, and they've been at it a long time. But they're still not very *good* at it. Raffles bungles most of the jobs. Bunny is still dense—something Raffles points out, "lovingly," at every opportunity. He shows no remorse at having left his friend behind and no interest in Bunny's time in prison. When Raffles tells Bunny what happened after he jumped off the ship, it's full of romance and tragedy on the scale of a Puccini opera, the sort of adventure most men dream about but is presented to Bunny to make him realize how lucky he was to simply go to prison. Raffles' time away does have one negative consequence, however. He has managed to get on the vendetta end of the Camorra, Naples' version of the Sicilian Mafia.

The Black Mask is richer, more complex, and more satisfying than *The Amateur Cracksman*. The stakes are higher. The fun and games are a thing of the past. Raffles' ability to justify murder or worm his way out of feeling responsible for deaths, has grown. The two move through London under a perpetual cloud of hunger and paranoia, forever wary that the police might get on to them or the Camorra might track them down. The collection wraps with "The Knees of the Gods," in which Raffles and Bunny, bored stiff in a London suburb, are swept up in a wave of patriotism and enlist to fight in the Boer War. Their adventure in South Africa is harrowing. Bunny is left with a permanent limp and a decidedly unromantic opinion about the nobility of war wounds. Raffles fares worse, his past having caught up with him once again and his only course of action, as he sees it, being a heroic, suicidal exit from the earthly stage.

A third collection of Raffles stories, *A Thief in the Night*, was published in 1904 despite the fact that, once again, Raffles had died. Most of the stories are set at periods before the final curtain of "The Knee of the Gods." Hornung wrote one more Raffles adventure after that, the novel *Mr. Justice Raffles*, in 1909. By then critics, readers, and even Hornung himself admitted that there was no longer any sport in the game. Raffles may be a narcissist. He may be passively-aggressively abusive toward Bunny. And he and Bunny are, for the most part, pretty bad at stealing things. But the stories are enjoyable, each one short enough to read in less time than it takes to finish a snifter of brandy. They set the standard for the coming deluge of gentlemen thieves, some of whom seized on the light-hearted "What if Bertie Wooster was a cat burglar" breeziness of the stores (granted, P.G. Wodehouse didn't write his first "Jeeves & Wooster" story until 1915) while others delved much deeper into the darker areas that were hinted at from time to time.

Hornung passed away in March 1921, having lived long enough to see his enduring creation brought to life in the new medium of motion pictures. A silent feature, *Raffles, the Amateur Cracksman* was released in 1917.

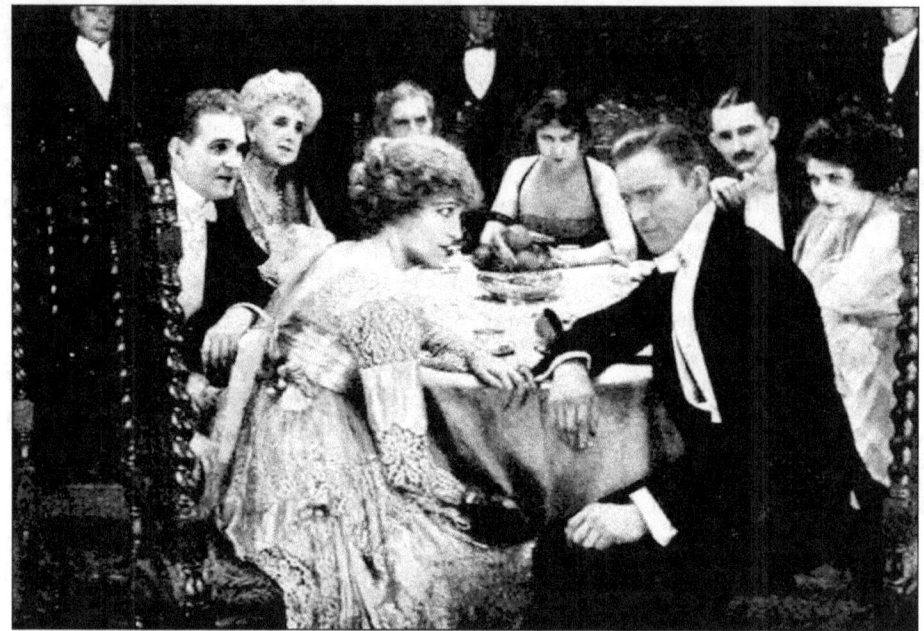

RAFFLES ON THE SCREEN—*John Barrymore in 1917's Raffles, The Amateur Cracksman*

First Crack

The rise of A.J. Raffles, gentleman thief, was perfectly timed to take advantage of the rise of motion pictures. Still fresh in the memory of readers, Raffles made his earliest known screen debut in 1905. Although no print of this film exists, one can safely assume, based on its vintage, that it's relatively short and simple in construction. The history of *Raffles* films in the 1910s is murky, bizarre, and from the vantage point of someone with little information beyond a title and release date, frequently amusing. For example, there is a Danish Sherlock Holmes film from 1908 in which a character named Raffles reportedly appears (despite the close relation of their respective creators, Raffles and Holmes never crossed paths in any story written by Doyle or Hornung). There are several shorts in a series called *Pimple*, in which Raffles, played by Joe Evans, is listed as appearing alongside the unfortunately-named Pimple, though how sanctioned those appearances were is suspect. There's also a *Baffles* series from around the same time starring Wilfred Lucas. *The Burglar and the Lady*, a play written by Langdon McCormick in 1905, again pitted Raffles against Sherlock Holmes and was adapted into a film 1914, but McCormick didn't bother to secure the actual rights to use Holmes or Raffles.

Cutting through the clutter of comedic shorts, spoofs, and unsanctioned appropriations, the first true *Raffles* film was released in 1917. Like subsequent Raffles films, it was based on the stories "The Ides of March" and "Gentlemen and Players" which had been adapted into a stage play by Eugene W. Presbrey in 1910. The 1917 film stars an actor who would become one of the most iconic American actors of the golden age.

Before he was the Great Profile, before he was the Beloved Rogue, before he was the man who typified the virtues and vices of Old Hollywood, John Barrymore was just another actor struggling to emerge from the shadow of famous parents. His father was acclaimed stage actor Maurice Barrymore, who, along with friend and fellow actor Ben Porter, was once shot by a notorious gunman during a game of cards. Porter was killed; Maurice was shot in the chest but survived. John was the youngest of three siblings, all of whom went on to great acclaim and established the Barrymore family as the preeminent American acting dynasty, one that endures still in the person of John's granddaughter, Drew, and is so complex and produced so many famous people that their family tree has its own Wikipedia page.

The three children of Maurice—Lionel, Ethel, and John—witnessed their father's collapse into madness (later attributed to syphilis). During a 1901 performance on the burgeoning New York vaudeville stage, Maurice stopped mid-monologue and launched into a tearful, hysterical antisemitic screed. He was committed to a sanitarium shortly thereafter, John being given the task of luring their mad but physically imposing father to Bellevue hospital. Maurice was later transferred to a sanitarium in Amityville on Long Island, where he remained until his death in 1905.

John's mother, Georgina Drew, was a member of another acting dynasty. Her parents and most of her siblings were actors of no small acclaim. She met Maurice while both of them were starring in a New York production of the play *Pique*. They married in 1876. As is often the case when actors marry actors, it was an unstable relationship. Maurice was frequently accused (and guilty) of extramarital dalliance. Georgina enjoyed success on-stage, but her career was cut tragically short when she contracted tuberculosis in 1891. She passed away in 1892, at the age of 36.

The death of Georgina—by most accounts, the more responsible party in the marriage—threw the family into disarray, even though young John had hardly known her (or his father) due to the incessant touring demanded of a professional actor. Financial difficulty led Lionel and Ethel into careers as professional actors, carrying on the family names, but John, being the youngest, rebelled against the idea of becoming an actor. In fact, he rebelled against pretty much anything, continuously enrolling in then dropping out of or being expelled from a steady procession of schools. He dreamed of becoming an artist, but the gravitational pull of acting was strong, and he occasionally found himself on stage, usually in bit parts, as a substitute for some actor or another alongside either Lionel or Ethel. These brief forays onto the stage rarely went well. In 1901, having attended more schools than one could reasonably be expected to remember, it was young John who bore the brunt of their father's descent into madness. That same year, he began a romance with a woman who was already doing time as the mistress of a married man. That woman, Evelyn Nesbit, was often tagged as "the most beautiful woman in the world" and is sometimes regarded as the first "supermodel." Her life, however, was even more outrageous and complicated than that of the Barrymore clan.

Nesbit, aged 14 or 16 at the time, was working as a model and chorus girl when she caught the eye of Stanford White, whose official career was architect but who excelled more as a sleazy rakehell. White, then 47, pursued the teenage girl, wooing her with lavish luncheons, displays of his material wealth, and, ultimately, getting her drunk on champagne and raping her in a room that was covered, floor-to-ceiling in mirrors. Times being what they were, his predatory behavior was, rather than criminal, the beginning of a relationship between Nesbit and the older, married man.

Coincidentally, it was at a party thrown by White that Barrymore met Nesbit, though it was not the first time he had seen her. By then, she was one of the most photographed and painted models in the country. John had seen her on stage in a revue titled *The Wild Rose* and became so smitten with her that he saw the show multiple times. In John, Evelyn found a friend who was, unlike White, her own age (more or less; John was 21 at the time) and to whom she could relate much more. She and John launched into a brief but passionate romance. When White and Evelyn's mother found out, they maneuvered to sideline the dashing young Barrymore, primarily because he was eking out a living as a struggling cartoonist at the time, and both White and Mrs. Nesbit felt Barrymore too impoverished for Evelyn.

John proposed, Evelyn said no, and at that point their relationship becomes a thing of bizarre conjecture, as shortly thereafter Evelyn traveled to Europe for an emergency medical procedure which was officially named as an appendectomy but which many suspected was an abortion. In fact, it would have been Nesbit's third "appendectomy."

Her life continued to get more bizarre. She was pursued by another fan of *The Wild Rose*, Harry Kendall Thaw, the mad scion of one of Philadelphia's richest industrialist families. After lavishing Evelyn anonymously with gifts, the man—with a long history of mental instability—revealed himself to Evelyn and ingratiated himself to White and Mrs. Nesbit. At least initially. Contriving to join Evelyn on her medical trip to Europe, Thaw pressured mother and daughter into a whirlwind tour of the continent which concentrated, in particular, on shrines to virginity and virgin martyrs. Female virginity, it turns out, was a keen obsession of Thaw's.

The intensity of the travel exhausted the recovering Evelyn and alienated her mother, who eventually threw her hands up and returned to America, leaving her daughter in the thrall of Thaw. While in Paris, Thaw's demand of marriage brought out the fact that Evelyn was not a virgin, and that she had been raped by White. Nesbit suffered a breakdown during her interrogation by Thaw, and Thaw became apoplectic, condemning both White and the mother who had so willingly pushed her daughter into dubious situations. But that was nothing compared to what he had in store for poor Evelyn Nesbit.

In a scene that seems like it could have come from one of John's more ghoulish film roles, Thaw spirited Evelyn away to Austria, where he imprisoned her in a castle and spent two weeks ranting at her, raping her, and subjecting her to whippings and other tortures. After the horrifying ordeal, Nesbit could find few people to whom she could confide. Other than John Barrymore, who her mother and Stanford White had conspired to exile from her life, she had only ever known older men and fellow performers. With no friends, with her mother not speaking to her, the bewildered young woman found herself once again pressed for marriage by the deranged Harry Kendall Thaw. Thaw, unbelievably, said he forgave Evelyn for the incident at the castle; that it was the influence of Stanford White that has caused her to turn out so wicked that he, Thaw, had to indulge in that bit of sordid insanity. Nesbit, utterly alone, her reputation tattered, and facing a life of poverty, married her tormentor in 1905. It didn't go well.

Thaw, descending further and further into madness and paranoia, constructed an elaborate conspiracy theory for himself in which his nemesis, Stanford White, had hired legions of underworld thugs to hunt down and murder Thaw. His mania boiled over on June 25, 1906, when Thaw confronted White at the rooftop theater of Madison Square Garden, stepping up to White's table during the finale of the evening's show and shooting the man three times, killing him instantly. The ensuing trial was a sensational media frenzy, the first "trial of the century" and the first time a US jury was sequestered.

Front and center, much to her dismay, was Evelyn Nesbit, who Thaw claimed he was avenging when he shot White. Nesbit was put through the wringer yet again while being examined on the witness stand, forced to make public her rape at the hands of Stanford White and subsequent relationship. The press commented primarily on her looks, or rather, how her recent ordeal had taken their toll on them. Articles ran the gamut from salacious, to empathetic, to judgmental of Evelyn Nesbit, a girl who had since her early teenage year been offered up by a conniving mother as a tool to achieve financial stability. John Barrymore himself feared he would be called as a witness, forced under oath to admit whether or not he had sent Nesbit to Europe to seek an abortion.

SHERRY COBBLER

- 2 ½ oz Brandy
- 4 oz Amontillado Sherry
- ½ oz Simple Syrup
- 1 Orange Wheel
- 1 Lemon Wheel

Add all ingredients to a shaker. Add ice. Shake well. Strain into Collins glass filled with crushed ice. Garnish with lemon wheel and fresh berries. Serve with a straw.

PIMMS CUP

- 2 oz Pimms No. 1
- 3 oz Ginger Beer
- 1 Cucumber Slice
- 1 Strawberry, Quartered
- ½ Orange Slice
- 1 Lemon Slice
- 6 mint leaves.

Add all ingredients to a highball glass filled with ice. Stir well.

SLOE GIN FIZZ

- 2 oz Sloe Gin
- ½ oz Fresh Lemon Juice
- 1 tsp Sugar
- Club Soda

Add all ingredients except club soda to a shaker filled with ice. Shake well. Strain into a highball glass filled with ice. Top with club soda. Garnish with a lemon wedge and a cherry.

TEMPTER

- 1 oz Apricot Brandy
- 1 oz Port Wine

Add all ingredients to mixing glass. Stir well. Strain into chilled cocktail glass.

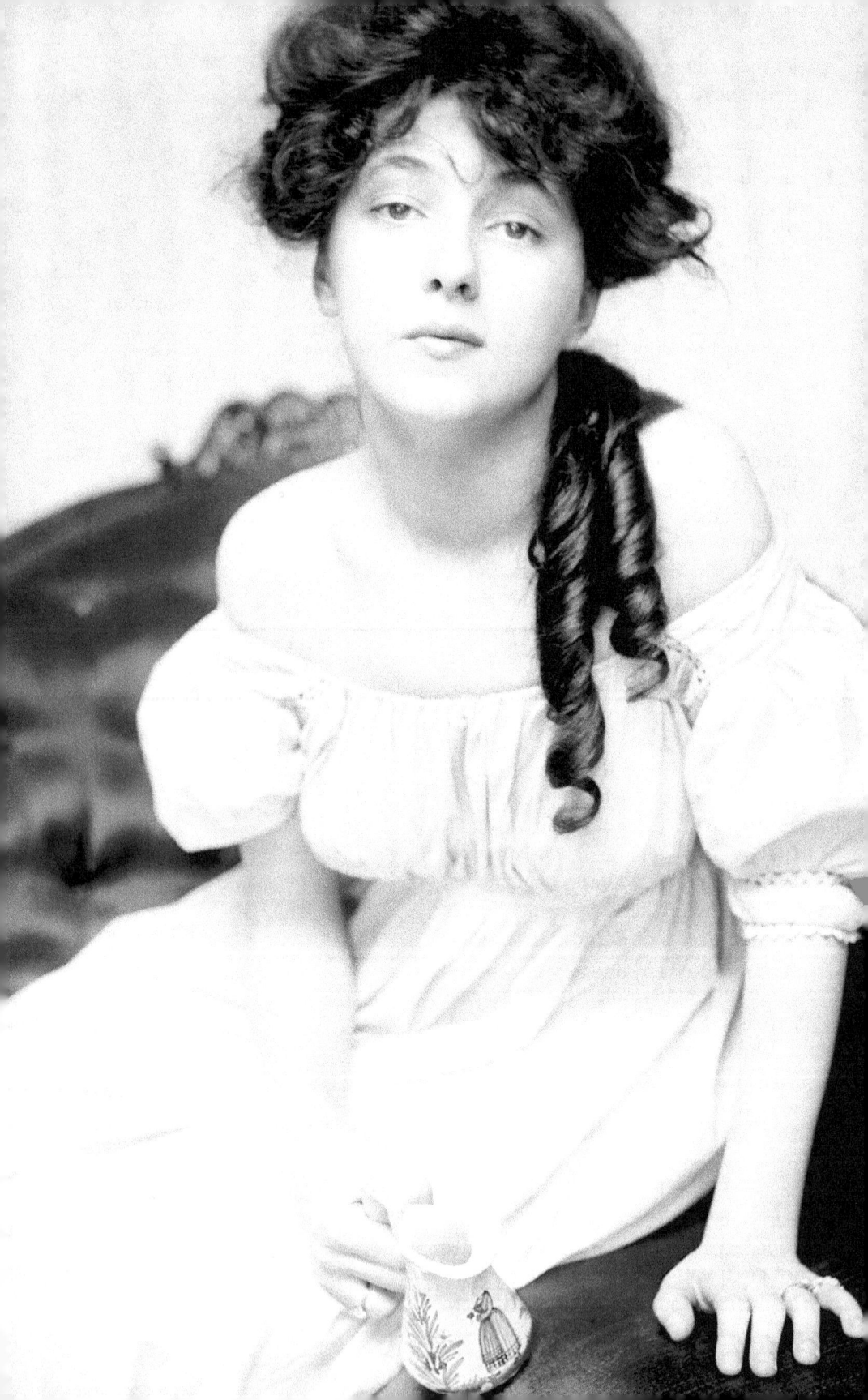

In the end, Harry Thaw was tried twice, the second jury finding him mad and sentencing him to an asylum for the criminally insane, one from which he escaped once and was, in 1915, released from, having proven himself sufficiently recovered. He and Nesbit divorced, though she bore him a son, Russell William Thaw, who became a pioneering aviator and flying ace. Nesbit made ends meet by working in silent film and the small stage, and was later hospitalized for an addiction to morphine. She married again, but it didn't last. In her later years, life settled down, and if it seems anti-climactic, one must remember that, for a life as torturous and full of horrors as was Evelyn Nesbit's, "a quiet, uneventful rest of her life" was a triumph.

As for John Barrymore, his life would develop its own complications. "It looks as though I'll have to succumb to the family curse: acting," John Barrymore once lamented. Despite his professed disdain for the stage, he was slowly having to face up to the fact that he wasn't cutting it as a cartoonist and illustrator. Desperate for money, he reached out to his mother's old agent, Charles Frohman, and soon found himself playing bit roles on a Midwestern tour. As he gained experience, he moved up in the ranks, mostly in comedic roles, debuting on Broadway in 1904 and finding a mentor in actor William Collier. Collier took on the task but found Barrymore, an advanced alcoholic even at that young age, difficult at times to work with. Still, through all the struggles, Barrymore continued to hone the craft he did not want. In 1907, he finally scored his first lead role, though his drinking and general undependability continued to undermine his success and frustrate his sister, Ethel. He received as many good reviews as bad, and several times was compared to his uncle, John Drew. From time to time, it was pointed out that young John tended to be a bit of a ham.

Sometime around 1912, Barrymore began supplementing his stage actor's income with work in short films, most of which have been lost over time. 1914 saw the release of his first confirmed feature, and it would seem from reviews that the tendency toward overplaying things on stage served Barrymore well in the exaggerated world of early motion pictures. The money was better, but Barrymore remained committed to the stage—odd for a man who multiple times professed that he was in it only for the money. He began to explore dramatic roles, usually to similarly mixed reviews as his comedic work. He frequently worked alongside his brother, Lionel, and while working as a duo, finally started collecting more good notices than bad. The brothers appeared in a stage version of George du Maurier's novel *Peter Ibbetson* in 1917. That same year, on screen, John Barrymore stepped into the shoes of A.J. Raffles.

As would be the case with many subsequent Raffles movies, this version is based largely on the stage play, an adaptation of "The Ides of March" and "Gentlemen and Players." It makes sense. In terms of what one thinks of when one thinks of "A.J. Raffles, gentleman thief," those two are the most Raffles of the Raffles stories, full of snappy action and fun. The film also throws in scenes from two more Raffles short stories: "The Gift of the Emperor," transforming it into an action set piece prologue rather than a climactic death scene; and "The Return Match," which makes sense as it's a direct continuation of events in "Gentlemen and Players." The film opens with Raffles orchestrating the heist of a necklace from a society boor (rather than a German military envoy) on an ocean liner. He is found out but escapes with a dramatic dive over the side of the boat, returning to England some time later to legends of "the amateur cracksman" but without suspicion falling on him.

That is, until he agrees to travel to the estate of Lord and Lady Amersteth, which he sees as an excellent opportunity to nick a bauble or two from some people who deserve it. A wrench is thrown into his scheme when he discovers also in attendance is a Mrs. Vidal (Christine Mayo), who happened to be on that fateful cruise and can identify Raffles as "the amateur cracksman." She intends to use the information to blackmail Raffles into a romance. Raffles finds the woman insufferable and only has eyes for pretty young Gwendolyn (Kathryn Adams), Lord Amersteth's ward. As if the situation wasn't complicated enough, Raffles discover another man, an old school acquaintance named Bunny Manders (Frank Morgan) is also vying for the young woman's affections. A romantic tangle and the threat of being exposed by a vindictive society dame aren't enough to deter Raffles from pulling a heist which, as with the same in the short story, is made more challenging by the presence of the thief Crawshay (Mike Donlin) and detective Bedford (Frederick Perry).

Although the movie follows the short stories fairly faithfully, there are some significant changes, at least one of which was brought about in efforts to assuage censorship boards. Raffles' "teach society snobs a lesson" vindictiveness is gone. Also gone is his willingness to profit from his crimes. Instead, he is a modern-day Robin Hood who never keeps what he steals and always takes from the rich to give to the poor. Or more accurately, who takes from the rich and later gives back to those same rich after he's had a good laugh and an opportunity to dive through a few windows. Also jettisoned is any concern on the part of Raffles or Bunny that being exposed as charming criminals will ruin their station in society. When the jig is finally up, rather than resulting in anxiety or disgrace, it seems only to add to the allure of Raffles. Even Bedford excitedly exclaims "He's splendid!" and is overjoyed that Raffles has escaped, since it gives Bedford himself a sporting bit of adventure to look forward to as the two friendly rivals continue to match wits.

Of course, in the novels, Raffles and Bunny are ruined by the public revelation of their side hustle, and Bedford/Mackenzie never warms to the duo. However, recasting Raffles as a beloved rogue was in tune with how the concept of the gentleman thief had evolved since the debut of Raffles. The next major gentleman thief in literature to sneak in through the window, Arsène Lupin, went a long way to advancing the dashing, lovable nature of the thief and the friendly rivalry between cop and criminal.

Added to the mix is the romantic angle, considered a necessity for the screen but absent from the short stories. Sequences of events are rearranged, but that's of less consequence. Bunny confides his financial predicament to Raffles at the

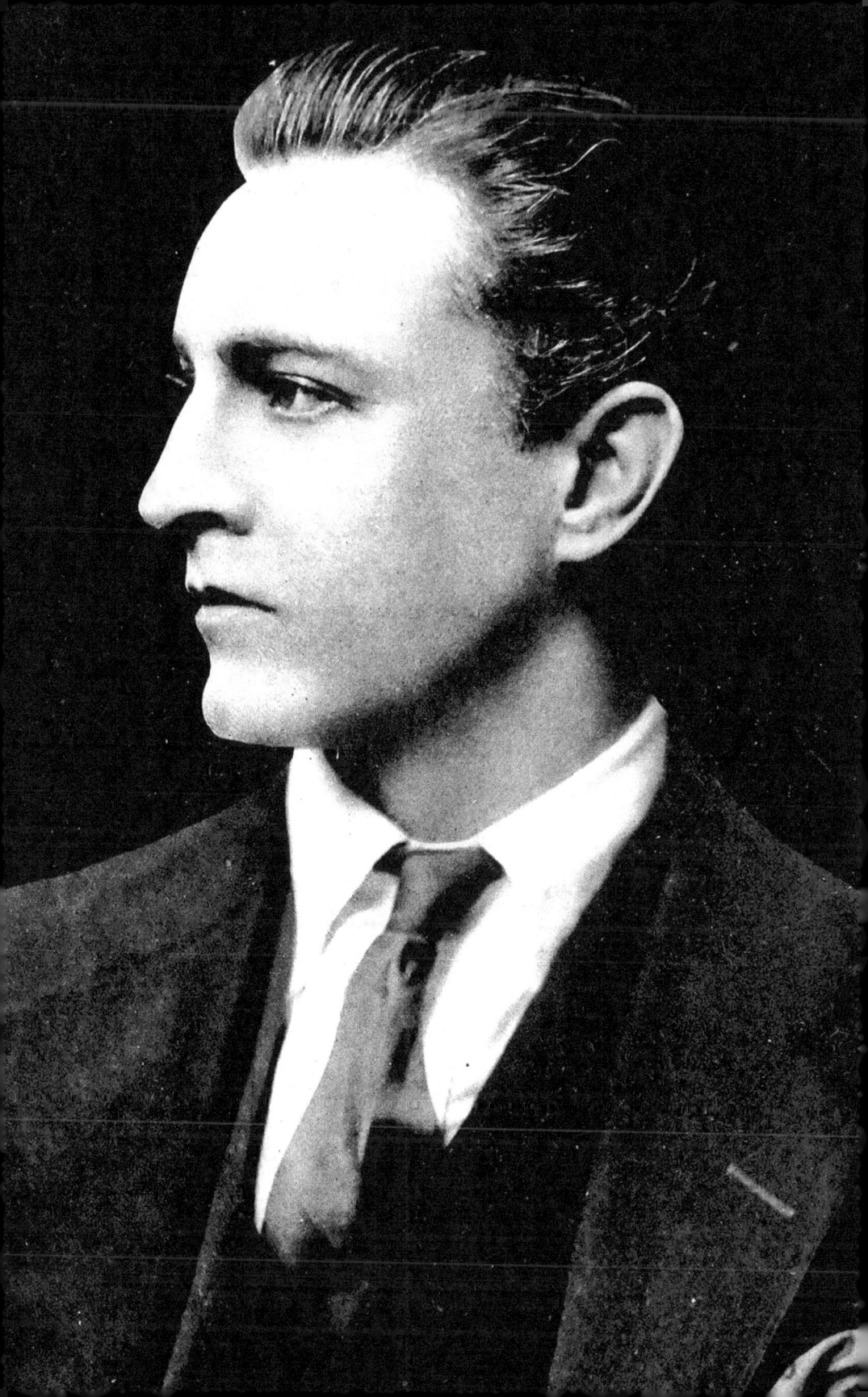

Amersteth estate rather than in Raffles' apartment, and instead of a separate crime to cover Bunny's debts, that's all rolled into the "Gentlemen and Players" heist. The final third of the film, based largely on "The Return Match," tweaks things so that there's a thrilling finale, a revelation, a few jokes, and Raffles once again diving through a window. These changes to Raffles, both in character and story, aren't necessarily for the worse. They make for a cohesive narrative (at a time when a fractured, episodic narrative would have sufficed) that moves at a brisk pace and gives Barrymore ample opportunity to strike dramatic poses, show off his comedic skills, and perform a number of stunts.

Despite the film language and technological innovations of epics like *Cabiria* and *Birth of a Nation*, *Raffles* sticks to limited, static camera set-ups and, except for the opening aboard the ship and a few scenes of gardens and fields, only a few sets. Still, it *feels* like a dynamic film because Barrymore and his supporting cast fill the screen with energy. Barrymore's style is well-suited for Raffles, imbuing the character with mischievous charm. Frank Morgan is an excellent Bunny Manders, capturing all of that character's confusion and enthusiasm (though, in alignment with the overall tonal simplification of the movie, skipping over the moral conflict). Morgan, like Barrymore, was quite a drinker, and later in his career was known to carry a briefcase with him that folded out into a fully-stocked mini-bar. While his name might not be well-remembered, one of his characters is. In 1939, when negotiations with W.C. Fields fell through, it was Frank Morgan who stepped into the titular role in *The Wizard of Oz*.

1917 was a transitional time for silent film, as the industry was really getting its feet under itself. New techniques were constantly being introduced, and the ramshackle studios that had pioneered the industry were beginning to figure things out. A star system was formed. Magazines were published in support of the movies. Cinematic style advanced in leaps and bounds. *Raffles, The Amateur Cracksman* possesses enough artifacts of the early silent era to keep it from being as much as it could have been, but it also contains enough of the new (primarily in its sprietly performances) to keep it fun for viewers used to the static conventions of the era. It won't convert anyone to the cause of silent cinema, but it will probably satisfy fans already seasoned in the limitations of 1917.

> "The sop to the powers that be, namely, that Raffles stole to help the poor, is the only discord in the whole piece. A fictionary thief as fascinating as Raffles needs no other raison d'etre than his entertaining self."
> — Motion Picture Magazine, March 1918

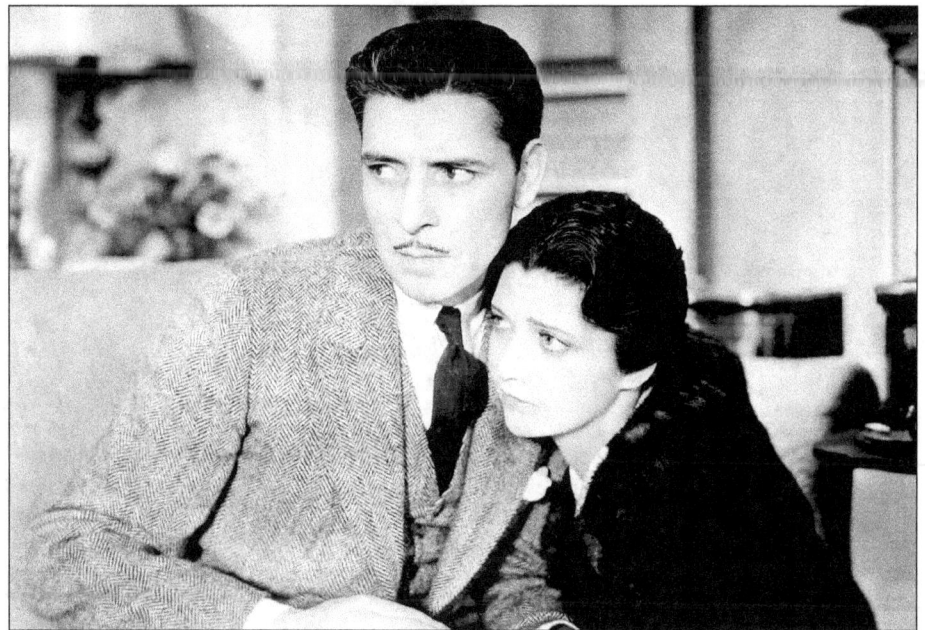

DEFINITIVE EDITION—Ronald Colman and Kay Francis in the wonderful 1930 version of Raffles.

Raffles Steals the Silver Screen

It would have been interesting to see a Raffles film that reinstated the literary Raffles' cruel streak, his temptation to murder, and his hatred of and addiction to upper class society. But by 1930, that just wasn't going to happen. The dashing stage version, stripped of his social grudge and darker tendencies, had supplanted the original in the minds of audiences in much the same way the lighter cinematic version of James Bond would come to supplant Ian Fleming's moodier original. As such, it's a harmless, breezy crime-comedy for the amateur cracksman first foray into talking cinema, but when that movie stars Ronald Colman and Kay Francis, it's hard to be upset. 1930's *Raffles* remains the definitive screen version of the character: dashing, witty, romantic, and enthused despite himself by the prospect of a little thievery. Ronald Colman was born to play Raffles, just as he was born to play Bulldog Drummond (and did, just one year prior, in 1929). Drummond and Raffles are practically the same man. Granted, Drummond falls on the side of solving crimes rather than committing them, but for the chance of a crime to be cracked presenting itself before one to be perpetrated, Drummond could have just as easily become another amateur cracksman.

Colman was a veteran of the Great War who had a permanent limp after taking shrapnel in the leg during the Battle of Messines. He cut his teeth on the stage, which meant when the rapid switch to sound came in 1929, he was well-positioned to transition from silent cinema (where as many stars of the silent era were unable to make the switch). With his perfect hair, athletic build, and expertly-crafted pencil-thin mustache, Colman was the very picture of an adventurous

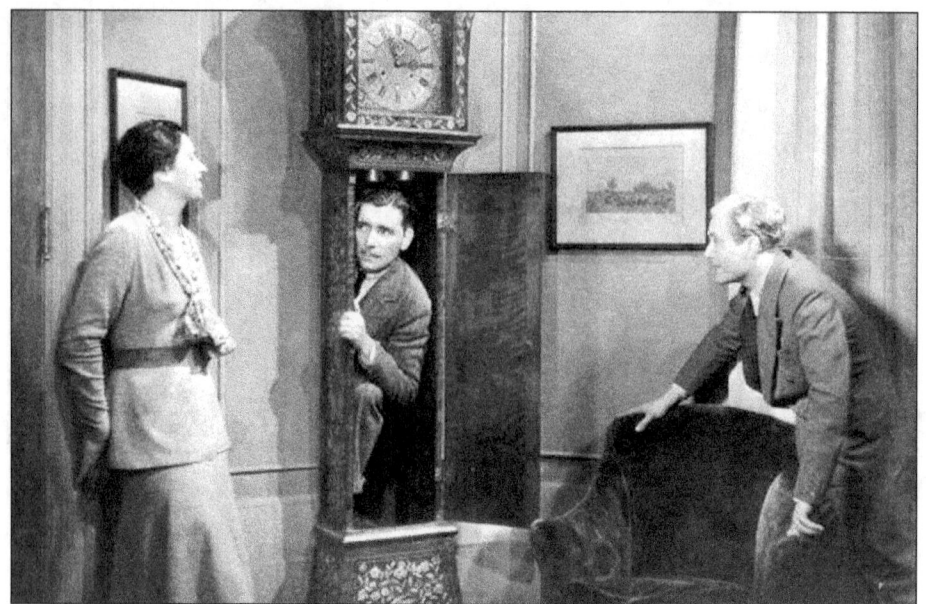

English gentleman (it's a little shocking he never played Richard Hannay, hero of John Buchan's adventure novel *The 39 Steps*). He hit the big time in the role of Hugh "Bulldog" Drummond in 1929, one of the earliest talkies. Producer Samuel Goldwyn was keen to capitalize on Colman's sudden fame. The amateur cracksman looked to be a perfect fit. And it was. Colman slips effortlessly into Raffles' top hat and tuxedo, bringing a near-overwhelming amount of sex appeal and charm to the role as he cuts a dashing swathe through polite society, relieving them of their diamonds when the opportunity arises.

Goldwyn rushed the film into production to make the most of Colman's popularity. On a tight schedule, screenwriter Sidney Howard had to pare down the story, although once again the changes were not necessarily for the worse. Gone was the silent 1917 version's shipboard prologue, and gone with it was the character of Mrs. Vidal, the spinster who knows Raffles' secret. With her out of the way, the 1930 version has more time to concentrate on the romance that was, of course, not present in the original stories but had been part and parcel of *Raffles* since the stage play—though this version thankfully drops any pretense of a love triangle (Bunny has his own girl).

Another notable change is the involvement of Raffles in the theft of the diamond necklace that causes so much consternation. In the Barrymore version, Raffles intercepts it as a crooked maid is passing it off to professional thief Crawshaw. Here, Raffles is more involved with the theft and with assisting the escape of Crawshaw from Inspector McKenzie (David Torrence). In fact, Raffles is so involved with the crime that it really makes no sense. He reveals himself to Crawshaw for no good reason beyond a sense of fair play and camaraderie, thinking that since he has bested Crawshaw, the least he can do is try to help the man escape. Which is to say, it doesn't matter that it makes no sense from a logical perspective. Raffles isn't acting from a logical place. It's all about the *sport* for him. Revealing his secret identity to Crawshaw is just one more way to keep the game interesting. It's also likely that as much as Raffles disdains the approval of high society, he craves the approval of the criminal element. He wants a seasoned hand like Crawshaw to know what he did and nod in admiration. Raffles is a little kid desperate for the approval of criminal parents.

Otherwise, the plot is much the same as the 1917 version. Slinking into the role of Gwen was one of the great icons of the pre-Code era. Kay Francis was still formulating the persona that would make her the envy of many an American woman during the 1930s, but you can see she's well on her way. Francis was an Oklahoma City girl who grew up in the tough world of touring performers. Her mother was a struggling actress. Her father was gone, abandoning the family when Kay was only four. She dabbled in school, married, divorced, and moved to New York to pursue a Broadway career despite a slight speech impediment. She made her Broadway debut in 1925, and split her time between New York and a touring troupe in the Midwest. In 1928, she took to the stage for what would become her final theater performance, in a play called *Elmer the Great*. Her costar, Walter Huston, was so impressed by her acting that he brought her with him to the Paramount Pictures headquarters in Astoria, Queens. A year later she debuted in her first two films: *Gentlemen of the Press*, alongside Walter Huston; and *The Cocoanuts*, alongside the Marx Brothers.

It didn't take long for Francis to establish herself as one of the premier stars of the talkie era. With her tall, slender frame, dark hair, and smoky good looks, she could have fallen into the role of *femme fatale*. Instead, she usually played witty, urbane, liberated women—thoroughly modern and unconventional and, in a break with the films of the 1920s, never punished for being so. Her height meant studios wouldn't cast her alongside many popular male stars (for fear of exposing their modest stature), but she works fantastically alongside Ronald Colman (and, later, William Powell). Her chemistry with Colman is palpable, but she seemed to have chemistry with just about everyone. Costumers loved her, too, and draped her in a stunning array of *haute couture*. In an era defined by the Great Depression, Kay Francis was the glamorous, shimmering dream.

Colman and Francis are joined by Bramwell Fletcher (who later went mad at the sight of a revived Imohotep in Universal's 1932 classic *The Mummy*) as Bunny Manders. Unfortunately, as much as Fletcher looks the part, development of his character is sacrificed on the altar of expediency. This version has even less time for side characters than the 1917 version. Poor Bunny, such an important part of the Raffles books, is relegated to a glorified cameo. The subsequent 1939 remake would manage to marginalize Bunny even further. He deserves better, the poor abused clod, and maybe one day he'll get it. On the other hand, Bunny getting shafted yet again is par for the course in the world of Raffles.

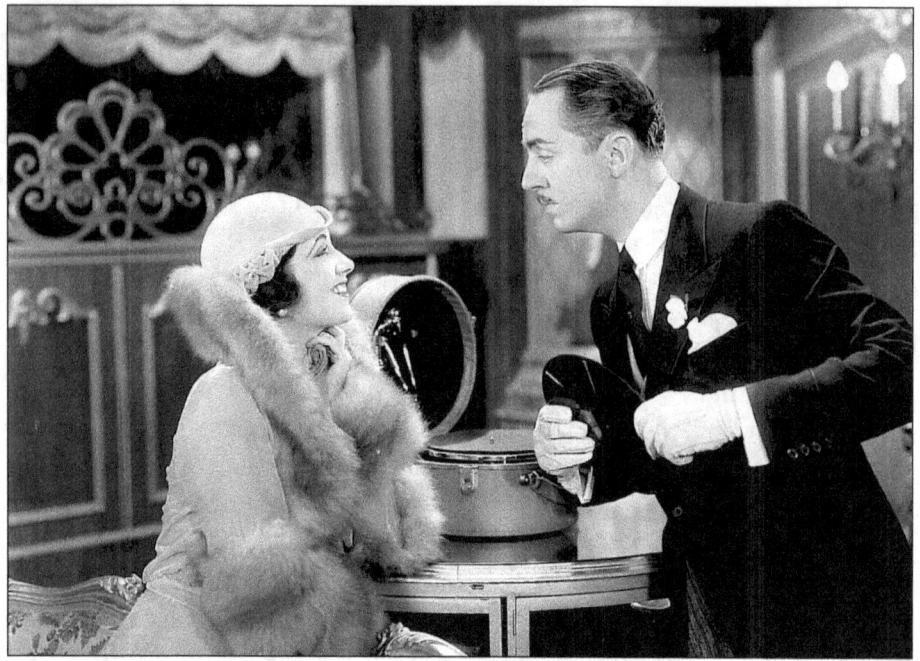

THIEF OF HEARTS—Kay Francis and William Powell flirt in 1932's Jewel Robbery.

Smoke Smoke Smoke that Cigarette

As well as she clicked with Ronald Colman and *Raffles*, Kay Francis wasn't one to limit herself to a single gentleman thief. In 1932, she romanced not one but two charming scofflaws. Ernst Lubitsch's *Trouble in Paradise* is considered by many to be one of the greatest comedies of the 1930s, and indeed it lives up to its reputation. But in its shadow was another snappy gentleman thief movie, *Jewel Robbery*, pairing Francis up with William Powell. A more modest but no less enjoyable affair, *Jewel Robbery* is especially interesting as an example of what clever filmmakers were able to get away with before more vigorous enforcement of the beast that became known as the Hays Code. From slinky costumes to bubble baths, sexual innuendo so overt that it hardly qualifies as innuendo, triumphant criminals, and of course adultery, extramarital sex, and William Powell's dashing gentleman thief getting everyone all blissed out on weed, *Jewel Robbery* is such a gleeful, unabashed collection of shattered taboos that it's surprising it was made even in the (relatively) liberal year of 1932.

Calling a film "pre-Code" can be misleading. Although people often mean it to refer to films made roughly between the end of the silent era and 1934 when they got serious about enforcing the guidelines, all of the films made during that era were, in fact, made under the Production Code. Will Hays (whose name became synonymous with the code) and the Motion Picture Producers and Distributors of America introduced the self-imposed set of decency standards in 1930 in response to criticism regarding the unsavory content of movies (a similar set of "don'ts" and "be carefuls" was drafted in 1927). Enforcement of the Code was not exactly optional, but it was applied in a very uneven manner. Suggested changes to a film script based on the Code were often ignored by the studios. Others would submit scripts containing scenes so outrageous that there was no question that the Hays Office would reject them, leading to them ignoring other, mildly less salacious material. "At least it isn't as bad as that one scene." That's what makes films produced during this phase of the Code "pre-Code." In 1934, under mounting criticism that the Code was about as useful as the League of Nations, William Breen was appointed to enforce its, which put the kibosh on all sorts of fun. It also ushered in an era of creativity when it came to circumventing the Code.

All of which is to say, unbelievable as it may seem given the contents of the film, *Jewel Robbery*'s script was subjected to review before it went into production. Somehow, this film about a dashing jewel thief (William Powell) who lights up elegant Kay Francis' libido was passed intact with only a few notes that local censor boards might have a problem with the use of guns, the depiction of successful crime, and the obvious allusions to adultery. Oh, and maybe Powell's "special" cigarettes. But none of these suggestions were made forcefully, because the film was a comedy and no one reviewing the film for Code violations thought audiences would take it seriously. How could one be offended by such a wink-wink film?

Of course, people *were* offended, because that's how people are, but for the most part, *Jewel Robbery* ran into no significant issues during its initial release. When Warner Brothers tried to re-release it, however, after Breen took over the Production Code office, it was flat out denied a certificate—with the reasons cited being the very reason it was passed a few years earlier: that it was breezy, comedic, and made crime look fun and glamorous and not at all serious.

Which is a fair assessment, if not a reason for censorship. *Jewel Robbery* does make crime look fun and glamorous. It's one of those movies you wish you could live in, where no one has any real cares, where everyone is sophisticated and liberated. Powell and Francis were a powerful on-screen pair, having first worked together in 1930's *Behind the Make-Up*. They starred opposite one another in seven films altogether. In 1932, both Powell and Francis were at the top of the game (though Powell would go on to even greater fame when he paired with another fantastic actress, Myrna Loy, in *The Thin Man*). Francis was one of the most popular female stars of the era, thanks to a series of films that cast her as an urbane, modern woman, quick with a one-liner, in charge of her own life, and ready for romance only if it came on her terms—and then, not always with eye toward marriage (or, if she was already married, fidelity). Draped in stunning, at times outrageous fashions, she was an aspirational figure, someone to inspire former flappers who found themselves forced back into conservative society and young girls who, with few prospects as the Great Depression smothered the country, could for an hour or so imagine themselves as this unabashed, intelligent, and defiant woman.

Powell, meanwhile, had risen rapidly to become one of Hollywood's most beloved leading men, the perfect on-screen match for Francis. Like her, he was quick with a joke, always had a trick up his sleeve, and was impeccably dressed—but also possessed an everyman quality that made him more relatable than other marquee idols, even when he was pulling unbelievable heists and trading expertly crafted *bon mots* with stylish women at luxurious cocktail galas.

In *Jewel Robbery*, Powell has no name. He is simply the Robber, a thief who pulls heists with the utmost politeness and consideration for his victims (usually jewelry stores catering to the upper strata of society). The film begins with a proud security expert explaining the foolproof system he's recently installed, which of course signals that the Robber is going to show up seconds later and rob the place. He likes to keep everyone entertained by turning on the phonograph and playing the greatest hits of the 1920s and '30s. Despite the fact that he and his gang are armed, his most potent weapon is a pack of "special" cigarettes he offers to his prey. A few puffs and they're giggling, smiling, wandering around, and will, according to the Robber, eventually come to their senses with nothing more than "a marvelous appetite."

Upon completion of the robbery, and with a jaunty tip of his hat, the Robber and his gang make their getaway. When the Baroness Teri (Kay Francis) hears about this heist, she's worried it might have occurred at the store where her dull but financially-generous husband has a diamond necklace waiting for her. Their marriage is stable one, but passionless, and the Baroness is unapologetic about her attraction to the wild life, planning potential trysts while and remarking that the necklace she is to be receive is beautiful enough that it could convince a woman to tolerate her husband.

When she and her entourage arrive at the store to pick up the jewels, the Robber is no more than a few minutes behind. In an extended sequence, he and his gang secure or incapacitate (by liberal offering of magic cigarettes) everyone but the Baroness, who refuses to be bound or penned up in a safe. She can also barely

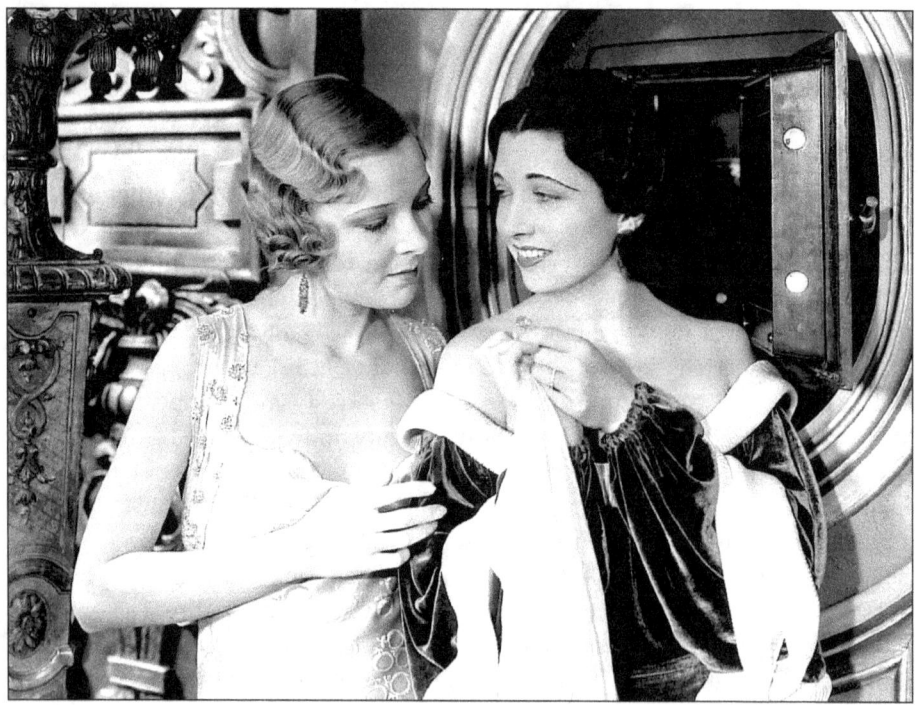

LADIES' NIGHT—Kay Francis and Helen Vinson shine brighter than diamonds.

COCKTAILS & CAPERS

contain her arousal as she watches the Robber go about his business. She flirts, fidgets, and has a look on her face somewhere between amusement at such an adventure and pure animal lust for a man who has, finally, enthralled her both physically and mentally. The Robber isn't one to miss so obvious a signal and is more than happy to reciprocate with innuendo-laden banter of his own. It seems a few times like they're on the verge of just dropping to the floor right then and there, yet the scene never crosses into the vulgar. It's obvious, sure, even naughty, but it's also playful. It's the sort of erudite courtship one wishes they were capable of, instead of what one can usually muster.

Sex must wait, however, because the Robber does have a task to complete, though he certainly seems open to the idea of encountering the Baroness again. He agrees to leave her untied and unconfined (symbolic indeed) as long as she promises not to tattle. Amused and aroused by the entire affair (so to speak), and looking forward to another encounter in a more intimate setting, Baroness Teri agrees. And of course, they *will* have another encounter. Or two. As the Robber says, "Night is before us, and if you wish, by dawn we shall have a secret behind us." A more elegant line than when Kay asks to see his jewels.

1932 was a hell of a year for Kay Francis. Aside from *Jewel Robbery*, she starred in *Man Wanted*, which many consider one of her best films (and which, like *Jewel Robbery*, was directed by William Dieterle), and Ernst Lubitsch's masterpiece *Trouble in Paradise*. *Jewel Robbery* doesn't quite rise to the genius of Lubitsch

WHIZZ-BANG
- 2 dashes Absinthe
- 2 dashes Grenadine
- 2 dashes Orange Bitters
- ¾ oz Noilly Prat Dry Vermouth
- 1 ½ oz Single Malt Scotch

Add all ingredients to a shaker filled with ice. Shake well. Strain into a cocktail glass.

FLAPPER
- 1 ½ oz Rum
- 1 ½ oz Noilly Prat Dry Vermouth
- ½ oz Demerara Syrup
- 2 dashes Angostura Bitters

Add all ingredients to a mixing glass. Add ice. Stir well. Strain into a chilled cocktail glass. Garnish with a lemon peel and brandied cherry. If you don't want to make Demerara syrup, you can use grenadine.

ANGEL FACE
- 1 oz Dry Gin
- 1 oz Calvados
- 1 oz Apricot Brandy

Add all ingredients to a mixing glass. Fill with ice. Stir well. Strain into a chilled cocktail glass. Garnish with an orange peel.

BRAMBLE
- 2 oz Dry Gin
- 1 oz Fresh Lemon Juice
- ½ oz Simple Syrup
- ½ oz Crème de Mure

Add all ingredients except crème de mure to a shaker. Add ice. Shake well. Strain into a chilled rocks glass filled with crushed ice. Top with the crème de mure. Garnish with a skewered blackberry.

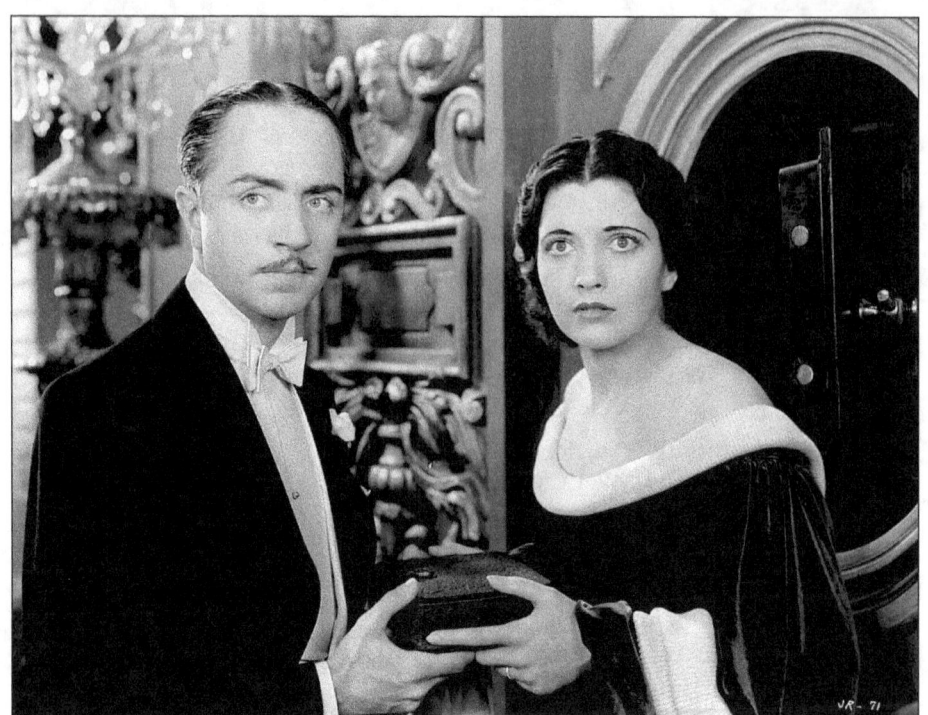

or challenge gender roles quite as bluntly as *Man Wanted*, which casts Kay as a workaholic career woman with no interest in marriage or children, but it's a fun film buoyed by the chemistry between the two leads. As the archetypal gentleman thief, William Powell is charming, debonair but approachable, a man who has learned the ins of society while operating on its outs, and who knows how to pitch powerful woo the way of a woman as grand as Kay Francis.

Kay is almost so glamorous that it hurts. Powell may be the man with the gun, but there's no doubt it's Francis who has the power. He's the subject of her desire. A perfectly compliant subject, sure, but who can blame him for happily surrendering to Kay Francis? In an ever-changing array of fabulous outfits by the legendary Orry-Kelly, she slinks like a cat across the screen, crackling with confidence and barely contained erotic energy. When the two of them are together, never has it felt so much like two characters are in the throes of lovemaking when all they're doing is sitting on a couch.

Powell and Francis shine so bright that it's easy to forget there's anyone else in the film. Indeed, director Dieterle and screenwriter Erwin Gelsey seem perfectly aware of this. The rest of the characters, though all ably played, fade into the background as the two leads command the screen. Helen Vinson, in her first credited screen role, gets in a few good moments as Teri's best friend and confidante. Together, the two of them laugh, dress, undress, bathe, and generally bemoan the sorry state of the average male. She pairs well with Francis. Both women were tall, or at least taller than many of the leading men at Warner Brothers. Francis was listed at 5'9" while Vinson was 5'7". No giant, she, but certainly taller than actors like Edward G. Robinson and Jimmy Cagney. But where Kay Francis used her height to her advantage in a series of roles where she commanded the attention of everyone and was meant to dwarf the sad, lame men who sought to saddle her with domesticity and conservative behavior, Helen Vinson's height worked against her, and leading lady status never came her way. She did turn in rather a good performance in *In Name Only*, playing alongside Cary Grant (6'2"), Carole Lombard (5'6"), and once again, Kay Francis—it was a tall person film. She married British tennis star turned fashion designer Fred Perry, though their marriage was brief. In 1945, at the behest of her third (and final) husband, she retired from acting. Her last role, as fate would have it, was alongside William Powell in *The Thin Man Goes Home*. As for the supporting male players in *Jewel Robbery*...seriously, who can remember them? The entire point is that they're all, at best, pleasantly bland.

Several state censorship boards took exception to *Jewel Robbery*'s dismissive attitude toward fidelity and the institution of marriage. Kay Francis' Baroness Teri is not ashamed of her philandering nature, nor does the film condemn her for it any more than Powell's Robber is punished for a life of crime. Instead, marriage is regarded as something that women are often forced into, either by circumstance or social pressure. Monogamy is tantamount to ownership, and the Baroness will not be someone's piece of property, regardless of how harmless the steward may be.

The husband who bores her to tears is never presented as a blow-hard or rotten human being. He's basically OK in his way; just not for her. The film doesn't paint him as a buffoon in order to easily justify her infidelity, though he is prone to bouts of self-important chest-pounding. *Jewel Robbery* expects the viewer to be sophisticated enough to juggle these two concepts, that a person can be unsatisfied with someone who is perfectly fine, and that perhaps one shouldn't be overly righteous about judging the adventurous nature of others, especially during a time when marriage was more an obligation than a choice.

As a heist film, *Jewel Robbery* is ridiculous. That's what helped it pass muster when under scrutiny by the Hays Office. Anyone who looked toward William Powell's crimes as blueprints for their own wouldn't get very far. There's not the slightest effort made to portray crime in a believable fashion. The Robber runs roughshod over the jewelry stores of Vienna, his face uncovered, more than willing to chat up the people from whom he is stealing, yet no one can identify him. The movie is content to shrug and excuse it as a byproduct of the Robber getting everyone high. It's a heist fantasy, with the crime serving no purpose other than to ignite sparks between Powell and Francis. Still, as purposefully silly as it is, the criminal angle does provide for a number of exciting sequences, including the big robbery and a rooftop chase.

Mostly, however, *Jewel Robbery* is here to deliver double entendres and cast smoldering gazes while wearing incredible clothes. A couple of years later, the Code would get strict. The fun would get shooed off the screen, and the complex feminist roles at which Kay Francis excelled would become *verboten*. But if 1932 was a final fling, what a fine final fling it was.

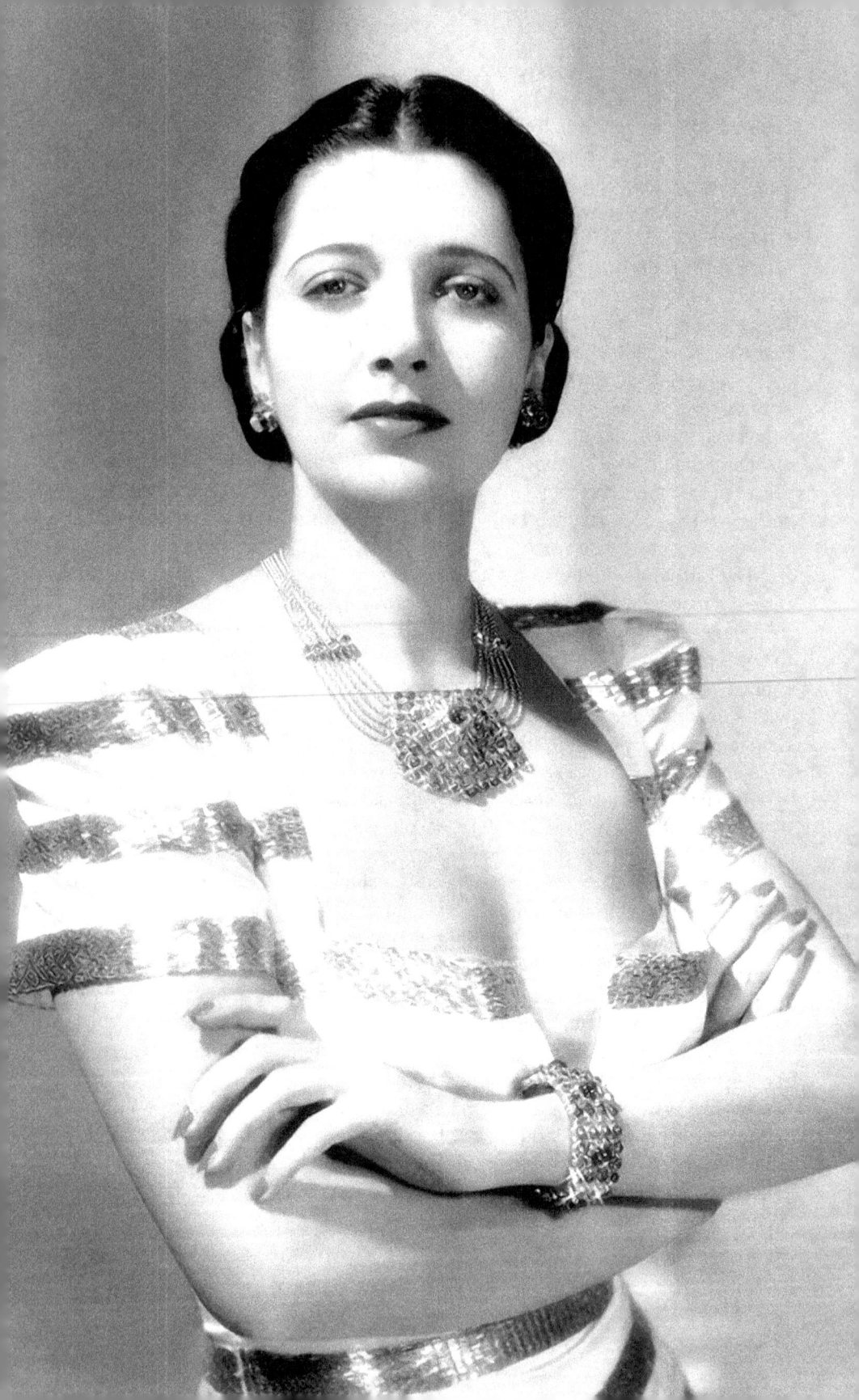

The Playlist: Cocktails with Kay

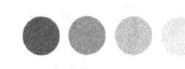

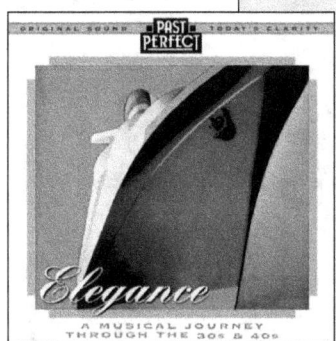

ELEGANCE
SOPHISTICATION
THE AGE OF STYLE
Various Artists, 2008-2010

OK, so perhaps it's a bit of a cheat to rely entirely on compilations from a single record label, but this is *Kay Francis* we're talking about. A little cheating is sometimes called for. And really, do you want a long-playing compilation to accompany your night together, or do you want to interrupt the mood every few minutes to get up and flip over the 78?

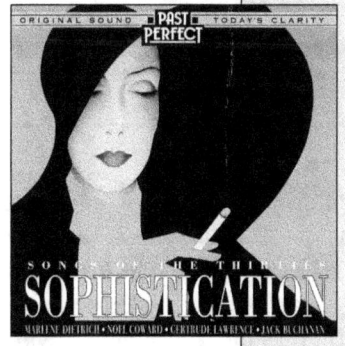

British label Past Perfect has perfected the art of putting together expertly-curated compilations of music from the 1920s, '30s, and '40s that fit a certain mood or theme. Need the songs that got the Allies through World War II? They've got you covered like the Royal Air Force. Need music for your speakeasy? No problem. You are spoiled for choice. In the case of entertaining the likes of Kay Francis for an evening, rely on the entries with names that capture her essence: Elegance, Sophistication, and Style.

There are two volumes of *Elegance* and three of *Sophistication*. *The Age of Style* is a double set, so between them all, they should see you through to the morning, at which time, if you played your cards right, you will in the words of the Robber share a secret. Being British in origin but readily available in the U.S. means you'll find a good selection of big band, swing, and jazz hits from both sides of the Atlantic, which perhaps you're traversing on a glamorous steamer.

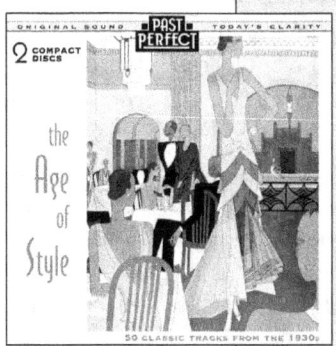

Familiar names include Ruth Etting, Fred Astaire, Noel Coward, Django Reinhardt, Nat King Cole, Glenn Miller, Marlene Dietrich, Al Bowlly, Marion Harris, and Ginger Rogers. There's a good many less-familiar names included as well, but none that don't deserve their place on this bandstand of cool, romantic music. Together, these albums are the soundtrack for moonlit nights, champagne cocktails, art deco interiors, knowing looks, easily-removed silk attire, and that coy fade-to-black as the bedroom door closes.

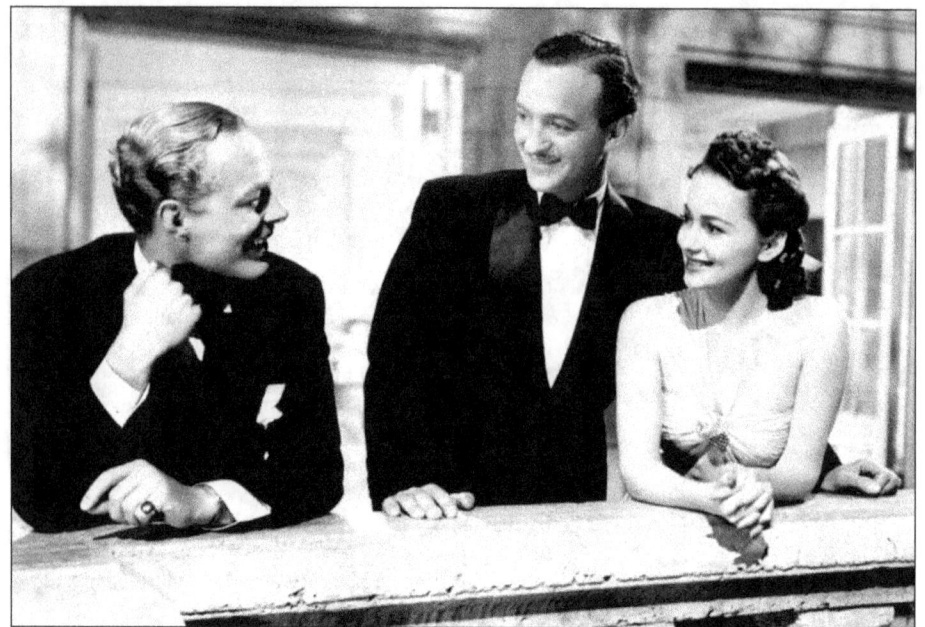

RAFFLES VS. THE CODE—David Niven grapples with Joseph Breen for the 1939 version.

He Stole My Pearls! He Stole My Heart!

How would the cracksman fare under the stricter enforcement of the Production Code ushered in by Joseph Breen? That was the question in 1939, when they dusted off the gentleman thief for one more go-round the same track. The Code was in existence well before 1934, but that year the office was taken over by Breen amid an atmosphere of increased scrutiny by and pressure from moral watchdogs who wanted to put a damper on the sex and violence rampant in horror and gangster films (the box office returns expose that, as usual, the professed outrage of society did not necessarily align with their movie-going habits). Breen vowed to make good on the promise of the Code, which until then had been at best mildly enforced, with studios having devised a number of ways to circumvent its restrictions. Under Breen's stewardship, things got tough. Movies like *Frankenstein* and *Scarface* were no longer going to slip by.

Among the chief tenets of the Code was the demand that crime must not pay. Criminals should always be punished for their transgressions. But, one wonders, does that apply even to dapper, good-natured gentlemen thieves like A.J. Raffles? In Hornung's original stories, Raffles paid for his life of crime, including, in the end, the ultimate price. But that business was in the past. Audiences had been thrilling to a light-hearted version of Raffles since the stage play. Would anyone want to see the playful, charming Raffles of John Barrymore, Ronald Colman, or as the case was in 1939, David Niven pay for his crimes? Probably not, but that didn't mean the Hays Office wasn't going to insist upon it anyway.

Once again, we're getting the same old story. There was a point to remaking it in 1930, when the technology of movie making had advanced so much since the 1917 version (the lamentable 1925 version, was actually a step backward in sophistication from the 1917 version), but what was the point of trotting out the same ol' Raffles movie yet again when the previous version was so recent and so good? This is especially puzzling given that so much of what is done in 1939's *Raffles*, from mannerisms to camera set-ups to the very way lines are delivered, is almost identical to what was done in 1930. Screenwriter John Van Druten does little more than take Sidney Howard's script from 1930, tack on a stinger ending, and sign his own name.

However, taking into account the more forceful application of the Production Code, the 1930 version of *Raffles* probably would not have been certified for redistribution after 1934. Any film approved before that had to be resubmitted if the studio wanted to put it back in circulation (and most films from the first half of the 1930s were re-released in the second half to meet the demand for programming). Given that Raffles executes a dramatic escape at the end of the film and does not "pay for his crimes," it would be difficult for the Colman-Francis version to secure a certificate under the new regime. Easier to just remake it and graft a Code-friendly ending onto the thing.

So as a result, what we get is a somewhat spiritless film saved by the boundless energy and debonair charm of David Niven. Niven made a career out of playing dashing gentlemen. He's not quite the Raffles Ronald Colman was, but he's a damn good second place and has at least as good a pencil-thin mustache.

Given the wealth of Raffles stories at the disposal of filmmakers, it's unfortunate that they kept going back to the same one again and again. One can only imagine what could have happened had they delved into the amateur cracksman's vendetta with the Camorra. It's a bit tiresome to watch the movie go through the same old plot points, but David Niven makes it all right.

Just as had been the case with the Colman version, the 1939 film was rushed into production, this time to take advantage of Niven's contractual obligation before he departed Hollywood to fight the Nazis. Given the undertaking on which he was about to embark, one could forgive Niven if he was distracted or not entirely invested in the role. But that's not the sort of man David Niven was. He gave a spirited performance as the amateur cracksman, buttoned his top coat, and then left to give a similarly spirited performance in the war, during which he served with the British Commandos as part of the "Phantom Signals Unit." As to the particulars of his wartime exploits, he was as tight-lipped about them as a fellow British actor and commando, Christopher Lee.

It's unfortunate that the rest of the movie isn't up to Niven's effort. Olivia de Havilland, one of the icons of Hollywood, is fine as Gwen, but she lacks the spark of Kay Francis and has less chemistry with her lead. Part of that can be chalked up to different eras. Francis was allowed to be sexy. She and Colman seemed like they might collapse into a fit of lovemaking at any moment. That liberal attitude toward grown-up fun wasn't acceptable in 1939, so de Havilland, though gorgeously dressed, is bundled in enough fabric and kept at a safe enough distance to satisfy the most sour-faced of prudes.

The rest of the cast suffers from a case of "like the ones in the previous film, only less so," which is an odd instance of history repeating itself not just in the plot of the film, but also in that the 1939 version is inferior to the 1930 version in the same way the 1925 version is inferior to the 1917 version. The only improvement over the previous one is the addition of E.E. Clive as Raffles' valet. In much the same way Ronald Colman was born to play A.J. Raffles, E.E. Clive was born to play a butler (and frequently did).

What really causes the film to falter, though, is the clumsy tag ending meant to fulfill the demands of the Production Code. No one but Joseph Breen would want to see Raffles arrested. And yet, after the familiar showdown between Raffles and McKenzie, after Raffles' escape through a false grandfather clock, the film is saddled with an awkward epilogue in which Raffles visits Gwen one last time and announces that, so impressed is he with McKenzie, that he has decided to turn himself in. It's obvious the ending is there as an afterthought. Again, who wants their gentleman thief to turn into a responsible citizen lecturing us all on morals in the final minute of the film? The film's heart isn't in it any more than horror films were when they were forced to placate the censors by tacking on an "all's well that ends well" final shot so incongruous with the rest of the film that at times they play like knowing jokes.

The 1939 *Raffles* is a reasonably enjoyable affair despite its flaws. Director Sam Wood, who previously directed the Marx Brothers in *A Night at the Opera* and *A Day at the Races*, and would win an Oscar for his work on *Gone with the Wind*, was too accomplished to let the film drag. He fills it with the wit and action we want, and it's not his fault he couldn't also give us the sex appeal and had to satisfy "crime doesn't pay" edict of the Code. Seconding him (one presumes he was distracted by *Gone with the Wind*) as an uncredited director was William Wyler, a man of no small accomplishment himself. He went on to direct, among other things, *Roman Holiday*, *Ben Hur*, *Funny Girl*, and in 1966, another gentleman thief classic, *How to Steal a Million*, starring Peter O'Toole and Audrey Hepburn. Together, Wyler and Wood keep *Raffles* springing along amiably enough, boosted by the can-do attitude of consummate professional David Niven. §

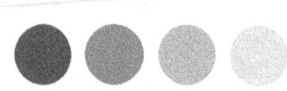

"Oh, his cleverness! His fiendish cleverness! Had he fallen back on threats, coercion, sneers, all might have been different even yet. But he set me free to leave him in the lurch. He would not blame me. He did not even bind me to secrecy; he trusted me. He knew my weakness and my strength, and was playing on both with his master's touch."

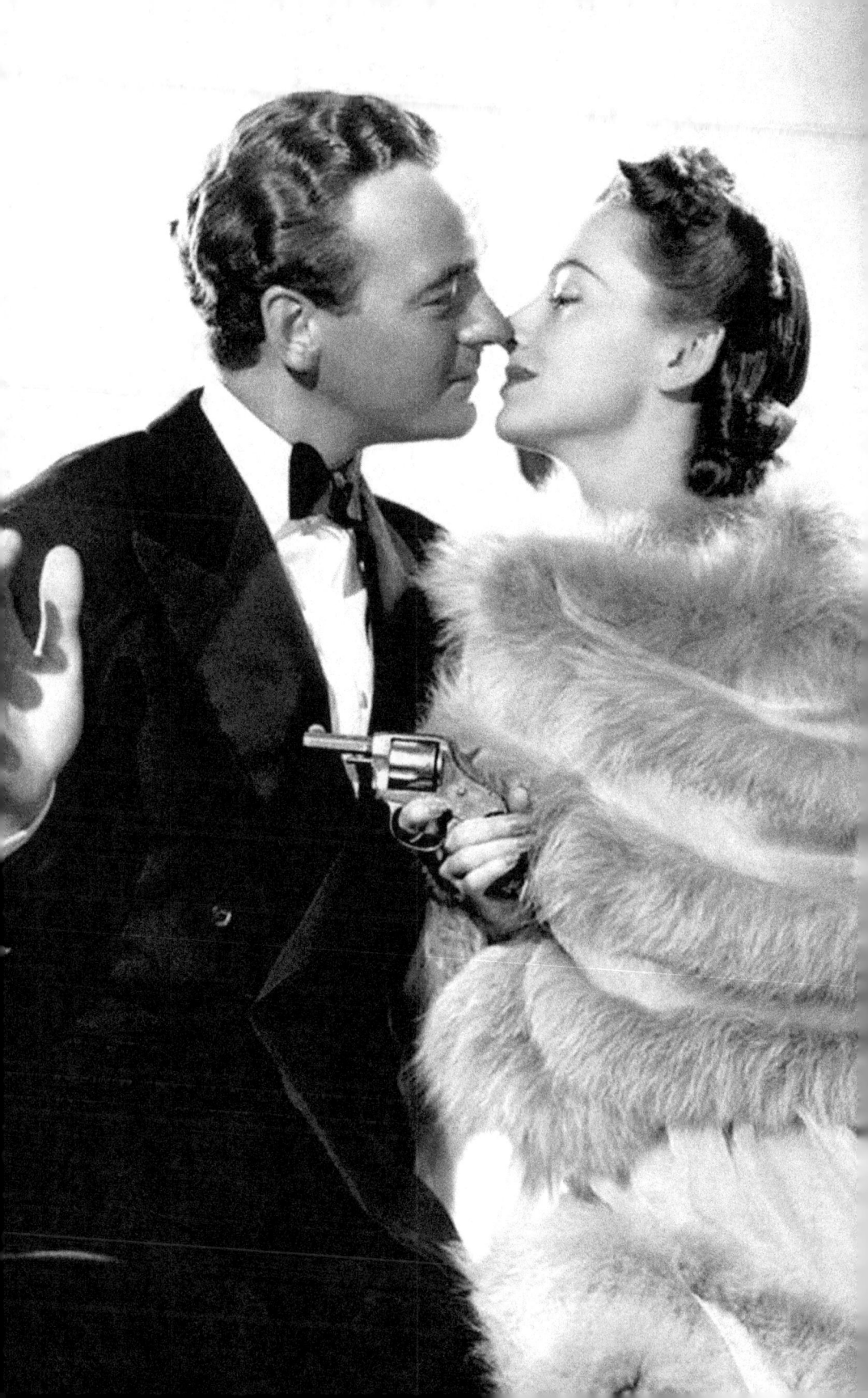

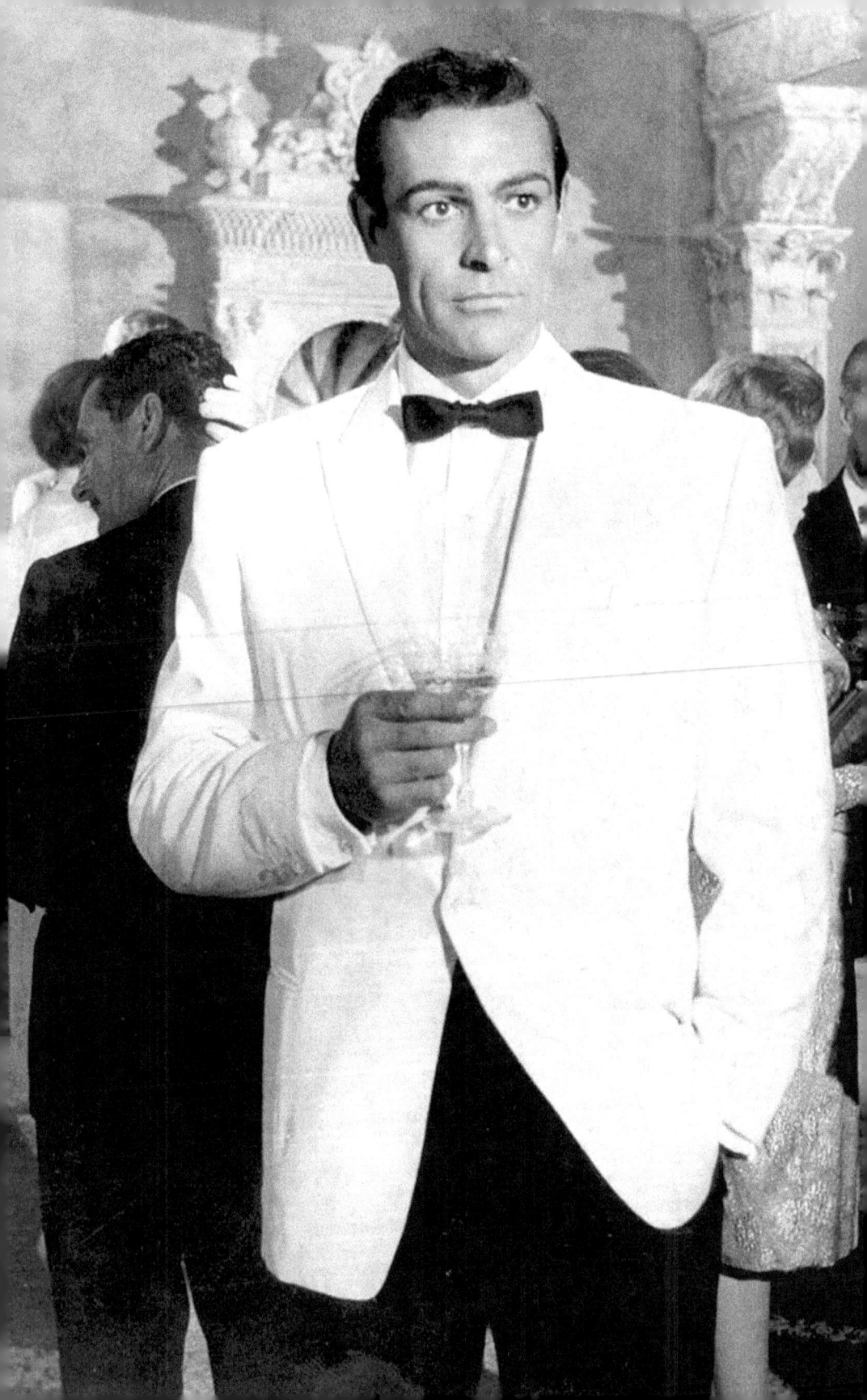

03 MYTHS OF THE MARTINI

The confused history of one of the world's most iconic cocktails and how James Bond came to prefer his shaken with vodka

The Martini has been around since the 1800s. It existence spans the Industrial Revolution, two World Wars, Prohibition, the Great Depression, Swinging London, the Summer of Love, disco, punk, and East German funk. It's been in style, out of fashion, and subject to the peculiar, not-always-trustworthy whims of the American drinker. Its ingredients have changed over the decades to compensate here for a shortage of one ingredient, there for an overabundance of another, before it settled down into a more-or-less agreed-upon recipe...that was immediately tweaked. Like many famous cocktails, the soul of the Martini is simple: gin and vermouth, with an olive or twist of lemon peel for garnish. Nothing more. Yet as simple as that recipe is, few cocktails have as many variations and corruptions as the Martini. Chocotinis, appletinis...*bacontinis*.

Even restricting oneself to the most basic definition of a Martini offers no respite from debate. Imbibers will argue about the amount of vermouth (three-quarters of an ounce? Half an ounce? A wash? Have the bartender inhale vermouth vapor and whisper the word "vermouth" at you as you walk into the bar?) and the type (dry or sweet). With so much time and alteration under its belt, the idea of pedantry in regards to the Martini seems a little misplaced, but then pedantry usually *is* misplaced.

So here we are, with a cocktail that inspires sometimes comically vicious debate. Often at the center of the debate is James Bond's shaken vodka Martini. After its appearance in the Bond movies, the Martini became synonymous with classic cool. There are drinks Bond consumes with greater frequency, but none of them have attained the status of the Martini. The

Martini glass (designed the way it is either because the shape helps bring out the bouquet of the gin while keeping the ingredients from separating, or because the wide opening made it easy during Prohibition to dump the drink quickly if the police came raiding) became the international symbol for "alcohol served here." Every novice drinker makes the social *faux pas* of ordering their first Martini by saying, "a vodka Martini, shaken not stirred." More committed Bond aficionados will hit the bartender with the full set of instructions from *Casino Royale*, and more than a few bartenders will know what you mean when you simply ask for a Vesper. Ah yes, the Vesper. Despite being the signature cocktail of the Bond universe, no screen Bond ever ordered a Vesper until 2006. Other than the farcical 1967 send-up *Casino Royale*, there had never been a Vesper Lynd to inspire its creation.

At the time it was written, there was no bidding war for the rights to *Casino Royale*. The first to give it a go were American television producers, who filmed the story in 1954 for the series *Climax!* In that early adaptation, James Bond became American agent Jimmy Bond, played by Barry Nelson. Bond orders only one drink in the episode: a scotch and water, which he never actually consumes. He and Le Chiffre (Peter Lorre) are far more excited by plain water. "Le Chiffre…can I have some water?" Bond inquires, to which Le Chiffre responds enthusiastically, "Oh yes, with pleasure. Basil, give him all the water he wants. Get me some water, too."

The film rights to *Casino Royale* were sold again in 1955 for $6,000 to actor-director Gregory Ratoff, but he never got around to making a movie. After Ratoff's death in 1960, the rights ended up with American producer Charles K. Feldman. Feldman, too, was slow on the draw. By the time he was ready to go into production, the Bond books had become sensations, and EON Productions, a partnership between British producer Albert "Cubby" Broccoli and American producer Harry Saltzman, had sewn up the rights to all other current and future James Bond novels. Feldman tried to sell *Casino Royale* to EON, but they weren't interested. Compared to *Dr. No* and *From Russia with Love*, *Casino Royale* is slow. Feldman decided that, rather than produce a competing James Bond film, he would make *Casino Royale* a farce. Despite the end product containing no fewer than seven James Bonds and at least one Vesper Lynd, not a single character drinks a Vesper. And so it would remain until the 21st century.

By the end of 2002's *Die Another Day*, filmgoers were exhausted by the bloat that had crept into the series. Bond films took time off and re-evaluated what it was to be James Bond. In that time, things changed in the drinking world. There was a resurgence in cocktails from the dusty archives of drinking history. The Internet made sharing information and enthusiasm easier. Bartenders started experimenting with the past. The craft cocktail boom was born.

The answer for what to do with 007 was the same one they come up with time and again: strip down, back to basics, "back to Fleming." Although they'd not been interested in *Casino Royale* in the 1960s, EON was interested by the 1990s. But the current rights holder, Sony, wasn't interested in selling. So began years of haggling that ultimately culminated in Daniel Craig, Eva Green, and 2006's *Casino Royale*. After nearly half a century of wandering the desert, the very first James Bond novel could finally come home. 007 finally got to order a Vesper.

The recipe (served in a champagne goblet rather than a Martini glass) is, to quote Fleming's original novel and to which Daniel Craig sticks: *"Three measures of Gordon's, one of vodka, half a measure of Kina Lillet. Shake it very well until it's ice-cold, then add a large thin slice of lemon peel."*

Fans of the books were happy to see the Vesper assume its rightful place in the canon of Bond films. However, there were a couple problems, all of which arose from the fact that over fifty years had passed since Fleming first committed the recipe to page. In that time, the proof of Gordon's gin dropped, and Kina Lillet hadn't been available for decades. They dropped the "Kina" (which referred to quinine added to the spirit). Meaning, if you order a Vesper using Bond's specifications, you will get a different cocktail. The ship can be righted somewhat by replacing Gordon's with the higher-proof Gordon's Export. As for the Lillet, you can use Lillet Blanc with a dash or two of bitters, or Cocchi Aperitivo Americano.

However, not getting the same drink as James Bond might be a good idea. Kingsley Amis, the man hired to continue the Bond books after Fleming's death, also wrote a literary study of Bond, 1965's *The James Bond Dossier*. Amis posits Fleming got his Lillets confused. Kina Lillet would have been too bitter. The Vesper is a variation of the Martini, so Fleming probably meant Lillet vermouth.

And while we assume Bond never orders it again because of Vesper's betrayal, perhaps the reality is more mundane; maybe he took that first sip and realized he'd made a terrible mistake. Fleming himself, in a letter to the *Manchester Guardian*, wrote of the Vesper: "I proceeded to invent a cocktail for Bond, which I sampled several months later and found unpalatable."

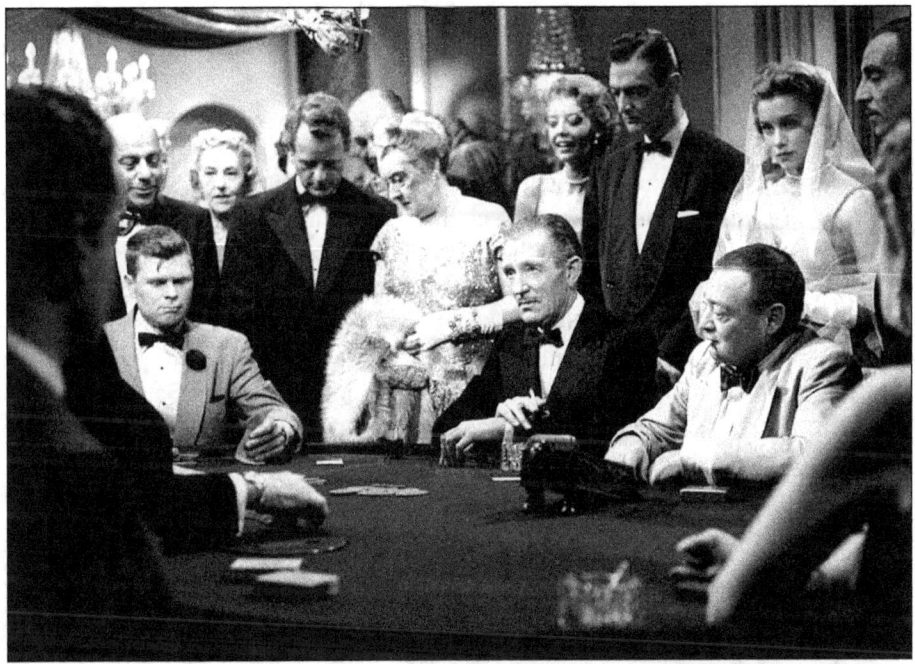

DEAL ME OUT—The 1954 television version of Casino Royale, featuring a lot of water-drinking.

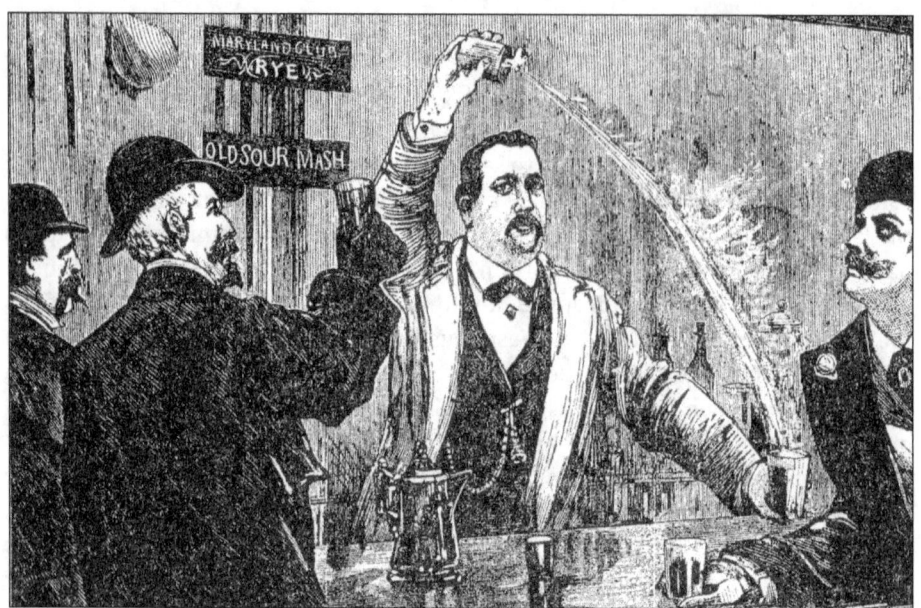

HOW'S YOUR DRINK—It's that one illustration of Jerry Thomas everyone uses!

California Cocktail Courts

For such a simple drink there is a tremendous amount of debate surrounding the Martini, including where it was invented, what you should put in it, and how the ingredients are mixed. Insisting on this way or that way being the proper way, or the only real way, to make a Martini can take on the pseudo-religious fervor of a Sean Connery-versus-Roger Moore debate. How did we come to such a contentious state? How can such a simple drink cause so much controversy? Will knowing the history of the Martini help us understand why it inspires so much impassioned debate? No, it won't, because the cocktail's history is every bit as murky as an overly dirty Martini.

Many of the best-known cocktails have a clearly-defined pedigree, including when, where, and by whom they were created. That's not the case with the Martini. The first published record of the drink was in bartender Jerry Thomas' *The Bar-Tender's Guide* (also known as *How to Mix Drinks or: The Bon-Vivant's Companion*) from 1862, one of the first published collection of cocktail recipes. Its appearance in the book often causes the Martini to be attributed to Thomas, and to the bar at the Occidental Hotel in San Francisco, where Thomas plied his trade. San Francisco is adamant that it was the birthplace of the Martini, but others are not so acquiescent to San Francisco's claim.

About forty miles from San Francisco is the town of Martinez, which also claims to be the birthplace of the Martini. As they tell it, a miner who had just struck gold entered a local watering hole and asked the bartender to make him a drink so that he might celebrate his bonny luck. The bartender threw together what he had on hand: fortified wine (vermouth) and gin. The drink was a hit with the newly-wealthy miner, who referred to the drink by the name of the town—

Martinez—at least until such time that he was so drunk he slurred the name into something vaguely resembling "Martini." The town of Martinez even uses San Francisco's own claim against it. Jerry Thomas' bar guide refers to the drink as a "Martinez." Even *he* knew it came from the town of Martinez, right? Ah, but not so fast!

As San Francisco tells the legend, the miner walked into the Occidental and ordered the drink, and when asked by Jerry where he was headed next, the miner said he was going to return to Martinez. So Jerry named the drink in honor of the man's next stop. To San Francisco's credit, they at least have a historically-verified name and a place associated with the event. There is no name associated with either the bar or the bartender who allegedly invented the drink in Martinez, though a Martinez mayor, Rob Schroder, said in a 2013 interview with *Esquire* that the bar was owned by a man named Julio Richelieu—the name of a Bond villain if ever there was one.

The feud between Martinez and San Francisco became so absurd that San Francisco convened a special hearing to settle the question once and for all. The Court of Historical Review determined that the Martini was indeed invented in San Francisco. Which might have settled things but for the small detail that the Court of Historical Review was *in* San Francisco. Citing a conflict of interest and claiming the judge had sampled too much evidence, Martinez appealed the decision. The appeal, which took place in a court in Martinez, shockingly overturned the San Francisco verdict. But then came yet another shocking twist. In Italy, the company Martini & Rossi was claiming

JERRY THOMAS' MARTINEZ
- 1 dash Boker's Bitters
- 2 dashes Maraschino Liqueur
- 1 pony of Old Tom Gin
- 1 wine glass of Vermouth
- 2 Small Lumps of Ice

"Shake up thoroughly, and strain into a large cocktail glass. Put a quarter of a slice of lemon in the glass and serve. If the guest prefers it very sweet, add two dashes of gum syrup."

MORE MODERN MARTINEZ
- 1 ½ oz Old Tom Gin
- 1 ½ oz Sweet Vermouth
- ¼ oz Maraschino Liqueur
- 2 dashes Angostura Bitters

Add all ingredients to a mixing glass. Fill with ice. Stir well. Strain into a chilled coupe glass.

COFFEE COCKTAIL
- 1 oz Cognac
- 2 oz Tawny Port
- ½ oz Simple Syrup
- 1 whole egg

Add all ingredients to a shaker filled with ice. Shake well. Strain into a chilled old fashioned glass. Garnish with grated nutmeg.

MORNING GLORY FIZZ
- 2 oz Blended Scotch
- ½ oz Fresh Lemon Juice
- ½ oz lime juice
- ½ oz Simple Syrup
- 1 egg white
- 3-4 dashes Absinthe
- Club Soda

Add all ingredients to a shaker. Shake without ice. Add ice and shake again. Strain into a chilled highball or old fashioned glass. Top with club soda. Garnish with an orange peel.

that *they*, or at least *some* Italian bartender, had invented the Martini, and that the name "Martini" derived from the trend of asking for a cocktail by the name of the primary ingredient. Thus, a cocktail based on Martini vermouth would simply be ordered by asking for "a Martini cocktail." Hell, it's as good a claim as any.

Whatever the case, there are some key differences between the Martinez and the Martini, and few Martini people, when presented with a Martinez, would recognize it as anything related to a Martini. For starters, the Martinez calls for Old Tom gin. Old Tom is not a brand of gin, but a style, a little sweeter than the more prevalent London dry. As legend has it (you'll notice that a lot of what passes for booze history begins with the qualifier "legend has it"), Old Tom gin got its name from the "old tom"cat-shaped signs that hung above many public houses in 18th-century England. The stories claim that, because gin was against the law at the time, enterprising pub owners would distill their own gin, which would then be pumped through a hose and out of the cat, where waiting gin fans could sneak a nip since nothing is less conspicuous than sucking a shot of gin out of a wooden cat sign. Old Tom gin eventually fell out of style, until the craft cocktail renaissance of the 21st century sent distillers digging through old records and recipes so they might recreate a lost spirit, though without the need to suck it out of a cat's butt.

Jerry Thomas passed away in 1885, blissfully unaware that the future would hold so much controversy. The Occidental was destroyed during an earthquake in 1905. It is unlikely, despite kangaroo cocktail courts (incidentally, the original name for a vodka Martini was the "kangaroo cocktail") and marketing material, that the origin of the Martini will ever be properly determined. With so much about the Martini's genesis existing purely in the realm of hearsay and "legend has it," modern drinkers are better off hearing the stories, filing them away, and simply enjoying the drink. Still, one wonders how the Martinez became the clear, minimalist gin and vermouth concoction synonymous with James Bond, Don Draper, and mid-century cocktail culture. Part of it was simply changing tastes. Old Tom gin was replaced by London dry. Affinity for sweet vermouth was replaced with a preference for dry. It's around this time that New York gets in on the debate. This legend comes courtesy of the *New Yorker* magazine, in an article that contains little in the way of supporting evidence. In 1911, the head bartender at the Knickerbocker Hotel was Martini di Arma di Taggia. With London dry gin becoming popular, it was purportedly Martini who mixed the first dry Martini and lent his name to the cocktail. It's also been claimed that the drink was invented for or soon became the favorite of John D. Rockefeller. This claim, at least, is exceptionally dubious since Rockefeller was a well-known teetotaler.

Gin's popularity grew during Prohibition. Unlike good whiskey, gin didn't need to be aged, so it could be produced quickly, in large quantities, and cheaply. As gin's stock rose, the Martini transformed from a vermouth-forward cocktail into a gin cocktail. When Prohibition ended, the gin Martini as it is known it today emerged as the preeminent star of the cocktail world, especially once bathtub gin could be replaced with a quality spirit. Exactly when and where the olive came into the mix is, you can probably guess by now that nobody knows for sure...*but there are some legends.*

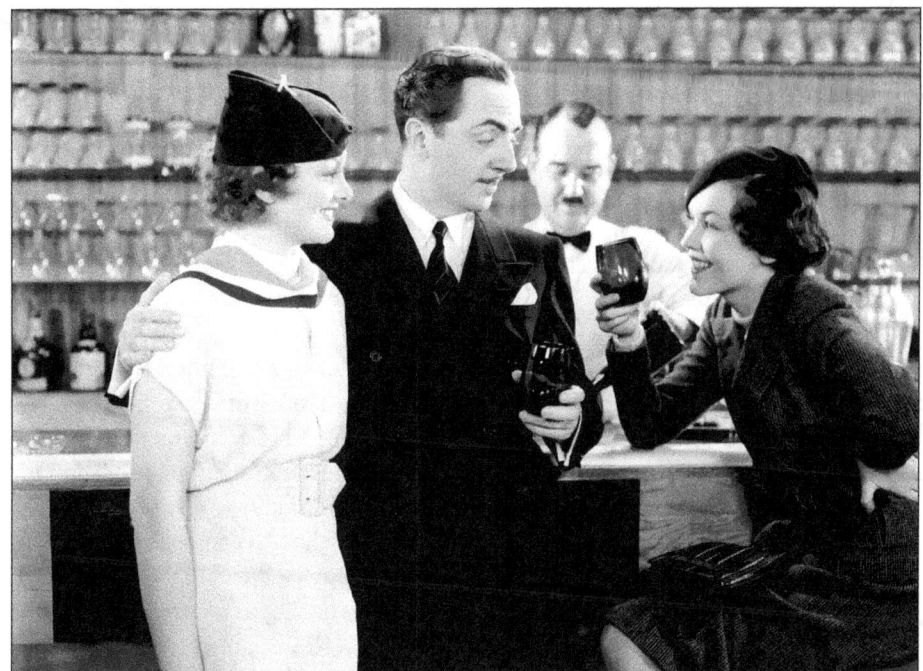

WALTZ TIME—William Powell and Myrna Loy as Nick and Nora Charles, fans of shaken Martinis.

Shaking Things Up

Ordering a Martini can be needlessly complicated. Granted, you can walk into pretty much any cocktail bar and just order a damn Martini, and the bartender will nod and make you a drink (etiquette suggestion: do not walk up to a bartender and *literally* order "a damn Martini" unless you are Lee Marvin). But the drink that bartender makes for you—well, it could contain any number of ingredients in any number of combinations. Gin and vermouth, right? Some people are iffy on the olive and prefer the more classic lemon twist. And what kind of vermouth? How much? Ah, you want vodka, not gin? Oh, you're James Bond and you want vodka *and* gin? Straight up? Straight up with a twist? Perfect, extra dry, dirty, down? Or, you want a Martini, but you want it made with Disaronno? Come on! A line has to be drawn *somewhere*!

A *basic* Martini—the gold standard, no screwing around—uses gin and dry vermouth in a 2:1 ratio, stirred over ice, then strained into a tall, stemmed glass containing no ice ("up") and garnished with either a twist ("up with a twist") of lemon or olives. A *perfect* Martini splits the vermouth 50/50 between dry and sweet. An *extra dry* Martini cuts the amount of vermouth by half. A *dirty* Martini adds brine from the olives to the mix. A Martini served "down" is in a tumbler or rocks glass (that's how they make them at one of Ernest Hemingway's favorite bars, Harry's New York Bar in Paris). If you want cocktail onions instead of a twist or olives, you can do that, too; ask for a Gibson. Now...do you shake it or stir it? Ah, there's a question. In an episode of the television show *The West Wing*, President Josiah Bartlet (Martin Sheen) says "Shaken, not stirred, will get you cold water with a dash

KNICKERBOCKER MARTINI

- 1 ½ oz Dry Gin
- 1 ½ oz Dry Vermouth
- 2 dashes Orange Bitters

Add all ingredients to a mixing glass filled with ice. Stir well. Strain into a chilled cocktail glass. Garnish with a twist of lemon.

NICK & NORA MARTINI

- 2 ½ oz Dry Gin
- ½ oz Dry Vermouth
- 1 dash Orange bitters

Combine all ingredients in a mixing glass. Fill with ice. Stir well. Strain into a Nick and Nora glass.

BRONX

- 1 ½ oz Dry gin
- ¾ oz Dry Vermouth
- ¾ oz Sweet Vermouth
- Juice of ¼ orange

Add all ingredients to a shaker. Shake well. Strain into a chilled cocktail glass. Garnish with orange wheel.

BROOKLYN

- 2 oz Rye Whiskey
- 1 oz Dry Vermouth
- ¼ oz Maraschino Liqueur
- ¼ oz Amer Picon

Add all ingredients to a mixing glass filled with ice. Stir. Strain into a chilled cocktail glass. Garnish with a cherry.

MANHATTAN

- 2 oz Rye Whiskey
- 1 oz Sweet Vermouth
- 5 drops Angostura bitters

Add ingredients to a mixing glass filled with ice. Stir well. Strain into a chilled cocktail glass. Garnish with a cherry.

---

of gin and dry vermouth. The reason you stir it with a special spoon is so not to chip the ice. James [Bond] is ordering a weak Martini and being snooty about it." But then, Bartlett also said, "To be called bourbon it has to come from Kentucky, otherwise it's called sour mash," so the guy's know-it-all game is worse than Bond's. But why shaken at all? Ian Fleming (who, as befits all great storytellers, is not the most reliable source when it comes to his own life) has his own story about how he, and thus James Bond, came to prefer his Martinis shaken. As the story goes (different than "legend has it"), Fleming was in Berlin after the end of World War II, working as a correspondent for Kemsley Newspapers, which allowed him to indulge his taste for travel and adventure. While there, he encountered a bartender by the name of Hans Schroder, who shook the Martinis. Fleming adored them.

By the end of the Fleming era, Bond had still shown no preference for vodka or gin martinis, and except on occasion, he doesn't seem to mind whether they are shaken or stirred. In fact, he drinks more bourbon than Martinis, shaken *or* stirred. The first utterance of "A Martini. Shaken, not stirred" comes in 1956's *Diamonds Are Forever*, but it is the third person narrator who says it, not Bond himself. In 1958's *Dr. No*, 007's diabolical captor offers Bond a Martini, "shaken and not stirred." It wasn't until the movies that Bond's preference for shaken (and vodka) was entered into the public record, to be forever repeated by corny barflies doing their worst Sean Connery impersonation. However, even Connery doesn't utter that line until the third of the films, *Goldfinger*.

Bond wasn't the first cinematic drinking icon to prefer his Martinis shaken, however. Before 007 became synonymous with cocktails and killing, the world's premiere booze icons of page and screen were Nick and Nora Charles. Although introduced in Dashiell Hammett's 1934 book *The Thin Man*, the definitive version of the characters (like James Bond) were their cinematic personifications, embodied by William Powell and Myrna Loy. Before the Hays Office came down on the series and switched out their booze in favor of milk or non-alcoholic cider and their glamorous partying and nightclubbing in favor of raising a child, Nick and Nora were the very last word in Jazz Age glamor and wit, sipping cocktails and solving the occasional murder. One Martini recipe even bore the moniker "The Nick and Nora," and there's a piece of glasswear, the coupe glass, that is commonly referred to as "the Nick and Nora glass." Most recipes for a Nick and Nora Martini specify mixing the drink, but *The Thin Man* is one of the first film appearances of the Martini, "shaken, not stirred."

From the mouth of Nick Charles: *"The important thing is the rhythm. Always have rhythm in your shaking. Now a Manhattan you shake to fox-trot time. A Bronx to two-step time. A dry Martini you always shake to waltz time."*

Nick wasn't alone in prescribing shaking for the Martini. Harry Craddock's seminal 1930 bartenders' guide *The Savoy Cocktail Book* instructs drink makers to shake Martinis (but does not specify to which beat). So why exactly is it that so many Martini enthusiasts blanch at the idea of a shaken Martini, or insist that a shaken Martini can be a delicious drink, but it's not a Martini; it's a Bradford? The most common reason you'll hear is that shaking "bruises" the gin, which means the agitation causes it to become overly bitter. Another complaint is that shaking causes the ice to chip, diluting the gin, causing the drink to go slightly cloudy, and changing its flavor. You will also hear that shaking over-aerates the drink, that traditionally cocktails that are all spirit, as is the case with a Martini, should be stirred, while cocktails with a juice mixer should be shaken.

In the end, we come to that most common of conclusions: you order the cocktail the way you want it made. If someone turns their nose up at you for wanting it shaken, not stirred, you can rest assured that James Bond, Nick Charles, and Harry Craddock have your back. I'd take them over that *West Wing* president any day.

Now as for Bond's preference for vodka instead of gin...

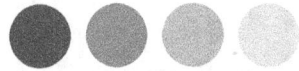

"A perfect martini should be made by filling a glass with gin then waving it in the general direction of Italy."
—Noel Coward

The Playlist: Martinis on the Menu

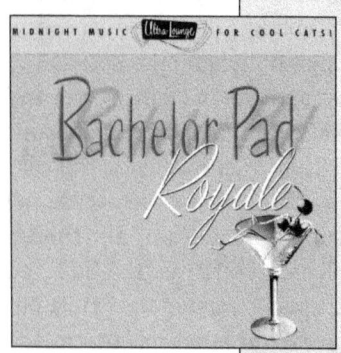

BACHELOR PAD ROYALE
Ultra-Lounge, 1996

Another collection of cocktail culture hits from the Ultra-Lounge series. It opens with Nelson Riddle's "Theme from Route 66" and spirits you along on a sexy journey guaranteed to quell any debate about Martini minutiae in favor of just pouring another one. If your interlude is interrupted by the spy guitar of Elliot Fisher's "Theme from Our Man Flint," well that's really part of the life, isn't it? Don't worry; after that assassin has been dispatched, an arched eyebrow and Cy Coleman's "Playboy Theme" will get the night on track. "Now then, where were we?"

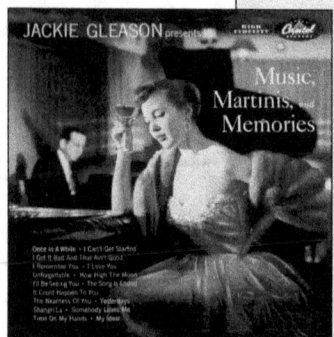

MUSIC, MARTINIS, AND MEMORIES
Jackie Gleason, 1954

It's right there in the title! How can you go wrong with the romantic moods of Jackie Gleason, regardless of how little he may have had to do with arranging the music attributed to him? No matter, because what you get is a platter of misty-eyed easy listening. Gleason evokes scenes of lonely cocktails at an empty bar, or romantic trysts on a patio overlooking the midnight sea, or maybe a silk cocktail dress sliding elegantly to the floor in front of a roaring fireplace. Alone, with another, or maybe there's three. It doesn't matter. This album takes care of all your situations.

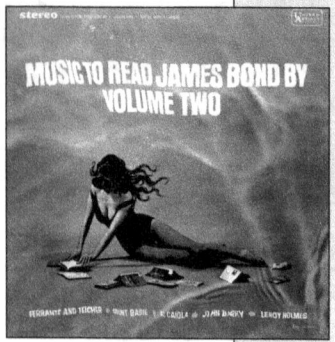

MUSIC TO READ JAMES BOND TO, VOLS. 1-2
Various Artists, 1965-1966

Well obviously there has to be *some* James Bond music in rotation. In the wake of *Goldfinger*, the market was flooded with Bond cash-in albums of wildly varying quality. The two volumes of *Music to Read James Bond By* are among the better examples. Like many of these albums, they're a mix of John Barry themes, covers, and originals inspired by James Bond. There are some heavy hitters of the cocktail era, including highlights such as Perez Prado's Latinesque versions of "Goldfinger" and the "James Bond Theme," Al Caiola's twanging surf guitarish cover of "From Russia with Love," and Count Basie's swinging take on "007."

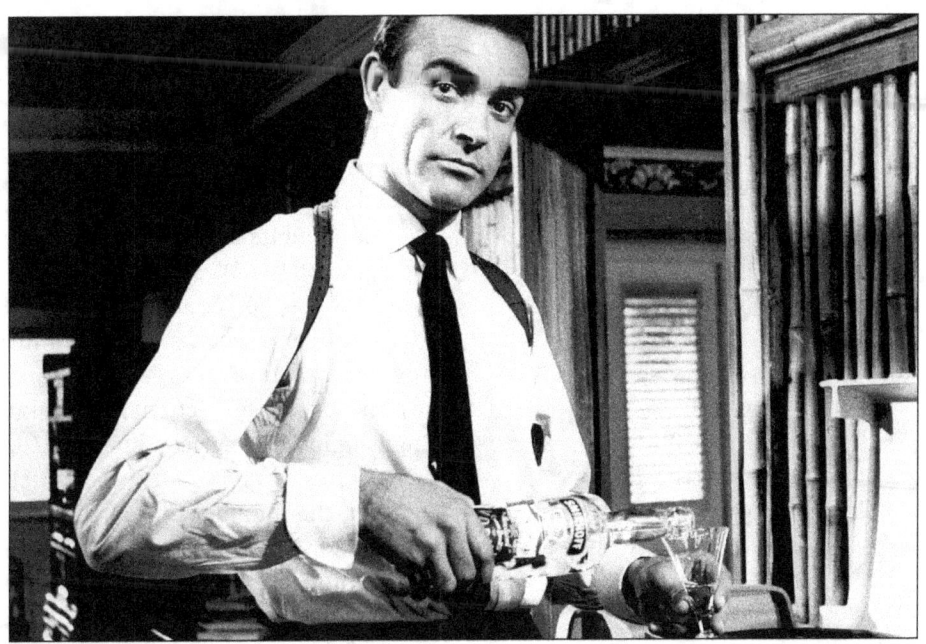

Russian Revolution

There are a couple theories as to why James Bond preferred vodka Martini over the more traditional gin, aside from him simply being an iconoclast. Chief among them is that Smirnoff was a sponsor of *Dr. No* and leaned on producers to make sure the product was featured prominently. Indeed, it is front and center. There are three famous stills from that film. The first is James Bond sitting at the casino table—the first time we see him. The second is Ursula Andress on the beach in her white bikini. The third is of Bond pouring himself a drink from what the camera makes sure you know is a Smirnoff bottle. But the notion that the vodka Martini came to be because of some behind-the-scenes deal doesn't hold water (or vodka, for that matter). The vodka Martini made appearances in the books predating the movies. People were drinking them before Sean Connery. Vodka distillers were already making advertising pushes in the United States, selling mid-century America vodka as a cooler ingredient than gin in a Martini, among other cocktails they hoped to coop. James Bond certainly helped, but *Dr. No* was part of an extended strategy rather than the whole game. It's likely Bond would have ended up drinking a vodka Martini sooner or later regardless of whether Smirnoff slipped him an envelope full of used, non-sequential hundred-dollar bills. But getting to that point took some work. Vodka needed an agent, and not a secret one.

When Ian Fleming started publishing Bond novels, vodka was *persona non grata* in the West. The Cold War had its first flare-up in 1950 with the outbreak of the Korean War. The same year that war ended, *Casino Royale* was published. England and the USSR may have been uncomfortable allies during World War II, but the subsequent decade put a chill on the working relationship. Then came the Cuban Revolution, the 1961 Bay of Pigs invasion by the United States, and the Berlin Wall.

GIBSON

- 2 ½ oz Dry Gin
- ½ oz Dry Vermouth

Add all ingredients to a mixing glass. Fill with ice. Stir well. Strain into a chilled cocktail glass. Garnish with a cocktail onion.

INCOME TAX

- 1 ½ oz Dry Gin
- ¾ oz Dry Vermouth
- ¾ oz Sweet Vermouth
- Juice of ¼ of an orange
- 2 dashes Angostura bitters

Add all ingredients to shaker filled with ice. Shake well. Strain into a chilled cocktail glass. Garnish with an orange peel.

CLASSIC MARTINI

- 1 oz Dry Vermouth
- 2 oz London Dry Gin

Add ingredients to mixing glass. Add ice. Stir well. Strain into a chilled or Martini glass. Garnish with a lemon twist.

VODKA MARTINI

- 3 oz Smirnoff Vodka
- 1 oz Dry Vermouth

Add ingredients to a shaker filled with ice. Shake well. Strain into a Martini glass. Garnish with a lemon twist.

IMPROVED VESPER

- 3 oz Gordon's Gin
- 1 oz Smirnoff Vodka
- ½ oz Cocchi Aperitivo Americano

Add all ingredients to a shaker filled with ice. Shake well. Strain into chilled coupe glass. Squeeze a strip of lemon zest over the drink then add as garnish.

In 1962, the world sat on edge during the Cuban Missile Crisis. The first James Bond movie, *Dr. No*, was also released that year. It was an odd combination to have a blockbuster movie about a suave British secret agent who swilled endless amounts of vodka.

Most of the Western world, like Bond's boss, M, considered vodka "dreadful communist swill,' certainly nowhere near as respectable and sophisticated as Scottish whisky, English gin, or American bourbon (or even wine, as long as it was claret). And yet, the moment that iconic shot of Sean Connery pouring from a bottle of Smirnoff hit movie screens, once *запрещенный* vodka was suddenly in vogue, Cold War be damned. Even more audacious, it became an alternative to good ol' English gin in that most iconic of cocktails, the Martini.

The Martini proper makes its first literary appearance in the second Bond book, *Live and Let Die*. Bond is relaxing in his room at the St. Regis Hotel in Manhattan when he is visited by his friend, CIA agent Felix Leiter, who mixes a couple gin Martinis. Later, when the two agents are at the hotel's King Cole Bar, Leiter orders Martinis for he and Bond, and once again they are gin Martinis (House of Lords gin, to be precise, with Martini & Rossi vermouth). The St. Regis still exists, on 5th Avenue at 55th Street. Designed in the *beaux arts* style prevalent at the time, and standing eighteen stories tall, the St. Regis was the tallest hotel in New York when it opened in 1904. Its owner was John Jacob Astor IV, a member of New York's premiere old-money family, and who perished aboard the Titanic in 1912. The hotel passed to his son, Vincent, who sold it to Benjamin Duke.

In 1932, Duke expanded the hotel, adding the King Cole Bar (anticipating the end of Prohibition). The bar took its name from a mural of King Cole hanging behind the counter. The mural was not a St. Regis original. It had previously hung in another bar: the one at the Knickerbocker Hotel.

Although the hotel, now the St. Regis-Sheraton, changed ownership multiple times and endured many renovations, the King Cole Bar is still there, waiting for savvy secret agents to slip in and have a Martini—although the King Cole is better known for another cocktail. Fernand Petiot was a Parisian bartender at Harry's New York Bar, where he created the Bloody Mary. During World War II, Petiot moved to New York, where he settled into a position at the King Cole and expected to put his famous Bloody Mary on the menu. The hotel's owners did not care for the name, however. Too graphic, they thought, and simply too *déclassé* for the King Cole's upscale patrons. What would that have made of a Sex on the Beach? Or for that matter, what would they have made of the juvenile sexual connotations later associated with the cocktail's new name, the Red Snapper? Or the juvenile secret rumored to be contained in the painting of King Cole from which the bar derived its entire identity (which was praised by none less than Salvador Dali)?

It is not until the end of *Live and Let Die*, when Bond is luxuriating with Solitaire, that the iconic shaken vodka Martini makes its first appearance. "I hope I've made it right," Solitaire remarks as she hands Bond the drink. "Six to one sounds terribly strong. I've never had vodka Martinis before." But Fleming presumably had. He spent a

FASCINATOR

- ⅓ oz French Vermouth
- ⅔ oz Dry Gin
- 2 dashes Absinthe

Add all ingredients to a shaker filled with ice. Shake well. Strain into a chilled cocktail glass. Garnish with a sprig of mint.

•••••••••••••••••••••••

FINE & DANDY

- 1 ½ oz Dry Gin
- ½ oz Cointreau
- 1 dash Angostura Bitters
- ¼ oz Lemon Juice

Add all ingredients to a shaker filled with ice. Shake well. Strain into a chilled cocktail glass. Garnish with a lemon twist.

•••••••••••••••••••••••

FITZGERALD

- 1 ½ oz Dry Gin
- 1 oz Simple Syrup
- ¾ oz Fresh Lemon Juice
- 2 dashes Angostura bitters

Add ingredients to a shaker filled with ice. Shake well. Strain into old fashioned glass. Garnish with a lemon twist.

•••••••••••••••••••••••

MOSCOW MULE

- 2 oz Vodka
- 3 oz Ginger Beer
- 1 oz Fresh Lime Juice

Add all the ingredients to a highball glass filled with ice. Garnish with a lime wheel.

•••••••••••••••••••••••

MONKEY GLAND

- 1½ oz Dry Gin
- 1½ oz Fresh Orange Juice
- 1 tsp Grenadine
- 1 tsp Simple Syrup
- 1 tsp Absinthe

Combine ingredients in a shaker with ice. Shake well. Strain into a chilled cocktail glass.

MYTHS OF THE MARTINI

considerable amount of time in Moscow as a reporter for the Reuters News Agency, covering the trial of six British engineers accused of espionage in 1933. The trial was a sham, using confessions from tortured prisoners who would recant on their confessions, then go back to sticking by them after some additional time in the hands of Soviet police. Two of the engineers received light sentences; one was acquitted entirely; and two were expelled from the Soviet Union. The leniency in sentencing was attributed by many to the reporting of Fleming, whose diligent accounts of the trial caused international uproar at the bald-faced corruption of the Soviet justice system.

Years later, Fleming found himself in Moscow again. This return, in 1939, was at the behest of Great Britain's Foreign Office, which wanted to take advantage of Fleming's easy social demeanor, proficiency in multiple languages, and reputation as a reporter. It was while serving in this capacity that he came to the attention of Rear Admiral John Godfrey, the man who would recruit Fleming for Naval Intelligence. It's also when Fleming had his first drink of vodka. It's likely that, in the Soviet Union, Fleming had his fair share of Martinis that substituted vodka for gin. The two spirits are about as similar as they are dissimilar (both are clear and distilled, but vodka does not have any of the juniper and botanical flavor of gin), but as pre-war vodka would have been the burlier of the two spirits, it's better suited for being shaken.

Once Bond put the seal of approval on the vodka Martini, it became *the* Martini. The tables turned, and where once you had to specify a vodka Martini if that was your druthers, you now had to specifically request a gin Martini if that was what you had in mind. Ironically, as vodka's stock continued to rise, the Martini did not come along for the ride. By the end of the 1960s, drinks like the Martini were regarded as old-fashioned by the younger generation. Though the 1970s saw a return of cocktail culture, it was an extremely different scene than it had been before the Summer of Love. Vodka was the superstar of the next two decades, but as a largely flavorless ingredient in fruit juice cocktails like the Harvey Wallbanger. Roger Moore's James Bond preferred champagne, expressly avoided Martinis of any type to differentiate him from Sean Connery.

The shaken vodka Martini resurfaced during the Pierce Brosnan films, though Finlandia replaced Smirnoff as the film's official vodka. Outside of the films, in the 2000s, the proper gin Martini—and the Martinez, as a matter of fact—enjoyed a comeback. Like a retired prize fighter proving he's still got it, the gin Martini reclaimed the name "Martini." Vodka, of course, remained extremely popular, mostly in flavored form, in fruit-flavored takes on the Martini, and in something to do with Red Bull energy drink. Say what you will about both the Roger Moore and Timothy Dalton's tenures as Bond during those dark decades of cloying concoctions—at least both of them had the good sense to never, *ever* walk up to the bartender and ask for, "a Harvey Wallbanger...shaken, not stirred." §

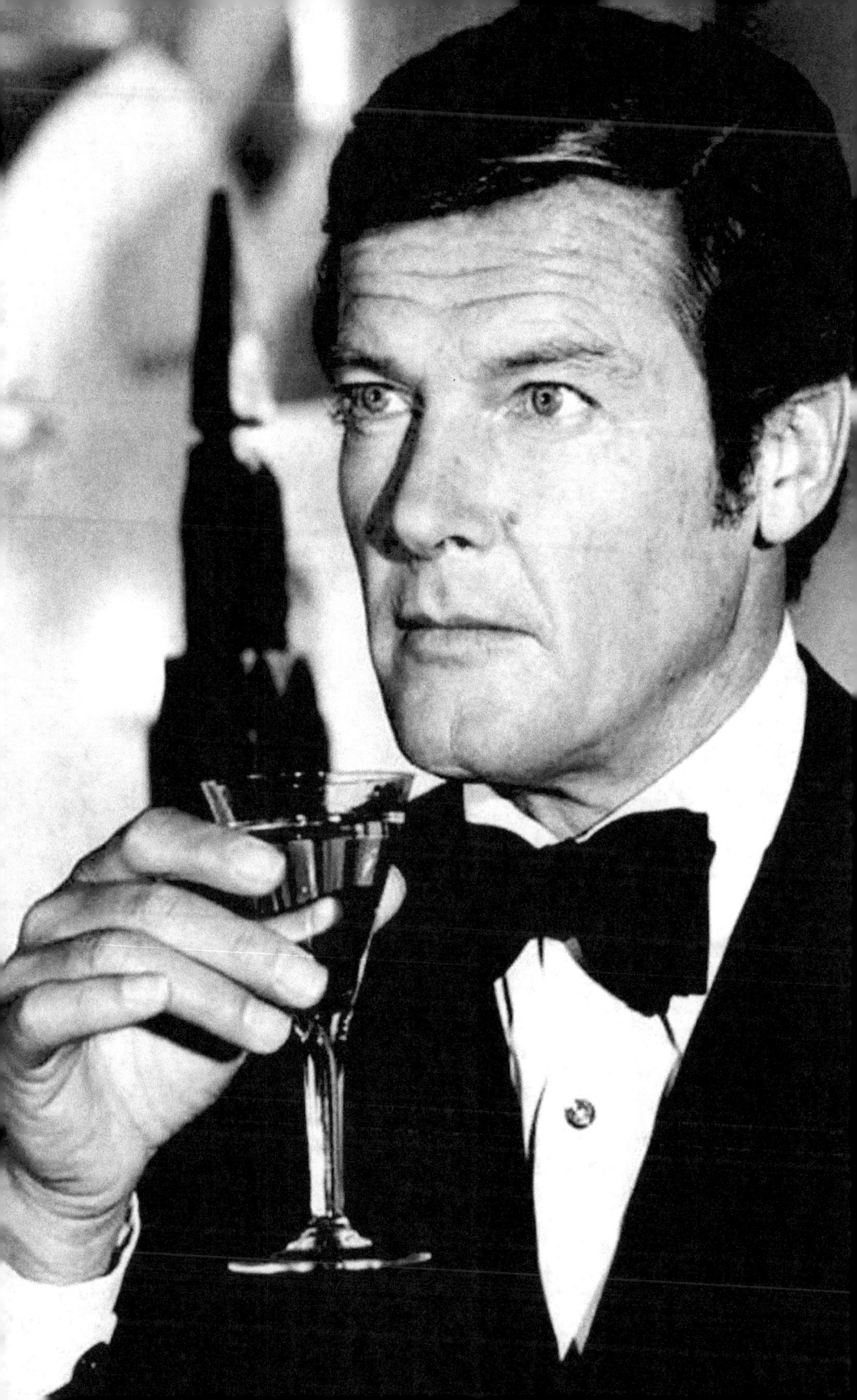

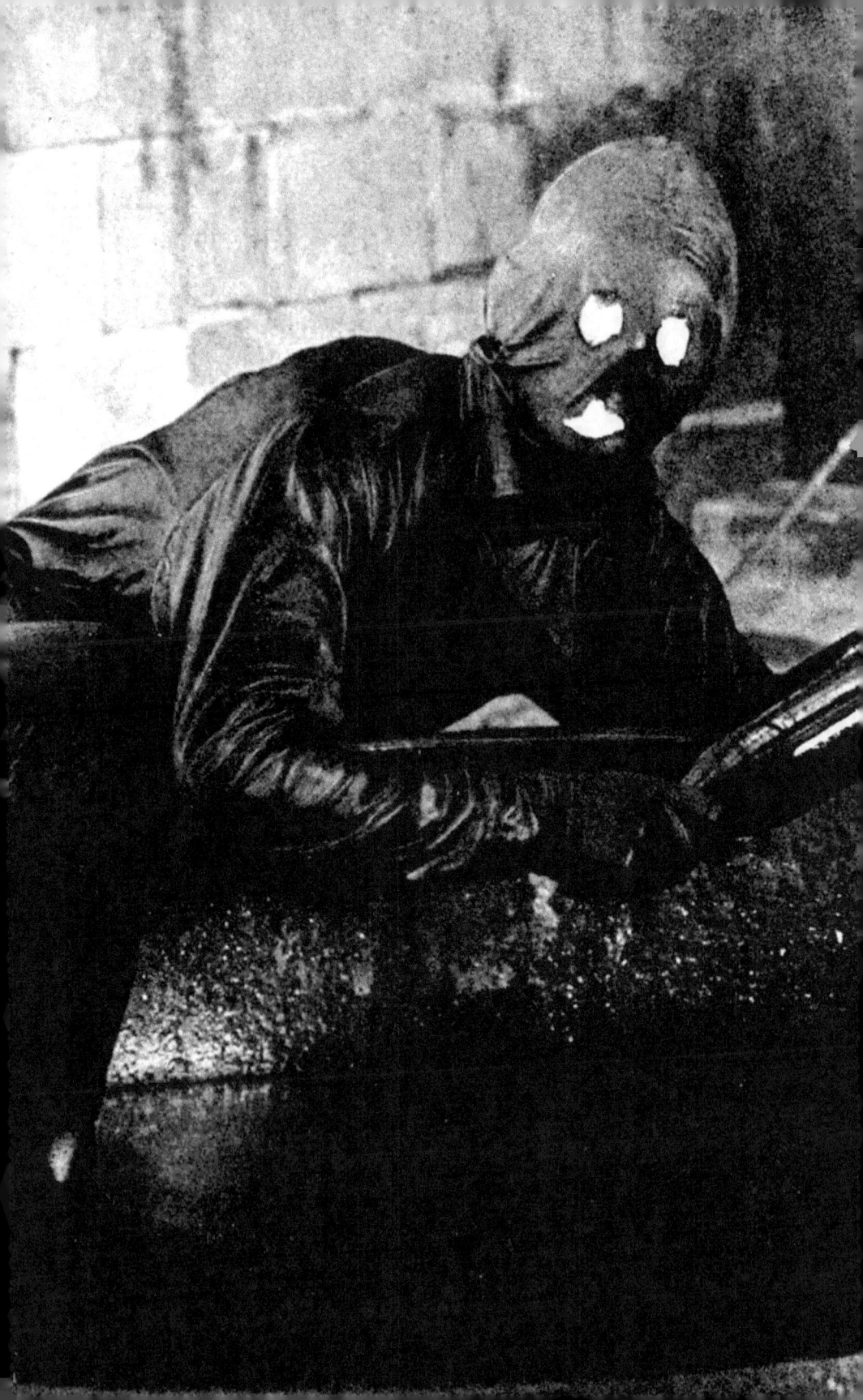

04 IL FAIT PEUR!

Louis Feuillade, Musidora, and the strange, sinister world of Fantômas and Les Vampires

Night falls. With it comes a hush. The good people of Paris are scurrying home to the smell of dinner, the warmth of family, the safety of their homes. But not all the people of Paris are good.

A lone figure—thin, lanky, almost a wraith—skulks across the rooftops. It is a black shadow in a black hood, creeping through a black night on an unknown mission undoubtedly diabolical in nature.

A woman undresses, safe she thinks in the sanctum of her bedroom with the night safely locked away behind the windows. She does not see the black-gloved hand emerging slowly from behind the curtain, holding a slim dagger poised to plunge into her back.

Two men, their flat caps pulled low, struggle with a heavy cloth sack that has been tied shut. As they haul it down a stone dock and let it slide with a splash into the Seine, one could swear something inside the sack was kicking.

On the rickety stage of a seedy Montmartre cabaret, a dancer winks at the hooting crowd as she hoists up the hem of her dress and unfastens a garter. A man with his collar turned up nods imperceptibly to the dancer as he makes his way through the smoke-filled room. He strides down a narrow hall that dead-ends...or so it seems, until the man presses a signet ring into a small depression in the wood. The wall slides open, revealing a stairway. The man steps across the threshold, and the wall creaks shut behind him. The scream that bubbles up from the darkness below cannot be heard over the din of the striptease out front.

Strange things were happening in Paris in 1913.

In February of that year, trials began for the members of the infamous Bonnot Gang, a group of anarchists who cut a swathe of terror across France and Belgium. In December, an Italian named Vincenzo Peruggia was arrested in Florence after trying to sell a painting to Alfredo Geri and Giovanni Poggi, directors of the illustrious Uffizi Gallery. The painting was the Mona Lisa. Peruggia had stolen it from the Musée du Louvre, where he had been employed, in 1911. It was a crime that could have been called "brazen" had he done more than stroll through the workers' entrance, take the painting off the wall, throw his smock over it, and walk back out the same way. Peruggia claimed he was motivated by patriotism and wanted to return the painting to its rightful place in Italy after it had been stolen by Napoleon. He did not know, it would seem, that Leonardo Da Vinci himself had sold the painting to a Frenchman. Many others claimed Peruggia did it for the money, though there's no reason it couldn't have been patriotism *and* greed.

One theory, advanced by *Saturday Evening Post* writer Karl Decker in 1932, claimed Peruggia was working at the behest of a criminal mastermind named Eduardo de Valfierno, who commissioned art forger Yves Chaudron to create six perfect copies of the Mona Lisa. After the heist of the actual Mona Lisa, de Valfierno could sell the forgeries to six different people around the world, each one thinking they were buying the stolen original (these scheme was later used in the 1966 Eurospy caper film *7 donne d'oro contro due 07*, aka *7 Golden Women vs. Two 07*). No one would catch on, because no one could come forward and claim they had the Mona Lisa without getting busted. No one, including Peruggia, corroborated the story, which Decker claims was told to him by Eduardo de Valfierno himself, who then swore the reporter to secrecy, extracting from Decker a vow not to tell the story until after de Valfierno had died. No one else ever came forward. None of the supposed forgeries were ever found. Karl Decker's primary source for this story seems to have been Karl Decker. But then, a criminal mastermind wouldn't leave an easy trail to follow, *would he*?

Between these sensational events, on May 29, the audience at the Theatre des Champs Elysee came to blows. Or so it was claimed: "Many a gentleman's shiny top hat or soft fedora was ignominiously pulled down by an opponent over his eyes and ears," an orchestra member allegedly reported to conductor Pierre Monteux, "and canes were brandished like menacing implements of combat all over the theatre." The cause? The premiere of Igor Stravinsky's *The Rites of Spring*, a discordant modernist ballet under the direction of Ballets Russes choreographer Vaslav Nijinsky. Exactly what happened that night remains unclear. Reports of the incident became more fanciful with each telling. Suffice it to say that *Le Figaro* music critic Henri Quittard did not enjoy the performance, at least the one on stage, dismissing it as "an exercise in puerile barbarity."

Across town in Montmartre, the famous Moulin Rouge was parading can-can kicking legs across its stage. A few minutes away, down a sinister-looking *cul-de-sac* called Cite Chaptal, one could revel in the madness and gore of a play at Le

Théâtre du Grand-Guignol, opened in 1897 by former policeman turned struggling playwright Oscar Méténier. He purchased the defunct chapel in Paris' Pigalle district and intended to stage plays there in the Naturalist style of Émile Zola. Naturalism eschewed poetic dialogue and historical characters in favor of focusing on the underbelly of society: pimps and prostitutes, thieves and tramps, killers, con-men, and cops, all rendered as realistically as possible. Méténier background with the police department provided him with plenty of inspiration for the plays he wrote and directed at Le Théâtre du Grand-Guignol, a moniker that paid tribute to a popular satirical character in puppet theater. Méténier's little theater (the littlest in Paris at the time) quickly earned a reputation. His play *Mademoiselle Fifi*, based on a story by Guy de Maupassant, was shut down for the shocking crime of having prostitute as the main character.

In 1898, Méténier turned directorial duties over to Max Maurey. Under his direction, the Grand-Guignol cemented its reputation as a "house of horrors" and the "Chapel of Gore & Psychosis." Maurey tapped into public fascination with that which revolted. He would capitalize on the desire of audiences to witness things that repulsed them. From 1898 until 1914, Maurey's productions reveled in murder, betrayal, and wickedness. He was particularly fond of plays that explored madness and psychosis.

Maurey didn't care if people were outraged as long as they kept buying tickets. And buy tickets they did, subjecting themselves to all manner of depraved acts and salacious displays. Maurey pioneered the sort of publicity stunts and ballyhoo that became the stock in trade of exploitation filmmakers such as Dwain Esper in

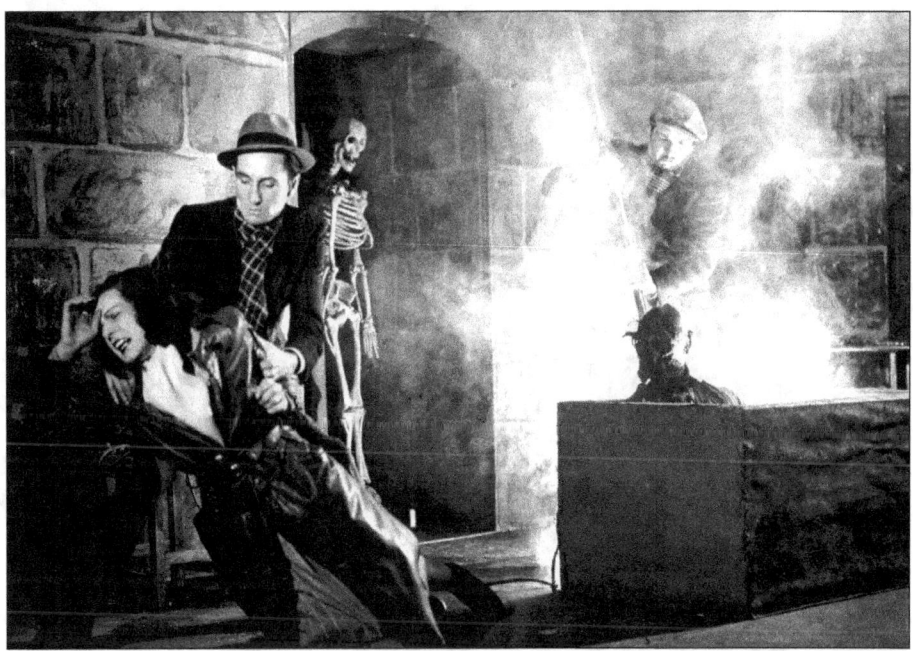

HOUSE OF HORRORS—Just another night on the stage of the Grand-Guignol.

the 1930s and William Castle in the 1950s (Esper's *Maniac* is practically a Grand-Guignol play turned movie, right down to a shared infatuation with madness and perversion). Maurey's PR touted the dangers of fainting during the shows. He even hired "doctors" to be on hand in case anyone suffered a heart attack or other fear-induced malady.

In 1901, he hired André de Lorde, a librarian in the Bibliothèque de l'Arsenal, as the Grand-Guignol's playwright. De Lorde, often collaborating with psychologist Alfred Binet, plumbed the depths of human madness for his material. The cramped interior of the theater, festooned with glowering angels and other accoutrements from its time as a church, only served to intensify the fear. De Lorde became known as "Le Prince de la Terreur." In 1914, Max Maurey retired and turned Le Théâtre du Grand-Guignol over to Camille Choisy, a man obsessed with, among other things, special effects. He pioneered the theater's use of gore effects, reveling in the spectacle of sex and violence that continued to keep audiences shocked and in attendance, even with the horrors of World War I bearing down on them.

The theater was infamous not just for its lurid tales of the macabre, but also for the behavior of the audience which, though a mix of both low and high-brow attendees, was prone to treat their chairs like the back seat of a Camaro at a drive-in theater. Couples out for a night or in the midst of a clandestine tryst were more than willing to let their fear lead to their arousal, and their arousal lead to...or so the reports would have you believe. The theater was happy to foster those rumors. Choisy hired actress Paula Maxa in 1917, the world's first "scream queen." She appeared in countless productions and was always game to endure grotesque

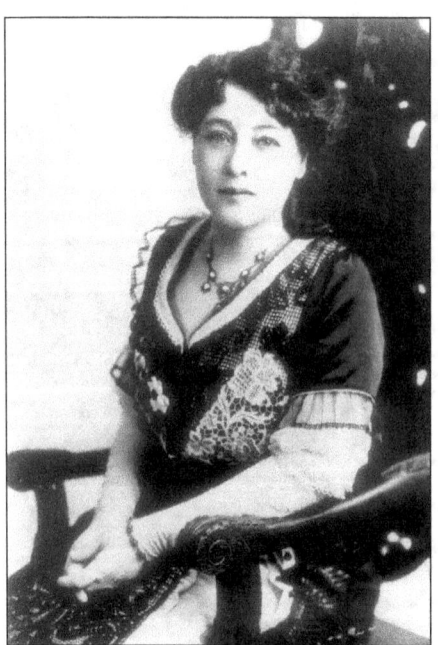 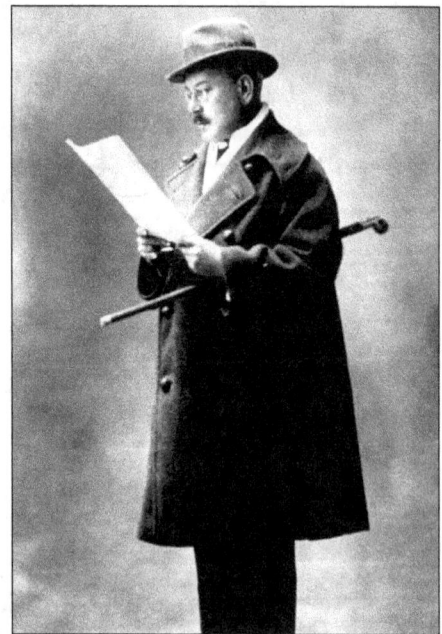

QUEEN AND KING—Alice Guy-Blaché and Louis Feuillade, pioneers of early cinema.

and terrible fates. Her catalog of suffering—scalped, disemboweled, raped, beheaded, dismembered, stabbed, poisoned, whipped, strangled, flayed, burned, and even eaten alive by a puma—earned her the title "the Sarah Bernhardt of the Impasse Chaptal," or more fitting, "the most assassinated woman in the world." She was the undisputed queen reigning over the blood-soaked stage of the Grand-Guignol.

A few minute's stroll from the Grand-Guignol, down the seedy Boulevard de Clichy, audiences were turning out in record numbers at the Gaumont Palace to marvel at the exploits of a screen villain who would have been at home on the Grand-Guignol's stage. Opening on May 9, this 54-minute film was a celebration of everything causing the average Parisian anxiety. The title character was a thief, murderer, criminal mastermind, anarchist, and probably enjoyed *The Rites of Spring*. He definitely wasn't above pulling down your hat and skewering you with a cane. Embodying everything people feared and to which they secretly thrilled was this enigmatic masked man. He was Fantômas, and he had been unleashed by a man named Louis Feuillade.

During his time at the Gaumont production company, Feuillade made hundreds of films, but he is best known for a trio of serialized thrillers: *Fantômas*, *Les Vampires*, and *Judex*. Although not connected by narrative, these films *seem* to take place in the same dangerous, seductive world. His films, like the plays of the Grand-Guignol, drew audiences from all strata of society. Everyone wanted to be in the thrall of Feuillade's murderous fiends, merciless cutthroats, and sensual *femmes fatale*. They laid the groundwork for what became *cinema fantastique*, a blend of horror and wonder, nightmare and dream, romance and revulsion. Feuillade's thrillers paraded images of the grotesque and horrific across screens, mixing them with a surrealism born from his attention to shock and spectacle at the expense of a coherent narrative.

Born in 1873, Louis Feuillade showed an early interest in writing. Before the age of twelve, he was scripting his own vaudeville shows, submitting poetry to local newspapers, and even had a few published articles (about bullfighting). After a stint at a Catholic seminary and a period of military service, Feuillade married and, in 1902, moved to Paris to pursue his dream of being a writer. Success, however, was slow in coming. It wasn't until 1905, after submitting screenplays to the Gaumont Film Company, that his career picked up.

Gaumont was founded in 1895 by inventor Léon Gaumont working in partnership with astronomer Joseph Vallot, engineer Gustave Eiffel (he of the Tower), and financier Alfred Besnier. It's the world's oldest film production studio, preceding by a year the other titan of French cinema, Pathé Studio. Gaumont worked most of his life as an engineer and had a keen interest in photography. In 1897, he founded the company's motion picture division, ostensibly as a way to promote their motion picture cameras. Léon appointed his talented secretary, Alice Guy, as Head of Production at this new film studio, a position she filled

1789
- ½ oz Bonal Quina
- ½ oz Lillet
- 1 ⅓ oz Brenne Whiskey

Add all ingredients to mixing glass with ice. Stir well. Strain into a chilled Martini glass. Brenne is recommended here. It's a French single malt finished in old cognac barrels.

THE ROSE
- 2 oz Dry French Vermouth
- 1 oz Kirschwasser Cherry Brandy
- 1 Cucumber Slice
- 1 tsp Raspberry Syrup

Add ingredients to a mixing glass and fill with ice. Stir, well. Strain into a chilled cocktail glass. Garnish with a brandied cherry.

KIR ROYALE
- ¾ oz Crème de Cassis
- 5 oz Champagne

Pour chilled Champagne into a wine glass. Slowly add the crème de cassis.

LE FORUM
- 1 ½ oz Dry Gin
- 2 tsp Noilly Prat Vermouth
- 4-5 drops Grand Marnier

Add ingredients to a mixing glass. Stir well. Strain into chilled cocktail glass.

TEMPTATION
- 1 ½ oz Canadian Whiskey
- 2 dashes Triple Sec
- 2 dashes Dubonnet
- 2 dashes Absinthe

Add ingredients to a shaker filled with ice. Shake well. Strain into chilled cocktail glass. Garnish with a twist of lemon and an orange peel.

from 1897 until 1907. She worked as a director and overseer of the studio's other writer and directors. Previously, she had been employed at a photography company that went out of business. Gaumont bought the defunct company's remaining stock of film and, finding Alice there, offered her a job. She was a quick learner.

When she assumed the role of director and Head of Production, she became not only the first female director of motion pictures, but could also be considered one of the pioneers of the narrative movie. These were the early days of filmmaking, and Alice Guy was at the forefront alongside Auguste and Louis Lumière (whose fifty-second-long *Sortie des Usines Lumière à Lyon* was projected at the Salon Indien du Grand Café in 1895), stage magician turned special effects genius Georges Méliès (who directed his first motion picture, the minute-long *Une partie de cartes*, in 1896), and in the United States Thomas Edison, who kicked off everything in 1891 when he debuted the Kinetoscope. In 1906, Alice made *La vie du Christ*, a 33-minute narrative feature with a cast of over 300. She was one of the first directors to experiment with sound, using Gaumont's "Chronophone" system, which synchronized pre-recorded sound effects with a film during exhibition.

In 1905, Guy received two scripts from Louis Feuillade and decided not just to produce them, but also to invite Feuillade to Gaumont so he could direct them himself. Feuillade, unsure of the fiscal viability of movie making, declined the offer to direct, choosing to remain semi-employed as a journalist. By 1906, however, he'd had enough of that and joined Gaumont as a writer and director. In 1907, Alice Guy moved to the United States, where she worked as the head of the American outpost of Gaumont before founding her own movie production studio, The Solax Company, in 1910 with her husband Herbert Blaché and partner George A. Magie. It was for a while the largest film studio in America. Before she left, She promoted Feuillade to Artistic Director.

In 1910, Feuillade had his first hits with the comedic *Bébé Apache* series, about the exploits of a precocious four-year-old child. He repeated the formula, and met with similar success, with the *Bout de Zan* series in 1913. Both were built on the sound assumption that people love watching children kick cops in the ass. There were ninety films in the *Bébé Apache* series and sixty-two *Bout de Zan* films, but Feuillade's output wasn't all little kids wearing fake mustaches and smoking cigars. In 1911, prefaced by the release of an artistic manifesto (as these things often are), Feuillade introduced *la vie telle qu'elle est*: "life as it is." Under this philosophy, sort of a protean version of neo-realism, Feuillade made fourteen serious, realistic films. However, something a little more anarchic was percolating in the back of his brain.

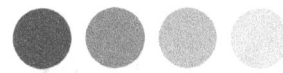

Feuillade thought himself a moral man, not given over to the baser temptations of human craving. But he also considered himself a commercial filmmaker. Inspired by the success of the American serial *What Happened to Mary*, Feuillade began working on a serial of his own. It introduced one of the all-time great madmen of the silver screen: Fantômas, the murderous thief who hid his identity behind a series of disguises and hid the corpses of his many victims in whatever wicker trunk was handy. Feuillade may have meant his films to condemn wicked behavior, but that's not how things worked out. His second serial, *Les Vampires*, was even more outrageous, and even less successful in making crime look anything but exciting and cool. It was a phantasmagoric orgy of criminal mischief and boiling sexuality, a gleeful, if unintended, celebration of everything Feuillade hoped it would condemned. But before Feuillade's madmen (and women) could rampage through Paris, someone had to invent the serial. That person lived in the United States.

"Fantômas."

"What did you say?"

"I said: Fantômas."

"And what does that mean?"

"Nothing.... Everything!"

"But what is it?"

"Nobody.... And yet, yes, it is somebody!"

"And what does the somebody do?"

"Spreads terror!"

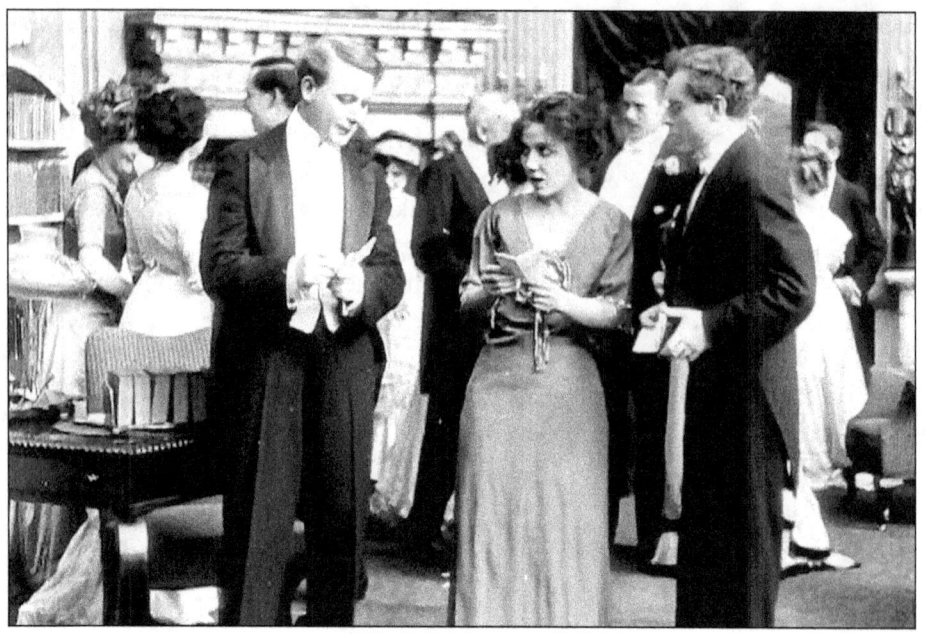

Sinister Silence

Serialized films can be traced to 1912, when a production from Edison Studios decided to tell the growing American movie audience *What Happened to Mary* (no question mark, despite how it is sometimes referenced). Like all early movie studios, Edison was always looking for new ways to exploit emerging motion picture technology and expand the variety of picture types.

Between 1912 and 1916, the movie industry was a very busy place. Although such things are difficult to pin down, since nothing evolves overnight, those years roughly represent the point at which the "primitive" stage of filmmaking ended and the more technically adept, savvy "early" period began (the fully realized "modern" era began around the turn of the decade). As a result of so many things happening so quickly, timelines become confused. Teasing out who came first, or who did it next and better, or who got most popular doing it, can be daunting.

Companies such as Gaumont and Pathé extended their reach across the globe, so that even in far-away places like Japan, their films seemed like local products. Open up a Japanese movie fan magazine from 1915, and there's American serial queen Pearl White staring at you. Most of the studios at the time were within arm's reach of one another, clustered in Fort Lee, New Jersey, or scattered around urban centers New York and Paris. After all, you had to make it easy for your actors to get to and from work, and most of the early stars of the silent era came from the stage. The clustering of movie production studios around major cities also makes sense not just because it's where the engineering was taking place, and not just because it provided a filmmaker with an ample pool of talent; it also made sense because people as a whole were moving toward urban centers and away from agrarian sprawl. The Industrial Revolution changed everything about the developed world, but poverty still ground people down. A city is a complicated machine, and it takes a lot or manpower to make it work. More manpower than men could provide. It's not like women hadn't always been a part of the workforce in one way or another, but as populations gravitated toward cities, women found themselves in a variety of new jobs, sometimes because of opportunity, often out of necessity. As they entered the urban workforce, women began to flex more independent muscle. By 1912, the year that the world's first adventure serial hit movie screens, women were no longer just wives, mothers, and farmhands. They were integrated into the city, and they were often at the forefront of influential social and political movements of the time. Labor, suffrage, even temperance. As women pushed for more liberty, more freedom, more independence, they also started to earn higher wages.

Filmmakers were keen on courting this new kind of women, and if at all possible, parting her from at least a little bit of the money she was making. At the same time, film studios were experimenting with new forms of motion picture. Longer films. More complex films. Serialized films. Films that starred women in athletic, adventurous, non-traditional roles. During a meeting between Charles Dwyer, editor of a magazine called *The Ladies' World*, and Horace G. Plimpton, manager of Thomas Edison's Kinetoscope Company, the duo came up with an idea. Serialized stories—that is, long stories published in short monthly installments—had been a staple of magazines since at least the penny dreadful days. So why not mimic the format on film? Furthermore, why not adapt a serial for film and release it to theaters concurrent with the publication of each new installment in the magazine? Plimpton and Dwyer figured it would benefit them both by bringing readers into theaters and convincing moviegoers to buy the magazine. Plimpton was interested in adapting a soon-to-be-published serial called *What Happened to Mary*, about the adventures of a young woman from a small town who moves to New York City.

It only took a couple of days for Plimpton and Edison Studios to secure the rights and hash out the release and promotion schedule with Dwyer and *Ladies' World*. In short order, *What Happened to Mary* became the world's first cinematic serials or "chapter plays." Edison Studios made twelve one-reel episodes, released every month beginning on July 26, 1912. The first chapter established the premise: Mary, an abandoned baby, is discovered on the doorstep of a small-town shopkeeper. In the basket alongside the foundling is $500 and a note promising the shopkeep $1,000 more for raising the child and seeing that she marries a good man. The story then skips ahead eighteen years, with Mary grown up, growing increasingly bored with small-town life, and increasingly irritated at her adoptive father's efforts to push her into marriage. When she discovers the old note explaining her situation, she decides enough is enough and heads for New York where, if content can be divined from the titles of chapters, she spends a lot of time escaping from kidnappers as she seeks to uncover the mystery of who her real parents are.

Most of the chapters were directed by actor-director Charles Brabin, who joined the Edison Manufacturing Company around 1908. Unlike what would become the case with many subsequent serials, these were not "cliffhangers" that left the heroine dangling in some precipitous situation. Although there was an emphasis on thrills, each chapter was self-contained, wrapping up its story by the end of the reel.

It was a huge success, bringing in not just the working-class women targeted by *The Ladies' World*, but also a large cross-section of urban cinephiles. The August 1912 issue of *Moving Picture World* described the crowd at a screening of the second chapter as "a mixed audience of Chinese, Italians, Greeks and Syrians." Knowing they had a bona fide sensation on their hands, Edison wasted no time exploiting *What Happened to Mary*'s overnight popularity. A theatrical version was produced by Leigh Morrison, with actress Olive Wyndham assuming the role of Mary. It played to packed houses beginning in February of 1913. Edison created tie-in products like hats and jigsaw puzzles. They hired lyricist Earl Carroll and composer Lee Orean Smith to write a Tin Pan Alley tune (called "Mm, What happened to Mary? Mm, What happened to Mary?" and with lyrics like "Mary had a dainty little fad, Of making boys feel very kindly t'ward her, Ruby lips, That Cupid created, Baby eyes, But so educated, Mary was a very wary fairy, So nothing ever happened to her.") *The Ladies' World* ran a contest challenging its readers to guess "what happens to Mary," predicting the finale, the winner of which received a $100 prize.

At the time, there was no clear-cut definition of what was or was not a serial versus, say, a series of films. It's hard for the first of something to follow all of the rules that emerge in its wake. *What Happened to Mary* doesn't have the cliffhanger endings that would become the norm for serials. It does, however, establish a number of conventions that would be followed by many serials of the 1910s. It's action-oriented, or at least contains some action and stunts. It focuses on a woman. And perhaps its most pervasive contribution of all to the format: it presents marriage—or the threat of marriage—as an impending death sentence for a woman's free-spirited days of adventure, though it also presents marriage as ultimately desirable. This was true both for the character and the woman playing her. In the 1920s, stars were portrayed as living glamorous lives in glamorous clothing, but in the 1910s, almost every studio sold their top star as much more down-to-earth and domestic. They may battle evil swamis and escape lions by day, but by night they enjoyed reading the Bible, gardening, and being married.

What Happened to Mary was such a huge success that a sequel series, *Who Will Marry Mary?*, was released the following year. Alas both it and *What Happened to Mary* are currently assumed to be lost (though some 8mm and 16mm reels of some *What Happened to Mary* chapters reportedly still exist).

Also lost, for a very long time, was the serial's star, Mary Fuller.

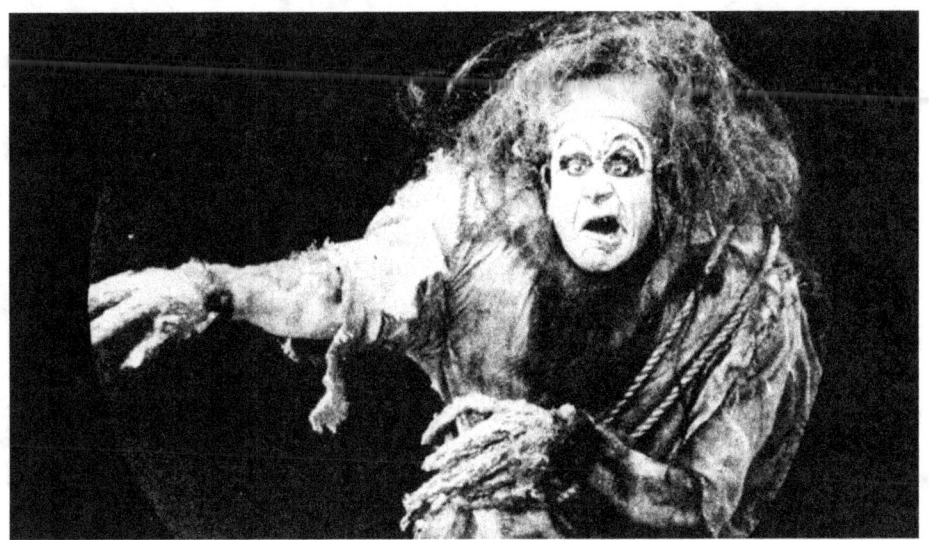

Mary and the Monster

"They say that some of Mary Fuller's ancestors were born 'neath Italy's sunny skies, If such be true or no, I know not; but this I know is so – she has the most thrilling eyes that one can ever hope to see; eyes that set one a-dreaming of Venice, and of the days when Rome was mighty and her dark-eyed maids walked in soft melancholy down marbled avenues, thinking of some tall sons of Rome afar upon the frontiers with the legion." – Colgate Baker, "The Girl on the Cover." *Photoplay*, June 1915.

If Colgate Baker's appraisal of Mary Fuller seems a tad flowery, he can rest assured he was not alone. The movie fan magazines of the day were stuffed with letters and poetry from adoring fans of Mary Fuller. Photos of her appeared just as frequently, and advertisements hocking movie star photos never failed to mention her or illustrate their ad with her face. Outside of the movie magazines, you could even buy Mary Fuller makeup, guaranteed(ish) to give you the same healthy, youthful beauty of Mary Fuller. And she wasn't just an actress and subject of features; she was also writer, penning articles for a number of magazines when she wasn't busy writing scenarios and scripts for serials and features, including some with enticing names like *The Golden Spider*, *The Viking Queen*, and *A Princess of the Desert*. *Motion Picture Magazine* published a series of "Extracts From the Diary of Mary Fuller" throughout 1916, featuring such choice recollections from the star as "April 6th. — They blew me up with a Black Hand bomb today, doing 'Dolly of the Dailies' (No. 7). The charge of dynamite was very heavy. The shack was wrecked, my clothes were torn and blackened, and blood ran from a scalp wound. It was exciting."

For a brief period in the first half of the 1910s, she was consistently ranked as one of the most popular actresses in the country, second only to the undefeatable juggernaut that was Mary Pickford. By 1918, she had vanished. She was born in Washington, DC, and like most movie stars of the day, started her career on stage before seeking employment as a screen actress, first at Brooklyn's Vitagraph, then later at the Edison Film Company. It was at Edison that she became one of the most popular players in America, appearing in many of the company's shorts, including 1910's groundbreaking *Frankenstein*. It was one of the first, if not the first, horror films ever made, provided you don't count Georges Méliès' *Le Manoir du Diable* from 1896, which ran a little over three minutes and featured a man menaced by a devil, ghosts, a skeleton, and lots of vanishing/reappearing camera tricks. Méliès' short contains all the trappings of a nascent horror genre, but they're presented more as gags. Méliès' stock in trade was mischievous ghosts, capering devils, dancing fairies, and guys who just can't stop juggling their own head. There's no attempt to build tension or elicit screams in any of his films. They were there to amaze, the cinematic conjuring tricks of a lifelong stage magician.

Japanese director Shirō Asano made a duo of ghost films in 1898, *Bake Jizo* (*Jizo the Spook*) and *Shinin no sosei* (*Resurrection of a Corpse*), but both are lost films unavailable for assessment. Gaumont's Alice Guy made a single-reel adaptation of *The Hunchback of Notre Dame* called *Esmerelda* in 1905, but despite Quasimodo's deformity, there's not much in the way of horror. In that regard, the honor of "first horror film" still goes to *Frankenstein*, though at the time its makers did everything in their power to convince censorship boards (who weren't too pleased in general with the motion picture business, what with its dangerous content and, more importantly, the fact that it facilitated the gathering of men and women in dark theaters where who knows what sort of hand-holding and sin could occur) that there was nothing offensive or blasphemous about their adaptation of Mary Shelley's classic. But really, when you make a movie about a creature stitched together from the parts of various corpses and reanimated by a mad scientist, the horror is going to come through regardless. The film glosses over the collection of

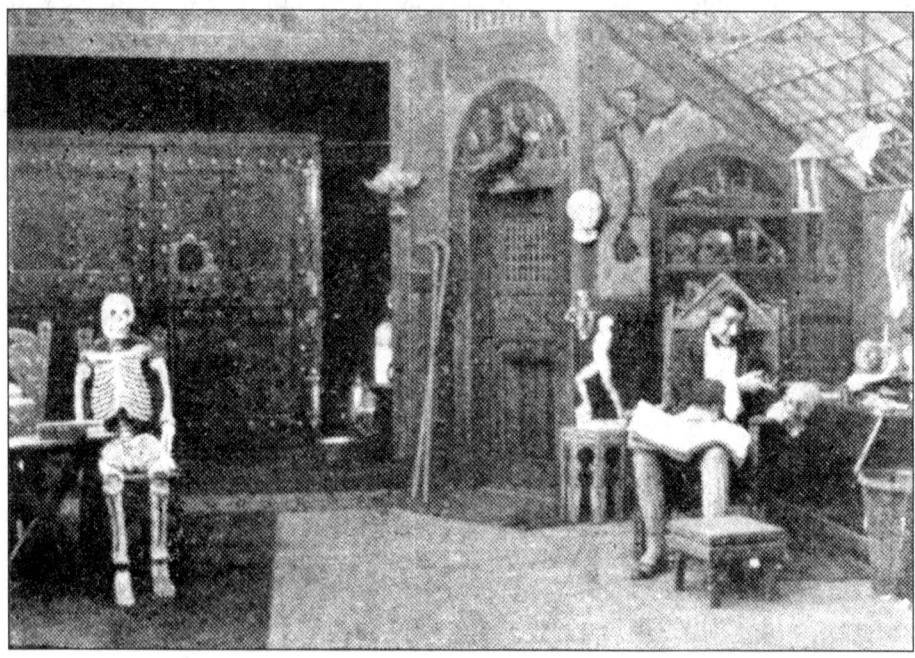

body parts and requisite "dabbling among the unhallowed damps of the grave," but in the end, it's still a living creature created out of the dead (and Frankenstein's lair is still strewn with skeletons). Despite Edison's reassurances, the film came out looking suspiciously like a horror film.

The single-reel "not a horror" movie took a lavish three days to complete at a time when such things were usually completed in under a day. It was filmed at Edison's newly opened Bronx studio, which replaced their facility on 25th Street in Manhattan once that space became too small to house their fast-growing film production unit. It was directed by Edison regular J. Searle Dawley (despite being known now as "Edison's Frankenstein," Thomas Edison wasn't involved in its making; he just owned the studio). Dawley was a competent but old-fashioned director who shot the film in a static, stage production-like style much like the films of Méliès but also much on the way out of fashion. The role of the monster went to staple Edison Player Charles Ogle, while Dr. Frankenstein was played by Augustus Phillips. The makeup Ogle devised for the creature was a harrowing mixture of the pathetic and the terrifying, the nightmarish and the absurd, based reportedly on the appearance of the monster as played on stage by Thomas Porter Cooke in the 1823 production *Presumption; or the Fate of Frankenstein*. Into the role of Frankenstein's bride Elizabeth stepped the young, up-and-coming Mary Fuller.

While Dawley's directorial style is old-fashioned, the special effects he devised for the film's famous monster creation scene were remarkable and still remain disturbing and mesmerizing. The effect was achieved by building a puppet with a fake skeleton structure, then setting the whole thing on fire. The resulting footage was then put into the final film backward, achieving an eerie, at times even grotesque effect of watching the creature form out of the stew of raw materials Frankenstein has dumped into his cauldron. Speaking of which, it *is* a cauldron rather than an assemblage of mad science laboratory gear, and the creation of the creature is rooted much more in alchemy than science. Although there are no overt occult symbols, Frankenstein employs a series of gestures somewhere between the ritual and stage magic, and his creature is concocted in what is basically a witch's cauldron. As such, 1910's *Frankenstein* isn't just the first horror movie; it's the first filmed golem story, predating the three most famous golem movies: 1920's *Der Golem, wie er in die Welt kam*, 1927's *Metropolis*, and 1931's *Frankenstein* (the Boris Karloff one).

At first, the 1910 *Frankenstein* plays coy with the doctor's abomination. After the phantasmagorical creation scene, which stops short of showing the fully-formed creature, we see the monster only as a horrifying, dead-looking, clawed arm reaching out toward Frankenstein from behind a heavy metal door. Once again, any Edison company claims that this isn't a horror film become ridiculous. This is horror, pure and simple, and one can only imagine how audiences reacted to that hideous, withered arm groping out from that alchemical furnace.

Dr. Frankenstein himself certainly reacts poorly to it, throwing up his arms in unholy terror and fleeing to his bedroom, where he promptly faints for the first of what will prove to be a surprising number of times for so short a film. The creature, knowing no better, follows the doctor to the bed chamber, and in another truly disturbing scene, emerges slowly from the shadows to stare at its unconscious creator. And it is then that we see, for the first time in cinema history, Frankenstein's monster.

Ogle's monster is topped with a ragged mane of hair the likes of which wouldn't be seen again until Larry Fine became famous as part of the Three Stooges. It's head is deformed, the jaw seemingly incorrectly hinged to the rest of the skull. The face is pallid, the lips blackened with rot. Its arms are withered and end in clawed fingers. Its body is hunched and contorted, and its bandage-swathed feet are almost comically huge, like a clown. And perhaps there is more than a little of the clown about this creature—Ogle was an old vaudevillian, after all—but it is a nightmare version of a clown, a clown that has been hacked apart and inexpertly reassembled. When Frankenstein's monster next made it to the screen in Universal's 1931 classic, makeup artist Jack Pierce obviously didn't look to (or possibly even know about) Ogle's creature, but one can see an echo of it, if perhaps only coincidentally, in the makeup used on actor Christopher Lee when he portrayed the shambling monster in Hammer Studio's 1957 film *The Curse of Frankenstein* (though Hammer wisely opted out of wild hair, at least until 1974's *Frankenstein and the Monster from Hell*).

Post-production on Edison's *Frankenstein* took two more weeks, much of which was spent color-tinting some of the scenes, a process that was common during the silent era and which was pioneered by Thomas Edison in 1884 after he filmed dancer Annabelle Moore, whose "Butterfly Dance" stage performance incorporated color projection of a stereopticon. On Friday, March 18, 1910, *Frankenstein* escaped from the Edison labs and rampaged through the population. Based on the remaining articles by film critics of the time, the film was respected for its technical merits and thematic complexity. Ogle's monster is not a rampaging beast, although it and Dr. Frankenstein are prone to bouts of grappling whenever Dr. "Faintenstein" can go more than a few seconds without being felled by the vapors. Instead, the monster is an abandoned pet, an unloved child who cannot comprehend its father's rejection and love for someone else. Dr. Frankenstein sees not so much a grotesque fiend that must be destroyed, but rather a vision of his own darker, more primitive side; the kind of side you generally don't want to show to your fiancée. In a poignant, poetic finale, the monster realizes and is horrified by its own hideous nature and gives up, fading away into nothingness and leaving behind only its reflection in a mirror—a reflection Dr. Frankenstein finds is his own.

But whatever merits critics found in the film, and however much we might recognize its importance with the benefit of historical context, audiences did not like *Frankenstein*. Perhaps they found Dawley's direction too outdated. Perhaps this "I swear it's not a horror film" horror film was simply too revolting, with its reanimated dead flesh, alchemical magic, stalking ghoul, and frequent man-on-monster fisticuffs. Whatever the case, *Frankenstein* was a flop. After its initial run, it was withdrawn from circulation and, unlike other titles in the Edison library, never released again.

Its female lead, limited though her role is, moved on with the rest of the world. In the many interviews she did once she became one of the most famous stars in the country, Mary Fuller doesn't seem to ever mention *Frankenstein*. Why would she? Who knew that, some two decades later, Frankenstein would become one of the most iconic monsters in movie history? By then it's likely no one even remembered Edison's single-reeler. Once they stopped showing it, the studio destroyed the prints—common practice at the time, since no one imagined there'd be a need to preserve such disposable entertainment. Film stock contained valuable silver, after all. By the time Boris Karloff's creature stomped onto screens, 1910's *Frankenstein* was a lost film. It was not until decades later that a press release for the film, featuring a picture of Charles Ogle's cockeyed creature, was discovered and anyone remembered that the film had existed at all.

For years after that, the film existed only as that one still, though that still showed up in just about every monster movie book that was published in the 1960s and '70s. It might have stayed that way had not a guy by the name of Alois F. Dettlaff discovered in the 1950s that his mother-in-law, an avid film collector, had somehow ended up owning a print of the film. Even then, it wasn't until the 1970s that he realized what he had, and then it wasn't until 2010 that a cleaned-up version of the film was finally released. A hundred years after it had been made, *Frankenstein* walked again.

After *Frankenstein*'s unremarkable performance, Mary Fuller just kept on working, becoming the *de facto* leading lady at Edison. With the release of *What Happened to Mary*, she became a superstar. She starred in another adventure serial for the studio, 1914's *The Active Life of Dolly of the Dailies*, but thereafter her relationship with Edison began to fray. Before the end of 1914, she parted ways with

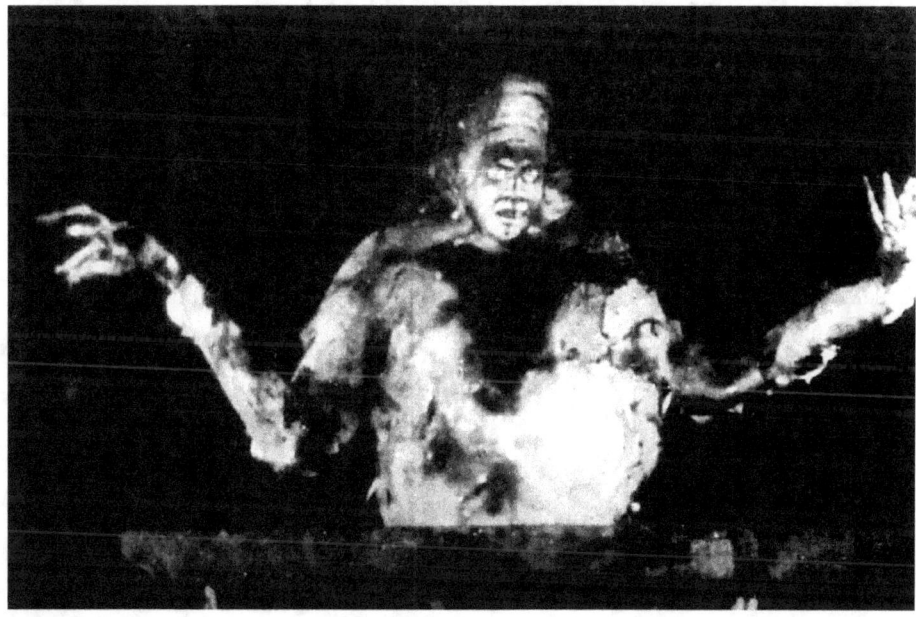

Edison and joined Universal, the very studio that would make *Frankenstein* in 1931. Universal promoted Fuller throughout 1914 and 1915 as their own Mary Pickford, and indeed Fuller delivered. Few and far between were the women who could go toe-to-toe with "America's sweetheart" (who would also become one of the most powerful and influential people in the American motion picture industry). Fuller was at the top of a very elite pack which included D.W. Griffith favorite leading lady, Lillian Gish and Fox Studio's raven-haired *femme fatale*, Theda Bara. After making some fifty or so films at Universal, including her first full-length feature (1915's *Under Southern Skies*), Fuller moved to another studio called Famous Players.

But by then, things were starting to change. Although the movie business was run almost entirely by men, many of the highest-paid and most-popular stars were women: Fuller, the Gish sisters, adventure serial queen Pearl White, and of course Mary Pickford. As the new decade approached, studios began to scheme regarding how they could clear themselves of women they felt were too powerful and commanded too high a price. According to Louise Brooks, an icon of the 1920s who later became a film studies writer and historian, studios conspired to undermine their own leading actresses, saddling them with inferior films then pointing at the (self-inflicted) disappointing box office as proof that such-and-such actress was past her prime and no longer deserved so high a salary.

Whatever the case, the film industry underwent a massive purge of top female talent at the close of the 1910s. A few persevered. Gloria Swanson soldiered on. And of course there was the indefatigable Mary Pickford, who just said screw it and formed her own studio alongside Charlie Chaplin, D.W. Griffith, and Douglas Fairbanks. Among the casualties though was Mary Fuller. At one-time (that time being just a few short years prior) she was one of the top stars in the world. In 1917, she made a single picture, *The Long Trail*. And then she was gone. She resurfaced briefly in 1926 and attempted a comeback, but there was no work to be had. After that, she disappeared entirely. It was decades before anyone knew what became of her. What they discovered was tragic. After the rapid demise of her film career and inability to find work on stage, she began an affair with a married opera star. When he broke off their affair, Fuller suffered a nervous breakdown that left her in a haunted state. She lived a quiet, reclusive life in her mother's house in Washington, DC.

When her mother passed away in 1940, Fuller suffered another, more severe breakdown that left her in a state of increasingly fragile mental health. Her sister tried to care for her, but it become too much to bear. On July 1, 1947, Mary Fuller was admitted to St. Elizabeth's Hospital in Washington, where she remained for 26 years. She died on December 9, 1973, with no known relatives, at the age of 85. Today, almost the entirety of her body of work has been lost. But pieces remain, here and there, and in time curious cinephiles started digging around and rediscovered, if not the films of Mary Fuller, then certainly her story, tragically though it may have ended. Today, her grave in the Congressional Cemetery in Washington DC is no longer unmarked. Her name is no longer forgotten.

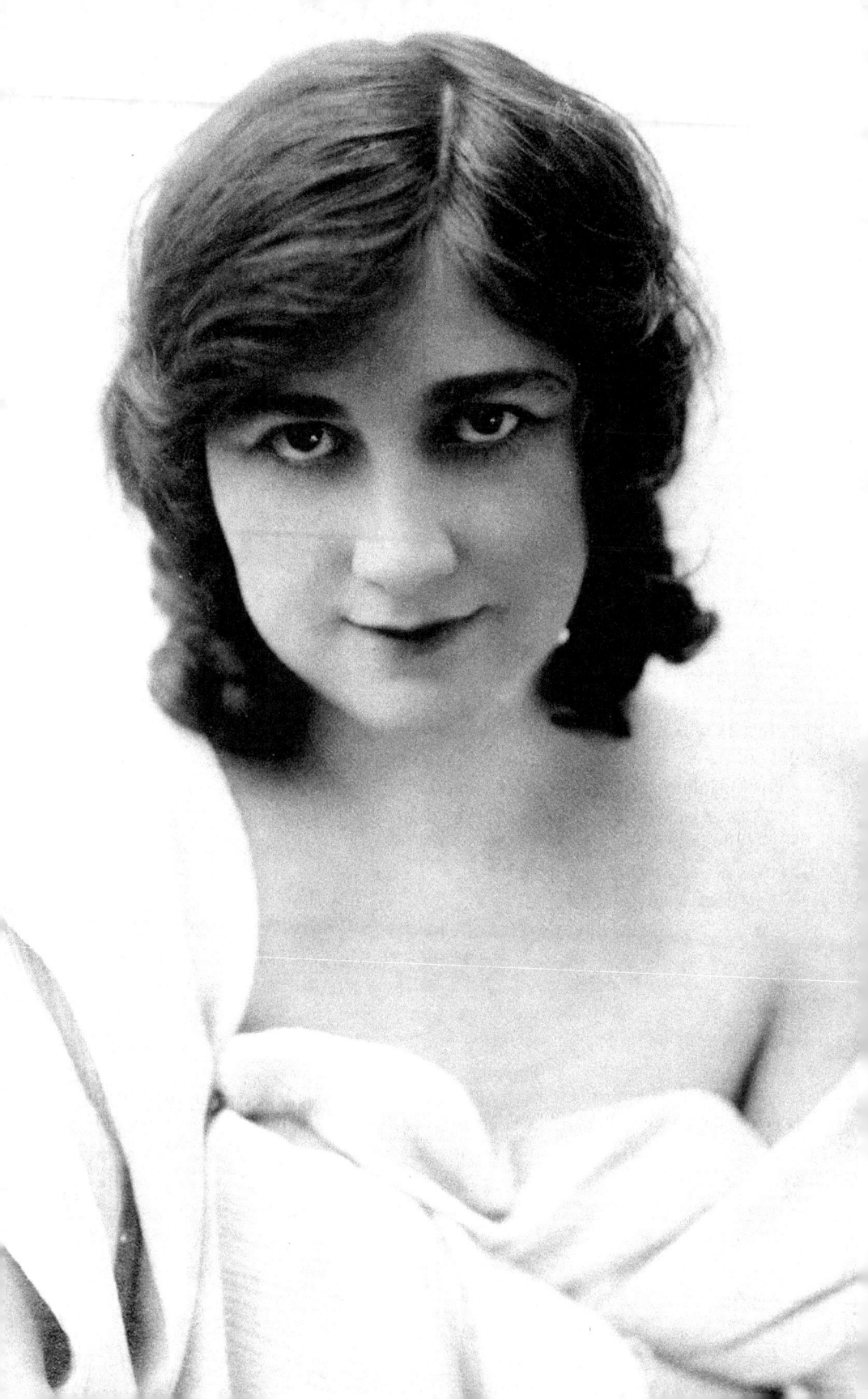

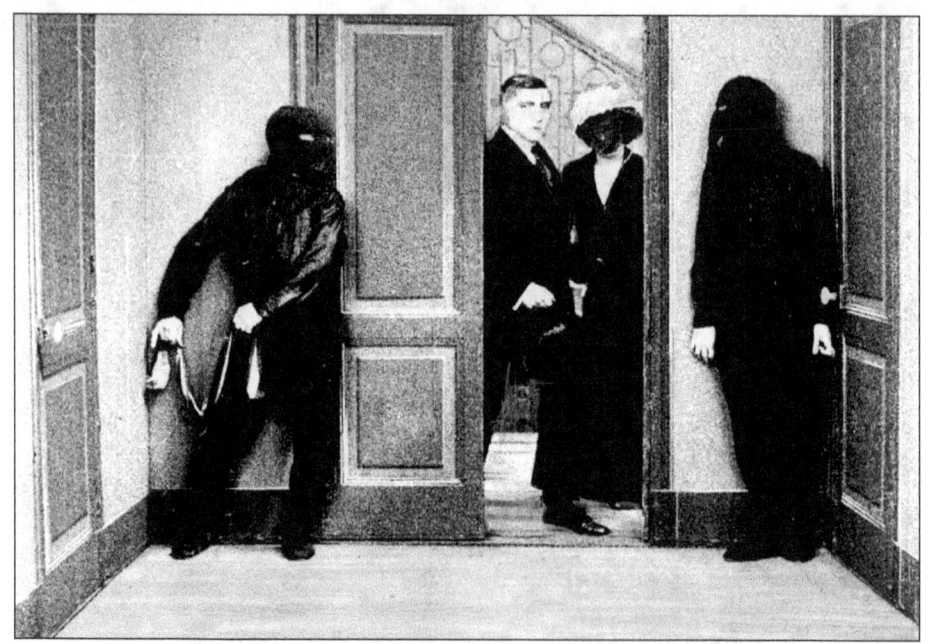

An Ungentlemanly Thief

On July 15, 1905, the magazine *Je sais tout* published the story *L'Arrestation d'Arsène Lupin*, the first of a long-running series of novels by Maurice Leblanc. Perhaps it was a bit odd to kick off the illustrious career of a gentleman thief with a story in which he is arrested. But as Leblanc would go on to show, France never did build a prison that could hold the man who would become one of their most enduring literary creations and, even more than the mercurial and manipulative A.J. Raffles, the very model of the gentleman thief.

Leblanc had reportedly never heard of A.J. Raffles, despite the similarity between the British cricketer/thief and Leblanc's own gentleman thief. Just like Raffles, Arsène Lupin was inspired by Sherlock Holmes, if only the financial success of Sherlock Holmes, which inspired the editors of *Je sais tout* to demand a detective story from Leblanc, at the time a struggling nobody with several stories and little success under his belt. Like E.W. Hornung, Leblanc thought it would be fun to explore the world of detectives and criminals from criminal side of things. So, reportedly using French anarchist Marius Jacob as his model, Leblanc created Arsène Lupin, gentleman thief.

Marius Jacob led a life worthy of the pulps he inspired. Born to a working-class family in Marseilles, by age twelve he was working as an apprentice sailor. That job took him to Australia (another coincidental parallel to E.W. Hornung), where he promptly deserted, kicked around a little, and eventually fell into a life of piracy. He abandoned that life, thinking piracy was simply too cruel, and returned to Marseilles, where he began attending meetings of the local anarchist society. After doing time in prison for possession of explosives, Jacob developed his philosophy of "pacifistic illegalism." It was the golden age of French anarchism, and as befits a philosophy like Anarchism, there were multiple schools of thought publishing newspapers, holding meetings, and furiously writing manifestos. Among these diverse forms of anarchism was Illegalism, very much a "might makes right" way of thinking; or perhaps more accurately, an early form of "wickedest man alive" Aleister Crowley's most famous quote: "Do what thou wilt shall be the whole of the law."

Proponents of Illegalism committed crimes for no higher reason than to satisfy their own personal desires. The philosophy arose from the unrest of the 1890s, and at least some its proponents couched their criminal mischief in the language of revolution, justifying (through manifestos) their crimes by claiming the right of Robin Hood to steal from the rich, or claiming that their crimes would inspire others to acts of civil disobedience that would lead to the always nebulously-defined "revolution." Illegalism would later inspire *Fantômas*, but Marius Jacob interpreted Illegalism a bit differently. For him and his crew, nicknamed "the workers of the night," there was a strict code of behavior. They were not to kill, except in self-defense, and then very selectively. They would steal only from the rich and powerful, never from the working man, tradespeople, or anyone they thought was a productive member of society. They targeted magistrates, police, and other member of governmental, law enforcement, and legal professions.

In pursuit of his revolution-through-crime, Jacob acquired a number of useful skills, including lock-picking, safe-cracking, and a system of gaining illegal entry by drilling through the ceiling from the floor above, using an umbrella slipped through a small hole in the floor then opened to catch falling debris (a trick that would later show up in the French noir *Rififi*). Jacob and his gang pulled well over a hundred jobs before his career as a gentleman burglar went off the rails. On April 21, 1903, a police officer was killed during a botched heist, and Jacob was apprehended. He was sentenced to life in prison, from which he frequently tried to escape. Unlike Arsène Lupin, however, none of Jacob's attempts were successful. However, an escape of a different kind resulted in his return to freedom, when France abolished the punishment of enforced hard labor. Although he retired from crime after his release...*as far as anyone knows*...he never renounced his methods or expressed remorse for his years as a thief.

Lupin and Raffles share a profession and a flare for the gentlemanly, but the two differ in as many ways as they are similar. Lupin's story begins as Raffles' originally ended: with a heist aboard a luxury cruiser that ends in exposure. But where Raffles dove dramatically off the side of the ship, presumably to his doom until he was resurrected for the second volume of stories, Lupin is arrested and affects a similarly dramatic escape from prison. Lupin shows a much more developed skill at plotting a scheme, sometimes working months to lie the groundwork for some bit of trickery, where Raffles, for all his claims to careful planning, rarely executed his plans with the same rate of success.

Both men, however, harbor a dark streak and a grudge against high society, but where Raffles is addicted to Society even as he seeks to undermine it, Lupin is much more committed to the cause and has, it is revealed in the short story "The Queen's Necklace," a rougher, more impoverished background. Raffles' motivation to prey on high society is largely born of not being included in it, except as an entertainer/

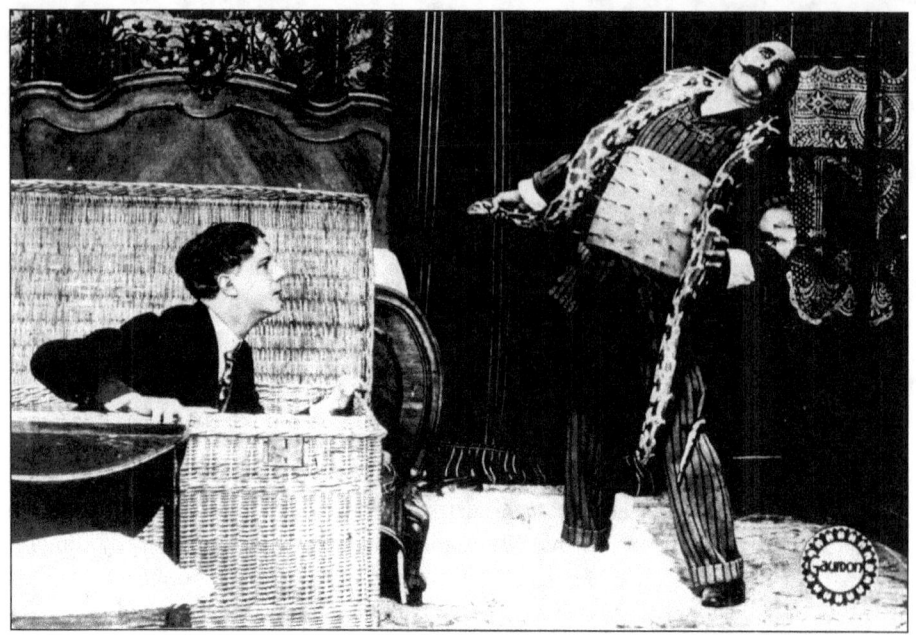

sportsman. Lupin's grudge is deeper, stemming from a hard life as the son of a washerwoman who was harried and mistreated by her employer (against whom, Lupin mounts an incredibly long-con revenge). And yet Lupin seems a lighter character, not haunted by the temptation to murder or defined by the narcissism that exists at the core of A.J. Raffles. Lupin has no Bunny to emotionally abuse and manipulate, though he does later pick up a chronicler who finds himself in the middle of one of Lupin's schemes. That story, "Seven of Hearts," also takes Lupin into the realm of international espionage, marking one of the first forays for pulp into a genre that would become increasingly important.

When Maurice Leblanc wrote the first Arsène Lupin story, two years after Jacob was arrested, he assumed it was a one-off to fill some space and cash in on the popularity of Sherlock Holmes. Neither he nor his publisher anticipated the success the story would experience. No sooner had it been printed than Leblanc was commissioned to write a follow-up, and another after that, and so on. As Lupin's popularity soared, so too did Leblanc's resentment for the character which, like both Doyle and Hornung before him, Leblanc felt had painted him into a professional corner from which there was little hope of escape. Nothing he did outside of Arsène Lupin met with much attention, so he found himself, again and again, forced to return to the gentleman thief.

He wrote short stories and novels, and where E.W. Hornung never gave in to the temptation to pit Raffles against his brother-in-law's famous consulting detective, Leblanc showed no such reservations. In June of 1906, Lupin's paths crossed with those of Sherlock Holmes in the story "Sherlock Holmes Arrives Too Late." It's a fun Lupin story in which Holmes, as one might infer from the title, arrives too late to foil the thief's scheme. But the two rivals develop a healthy appreciation for one another's skills. That mutual admiration did not cross over to Doyle for Leblanc.

Leblanc hadn't bothered to secure permission to use Sherlock Holmes, and Doyle was displeased about the unsanctioned appearance. Leblanc and *Je sais tout* were forced to republish the story with Holmes removed and replaced by a character with a different name.: Herlock Sholmes.

While Lupin was a kinder, more gentlemanly gentleman thief, there was another Frenchman who wasn't so refined. Like Lupin, Marcel Allain and Pierre Souvestre's Fantômas was a thief. But he was far from the gentleman thief Lupin was. Fantômas was sociopathic and perfectly happy to murder anyone who got in his way; actually, he's perfectly happy to murder even people who weren't in his way, just in case he needed a spare corpse for one of his schemes later on down the line. Fantômas was unrepentantly villainous yet still the center of the reader's fascination. He was the prototype for the anti-heroes that became so popular in the Italian *fumetti* (comic books) of the 1960, the father of nasty customers like *Diabolik*, *Kriminal*, and *Killing*.

Fantômas, in any of his disguises, was a villain. The darkness that occasionally flashed across the face of A.J. Raffles was, in Fantômas, the sum of his being. The reader is never invited to root for Fantômas or to identify with him in the same way one would have Raffles or Lupin. Instead, we are on the side of the law as we follow the progress of police inspector Juve and his sidekick Fandor. In both the Raffles and Lupin stories, the detectives were, at best, supporting characters, there to provide moments of dramatic tension but never presented as the ones for whom we should be rooting. In *Fantômas*, it's Juve and Fandor who occupy the bulk of the narrative. Yet no matter how vile his actions, the reader never *really* wants to see Fantômas get caught. That would mean the end of the series. Or, it would if Fantômas wasn't so good at escaping from prison. That, at least, he had in common with Lupin.

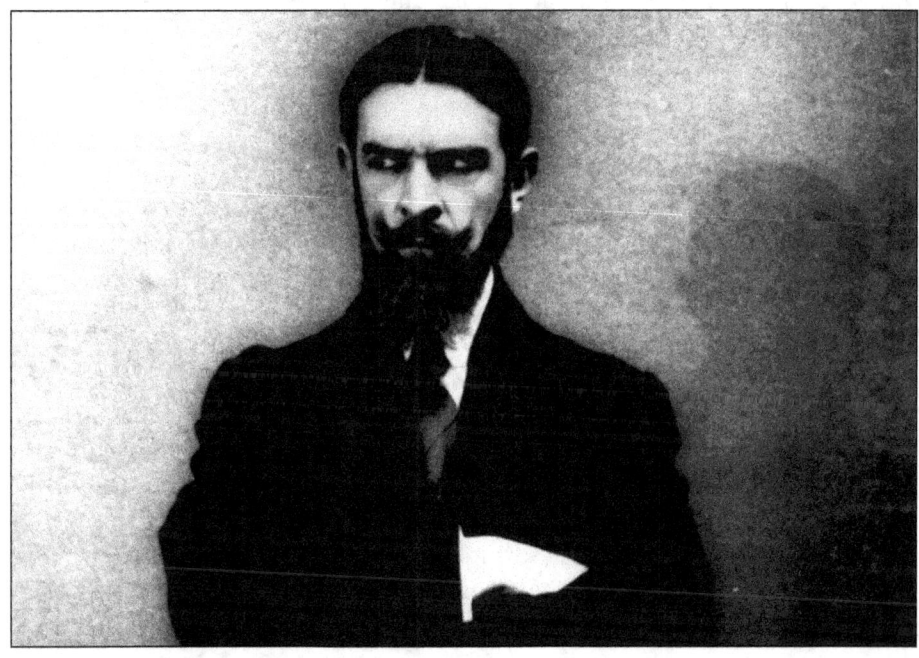

Having the benefit of years of gentleman thief adventures behind it, Allain and Souvestre's debut novel, *Fantômas*, is a lean, twist-filled thriller that keeps one's attention even if the eventual reveal is obvious. Young gentleman Charles Rambert is attending a dinner party hosted by the Marquise de Langrune, where the gossip inevitably turns to the exploits of black-hearted villain Fantômas, who has been on a crime spree that has the whole of France gripped by fear and fascination. Most recent in his catalog of accomplishments is the kidnapping of a Lord Beltham.

Some guests doubt Fantômas exists at all, or assume that even if he does, a number of crimes attributed to him have been assigned mistakenly and were, more likely, the work of more common criminals. Perhaps, it is even surmised, the sinister spectre of Fantômas is something created entirely as an excuse for the police when they cannot solve a crime. Rambert is entranced by this talk, but he's equally entranced by Thérèse, the granddaughter of the Marquise. He's also preoccupied with the impending arrival of his long-absent father, Etienne, who has been abroad for so long that Rambert can scarcely remember the man's appearance. This reunion, and Charles' romance, are cast in a gloom when, shortly after the elder Rambert's arrival, the Marquise is discovered dead—*murdered*—and all fingers, including his newly-arrived father's, point to Charles. The case looks cut-and-dry, and Charles seems fated to have his neck lengthened by the hangman. Only one man suspects there might be more to the case, and more to Etienne Rambert, than is apparent.

Inspector Juve, whose life's obsession is the capture of Fantômas, catches a whiff of the arch-criminal's style about the affair and sets about proving the murder to be the work of the shadowy mastermind. By the end, we will have learned much about Fantômas' true identity—*maybe*. Or perhaps we learn much about last victim of Fantômas' identity theft. It's difficult to say when it comes to Fantômas. Whatever the case, even exonerated, the scandal leaves poor Charles Rambert's life in shambles, inspiring Juve to create for the hapless young man a new identity: Fandor, a dogged rookie investigative reporter. It is at this point that the first of Feuillade's movies picks up the thread.

Allain and Souvestre wrote thirty-two entries in the Fantômas series (Allain continued the series alone after Souvestre's death, starting with 1925's *Fantômas est-il ressuscité?*). The final Allain and Souvestre story came out in 1913. That same year, Louis Feuillade went into production on the first of his five *Fantômas* movies, *Fantômas: À l'ombre de la guillotine* (*Fantômas: In the Shadow of the Guillotine*). As his biography is eventually laid out, Fantômas is Archduke Juan North, a philanderer who ends up in a German prison, from which he escapes and flees to India, and later the United States, Mexico, and South Africa, where he fights in the Boer War under the name Gurn. No word on whether he served alongside A.J. Raffles. In South Africa, he meets Lady Maud Beltham. At this point, with Fantômas masquerading as Gurn and courting Lady Beltham, both the first novel and the first movie pick up the mysterious swindler's story.

True to the novels, Feuillade's Fantômas (René Navarre) is a thief, swindler, and murderer. "He creates fear!" one character exclaims. The first film, which skips a lot of backstory under the assumption that the audience has already read the

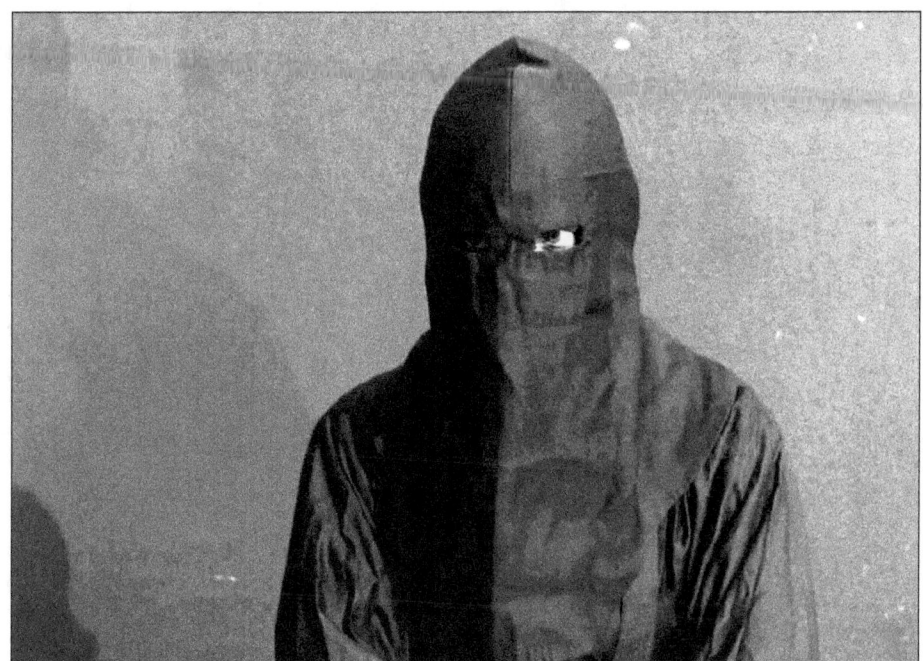

book, runs fifty-four minutes and begins with Fantômas living life as Gurn until he commits a murder in rather a sloppy fashion. This leads to his arrest by Juve (Scotsman Edmund Breon, whose long career included films as varied as Feuillade's *Fantômas* and *Les Vampires*; the Academy Award-nominated *Goodbye, Mr. Chips*; Basil Rathbone's final Sherlock Holmes film, *Dressed to Kill*: and the Howard Hawks science fiction horror film *The Thing from Another World*).

Prison doesn't stop Gurn/Fantômas from scheming. He corrupts a guard, and with the help of Lady Beltham (Renée Carl, who appeared in both this and *Les Vampires* as well as the 1925 production of *Les Miserables* and the 1937 French noir *Pépé le Moko*), conspires to escape and replace himself with a hapless actor who has made himself up to look like Fantômas for a stage show. In the second film, *Juve contre Fantômas*, Juve is hot on the trail of the escaped criminal, assisted by Jerome Fandor. None of Fandor's backstory as a man framed by and possibly related to Fantômas is in the films, the assumption being once again that you read the book. Assisting Fantômas is Lady Beltham, though this time around she realizes Fantômas is a madman, and that she is in over her head.

The series ran for three more movies: *Le Mort Qui Tue* (the longest of the bunch, at 90 minutes, and the first to feature Fantômas donning his signature black satin hood), *Fantômas contre Fantômas* (which features the classic scenario of a masquerade ball in which multiple people show up dressed as Fantômas—including the actual Fantômas), and concluding with *Le Faux Magistrat*, released in 1914 on the eve of the Great War. Intellectuals, lead by the Impressionists, turned up their noses at the *Fantômas* films, considering them visually bland and Feuillade too commercial to be worthy of artistic praise. Which isn't a totally unfair assessment, but Feuillade did not regard film with the same eye for the quixotic and esoteric as

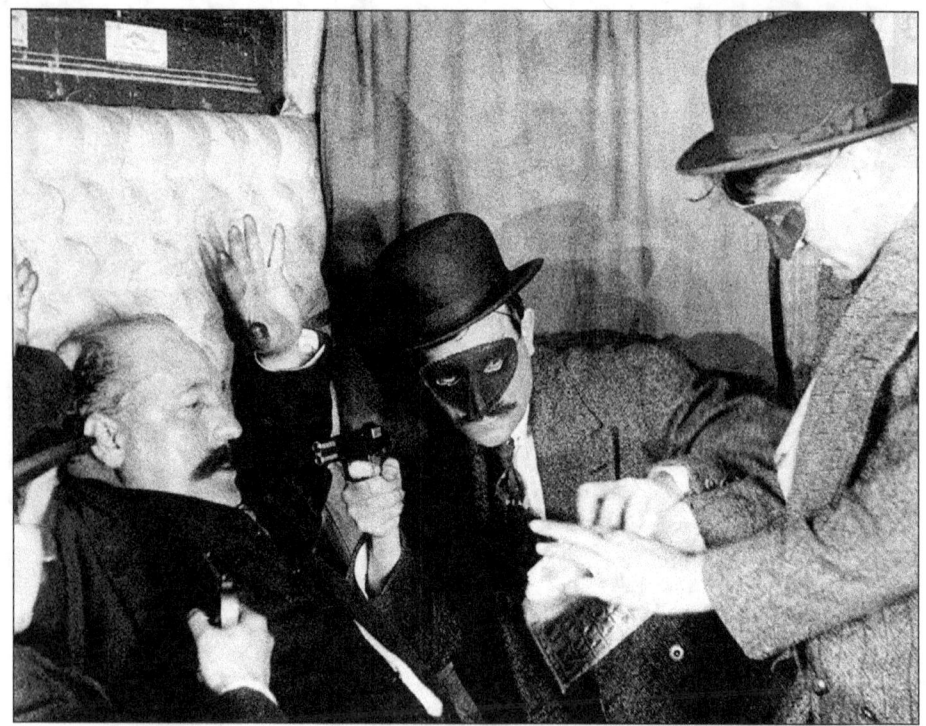

did the Impressionists. High art was not his goal, as he once explained: "A film is not a sermon nor a conference, even less a rebus, but a means to entertain the eyes and the spirit."

Arbiters of good taste and social decency also turned up their noses, charging that Feuillade's violent potboilers glamorized crime, pretending to condemn Fantômas while undermining their own moral message by making audiences thrill to and demand more of the fiend's bloody exploits. Critics branded the films "*plates, sottes, et cyniques*"—flat, foolish, and cynical. Dismissed by both the intelligentsia and the moral watchdogs, Feuillade had to settle for being wildly popular with the public, a consolation with which Feuillade was perfectly fine.

Although still in its infancy, one can see the evolution of cinema in the frames of *Fantômas*. Feuillade's plots make little sense, but they are also complex and full of twists, a far cry from the days when the plot of a moving picture was "a guy sneezes." Although his camera remains static, Feuillade was doing more than "filming a stage play," as films from this era are often accused of doing. Scenes are intricately composed, even when they are of a *tableau* style, often with important action taking place in both the fore and background. He frames odd geometric patterns and layouts and plays with close-ups. He also includes a fair amount of stunt work. His style is somewhere between the primitive films of the previous decade and the sophisticated filmmaking that emerged in the '20s. Feuillade depicted the fantastic taking place on the landscape of the mundane. Unlike French Impressionists or later German Expressionists, Feuillade did not use abstract or stylized sets. He did not use special effects, even though his mentor Alice Guy studied the work of Méliès and used some of his techniques in her own films. Instead, Feuillade shot his films on the streets of Paris, in very normal apartment sets, and in sparse basements and cellars. It was a familiar world, the world of the average Parisian. Yet against these recognizable locations and bland settings, Feuillade staged some truly mad storytelling. The *Fantômas* movies populate these everyday locations with sadistic murders and a hooded madman who commands an army of bloodthirsty cutthroats; with bombs and guns and knives and an endless supply of wicker baskets in which one can hide. Or hide a body.

In bringing the fantastic and the dangerous to the streets of Paris, *Fantômas* reflected what was happening on those same streets in real life. The 1910s were a tumultuous time for France, not just because they were looking down the barrel of a German invasion. Anarchist gangs were roaming the city. Stiletto-carrying assassins. Bombers. And Fantômas, a man described as a master criminal but whose primary concern seems to be nothing more than sowing mayhem. It's not a coincidence that most of Fantômas' disguises position him among the moneyed. He is a doctor, a banker, here a lord and there a money lender. He assumes their identities because he knows, like Raffles, it is easier for a rich man to get away with crime. It is easier for a rich man to rob other rich men. Most of his schemes are inept and easily-solved but leave a trail of bodies and burning buildings in their wake. He is less concerned, it would seem, with "getting away with it," than he is with creating as much chaos as possible. Sure, he wants the jewels, the pearl necklaces, and the francs. But mostly, Fantômas just wants to hurt people.

The scripts often pick up Fantômas mid-scheme, totally unconcerned with the mechanics of how, in the span of a few days, Fantômas has been able to amass a fortune, a chalet, the identity of some count or lawyer, and dozens of friends who seem to have known him under his false identity for years. Like Fantômas, Louis Feuillade isn't concerned with the details or realism of his schemes. It's the maniacal ride and the gory aftermath about which he is passionate. There is a sense

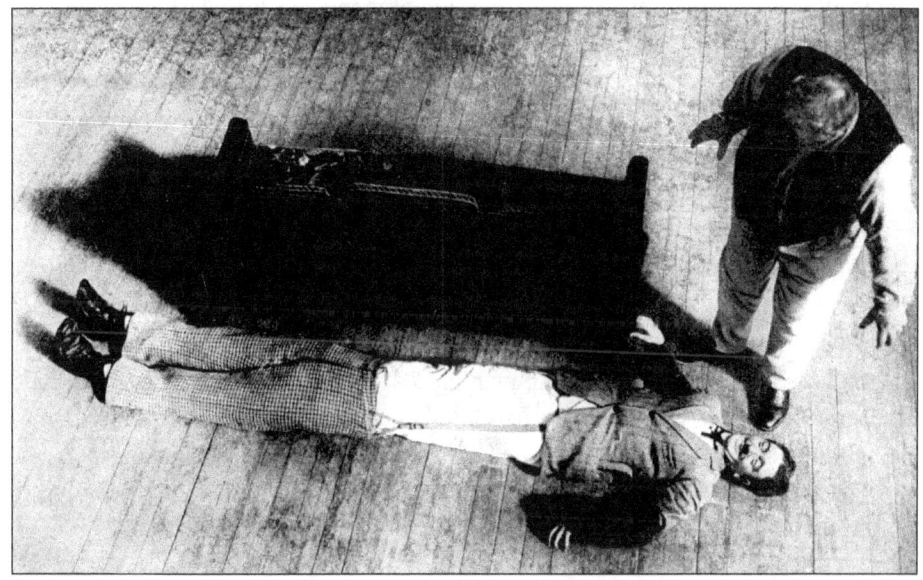

of anarchism in the plotting of Fantômas, though this might have less to do with Feuillade wanting to craft a narrative simulation of anarchism and more to do with production schedules and the fact that Feuillade made something like 800 films in his career. He operated under the assumption that most audience members were familiar with the Allain and Souvestre material. Screenings of the films were accompanied by supplemental materials that included a synopsis of the story and guides to which characters were played by which stars. If Feuillade left out chunks of plot, viewers would fill in the gaps.

Other gaps in logic, however, cannot be chalked up to "well, they read the book." It may be that audiences simply did not care and were happy to go along on such a fun, macabre ride. It didn't matter if the "big picture" failed to make sense. The entire premise of *À l'ombre de la guillotine*, for example, is patently ludicrous: that Fantômas could sneak in and out of jail at will, and that he could successfully replace himself with an actor in a dodgy wig and obviously-fake mustache and an entire precinct full of cops wouldn't notice. Fantômas' donning of his black hood and tights is itself without clear function. He often puts on and removes the hood in the same scene, sometimes in front of the person from whom Fantômas would be wearing the hood to obscure himself. Subsequent schemes seem to be even less plausible and make even less sense, as if Fantômas enjoys complexity simply for the sake of complexity. Feuillade is more than happy to accommodate the man's sociopathic over-indulgences.

But Fantômas isn't the only one hatching loony schemes. Juve matches his arch-nemesis loony-for-loony with such plans as capturing Fantômas by helping Fantômas escape from prison and taking his place in confinement. Then there's the bizarre scene in which Juve, having been threatened with murder by a vengeful Fantômas, protects himself against assassination by wrapping himself in a suit of spikes (which, sadly for Juve, proves ineffectual against the assassin Fantômas sends after him: a python). The masquerade of many Fantômases hardly makes a lick of sense either.

And no one cares. Why would they? The viewer is convinced to surrender any sense of logic. They willingly play along because Feuillade so deftly convinces us the world of Fantômas is not bound by plausibility. It may *look* like the real Paris, but it's not. It is this subversion of the familiar that lends *Fantômas* an additional air of menace and fantasy. In *Fantômas*, and even more so in his next serial, Feuillade taps into the same sense of the uncanny as would later be used so effectively by horror films, and by directors who made films with one foot in horror and the other in thrillers, like David Lynch, with his propensity for twisting the ho-hum veneer of small-town America into something nightmarish. Feuillade's "fantastic realism" warped the familiar world and tapped into concepts Sigmund Freud described as being at the core of feeling unsettled. Feuillade made the mundane dangerous; he brought into the plain, once-secure embrace of daylight the "things that ought to have remained in the shadows."

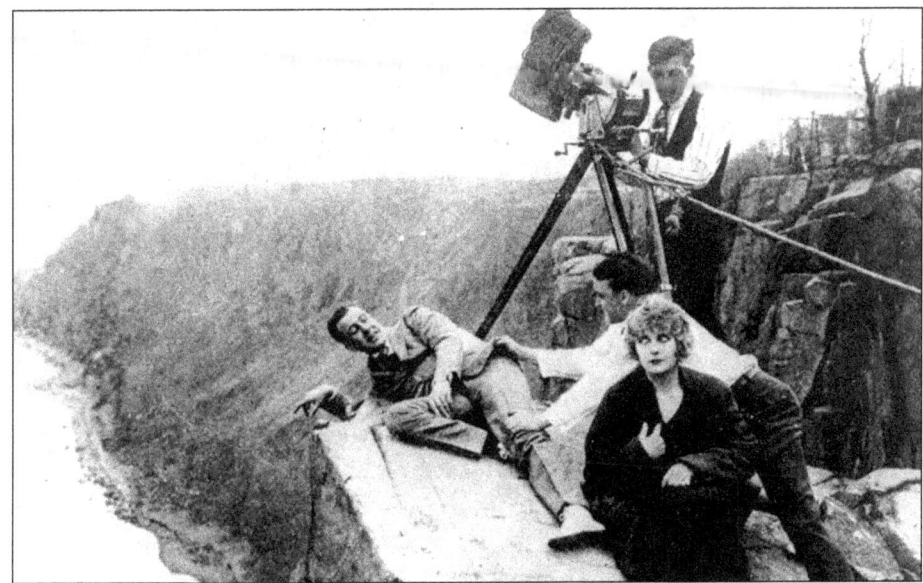

CLIFFHANGER: Pearl White and crew prepare for a literal cliffhanger in New Jersey's Palisades.

The Stunt Sweetie and the Vampire Queen

Needing to compete with a new slew of thrillers, notably Pathé's *Les Mystères de New York*, Feuillade threw himself into production of a new serial immediately after wrapping *Fantômas*. Pathé was founded a year after Gaumont, in 1896, by four brothers: Charles, Emile, Theophile, and Jacques Pathé. Like Gaumont, it began as a film equipment company, even acquiring the patent portfolio of motion camera pioneers Auguste and Louis Lumière. Charles Pathé steered the company toward motion picture production, and soon Pathé struck a deal with American exhibitor Mitchel Mark, who along with his brother, Moe, opened one of the world's first movie houses, the Vitascope Theater in Buffalo, New York, in 1896. Pathé grew rapidly, becoming the world's biggest motion picture equipment company and opening a string of theaters and production studios around the world. In 1914, at their satellite production facilities in Fort Lee, New Jersey, Pathé entered the serial business, producing two of the most popular serials of the early silent era and creating one of its biggest stars, a vivacious Midwestern belle named Pearl White.

Born in Missouri in 1889, Pearl White was on stage as early as age six, performing in a Springfield production of *Uncle Tom's Cabin*. She worked an increasingly incredible series of jobs—some say *un*-credible, and that much of her biography was manufactured by the studio, as was pretty common in the day (just ask Pearl's fellow Midwesterner, Theodosia Goodman). As the stories were told, Pearl worked as a trick rider in a circus, dropped out of high school, and eventually found herself on stage as part of a theater troupe called the Trousedale Stock Company. She toured through the Midwest, South America, and according to her own telling of her life, even worked as a dance hall queen in Cuba under the stage name Miss

IL FAIT PEUR!

Mazee. When her voice began to give out, White decided to try her luck in the movies. 1910 brought her to New York, where her athleticism, energy, all-American good looks, and willingness to put her own physical well-being at risk helped her secure roles. She became an able physical comedian and stunt woman. By 1912, she was headlining shorts. In 1914, she became a superstar when she made the move from shorts to serials and appeared in director Louis Gasnier's adventure series, *The Perils of Pauline*, financed by Pathé.

Based on a script by Broadway playwright Charles Goddard (whose play *The Ghost Breaker* had just been adapted for the screen and directed by Cecil B. DeMille), *The Perils of Pauline* was custom-made for Pearl. It's the story of a young woman who inherits a great deal of money but can only have it after she marries. Not in the mood to settle down, Pauline decides instead to pursue a career as a writer. In order to prepare herself for her chosen profession, she figures she should have as many adventures as possible. The executor of Pauline's inheritance wants her money for himself, and so spends all of his time attempting to murder her by sabotaging whatever adventure she's on.

The plot is really just a means to deliver thrills and stunt work, most of which was performed by Pearl White herself. Week after week, the hapless heroine was placed in increasingly outrageous predicaments. The series was filmed primarily in New Jersey, where the rocky Palisades provided cliffs off which Pearl could hang. The stunt work was not exactly what one might think of as safe, resulting in more than a few close calls. One of the most famous stunts gone wrong occurred when White was in a hot air balloon that got swept away by a fast-approaching storm. She was blown for miles before she managed to wrangle the balloon back to the ground.

Of *The Perils of Pauline*'s twenty episodes, none exist in their original format. All that remains today is a truncated version that compressed the serial into a nine-chapter, 214-minute feature released in Europe, where the series was as tremendous a hit as it was in the U.S. Pathé produced a follow-up that same year, *The Exploits of Elaine*, released in France as *Les Mystères de New York*. It was based on the literary series *Craig Kennedy, Scientific Detective* by Arthur B. Reeve, an early example of the use of scientific investigation in detective fiction: fingerprinting, chemical analysis, that sort of thing.

The Exploits of Elaine was similar to *The Perils of Pauline* in. The entire point was to be to put Pearl in horrible danger or have her perform a daring stunt every week. Her characters were one of the first examples of—and one of the earliest subversions of—the "damsel in distress." Both Pauline and Elaine frequently found themselves in need of rescuing, but just as often, they did the rescuing, or escaped from a predicament by their own cunning. They were also young, unmarried, and without children. *The Exploits of Elaine* distinguished itself with the inclusion of the Clutching Hand, the archetype for hooded fiends. The Clutching Hand lent the otherwise straightforward series a more sinister air, in much the same way mystery writer Edgar Wallace infused his novels with an surreal air by trotting out outlandish masked criminals. And speaking of sinister...

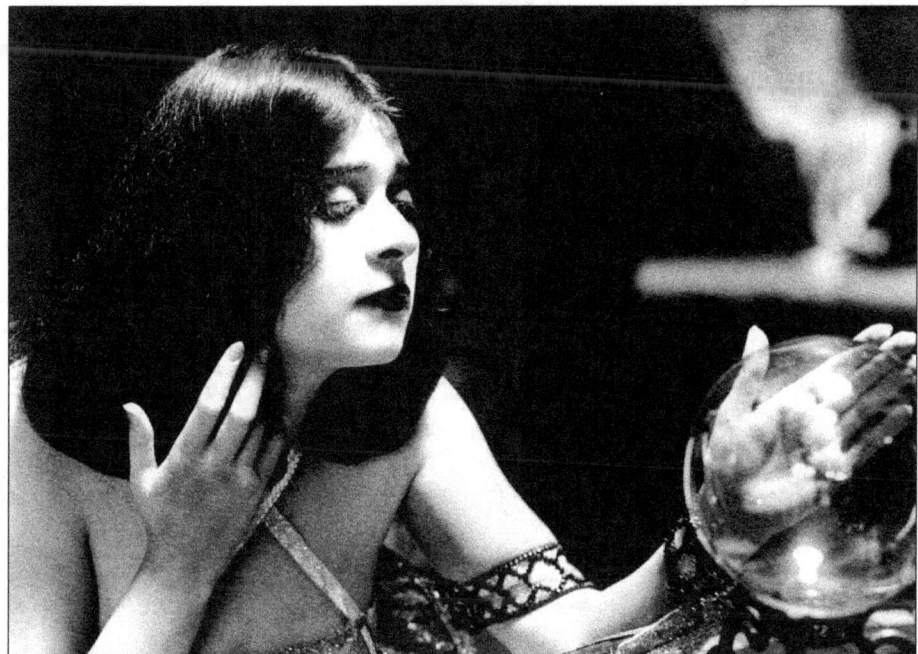

ARAB DEATH: Theda Bara, the template for all the vamps, man-eaters, and femmes fatale who followed.

While Pearl White was hanging off cliffs and jumping onto moving trains, another young actress was also busy making her mark in the burgeoning Fort Lee cinema scene. She was a woman altogether unlike Pearl...or anything Americans had seen anywhere other than in their darkest fantasies. The air around this woman, Theda Bara, was thick with incense. She was a raven-haired beauty from "the mysterious East," the daughter of a French actress who had been seduced by an Italian sculptor "beneath the shadow of The Sphinx." Reporters who were granted access to this strange, alluring woman, would find her reclining amidst silks, curtains, and all the accoutrements of Orientalism that Westerners imagined comprised the East. Scattered amongst these artifacts was occult and Spiritualist ephemera: a crystal ball, a tarot deck, perhaps even a human skull.

If Pearl was the blonde-haired pretty face of a new, can-do America, Theda Bara was its shadow. Dark, mysterious, dangerous. If Pearl plucked you from the jaws of death, Theda was the woman who would sacrifice you to them. Her dark, kohl-smeared eyes enticed you, and she laughed as you willingly destroyed yourself for her. And yet America loved her as much as they feared her.

Pearl White bucked traditional notions of feminine helplessness and subservience, but Theda actively attacked them, preyed on male weakness and exploited it, never with the altruistic sense of adventure and do-goodism that defined Pearl. For a young film industry that needed a foil, and a way to capitalize on the popular interest in Spiritualism, the Orient, and Egypt, Theda Bara was perfect. There was only one problem: it was all bullshit. Theda Bara was actually Theodosia Goodman, a Midwestern blonde from a nice, normal Jewish neighborhood in

MARY PICKFORD

- 1 ½ oz White Rum
- 1 ½ oz Fresh Pineapple Juice
- 1 tsp Grenadine

Add all ingredients to a shaker filled with ice. Shake well. Strain into a chilled cocktail glass.

BEE'S KNEES

- 2 oz Dry Gin
- ¾ oz Fresh Lemon Juice
- ½ oz Honey Syrup

Add ingredients to a shaker filled with ice. Shake well. Strain into a chilled cocktail glass. Garnish with a lemon twist.

BLOOD & SAND

- ¾ oz Single Malt Scotch
- ¾ oz Sweet vermouth
- ¾ oz Heering Cherry Liqueur
- ¾ oz Fresh Orange Juice

Add all ingredients to a shaker filled with ice. Shake well. Strain into a chilled coupe glass. Garnish with an orange peel. For a smoky twist, use a peated scotch, such as Ardmore.

BARRYMORE ROOM

- 1 ½ oz Bourbon
- ½ oz Sweet Vermouth
- ½ oz Lime juice
- ½ oz Simple Syrup
- ¼ oz Egg White
- 1 Strawberry

Muddle strawberry and simple syrup in a shaker. Add remaining ingredients. Shake without ice. Add ice. Shake well. Strain into a chilled cocktail glass.

DEATH IN THE AFTERNOON

- 1 ½ oz Absinthe
- 4 oz Champagne

Pour the absinthe into a coupe glass. Top with the Champagne.

Cincinnati, Ohio. From an early age, she wanted to perform. Accounts of her early life have her assembling neighborhood kids as an audience for her one-woman show featuring her favorite stock character, the "Dirty-Faced Brat." Acting being an art and a craft that respectable people viewed to be cultured but never to be pursued as a career, Theodosia's mother curbed her daughter's craving for the stage, eventually sending her off to college. It didn't stick. Before graduating, Theodosia had packed her bags and, like so many others, sought the bright lights of Broadway. And like many other hopefuls, she found it rough going.

She sustained herself with minor stage roles until William Fox, having just started his own movie studio, started sniffing around the peripheries of the New York theater scene for some stars around which he could build his fledgling company. Fox was a Hungarian immigrant who, by some accounts, was tricked into the motion picture business when he purchased, in 1903, a Brooklyn theater, a transaction into which he might have been swindled. Whatever the case, Fox was clever enough to seize on the new medium of motion pictures. By 1907 he owned fifteen movie houses and founded the Box Office Attractions Film Rental Company. Then he fought a war against "the Wizard of Menlo Park," inventor and enthusiastically-litigious filer of patents, Thomas Edison.

Edison had assumed the future of the technology he derived from the early European motion picture cameras would be applied primarily in the form of Kinetoscopes, which were single-viewer machines. When it became obvious that projecting moving pictures onto a screen for an audience was going to be the dominate way viewers consumed movies, Edison leapt into action in the way for which he had become famous: by claiming all motion picture projection equipment was derived from his technology, which was patented, and threatening to sue anyone who did not pay up. Not wanting a showdown with Edison in court, most movie studios obliged, forming a collective called the Motion Picture Patents Company. Notable by his absence was William Fox, who elected to take on Edison in court, claiming that the Motion Picture Patents Company constituted an illegal monopoly. The courts agreed, and as part of his victory lap, Fox bought a studio lot in Fort Lee and entered into the motion picture production business. The Fox Film Corporation's first film, *Life's Shop Window*, was released in 1914 to tepid reviews and lackluster business. If he was going to cement his position in the industry, Fox needed something—or *someone*—sensational. He didn't want a star with an established following; no recognizable luminaries of stage or screen. He wanted a new face he could mold into whatever image he wanted without an existing biography.

At Pathé, where they were cranking out Pearl White adventure serials, director Frank Powell was wrapping a film called *The Stain*. Powell had cast struggling actress Theodosia Goodman, now trying to make it in the business for nearly a decade and pushing thirty—the age at which an actress' bankability, wrong though it was (and continues to be), began to wane. Fox wanted Powell to direct his next feature, a salacious film called *A Fool There Was*, adapted from a play by Porter Emerson Browne who in turn had based his script on a poem by Rudyard Kipling titled *The Vampire*. It was a pretty standard morality tale about the dangers of loose, liberated women. Powell agreed and told Fox that he wanted Goodman as his star, the titular "vampire" (so named because of her tendency to figuratively, not literally, suck the lifeblood from a man). It was a cheap, rushed production shot in New Jersey and Florida. Goodman, her hair dyed black because she thought she might find more roles if she wasn't a blonde, was thrust into the role of a leading actress without much in the way of preparation. By the end of it, however, she was no longer Theodosia Goodman.

Fox wasn't going to rely merely on tantalizing subject matter. Even this early in the film industry, they knew success required a certain amount of carnivalesque ballyhoo. Fox hired newspapermen Al Selig and Johnny Goldfrap for the job. The duo cribbed from two sources to craft the persona of the woman who became Theda Bara. First, there was good ol'-fashioned hokum, the sort of transparently overblown carnival barker nonsense that had been parting rubes from their money and luring them into disappointing sideshows since time immemorial. This sort of bait-and-switch razzle-dazzle was already part and parcel of the motion picture business, mostly in the form of turgid morality dramas about unexpected pregnancy, prostitution, and venereal disease that were, in defiance of the actual contents of such

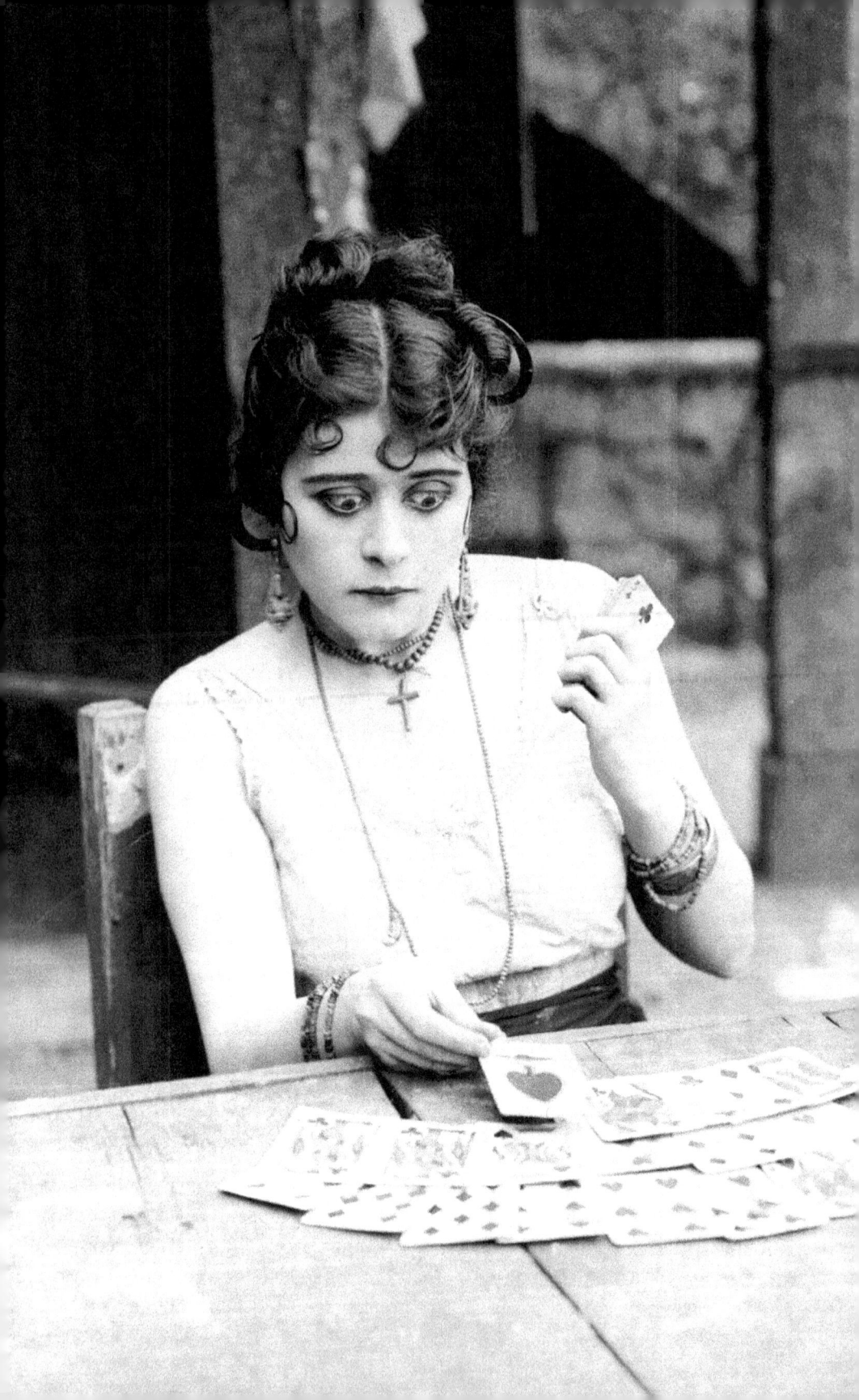

films, advertised via lurid posters promising unflinching portrayals of wantonness, sin, temptation, and damnation. Films such as *Traffic in Souls* promised moviegoers all sorts of vice and reassured moral watchdogs that the film was a cautionary tale in which sinners got their comeuppance, so everything was cool. That the film itself, like most such dramas, was dreary and boring, seemed beside the point. This sort of flim-flam was perfected by the next generation of talented con artists, and men like Louis Sonney, Kroger Babb, and Dwain Esper became the first true mavens of the exploitation film. But the practitioners in the 1910s were already pretty adept at knowing what to do.

The second source from which Selig and Goldfrap drew to craft Theda Bara was famed stage actress Sarah Bernhardt. Almost everything they put into Bara was lifted from Bernhardt. Capitalizing on the European fascination with the East and occultism that sprung up in the Victorian era, Bernhardt was frequently depicted couched in the artifacts of esoterica. She had a strange past, a string of wealthy lovers, and slept in a coffin because, she claimed, it helped her better understand tragedy. In fact, Selig and Goldfrap actually had to tone *down* Bernhardt's weirdness when they borrowed it for Theda Bara. The sort of libertine eccentricity permissible to the most acclaimed stage actress in the world exceeded what was permissible for a star of the American motion picture industry. So while they devised the mysterious persona of Theda Bara and draped her in token symbols of the East and the Occult, they were also aware of the fact that the trend was to market movie stars as pure and committed to God, America, and family. They walked the line with Bara, exploiting the on-screen image while, in interviews, making sure she mentioned that even the vamp just wanted a good husband, lovely children, and a nice home in the country.

Reporters recognized it as a load of bunk: her phony accent, her fluid biography, the camp faux-Oriental setting. It didn't take much digging to discover that Theda Bara was just a gal from Ohio. Some magazines called it out. Others played along, if with a tone of knowing tongue-in-cheekiness. Theda Bara was a magician's trick. You know the magician can't *actually* teleport, that the woman isn't *actually* sawed in half. But for the duration of the show, it's more fun to play along, to let yourself be deceived for the sake of good entertainment. As over-the-top and transparently fabricated as Fox's publicity around Theda Bara was, it worked. *A Fool There Was* was a shoddy production, even for 1915. D.W. Griffith had just made the racist epic *Birth of a Nation* while Italian director Giovanni Pastrone had more-or-less invented the big-budget spectacle with *Cabiria*. Charlie Chaplin was America's biggest movie star (if not the world's). Lillian Gish was an up-and-coming star, and "America's sweetheart" Mary Pickford was on the verge of ascending to her role as the most popular, most powerful woman in show business. Compared to these films and these stars, *A Fool There Was* was a cheap, amateurish film, small in scope, stiffly acted, and containing scenes that looked more like rehearsals than finished takes. But it didn't matter.

The story was, like so many other morality movies, about a vamp (Bara) who has left a trail of broken men in her wake. One is in prison. Another is a shattered husk of a man hustling for spare change. A third, her current, has gone from promising young man to feeble-minded drunkard as she strings him along and drains him of his money. When she learns about a well-to-do diplomat traveling to Europe, she ditches her current mark and sets her sights on new prey. And he *is* prey. There is a scene in which Bara almost supernaturally senses her quarry's arrival on a ship. She sniffs the air like a predator scenting blood, her chest heaving like someone in the throes of passion...or bloodlust. Less a seductress and more a beast. She might not be a vampire in the mold of Count Dracula, but there is something in her performance that anticipates the sexualized, animalistic portrayal of supernatural vampires. When the vamp's spurned lover tracks her down before the ship disembarks, she reacts to his shoving a gun in her face with icy cool, tempting him, taunting him, uttering the immortal line, "Kiss me, my fool." When he turns the gun on himself, she simply laughs, much to the horror of a ship's steward, as the man takes his own life.

As crudely-made as *A Fool There Was* is, director Frank Powell manages to tap into a certain bestial vitality, thanks largely to Theda Bara. Her first appearance sets the tone not just for her character, but for her entire career. A man steps on screen, romantically sniffing a rose. When he places the rose on a pedestal, Theda Bara enters the scene, picks up the rose, laughs, and crushes it. Although the Edwardian *vetements* on the women are more conservative than what would become the norm during the 1920s, Bara still manages to exploit her curves. Where other women are wrapped in stout, conservative dresses and coats, Bara's vampire is draped in close-cut, clinging silks and satins or in a nightgown that puts little effort into not slipping off her shoulder, constantly threatening to expose a bare breast.

Her character is the villain, a warning to men against the temptations of a wanton woman, Although later readings of Theda Bara and the vamp archetype cast her as a sort of proto-feminist rebellion against a fast-withering patriarchal tradition that prescribed for women a subservient and domestic role, such subversion wasn't necessarily the intention. Like the interviews that portrayed Theda as both the exotic vamp and the demure woman longing for domesticity, *A Fool There Was* is a film of mixed messages. It's hard, from a vantage point in the 21st century, not to root for her just a little bit. The lives in which she is meant to stand in stark contrast are so exceedingly *dull*. One thing, however, was exceedingly clear: by the time the film ends—a shocking ending, in which Bara's vampire laughs as she stands triumphant over the husk of her dying conquest, blithely tossing flower petals on what is sure to become his lifeless corpse, the vampire having suffered no consequences or comeuppance for her sin—Theda Bara had *arrived* and brought the whole of Fox with her. The film was a smash. Theda was Hollywood's first overnight superstar, joining the ranks of Pickford and Chaplin as one of the most popular stars of the 1910s. Unfortunately, it didn't last.

After *A Fool There Was*, she starred in two of Fox's most opulent productions, both times playing "historical vamps," first in 1917's *Cleopatra* and then in 1918's *Salome*. Both are lost films, not seen in nearly a century. Almost *every* film in Bara's catalog—films with tantalizing, scandalous titles like *When a Woman Sins*, *The Vixen*, *Siren of Hell*, and *The She Devil* as well as historical dramas like *Romeo and Juliet*, *Carmen*, *Madame Du Barry*, and *Camille*—are gone. Film preservation was not a priority in the early silent era, with films frequently being destroyed to recycle the stock or because nitrate was highly flammable (much of the early Fox library was lost in a fire). Luckily, the publicity machine around Bara was so intense that many photographs of her in costume and on-set still exist. Not only did she terrorize morality as a vamp, she did it wearing some of the skimpiest, most salacious costumes of the era. The costume conservatism of *A Fool There Was*, not to mention the production values, was made quaint by *Salome* and *Cleopatra*, in which Bara was clad...*barely*...in costumes that exposed as much flesh as possible and sent her slinking through lavishly-appointed sets. Fox was willing to court controversy as long as it brought in money, and for the latter half of the 1910s, Theda Bara did just that. Undressing her in costumed dramas meant they could hide behind a veneer of theatrical authenticity, framing Bara not just as a screen starlet, but as a giant of the legitimate theater, the cinematic equal of Sarah Bernhardt. Nonsense, of course, but that didn't matter. Until it did.

Bara's star fell almost as rapidly as it rose. By 1920, what had been sensational in 1915 looked old-fashioned. The dawn of that decade saw the rise of a new kind of woman, dubbed in the press as flappers, who brought with them a new attitude and new style: slimmer, younger, wilder, and clad in flashier clothes. Suddenly, Theda Bara looked dowdy, matronly even. Cautionary tales about female empowerment gave way to women who were *actually* empowered, fighting for property rights,

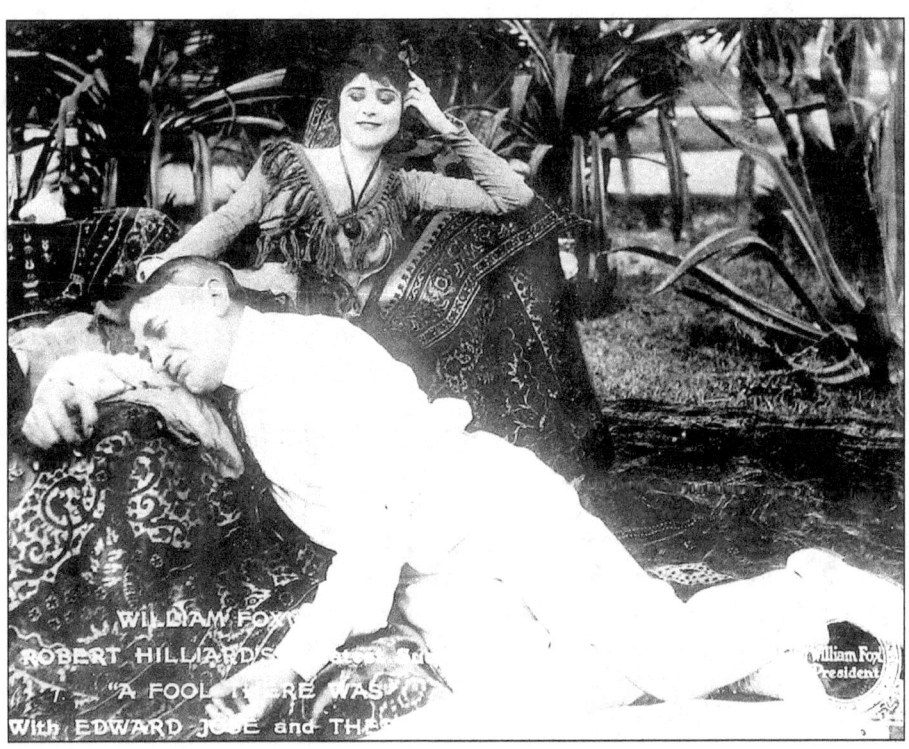

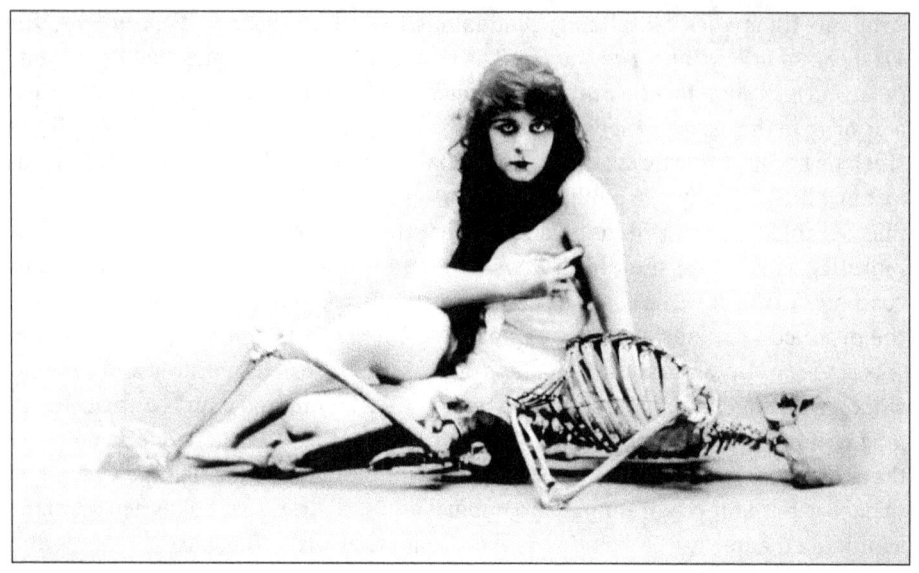

establishing businesses, seizing the right to vote. With so many men devoured by World War I, women stepped into new roles, enjoyed new freedoms—and they were not willing to let go of them once the war was over. By the end of the 1910s, the vamp in general and as played by Theda Bara in particular had been squeezed for all she could give. Audiences were tired of vamps, or demanded more complex, sophisticated portrayals of vamps than soulless destroyers cackling at the demise of weak-willed men. Bara herself was as weary of playing the vamp as audiences were of seeing her do it. Alas, her attempt to break out of the role might have been what did in her career for good.

In 1919, Bara thought an adaptation of the poem *Kathleen Mavourneen* would be her ticket out of the vamp trap. By then, her fictional biography had been debunked from top to bottom, and her real background was common knowledge. And that is, according to many, what sunk the film and turned it from her second coming into the final nail. At issue was not that an American actress was playing a beloved Irish character, but that a *Jewish* actress was playing her. Irish and Irish-American organizations also objected to the portrayal of Ireland as impoverished and full of peasants. Bara's reinvention crashed and burned. The one comfort she could take from the debacle was that the director, Charles Brabin, became her husband.

Bara wasn't the only casualty among the stars of the early silent period. For the most part, the first generation of screen sirens, like Mary Fuller, were banished to obscurity during the '20s. Mary Pickford persevered on the screen, behind the camera, and as one of the founders of United Artists. But then, she was Mary Pickford; people like her don't come around very often. Bara made her final feature, *The Unchastened Woman*, in 1925, but nothing she did in the 1920s caught fire. In 1926, she appeared in a comedic short called *Madame Mystery*, directed by Richard Wallace and Stan Laurel and starring Laurel's long-time stage and screen partner, Oliver Hardy.

But, for the most part, after the disaster of *Kathleen Mavourneen* Theda Bara lived a quiet, domestic life; the kind, perhaps ironically, she had always wanted and which her characters had so often destroyed. Feature films belonged to the next generation, to Louise Brooks, Clara Bow, Marion Davies, Norma Shearer, and Greta Garbo. In 1936, audiences who remembered Theda Bara heard her voice for the first time, when she appeared in a radio adaptation of *The Thin Man* alongside movie series stars William Powell and Myrna Loy (who had been directed by Bara's husband, Charles Brabin, in 1932's *The Mask of Fu Manchu*). Bara never made a talkie. On April 7, 1955, stomach cancer claimed Theodosia Burr Goodman, the woman the world would know as Theda Bara.

Bara was the embodiment of the vamp, but she was not alone. Universal promoted Louise Glaum as a vamp. Valeska Suratt was another Fox actress whose persona was crafted in a way similar to Bara, right down to publicity photos of her with a skull. Fox also promoted Virginia Pearson as a vamp. Like Bara, both Pearson and Suratt were Midwesterners. Suratt hailed from Indiana while Pearson was born in Anchorage, Kentucky, just down the road from the birthplace of D.W. Griffith.

The vamp wasn't just an American phenomenon. In fact, despite Bara's position as "queen of the vampires," it was a woman in France, another queen of a very different sort of vampires, who might have set the template for the generation of *femmes fatale* to come.

Pearl White fared little better. As her interest in serials waned, she signed on as a player for Fox, with the goal of

GIN & SIN

- 2 oz Dry Gin
- 1 oz Fresh Orange Juice
- 1 oz Fresh Lemon Juice
- ¼ oz Grenadine

Add all ingredients to mixing glass with ice. Stir well. Strain into a chilled old fashioned glass. Garnish with an orange twist.

....

BLACK ROSE

- 2 oz Bourbon
- 2 dashes Peychaud's Bitters
- 1 dash Grenadine
- Fill a glass three-quarters full with ice. Add the bourbon, grenadine and bitters. Stir and garnish.

Add ingredients to a mixing glass and fill with ice. Stir, well. Strain into a chilled old fashioned glass. Flame a lemon peel over the drink then add as garnish.

....

FRENCH PEARL

- 2 oz Plymouth Gin
- ¼ oz Pernod
- ¾ oz Fresh Lime Juice
- ¾ oz Simple Syrup
- 1 sprig spearmint

Add lime juice, simple syrup, and mint sprig to a shaker. Muddle the ingredients. Add Pernod and gin. Fill shaker with ice. Shake well. Strain into a chilled cocktail glass. Garnish with a lime wheel and mint sprig.

....

SERENDIPITI

- 1 oz Calvados
- 1 oz Fresh Apple Juice
- Champagne
- 1 Sprig of Mint

Add calvados and mint to an old fashioned glass. Muddle lightly. Add ice. Add apple juice. Top off with Champagne. Garnish with mint sprig.

making features. But a feature film career never panned out. In 1922 she returned to stunt serials with *Plunder*, but the death of her double during a stunt gone wrong exposed the widespread use of doubles for dangerous stunts and the risks these doubles took. The accident put Pearl off serials for good. After the completion of *Plunder*, she moved to Paris and remained there for the rest of her life. She made her final screen appearance in the 1924 French production, *The Perils of Paris*. She briefly returned to the stage in 1925, appearing at London's Lyceum Theater and commanding a whopping $3,000 a week salary. Although no Mary Pickford, it turned out Pearl White was pretty good with the business end of show business. By the time she retired from the screen, she had a fortune in excess of $2 million. She bought race horses. She opened a resort and casino. In the company of Greek tycoon Theodore Cossika, she traveled the world, even buying a home in Egypt. But health issues plagued her. Medication, including alcohol, used to manage pain stemming from injuries during her years making adventure serials wreaked havoc with her liver. In 1937, she quietly began setting her affairs in order. In June of 1938, she checked herself into a hospital. On August 3, she passed away at the age of 49.

In 1914, Louis Feuillade set about making his follow-up to *Fantômas*. Everything he did with *Fantômas*, Feuillade would outdo with this new serial. It was bigger. It was longer and more complex. It was most definitely weirder. Where *Fantômas* was criticized for a glorification of crime it did not exactly deliver, the new serial made the life of a mysterious *apache* gang seem very attractive indeed, so full was it of drinking and revelry and dangerous women in black silk catsuits. Feuillade called it *Les Vampires*. That same year, on August 3, 1914, Germany declared war on France.

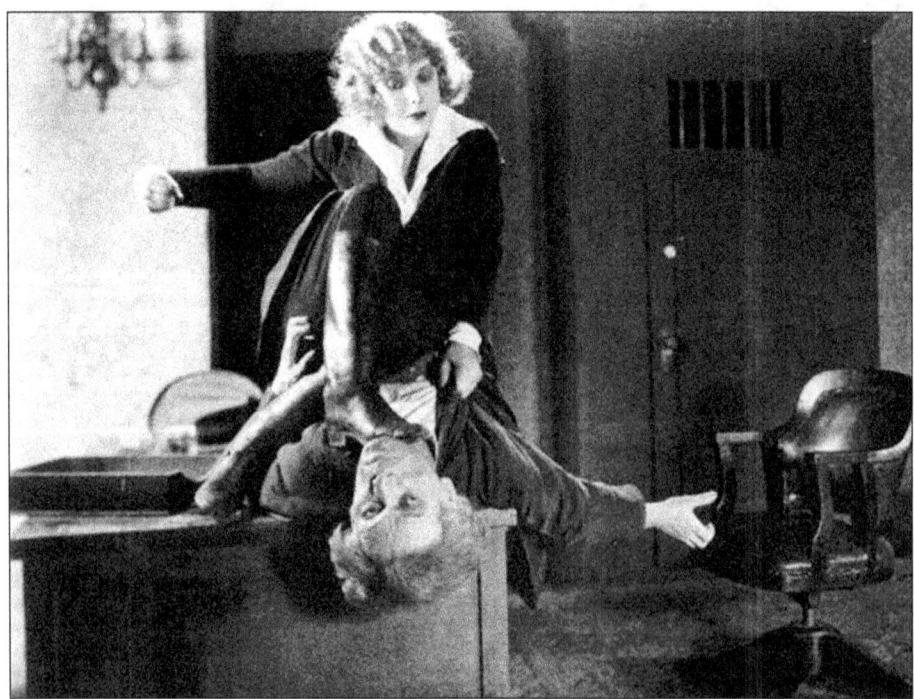

DON'T MESS WITH HER—Pearl White lays down the law in Plunder.

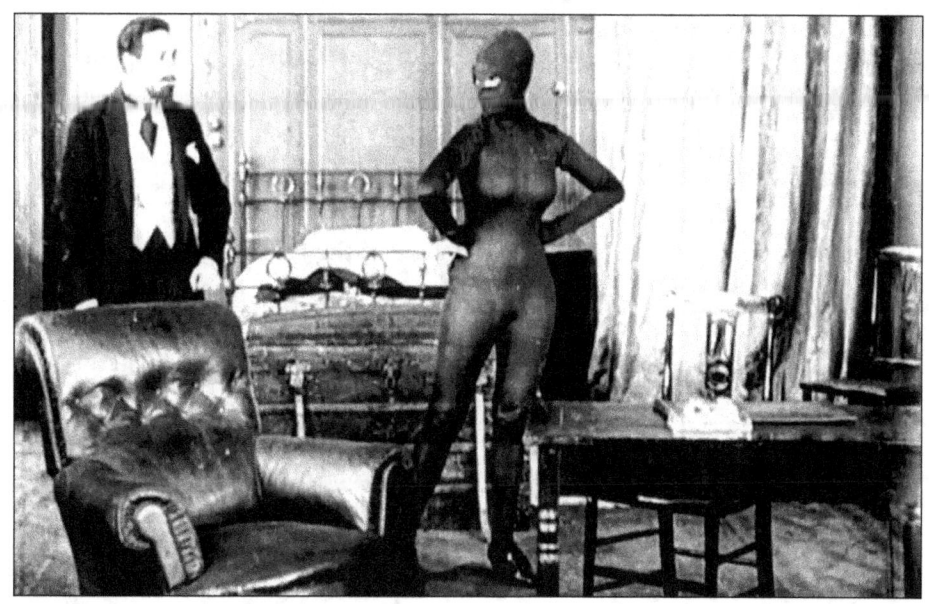

Qui? Quoi? Quand? Où...?

In August of 1914, German forces planned for a swift, overwhelming victory over France by circumventing the bulk of the French forces amassed along the Franco-German border, instead storming across the border with Belgium. Belgium, however, had a pact with Great Britain, so that the first German soldier who set foot in Belgium brought Great Britain into the war. The German advance bogged down. Soldiers on both sides of the struggle began digging in, using a series of trenches to shield themselves from enemy fire. The Great War began, and with it, a grueling stalemate that lasted until November, 1918.

Behind the lines of the Western Front, in perpetually-threatened Paris, Louis Feuillade began work on *Les Vampires*. It wound up very closely reflecting the confusion and anxieties seizing Parisians as the streets of their city were overrun by chaos and the country's men marched off to war. If the Anarchists gave the police and the *bourgeois* heart palpitations, at least they tempered their hijinks with a veneer, however thin, of political idealism. In *Les Vampires*, the inspiration for the gang of criminals running roughshod over Paris were the less politically-motivated *apache* gangs. Questionably-named for the savagery Europeans thought was displayed by American Apaches, these gangs were the bane of early 20th century France. Who exactly coined the phrase remains unknown, but by 1900, it was being used in print, mostly in the popular, sensationalist *feuilliton*, "true crime" periodicals of 19th and early 20th century France. Apache gangs even had their own signature weapon: an amazing, impractical tool that combined a pistol, a shiv, and brass knuckles.

Unlike *Fantômas*, *Les Vampires* was an original work by Feuillade, not an adaptation of an existing property. However, to say Feuillade "wrote" it is stretching the definition of what it is to have written something. Let's say he conceived it.

The script with which actors were presented was skeletal. Actors were relied on to improvise. Feuillade invented new scenarios and tangents as he was filming. *Les Vampires* is a serial after all, and pulp serials often ran so long that the author would lose the strands of the plot, or repeat themselves, or introduce contradictions. *Les Vampires* recreates, for the same production reasons, that rambling, sometimes confusing structure.

In this regard, Feuillade is the forefather of the lackadaisical approach to scripting that became the hallmark of European cult film directors such as Jean Rollin (whose *oeuvre* seems heavily-influenced by Feuillade) and Jess Franco. Perhaps by accident, Feuillade's seat-of-the-pants production style birthed the attitude toward logic and reality that typified continental European horror for so much of the 20th century. Logic and reality are inessential, not even worth paying attention to during the creative process. Scripts, if they existed, should be willingly sacrificed on the altar of creating a dreamy (or nightmarish) mood in which events do not proceed with the same explainability, the same logic, as they would do in waking life. Where American and British horror films concerned themselves with scientific explanations and rational deduction—the "why" of an otherwise fantastic situation—European horror just figured "why not?" Who cares? Who wants a rational dream?

The theoretical main character of *Les Vampires* is intrepid newspaper man Philipe (Édouard Mathé, who played major roles in Feuillade's subsequent thrillers *Judex*, *La nouvelle mission de Judex*, *Tih Minh*, and *Barrabas*). "Theoretical" main

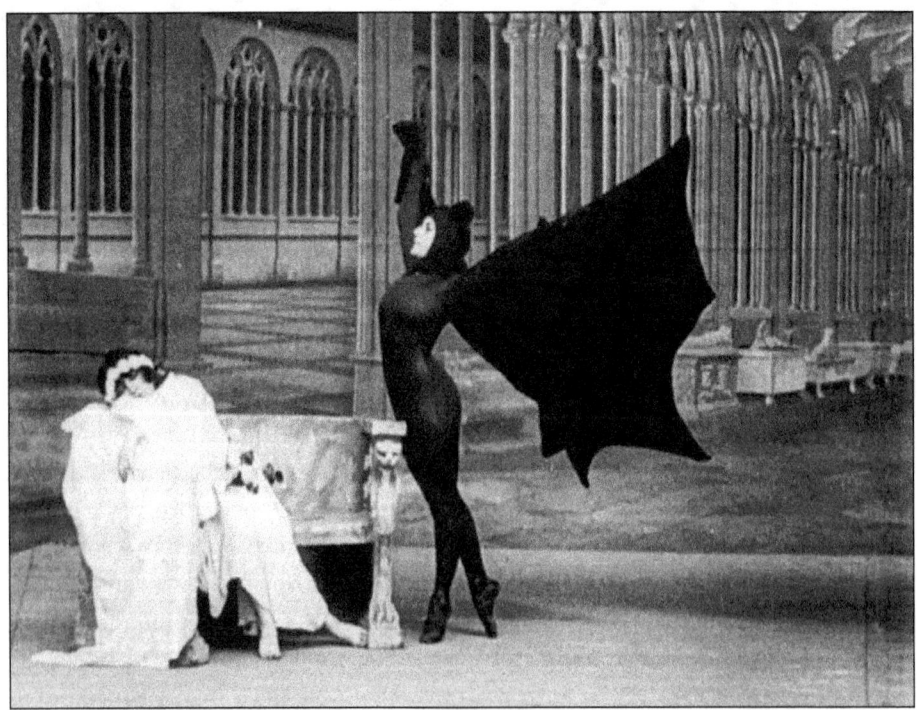

character because, while Juve held his own against the flamboyant Fantômas, Philipe Guérande is hopelessly outclassed by *Les Vampires*' villains. Uninspiring though he may be, it's Philipe who engages in the bulk of investigating and tracking down the notorious apache gang Les Vampires (no word on whether they allowed Bebe Apache to join, but one assumes every gang of cutthroats needs at least one cigar-smoking baby) since there is almost no police presence in *Les Vampires*. They show up from time to time to make an arrest or cart off a corpse that has come tumbling out of a hidden chamber, but only after Philippe has done all of the detective work. It's a statement of the disillusionment with the efficacy of state authority in the face of anarchists and apache gangs running wild, and a reflection of the harrowing reality that Paris had been drained of so many men as wave after wave was sent to the meat grinder of the Western Front. Philipe is assisted by a comical, reformed Vampire named Mazamette (Marcel Lévesque, also in *Judex* and *La nouvelle mission de Judex*), whose shtick is, surprisingly, usually funny and consists mostly of Mazamette dramatically removing a hood or hat or other disguise in a way that shouts "Hey! It's me! Mazamette!"

From the title of the first episode in the lengthy series, "The Headless Corpse," it's evident that *Les Vampires* is bringing something to the screen in addition to the violence that permeated *Fantômas*: gruesomeness. For the first two episodes, Philipe matches wits with the Grand Vampire (Jean Aymé, who later played the judge in Carl Dreyer's silent masterpiece, *The Passion of Joan of Arc*). That changes for the better in the third episode, "The Red Codebook." In and of itself, it's not a particularly outrageous entry in the series, especially not after the previous two episodes confronted audiences with a mutilated cop and a gorgeous scene in which Philipe's fiancée, a dancer named Marfa Koutiloff (Stacia Napierkowska), performs a surreal ballet in a bat costume meant to be reminiscent of the signature black body stockings donned by the Vampires. She moves with balletic grace across the stage, menacing a slumbering young woman (perhaps a reference to Sheridan Le Fanu's famous "lesbian vampire" story *Carmilla*?). That grace transforms to terror when she begins to choke, convulse, and then dies on stage, poisoned by the Grand Vampire! If *Fantômas* and *Les Vampires* teach audiences anything, it's that you shouldn't dress up like a famous criminal for your play.

"The Ring that Kills" reveals that the Grand Inquisitor of the Vampires is a justice of the supreme court. Add a couple pretty good Mazzamete jokes, and it's a hard act to follow. One doesn't expect that the Grand Vampire is about to experience a dramatic fall from power, or that it will come from within his own ranks, or that it isn't actually a function of the plot. No, the Grand Vampire seems an able foil for the crusading Philipe. But then, at one point in "The Red Codebook," Philipe visits a cabaret in pursuit of clues. That's when Irma Vep steps on stage.

Played by the enigmatic Musidora, Irma Vep's introduction into *Les Vampires* is a conscious contrast to poor Marfa Koutiloff. Marfa was part of the classical arts; Irma performs at a run-down dance hall. Marfa performed for the elegant and rich;

Irma sings and dances for the city's thieves, cutthroats, cast-offs, and undesirables. Marfa's dance was graceful in its sensuality; Irma Vep's dance is not graceful or sensual—it's sexual and full of thrusting. It's aggressive, brazen, even raunchy by the standards of the day. In short, it establishes her as a vamp and a Vampire to be reckoned with, a threat to men, to patriarchy, to the idea of what a woman should be. It's similar to the scene of Theda Bara, in *A Fool There Was*, zeroing in on her next victim with a palpable, bestial lust. However, where Bara's vamp hungered for power and achieved it through sex, Musidora's variation on the vamp hungers for power and achieves is mostly by shoving guns and knives at people.

Irma Vep is no respectable lady or demure coquette. She is a bold, liberated, *dangerous* woman, one of the screen's first true *femmes fatale*. She is not the Grand Vampire's girlfriend. She's not a tag-along. She's not there to tend to the clubhouse while the boys have all the bloody fun. She's a Vampire; an equal. In fact, she quickly becomes a superior, in screen presence if not in rank. Neither Philipe nor the Grand Vampire dominates the audience's attention the way she does. As soon as Irma shows up, *Les Vampires* becomes her show.

The daughter of a feminist and a socialist, Jeanne Roques, as she was named, entered into the arts early. She began writing and, in her teens, acting. She struck up a lifelong friendship with novelist Sidonie-Gabrielle Colette, better known simply as Colette, writer of *Gigi* and no stranger to controversy. Happy to flaunt her bisexuality, Colette wrote and performed a pantomime skit called "Rêve d'Égypte" at the Moulin Rouge. The lesbian kiss exchanged during the performance between

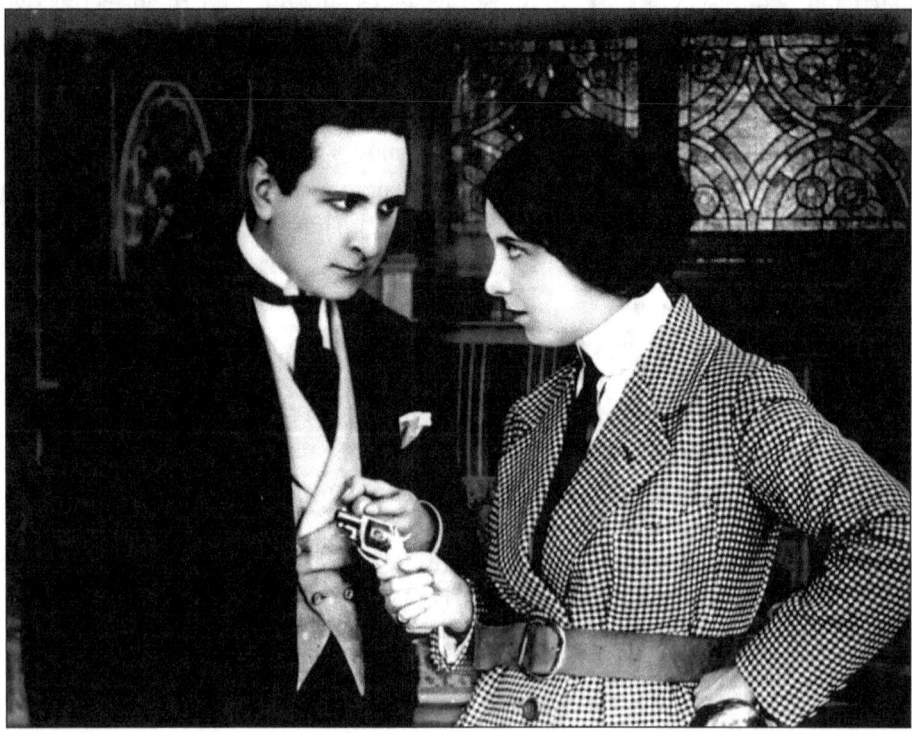

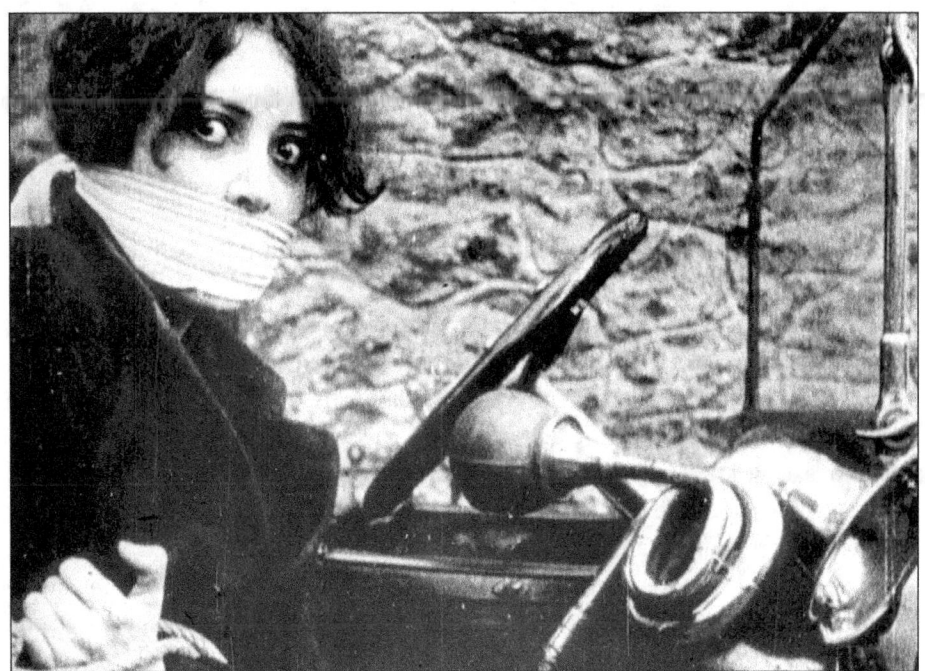

her and her then girlfriend Mathilde de Morny precipitated a small riot, the arrival of the police, and the shuttering of the play (France isn't always so liberal as its reputation would have you believe). She was also romantically involved with Italian writer and madman Gabriele d'Annunzio, a leading light of the Italian "Decadence" movement and in his spare time leader of his own private army. Despite the scandalous life of her best friend, Musidora and Colette were never romantically linked to one another.

Jeanne Roques debuted in film in 1914, but it was her appearance in *Les Vampires* that made her a star, that made her Musidora—the gift of the muses. She certainly makes a striking first impression in *Les Vampires*. Throughout the serial, she remains a constant threat to poor ol' Philipe, hatching scheme after scheme that the reporter and Mazamette must try to foil (often not entirely successfully). The gang loses leaders to assassination and prison with shocking rapidity, but Irma Vep remains, the unspoken foundation of this unruly gang of cutthroats. The enduring image of *Les Vampires* is Musidora clad in the signature black silk body stocking favored by her gang. It fits her substantially better than it does the Grand Vampire, and certainly better than it does Mazamette, who looks likes he got saddled with a body stocking two sizes too large.

The more critics condemned it or reporters wrote about it, the more scandalous it became. Breathless "naked beneath her costume" hyperbole abounded. There were some shots where tricks of lighting and shadow make it look as if the suit is sheer. The suggestive nature of the costume is a contradiction, revealing yet covering her from head to toe, sexual but concealing, a fetishistic indulgence that accentuates her womanhood while depriving men of it, identifying her as unrepresentative of what society expects from woman but representative of what it might want (or want to be). By the time the press was done, one could be forgiven, had one not seen the movies, for thinking Musidora was slinking around the streets of Paris fully nude. She wears this *maillot de soie* sporadically, a few minutes spread throughout the serial's epic run time of nearly seven hours, yet that is—not undeservedly—the indelible image not just of *Les Vampires*, not just of Musidora, but of Louis Feuillade's entire career.

The criminal Moreno (Fernand Herrmann) is introduced in the serial's fourth installment, "The Spectre," working the same con as Irma and the Grand Vampire. Philipe's crusade against the Vampires takes a back seat to the war between the Vampires and Moreno, who leads of a rival gang nearly as feared (and better dressed, except for Musidora) than the Vampires. Moreno's gang is just as vicious as the Vampires, but they seem higher class; less apache, more Lucky Luciano. They selected smart pinstripe suits over silk body stockings. Philipe and Mazamette disappear for long stretches of time during these installments. The movie concentrates instead on the Vampires and Moreno. Moreno ends up on the wrong side of a frame-up involving a complicated real-estate scheme, a corpse, and a safe with a false back.

Moreno swears vengeance against the Vampires. Philippe pops up occasionally to remind us that we shouldn't be rooting for either side in this struggle. But it's hard to care about the right side of the law when the viewer is engulfed by such phantasmagoric lunacy as Moreno's mesmeric powers, which he uses to put Irma Vep in his thrall, enlisting her in killing the Grand Vampire. *Fantômas* kept Juve at the forefront, but here, the heroes are lost among the madness of these criminals. When they resurface, there's an interesting subversion of expectations. Since this middle portion lacks a female character to play the damsel in distress, it's Philipe who spends these episodes getting captured, and it is Mazamette who usually comes to his rescue.

In *Fantômas*, even when Juve was not on screen, it was obvious he'd soon be back and that, despite the title of the serial and the outlandishness of the villain, Juve was the focus. Here, however, by the time Moreno and Irma involve themselves with Satanas (the "real" leader of the Vampires), one can't be blamed for having forgotten that one is supposed to be on Philipe's side, or that Philipe is even in the movie. He can't hope to compete with the likes of Irma Vep and Moreno and is decidedly dull compared to the criminals. In fact, he's pretty dull compared to Juve, who kept the good guys interesting by being just as willing to hatch insane schemes and don elaborate disguises as was Fantômas.

As with *Fantômas*, viewers are thrown into the story in the middle of things. The discovery that this vicious gang that calls themselves "les Vampires" have murdered and decapitated someone (a policeman, no less, further signifying the inefficacy of the police) and stolen the head is just one of many atrocities they've perpetrated, and that's all the information needed for viewers to hit the ground running. Feuillade even rolls out the head in a scene that seems right out of the Grand-Guignol, during which you can practically hear audiences gasp and faint. At least there, the horror was contained to madhouses, crypts, and the stage. *Les Vampires* roamed throughout Paris with complete disregard for boundaries. It was one thing for crimes to be committed in the disreputable parts of town, or for Fantômas' house to be riddled with traps. It's quite another thing when, as it is in *Les Vampires*, such things can happen anytime, anywhere.

Although not the blood-drenched horror show of the Grand-Guignol, *Les Vampires* certainly exploits deep-rooted psychological fears to heighten its impact. Nowhere is safe. The whole of Paris is under assault from these degenerate brutes. Every building seems to contain a secret passage, every floor a trap door, and every closet a corpse. Every rooftop seems to have no purpose but to facilitate the egress of these fiendish ghouls. It is these scenes, in particular one in which a member of the Vampires eludes capture by taking to the rooftops, that Feuillade creates some of his most striking images. A combination of limited film technology, costume, and the actor's body language combine to create an unnatural apparition, an inhumanly elongated and contorted revenant stalking across the rooftops of Paris. Although this Vampire is no vampire, not the stuff of Le Fanu or Bram Stoker, it's easy to see the resemblance between the creeping

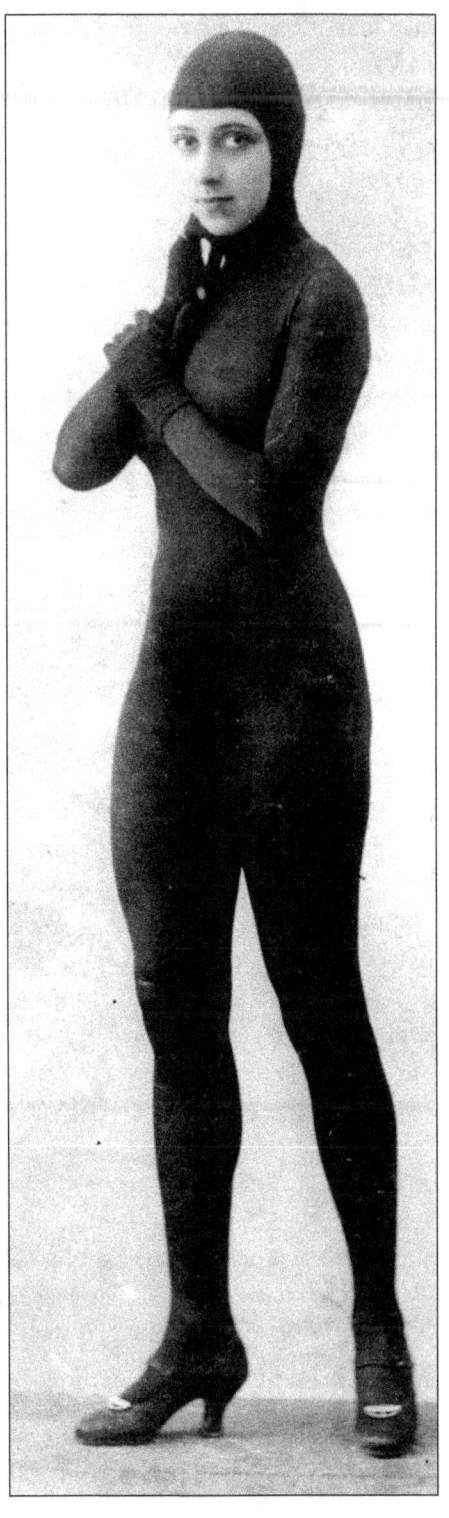

IL FAIT PEUR!

criminal of *Les Vampires* and later unholy apparitions, especially Conrad Veidt's lanky, tortured somnambulist (himself rather fond of black bodystockings) stalking the warped, Expressionist streets of 1920's *The Cabinet of Dr. Caligari*.

The eighth episode of *Les Vampires*, "The Thunder Master," features one of the series' best scenes: Irma Vep's triumphant return to the Howling Cat Cabaret after narrowing escaping imprisonment in an Algerian labor camp. Charges that Feuillade was glamorizing the lives of scoundrels are lent credence by how easy it is to cheer along with the audience full of rabble and rascals when Irma Vep returns. But "The Thunder Master" also marks a turn in the focus of the series toward a more melodramatic structure. It begins when we meet Eustache, Mazamette's ill-mannered son who is immediately enlisted in the effort to capture Satanas. No one ever claimed Mazamette was a good parent.

The Vampires had previously fired shots at domestic bliss: the murder of Marfa, for example, and the unholy union of Irma and Moreno. But with the introduction of Eustache, *Les Vampires* puts Philipe and Mazamette back in the spotlight. The Vampires become less about reigns of terror and more about upsetting the domestic life of Philipe, who suddenly has a new fiancée. It culminates in "The Terrible Wedding," in which Irma is to wed Venomous, yet *another* "real" leader of the Vampires. For over six hours of film, Irma the Vampires have run roughshod over the law, but when they profane the holy institution of marriage, things come to a boil.

It's not surprising that in the end the good guys and social norms prevail. Feuillade was a commercial filmmaker, so it's not surprising that *Les Vampires* spent seven hours reveling in the exploits of criminals and falling in love with the diabolical Irma Vep before the "good conquers all" message necessarily exerted itself. Feuillade knew you could get away with a lot for 99% of your film as long as that last 1% featured the triumph of the forces of morality. The road to the final showdown is strewn with corpses, murders, trap doors, secret chambers, suicide pills, bombs, poison gas (the preferred method of attack in the final two episodes, reflecting its introduction on the Western Front around the same time), Irma Vep ruling over all, Mazamette punching a cop, and wholesale mayhem. Each episode moves at a spry clip, denying viewers the chance to sit and wonder about logic. Like Fantômas, the Vampires are able to conjure ruses with complicated back stories in a matter of hours and at a cost that seems substantially more than what the gang would net should the scheme succeed. Events never demand or offer an explanation; they simply happen. If none of it makes sense, don't worry. Just when you start to wonder about the feasibility of such schemes, a corpse will tumble out of a basket or Musidora will dive out of a window, and all is forgiven.

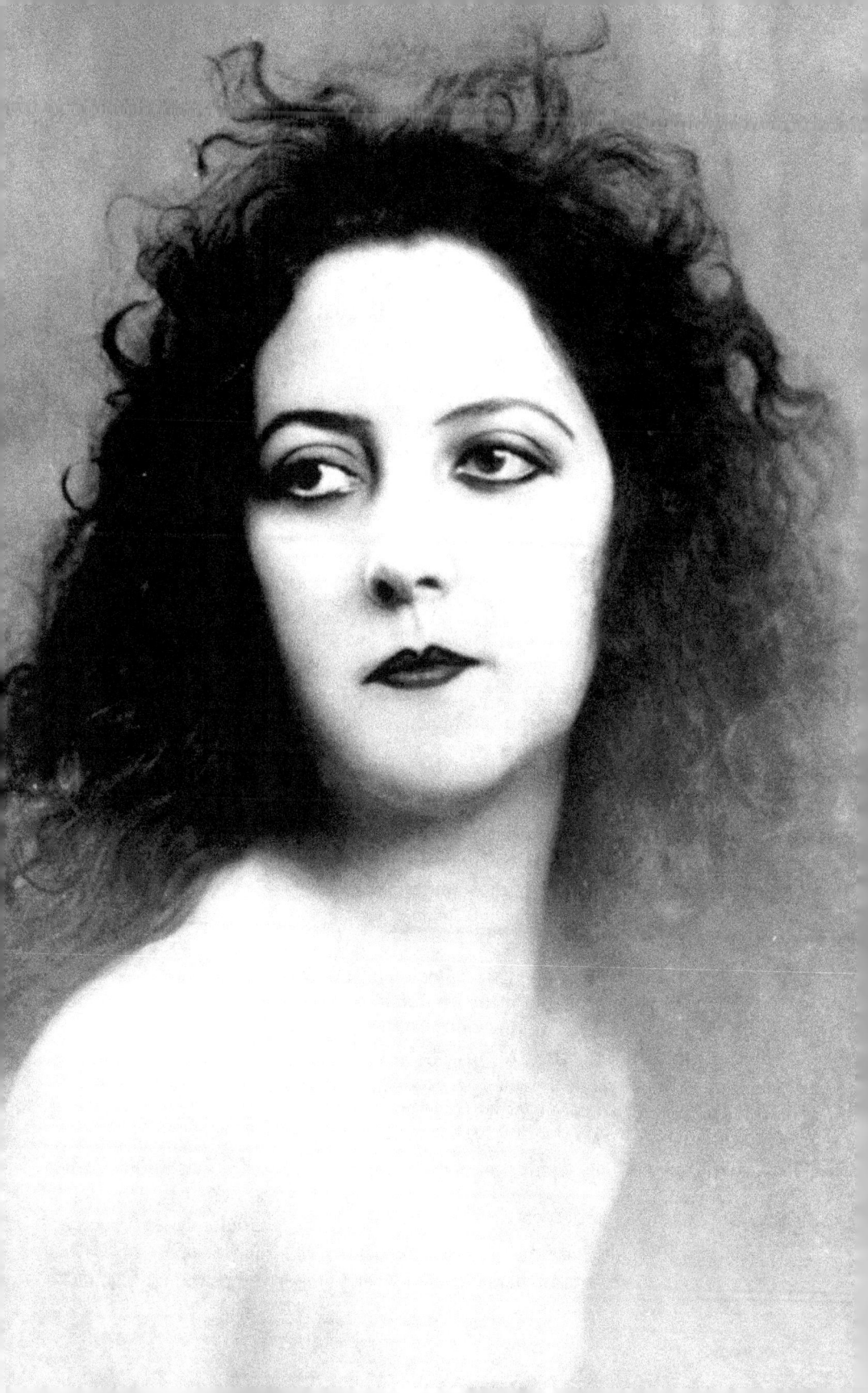

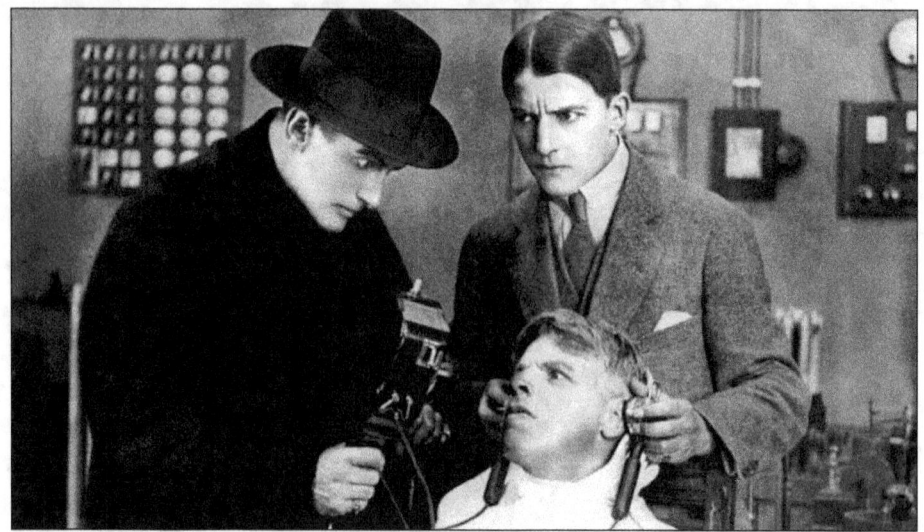

AVENGING CONSCIENCE—Feuillade's third big serial, Judex, is the least of the bunch.

Back Into the Shadows

After the madness of *Fantômas* and the phantasmagorical genius of *Les Vampires*, Feuillade's third series was, through no fault of its own, saddled with the unenviable task of following up two works of art that so resonated with audiences that they're still analyzed, and enjoyed over a hundred years later. *Judex* was in production as early as 1914, shooting concurrently with *Les Vampires* and using most of the same cast, including Musidora. Upset, at least to whatever degree the profits couldn't offset, that *Fantômas* was seen by many to glorify crime and violence, Feuillade decided *Judex* would be the flip side of the coin. Even as he was shooting *Les Vampires*, which would take depiction of crime and perversion to a level far beyond what had been done in *Fantômas*, he began working on the story of a noble avenger, a man working outside of the law but still in the name of justice and, more importantly, in the name of protecting family. Because of the War, however, the release of *Judex* was delayed several years.

In November of 1918, at "the eleventh hour of the eleventh day of the eleventh month," the war that had claimed so many finally ground to a halt. There is a story about an event that occurred in the final minutes of this titanic, heartbreaking conflict. As recounted in Paul Fussell's 1975 book *The Great War and Modern Memory*, troops from the British Fourth Army were startled by machine gun fire coming from the German trenches. "At two minutes to eleven," Fussell wrote, "a machine gun, about 200 yards from the leading British troops, fired off a complete belt without a pause. A single machine gunner was then seen to stand up beside his weapon, take off his helmet, bow, and turning about, walk slowly to the rear." For anyone familiar with the history of what was then the War to End All Wars, but which is tragically known today as World War I, this finale is as suitably sentimental as it is devastating. By that time, between August of 1914 and November of 1918, nearly two million German soldiers had died. Over a million troops from the United

Kingdom had met the same fate, and something along the lines of 1.5 million French. Millions more were maimed, and millions more still would die from post-war epidemics such as the Spanish flu. Three empires—the Austro-Hungarian, the Russian, and the Ottoman—were wiped out. Three more—the German, British, and French—had been dealt severe blows. Entire countries ceased to exist, with new ones drawn, often hastily and without much regard for local considerations. The United States emerged from the conflict, which had joined much later than other combatants, stronger than when it entered. Japan also benefited from the war, handily taking over German possessions in the Pacific and adding to the prestige of having already trounced Russian at the beginning of the century. They began eying their neighbors on the mainland and wondered if, perhaps, it was time for a Japanese empire.

But in Europe, World War I left the countryside ravaged, the cities emaciated, and the people shell-shocked. It was a conflict unlike anything the world had seen and which only a few people had predicted would be as horrific as it ended up being. The wounds were deep. Much of Europe had been spoiling for a fight in the years leading up to WWI, but it was Germany that fired first. That aggression led to the Treaty of Versailles, an agreement that inflicted so many punitive measures on Germany that many considered it a guarantee of future hostilities. American President Woodrow Wilson was horrified by it. French general Ferdinand Foch thought the treaty attempted to severely punish Germany without providing the muscle to back up the measures. "This is not a peace," Foch proclaimed after the signing of the treaty in June of 1919. "It is an armistice for twenty years." World War II started twenty years and 64 days later.

In the two decades between the fall of the Kaiser and the rise of Hitler, Germany endured one of its bleakest economic periods. It also happened to be one of Germany's most profoundly creative periods. The war had been harrowing, and the men who returned from it were not the same men who marched to it. Artists from across Europe and the United States flocked to Berlin, attracted as they so often are by the macabre and melancholy state of the defeated capital. But that melancholy was not as melancholy as they thought. The end of the war ushered in the beginning of the Jazz Age. Many Europeans picked up a taste for this brash new American style of music that had been carried to their shores when the U.S. entered the war. Then there was Prohibition, which scattered American entertainers, artists, bartenders, and adventurers elsewhere in the world. Paris, the traditional home of such artistic enclaves, was in the grips of severe post-war social conservatism. But Berlin—defeated and disgraced Berlin—was suddenly in the throes of an apocalyptic abandon that ushered in an era famous for artistic accomplishments and stunning decadence. Cross dressers, torch singers, drugs and booze, strip clubs and prostitution, writers' circles and artists' schools, self-discovery and self-destruction; it was known as the Weimar era. As artists, hustlers, and dreamers flocked to Berlin, the nexus of important European filmmaking moved with them, shifting away from Paris. In this crucible, a new cinematic philosophy called Expressionism found its ultimate expression in Robert Wiene's 1920 masterpiece, *The Cabinet of Dr. Caligari*.

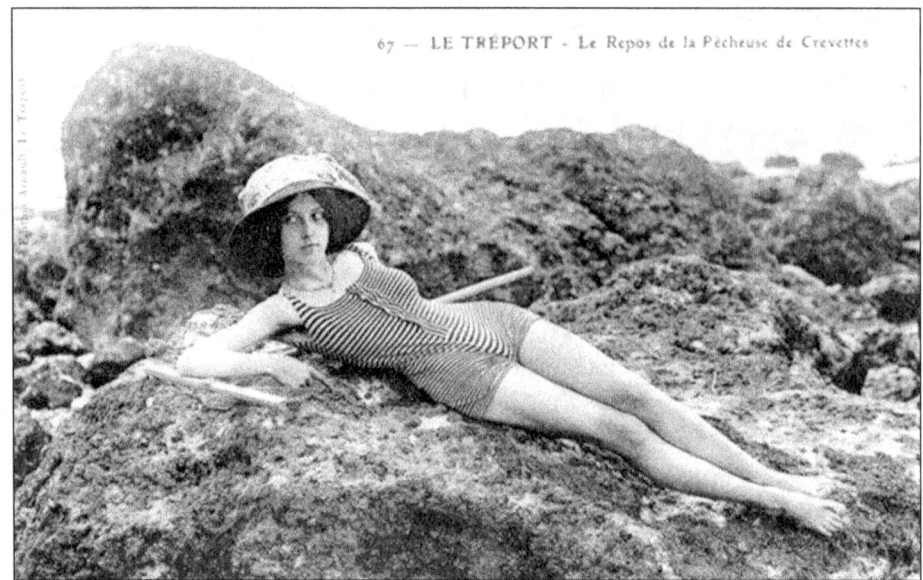
FEMME FRONT LINE—A Musidora postcard popular with French troops on the Western Front.

In 1925, at the age of just 52, Louis Feuillade passed away. Although his work faded from the limelight with the introduction of sound film, neither Fantômas nor Irma Vep spent much time in the "forgotten" category. They remained influential and popular, if only sporadically and among film fanatics. Fantômas was never long absent from the screen. There were more feature films, television shows, and in the 1960s a James Bond-meets-Diabolik makeover for a trilogy of slick caper/spy films. *Judex*, the least of Feuillade's "big three" was remade by director Georges Franju. If Feuillade built the foundation of *cinema fantastique*, Franju erected the cathedral. His eerie 1960 film, *Eyes Without a Face*, is widely regarded as the first French horror film. Irma Vep herself resurfaced in Olivier Assayas's 1996 arthouse film *Irma Vep*, starring Maggie Cheung.

Some of the first people to celebrate the work of Louis Feuillade and revive his films—particularly *Fantômas* and *Les Vampires* (no one seemed to enjoy the moralizing of *Judex*) as well as Pathé's *Les Mystères de New York*—were the Surrealists, whose art movement grew out of dadaism and the psychoanalytical theories of Freud. Surrealism stressed, by way of the ever-popular manifesto (this one written in 1924 by André Breton), the need to shed the shackles of structure, tradition, and rationality and pursue art that captured the true, often baffling process of human thought and dreams. In Feuillade's thrillers, they found something to champion, even though Feuillade considered himself a social and artistic conservative.

After her work with Feuillade, Musidora moved behind the camera, directing a number of films, of which only two remain in existence: 1922's *Soleil et Ombre* and 1924's *La Terre des Taureaux*. She produced and directed *La Flamme Cachee* in 1918, based on the writings of her friend, Colette. Her image on screen is often couched in terms of the erotic, but for her it was more about assertiveness. She was, in nearly every way, the sort of independent, modern woman she depicted and which so terrified those prone to being terrified by feminism and liberation. Though the role of Irma Vep caused her to frequently be compared to Theda Bara, in the end Musidora was much more a Mary Pickford, including a career as a writer, director, and crusader for actors' rights. Signed photographs and totems from Musidora were common among the personal effects of French soldiers hunkered down in the trenches during the War. The government, in the name of French pride and family values, might have wanted women to be chaste and pure Jacqueline, but the soldiers preferred Irma Vep.

Musidora wrote for film journals. She was one of the few stars at Gaumont who stood up to studio head Leon Gaumont, and she did it for the same reason Mary Pickford rebelled against her handlers. As part of a contract dispute, Gaumont decided to drop the practice of including the names of actors in a film's credits. Musidora was incensed, and confronted Gaumont in his office—an unheard of act! But for her, it was important that she not be Irma Vep or Diana or any of her characters. She loved them and embraced them, but they were not her. She was, then and always, Musidora.

In the 1950s, someone attending a screening at Paris' Cinematheque Francaise, one of the most famous film archives in the world, might have had their ticket taken by an aged woman with a passion for cinema and impressive knowledge of its inner workings and history. It might not occur to the attendees to wonder about the woman. Just another senior citizen volunteer, nothing out of the ordinary. They would not suspect that, if they were watching one of the revival screenings of *Les Vampires*, the old woman who had sold them their ticket was up there on the screen, decades younger, creeping across the rooftops of old Paris in her iconic *maillot de soie*. §

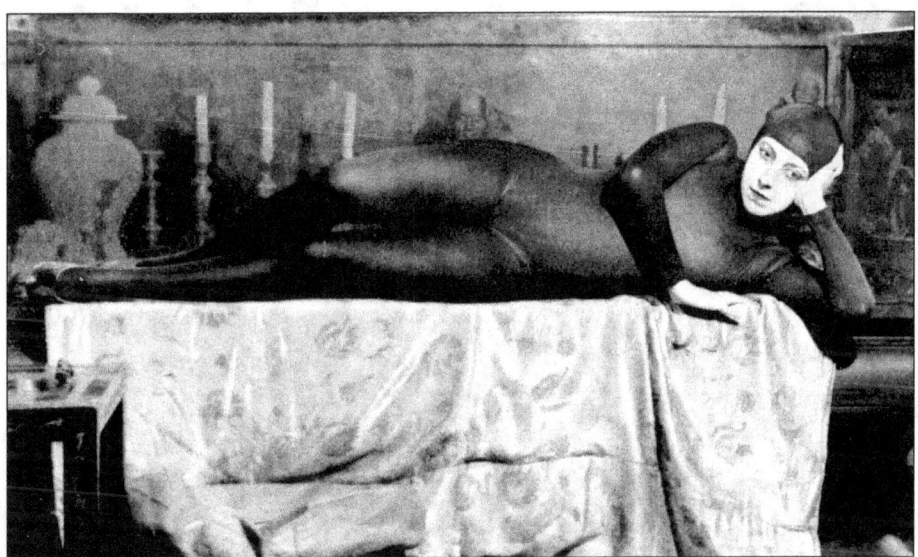

FEMME FEUILLADE—*Musidora as Irma Vep, in Les Vampires' most famous publicity still.*

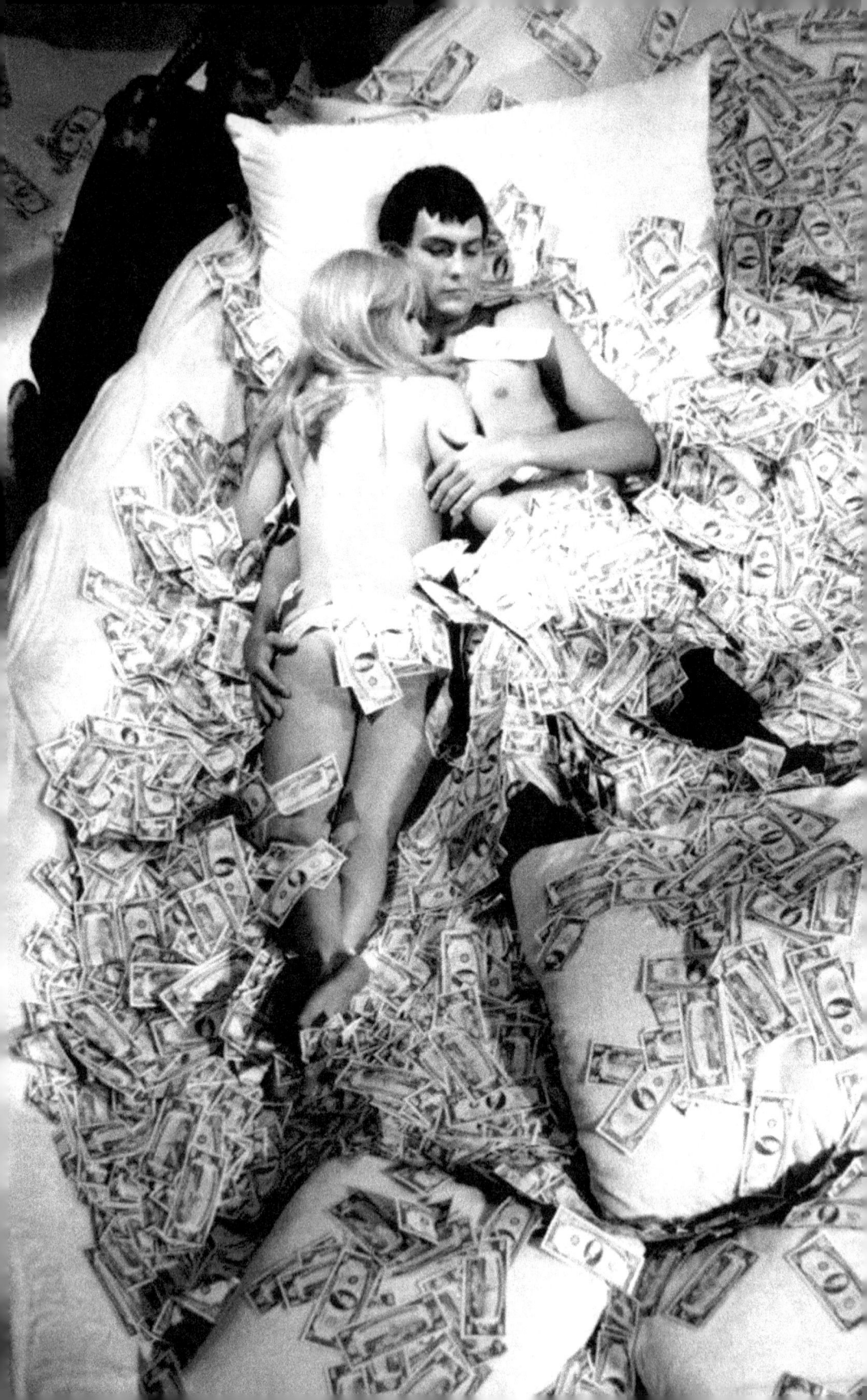

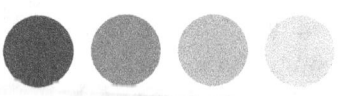

05 DEEP DEEP DOWN

The wonderful, sleazy world of Italian comic books, Diabolik, and Luger-waving madmen dressed as skeletons

F*umetto* is the name applied to Italian comic books and strips, an odd term to mean what it does, in the same way *giallo* ("yellow") came to refer to a line of murder/thriller novels and, later, a style of film. Giallo acquired that meaning because a series of mystery novels were released by a publisher all bearing the same striking yellow cover design. "*Fumetto*" translates to "little puff of smoke" and was derived from the word and thought bubbles used by comics. Like giallo or pulp, *fumetto* can refer to different things for different people. Often, all those concepts get mixed up into one big, difficult-to-separate stew thanks to the fact that they all evolved from pretty much the same source material: penny dreadfuls, French crime novels like *Fantômas*, and the adventure novels of authors such as Alexandre Dumas and Edgar Rice Burroughs.

Early Italian comics were translations of American strips. During World War II, many of these were forced to suspend publication. The Fascist propaganda comics that took their place probably weren't as much fun as *Felix the Cat*. After the War, American comics flooded back into the market. By then, comics had changed dramatically. A new generation of characters and creators arose during the War years, as had a new way of delivering comics. Newspaper funny pages were still around, full of adventure serials featuring costumed heroes with strange powers and names such as *Mandrake the Magician*, *Flash Gordon*, *Dick Tracy*, and *The Phantom*. But there was also a trend to move away from newspaper strips and toward comic books, where "super" heroes such as Captain America, Wonder Woman, Superman, and Batman, staked out their place in pop culture history. And then there were the pulps, introducing a generation of dark, mysterious heroes were being developed in magazines, radio, and movie serials.

Although American comics were popular during Italy's lean post-war years, as Italy got its feet back under it, there was a call for home-grown heroes. Many of the Italian properties created during this period hedged their bets by using classic American settings and archetypes. Gian Luigi Bonelli and Aurelio Galleppini's *Tex Willer*, which debuted in 1948, was about an American cowboy. In 1961, Sergio Bonelli and Gallieno Ferri created *Zagor*, a Native American protector of the forest. Italian creators also started poking around the dark alleys populated by the Shadow, the Spider, and antiheroes who operated outside of the law.

Then there was the new breed of superheroes, who were not exactly super and definitely not heroes. Although inspired by American superhero comics, Italian creators were attracted primarily to the darker spectrum of characters. In Batman's origins, in particular, are many traits that would become common among the *fumetti* anti-heroes of the 1960s: the tragic past, the vengeful mindset, the playboy alter ego, a lack of superpowers compensated for by superhuman levels of training and the willingness to maim and kill the guilty.

In 1962, a combination of Batman and Fantômas crossed with James Bond resulted in *Diabolik*, the creation of sisters Angela and Luciana Giussani. *Diabolik* was a thief, a master of disguise, and an ace at killing anyone who got in his way. His mayhem struck a chord with readers. Others would follow, each one trying to be more outrageous and offensive than the last. The *fumetto nero* was born.

Among the characters inspired by *Diabolik* was *Kriminal*, created by Luciano Secchi under the pseudonym Max Bunker. Kriminal whose alter ego was Anthony Logan, was a thief from England, notable for his choice in clothing: a black and yellow skeleton suit. Like Diabolik, Batman, and Fantômas, Kriminal had no superpowers. If he needed to kill you, he did it with a Luger. *Kriminal*, did its best to one-up *Diabolik*, exhibiting absurd levels of cruelty and violence and a parade of scantily-clad females. The potent combination of sex and violence got *Kriminal* in trouble with critics and censors—and made it a hit. In time, as with *Diabolik*, *Kriminal*'s sadistic streak was softened, until eventually he only killed those who were asking for it, though he never did get over his need to menace buxom babes whose blouses were falling off.

No worries about Kriminal growing soft though, because another skeleton suit wearing anti-hero was waiting to take up the slack and commit depraved acts of which even Kriminal couldn't approve.

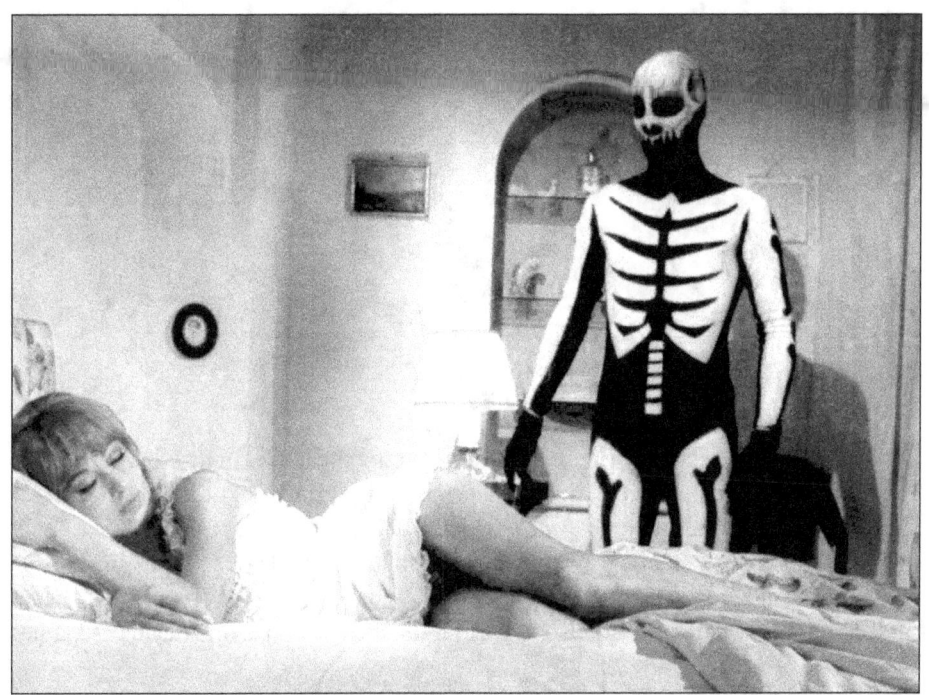

Skeleton Crew

Although he followed in the footsteps of Diabolik in print, Kriminal beat him to the big screen. *Kriminal*, an Italian production directed by Umberto Lenzi, was released in 1966. By that time, Lenzi was a seasoned pro of the cut-throat Italian exploitation industry, working in whatever genre was popular at the time. He dropped out of law school to pursue filmmaking and, in his spare time, worked as a journalist, including a stint with *Bianco e Nero*, the oldest film magazine in Italy. In 1958, he directed his first film, a Greek production called *Mia Italida stin Ellada or Vacanze ad Atene*. It was never released, but Lenzi recovered and, in 1961, scored his first legitimate directing credit with the swashbuckling adventure *Le avventure di Mary Read* (*Queen of the Seas*). He settled into a groove, directing several adventure films that ranged from swashbucklers and historical hellraisers to sword and sandal spectacles, enabling Lenzi to hone his skill at crafting exciting action scenes and competently-mounted productions with minimal time and budget. In the 1960s, with the success of James Bond, spy films became all the rage, and with them the variation on the formula. Lenzi was on hand to direct.

Like the silent *Fantômas* series, *Kriminal* begins with its titular villain (played by handsome Dutch actor Rolf Boes under the pseudonym Glenn Saxson) about to be executed in London as the powers-that-be, including his arch-nemesis Scotland Yard inspector Milton (because all costumed villains need an arch-nemesis at Scotland Yard), wait anxiously for confirmation that the dastardly devil is dead. Naturally, that confirmation doesn't come. As the lever is pulled and Kriminal is about to hang, the rope breaks, the lights go out, and Kriminal vanishes. The officials are aghast—except for Milton, who planned the whole thing. It turns out Kriminal had stolen

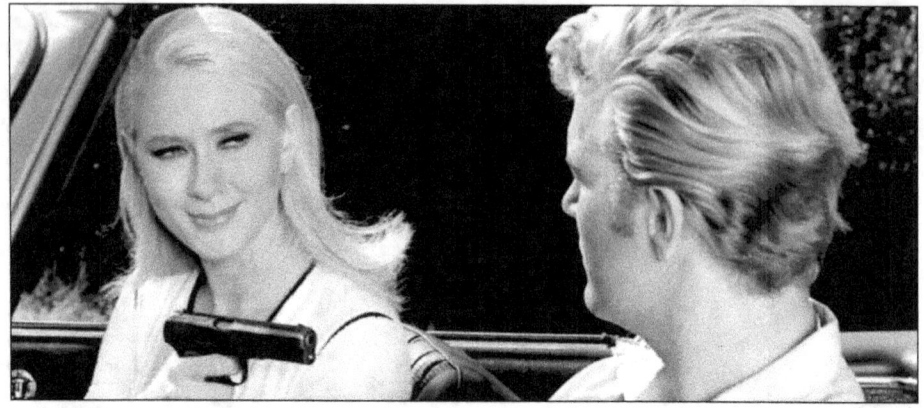

the Queen of England's crown and is willing to take the secret of its whereabouts to the grave. Milton engineers Kriminal's escape so that they might follow him to the crown, recover it, and then recapture Kriminal. Obviously, plans of this nature never go well, and before too long Kriminal has eluded his tail and is free to resume his life of crime, though he does politely return the crown to Milton as a "thank you." Never let it be said that Kriminal isn't a class act (well, until he starts murdering old ladies for their insurance money).

Kriminal's first action as a free man is to pay a visit to his ex-wife, which he does the only way he knows how: by slipping into his signature skeleton suit and creeping in through the window. Like Fantômas' hood, this skeleton suit serves no real purpose, and in fact works to Kriminal's detriment since a bright yellow suit contributes little to a cat burglar's need to hide in the shadows. Also, everyone in law enforcement knows who Kriminal is, and he frequently takes off his mask in front of people he should be menacing, just like Fantômas would take off his own mask, taunt a victim, then put the mask back on. Like Fantômas, Kriminal is less a master of disguise and more a master of fake mustaches, a skill that serves them far more effectively than the penchant for outlandish get-ups.

Still style counts, and as absurd as the skeleton suit is on the surface, somehow actor Glenn Saxson doesn't look totally ridiculous in it, as long as you don't pause for one moment to think about the inherent silliness. It *does* look cool, and it does look creepy, and if it doesn't make a lick of sense, one need only remember that this is a comic book world where a villain can build a bomb the sole function of which is to blow the shirt off a beautiful woman.

Kriminal's ex-wife (played by Maria Luisa Rispoli, who didn't have much of a career in film but does pop up in a few other Eurospy films, including the pretty good *Desperate Mission* and a Franco and Ciccio comedy called *Oh! Those Most Secret Agents*) wants nothing to do with her felonious former, but Kriminal isn't the kind of skeleton leotard-clad brute to let that go without working his sensual magic. He also wants to steal some information from her, since she works for a bonded courier about to transport a fortune in diamonds. Like everything in this film, the company's plan to protect against theft is ludicrously complicated when all they really needed to do was send one very attentive and focused courier accompanied by a small retinue of muscle. Instead, they hatch a loony scheme in which a glamorous young woman (cult cinema icon Helga Liné) will travel alone with the diamonds, except she has an identical twin who will be on a different airline, so no criminal (or Kriminal) will know which woman to rob. This complex scheme full of multiple points of failure is made even more confusing when it turns out Kriminal is not the only cat in town with a notion to steal the diamonds, and indeed some of the others are working an angle from the inside. As is the way with such films, stealing the diamonds will require Kriminal to travel to multiple exotic locations, bed multiple beautiful women, and kill a good many people, all while being pursued by the indefatigable Inspector Milton.

When Lenzi is at his best as director, his films are snappy and crisply paced, and *Kriminal* is Lenzi at his best. It never slows down, but it never goes so fast that you can't stop to luxuriate in all the location work or admire all the swank 1960s fashion. It's a more down-to-earth film than *Danger: Diabolik*, which two years later elevated the genre to absurdist pop-art masterpiece. Being less phantasmagoric than *Danger: Diabolik* leaves plenty of room for swingin' style, though, and *Kriminal* has it in spades. Working with cinematographer Angelo Lotti, Lenzi mounts a gorgeous production. It's not quite James Bond opulence, but there's no doubting *Kriminal* is several cuts above similar films being made at the same time. Lenzi's experience shooting budget-conscious epics prepared him well for *Kriminal*. It never feels small, and Lenzi is happy to indulge in sun-drenched travel footage for the benefit of viewers who might not have a chance to get to Spain or Istanbul. Lenzi was always a straightforward director, and that remains so here. The only stylistic indulgence is the occasional transition from live-action to comic book style illustrations. Romano Mussolini provides a swinging fusion of jazz and lounge music to keep everything peppy. It's true the plot meanders and, at times, almost loses itself inside the ill-defined web of double- and triple-crosses, but the pace is such that one can easily shrug off the convoluted details and just go along for the ride assured that, in the end, all that matters is Kriminal *wants those diamonds*!

Helga Liné was one of the great fixtures of Italian cult cinema, appearing in, among others, *Hercules and the Tyrants of Babylon*, *Mission Bloody Mary*, *Special Mission Lady Chaplin*, and *Password: Kill Agent Gordon*. She was even in another

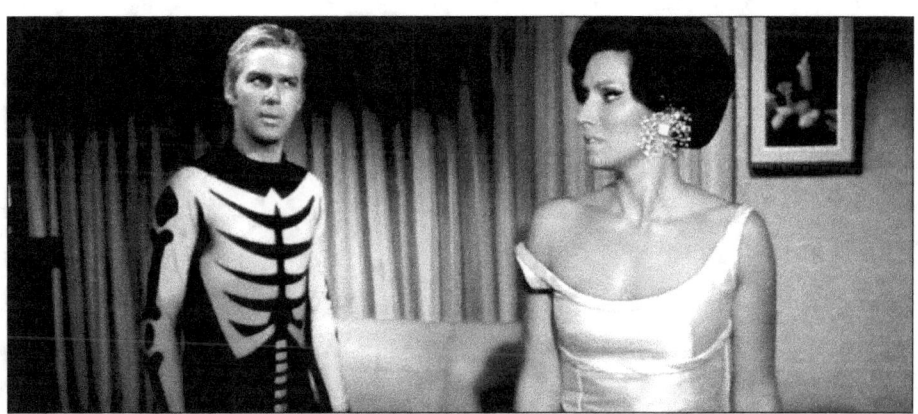

fumetti-inspired comic book adventure, 1968's *Avenger X*, as well as Mexican superstar El Santo's luchador/Eurospy crossover, *Doctor of Death*. She also made a lot of horror films in the '70s, including *Vampire's Night Orgy*, Antonio Margheriti's *Nightmare Castle* (alongside Barbara Steele), and some of the rare Paul Naschy films where he *doesn't* turn into a werewolf. Born in Germany but Spanish and Portuguese by heritage, Liné's family fled Nazi Germany in the 1930s and settled in Portugal, where the young Helga worked as a dancer, circus acrobat, child actress, and eventually a model. The cross-cultural collaborative nature of post-war European cinema led her to Italy, where she worked, like most, in whatever genre was popular, making a name for herself first in Eurospy and spaghetti westerns then later becoming a staple of Euro-horror. She twice worked with respected art house director Pedro Almodóvar, on *Labyrinth of Passion* in 1982 and *Law of Desire* in 1986.

Glenn Saxson is a bit stiff as an actor but looks dashing as the lady-killer (among others he kills) supervillain. He'd previously starred in Alberto De Martino's spaghetti western *Django Shoots First* (De Martino, incidentally, directed a number of great films, including the top notch Eurospy capers *Special Mission Lady Chaplin* and *Operation Kid Brother* starring Neil Connery, Sean's brother). He went on to star in the *Kriminal* sequel, a couple other actioners, and then a string of saucy '70s erotica with titles like *The Hostess Also Likes to Blow the Horn* and *School of Erotic Enjoyment*. He's perfectly suited for the role of Kriminal, and somehow he manages not to look completely ludicrous when he's strutting around with his mask off and the rest of the skeleton suit still on. Supporting him is a cast of Italian exploitation stalwarts lead by Umberto Lenzi regular Andrea Bosic as the harried Scotland yard inspector. This version of Kriminal is relatively soft. He kills people, but those people are usually trying to kill *him*, so turnabout is fair play. As fun as it is, though, *Kriminal* is just the appetizer for what came next. It was time for Diabolik to make his move.

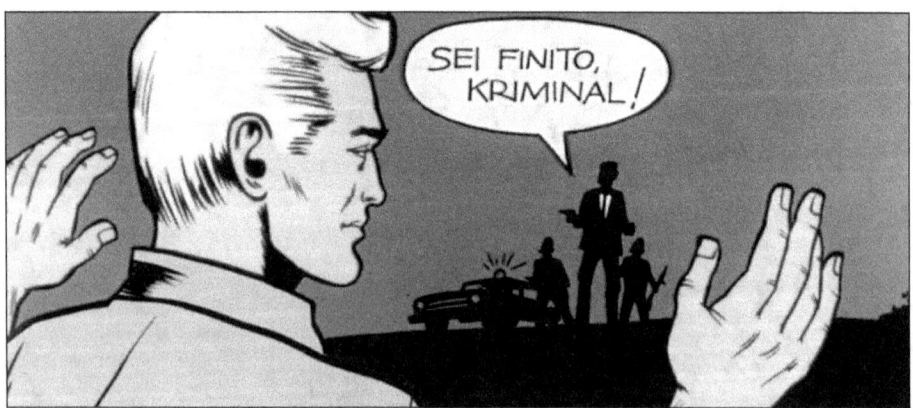

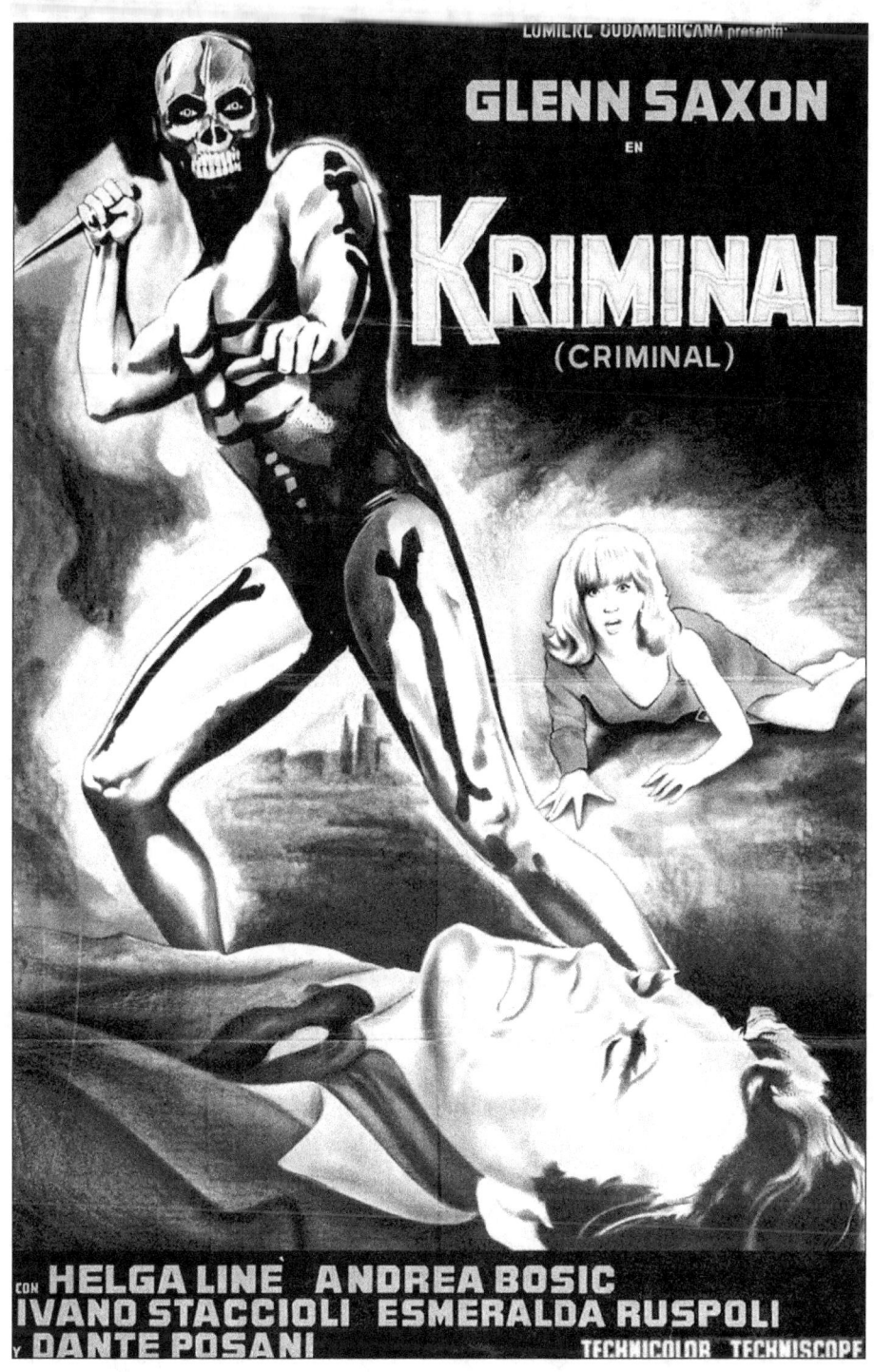

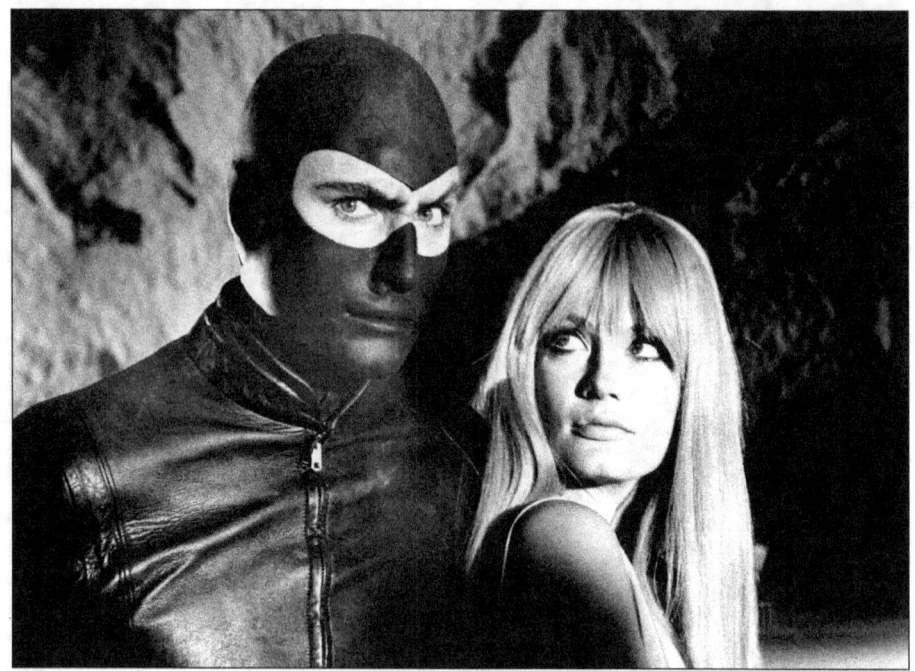

Bava and the Burglar

In 1968, director Roger Vadim gave the world a zero-G striptease by his then-wife Jane Fonda in *Barbarella*. Dino De Laurentiis, famous for throwing big budgets at low-budget genres, produced this phantasmagoric Technicolor acid trip adapted from a French comic strip about a sexy space agent plying the galaxy in search of missing scientists and lustful encounters. It was such a hoot that De Laurentiis decided more of the same would be in order. Again he turned to European comic strips for his source material, this time setting his sights on *Diabolik*, the ongoing saga of a master criminal who confounds both the police and the established criminal underworld.

On paper it was supposed to be a spiritual if not narrative follow-up to *Barbarella*. De Laurentiis snagged Mario Bava to direct, and it couldn't have been a better choice. Since his first color film, Bava had proven himself a master of playing with light and creating surreal atmospheres on the tiniest of budgets. Films like *Blood and Black Lace* (1964), *Planet of the Vampires* (1965) and *Kill, Baby...Kill!* (1966) continue to influence films to this day thanks to their bold, convention-bucking use of color and lighting (not to mention violence). With *Diabolik*, Bava would be allowed to indulge his sweet tooth for candy-colored psychedelia equipped with a budget that dwarfed anything with which he'd previously been supplied. Not that the bigger budget mattered to him. Although De Laurentiis gave him $3 million, Bava brought the film in for $400,000. You'd never know it. The film looks like he spent the full budget, and one can only imagine how out-of-this-world it would have been had Bava not been so conditioned to make the most of every single cent.

Audiences may have had to wait for the cinematic debut of Diabolik, but when it hit, boy did it hit...without actually being a hit. Mario Bava's lavishly colorful romp features, among other notable accomplishments, what is without a doubt one of the most wonderful moments in all of cinema. Having just completed a major heist, cool-as-liquid-nitrogen antihero Diabolik returns to his sprawling, space-age underground lair full of pop art furnishings, where he and his staggeringly beautiful girlfriend proceed to make love on a gigantic rotating bed covered in piles of the money he's just stolen, all as Ennio Morricone's lush, romantic, yet thoroughly absurd soundtrack sighs and growls and wah-wahs in the background.

French star Jean Sorel was slated to portray Diabolik. Catherine Deneuve was to star as his partner and lover, Eva. Mere days into the production however, Bava determined that Sorel simply wasn't right for the part. He was replaced by John Phillip Law, who had starred as the blind angel Pygar in *Barbarella*. Law was a hunk with near inhuman good looks, but he was never the greatest actor on the block (though many claimed his acting resembled a block). Still, since the idea behind *Diabolik* was not style over substance but rather, as with *Barbarella*, style *as* substance, he fit the bill because he *looked* the part, especially his eyes, which were a dead ringer for the comic book version of Diabolik and which were important for a character who spends so much time in a mask that obscures the rest of his face. Law's reserved acting works for the character, a man so far removed from traditional human morality that he seems at times almost unable to act human.

Casting woes continued. Deneuve refused to do the nudity required in what became one of the film's signature scenes. Bava always thought more of concealing than revealing, and while there is certainly plenty of flesh (both male and female) on display in the scene, there is no actual nudity *per se*. All the areas proscribed by moral watchdogs as naughty were suitably and strategically covered. But the scene had to be shot with both actors in the buff, and Deneuve was uncomfortable with the prospect. She was replaced by Marisa Mell. Like John Phillip Law, Mell was born to play the part and bore an uncanny resemblance to her comic book doppelganger. She was a beauty so great as to cause folks to drop to their knees and weep. An auto accident in 1963 had left her partially disfigured, and after years of rehabilitation and reconstructive surgery, she emerged with the only lingering side effect of her accident being a quirky upturn at the side of her mouth.

For the role of Diabolik's foils on both sides of the law, Bava cast French actor Michel Piccoli as dogged Inspector Ginco and robust Italian character actor Adolfo Celi, still fresh off his memorable turn as the villain Emilio Largo in the Bond film *Thunderball* (1965), as flamboyant Mafia boss Valmont. Bava drops everyone into a world that isn't quite real. One of Bava's great strengths, and the element that perhaps made his horror films so successfully eerie, is his ability to warp the familiar, to twist the mundane into something foreign and menacing. In *Diabolik*, he's pulling the same stunt, but purely for laughs. The world of *Diabolik* is not the world in which we live, though it bears a striking resemblance. It is instead a campy pop-art extraction. Money is transported in bags marked with huge dollar signs on the front, for example. It is also Bava at his most playful, with only a slight hint of the bite that would inform the humor of his later *Bay of Blood*.

The story is a series of vignettes that are eventually stitched together, somewhat loosely. Diabolik pulls heists that get him on the bad side of both the police and the crime syndicate. Chief Ginco sets traps for Diabolik, but each time Diabolik outsmarts the inspector and makes his getaway with the loot. When Diabolik crosses crime boss Valmont, Ginco hatches an unholy alliance with the Mafia to catch the thorn in both their sides, building toward Ginco's preposterous plan to melt down the whole of France's gold reserve in order to lure Diabolik into a trap. The heists are exciting and outlandish, this again being a fantasy in which the standard laws of common sense and logic do not apply. In his quest to steal a priceless jeweled necklace, Diabolik defeats the inspector's trap by pulling the "stick a photo in front of the security camera" gag. He later smuggles the jewels to safety by fashioning them into bullets, using them to kill an opponent, then posing as said opponent's relative to collect the jewels after cremation.

We're not meant to take anything seriously or worry about realism. This is part of the reason it's also easy to accept Diabolik as the hero of the story even though he is, without a doubt, a villain. He kills cops. Not corrupt cops, but regular guys just doing their job. He has no concern for anyone but himself and Eva. When he dynamites the nation's tax records, he doesn't do it out of any sense of Robin Hood-esque duty to the poor and oppressed masses. He simply wants to screw with The Man — which leads to one of the film's funnier moments, in which the Minister of Finances (a cameo-ing Terry-Thomas) makes a public plea to all the outstanding citizens to come forward and voluntarily pay the taxes they owe. Comedic touches

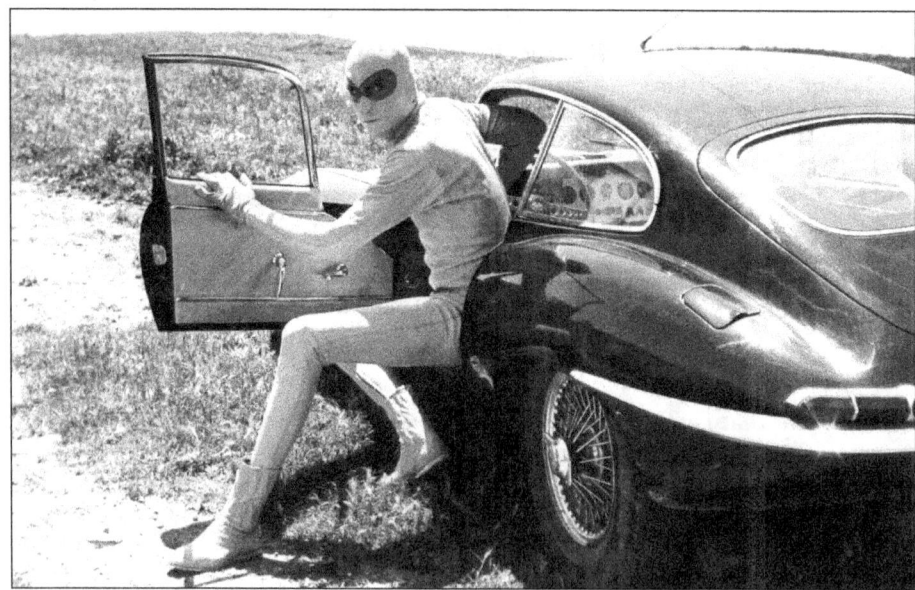

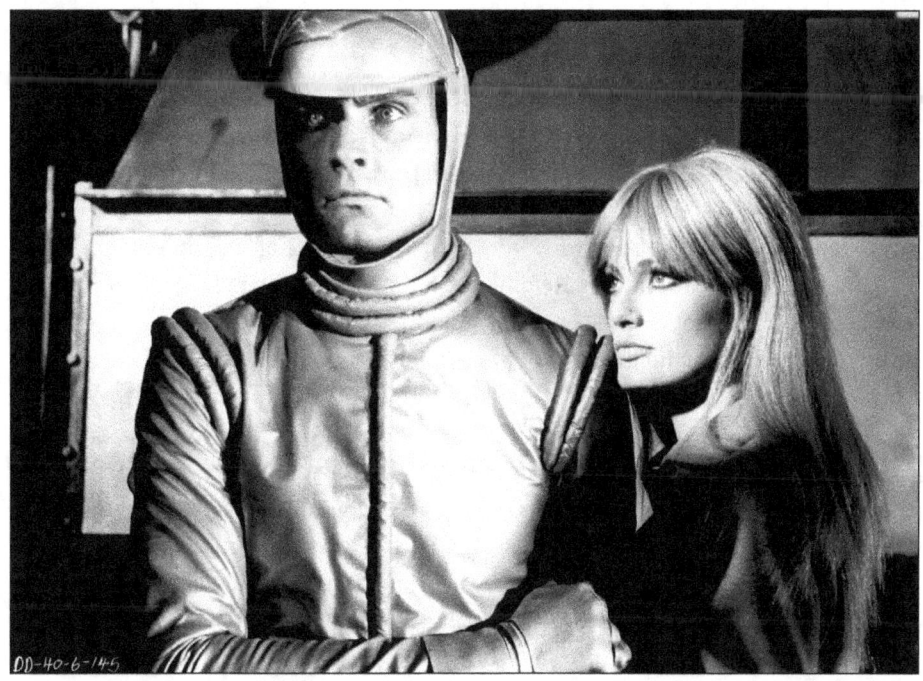

like this, along with the purposeful disregard for realism, keep the movie light-hearted even when Diabolik is committing acts of a most heinous nature.

It's not that Diabolik is *im*moral, however; he is *a*moral, rejecting the standards by which society judges the concepts of good and evil. He's *not* evil, or at least maliciously so. He's even likable, almost childlike. At his heart, he is an embodiment of 1968. He is the social upheaval, the youthful rebellion engulfing countries across the globe. It's no coincidence that the forces most opposed to him are established law and established crime, two sides of a coin in which Diabolik sees no difference. They are the old guard; the outdated, out-of-touch generation whose lack of modern sophistication is best exemplified by the fact that Valmont and his thugs abuse women and dress anachronistically, acting like something out of a 1930s gangster movie. They don't understand Diabolik's approach to crime, his use of modern technology, or his embracing of modern, liberated ideas. On the other side of the coin is Inspector Ginco, a man who respects Diabolik in a way. It's possible that Ginco *could* catch Diabolik if only the inspector was capable of breaking away from the rote way of thinking. Unfortunately, he is a man too mired in the old ways, a general fighting the previous war, destined always to be one step behind Diabolik. If only he could escape the constant supervision and micro-managing of the bureaucrats, Ginco could make progress. He must envy Diabolik his freedom of thought.

It is in this way, more than through the story itself, that *Diabolik* achieves the depth many people claim it lacks. It is a tale of a super criminal versus the cops on one level, but on a deeper level it is a tale of the generation gap, of the culture conflict between young and old. Diabolik and Eva are the new way, feared and misunderstood by their elders. They are iconoclasts, more symbols than actual people, as is Valmont. Ginco is the man in the middle. He knows times are changing, that they must change, but not by the methods employed by Diabolik. Ginco is, despite being the foil to Diabolik, the most sympathetic and human of the characters. He is most of us: dissatisfied with the establishment but still committed to some sense of orderly society.

The relationship between Eva and Diabolik is further example of the film's hidden depth. They are in love, deeply and passionately. Ginco forgoes romance in favor of duty. Valmont can see women as nothing more than objects to be verbally abused. The woman hanging around him and his crew shows flashes of being smart and capable, but she is immediately shut down by Valmont delivering a sexist insult. Eva and Diabolik are liberated and modern. They are attractive and have an insatiable appetite for one another, but they are also in love. Unlike Valmont, Diabolik regards Eva as an equal partner. His schemes do not succeed without her, and her part in them is never a minor one. He steals for Eva, but Eva does not stay with Diabolik because he steals; she stays because she loves him. Stealing is simply *what they do*, a game and an amusement. It's another way for them to thumb their noses at the generation that does not understand them. In the face of a world that wants to rub them out, they have each other. Sometimes, they have each other on a rotating bed covered in money.

That Mario Bava pulled off *Diabolik*'s gorgeous design on a self-imposed minuscule budget is unbelievable. With the possible exception of the Bond adventures of the '60s, few films look as sleek and sophisticated as *Diabolik*. The fashion is impeccable, like some crazy kind of pop art dream come true. Every outfit donned by Marisa Mell is gorgeous enough to make you cry, especially when it's draped upon someone as beautiful as she was. Likewise, Diabolik's fetishistic head-to-toe leather outfits are beautiful, leaving as they do only John Phillip Law's intense and deep eyes visible. Their underground lair is a sight to behold as well, as are the '67 Jags they both drive. *Diabolik* is, indeed, a mod-futurist fan's dream, even more so than the more outlandish *Barbarella*. After all, someone out on the town dressed as Barbarella would turn heads but look kind of silly; someone out dressed in the mod fashions displayed by Marisa Mell would simply look breathtaking. Someone dressed in Diabolik's leather catsuit is probably on his way somewhere special.

Dino De Laurentiis was so pleased with the fact that Bava brought the movie in $2.6 million under budget that he practically begged for a sequel. Unfortunately, the mild-mannered Bava could not bear the oppressive, dictatorial producer, so no sequel ever came about.Ultimately, of course, Diabolik is a criminal and must pay for his crimes. Sort of. The film's ending is vague in its resolution but fitting. Ginco must prevail, after all. The exuberance and reckless abandon of youth must be tamed, at least temporarily.

And so we are left with Diabolik encased in a gold coffin forged out of his own indulgence, a prison from which he cannot escape...or *can* he?

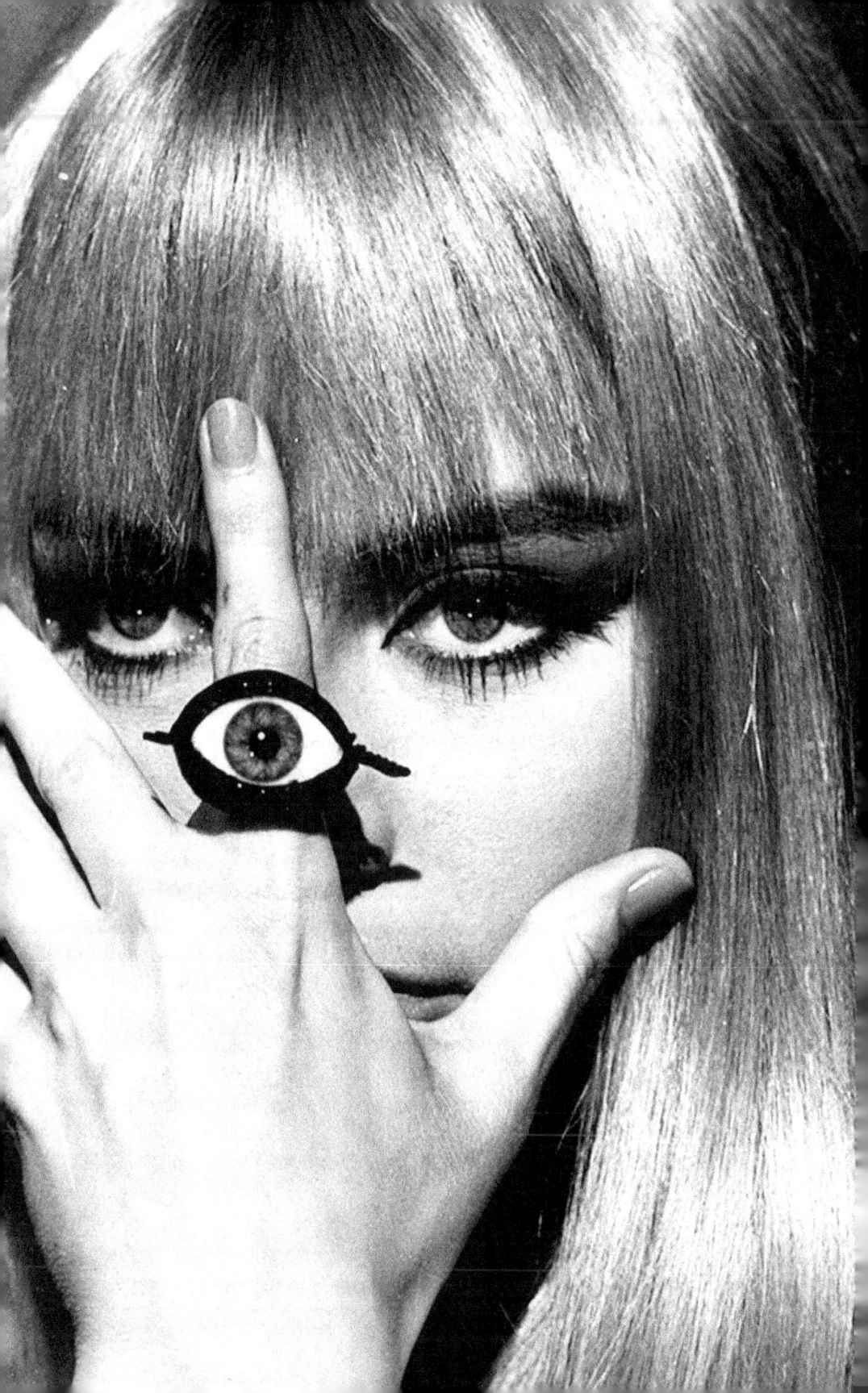

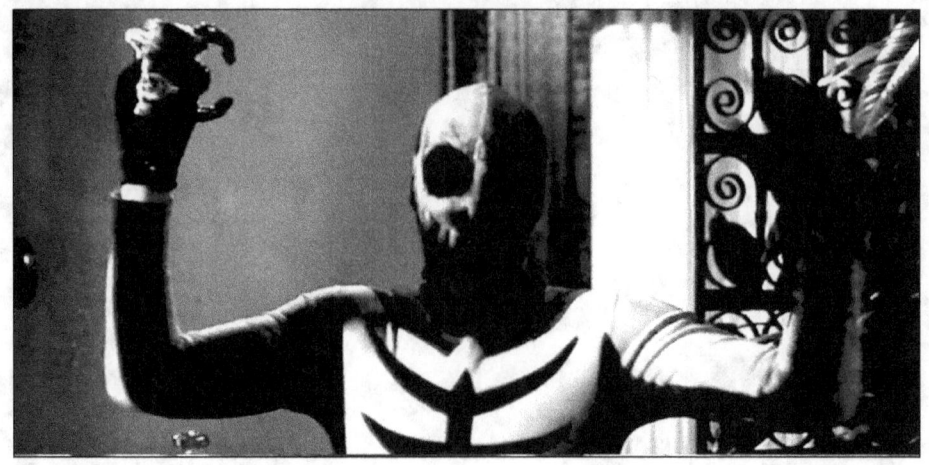

You Can't Keep Kriminal Down

Despite the fates of both Inge and Trudy in *Kriminal*, Helga Liné returned, along with Glenn Saxson and Andrea Bosic, for the sequel, *Il Marchio di Kriminal*, in 1968. Absent from th sequel was Umberto Lenzi, who spent that year in the Middle East and Spain working on the war adventure *Desert Commandos* and the spaghetti westerns *Go for Broke* and *A Pistol for a Hundred Coffins*. In fact, *Kriminal* was Lenzi's final entry in the broadly-defined Eurospy genre. In 1969, he directed two thrillers, *Paranoia* and *So Sweet... So Perverse* (both starring Hollywood exile Carroll Baker,) and in 1973 made the crime film *Gang War in Milan*. For the rest of his career, Lenzi worked within the genres of horror and Eurocrime, leaving directorial duties for the *Kriminal* sequel to Fernando Cerchio and Nando Cicero, a couple guys better known for sex comedies and sword and sandal adventure films.

Kriminal ends with the master thief foiled and in the custody of Turkish police. *Il Marchio di Kriminal* (*The Mark of Kriminal*) picks up right where *Kriminal* left off and delivers, pretty seamlessly, more of the same. It begins with a reassurance that London and Inspector Milton have been enjoying their respite from the rogue's capers. That doesn't stop the skeleton suit-clad baddie from slipping through the window of an old woman's bedroom. He then proceeds to terrify the shocked senior into a heart attack. Yes, Kriminal is back, and he's murdering old ladies as part of an insurance scam, which returns the character to meaner, more repugnant behavior of the early comics. At the same time...well, come on! Scaring old ladies to death? That seems like a low crime, even for Kriminal. How did the jet-setting master-thief end up running such a lame con? How is he free and terrorizing pensioners when everyone thinks he is in prison back in Turkey? Where is he getting so many skeleton suits? Is he eventually going to set his sights on a prize more worthy of his reputation? Probably, but killing senior citizens means that this time around Kriminal is less anti-hero than he is villain. That, along with the overly elaborate set-up it takes for him to execute the plan, places him once again in the company of silent-era malcontent Fantômas. Fantômas often devised elaborate heists that required an absurd amount of set-up and almost certainly cost more than they ever could have netted in ill-gotten gains. Similarly, for Kriminal to pull off his "kill old ladies for their insurance money" scheme, he (Glenn Saxson) has to purchase a retirement home, establish himself as a respected doctor, get himself licensed as a mortician, hire an accomplice to apply for life insurance under the identity of whoever their next mark was going to be, wait for months so that it wouldn't seem suspicious when the marked died, then come up a way to collect the insurance money without drawing the attention of inspectors — all while being careful not to get noticed by Scotland Yard and Milton, who thinks Kriminal is in prison and would react poorly to seeing him strutting around London. How Kriminal is managing to break even on this scheme, let alone turn a profit, is anyone's guess. But, like Fantômas, maybe it's not the profit that is important. Maybe he just likes messing with people.

Through a series of coincidences, Kriminal acquires a confession and a fragment of a map purporting to show the location of a couple of stolen priceless works of art. This being a cooler scheme than geronticide, Kriminal throws himself into it, hoping perhaps that we'll just forget what he'd been doing previously. Unfortunately for Kriminal, he doesn't get out of the grandma-killing business without raising the suspicions of Inspector Milton who, through a series of coincidences of his own, learns than Kriminal has managed to escape from prison by swapping places with another prisoner (who looks nothing like him and yammers like a madman). Postponing his own wedding like Bulldog Drummond with a new mystery to solve (which is interrupted by Kriminal showing up to deliver a gag murder-gift anyway), Milton follows the trail of corpses, little blue Buddhas, and confused socialites as the hunt for the stolen

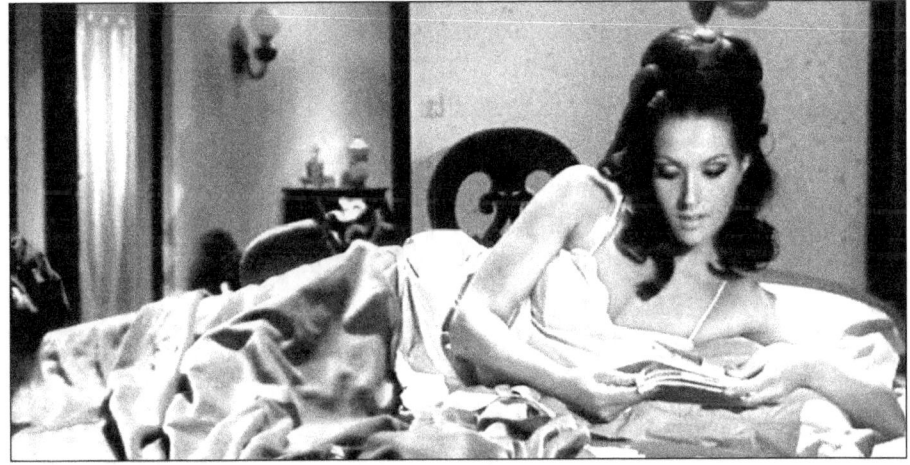

paintings leads, once again, to Spain and to Helga Line, though she's not playing the same character as she did in the first film. This time she's a Spanish dancer who has one of the pieces of the map and who, like several other characters, might know more about what's happening than she lets on. From there, the action moves to a cruise ship, the swinging city of Beirut (so it was at the time), and the fabled ruins at Baalbek.

Co-directors Fernando Cerchio and Nando Cicero never became notable names in Italian cult cinema. At the time they took over for Umberto Lenzi on *Il Marchio di Kriminal*, neither of them had much experience with action cinema or the Eurospy genre. Cerchio was the best prepared of the two, having previously made a spy film (1967's *Top Secret* starring former Tarzan and peplum star Gordon Scott) and quite a few sword and sandal spectacles, including *Desert Warrior* starring a young Ricardo Montalban, *Cleopatra's Daughter* starring Debra Paget, *Nefertiti, Queen of the Nile* starring Jeanne Crain and Vincent Price, and a trio of *peplum* spoofs starring popular Italian comedian Toto.

But where Umberto Lenzi's period adventures had been action-oriented, Cerchio's films were inspired by Hollywood Biblical epics more than rough and tumble swashbucklers and Hercules films. *Il Marchio di Kriminal* was his second-to-last film before retiring in 1969. His experience with ancient world epics, like Lenzi's, equipped him to make the most of the widescreen format and exotic locations. Indeed, as with the first film, *Il Marchio di Kriminal* is beautiful. Cerchio also enjoyed the services of Angelo Lotti, who worked frequently with Lenzi and shot *Kriminal*.

Nando Cicero was less qualified to helm such a large picture, having before *Il Marchio di Kriminal* made only a few films, including a trio of obscure spaghetti westerns: *Last of the Badmen*, *Professionals for a Massacre* (both 1967) and *They Were Called Graveyard* (1968, starring Antonio Sabata and Klaus Kinski). Given the way the Italian film industry works, it's likely Cicero was apprenticing with the older Cerchio on this second *Kriminal* movie, but the world of swinging spies and super-villains didn't prove to his liking. He spent most of the rest of his career directing sex comedies. Given that he worked with Michela Miti, Gloria Guida, and Edwige Fenech, that was probably fine with him.

Together, the duo made a film that retains all of the thrills of the first *Kriminal* but boasts a harder edge owing to Kriminal's more diabolical indulgences. In the end, the villain is seemingly done for, but given how often these *fumetti* anti-heroes/villains escape death by simply proclaiming "I have escaped!" at the end of one film or beginning of the next, nothing is guaranteed.

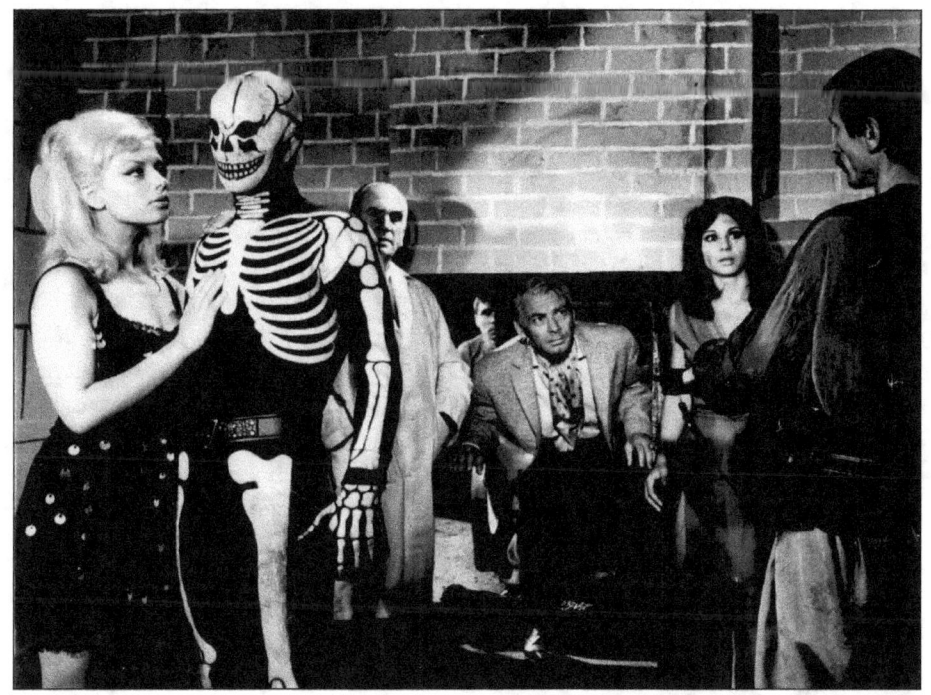

The King of Rogues

If *The Mark of Kriminal* was the last Italy had to do with skeleton suit wearing villains, the same didn't hold true for the rest of the world. As Kriminal was skyrocketing to fame and the nasty edge that had made him so popular and controversial softened somewhat to make him more palatable to a wider audience, another character in basically the same skeleton get-up arrived on the scene to make sure critics and censors were still incensed. That psychotic terrorist was known appropriately enough as Killing. Created in 1966 by Pietro Granelli, Killing was a reprehensible brute on his best days. The things he did were extreme even by the standards of Kriminal. That *Killing* relied on the photonovel format—using photography of staged scenes—made the salacious nature of his sexy, hyper-violent adventures even more risqué.

With *Killing* having no redeeming values, people once again ate it up as eagerly as censorship boards and parents denounced it as this gun-toting madman in a skull mask lorded over it all, laughing evilly as he stood on top of an overpass with arms akimbo. Unhappy with seeing his designs hijacked, but unsuccessful in court, *Kriminal* creator Luciano Secchi countered with a new character: *Satanik*, a disfigured woman who takes a serum to become beautiful then spends her time killing people. It was made into a movie, but unlike *Kriminal*, it plays out like a horror movie. Don't let the *Diabolik*-inspired outfit that shows up in all the poster artwork fool you; that's in the movie only for a few seconds. But the joke was again on Luciano Secchi. As *Killing* was exported, finding particular purchase in Argentina, for one reason or another, it got retitled with a whole host of new names, including *Sadistik* and, yes, *Satanik*.

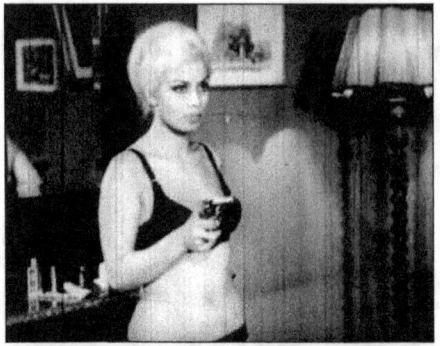

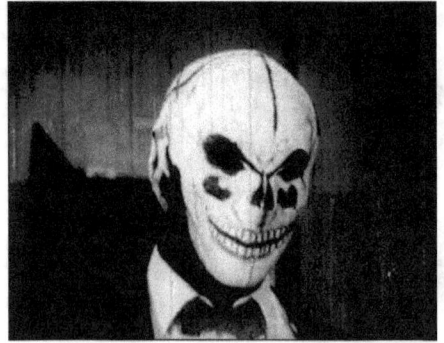

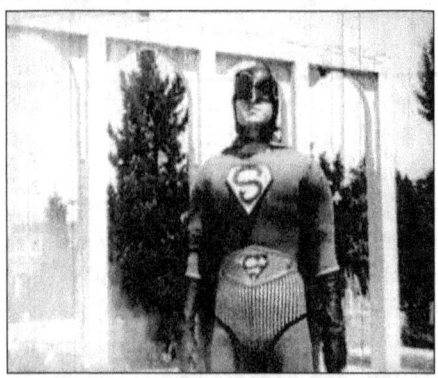

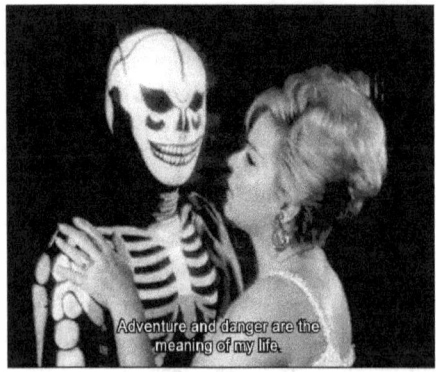

Adventure and danger are the meaning of my life.

Kriminal was partially set and filmed in Istanbul. Inspired by what they saw, Turkish filmmakers decided if the Italians could rip off their own guy in the form of Killing, then the Turks could rip off the rip-off, and that would just be awesome. So Turkish producer-director Yilmaz Atadeniz commenced filming of his own Killing movie, 1967's *Kilink Istanbul'da*. Stylistically, it's somewhere between early Mexican *luchador* movies and old American horror serials. The opening scene, in which a mummy in a spooky room is revived and unwrapped to reveal the hideous skeleton below, is straight out of a serial. The spookiness ends there, however.

The mummy-skeleton is Kilink (Yildirim Gencer if that matters—it's not like he ever takes off his skull mask), who springs out of his coffin and starts slapping asses, calling women "baby," and ranting about his need for a secret formula to complete the doomsday weapon that will help him rule the world. So the plot is straight out of the old serials as well, with Kilink trying to get the secret formula from a parade of scientists whose only contribution to the world besides creating weapons of mass destruction is uttering the line, "I'll never tell you the location of the formula!" before being shot by a skeleton.

When the dastardly Kilink murders one particular scientist, the scientist's son, Orhan (Irfan Atasoy), swears revenge but bemoans the fact that a normal man could never hope to foil the mad schemes of a villain as diabolical as Kilink. The ancient god Odin suddenly appears and grants Orhan super-powers that activate whenever he yells "Shazam!" Seriously.

Shouting this magic word (which the makers of this film made up all on their own) transforms Orhan into Uçan Adam, a guy in an unconvincingly-padded Superman outfit with striped underwear and what looks to be a slight variation of the Batman cowl worn by Adam West. As Uçan Adam, Orhan can throw marble slabs around, shrug off bullets, jump over stuff, and superimpose himself onto footage of clouds in order to fly. Armed with these superpowers, Orhan feels he is finally a match for the wicked Kilink, whose main superpower is the ability to surround himself with gorgeous henchwomen.

In *fumetti*, actual superpowers were rare. Most of the big stars of the 1960s were cut from the Batman mold, meaning that they have no superpowers but have trained so hard that they seem capable of superhuman feats. Kilink himself is very much in this vein, though perhaps a little more Joker than Batman, since he doesn't seem all that great in a fist fight and most of his training is just ass-slapping and breast-grabbing. As soon as an ancient god pops up in the cemetery and turns some guy into a superhero with pillows stuffed down his shirt, *Kilink Istanbul'da* starts to resemble something different than the *Kriminal* and *Killing* stories that inspired it. Kilink himself is also different from Kriminal in ambition if not sense of style. Kriminal was interested in stealing, while Kilink is interested in conquering the world. Kilink also has a gang of useless henchmen decked out like Father Guido Sarducci, whereas Kriminal worked alone save for the occasional beautiful accomplice (which Kilink was wise enough to keep in place as well). Additionally, one is meant to sympathize to some degree with Kriminal, but Kilink offers no such hook. He is the bad guy, at least in this outing, and one is never (or is not *meant* to be) tempted to root for him. Kilink has one bony foot in the madmen of the old serials and another in the world of megalomaniac James Bond villain.

If a gun-toting murderer dressed as a skeleton fighting a superhero in a poorly-stuffed suit sounds like fun, then *Kilink Istanbul'da* isn't going to let you down. The screen is never devoid for more than a few seconds of scantily-clad women. Near the end, when Kilink leaves the suburbs and goes to his secret island lair, he walks into his new throne room and there are already half a dozen women in bikinis just standing around in alluring poses. The man has his priorities. Suzy (Suzan Avci) leads a parade of beautiful women, including Pervin Par as Orhan's fiancée Guile, Mine Soley as one of the scientist's secretaries and eventual Kilink sidekick, and whoever it is that plays Orhan's younger sister. None of these women can go for more than a few minutes without their tops falling off, or their skirts being hiked up, or them just walking around in a slinky bikini because hey, why the hell not?

Like any good old-fashioned serial, *Kilink Istanbul'da* ends on a cliffhanger, with Orhan trying to track down Kilink, who has kidnapped Guile and her father, while Kilink himself gets it on with the traitorous secretary and unveils his super weapon: a smallish laser beam. Some people have nuclear and biological weapons. Kilink has a small laser gun in a cave off the coast of Turkey. The super weapon this whole movie is about is a little laser cannon that looks like, at it's most effective, it could be used to take out one guy, *maybe* two if the second guy is patient. Maybe when Kilink turns it on, it will be more impressive. Probably not.

After all, despite his cool set-up, Kilink is a bit of a buffoon. He lives in the suburbs in a house with cheap wood paneling; he only has like four guys working for him; and anytime he has to fight someone more capable than a passed-out woman, he ends up running away. He can barely handle terrorizing a couple of scientists, and the only reason he captures anyone is because they keep coming home to the same unlocked houses even though they know Kilink is after them. A cop keeps popping up to remind us, over and over, how amazingly evil and dangerous Kilink is, lest evidence on-screen lead us to a contrary conclusion. When Kilink does something as simple as pick the lock on a window, the inspector is there an hour later to slam his fist into his palm and proclaim Kilink the most diabolical evil genius who ever lived.

Despite Kilink's dubious crowning as the King of Rogues, *Kilink Istanbul'da* is top-notch entertainment. The episodic structure keeps it from getting dull, and there's usually not more than a minute or so before a skeleton is ripping off a woman's top or a superhero is punching a villain's car. As silly as the idea of a grown man dressing up like a skeleton and demanding to rule the world may be, it works in the fantastical context created by films like this. Kilink looks good in action, too. Uçan Adam is a little less spry in his action scenes, but that's just because all the foam stuffed into his shirt means his mobility is restricted to little more than walking like a stiff-jointed bodybuilder while guys pointlessly shoot at him over and over. Irfan Atasoy as Orhan is a fine-looking man with classic matinée idol looks. But when you're a regular Joe, even one who turns into Shazam, surrounded by a dude in a skeleton suit and a bunch of *femmes fatale* in slinky cocktail dresses, bikinis, and underwear, you tend to get lost in the shuffle. Of course, there's the whole business of the film ending right in the middle of the action. Luckily, the second film, *Kilink Uçan Adama Karsi*, was waiting in the wings to pick up the action immediately where the first one leaves off.

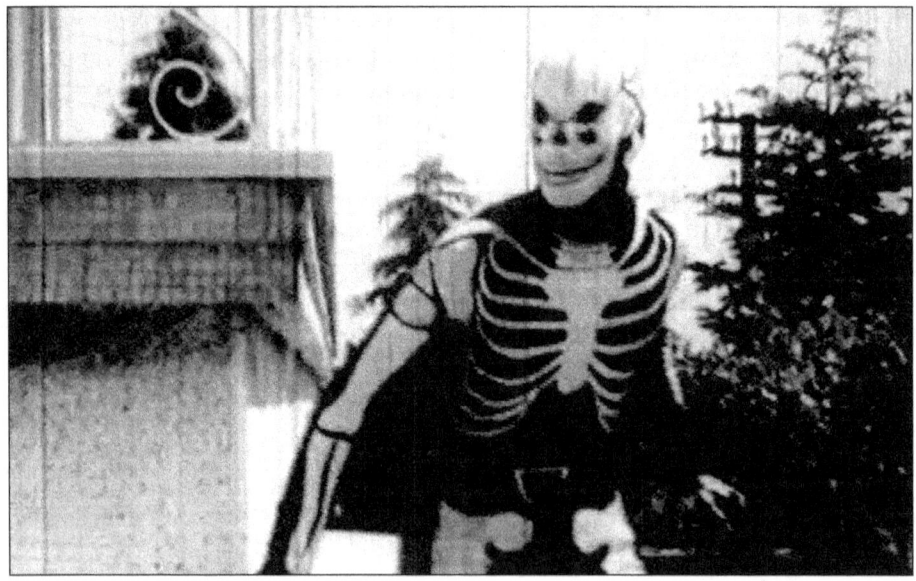

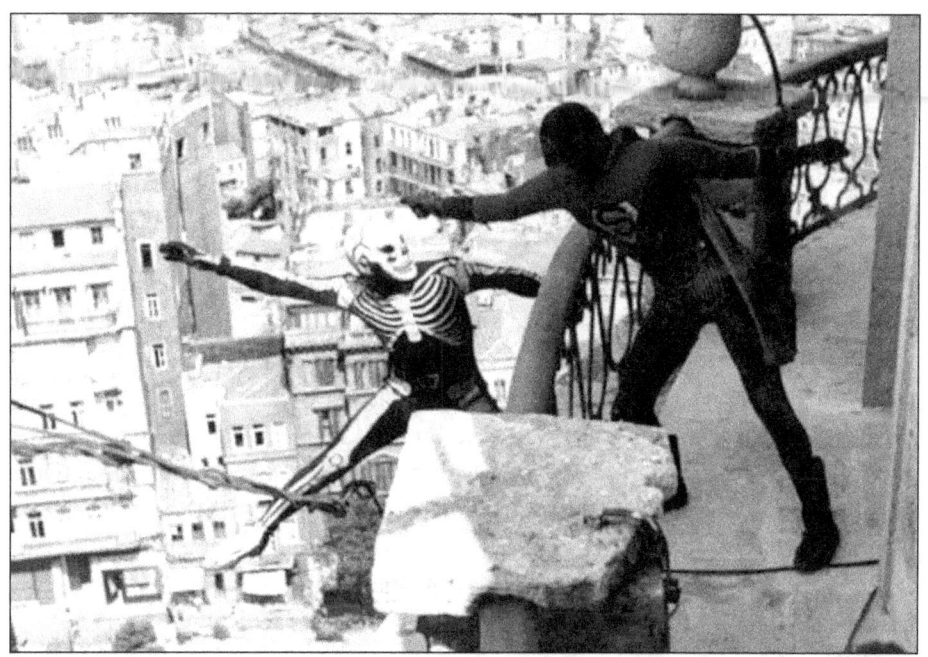

Kilink Strikes Again

Kilink Istandbul'da sets us up for the main event in *Kilink Uçan Adama Karsi*, in which our two main characters finally battle one another. Until this point, Kilink and Uçan Adam have only met face to face once, and that showdown ended with Kilink swapping identities with a doorman who he somehow convinced not only to wear a skeleton outfit, but also to try and escape from the combined forces of Uçan Adam and the Istanbul police force via a slow-moving dumb-waiter. One can assume, based on the title of this entry in the *Kilink* series, that we'll finally be getting the *tête-à-tête* between the villainous madman and the guy in the padded leotard and striped panties. And we would have, if that footage still existed.

When last the dastardly Kilink was seen, he was in his secret island lair, well-stocked with randomly-placed, artfully-posed bikini girls, bragging about his super-weapon (a rickety-looking laser gun) while harassing a scientist and the scientist's beautiful daughter, who just happened to be the fiancée of a man whose own scientist father was murdered by Kilink, causing the man to swear vengeance and be granted super powers and a bad costume by a crazy hobo in the cemetery. Got it? If you didn't, no worries, because the cliffhanger ending of *Kilink Istanbul'da* springboards us immediately into the sequel, *Kilink Uçan Adama Karsi* (*Kilink vs. Superman*), but not before the second film takes twenty minutes or so to recap the events of the first movie. Calling *Kilink Istanbul'da* the "first" film is misleading. They are really just one long movie chopped into two episodes. The Kilink movies were drawing influence from old American adventure serials, thus the serial-like cliffhanger ending—although to be fair, the final shot of the first part, with Kilink hanging out in his living room while the good guy stands on a pier is somewhat less thrilling than many cliffhangers tended to shoot for. The recap of the previous "episode" is another trick straight out of the serials. The summary is nice, however, because it contains pieces of footage that were lost from the existing print of *Kilink Istandbul'da*, so if you want to get a glimpse of some Saddam Hussein-looking guy laughing as he turns a knob, this is your chance.

In part one, viewers are meant to root for Uçan Adam. This has a lot to do with the Turkish film-going population's preference for identifying with a strong, black-and-white hero. Uçan Adam is both strong (see how he throws those concrete slabs around in the first film, a brute display of strength that was probably unappreciated by the employees who came in later and had to clean up the mess) and his film is in black and white, so the Turks were in luck! But it's kind of cheating on Uçan Adam's part to use the assistance of a randomly-appearing god disguised as a homeless hippie and granting superpowers. Kilink has no superpower other than the ability to prance around in a ridiculous skeleton costume without looking ridiculous. Part two continues to position Uçan Adam as the ostensible good guy, but things are already starting to slide. Kilink is just so much more fun, after all.

Part two opens with Orhan trying to find a ride to Kilink's mysterious secret island, which can't be too secret if every fisherman in Istanbul knows where it is and that it's crawling with guys in genie pants and some dude in a skeleton suit running around on the beach. Eventually, Orhan finds a boatman willing to take him to the island, even though...hey, wait! Isn't Orhan possessed of super powers that allow him to, among other things, *fly*? Maybe he's just such a good guy that he doesn't want to use his superpowers when he could help out the local economy by hiring a boatman (and putting the guy in mortal peril by making him sail out to Kilink's island of doom).

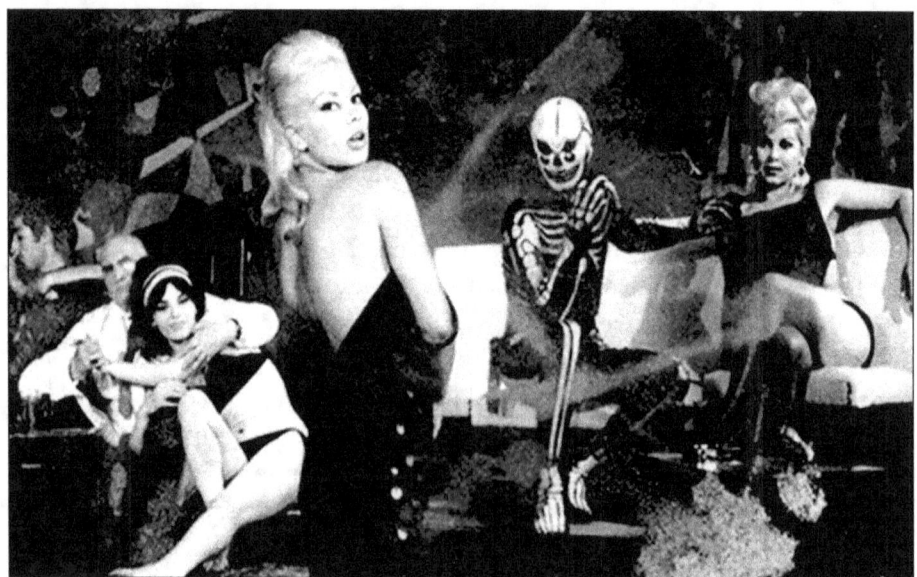

Kilink is splitting his time between making love (while still in his skeleton outfit) to beautiful women and showing off the awesome might of his laser gun. When he finally fires his weapon, the result is ...well, maybe he would have been better off if he invested his time in trying to steal an atom bomb, because the laser cannon isn't too impressive. He blows up a boulder with it, and later on he'll use it to mildly inconvenience Uçan Adam, but other than that, one can't see the world quaking in fear at the skeleton-bootied feet of Kilink just because he has a laser cannon, especially given that everyone seems to know where Kilink is, and they could just drop a bomb on his lair and be done with things. They must have plenty of bombs, because Kilink didn't try to take any of *those*.

The action on Kilink's island is boss even if his doomsday weapon isn't. He's got bikini girls, and although he talks big about conquering the world, he seems more interested in lounging around, letting his secretary strip while Suzy massages his shoulders and guys in Genie pants and vests with a giant "K" on them lean on their machine guns. Maybe the world *should* give Kilink a chance to run things. His primary vision for the world seems to be one full of half-naked people, of slinky cocktail dresses, smart suits, skeleton bodystockings, groovy music, and guys with Rollie Fingers mustaches and genie pants. That doesn't sound so bad. Sure, he has a tendency to walk up to random henchmen and say, "Don't disappoint me, or I'll kill you," even though nothing is going on at that moment, but whatever. What world leader doesn't have his idiosyncrasies?

Orhan arrives to change into Uçan Adam and smash things up. Kilink unleashes the power of his laser beam, which is now suddenly a flamethrower and which causes Uçan Adam to have to sort of suck it in (hard when your body mass is composed primarily of pillows stuffed into long johns) and stand against the wall for a little bit. It buys just enough time for Kilink to make his escape in classic third-world dictator form. Actually, maybe those guys commandeer a jet at the airport or get a free ride from some other country's government. Kilink, on the other hand, makes his escape in a rowboat. Ahh, but it's not really Kilink at all! It's a fat, old scientist who, when disguised as Kilink, suddenly becomes a fit, muscular man. Kilink himself slips out the back door and begins plotting a decidedly less Bond-villainy, more Kriminal/Diabolik scale caper: stealing jewels from a princess.

Unfortunately, we only get the gist of things here, as the latter half of *Kilink Uçan Adama Karsi* has been lost. That's a shame, but what remains is fun. The showdown between Kilink and Uçan Adam on "Kilink's island of pleasure and certain death" is high-spirited and energetic with some great fights and plenty of action. The world is better off for having seen at least this small surviving sliver of the film. And luckily, Kilink never stops to take a breath. No sooner is he lying dead on the street after the final fight with Superman than he is taunting people via some inexplicable public address unit, promising to return. And return he does.

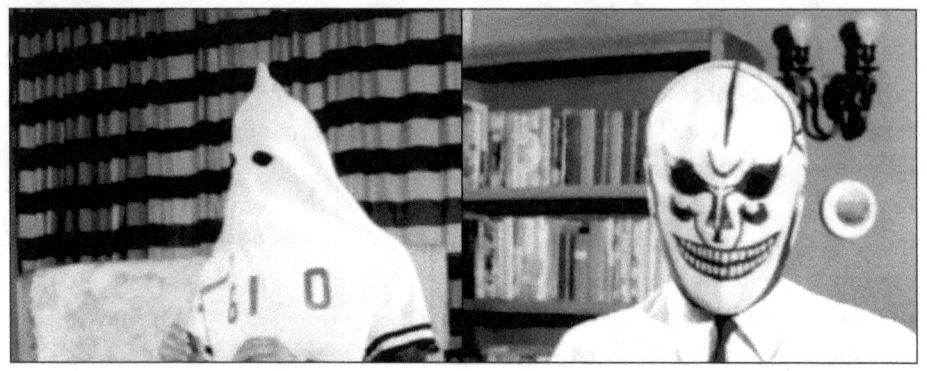

Strip and Kill

Strip and Kill continues, against the better efforts of the first two movies, to follow the same trajectory as Kriminal, with the King of Rogues becoming a celebrated anti-heroes no matter how dastardly and devious his schemes may be. In the first two films, one knew who the hero was (Orhan), and one knew one was going to root for the hero, however silly his striped panties may be. One also knew that, despite all obstacles thrown into his path, Uçan Adam was going to triumph. Kilink was evil. He was pitted against a do-gooding magical flying superman in striped undies. There was no doubt that you were supposed to be rooting for Uçan Adam. However...

Europe was cranking out films infused with paranoia and distrust of authority figures, showing disillusionment with the concept of clear-cut good and evil. That meant old-fashioned do-gooders like Uçan Adam were falling out of favor. Less socially important, but perhaps more likely the cause of the shift in sympathies, Kilink was just *cooler* than Uçan Adam. Sure, Uçan Adam had Batman's mask and a suit with pillow muscles stuffed into it. And he had those striped panties purchased at the Phantom's last Skull Cave rummage sale. And he could fly and lift large slabs of granite in order to impress Odin or whoever. But the problem Uçan Adam faced, and the problem many superheroes face, is that it's more fun to explore the bad guy. Uçan Adam may have been the super hero, but the movie was called *Kilink Istanbul'da*. Uçan Adam got his name mentioned in the second film's title, *Kilink Uçan Adama Karsi*, but it was almost an afterthought. People were coming to the theater to see Kilink.

And why not? Uçan Adam behaved properly and, when not flying, lived a quiet, typical life, so long as "quiet, typical life" includes being friends with scientists who have a tendency to be stalked by murderous madmen in skeleton costumes. While Uçan Adam was busy sitting in a living room, drinking tea and making plans for a picnic, Kilink was dressed up as a skeleton, making love to a procession of gorgeous ladies, watching talented dancing girls, kidnapping scientists, and shooting chumps with his Luger. You sort of hit a dead end exploring a one-dimension good guy, but a bad guy? There's almost no end to the wild exploits in which you can involve the bad guy. Of course, then arises the question of at what point does the bad guy stop being the *bad* guy? In the case of Kilink, it happens with *Strip and Kill*. The Kilink we meet in this film, while still the same man, suddenly only kills other criminals. He's still out to steal gold and foil the cops, but the days when he was kidnapping the hero's pretty wife and slapping her around are behind him. With this transformation of Kilink, Uçan Adam disappears entirely. *Strip and Kill* picks up immediately after Kilink's apparent death at Uçan Adam's hands, but there is no mention of Uçan Adam. It is as if he never existed and Kilink just fell off a tower of his own accord. Even though he's still dressed as a skeleton and calling women "baby," the protagonist this time around, and the obvious focus of the film, is Kilink.

The story for *Strip and Kill* was lifted from an issue of the *Killing* photo-comics. Kilink falls to his death yet still manages to taunt people via a public address system that seems to have been set up specifically so Kilink could taunt people. There is, as best as anyone can tell, no way Kilink could have escaped his fate. He is fighting Uçan Adam. He falls to his death in the middle of a gathering of onlookers. The police are already on the scene and examining Kilink's body. And yet all of a sudden, Kilink is somewhere else, laughing into the PA system, pulling a Reichenbach Falls of his own, and probably intentionally causing it to emit ear-piercing feedback, because that's just how evil Kilink is, baby! Oh well, if the impossible fall worked for Sherlock Holmes, why not Kilink? *Strip and Kill* sees no real reason to reconcile Kilink's apparent escape from death with any sort of serial-like unseen twist. It simply assumes that the best thing to do provide no explanation for how he goes from being a corpse getting poked at by cops to being a guy sitting in his posh living room, drinking Martinis with his sexy girlfriend, Suzy. Do you want a convoluted explanation of how Kilink escaped, or do you just want to watch a guy dressed as a skeleton punch out a dude with an eyepatch?

Having narrowly escaped death, Kilink attends a conference in New York of a secret criminal society whose members all wear hoods when they gather, even though they already know each other, and they all take their hoods off as soon as the meeting is adjourned. Kilink, it seems, was not invited to the criminal pow-wow, but that doesn't stop him from showing up, killing one of the members, and taking his place. This mysterious group is determined to steal microfilm that details the location of Turkey's various missile defense installations. Kilink take personal offense at this, even though he just spent the entire last two movies menacing Turkey with a flame thrower. Perhaps he assumes threatening Turkey is *his* birthright,

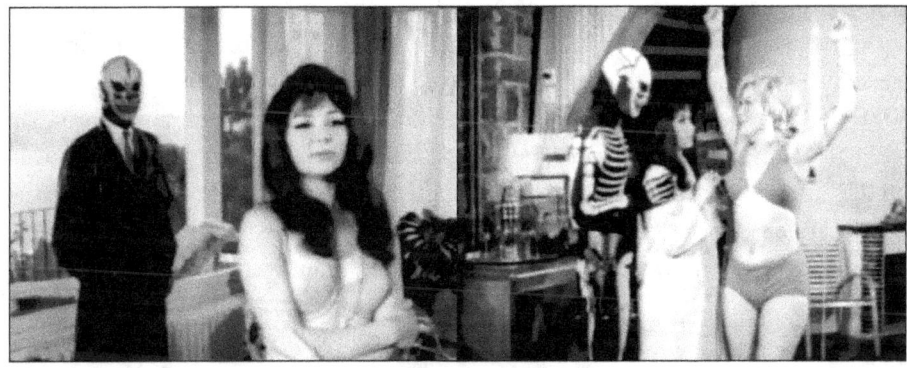

and he's not going to let some uppity bunch of outsiders intrude on his turf. As for the country of Turkey itself, if you spent the last two movies being terrorized by a guy dressed as a skeleton, having your next threat be from a group of regular old gangsters, hooded meetings notwithstanding, seems underwhelming. A rival Turkish crime boss gets in on the picture, introducing a subplot about stolen gold that Kilink is going to be wanting for himself. The entire thing ends up with Kilink playing the good guy as he systematically dismantles and destroys both criminal/spy rings — and by "systematically" I mean he disguises himself, then a few seconds later rips off the disguise and yells "Kilink is here!" while diving off a hill.

Unlike the previous films, which existed within the realm of superhero fantasy thanks to the presence of Uçan Adam, *Strip and Kill* is pure Eurospy/*fumetti* adventure. There are no magic powers, no ancient gods appearing in a puff of smoke; just a dude in a skeleton suit scheming against a bunch of guys in skinny ties, well within the realm of James Bond and Diabolik. The series benefits from this change to the formula. Injecting a Uçan Adam into the mix was fun on a purely "what the hell" level, but it just didn't click. Uçan Adam seemed like a guy who wandered in from an entirely different movie. When your character is invincible and super-strong, fighting henchmen whose sole power is to wear genie pants and shirts with a giant "K" taped to them doesn't make for especially thrilling action sequences. You're mostly going to see a shot of someone throwing something at Uçan Adam, followed by a shot of that object bouncing harmlessly off his chest. With the yoke of superpowers removed, *Strip and Kill* is free to cram itself full of kinetic fight scenes involving Kilink kicking people and jumping off overpasses.

Neither of the previous films were short on action, but with the super-powered guy discarded, and along with him the lengthy domestic scenes that accompanied his human identity, *Strip and Kill* can get down to some serious, no-nonsense skeleton guy action. Kilink handles the killing, while the stripping is left to his usual procession of beautiful women he can't help but menace and make love to, although this time he only goes so far as to menace and make love to the *evil* ones. In a departure from the last film, he even gets angry when his rivals kidnap an innocent woman and her child. He also still has ever-faithful Suzy and her vast array of slinky cocktail dresses and revealing bikinis by his side.

If there is a weakness in *Strip and Kill*, it is the final scene, which is a bit of a let-down after a film that included car chases, foot chases, a big fight in a cemetery, various fights along the road, and all of the good stuff you expect from a movie with a title like *Strip and Kill*. All things considered, *Strip and Kill* generates more than enough goodwill to make up for the final scene of our lovable rascal surrendering to the police and expounding on their virtues, just as Raffles was forced to do in the 1939 version of his own film. At least with Kilink, you can see him turning the whole thing into a taunt for the opening scene of the next film.

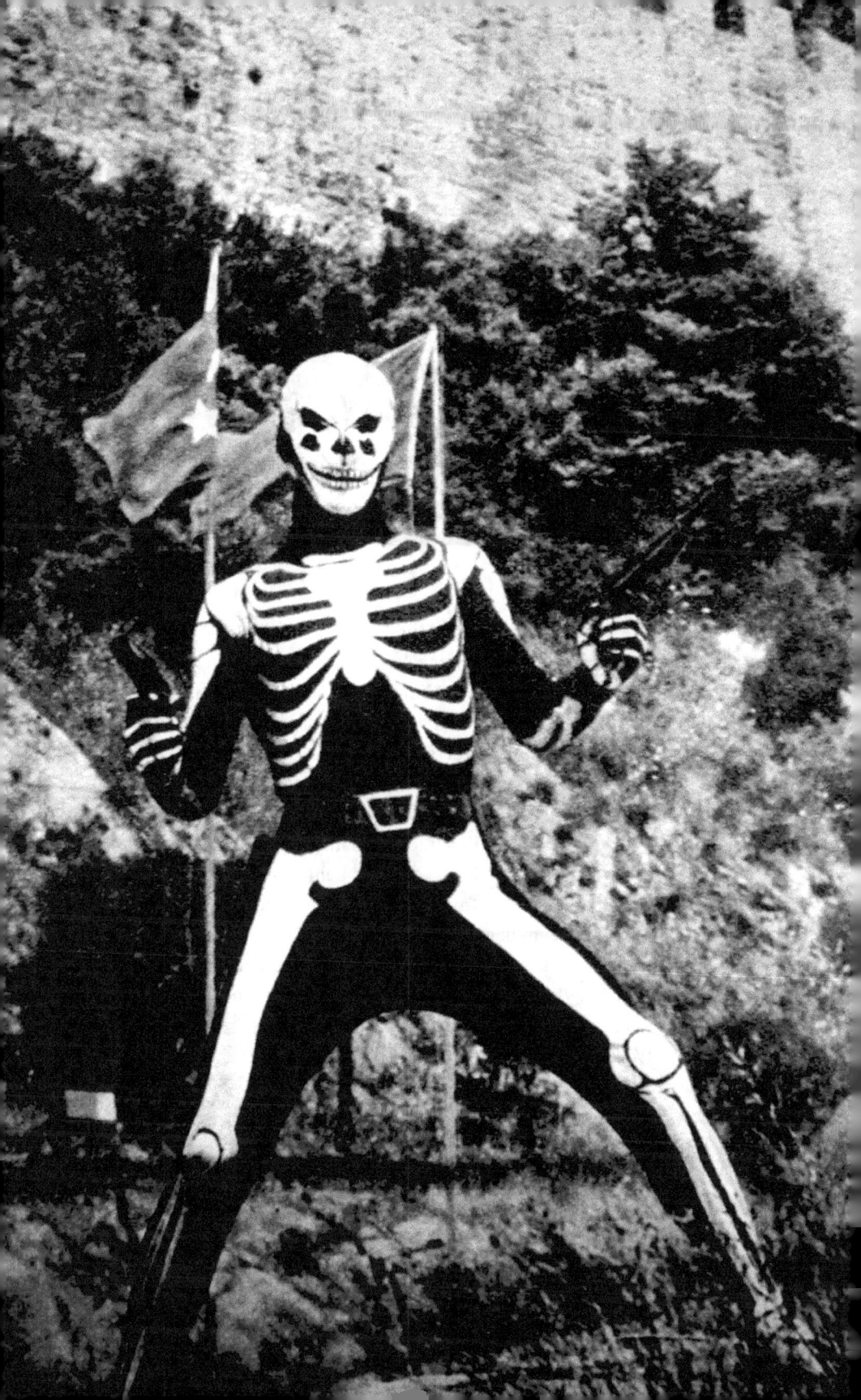

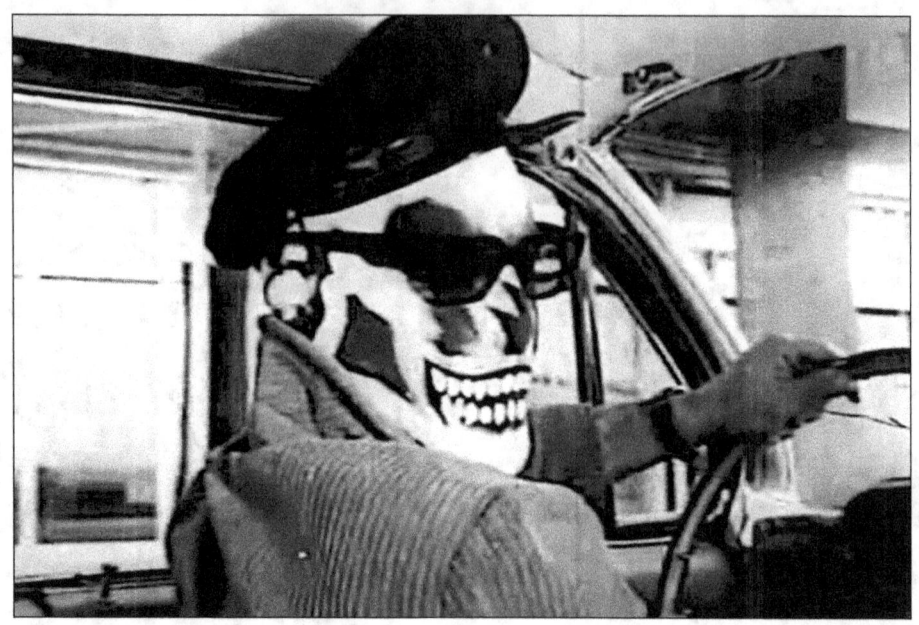

From Shazam! to Presto!

There is some sort of lazy justice in the fact that Kilink, the Turkish rip-off of Killing who was a rip-off of Kriminal, would inspire an even greater number of rip-offs ripping off the rip-off. Director Yilmaz Atadeniz and star Yildirim Gencer's four original Kilink films (the aforementioned *Kilink Istanbul'da*, *Kilink Uçan Adam Karsi*, *Kilink: Strip and Kill* and a fourth film, *Kilink: King of Criminals*, which is presumed lost), all made and released in rapid succession in 1967, inspired at least six other Kilink films made by different producers. Çetin İnanç was the highest profile name to get in on the Kilink game, releasing *Kilink Canilere Karşı*. İnanç was a filmmaker of immense popularity who was behind some of the best Turkish pulp films of the 1960s and '70s. Filmographies for Turkish directors can often be incomplete, but it would seem based on existing lists that *Kilink Canilere Karşı* was the first feature film from the man who would go on to create such films as *Iron Claw the Pirate*, *En Büyük Yumruk*, *Ölüm savaşçisi*, and perhaps the best-known Turkish film outside of Turkey, *Dünyayi Kurtaran Adam*, also known as *The Man Who Saved the World* but perhaps better known simply as "Turkish Star Wars" on account of its liberal pilfering of special effects shots and music. It's a shame that İnanç's Kilink film is presumed lost, as it doubtless would showcase the director's penchant for over-the-top action and stunts, and because it stars able and willing Yildirim Gencer, back under the skeleton mask for the fifth time.

Other Kilink films produced in that fecund year of 1967 include Yavuz Figenli's *Kilink Oluler Konusmaz* (*Kilink: The Dead Don't Talk*); Nuri Akıncı's tempting-sounding *Kilink Frankestayn ve Dr no'ya karsi* (*Kilink vs. Frankenstein*); Natuk Baytan's less tempting-sounding *Saskin Hafiye Kilink'e karsi* (*Silly Detective vs. Kilink*); and Aram

Gülyüz's much sought-after *Dişi Kilink*, which gender-swaps Kilink into a busty female in a bikini. Alas, given the Turkish film industry's tendency to regard film as disposable and not worth preserving (an attitude that was hardly unique to Turkey) and the fact that many of these films were produced for small regional markets, all of them are considered lost films, or at the best, missing in action. Every now and then, however, one of them turns up in the basement of a Greek television station or an Argentinian grandmother's attic. Such was the case with one of the final Kilink films of 1967: *Sihirbazlar Kralı Mandrake Kiling'in Peşinde*, also known as *Mandrake vs. Kilink*, directed by illustrator/opening credits designer Oksal Pekmezoglu.

Mandrake the Magician was one of the early heroes to appear in newspaper comic strips, created by St. Louis native Lee Falk and debuting in print on June 11, 1934, nearly two years before the debut of Falk's more famous creation, *The Phantom* (who appeared from time to time in Turkish films, such as *Kizil Maske*; how did Kilink never throw down against the Phantom?). Falk's biography highlighted the years he spent traveling through the "mysterious East," studying with mystics and swamis. In truth, Falk had never set foot outside of the United States. In fact, until he traveled to New York to pursue a career in comics, he'd never even set foot outside of St. Louis. Once he'd established himself as a successful comic strip artist, he did his best to make good on his fake biography's boasts, becoming a seasoned world traveler despite, as far as anyone knows, never penetrating the secret societies and cults of "the Orient."

Mandrake was inspired by Falk's fascination with stage magicians and is considered by many to be the first superhero of modern comics (Superman didn't debut until 1938; Batman in 1939). Mandrake's power was the ability to hypnotize anyone almost instantly, causing them to see illusions and other phantoms convenient to the foiling of crime. He was armed with an array of magical implements, including his wand, cape, and top hat, that possessed sundry properties. Setting the mold for many superheroes to come, Mandrake worked a day job (stage magician, naturally) when he wasn't off fighting crime. He lived in a high-tech superhero lair (in this case, a magnificent estate in the mountains of upstate New York). Like many long-running superhero, his powers evolved and expanded over the years. By the 1960s, the do-gooder magician had been known to levitate, turn invisible, teleport, and shape shift. Curiously, other than a serial released in 1939, Mandrake never made it to the big screen, except in Turkey.

Mandrake vs. Kilink begins with a woman fleeing from a gang of meandering assailants. She runs into a mysterious man in a trench coat whom she beseeches for help. He helps by gunning her down and chastising the gang for letting her escape in the first place. Then the opening credits play over the image of her lifeless corpse. And play. And play. For a film that clocks in at under an hour and was made on the cheap even by the standards of '60s Turkish cult cinema, *Mandrake vs. Kilink* has an awful lot it wants to tell you about who made it (when you remember that director Oksal Pekmezoglu was a credit sequence designer, the length of this opening—

though not their unimaginative nature—becomes easier to understand). Once the *Lawrence of Arabia* of Turkish skeleton guy movie credits finally wrap up, the film moves on to the arrival of a plane filled with VIPs, among them Mandrake himself (Güven Erte) as well as an Indian princess, played by Turkish cult cinema mainstay Mine Mutlu (who appeared in, among others, Yilmaz Atadeniz's *Yilmayan seytan*, aka *The Deathless Devil*).

Mandrake is on holiday with his sidekicks Abdullah (aka Lothar, if you are a fan of the comics, and played by a guy in full-body jet-black body paint) and Bircan (Hilal Esen). The princess attracts the attention of a nefarious-looking gang who have all carved a gory "K" into their faces, just in case the police ever need something to fill in on the "Distinguishing Marks" part of their arrest form. It certainly outdoes the previous henchmen, who just wore those billowing satin Kilink brand shirts.

The princess also attracts the attention of Mandrake, who in turn attracts her attention. The two engage in a bit of light-hearted flirtation that culminates in Mandrake "playfully" teleporting her priceless tiara into his own room, replacing it with a note informing her that she can swing by and pick it up in the morning. Unfortunately for Mandrake, his mystical prank backfires when Kilink sneaks into the princess' room and finds Mandrake's note. Mandrake might have a lot of amazing powers, but waking up while a grown man in a skeleton suit pokes around in his hotel room isn't among them. Kilink absconds with the treasure and leaves a taunting note of his own. Although breaking into Mandrake's hotel room and leaving him a dickish note is the sort of behavior we've come to expect from Kilink, this version quickly moves into much more unsavory territory than Atadeniz's Kilink.

His day job is running a sex slave ring and brothel where kidnapped women are routinely raped and forced into prostitution. This is a much more horrifying version of Kilink than the one that just liked to party, slap a few asses, and kidnap the occasional daughter of a scientist. Despite the comic book powers of Mandrake, Kilink and his gang operate more like straight-up human traffickers, albeit with a leader who likes to occasionally don a skeleton-motif bodystocking. And "occasionally" is the truth. Unlike previous incarnations of the character, this Kilink (played by handsome Sadettin Düzgün) unmasks frequently, like Kriminal, and only dons the skeleton wear when burgling or when it actively detracts from what he is attempting to accomplish. For example, he walks around in regular clothes for much of the film, but when it comes time to kidnap someone by posing as a cab driver, he wears his skeleton suit and mask but "disguises" himself by wearing a flat cap and raincoat.

This Kilink is also explicit in his own fetishes, with the scars across his back signifying that he enjoys receiving the occasional whipping session as much as he enjoys giving. He plays, at least at times, the submissive to his blonde girlfriend in a relationship pretty overtly colored with sadomasochism. In this regard, and despite the fantastical powers manifested by Mandrake, *Mandrake vs. Kilink* is a

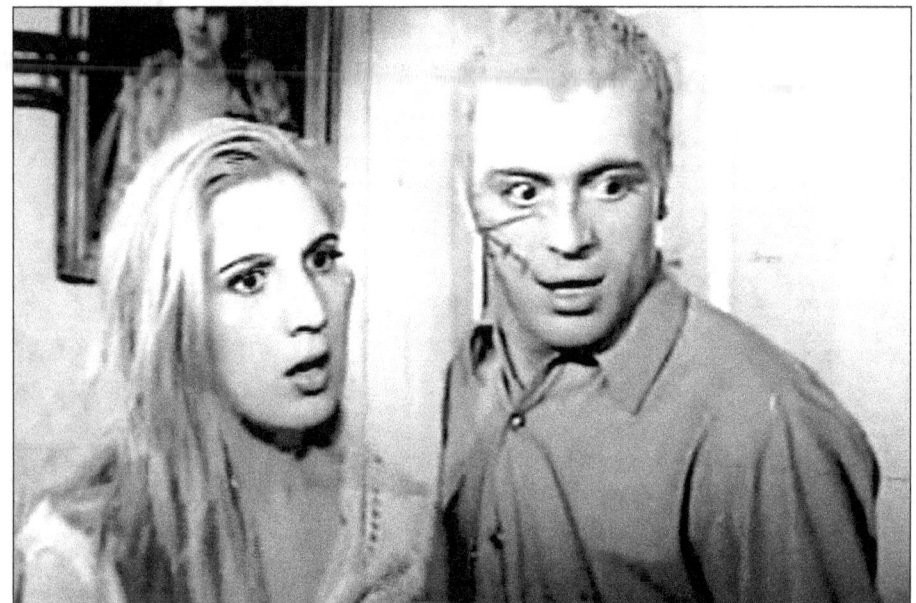

more adult, more faithful adaptation of the photo-novel character Killing than was the Kilink of the Yilmaz Atadeniz films, with his hopelessly absurd plans for world domination and his inability to concentrate on anything other than his living room full of strippers. No, this Kilink is mean, repugnant, and truly lives up to the sadistic portion of his description. Less so the "super criminal" portion, but that's what happens when an eccentric-but-human rapist/thief/pimp choses to tangle with a heroic magician who has supernatural powers.

Mandrake's powers mostly manifest as the ability to teleport or transmogrify items, a power which he uses not only to "steal" the princess' tiara but also to perform such feats as escaping from chains, stealing motorcycles and replacing them with bicycles (which leads to a pointless but amazing scene of Mandrake and Abdullah zipping down the highway while standing up on motorcycles), and, at one point, turning Kilink into a dog. Kilink never seems much of a match for Mandrake, even when he has the wizard in chains. Unlike Uçan Adam, who seemed to forget that he could fly, had super strength, and was impervious to bullets, Mandrake never misses a chance to use his powers.

Too bad one of his superpowers isn't performing well in fight scenes. There are a few and, while they are executed with the reckless energy one expects from Turkish action cinema of this vintage, they're not very good. The Atadeniz films had the benefit of Yildirim Gencer under the skeleton suit, and Gencer was an accomplished stuntman. No one in *Mandrake vs. Kilink* operates on the same level, and so the fights take on more of a slapstick comedy atmosphere. Yet, as bad as Guven Erte may be in the action scenes, he fares better in them than he does in the acting scenes. Erte reacts to pretty much everything by not reacting at all. Flirting with a pretty Indian princess? Discovering a corpse in the closet? Being whipped by

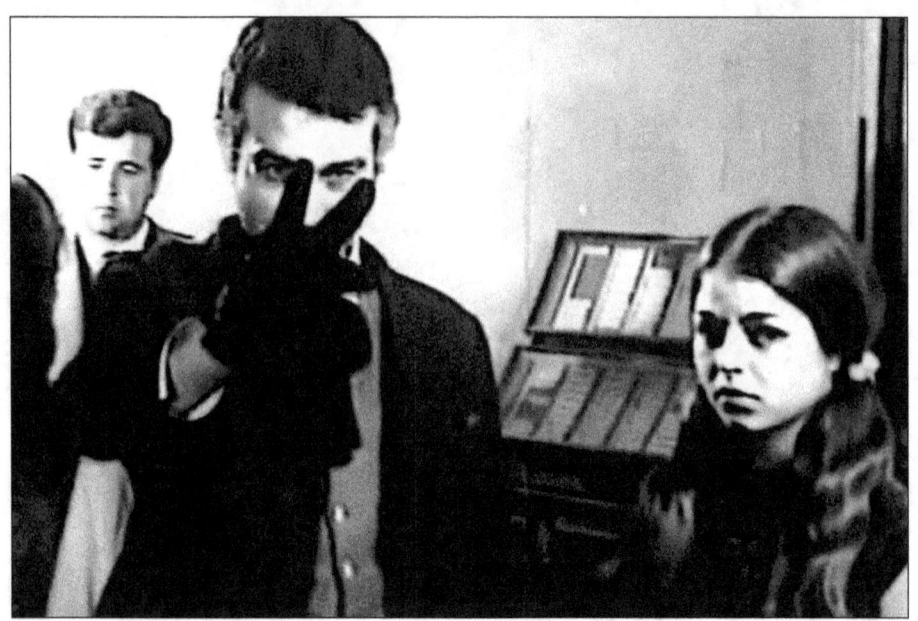

a henchman? Guven Erte handles these and all other situations with neutral-faced stoicism. Sure, as a wizard superhero he's probably seen it all, but even then you'd think *something* would elicit a reaction. This is especially detrimental to the film since, at only 55 minutes long in its existing form, Kilink doesn't appear (at least in his skeleton outfit) until the 20 minute mark, leaving the bulk of the film in the hands of Erte's Mandrake, Mutlu's princess, Abdullah (who spends every second of his screen time mugging for the camera and doing the typical too-hearty laugh), and Kilink's gang, anchored by the treacherous Mustapha (who bears an uncanny resemblance to Batman's Joker) and Salma, the latest in Kilink's long line of blonde bombshell *femmes fatale*. When Kilink finally skulks into the film, he gives a pretty good performance that delves deeper into the warped psyche of a man who enjoys dressing up in skeleton pajamas and getting whipped. He also performs better during the film's action scenes, at one point even swinging around an ax while shirtless and still wearing his Kilink tights.

Tansu Sayin, who plays Salma, was also no stranger to Turkish pop cinema, having appeared in *Kilink: Strip and Kill*, *Demir Pençe Casuslar Savaşı*, and a couple Zorro films. Her job is mostly to point guns at people, nod approvingly at Kilink's cruel tortures, and get jealous when it seems like Kilink might be developing the hots for the princess. The real prize for this cast goes to her frequent collaborator, head henchman Mustapha. His pale face, macabre grin, twitchy demeanor, and massive facial scar hint at a character far more disturbed than even the boss. If only we got a little about *that* guy.

In its present, and likely only remaining, form, *Mandrake vs. Kilink* is less than hour long. There is obvious damage to the print and some crude splicing in places. Records of the time show that censors demanded several cuts to the film to remove material even more salacious than what's been left in. Whether an "uncut" print ever existed anywhere but in what was submitted to the censors is uncertain. It's likely that even if a longer cut was released in 1967, nothing better than the 55 minute version will ever be found. At least we have that.

Mandrake vs. Kilink doesn't live up to the high-energy lunacy of the Yilmaz Atadeniz films, but it doesn't stick around long enough to wear out its welcome. That it delves into seedier territory and makes Kilink an overt sex trafficker means some of the fun of the other films is sacrificed, but the Mandrake stuff is so absurd and the film so gleefully daft that it possesses enough charm to get by. It gets weird, and not just because it lingers on Kilink's sadomasochism, and not just because it's about a super-criminal in a skeleton suit fighting a powerful wizard.

There are moments, sometimes fleeting, that elevate the film into the realm of the surreal. Why, for example, do Mandrake and Abdullah insist on riding their stolen motorcycles while standing up on the seats (because it looks cool). Why, toward the end of the film, is there suddenly a Bollywood musical number, complete with the Princess and Mandrake frolicking at the beach as they sing a decidedly Indian song? Were they hoping for some sort of crossover appeal? A Bollywood Kilink film—now *that* would have been something to see. Alas, we never got to see Dharmendra facing off against the diabolical super-criminal (though he did once fight Fantômas).

Brightly colored comic book movies had just about run their course by the end of the 1960s, and after Mario Bava put the exclamation point on the genre in the form of *Danger: Diabolik*, there just wasn't much point to continuing to dabble. Indeed the entire Eurospy genre, of which these films were a tangential part, was winding down, making way for spaghetti westerns and the grim cops and robbers films of the 1970s. Kilink continued to pop up in Turkish cult cinema well into the 1970s, even though Turkey followed Italy's lead and moved away from costumed super-criminals and toward more down-to-earth cops and gangsters films. Among these were *Special Squad Shoots on Sight* and *Four for All*, two Turkish-Italian co-productions directed by Yilmaz Atadeniz and Giulio Giuseppe Negri and starring Uçan Adam himself, Irfan Atasoy, alongside Italian cult cinema mainstays Gordon Mitchell and Richard Harrison. There were still a few freewheelin' spy classics to come, but more and more, the sharp suits and wild costumes were being retired in favor of roll-neck sweaters, brown corduroy flares, and thick mustaches.

But rest assured, dead though you may think these madmen, it's only a matter of time before you hear maniacal laughter ringing out and turn around to see, to your astonished horror, a man in a skeleton suit standing on top of a parking garage, arms akimbo, ready to do some more crimes. §

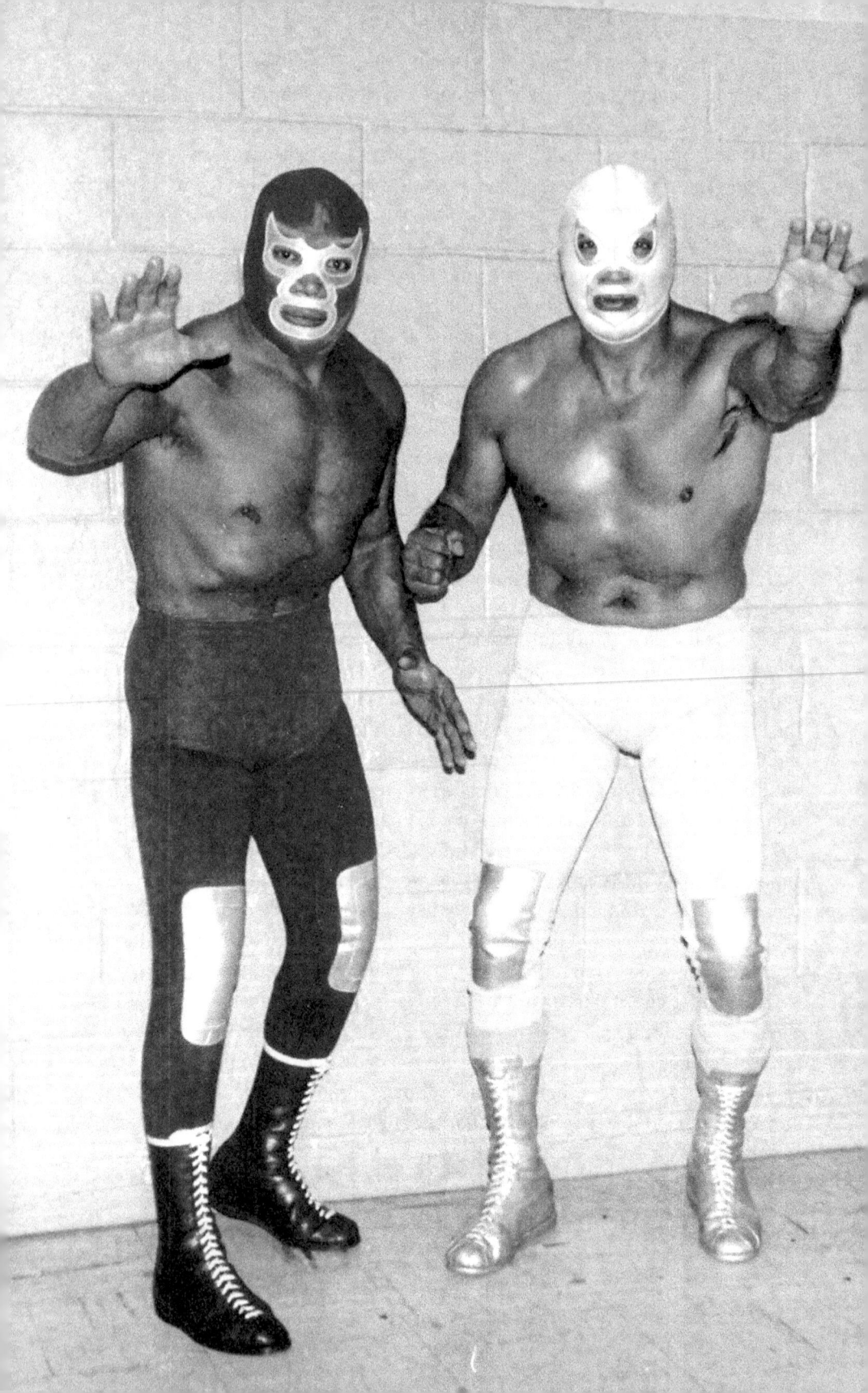

06 LEGEND OF THE MASK

How masks came to lucha libre, how lucha came to film, and how El Santo and Blue Demon came to punch Dracula

With Material by Todd Stadtman

Arena Coliseo, Mexico City, November 7, 1952. Known locally as "the Lagunilla funnel" because of the design of the spectator stands. The coliseum could seat just under 9,000 people, all of them cheering, jeering, and making merry—all the things that are part of the ritual of a live *lucha libre* event. And what an event they were getting. Four of the biggest stars were locking up in a tag team main event. Arena Coliseo was the spiritual home of *lucha libre*. One of the men striding to the ring that night in 1952 was also there the night the Arena opened on April 2, 1943. Back then, the *luchador* was a last-minute substitute. The main event was scheduled to be a title bout between Bill Longsan and Juan Humberto, two popular American wrestlers. Humberto, however, wasn't going to make it to the Coliseo in time. The promoters scrambled for a substitute for the arena's inaugural main event. They found a *luchador* who was wrestling under an identity he debuted just a few months earlier, when he took a new in-ring name and donned a silver mask. That night in 1943, El Santo ushered in the era of the Arena Coliseo.

Almost a decade later, he was still wrestling. He'd come a long way, become one of the biggest stars in *lucha libre*. There was a comic book coming out that cast him as a crime-fighting superman—even though El Santo wasn't a good guy in the ring. He was a *rudo* who won matches by cheating. But being a bad guy didn't mean you weren't also a popular guy. Audiences understood the importance of a *rudo*. There was no drama without them, no emotion to be harvested from a match-up of just good guys (*tecnicos*). You needed a *rudo* people loved to hate, someone who could milk every ounce of emotion.

Together with Gory Guerrero, their team known as La Pareja Atómica, El Santo was the sport's top *rudo*. The team they were facing that night in 1952 was Los Hermanos Shadows. The Shadow Brothers. One of them, Black Shadow, wore a black mask trimmed in white, a stark contrast to his frequent opponent El Santo's silver mask. The two had been going at one other for years. Tonight was the culmination of that lengthy feud.

Black Shadow's partner wore a mask of electric blue, a mask he started wearing in September 1948. Like the man in the silver mask—*el enmascarado de plata*—the man in blue—*el demonio azul*—was a big name, though the main draw of the match was the rivalry between Black Shadow and El Santo. The stakes were high. It was a *Luchas de Apuestas*, a mask-versus-mask match. The loser would be unmasked in front of the crowd. It was the ultimate humiliation for a masked wrestler and often signaled the end of that particular persona (if not the wrestler beneath the mask). For 70 minutes, the teams beat on one another. In the final seconds, through the devious methods of the *rudo*, El Santo triumphed and ripped off Black Shadow's mask. Black Shadow's partner was outraged. He swore vengeance against El Santo. The crowd went nuts. Like, really nuts. There had been heat before, but nothing like this. The promoters started planning for a new coliseum, because Arena Coliseo was too small to contain what happened that night. Black Shadow might have been defeated, but the feud between El Santo and Blue Demon had only just begun.

When El Santo became El Santo, he was wrestling for a promotion called Empresa Mexicana de *Lucha Libre*. EMLL didn't invent *lucha libre*, but they did organize it on a national level, turning it from a festival sideshow into a sport, or something like a sport. A representation of a sport, perhaps. Pro wrestling, be it American, Mexican, or Japanese, has always walked the line between sporting event and entertainment spectacle (something that has since become true of many sports). There is a script, yes, and a pre-determined outcome, and an attempt (albeit at times cursory) on behalf of those involved to deny the scripted nature.

This leads many to brand pro wrestling as "fake." Defenders counter that calling wrestling fake is like calling opera fake, or complaining that a magician tricked you and didn't *really* make that woman disappear. Today, most everyone acknowledges the scripted nature of pro wrestling. Promotions even use the script as part of the script, building controversy for certain wrestlers by constructing elaborate narratives in which they go "off-script," winning a match they were scripted to lose. Fans watch pro wrestling for the same reason they watch movies. For the drama. For the entertainment. For larger-than-life characters and, scripted or not, feats of often incredible athleticism.

Wrestling has been around since pretty much the dawn of history, and doubtless long before then. Over the centuries, different styles evolved, each with its own moves, rules, and origin story. Among these was "free wrestling." Free wrestling was a popular way to pass the time among soldiers. Over the years, bouts became more organized. They moved out of the barracks and onto the midway. Predictably, it's there that the scripted nature of the sport was introduced. Wrestlers would sometimes fight other wrestlers, but often they would challenge members of the audience. Go a certain number of minutes, win a prize! It was usually a safe set-up, but every now and then a proper athlete from the audience would find his way into the ring, or the wrong local would get injured, causing the performers grief. So the formula was tweaked. One of the architects of the new system was P.T. Barnum, in whose circus sideshows wrestling played an important role. Under the new system, hired men were planted in the audience. Inevitably, these "random strangers" would be chosen to compete against the wrestler, insuring that "the house" controlled everything.

Eventually, wrestling moved from the midway to the boxing arena. Being inside an actual gym or arena lent it an air of legitimacy. The fix was still in, but that didn't stop unsavory promoters from taking bets from unsuspecting audience members, most of whom regarded wrestling, with its Olympic and collegiate roots, as being as legitimate as professional boxing—ironic though that might have been, given boxing's checkered past. The practice of people in on the con maintaining the illusion of legitimacy became known as *kayfabe*, a carny term that means "keeping the secrets of the business," though its etymology is unknown. With arenas came a stability that enabled promoters to develop territories and in-ring performers to develop personae. Drama is a part of all sports—look at how much effort is spent manufacturing team rivalries. Pro wrestling began to exploit the ability to build characters: good guys and bad guys—or "faces" and "heels," as they became known. In Mexico, free wrestling became *lucha libre*. There was nothing like a league, and the matches weren't fixed (any more than any other sporting event). That changed in 1933. Salvador Lutteroth González was a veteran of the Revolution, fighting engagements against bandit-cum-insurgent Pancho Villa. After his military service, Lutteroth married, started a family, and settled in the border town of Juarez. There, he saw his first professional wrestling match, in El Paso's Liberty Hall.

He decided that his calling in life was to bring the sport-entertainment hybrid to Mexico, building on the regional popularity of *lucha libre* and mixing it with the scripted spectacle of American pro wrestling. In 1933, he launched Empresa Mexicana de *Lucha Libre*. They held their first show on September 21, 1933, at the Modelo Arena in Mexico City. Modelo Arena was a small, shabby facility, exactly the kind of place you'd want to be the birthplace of *lucha libre*. They did well there. EMLL held their first anniversary show for a sold-out crowd of 5,000. Not much is known about the card for this show, but what is known is exceptionally important to the development of *lucha libre*. American wrestler Corbin James Massey, who had been working for EMLL under the name Cíclon MacKey since the company began, stepped into the ring for the main event. On this night, Gonzalez needed someone new, so MacKey became La Maravilla Enmascarada, hiding his face under a black mask. Masked wrestlers were a common gimmick on the American wrestling circuits, but this was the first time a masked wrestler had performed in Mexico. It would not be the last.

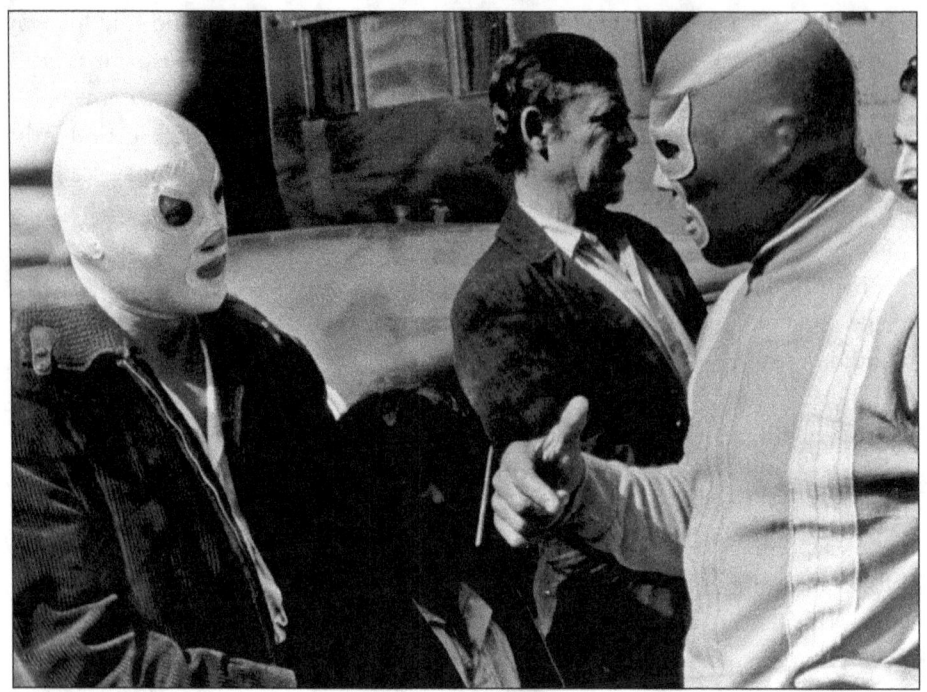

Behind the Mask

The history of masked wrestlers in Mexico comes with a lot of lore, almost all of which is bullshit. Granted, it's really good bullshit, and if you're going to accept the orchestrated drama of *lucha libre*, then there's no reason not to do the same when it comes to the history of the masks worn by so many of the sport's performers. The romantic version of the story is that the *lucha libre* mask is derived from either the long cultural history of masked theatrical performances or from the *ocēlōmeh*, or "jaguar warriors" of the Aztec era (or Olmec or Mayan, depending on who is writing the history). According to legend about these jaguar warriors, they would don jaguar masks (and often skins) before charging into battle, believing that in doing so they would be imbued with the strength of the animal. The line is often drawn directly from the masks of such performers and warriors to the masks of modern day *luchadors*, who adopted masks as way to uphold this ancient tradition. It's even been claimed that the simple, iconic mask of El Santo is an explicit tribute to the Olmec jaguar god. It's a great story, no less so just because none of it is true. Oh sure, there were jaguar gods and were-jaguars and jaguar warriors, but their role in the history of masked wrestlers was manufactured after the fact. Ironically, it's not even a history that begins in Mexico.

Though you can bet some ancient Greek probably showed up to a local bout with some manner of mask at some point, the first easily-located record of a masked pro wrestler is from France. *"Le veritable lutteur masque"* as he was labeled in periodicals of the day, or simply the Masked Wrestler, appeared on the scene sometime between 1865 and 1867. Some sources claim he debuted as part of a sideshow at the 1865 International Exhibition—the World's Fair—in Paris, which seems plausible except for the fact that in 1865, the World's Fair took place in Porto, Portugal. 1867 makes more sense, since there was a World's Fair in Paris that year, and rather a large one meant to celebrate the 100th anniversary of the storming of the Bastille and show off the military and cultural might of Napoleon III's new French Empire (the very same emperor who launched an invasion of Mexico in December 1861).

By all accounts, it was a lovely event, but it didn't do Napoleon much good. In 1870, the German Empire was looking to show itself off to the world too, but rather than host a World's Fair, they went to war with France. Germany won, portions of France were annexed, and Napoleon III was captured during the bloody Battle of Sedan. Having led the country into disaster, France proclaimed itself a republic (again) and Napoleon III was exiled to England, where he died in 1873 without anyone thanking him for having hosted such a grand International Exhibition a few years earlier.

At that International Exhibition, or so the story goes, a wrestling tournament took place. One of the entrants was a masked man, his identity unknown even to the event managers. The masked man won the tournament (who knows if it was fixed or not) and became a minor sensation around Paris, until people moved on to things like worrying about Otto von Bismarck and Prussian expansionism. The Masked Wrestler was never unmasked, so rumors started to spread. Who knows how many of these rumors were started by the tournament's promoters? Remember: this is a story told by circus men. The most lavish rumor was that this masked man was a famed French nobleman who wanted to test his mettle in the ring, but of course he could not reveal his true identity for fear of the damage it would do his reputation among the social elite.

Three men have been fingered as or claimed to be the Masked Wrestler. In December 1902, the *San Francisco Call* claimed that the Masked Wrestler, known also as "Bras de Fer," was a recent immigrant to San Francisco, where he opened a restaurant in the city's Latin quarter. The *Call*'s account of the Masked Wrestler is as exciting as an Alexandre Dumas story (though shorter by a thousand pages, give or take) and as dramatic as a fight promoter's dream. According to the *Call*, which cites no supporting documentation, Paris in 1862 was abuzz about a sensational wrestler in a brilliant scarlet mask who was taking on all comers. Harking back to tales of the Scarlet Pimpernel, gossips supposed the man in the scarlet mask was a slumming count or duke. The man in the scarlet mask vanquished all comers, and it seemed like no one could defeat him...until he received a mysterious challenge to a match at Paris' fabled Hippodrome. He accepted, though like the average citizen of Paris, he had no idea who the challenger was. On the appointed evening, the mysterious masked man strode to the ring, the cheers of the sell-out crowd showering down on him. And then, out came the challenger: another masked wrestler, clad entirely in black.

The paper describes the hushed awe that fell over the crowd and the ensuing two-out-of-three falls match, with the man in the scarlet mask winning the first fall and the man in the black mask claiming the second, driving the crowd insane. There's even a dramatic moment in the struggle for the final fall where the black mask comes loose, *almost* revealing the man beneath. As the man in black executed a shocking maneuver that pinned the man in scarlet, winning the fall and the match, the stunned silence of the crowd slowly gave way to the growing chant of "Bras de Fer!" One can't help but think that P.T. Barnum himself couldn't have devised a more effective spectacle.

So began the short, storied career of Bras de Fer, who took on the best France could throw at him, including a series of dramatic rematches with the man in scarlet. But no one could defeat him. Not content to leave his legend in the ring, stories began to surface about amazing feats of derring-do performed by Bras de Fer outside the ring. The paper relates a story about how a young, inconsolable, and probably drunk soldier returning from a gala threw himself into the Seine in a fit of depression. Suddenly, Bras de Fer emerged from a passing coach—wearing his mask, of course—and without hesitation dove into the river, saving the soldier's life then disappearing into the night. It's like someone was writing a Santo movie before Santo was even born.

Adding further to the mystique of the masked man was his pre-match ritual, in which he signaled to the same area of the Hippodrome. It was assumed he was just saluting God or Napoleon III or whoever, until one night Bras de Fer was locked once again in mortal combat with the man in the scarlet mask. It looked like this was the night Scarlet Mask would finally avenge himself. As he achieved what looked to be a sure submission, Bras de Fer was seen to bow his head toward a specific part of the arena and make his signature gesture. He then looked up, briefly, as the crowd grew quiet. And there, directly where he looked, stood a woman. A woman in the plain dress of the poor, who met the wrestler's glance and waved a white-gloved hand at him. In an amazing reversal of fortune, Bras de Fer then escaped certain defeat, slipping out of the hold and pinning Scarlet Mask.

Three months after his mysterious appearance, the masked Bras de Fer vanished just as mysteriously. He would have remained forever anonymous if not for someone strolling down the street in front of the home of a man named Alfred Perrier. This unnamed pedestrian was amazed to see Perrier in the yard, lifting massive amounts of weight as if it was nothing. Witnessing these feats of incredible strength, the stroller loitered, and in doing so caught a glimpse of a woman who appeared at the balcony to call Perrier's name. The pedestrian was astonished...for she was the very same woman who had waved to Bras de Fer on that fateful night at the Hippodrome! Although the witness immediately set about bragging, Perrier himself did not confirm the claim, though he did, by the newspaper accounts, enjoy a lucrative career as a strongman before moving to San Francisco and opening the restaurant—but not before he saved the lives of some people during a fire in London and, a little later, encountered a struggling widow and took her two sons under his muscular wing, teaching them to be great athletes like himself.

Historian Peter Briant once said, when commenting about the malleable nature of stories about the ancient world, "You must believe ancient history even if it's not true." You must believe in Bras de Fer, because true or not, it is a fantastic story. You must believe that Mexican wrestling masks were derived from Aztec jaguar warriors, even if it's not true. How could you not want to? Well, you could be a man named Professor Thiebaud Bauer, another of the contenders for "true identity of the Masked Wrestler of Paris."

Though Perrier's claim came some four decades after the exploits of the masked Wrestler were the talk of Paris, at least it comes with a great back story. In the case of Bauer, almost nothing is known about his life before he arrived in San Francisco in 1874. What is known though is that shortly after his arrival in San Francisco, Bauer began working as a professional wrestler, garnering quite a local reputation. In late 1874, Bauer was challenged by a guy named Professor William Miller, a well-known wrestler who claimed that Bauer had never been tested against anything other than local galoots. The two grapplers clashed in a series of bouts that saw them trading wins or ending in draws, until May 28, 1875 at San Francisco's Palace Amphitheatre they locked up in a "three falls out of five" match that would determine the final outcome of the rivalry.

The outcome was that the referee, after each wrestler had won two falls, called the whole thing off and announced that it had become apparent to him that Bauer and Miller were working together, that the whole thing had been a fix. Furthermore, it came out that Miller's dramatic arrival in San Francisco to challenge Bauer might itself have been a planned (or "worked") spectacle, as the two had apparently already known each other. This being the (theoretically) legitimate Greco-Roman circuit and not sideshow free fighting, the reputation of both men was ruined.

Luckily, news traveled slow back then, so Bauer and Miller were able to revive the act on the east coast. They were able to milk it for a while until once again being exposed. However, while the collaborative nature of their matches might have infuriated boxing and wrestling commissioners (if anyone was going to fix a fight, it was the commissioner), crowds didn't seem to care. Miller and Bauer still managed to pack arenas. In 1878, they even took the "act" to Cuba. When Bauer returned to the States, he found a new challenger waiting for him, a native of New York state named William Muldoon. Muldoon, who went on to be the state's boxing commissioner and a well-known crusader for cleaning up sports and getting rid of the fix, consistently defeated Bauer in a series of popular matches. Bauer's in-ring fortunes declined rapidly, and it's difficult to discern during this period how much of professional wrestling was legitimate and how much was faked. It seems pretty evident, however, that at least when Muldoon was in the ring, things got real. Bauer eventually returned to San Francisco and invested his wrestling money in property. Despite success as a landlord, his luck ran out. A bad drinking habit and possible brain damage from his rough career (even a fixed wrestling match hurts) left him debilitated in his later years. He died in January of 1902. Given his pioneering career as one of the early practitioners of scripted pro wrestling, it's entirely possible claims that he was the legendary Masked Wrestler of Paris were just part of the fiction. Who knows, and frankly, who cares? In the end, isn't it better that the true identity of the Masked Wrestler remain shrouded in extravagant claims and conjecture?

The first widely-publicized match featuring a masked man in the American wrestling ring happened in 1915 during a series of bouts in New York. By this time, classical Greco-Roman wrestling bouts, be they legitimate or fixed, were falling out of style. They could go on for hours, with minimal perceptible action (regardless of how titanic the struggle might have been for the participants), and often ended in a draw. Europe was settled into a protracted, largely static, horrific war in which one side never seemed to get the clear advantage over the other despite occasional explosions of violence, and it's possible no one wanted to see something so similar to the stalemated trench warfare of the Western Front played out in the wrestling ring, especially not when you could go see a thrilling Pearl White serial or a movie like *Cabiria*, which featured a strongman (Bartolomeo Pagano) partaking in breathtaking stunts rather than locking up in an almost immobile tangle for three hours. Greco-Roman bouts were beginning to lose their hold on the American public, and the more dynamic, flashier, and exciting freestyle or catch-as-catch-can style of wrestling was growing in popularity.

The United States, still in 1915 a neutral and a safe haven from the war, saw an influx of immigrants from eastern Europe, where the front was much different from the western front but still nightmarish in the amount of destruction and casualties being caused by the fighting. Among the refugees fleeing the destruction were quite a few experienced wrestlers. Most were practitioners of Greco-Roman style. Some were willing to adopt the wilder catch-as-catch-can style. Promoters, never ones to miss an opportunity, capitalized on this "rift," which allowed them to both mine narrative drama from the age-old "traditionalist vs. modernist" conflict while also using catch-as-catch-can to buoy shows that wouldn't have been very profitable with pure Greco-Roman cards.

It was during one of these hybrid shows (which, somewhat ironically, had the affect of pretty much killing off the popularity of Greco-Roman wrestling for good), that a man in a black hood stepped into the ring to help liven up the show, which was taking place, fittingly, at the Manhattan Opera House. With box office for the show starting to flag, the mask gimmick was suggested by an opera impresario Mark A. Luescher, who had previously concealed an opera diva in a scarlet mask (no doubt recalling the masked wrestler of the Paris World's Fair) and toured with the opera, billing her as "La Belle Dazle" to quite a bit of success. According to a December 1915 article in the *Brooklyn Daily Eagle*, Luescher suggested the gimmick to Ben Atwood, who was the press agent for the wrestling show at the

Opera House and was casting about for ways to remedy the faltering attendance. Atwood in turn passed the suggestion on to promoters Charlie Cutler and Jack Curley. They liked the sound of it, were probably willing to try anything at that point, and set about finding a man to put behind the mask. That man ended up being Mort Henderson, a wrestler hailing from upstate who was described by the newspaper as having worked as "a fireman, brakeman, policeman, pugilist and most everything that requires strength." Henderson appeared under the name the Masked Marvel and was a hit. Of course, most stories were less about his in-ring performances, which were apparently solid, than they were about the mystery of who he was. As with Bras de Fer so many years prior, the identity of the Masked Marvel was a closely guarded secret. To foil any newspaper men who tailed him after the matches, the Masked Marvel would take a cab to the Crescent Athletic Club and disappear into the club through the employees' entrance, allowing him to unmask and leave the gym through the front door like any other tough guy out for an evening.

They maintained the ruse until Henderson's manager, Ed Pollard, spilled the beans to the *Eagle*. Although he quickly retracted the statement, it was too late. This "unmasking" however didn't diminish Henderson's popularity as the Masked Marvel. Soon, other tournaments, promoters, and wrestlers were debuting their own masked wrestler gimmicks. As the sport of pro wrestling escalated in popularity, there was a proliferation of masked marvels, executioners, maniacs, and such popping up across the United States. It was one of these masked marvels that Salvador Lutteroth Gonzalez eventually saw. He recognized a good gimmick when he saw one, and soon EMLL had a growing stable of masked wrestlers. It was Lutteroth's EMLL that developed the mythology of the mask, linking it not just to individual wrestlers but to the ancient Mexican tradition of warriors donning masks before hunts and battles. The system also enabled EMLL to create a near infinite number of new wrestlers simply by taking one of their regular guys and slapping a new mask on him for the night. If he clicked with the crowd, he might continue wrestling under the new identity. If not, well, no loss. One of the ones that did click came around in 1942.

Rodolfo Guzmán Huerta had been wrestling professionally since the 1930s under a series of in-ring identities: Rudy Guzmán, El Hombre Rojo, El Demonio Negro, and El Murcielago II, the last of which landed Guzmán in hot water, as there was already a wrestler, Jesus Velazquez, who performed under the name The Bat and who did not take kindly to someone passing themselves off as an unofficial sequel. In 1942 manager and promoter Don Jesús Lomelí approached Guzmán with an offer to join a new stable of wrestlers he was putting together. The trio would all wear silver costumes and be known by evocative religious names: El Santo, El Diablo, and El Angel. On June 26, 1942 Guzmán donned a silver mask and stepped into the ring at the Arena Mexico for the first time under the name that would be his for the rest of his life. By the time his feud with Blue Demon began in 1952, El Santo was so popular that he was getting his own comic book. Which was representative of a growing concern among certain segments of the population about *lucha libre*: that its fans (mostly low income city dwellers, with a smattering of the middle class and a few "slumming" artists of note) often adored the bad guys. There was an interactive aspect to pro wrestling. At a baseball game, the gulf between spectator and player was wide. At the opera, the curtains parted and the performers were already on stage. But in pro wrestling, as in boxing, the wrestlers paraded down narrow aisles amongst the crowds, within easy touching distance. And if you were a *rudo*, within easy taunting distance. Soon taunting the bad guys became (and remains) one of the highlights of any night at a *lucha libre* event. After all, you can be way more creative with your heckling than you can with your cheering. Naturally, the *rudo*s would taunt back, sometimes even threatening to fight members of the audience. That interaction creates a bond, one that is often more intimate than the one between *tecnico* and fans. All you can do when a *tecnico* walks down the aisle is cheer and pat him on the back. Audiences want to see the *rudo* vanquished, but not right away. Souvenir masks are a staple of *lucha libre* merchandise stalls, and the masks of *rudo*s sell as well as *tecnico*s.

This adoration of *rudo*s concerned the government, which in the 1950s was attempting to inflict stricter controls on the moral fiber of the nation's entertainment. They didn't want Mexico's youth, especially its poor urban youth, swaggering around in imitation of popular *rudo*s. It presented a negative image of modern Mexico, they claimed. It also encouraged sass and rebellion and the sort of civil unrest that had plagued Mexico for generations. It was too drastic a step to ban *lucha libre* events, but the government could outlaw the television broadcast of *lucha libre*. Which is exactly what they did, under the time-honored aegis of "protecting the children."

In the U.S., professional wrestling found its way onto the movie screen, usually as low-budget dramas that followed a standard formula in which either a new guy struggling to make it or an old guy struggling to keep it is tempted to corruption, usually because of debts or to save an orphan or because of, you know, some dame. Mexico's film industry evolved alongside *lucha libre*, and it was inevitable that the two should meet. In the 1950s, under pressure that would see *lucha libre* banished from television but also aware of the fanbase *lucha libre* had, multiple film producers started working on ways to incorporate *lucha libre*.

In 1951, four films were jockeying to be "the world's first lucha movie," though it's doubtful any of the makers of these films thought of the situation as such at the time. Chano Urueta's *La bestia magnifica*, Fernando Cortes' *El luchador fenómeno*, Joselito Rodríguez' *Huracán Ramírez*, and René Cardona's *El enmascarado de plata* each came to the conclusion that it was time for *luchadors*, so popular in the ring but bit players in film, to step onscreen for the main event. *Luchadors* were, in effect, actors already, so the decision was whether to hire an established *luchador* to play himself or create a new one for the screen. Cardona was developing *El enmascarado de plata* for El Santo. El Santo would be the first *luchador* leading man. So, if that was the plan, then who the hell is Huracán Ramírez?

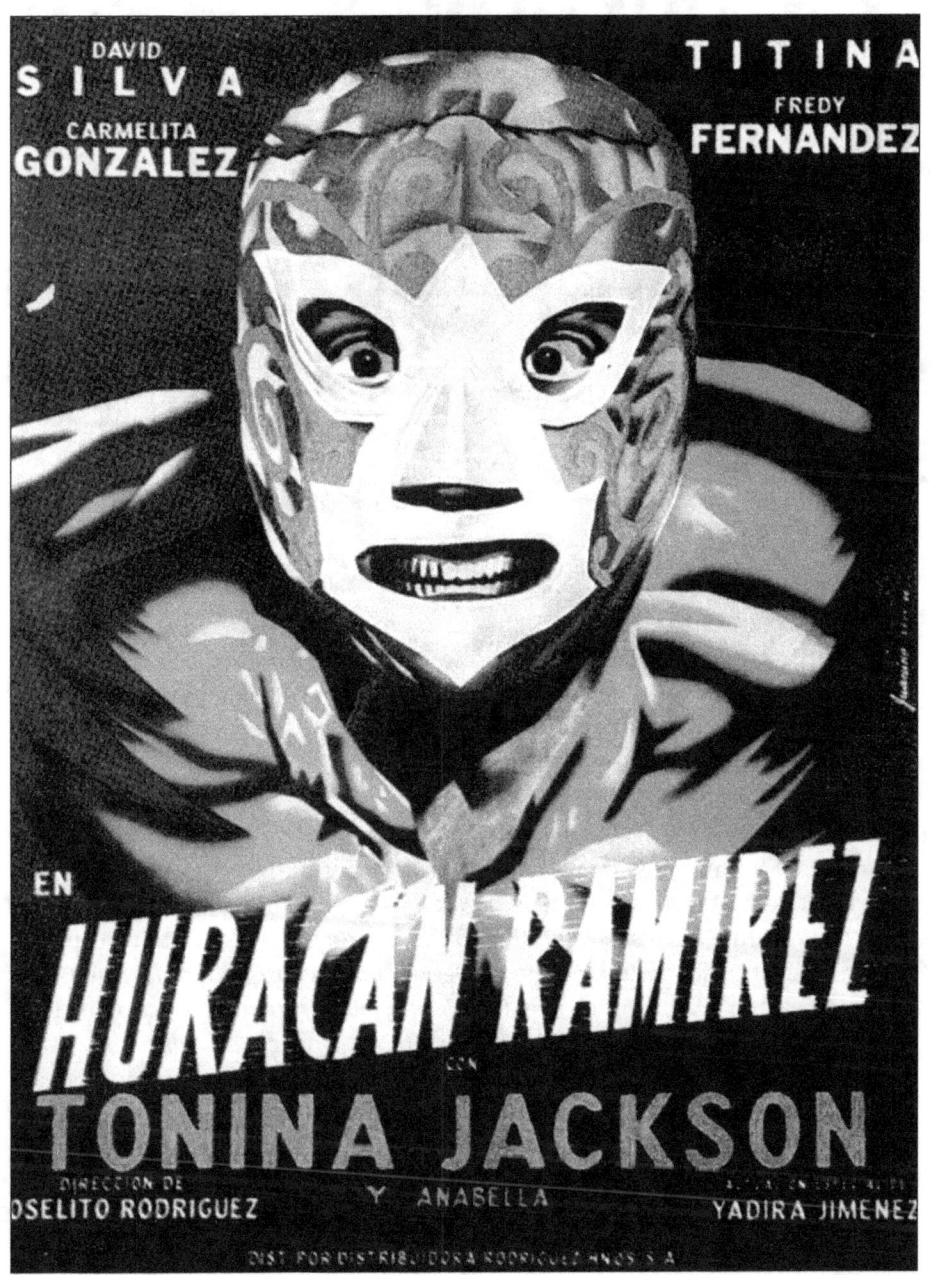

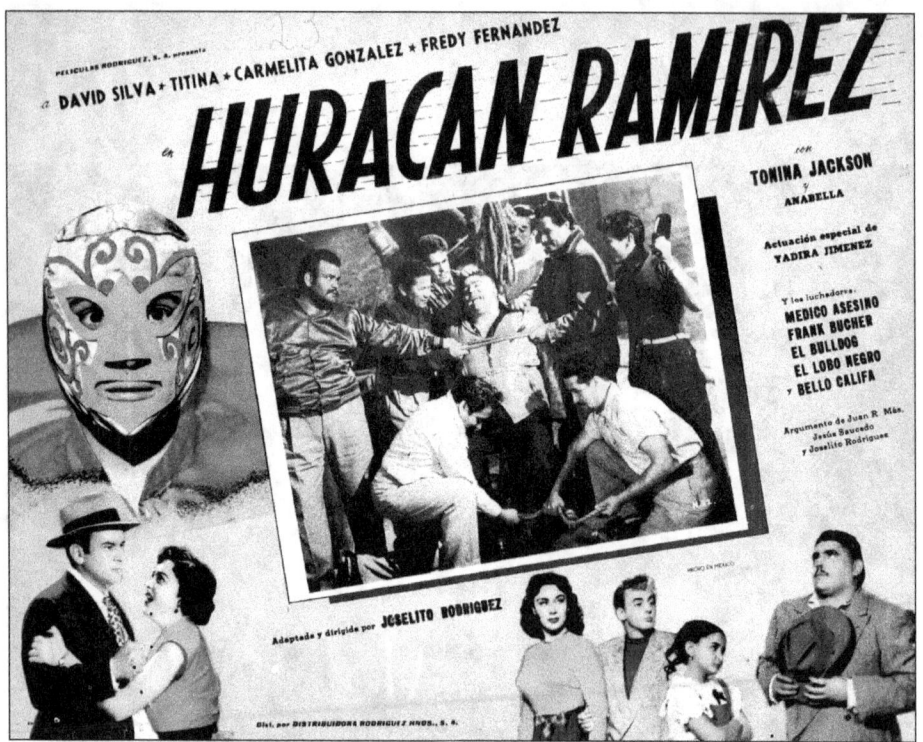

Hurricane Warning

Each of the four films that went into production in 1951 and 1952 contributed other aspects to the mythology of the lucha film apart from vying for the claim of being the first. *El luchador fenómeno*, released in October of 1952, was a screwball farce starring popular comedic actor Adalberto Martinez (who made a similar comedy about baseball that same year), but it also showcased a man named Wolf Ruvinskis, a Latvian whose family had fled Eastern Europe fearing Nazi persecution and resettled in Argentina. He would go on to appear as the masked wrestler-superhero Neutron in a series of films that were among the first to incorporate aspects of science fiction, horror, and old serial thrillers into the *luchador* film. Wolf also appeared in a substantial role in *La bestia magnifica*, in production in 1952 but not released until May of 1953. It was a more proper *lucha libre* film, in fact also known under the title *Lucha libre*. The film is molded after American sports dramas which were popular in the 1950s (especially with low-budget filmmakers) and were often set in the seedy underbelly of either the boxing or pro wrestling world and revolving around some hungry young contender or desperate old has-been being tempted by crooked promoters and shady gangsters.

Although there were movies about other sports, those two in particular appealed to filmmakers thanks not only to their long history of corruption and deception but also to their curious blend of the romantic and the grotesque. What other sports could so effectively lend themselves to triumph and tragedy, to violence and beauty and the criminal element? Those rings, be they boxing or wrestling, those sweat-soaked locker rooms, smoke-filled arenas, back door deals and hustling gamblers, made for good drama. Plus, they were cheap to shoot and a lot easier to manage than, say, entire baseball teams or horse races.

Written by the director Chano Urueta, based on a story by Neftali Beltrán, *La bestia magnifica* sticks pretty close to this tried and true sports drama formula. No vampires or sexy space ladies in the genre yet, though Urueta would go on to play an important part in the development of Mexican cult cinema, directing several key films, including 1954's *La Bruja* (*The Witch*), Blue Demon's "coming out" movie *Demonio Azul*, and two of Blue's best adventures, *Blue Demon contra cerebros infernales* and *Blue Demon contra las diabolicas*, both in 1968. Leading man Crox Alvarado went on to star in an early lucha-horror hybrid, 1957's *Ladrón de cadáveres* (*The Body Snatcher*) as well as a trio of early mummy horror movies: *La momia azteca*, *La maldición de la momia azteca*, and *La momia azteca contra el robot humano*. Also starring in *La bestia magnifica* was one of Mexico's most famously tragic actresses, Miroslava Sternova, billed only as Miroslava. Like Wolf Ruvinskis, she was born in then-Czechoslovakia and, as a child, fled the Nazis, settling in Mexico City. A remarkable beauty, she turned beauty pageant victories into an acting career, working the gamut of genres comprising the Mexican film industry at the time, including 1951's *Streetwalker*, directed by one of pioneering women in the industry, Matilde Landeta. She found occasional work north of the border and also appeared in a seminal Mexican horror film, 1953's *El monstruo resucitado* (*The Monster*).

Of the remaining two films in that first class, René Cardona's *El enmascarado de plata* is the more legendary of the two, primarily because of who was supposed to be in it versus who actually ended up in it. It's also the only of these first four *luchador* films to embrace Republic serial style thrills and fantastic elements right out of the gate. El Santo's growing profile in the ring and in comic books led to the development of the film with the assumption that he would accept the lead role. He considered the project but ultimately decided it was destined to fail. As a result, *El enmascarado de plata* was left without *el enmascarado de plata*. Burned by the wrestler's rejection, director René Cardona scrambled to salvage the film.

The revamped movie didn't hit screens until 1954, long after the other films that had gone into production around the same time. Cardona replaced El Santo with another *luchador*, El Médico Asesino, and as a dig at El Santo retained the film's original title and turned the man in the silver mask into a villain. *El enmascarado de plata* wasn't a failure, despite El Santo's prediction, but El Santo wasn't particularly concerned. Most of Mexico was watching the increasingly intense in-ring feud between him and Blue Demon. They thrilled audiences with a series of dramatic matches that culminated, finally, in Blue Demon's triumph over the scoundrel who had humiliated Black Shadow. Backstage, El Santo was furious with the direction of the feud, feeling that he was the better and more popular performer. Although they would later be teamed up many times on screen as allies, the men behind the respective silver and blue masks retained animosity toward one another for the rest of their lives.

It's the fourth of this first class of films, *Huracán Ramírez*, that claimed the right to call itself the first *lucha libre* film. Released in February of 1953, it beat both *El enmascarado de plata* and *La bestia magnifica* to the movie houses. True, *El luchador fenómeno* was released in October of 1952, but that was a sports comedy. And really, it's nice for *Huracán Ramírez* to garner that historical accolade, because there's not much else worth recommending about the film.

Like *La bestia magnifica*, it's a sports drama of sorts. In fact, it only *barely* qualifies as a sports drama, with only a couple scenes involving wrestling and the lead donning the iconic mask of Huracán Ramírez. Most of the film is occupied with meandering family drama and middling (at its best) comedy surrounding the story of a father (Tonina Jackson, aka Héctor Garza, who competed in the ring under the names Tonina Jackson and Héctor Lozano, as well as the nickname *Cara de niño*) who works as a *luchador* and forbids his son to do the same.

Tonina's particularly irritated by a muscular, athletic new wrestler named Huracán Ramírez, who hides his true identity under a mask and constantly dodges the older wrestler's challenges. What Tonina doesn't know is that Ramirez is his own son, Fernando (David Silva), pursuing the life of a *luchador* against his father's wishes. The rest of the family includes Fernando's two sisters, insufferably precocious eight-year-old Margarita (Titina Romay, who just happens to be director Joselito Rodríguez's daughter) and sixteen-year-old Cata (Anabelle Gutiérrez, who appeared alongside Miroslava in 1954's *La visita que no tocó el timbre*). Margarita's primary character trait is endlessly and "hilariously" admonishing everyone. Cata's primary trait is that she has a crush on her father's nemesis, Huracán Ramírez—unaware that the mysterious masked man is her brother.

When he's not moonlighting as a wrestler—and for the vast majority of the film, he isn't—he's a singer in a local nightclub, where he takes his pay and hands it over to *luchadors* to convince them to take falls for his dad, keeping the old man's career going. The only ones who know the truth about Huracán Ramírez are his waitress girlfriend Laura (Carmelita González, who despite becoming a very successful and respected actress always seemed to have time for a Huracán Ramírez film) and her obnoxious younger brother Pichi (Freddy Fernández), who also serves as Fernando's comic relief sidekick, trainer, and when the situation calls for it, a fake Huracán Ramírez. Comedy ensues since Cata has a crush on Huracan while Pichi has a crush on Cata. Inevitably all these masquerades lead to Pichi being mistaken for the actual Huracán Ramírez and, in a bid to win the heart of Cata, ratting Fernando out. Eventually, Fernando as Huracán Ramírez finds himself in the ring against his own father who, not knowing it's his son behind the mask, is duly impressed by Ramirez' in-ring prowess. They agree to form a tag team, facing off against a team of *rudo*s including El Médico Asesino, the masked wrestler with an evil doctor theme and who will play an important part in the history of *luchador* films when he replaces El Santo in *El enmascarado de plata*.

Before the big match, local thugs kidnap one of the sisters, lending Huracán Ramírez the only element of its plot that could tie it in any significant way to the rest of lucha cinema or even to the "seedy underbelly of sports" films that inspired it. The two *luchadors* head off to rescue the unfortunate girl, and Fernando/Ramirez is slashed in the leg during the ensuing brawl. Apparently not one known for his powers of deductions, Tonina doesn't figure out the ruse when he returns home and discovers Fernando being treated for exactly the same wound Huracán Ramírez suffered during the rescue operation.

Oblivious to the obvious, Tonina heads off for the big tag-team match and is angry when Ramirez no-shows. A substitute is found and the match progresses. Huracan eventually shows up to take his rightful place in the ring. Unfortunately, El Médico Asesino is an *evil* doctor instead of a good one, and rather than calling a halt to the match and tending to Huracán's wounded leg, he targets it (having been tipped off by a jilted chorus girl from Fernando's nightclub gig), eventually subduing and unmasking Ramirez. Realizing that it's his own son in there fighting the fight under the mask of Huracán Ramírez, Tonina storms the ring and clears house, saving his son and winning the match.

Two characteristics of what was to become the *luchador* film industry were developed during *Huracán Ramírez*. The first was the conflict between established *luchadors* as cinematic characters (El Santo, Blue Demon) and *luchadors* made up specifically for a movie (Huracán Ramírez). Second was the screen-to-ring crossover of these *luchadors*, regardless of whether they existed previously or were invented for a movie. Several wrestlers that were the invention of screenwriters, Huracán Ramírez among them, became actual *luchadors* competing in live events, sometimes inhabited by the same man (or men) who played them in the films and sometimes "sold" to a wrestler by whichever film company held the rights to the character. Fernando was played by David Silva, an actor who would go on to play a major role in Mexican cult cinema, including reprising his role as Fernando in a couple belated Huracán Ramírez sequels, the first of which, *El misterio de Huracán Ramírez*, came out a decade after the original. During the ensuing decade, Huracán Ramírez had proven more popular and more dynamic in the actual lucha ring than he had in the film. But that Huracán Ramírez, the one who set foot into the squared circle in front of live audiences, wasn't David Silva. It was Eduardo Bonada, who also happened to be the man who doubled for Silva in *Huracán Ramírez*' action scenes. As a tie-in to the movie, Bonada was contracted to appear at wrestling events as Ramirez, which is the one aspect of the movie that would become part and parcel of the strange world of *lucha* cinema: the idea that a screen persona could step off the screen and into actual wrestling events.

Subsequent lucha films are often compared to comic book superhero movies, with an array of masked strongmen matching wits against an army of outlandish villains and monsters. But what makes the lucha film unique is the commitment to the personae—the *kayfabe*, if you will—shown by the stars. In some cases, as with El Santo, it was an established wrestler who finds his persona adapted for the cinematic world. For others, like Huracán Ramírez, it's a character conceived for a movie then co-opted for the real world. It's a bit like if Chris Hemsworth was cast as Thor in *Avengers* but then, from that day on, lived his life as the character of Thor, never appearing out of costume or out of character. Or, from another angle, it would be like Batman going to his job at Wayne Industries every day not in the guise of Bruce Wayne, but as Batman, in full costume. Even during staff meetings and face-to-faces with clients.

It is this blurring of the division between screen and reality, however, that helped make the masked heroes of the lucha film so popular, and it's fitting that they be practitioners of professional wrestling, something that has itself always blurred the lines between fantasy (scripted outcomes, larger than life characters) and reality (the actual physical demands of being able to perform in the ring and endure a life that, behind the scenes, is every bit as harsh as that of and old time traveling vaudevillian). It's one thing to watch Huracán Ramírez in a movie. It's quite another, especially for a kid or people in a small town with very little else to amuse them, for this movie character to suddenly show up in your town, willing to perform for you in the ring. Rural some of these places might have been, but the people weren't unsophisticated. They knew they were getting a show, just like they knew later when they went to see El Santo movies that the flying saucers and vampire bats were hanging from strings; for them, as for later viewers, it was part of the fun. It was something to talk about.

Eduardo Bonada eventually gave up the Huracán Ramírez identity under the rationale that he was a pretty good looking guy, so it was a waste to hide that handsome face under a mask. To the horror of filmmakers José Rodríguez and his son Juan Rodríguez Mas, who had made *Huracán Ramírez* and thus owned the rights to the character and mask design both onscreen and in real life, Bonada revealed his true identity in public, announcing that he was through obscuring himself with a sweaty lucha mask and was ready to do business as Eduardo Bonada. Despite indeed being a handsome fellow, he didn't appear to enjoy much success once he came out from behind the Huracán Ramírez mask, appearing mostly as a henchman

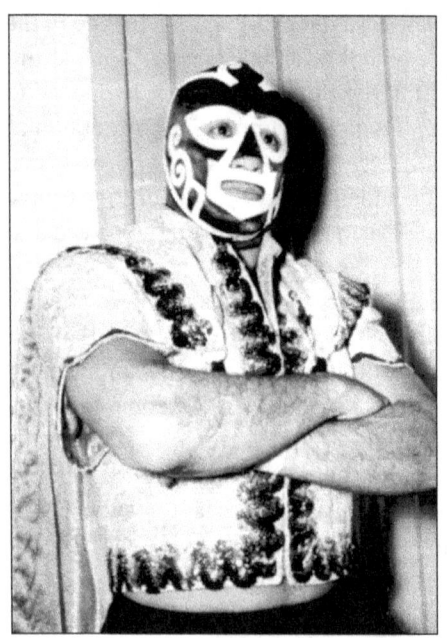
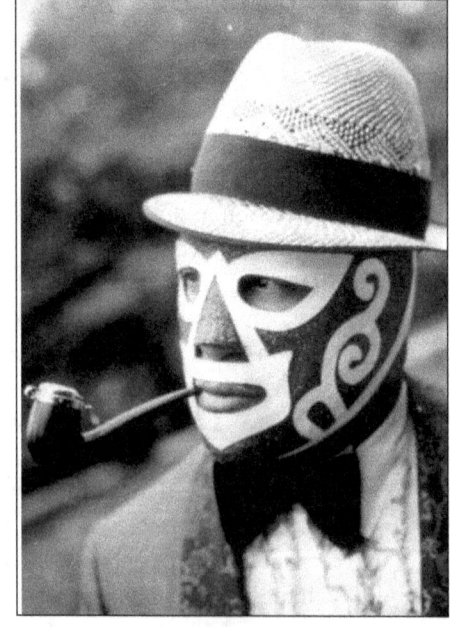

or a monster in a slew of lucha films including: *La venganza de la sombra* (1962), starring La Sombra Vengadora; the Santo films *Santo contra los zombies* (1962), *Santo vs. La Invasión de los marcianos* (1967), and *Santo el enmascarado de plata vs los villanos del ring* (1968); and the Blue Demon films *La sombra del murciélago* (1968), *Blue Demon contra cerebros infernales* (1968), and *Blue Demon y Zovek en La invasión de los muertos* (1973). Despite abandoning the persona, he also appeared in one more Huracán Ramírez movie, *El misterio de Huracán Ramírez*, but as a different, lesser character than the masked wrestler he helped create.

After Bonada's departure, the world of *lucha libre* suffered a flood of men claiming to be Huracán Ramírez, which the Rodríguez' fervently tried to stamp out. To stem the tide of false Huracáns, they held an open tryout to find the next, true Huracán Ramírez. The job went to a young *luchador* named Daniel García, though that was a closely guarded secret. Bonada's public unmasking had done damage to the mystique of the character but was nothing that couldn't be repaired as long as they closely managed the persona of the new Ramirez. Garcia as Huracán Ramírez made his in-ring debut against, fatefully, El Médico Asesino. With Garcia under the mask, Huracán Ramírez' popularity soared, thanks in no small part to an arsenal of high-flying acrobatic moves, the most impressive of which—the *huracanrana*—is still used by pro wrestlers looking to add something impressive to their retinue. Thanks to Garcia/Ramírez' popularity with crowds, and the rise in the 1960s of lucha movies stars like La Sombra Vengadora and El Santo, who skyrocketed to cinematic fame in 1962 with the triple punch of *Santo contra los zombies*, *Santo contra el rey del crimen*, and the landmark *Santo vs. las mujeres vampiro* (AKA *Santo vs. the Vampire Women*), in 1962 the Rodríguezes decided to make a new Huracán Ramírez film, *El misterio de Huracán Ramírez*.

By this time the more fantastical elements of lucha cinema were beginning to assert themselves. Not only was 1962 the year El Santo matched muscle against both zombies and vampire women; beneath the mask of Neutron, Wolf Ruvinskis was tackling cartoonishly over-the-top serial-style mad scientists and super-villains. La Sombra Vengadora had been delivering similar serial thrills since as early as 1954. Despite the trend toward more outlandish content, *El misterio de Huracán Ramírez* sticks to the original Huracan plan and is another straight sports drama, albeit one with more of what people expected from such films (namely, scumbag gangsters and *lucha libre* matches).

Right out of the gate, *El misterio* starts with a bang, as Ramirez is wrapping up a match when a thug in the audience suddenly stands up and opens fire, hitting Ramirez in the arm. The wound only enrages Huracán Ramírez, who gives chase to the fleeing hood. During a pretty good fist fight, the gun-toting gangster gets the drop on Ramirez and, holding him at gunpoint, demands the *luchador* unmask himself. Ramirez then proceeds to instruct the gangster on why, if you have a gun you should not stand within grappling distance of a guy who is well-trained in the art of unarmed combat. With Ramirez dangling from the side of the building, he finds time to reflect on the past and how he came to be in this precarious position. Cue the flashback and a clever transition that sees Ramirez hanging from the side of the building wavy fade to Ramirez hanging from the top rope of a wrestling ring.

All of which is a far better and more dynamic opening than the original. Under the mask of Huracán Ramírez, Daniel Garcia turns in a high-energy fight scene and, immediately afterward, a good wrestling match with a lot of acrobatic moves.

It's after this match that we're introduced to the gangster we eventually see taking pot shots at Ramírez. He's the Prince (Carlos Agostí), a gangster obsessed with discovering the identity of Huracán Ramírez. Prince and his goon squad even barge into Ramirez' locker room after the match and rough up his manager. The crafty *luchador* doesn't take kindly to Prince's strong-arm techniques, and at one point in the confrontation even pulls a gun of his own on the gangster. Prince, being a classic fist-shaking sort of fella, isn't one to let this slight go unavenged.

Prince's crusade to discover the secret identity of Huracán Ramírez reflects, with more sniveling and aggression, the position of the viewer. David Silva returns for the role of Fernando, but we soon discover that in the years since the first film he has retired, started a family, and sold Huracán Ramírez to a new wrestler who has done so well under the mask that he's purchased his own arena. Or *has* Fernando retired? Tonina Jackson, Carmelita González, Titina Romay and Freddy Fernández all return from the original film, and since this is still a Huracán Ramírez film, the action-packed, gangster-filled opening eventually gives way to a lot of goofy family comedy.

Although lucha film fans who enjoy watching wrestlers duke it out with robots and vampires will still be disappointed by the lack of phantasmagoria, as a more straight-laced sports 'n' gangsters film, *El misterio de Huracán Ramírez* is entertaining. A subplot sees Tonina and Fernando's karate student son getting involved in the wrestling world, which involves the son wearing an ill-fitting mask and little hat. Even under the shirt he wears in the ring, you can still tell he transforms from a slightly dumpy teenager into a physically fit young man during the wrestling scenes. Everything about *El misterio de Huracán Ramírez* is an improvement over the first. It's faster paced with more action, which is better staged and filmed than the meager action scenes in the first film. Prince is a great scumbag villain. This is also one of the only movies you'll see where someone is killed by laundry. The film also boasts the appearance of Nathanael León, the hulking bald wrestler who appeared in a truly staggering number of lucha movies, including a bunch of Santo and Blue Demon films as well as some of the *luchador*a—female wrestlers—movies, straight horror, spy movies, and even an episode of *I Spy*.

After *El misterio de Huracán Ramírez*, the Rodríguezes didn't wait as long for another sequel as they had the first time, though four years is still an awful long time in a genre where the top stars could appear in three four, even five or more movies in a single year. But it was 1966 before Huracán Ramírez returned to the screen in *El Hijo del Huracán Ramírez*. Once again the film eschews the monsters and Martians that had firmly become part and parcel of the lucha film, though *El Hijo* does open with a carload full of masked *luchadors* pulling an armored car heist. The whole gang is back again, including Pepe Romay as Fernando's son Panchito (who eventually inherits the mantle of Huracán Ramírez from his father) and Daniel García under the mask.

Sadly, despite the promising *luchador* heist opening, the rest of the movie is a big step down from *El misterio*, with a lot more bad comedy, uneven pacing, the return of undercranked action scenes, and Pepe Romay mugging for the camera in a way that is less Jerry Lewis, more Sammy Petrillo. There is a battle royale where all the wrestlers are dressed in drag (because who hasn't been hoping to see big Tonina Jackson in a dress?), but that's cold comfort for enduring the rest of the film. *La Venganza de Huracán Ramírez* followed the next year in 1967, the first of the series to be in color. It seems from the opening credit sequence that several years' worth of Santo and Blue Demon battling mad scientists and vampires has finally made an impact on Huracán Ramírez (who, despite being a big name in *lucha libre*, never appeared in a film with either Blue or Santo, or even Mil Mascaras).

As spooky horror movie music plays, the camera pans across all the accoutrements of a world-class mad science lair: jars of scorpions and spiders, gratuitous gila monsters, human skulls, and most important of all, beakers full of bubbling liquid. Unfortunately, there's also a splash of animal cruelty, including a dead dog being dragged around and a cat that gets a shot from a hypo and goes into a fit. Animal cruelty such as this isn't uncommon in cinema, especially in decades and countries where sensitivity to such acts was or is not as pronounced. One sometimes has to either grimace and bear it or elect not to keep watching. Whatever the case, it's an oddly exploitive bit of sadism for a series that has, up until this point, been relatively squeaky clean and family friendly.

The experiments are conducted by a trio of haggard looking weirdos, one of whom caresses a python. After that gruesome intro, we're in for one more shock as we cut to the now familiar diner set and discover that Panchito has grown into Pancho (Pepe Romay) and now sports a little mustache. David Silva and Carmelita González are on hand as well, as are Freddy Fernandez and Tonina Jackson in what would sadly be his final role (he died in 1969 at the age of 48). The *Huracán Ramírez* nightclub scenes have been replaced by go-go dancing, but other than that and despite that creepy, uncomfortable intro, the film quickly settles into familiar Huracán Ramírez territory. The mad science was a fake-out, just an attempt to synthesize a drug that would help the trio fix wrestling matches. When your next-door neighbor mad scientists in other films are resurrecting witch queens, fighting draculas, and sneaking werewolves into wrestling matches, common doping seem pedestrian by comparison.

As in past films, most of the comedy is middling at best, but the film does deliver a decent pie fight. Then, just as you think you're in for another slightly dull but moderately watchable Huracán Ramírez movie, the final match comes along and, out of nowhere, goes full lucha movie bonkers, complete with a Dr. Jekyll/Mr. Hyde twist. That, Pancho's new mustache, and the pie fight would have been enough to make this one slightly more entertaining than *El Hijo*, but it's difficult to reconcile the series' good humor (even if it doesn't feature "good" humor) with all the cat torture.

La Venganza was David Silva's final outing as Fernando. He went on to roles in some of the most important and confounding entries in the canon of Mexican cult cinema. He remained active in lucha films, even if not in the role that launched the entire genre. He appeared in the zany spy/superhero mash-up *Las Mujer Murcielago* (*The Batwoman*) with genre staple Maura Monti. He teamed up with *luchador* Mil Mascaras to stop mad Nazi circus leader (it's complicated) David Carradine in *Enigma of Death*. He commanded an army of superhuman dwarves that matched muscle with Blue Demon and Mil Mascaras in *Champions of Justice*. He played the police inspector in the classic psychotronic horror film *The Brainiac* (1961). But perhaps most notable, in the 1970s he worked with two of the leading luminaries of alternative cinema: Alejandro Jodorowsky, for whom he worked in *El Topo* and *Holy Mountain*; and Juan López Moctezuma, appearing in *Mansion of Madness* and *Alucarda*.

Despite Silva's departure, Huracán Ramírez still had two films under his belt: 1973's *Huracán Ramírez y la Monjita Negra* (*Hurricane Ramirez and the Black Nun*) and 1974's *De Sangre Chicana* (*Of Chicano Blood*). Despite being in color and attempting to tap into activist trends of the day to lend themselves an air of social *gravitas*, neither of these late entries have much to offer. Lucha films, by then, had run their course anyway. Despite this, in each appearances under the mask, Daniel García is fantastic. It's no wonder he became a sensation on the lucha circuit. He wrestled as Huracán Ramírez for decades, retiring in 1989, at which time the identity was supposed to be passed on to another wrestler—a bit like pulp hero the Phantom, whose persona is passed from one man to the next, creating the illusion of an ever-present and unaging hero. The transition did not go smoothly. The Rodríguez family retained rights to Huracán Ramírez, including all profits from action figures, replica masks, comic books, and other merchandise. Figuring he'd put three decades into the character, not to mention breathing life into the mask and turning Ramirez into an in-ring phenomena, Garcia thought he was entitled to a piece of the Huracán Ramírez profits after he hung up the tights. The Rodríguezes disagreed.

For all those decades, Huracán's true identity was a closely-guarded secret. When the Rodríguezes refused to cut Garcia in on royalties, he retaliated by unmasking in public, shattering the illusion and throwing the Rodríguezes plans into disarray. When Bonada unmasked, Huracán Ramírez was popular but not a superstar. With García in the tights, Ramirez became one of the legends of *lucha libre*, so it was more difficult to recover this time around.

In the wake of Garcia's retirement, a new wrestler would still assume the official mantle of Huracán Ramírez, but he would not enjoy the same level of success. In addition, there was another flurry of false Huracáns and unsanctioned Huracan spin-offs and cash-ins, including Huracán Ramírez II, Huracán Ramírez Jr., and el Hijo de Huracán Ramírez. 1989 saw the release of *Huracán Ramírez contra los Terroristas,*. Very few people were interested, though whether that's because of Garcia's public unmasking or because lucha films simply weren't en vogue anymore is debatable.

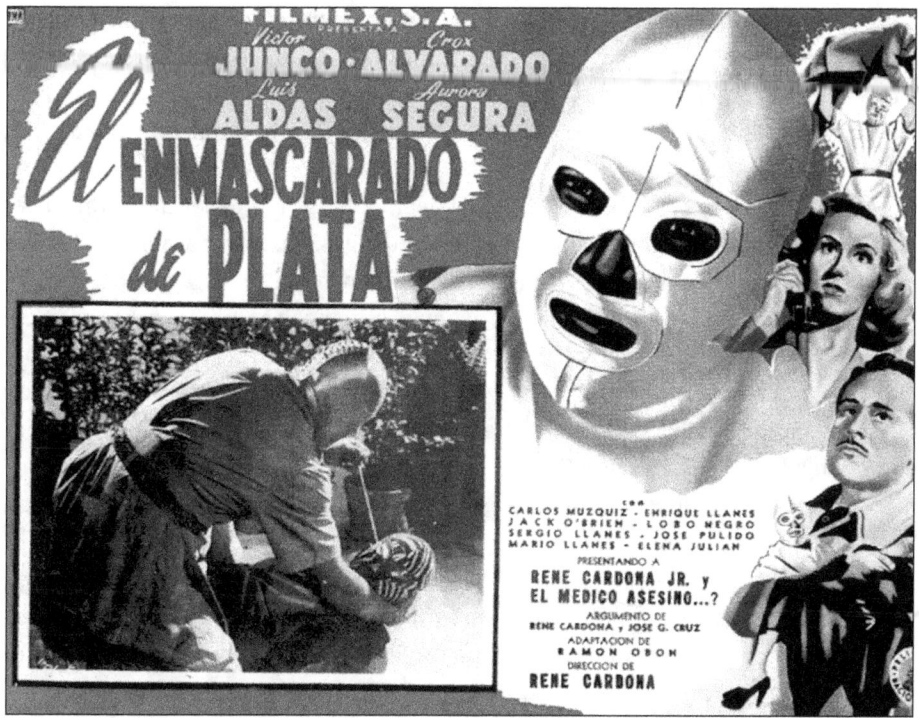

The Silver Maskless Silver Mask Serial

Besides being famous as the Santo film in which Santo decided not to appear, *El enmascarado de plata* contributed a few key elements that became common to many *luchador* movies to come. The most notable is the action-oriented plot. *La bestia magnifica* and *Huracán Ramírez* patterned themselves after sports dramas, but *El enmascarado de plata* looks to the serial thrills of series like *Spy Smasher*, *The Phantom Creeps*, and anything where a mysterious hero battles an equally mysterious villain and a science lab explodes. Serials had been around since the early 1910s, and even then the emphasis was on mystery and stunts. There wasn't a lot of character development you could do given the circumstances under which serials were created, but you could have Pearl White hang from a hot air balloon or Helen Holmes jump onto a moving train.

As the film industry grew more sophisticated, serials declined in popularity. They were still made throughout the 1920s, but it wasn't until the middle of the 1930s, with the advent of sound pictures, that serials enjoyed a true resurgence. As has been the case in the 1910s, the emphasis of this next generation of serials was on action and "cliffhanger" endings in which each episode ends with the apparent certain death of the hero. Serials were themselves an outgrowth of pulp magazines and comic books. Many of the biggest serials featured familiar faces from the page: Dick Tracy, The Phantom, The Shadow, even Batman and Captain America.

Besides stunts, serials were the first major science fiction productions in the US industry. Certainly, there were science fiction films made during the silent era, but most of those had been European. There was a smattering of science fiction in the

1930s, but for the most part, science fiction was the purview of the serials like *Flash Gordon* and *Buck Rogers* (both starring Buster Crabbe), and they embraced it with gusto. Even crime serials started integrating elements of sci-fi into their stories. Every gang of thugs owned at least one "mad science lair" or radio-controlled robot or other fanciful gadget.

They also borrowed a cliché that had been popular in the serials of the latter half of the 1910s: the hooded villain. Entire campaigns were built around audiences guessing the identity of the menacing masked villain in the 1910s, and what worked then worked equally well in the 1930s, when pretty much anything was a welcome diversion from grinding poverty and social collapse of the Great Depression. Curiously, the Mexican film industry never embraced the serial as a domestic product and produced very few of them, even as Mexican heroes like Zorro were swashbuckling weekly across US theater screens. When, in 1951, writer-director René Cardona started developing the story that became *El enmascarado de plata*, a lot had changed. For starters, the Mexican film industry was in a period of rapid decline after the "golden age" had been severely hampered by increased government censorship of controversial topics. Second, television was starting to impact the daily lives of many, exposing them to the episodic structure of television programming. Third, *lucha libre* had been chased off those same TV sets, not to return until the 1990s.

Citing the perennial "protecting the children," stewards of Mexican morality determined *lucha libre*'s ongoing battles between *tecnicos* and *rudos* to be inappropriate for children, especially given the human propensity for getting excited about the bad guy. What sort of image did it project to have a bunch of Mexican youths strutting around in imitation of their favorite *rudo*? Throughout the first half of the 1950s, the government began instituting regulations that effectively banned *lucha libre* from the airwaves. They couldn't shut down the live shows; that would be too drastic a step. But they could certainly make sure it wasn't beamed conveniently into homes and bars with TVs.

Filmmakers, however, weren't affected by the ban. Given the operatic *lucha libre* storylines, it seemed a great time to bring the masks to the screen. *La bestia magnifica* and *Huracán Ramírez* were content to treat the sport as a sport, and be movies about that sport, but Cardona decided to take a different approach. Instead of making a movie about *lucha libre*, he would take inspiration from the titanic struggles of good vs. evil that took place in the ring and combine it with the popularity of action-oriented comic books to cast *luchadors* as crime-fighting superheroes rather than as regular *luchadors*. For Cardona, a masked wrestler like Santo could be the equivalent of Batman or the Shadow. Cardona's movie wouldn't be about wrestlers wrestling; instead, it would adapt the look and personality of wrestlers but cast them as comic book heroes and villains. El Santo, the man Cardona wanted for his film, might wrestle, but his true vocation was fighting crime. There was just one problem: El Santo wasn't interested.

Depending on who is talking, the man in the silver mask turned down becoming "El enmascarado de plata" either because he wasn't convinced that he had screen appeal and so would be wasting his time, or he wasn't convinced that a superhero *luchador* movie would succeed and so would be wasting his time. Whatever the case, Cardona was flabbergasted to discover that he had a movie called *El enmascarado de plata* but didn't have the Silver Mask. Along with writing partners José G. Cruz and Ramón Obón, Cardona scrambled to rewrite the project, resulting in delays that allowed both *Huracán Ramírez* and *La bestia magnifica* to beat it to the screen. It wasn't until 1954 that Cardona completed and released *El enmascarado de plata*, and in that time a few notable things about it had changed. It was still called *El enmascarado de plata*, but the silver mask of the title was no longer the hero. In what everyone cites as a bit of revenge for Santo backing out, Cardona made the man in the silver mask into a villain. And not only that, he wasn't even the main villain, just a second in command who gets flung off a cliff about halfway through the film, leaving the remainder of the runtime to the film's boss villain, El Tigre. The mysterious masked hero was now played by a *luchador* named El Médico Asesino—the very man Huracán Ramírez locked up against in the finale of that film.

El Médico Asesino was one of a new generation of *luchadors* who had been created specifically to succeed not so much at live events as on television. The Televicentro promotion, a rival to EMLL, was by its very name dedicated to developing *lucha libre* for TV rather than live audiences (too bad *lucha libre* would find itself banned from TV shortly thereafter). The man who would become El Médico Asesino, Cesáreo González Manriquez, started in the business as a timekeeper and referee, but his size guaranteed that sooner or later, someone would think to put him in the ring.

That someone was *luchador* turned promoter Giraldo del Hierro. Cesáreo, like just about everyone, wrestled under a number of different personae before donning a mask for the first time and becoming El Asesino, clad all in black. Unfortunately, he lost the mask in a match, and his fortunes declined until Televicentro put a different mask on him, gave him a doctor's bag, and dubbed him El Médico Asesino. The Killer Doctor. He debuted in this new persona on February 9, 1952, teaming with *La bestia magnfica*'s Wolf Ruvinskis to beat Enrique Llanes and Tonina Jackson, who played the father in *Huracán Ramírez*. The weird gimmick was enough to garner him the popularity that had until then eluded him; to "put him over," as they say in the wrestling business. When Cardona came calling for a *luchador* to replace El Santo in *El enmascarado de plata*, the made-for-television persona of El Médico Asesino seemed as good a choice as any.

He wasn't. El Santo didn't miss much by not appearing in *El enmascarado de plata*, but one wonders what *El enmascarado de plata* could have been with El Santo. Or if Cardona has hired a more able performer than El Médico Asesino, someone like Wolf Ruvinskis, for example, or Fernando Osés (who would come to play a major role in the full realization of the lucha movie just a short time later).

El Médico Asesino was popular in the ring because the idea of a crazy wrestling doctor was so strange, and because he was a big guy. He was never considered a particularly dynamic wrestler. In *El enmascarado de plata*, he proves he's not much of a dynamic actor either. No one looks at Santo and praises his acting ability, but he certainly had *charisma* and screen presence. El Médico Asesino possesses no such presence. He's a lump in the middle of the screen, moving slowly and never generating anything approaching excitement. Later Santo films would sometimes cut from the plot to scenes of Santo in the ring, doing his job, since he was often still employed as a wrestler in the films. It's a shame this one doesn't cut from time to time to El Médico Asesino in the E.R., doing legitimate hospital work before getting called away on a mission. At least that would provide some amusement.

He fumbles through the fight scenes, which are frequent and uninspired, consisting mostly of rudimentary fist fights and guys sneaking up and hitting each other in the back of the head. The stunts, when they come, are mostly unspectacular as well, consisting of things like El Médico Asesino about to vault through a window or from a car then cutting to him pretending to land. His doctor's scrubs lend him none of the majesty that would come from Santo's wonderful cape or the lean athletic appearance of Wolf Ruvinskis (El Médico Asesino being neither lean nor particularly athletic). Instead, he looks like a *luchador* who showed up to the fight still dressed in his pajamas. He's the number one problem in *El enmascarado de plata*, but he's not the *only* problem. René Cardona structures the film like a serial, complete with fake "chapters" and cliffhanger "endings" (it was never actually

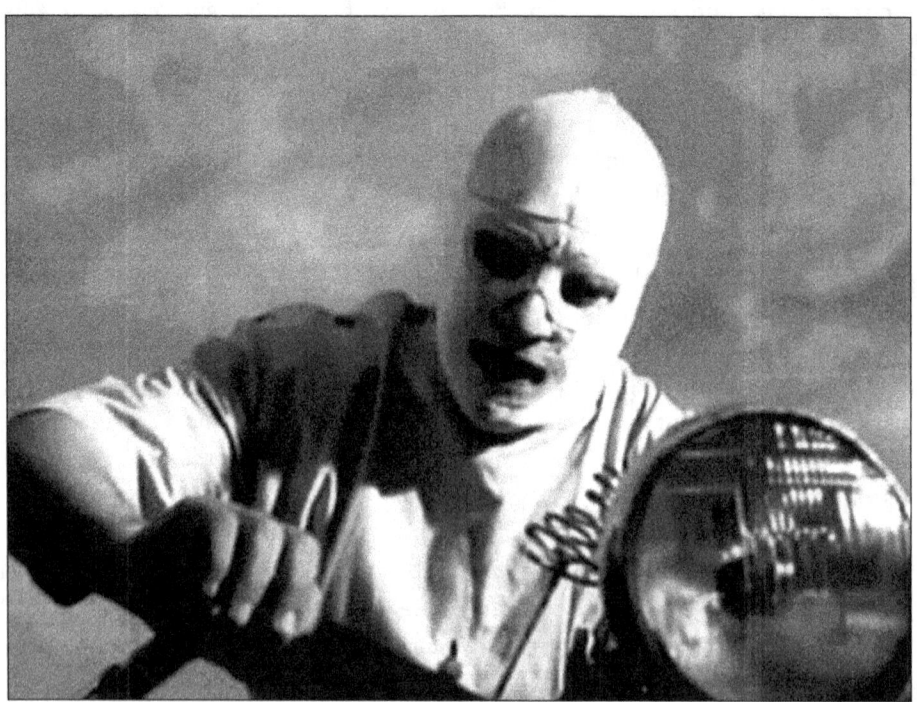

screened as a serial, though). The problem there is that serials are formulaic and often repetitive, and they depend on the passage of time between new episodes to help audiences forget that they're seeing more or less the same thing over and over. When that repetition happens within the confines of a feature film, however, it becomes much more noticeable. Plus, a cliffhanger ending only really works if you have to wait a week to find out what happens next. If you build to a cliffhanger, and then it's resolved in the next shot, it tends to lack any power, especially if the build-up isn't good at building tension. But the real nail in *El enmascarado de plata*'s coffin is the run time. Serials could be long because you were watching them spread out over many weeks. Cardona, in compressing a serial into a feature film, doesn't compress it enough. *El enmascarado de plata* is two hours long. Two hours long in a genre that often got its business finished in 70-80 minutes. And it's not two hours long because there's so much going on. It just is. It lumbers on with no real point, repeating itself, padding itself out, even switching villains part way through.

It's a shame, because the core of *El enmascarado de plata* is a potentially thrilling film, and René Cardona was no rookie. He should have made a better film. But given the monkeywrench Santo threw into the works when he decided to turn the movie down, perhaps we can cut Cardona and *El enmascarado de plata* a little bit of slack. Parts of it are entertaining, after all, and manage to successfully realize the thrills of serials. The movie opens with a mysterious gloved hand—and what a magnificent glove it is—controlling some sort of doomsday device that can disrupt the weather, destroy buildings, and accomplish sundry other diabolical acts. In short order, we learn the machine is the property of a nefarious gang of hoodlums who take their orders from a masked madman named El enmascarado de plata, the Silver Mask. The exploits of the gang, which also include kidnapping, are covered and occasionally foiled by two intrepid reporters named Alfredo (Víctor Junco) and Julio (Crox Alvarado, yet another alumnus of *La bestia magnifica*). The real thorn in the gang's side is the masked vigilante El Médico Asesino, who shows up more or less at random and sometimes from the strangest of places (emerging out of someone's bedroom without any explanation). The audience is supposed to wonder which of the two reporters moonlights as El enmascarado de plata even though neither of them looks a thing like him (totally different mouth and nose, to say nothing of physique). This means the movie has a lot of scenes of Médico lumbering off after a fight so that a minute later Julio or Alfredo can dash in, adjusting a tie and looking suspiciously disheveled.

Carlos Múzquiz plays a standard-issue gangster leading all the bad guys who don't have masks, and René Cardona, Jr., who would become a major player in Mexican genre cinema, co-stars as El Médico Asesino's teenage sidekick Pecas (and looks better in the fight scenes than El Médico Asesino). The titular Silver Mask, villain of the piece, gets dumped over the side of a cliff during a scuffle with El Médico Asesino at about the halfway point through the film. He's unmasked to no real circumstance, but before the heroes can celebrate their victory, yet another masked maniac pulls up and announces that he was the boss all along!

And then it all starts over again, but at least this new villain, El Tigre, is a sight to behold. Clad in a striking tiger stripe mask and accompanying gloves (that skirt awful close to furry mittens), El Tigre completes his look by donning a snappy fedora and, when he's out on the town, trenchcoat. Like El Médico Asesino, he has a science lab full of beakers full of bubbling liquid and Jacob's ladders and computers. And like El Médico Asesino's lab, it is never used as for actual mad science. It exists simply as a set that can be trashed, set on fire, and explode.

Despite the signature wrestling mask, El Tigre has almost nothing to do with *lucha libre* and is instead a villain straight out of the pulps. And really, if you're going to shroud your face, a lucha mask and trench coat seems much more versatile than a big pointy hood and wizard robes. The sheer spectacle of El Tigre almost makes up for El Médico Asesino's lack of charisma and fighting prowess, but it's still a long road to travel before reaching the end of El enmascarado de plata, and the drive often takes you through pretty dull territory. Like Huracán Ramírez and La bestia magnifica, El enmascarado de plata is watchable primarily because of its historical importance in the development of the genre. The first two brought the *luchadors*, while El enmascarado de plata brought the serial formula. El Médico Asesino, for all his weakness as a leading *luchador*, also has the honor of being the first ring-to-screen lucha star, as opposed to being a character created purely for the screen. Even if he was created primarily for the television screen, at least he was as a guy who wrestled in a wrestling promotion. There was, however, something still missing from the lucha formula. Something weirder, more sinister. Well, more sinister, anyway. It's hard to get much weirder than El Tigre strutting around in his fabulous mask, overcoat, and hat.

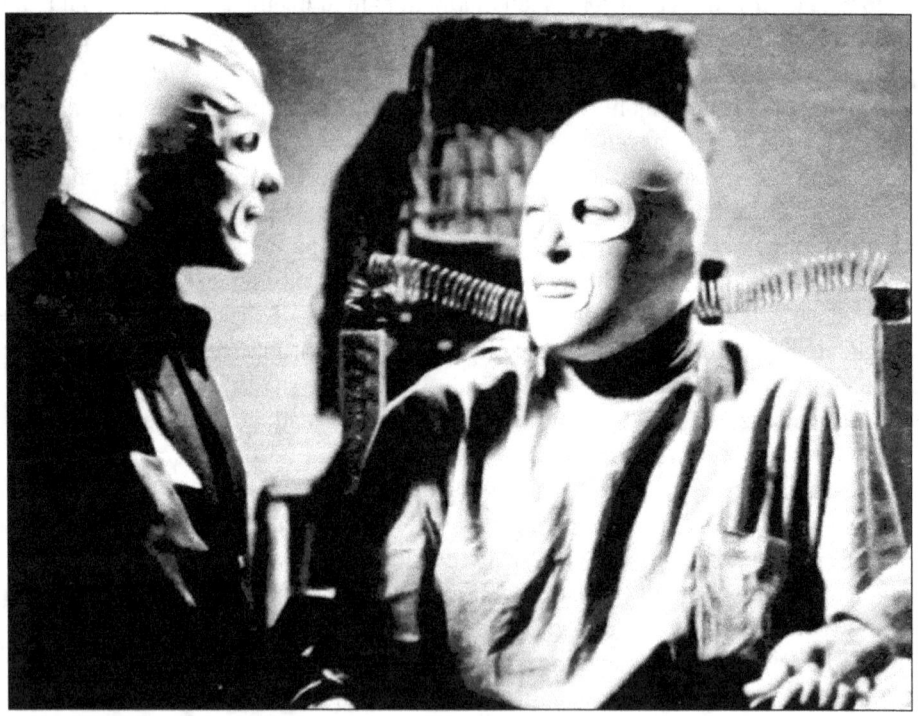

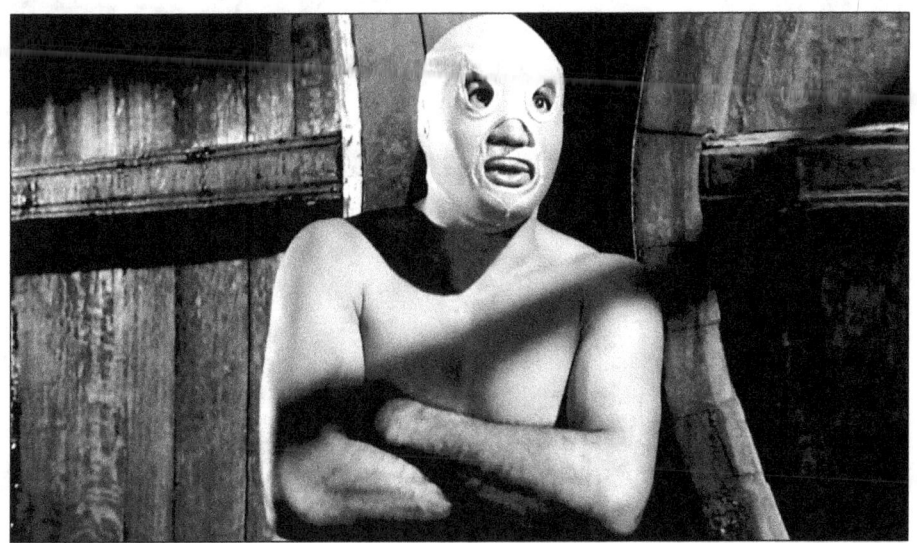

Cuba (Lucha) Libre

It wasn't until 1958 that El Santo found his way onto the screen after blowing off René Cardona in 1952. Another wrestler, Fernando Osés (who did not wear a mask), was looking to launch his own career with a series of films in which he played a masked super-cop named El Incognito with a similarly masked sidekick. Osés convinced El Santo to play the sidekick, and two films—*El Cerebro del Mal* (*The Evil Brain*) and *Hombres Infernales* (*The Infernal Men*)—were made in Cuba on the eve of the Revolution and released in 1958. Neither film made much of an impact. Relegated to a supporting role, El Santo failed also to make much of an impact. *Hombres Infernales* is a particularly brutal film in that 90% of it seems to be filler. Never has a film been so fond of showing you someone driving from the beginning of their route to the very end. Likewise, few films so enthusiastically embrace long, long close-ups of people "reacting"—usually smiling or doing the "oh no, not that" panic face. You want to watch someone eat dinner from appetizer to dessert? *Hombres Infernales* has you covered. Like watching guys nap in hammocks? Then this is the movie for you. For everyone else, including fans of El Santo, *Hombres Infernales* is worth watching purely for historic purposes, and even then it's not entirely worth the time. Somewhere beneath the incidentals is a story about drug smuggling and an undercover cop. El Santo, as an operative of some international organization, swims up to a dock every fifteen minutes or so to punch someone and look at the camera, almost as if saying, "I know, I know. But at least I just punched a guy."

If you want a glimpse at Cuba in the twilight of its pre-Revolution casino culture, you'll get a taste of that. Much of the film's inaction takes place around the Hotel Capri and it's associated casino. The Capri was infamous before the Revolution and it managed to stay infamous clear up to 2017. Opened in November 1957, it was one of the largest hotels and casino in Havana at the time, with American actor (with many a rumored tie to the Mafia) George Raft as its face. It was owned by legitimate businessman Santo Trafficante Jr. from Tampa. Trafficante was a guy with friends in low places, including Sam Giancana, boss of the "Chicago Outfit" and one of the attendees of the Havana Conference in December of 1946, which was organized at the behest of New York boss Charlie "Lucky" Luciano to sort out the Family business in the US and Cuba. Also in attendance that week was Frank Sinatra. In fact, the official story was that the conference was really just a birthday party for Frank, who arrived in Havana in he company of Charlie, Rocco and Joseph "The Fish" Fischetti, two guys from Chicago who also happened to be cousins of Al Capone. Luciano, then exiled from the United States, was in attendance along with his longtime friend and business associate Meyer Lansky, who was an owner of another famous Havana hotel and casino, The Macional, just down the block from the Capri, as well as being an investor in Benjamin "Bugsy" Siegel's mad gamble to turn the backwater town of Las Vegas into a gaming mecca. In fact, one of the many items on the agenda for Sinatra's birthday party was discussing what to do with Siegel and his desert boondoggle, The Flamingo Hotel.

Trafficante was too young to be at the Havana Conference, but he was in attendance at another major Mob meeting a decade later known as the Apalachin meeting (Frank Sinatra did not perform). Held in the sleepy town of Apalachin, New York, one of the primary purposes of the convocation was to decide how best to fill the power vacuum left by the sudden demise of a trigger man named Albert Anastasia, one of the bosses of a New York outfit known as Murder, Inc. Unfortunately, local police got curious about all the fancy cars with out-of-state license plates rolling through town and decided to pay a visit to the estate to which they were all heading, which happened to be owned by a guy named Joseph "Joe the Barber" Barbara. Finding the grounds crawling with known gangsters, suspected Mafiosos, and wanted felons, a raid took place, sending well-heeled mobsters scattering into the woods. But twenty of them proved not to be fleet enough of foot to elude the local constabulary, among them Trafficante, who had just opened the Capri in Havana. Unfortunately, just getting together and hanging around turned out not to be much of a crime. Every mobster arrested that day had their sentences overturned. Trafficante, though often suspected and several times arrested, always beat the system. He never served a day in prison.

While he was dealing with that, a Mexican-Cuban film crew was prowling around his crown jewel hotel shooting *Hombres Infernales*, in which Joaquín Cordero stars as a cop infiltrating a drug smuggling ring. El Santo appears—in mask and tights, which is never regarded by anyone as odd—as a fellow cop whose job consists mostly of extricating Cordero from precarious situations and picking up the remarkable number of matchbooks with secret messages scrawled in them that get scattered about in this movie. Santo doesn't get very much screen time, since the film's director, Joselito Rodríguez (who also directed the

Huracán Ramírez films), is far more interested in scenes of cars traveling down city streets and people sitting on patios looking at other people sitting on other patios. The film is boring, cheap, and shoddily made even by the standards of early Santo efforts. Joaquín Cordero became one of the most prolific actors in Mexican cinema, but no reason for his popularity could be mined from *Hombres Infernales*, though that's no fault of his. He's an able and handsome performer. It's just that, while he has much more screen time, the film doesn't have anything more for him to do than it does El Santo.

Better was *Santo contra cerebro del mal*, if not by much. Shot concurrently with the same cast and crew, it benefits from more Santo screen time, more action, and more of the trappings of lucha cinema, including a mad scientist, secret labs, and that genre staple, mind control. Don't worry, fans of long shots of cars slowly driving. They still got you covered, along with anyone who was a fan of the castanet-heavy floor show at the Capri, which is back for a second round. *Cerebro del mal* is also better because it throws a second *luchador* into the mix.

While Santo, Cordero, and Rodríguez were busy making their two movies, a revolutionary tidal wave led by Fidel Castro and Che Guevara was sweeping toward Havana, Cuban President Fulgencio Batista, and Sam Trafficante's still-new Hotel Capri. In December of 1958, the forces of Castro and Guevara won a decisive victory against the Cuban army, resulting in President Batista's panicked flight from the country, trailing behind him a steady stream of hustler, mobsters, and others who had been calling Havana their personal playground

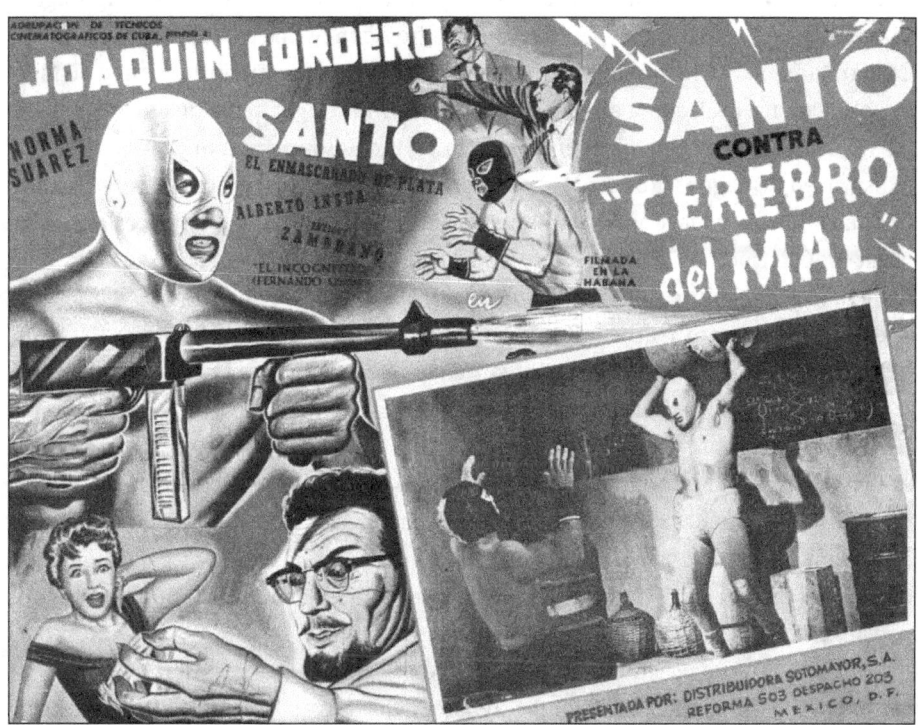

for decades. Suddenly victorious after a struggle that had begun in 1953 as little more than series of labor uprisings and guerrilla skirmishes, Guevara led Cuban revolutionary forces into Havana in January 2, 1959. A few days later Fidel Castro followed. Sam Trafficante's Capri had been open barely a year. It was nationalized by the Cuban government in October 1960, and the casino was closed. Since then, it has been renamed, closed, and reopened a number of times until 2014, when a Spanish company purchased it, undertook major renovations, and reopened it as the Hotel NH Capri La Habana.

The Capri served as home for a number of American who worked at the newly reopened US embassy, and in November of 2016, some of these Americans began complaining about mysterious headaches, dizzy spells, and other afflictions. Cuba-US relations, which were put on ice after the Revolution and had just began down the long road toward normalization under the Obama administration, suffered a setback when accusations were made that the Cuban intelligence service was using "sonic weapons" to sicken Americans at the Capri and the nearby embassy. No proof surfaced of such an attack, but that didn't stop tempers from flaring in the newly-minted Trump administration, resulting in the United States withdrawing over half of its embassy personnel and ordering the expulsion of fifteen diplomats from the Cuban Embassy in Washington.

Trafficante's post-Capri life was no less odd and filled with shady claims about espionage than that of the hotel and casino he was forced to leave behind after the Revolution. Like many mobsters burned by the overthrow of the Batista regime, Trafficante was reportedly approached by the CIA about assassinating Castro. CIA records (declassified in 1975) claimed the Agency hired Trafficante to poison Castro, though Trafficante himself denied the plot. In the quaintly named "Family Jewels" report that exposed shady CIA deals and illegal activities spanning the '50s-'70s, Trafficante shows up multiple times, including as part of a plot devised by a disgraced FBI agent, Robert Maheu, working for the CIA to recruit mobsters and Cuban exiles for covert actions against Castro. He acquired the services of a west coast mobster active in both Hollywood and Las Vegas to assist in the effort. That man, Johnny Roselli, would in turn introduce Maheu to two guys named "Sam Gold" and "Joe"—alias Sam Trafficante and Sam Giancana. The story of Roselli is itself one hell of a strange trip...perhaps better suited for a chapter about the Rat Pack.

Trafficante never returned to the Capri, though he did return to court many times, including to testify about allegations that he had facilitated the assassination of President John Kennedy in retaliation for both the failure to reclaim Cuba and for JFK's younger brother, Robert, making the Mafia into public enemy number one. That allegation came from Jose Aleman, a Cuban exile who claimed that, during a venting session about JFK, Trafficante dismissed a second term for the president on the grounds that "he is going to be hit." In the sort of mad storm of allegations, coincidental connection, and conspiracy theory that characterize the Kennedy assassination to this day, Trafficante was linked to everyone from

Lee Harvey Oswald to Jack Ruby to anti-Castro dissidents to pro-Castro Cuban hit squads looking to kill Kennedy in retaliation for all the poison, exploding cigars, and would-be assassins the CIA kept sending Castro's way. Trafficante dismissed all of it during hearings that ran throughout the middle of the 1970s. He did, however, confirm that he had been on the CIA payroll during 1960 and '61, but only, he claimed, as an interpreter for Roselli, Giancana, and Maheu (Trafficante speaking excellent Spanish and being well-versed in Cuban politics). As late as 1992, Trafficante was still being named in JFK conspiracy theories, including one that linked him to Teamster boss Jimmy Hoffa and another that claims Trafficante might not have orchestrated the Texas "hit" on the president but did try to have him assassinated once in Tampa.

Whatever the truth behind any of these claims—and such claims are dubious in the extreme—Trafficante certainly had his fingers in a lot of pies. His last high-profile go on the merry-go-round came in 1986, when he was swept up as part of an investigation into Brooklyn organized crime involving an undercover FBI agent named Donnie Brasco. But, as he always did, Trafficante escaped conviction, living out the rest of his life a free man until his death on March 17, 1987 at the age of 72. But he never did get to return to Cuba.

Neither, for that matter, did El Santo, who as a professional wrestler and entertainer probably had at least a passing acquaintance with some underworld heavies but was himself never implicated in anything unseemly (or anything any more unseemly than the sport of profession wrestling already is). Nor, alas, did the CIA ever seek out El Santo's help in overthrowing Fidel Castro and restoring the glory of the Capri and the Nacional, though El Santo would be enlisted in the cinematic espionage game in the wake of James Bond's success.

The final quality of his first two films didn't do much for the Saint, who doesn't even get called El Santo in either film; he's just "the masked man." The acting bug must have burrowed into him though, because despite the failure of the films he returned to the screen in 1961. This time he was the star, and the film eschewed the "sports drama" aspects of *Huracán Ramírez* and the "policeman's sidekick" approach and instead filled itself with elements drawn from science fiction, horror, and pulp serials. By now, there was no casting El Santo as a villain or a sidekick. Titled *Santo contra los zombies* and featuring Fernando Osés and Black Shadow in supporting roles, it marks the true arrival of what would become recognized as lucha cinema.

The plot is something that seems like it should feature Bela Lugosi. A doctor who specializes in the history of voodoo mysteriously vanishes shortly after returning from Haiti with his daughter Gloria (played by Lorena Velázquez, the queen of Mexican genre film). When the police are unable to turn up anything, Gloria does what any person would do: turn to pro wrestler and part time crime fighter El Santo. When three zombie-like thugs rob a jewelery store, El Santo begins to suspect there is a connection between them and the disappearance of Gloria's father. By an incredible stroke of luck, El Santo has a closed-circuit television that allows him to peer directly into the lair of a sinister hooded villain straight out of a Republic serial. Using all the powers of the surveillance state a pro wrestler is likely to have, El Santo watches as the mysterious fiend sends three hulking zombies out to steal children from an orphanage. Santo derails the attempted kidnapping but the hooded villain, possessed of his own incredibly powerful closed-circuit television, observes Santo's meddling and is able to trigger the zombies' self-destruct mechanisms before Santo and the cops can get their hands on them.

The plot thickens when the man the police think is responsible turns up dead and prints on a crowbar used by one of the zombies turn out to belong to a man executed eight years earlier. Annoyed by El Santo butting in and ruining his schemes, the hooded villain comes up with the plan to kill El Santo that will be used in countless movies for decades to come: putting a mind-controlling zombie hex on an in-ring opponent and commanding him to kill El Santo. When that fails, the hood shows he is determined to lay the groundwork for all the Santo movie clichés to come and kidnaps Gloria.

Made as a B-side by Churubusco-Azteca Studios, which in 1961 became the home of Mexican horror cinema with the release of the classics *The Brainiac* and *Curse of the Crying Woman*, *Santo contra los zombies* is a modest film but one that doesn't fail to deliver fun and excitement. The film keeps a fleet pace and is always anxious to throw something on screen to keep your attention. If it's not a wrestling match it's a scantily clad belly dancer. If it's not a zombie heist it's a car chase. Pile onto that Frankenstein-esque underground lairs, smoky nightclubs, seedy locker rooms, and El Santo's space age crime-fighting lab with the TV that apparently enables the masked one to watch any one of us at any time, no matter where we are, and you have a solid, swift "true" introduction to El Santo.

Not one to rest on his beefy laurels, El Santo appeared in two more films in 1962, including the legendary *Santo Versus the Vampire Women* which would make his film career. He made three more films in 1963. The skyrocketing popularity of the Santo films meant that the canny wrestler was, rightfully, looking for a higher salary. Producer Enrique Vergara, not wanting to find himself locked into an El Santo monopoly, went shopping for a second lucha film act and came up, predictably, with El Santo's number one in-ring rival.

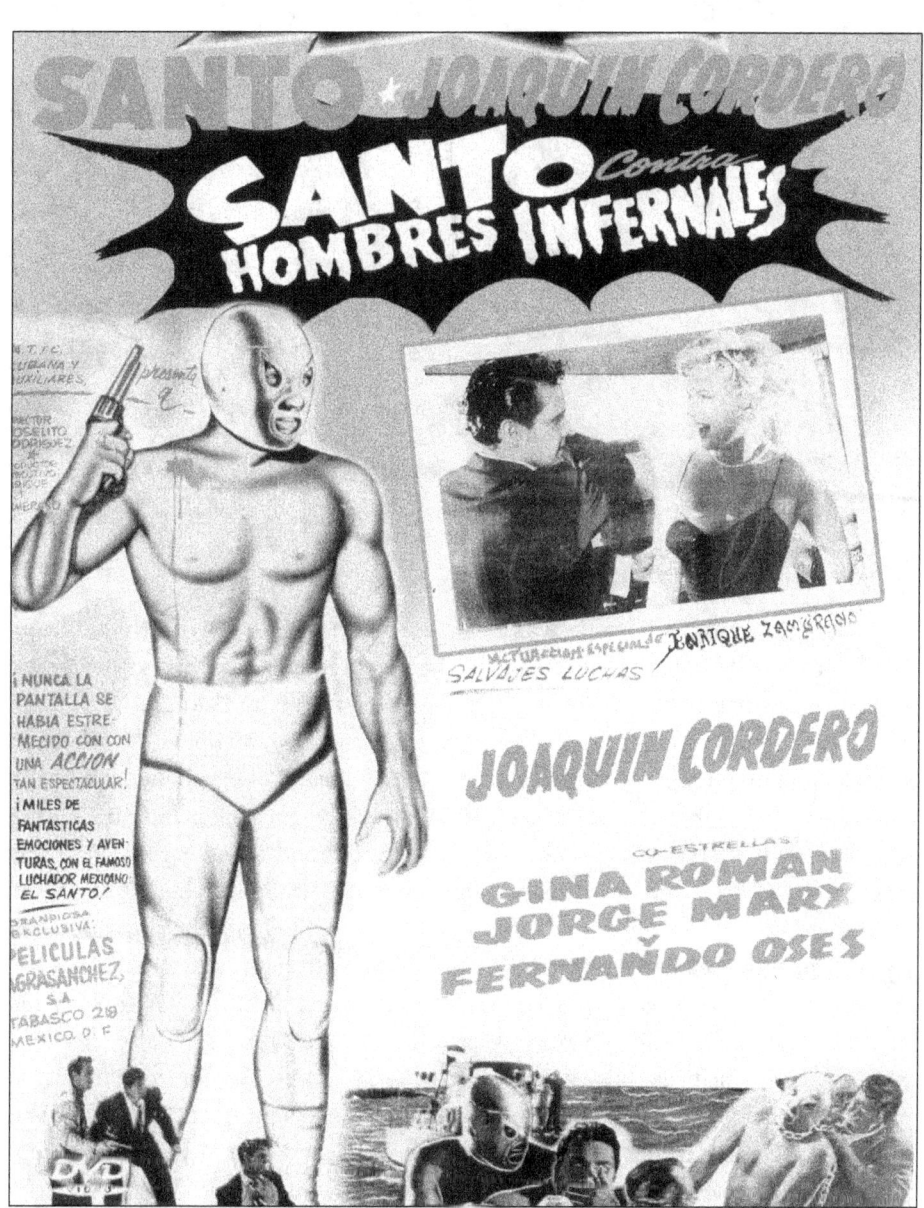

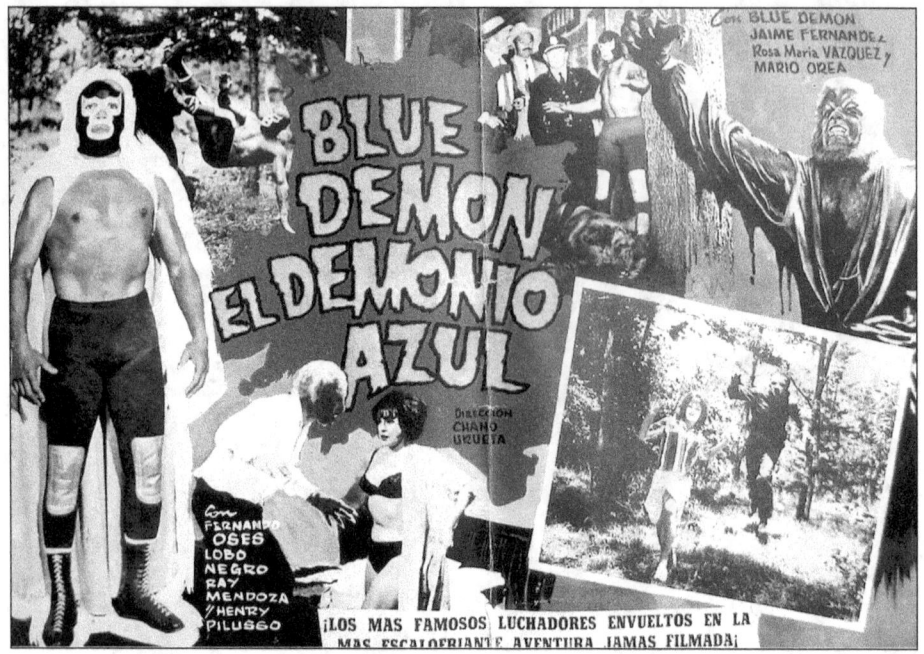

Devil with a Blue Mask On

Alejandro Muñoz Moreno was born April 24, 1922 in García, Nuevo León, Mexico, the fifth of twelve children born to a family of farmers. He worked for a while on the railroads in Monterrey, where he earned the nickname "Manotas" because of the massive size of his hands. One day, he met a wrestler named Rolando Vera, who piqued the railwayman's interest in *lucha libre*. Moreno headed north, to Laredo, Texas, where he wrested his first match—no mask—on March 12, 1948 against a cat named Chema Lopez. Soon after, he donned his signature mask. His first match as Blue Demon happened in Mexico City in September, 1948. A few years later, he was teamed up with Black Shadow, stepping into the ring against El Santo. And a few years after that, he was stepping onto the silver screen.

Just as Santo played second banana in Fernando Osés' 1958 films, so too did Blue Demon find himself relegated to little more than cameos for his first on-screen appearances, in *The Killers of Lucha Libre* and *Fury in the Ring*. But it wasn't long before Blue Demon scored himself a more significant movie victory. In 1965, he got a starring role in *Demonio Azul*, a film which pitted the *luchador* against a mad scientist who turns into a werewolf. Although not as well-paced as *Santo contra los zombies*, *Demonio Azul* is not without its considerable charms. For starters, Blue Demon is a much abler performer of stunts and choreographed fights than El Santo. It also marks the introduction of stylistic elements drawn from old Universal horror films. Rubber bats and spooky castles abound. Every walk through the woods is drenched in eerie mist and theremin music. Just as the hooded villain in *Santo contra los zombies* tries to kill El Santo by sending a zombie into the ring, so too does Blue Demon find himself surprised during a match when his opponent turns out to be a werewolf! Director Chano Urueta was no stranger to horror. He was the man who gave the world *The Brainiac*, among others, and he and Blue Demon would work together on many of Blue's best films, including *Blue Demon contra las diabólicas* and *Blue Demon contra cerebros infernales*. When it came time for the inevitable—the pairing of Blue Demon and El Santo in a movie—it was Urueta who directed. Released in 1966, the film was *Blue Demon vs. el poder satánico* (*Blue Demon vs. Satanic Power*).

Perhaps reflective of the salary dispute between Enrique Vergara and El Santo, perhaps because at the time Blue Demon was arguably as big a name as El Santo, this historic first cinematic outing to team the two men up is largely Blue's movie (this would not remain the case in subsequent films). El Santo appears only in a wrestling scene and in a locker room scene, where he pops in to congratulate Blue Demon. Not the most auspicious of team-ups, but knowing that they were going to be in the same film, both Blue and El Santo seem to up their game in order not to appear inferior to the other. Blue later finds himself fighting an evil mesmerist who escapes prison by feigning death. The fiend later uses his insidious powers for pretty predictable stuff like making a pretty lady strut around in her underwear. He also messes with Blue Demon's mind (which would become a hallmark of Blue Demon movies; the man was mind-controlled more times than can be counted) and causes the heroic wrestler to attempt suicide by jumping off the top of a building (thank goodness for ledges). Although not as *outré* as *Demonio Azul*, *Blue Demon vs. el poder satánico* is still kitted out with full Gothic ambiance, including more spooky castles, cobwebs, and lots of scenes of Blue Demon sitting in his eerie den reading books on occult power while still wearing his cape and mask.

Santo and Blue would team up many more times throughout the 1960s and into the '70s, usually with Blue forced to play second fiddle to the more powerful man in the silver mask. Their first proper team-up, one more substantial than having one wrestler walk by and flash the thumbs up to the other, came in 1969's *Santo contra Blue Demon en la Atlantida*. Some ten years into his film career, El Santo had already faced off against zombies, witches, mummies, mad scientists, vampires of both the male and female variety, hatchet-wielding ghosts, homicidal table lamps, and Martians. So it was only a matter of time before the denizens of Atlantis got to the front of the queue. Blue Demon had already starred in a series of successful films for producer Luis Enrique Vergara. And Santo, working for a variety of studios and producers—including, for a time, Vergara—had chalked up an impressive slate of twenty-plus features (though those, thanks to Santo's apparently indiscriminate practice of just following the paycheck, were wildly varying in quality).

There are a couple of things that all of Santo's pictures for Sotomayor have in common. One is that each bore a title promising content that was tragically beyond the filmmakers' means; a promise that those filmmakers then tried to make good on to the best of their ability and with the very limited materials they had on hand. After this fashion, the first film was called Santo contra Blue Demon en la Atlantida—aka Santo vs. Blue Demon in Atlantis, a title which, if nothing else, guaranteed that no one would ever have to ask what Santo vs. Blue Demon in Atlantis was about. In practice, however, the film was only able to deliver on its vision of a sub-aquatic battle royal by means of stolen special effects footage from *Atragon* and *Monster Zero*. Likewise, the last of the three Sotomayor Santo films, *El Mundo de los Muertos*, seemed to promise that Santo would be paying a visit to Hell itself, but in the end only gave us a red-tinted state park besieged by silent-era stock footage.

The other thing that the Sotomayor films have in common is that each teamed Santo with Blue Demon. These were the first films to do so, and they sparked a successful screen pairing that would last through eight films. Most people outside of Mexico who are familiar with the screen work of Blue Demon know him exclusively for these films, in which he basically plays Santo's sidekick. But the fact is that, in addition to being an iconic star of *lucha libre* in his own right, Blue had, by the time of making Santo vs. Blue Demon in Atlantis, already starred in nine films of his own. These included goofy monster-fests like *La Sombra del Murcielago* and *Aranas Infernale*s, and groovy spy capers like *Destructor de Espias*, as well as the colorful Batman-inspired camp exercise *Blue Demon contra Cerebros Infernales*. And though he may not have been as prolific as Santo, a number of these titles were every bit as much fun as Santo's best.

So when Sotomayor productions got the notion to properly team the two together in a film, it must have seemed like a formula for pure box office gold. The only stumbling block, however, was the small matter of a bitter rivalry between the two wrestlers that stretched back some sixteen years. The fact that Santo had lost his title to Blue in an ego-bruising defeat back in 1953 was reportedly something that still rankled El enmascarado de plata all those years later. Blue, for his part, may have found equal cause for resentment in the fact that, while he was arguably the superior athlete, he was perpetually relegated to the number two spot thanks to the iconic status that Santo enjoyed in Mexico, a status that was as much due to Santo's roles as a movie star and popular comic book hero as it was to his skill in the ring.

The dilemma for Sotomayor was that, because of this legendary rivalry, fans who paid to see Santo and Blue Demon in a movie together would come with the expectation of seeing them fight one another. The simple solution to this would be to cast one wrestler as the hero and the other as the villain, but the fact that both were presented as heroes in the ring and in their own movies made this problematic. After all, the conceit of lucha movies was that the wrestlers who appeared in them were not playing roles, but appearing as themselves, and the way that they were presented on screen was meant to carry over into how they were perceived off of it, and vice versa. The solution that producer/writer Jesus Sotomayor Martinez, his co-writer Rafael Garcia Traversi, and director Julian

Soler came up with would set the tone for many of Santo and Blue Demon's screen pairings to come. And that solution was to have Blue Demon start out as a good guy, and then, through circumstances beyond his control, become the slave of some otherworldly force that would cause him to turn against his pal Santo, in turn forcing Santo to repeatedly beat the living tar out of his good chum Blue Demon before, through heroic efforts, effecting his return to normalcy. Once that was achieved, both *luchadors* could clock out the film's remaining minutes with a united display of good guy derring-do—until the next film, at which point the process would start all over again. *Santo vs. Blue Demon in Atlantis* (or, more accurately, *Santo contra Blue Demon en la Atlantida*) is, in fact, the most honest in its presentation of this arrangement of all the films, as it is the only one to use "vs" in the title rather than "and."

In addition to marking the beginning of a successful screen partnership, *Santo vs. Blue Demon in Atlantis* also serves as evidence of a couple of distinct trends that were developing in Santo's movies as the sixties came to a close. American audiences who are familiar with Santo only through those few films that were dubbed into English by K. Gordon Murray (in which Santo was referred to as "Samson") might understandably consider his customary milieu to be one of Gothic horror. But while films such as *Santo vs. the Vampire Women* and *Santo in the Wax Museum* definitely represent a dominant strain in Santo's filmography, the sheer volume of his output practically necessitated that his cinematic offerings fall within a wide range of genres, including westerns, crime thrillers, science fiction, and even—ostensibly at least—comedy (which is to say, the less said about *Santo vs. Capulina*, the better).

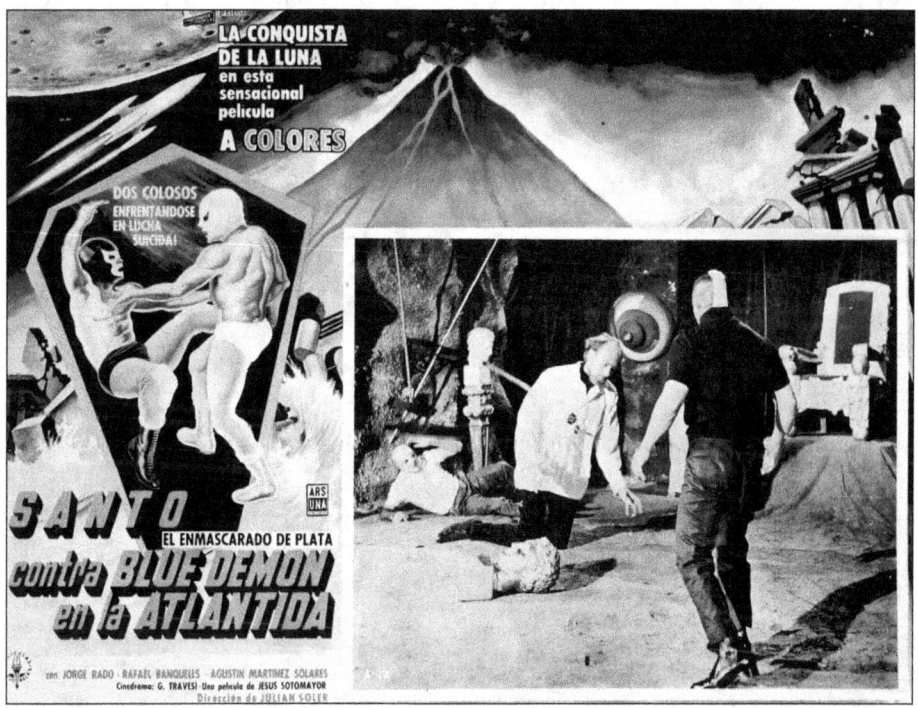

In 1966, a new genre was added to this list when, in an effort to cash in on the Bond craze, the studio America-Cima Films teamed Santo with a young pretty boy actor named Jorge Rivero for a pair of spy films titled *Operacion 67* and *El Tesoro de Moctezuma*. Though these films were never exported to the U.S. and remain virtually unknown here today, they are actually among the most well-appointed of Santo's films, blessed with obviously higher budgets than was the norm and boasting a slick, colorful look that easily put them in the league of the better funded Bond knock-offs coming out of Europe at the time. In addition to introducing Santo to the thrilling world of espionage—and, presumably, fans of such films to Santo— the Rivero spy films also effected a marked transformation in the masked one's on-screen persona. Up to that point, the Santo seen on screen had for the most part lived up to his name, as a saintly figure who existed only to help those in need. In fact, 1961's *Santo contra el Rey de Crimen*, one of the only films to refer to Santo as having any kind of conventional, superhero-type "origin," makes the ascetic aspect of his character fairly explicit. As represented in that film, Santo's mask was not meant to conceal his identity so much as obliterate it, thus removing the incentive for worldly rewards such as fame and personal adoration, and insuring that Santo's good deeds were performed out of only the purest motives. Following along these lines, almost all of Santo's early films positioned him as an adjunct to a traditional romantic lead, one who, when not putting scissor holds on zombies, would spend all of his time tooling around alone in his lab waiting for the call for help to arrive. He never got the girl, or even tried to, nor did he have much interaction in the social lives of the other characters.

Of course, when it came time to retool Santo for inclusion in a swinging sixties spy caper, that monkish demeanor would have to be done away with completely. And so, in *Operacion 67*'s opening minutes we were immediately thrust into a world in which a swimming trunks clad Santo necked on the beach with an adoring bikini babe, only to callously dispatch her with a snap of his fingers when duty called. From this point on, the saintly Santo of old was conclusively banished to the past, and no future Santo film would be complete without the masked one being provided with a love interest or a sexy girlfriend and would frequently include scenes such as the one in *Vengeance of the Vampire Women* where Santo can be observed lounging by the pool while being served by his voluptuous and revealingly attired maid.

In addition, *Operacion 67* and its sequel insured that, between battling with the usual vampires and werewolves, every third or so Santo feature from that point on would feature him as an agent of Interpol or some other secret organization, doing battle against the forces of international espionage. This path lead to its logical conclusion in 1973, when Santo starred in an actual Eurospy film, the Spanish-produced *Santo vs Dr. Death*, which had him rubbing elbows with such genre regulars as Helga Line and Mirta Miller. Of course, these later spy efforts weren't mounted on anywhere near as handsome a scale as the Rivero films, which brings me to that second trend that was taking hold in Santo's movies as the '70s dawned. As time went on, it seemed that Santo's film career was increasingly falling into the hands of producers whose primary goal was to create features without providing more than the absolute minimum of original content, a practice that resulted in films heavy with recycled and borrowed footage, as well as endless taxing minutes of soul-deadeningly aimless filler. This practice would become even more pronounced as the decade progressed, and dwindling audience interest in the lucha genre made it the provenance of independent producers and small time production companies who could only turn a profit on the films by churning them out as quickly and cheaply as possible. This resulted in the genre pioneering new lows in film padding, forcing audiences to watch their wrestling heroes performing the type of mundane tasks that are boring enough when one has to do them oneself, and no less so when observed being performed by Santo, Mil Mascaras or Superzan. (Though, granted, the practice did on occasion provide for some wonderful moments of unintentional surrealism.)

Not that Santo vs. Blue Demon in Atlantis comes anywhere near that level of slackness in its execution, of course. But the tendency is still well in evidence. And to helpfully illustrate that fact, the film kicks off with a dizzying seven minute montage of repurposed film stock—including newsreel footage, scenes from an old black & white science fiction movie, that A-bomb test footage you always see in movies from the Fifties, and, most strikingly, a number of Eiji Tsuburaya's special effects shots from Godzilla vs. Monster Zero. As one might expect in a film of this type, these events lead to a group of severe looking middle-aged men in crisp suits convening around a large conference table with some flags scattered about.

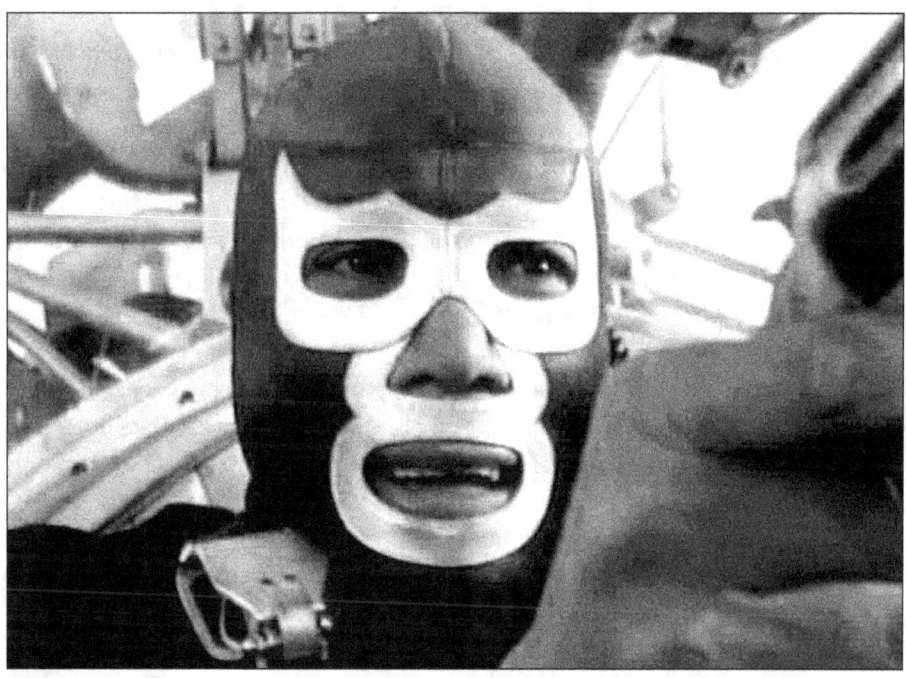

More stock footage is viewed on a projector, and the theory is put forward that Achilles, despite his apparent relative youth, is actually an escaped Nazi scientist who's still hung up on that whole "race of supermen" idea. One of the agents of the international organization that owns the conference table and projector, a scientist named Professor Gerard (Rafael Banquells), is apparently the only person with the know-how to put a stop to Achilles' plan, and it is decided to partner him up with the organization's key operative, the masked man Santo, aka Agent X-21.

A lengthy wrestling sequence follows featuring a match between Santo and Blue. This is a rarity in the Santo and Blue Demon films, because in subsequent films featuring the two, if the two were shown in the ring together at all, it would typically be in team matches in which they fought side-by-side. That said, this match is a particularly brutal one, comprised a lot more of bare-knuckled punches to the face than it is of the wrestling holds or flips you'd expect to see. In fact, though the whole Santo vs. Blue Demon feud may have been played up for drama, the fights between the two stars throughout Atlantis are pretty realistic, with both participants appearing, shall we say, particularly motivated. It's hard to imagine that both didn't bring home quite a collection of scrapes and bruises at the end of the shooting day. Another noteworthy aspect of this ring sequence is that it takes place in an actual arena with a live audience, whereas later Santo films would feature fights shot on a stage with dubbed crowd noise and an announcer commenting on the enormity of the crowd, the luxuriousness of the venue, the viciousness of the blows, Santo's fine fighting trim, and anything else that the evidence of the eye might contradict.

Somewhere during the course of the fight, some of Achilles' minions sneak into the arena and switch both Santo and Blue Demon's water bottles with drugged ones. Santo doesn't drink, but Blue does, and goes down like a well-oiled side of beef as a result. Disguised as ambulance attendants, Achilles' men then spirit Blue away to Atlantis, which appears to be in a shallow underwater cave just a few yards from the beach. A couple of shots from *Atragon* are inserted in an attempt to spruce things up a bit, but we soon see that Achilles' lair is basically just a rocky cavern decorated with some colored curtains and a couple of Roman-style busts on pedestals. Achilles (serial Santo supporting actor Jorge Rado), who looks like a hippy college professor, shows us some more stock footage—this time of Olympic gymnasts and sprinters—in an attempt to sell Blue on the whole master race idea. Then he has Blue fight a burly bearded minion in trunks in a scene that makes Santo vs. Blue Demon in Atlantis the closest thing to a peplum in either Blue or Santo's filmography. Still unable to sell Blue on how awesome life in Atlantis is, Achilles settles on simply strapping Blue to a table and hypnotizing him with a disco ball.

Now under Achilles' control, Blue calls Santo and arranges a meeting, saying he has information about Achilles. Santo jumps into his sports car and zooms off to the roadside rendezvous. However, soon after Santo has hopped into Blue's snazzy red Thunderbird convertible, he realizes that all is not right with his burly BFF—and when Blue refuses to pull over, begins to punch him repeatedly in the head, which is probably not the most advisable course of action given that they are speeding along a narrow and winding road overlooking a steep cliff. Blue finally pulls over and the two pile out of the car for a savage smack-fest that is eventually joined in by a gang of Achilles' henchmen. Just as it looks like Santo is about to have his ass permanently tied up in a nice little bow and handed to him, help arrives in the form of female Agent X-25 (Magda Giner) and her gun. Like most henchmen in Santo movies, Achilles' men came to the party only expecting a little wrestling and hand-to-hand, so when someone introduces bullets into the mix, they make their getaway with Blue in tow.

And then it's time for romance back at X-25's apartment. But first, X-25 must retire to her boudoir to slip into something more comfortable, which provides occasion for an astonishing two minute sequence during which Santo sits on X-25's plastic-sealed couch and stares blankly at her TV while a black & white musical number from an older movie plays out on it. X-25 finally comes back and the two begin to do a little necking on the couch. After a fade-out, we return to find that Santo has fallen asleep with his face embedded in X-25's armpit.

After that, *Santo vs. Blue Demon in Atlantis* goes on to exhibit further questionable judgment by knocking-off one of the most sloppily plotted sequences from You Only Live Twice. As James Bond did in that film, Santo sets out in a helicopter to locate the villain's hidden base of operations, and,

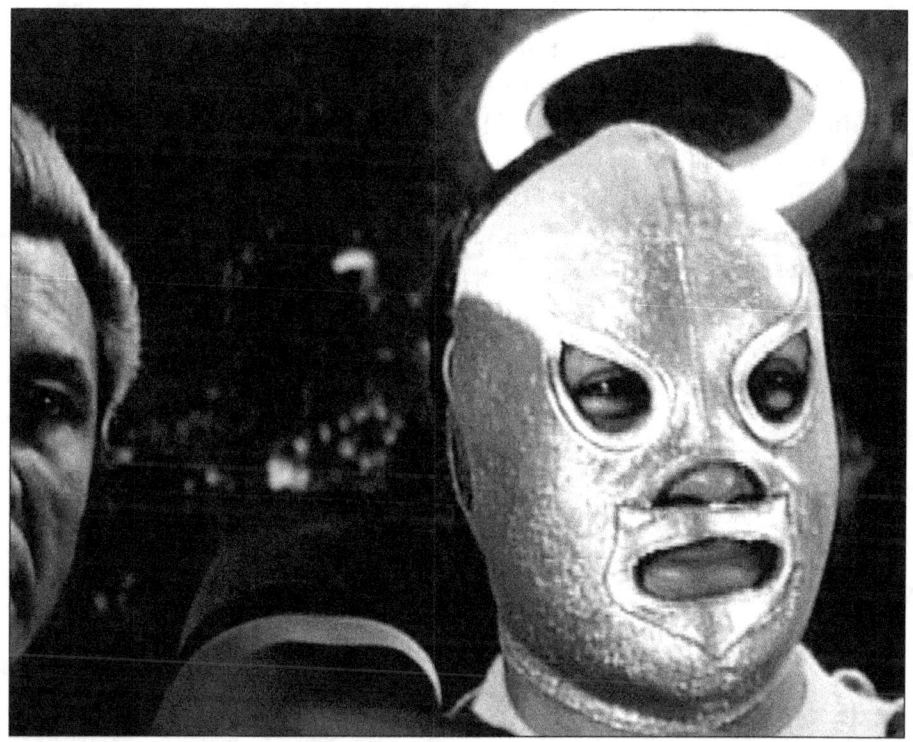

also as in that film, that villain sends out some attack helicopters that, while completely failing to kill the hero, helpfully alert that hero to the fact that he's very much on the right track, while just staying quiet might have been more advisable on the villain's part in terms of preserving the hidden-ness of his base. In a departure from the source, the attack helicopters here are just one helicopter playing two, one of which contains Blue Demon firing a pistol at Santo and a distressed-looking X-25. No helicopter battle would be complete without concluding with a fiery helicopter crash—but the crew of Santo vs. Blue Demon in Atlantis, not having recourse to the unconvincing miniature work of a more technically sophisticated film like, say, *Danger!! Deathray*, instead have one of the helicopters make a smooth, conventional landing and then blow up a charge in front of it, making it look like that gentle upright touchdown has somehow caused it to explode. Blue Demon, meanwhile, has parachuted to safety.

Santo, following the path highlighted by Achilles' foot soldiers, dives into the ocean and swims his way to Atlantis. Santo is captured and strapped to Achilles' disco ball hypno-table, by all appearances soon to become yet another pawn of the madman. And, sure enough, we next cut to Professor Gerard's lab, where an evil Santo barges in and starts wrecking the joint. But, wait! The actual Santo shows up and has it out with his double, finally skewering him on that old standby, the random pointy thing that's sticking out of the wall for no reason. It seems that Santo was rescued at the last minute. Professor Gerard de-hypnotizes Blue by shoving a light in his face while Blue displays a facial expression reminiscent of that worn by a dog being given a bath.

It's a fair enough film, but once again it lacks the out-and-out Universal monsters battiness many expect from a Blue and Santo team-up. That would be rectified, however, in their second film together. *Santo y Blue Demon contra los Monstruos* marked the 23rd screen appearance by El Santo. He was in his early fifties at this point, but, despite his prime wrestling years being behind him, his iconic status in Mexican popular culture was undiminished. In fact, he was still fairly early in his screen career at this point, with another couple dozen films ahead of him.

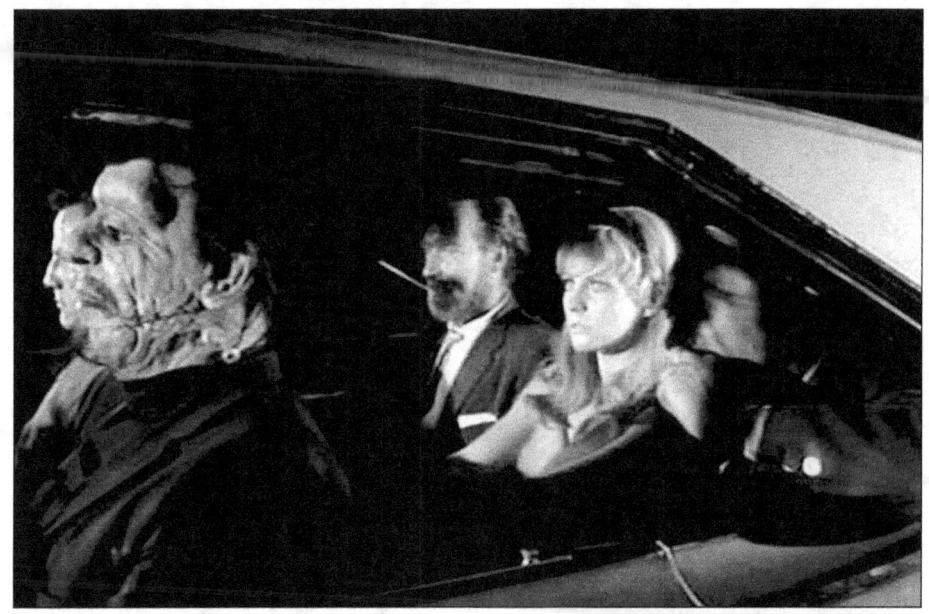

Monster Mash

Contra los Monstruos was also the second of three films, all made in 1969, that Santo starred in under the banner of the production company Producciones Sotomayor. Santo tended throughout his film career to follow the money, jumping over to whatever studio could provide the fattest paycheck, with apparently little regard for the quality of the movies that resulted. In the sixties this practice lead to him going from the relatively lavish ministrations of Filmadora Panamericana (where he made *Santo contra las Mujeres Vampiros*) to more hardscrabble outfits like Filmica Vergara (where he made *Profanadores de Tumbas*, a film in which Santo battles a lamp) and then to Sotomayor. Sotomayor had seen better days, and had a production history that went back well over a decade, but by the time of making *Contra los Monstruos* it had hit hard times. Given that, it was pretty much guaranteed that, no matter how much Sotomayor paid Santo for a film like *Contra los Monstruos*, his presence was going to be the only visible evidence of production value on screen.

Santo y Blue Demon contra los Monstruos begins like most of these movies do: with an eight minute wrestling sequence, half of which doesn't feature either Santo or Blue Demon. The story of *Contra los Monstruos*, then, begins with Santo and his buddy Blue Demon pondering the fate of a recently vanquished foe. If you didn't know better, you might think that *Contra los Monstruos* was a sequel to a nonexistent film in which evil scientist Bruno Halder (Carlos Ancira) has been killed, apparently at the hands of Santo and Blue Demon. Before dying, Halder has sworn to take vengeance upon the two *luchadors*, as well as upon his own brother, Otto (Jorge Radó), and Otto's lovely daughter, Gloria (Hedy Blue), who also happens to be Santo's girlfriend.

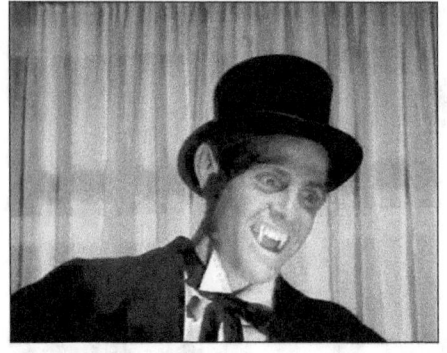

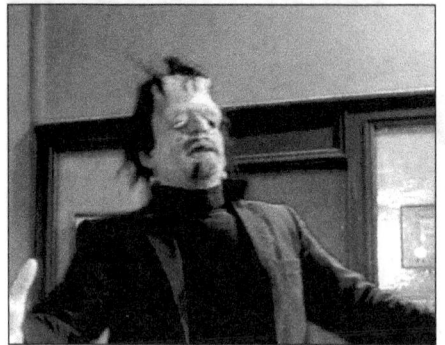

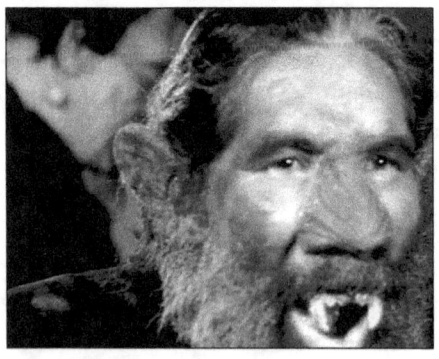

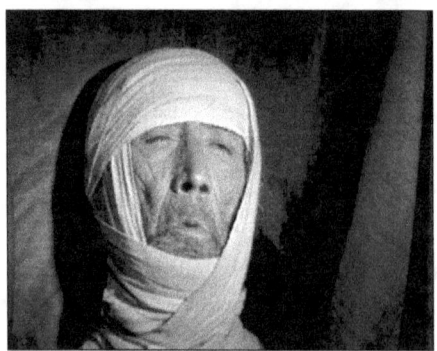

Santo has reason to be concerned about Bruno, because it seems his specialty was raising the dead, and Otto has somewhat stupidly followed his brother's wishes and not had the body cremated. And sure enough, Bruno's faithful hunchbacked dwarf assistant Waldo (Rafael Muñoz), aided by a covey of burly, green-faced zombies (in other words, wrestlers with green spackle on their faces), is in the process of exhuming Bruno as Blue and Santo speak. Still, Blue Demon teases Santo for worrying about Gloria too much, and then heads off on his vacation. That will turn out well.

On his way to wherever it is he's vacationing, Blue happens to pass by Bruno's creepy castle at the very moment that Waldo and his zombie slaves are carrying the mad scientist's corpse inside. Sensing that something is amiss, Blue follows them inside and witnesses the resurrection of Bruno amid much showering of sparks and flashing of lights. Blue is captured and strapped to a table, where he's subjected to the evil cackling and diabolical proclamations of Bruno and Waldo before being placed in a machine that makes an evil duplicate.

Bruno, it has been revealed, hails from Transylvania, a fact which is given as the reason for him having an interest in monsters. With zombies, Waldo and evil Blue Demon in tow, Bruno goes about breaking into crypts and haunted houses, gathering up every monster he can find. Soon, his infernal army of Godforsaken creatures of the night is assembled in his lab and ready to commit acts of unspeakable evil:

The Vampire! Frankenstein! The Wolf Man! The Mummy! Um.. Cyclops! Not to mention, after the Vampire has a chance to bite some strippers, the Vampire Women! But before you get too excited at the prospect of all of your old Aurora monster models and a Cyclops coming to life and having it out with a couple of colorfully-garbed Mexican wrestlers, let's have a look at those monsters. They're a notoriously shabby lot.

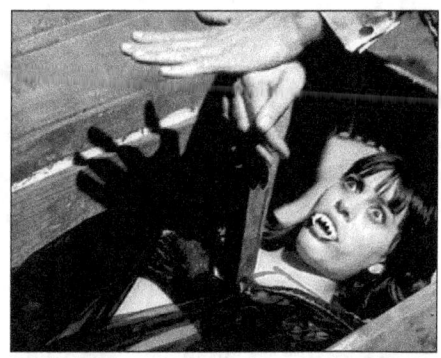

THE VAMPIRE!, for starters, is a nonthreatening-looking bald guy with Spock ears and vampire teeth whose wardrobe appears to have been borrowed from Jose Marins of Coffin Joe fame. Like the rest of the monsters in *Contra los Monstruos*, The Vampire looks like the type of thing you'd come across in a charity haunted house put on by a local church group. Such haunted houses, like *Contra los Monstruos*, are limited by their budget and materials but have the added restriction of needing to make sure nothing looks too scary. And much like a cut-rate haunted house spook, when The Vampire in *Contra los Monstruos* wants to be scary, he jumps up with his arms outstretched like bat wings and goes "RAAAR!" Which is about as scary as it sounds.

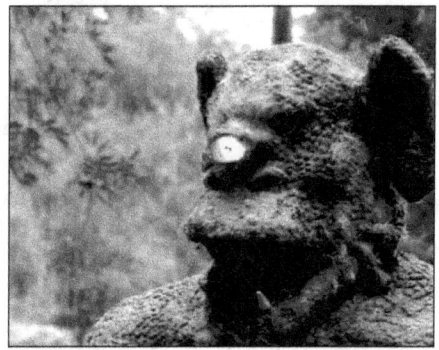

FRANKENSTEIN! (or Franquestain as the liability-averse credits list him) is realized with the help of what looks like one of those Don Post masks you used to be able to get from the back of *Famous Monsters*, but with the addition of a snappy mustache and goatee. Frankenstein was portrayed by the towering Manuel Leal, who would go on to become the masked wrestler

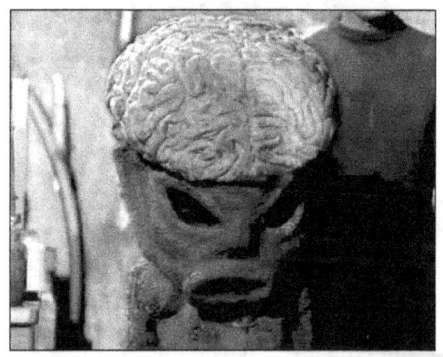

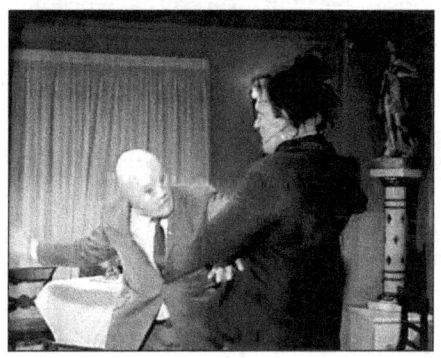

LEGEND OF THE MASK

Tinieblas (he would also play the lead mummy in *Las Momias de Guanajuato*). Even though he never got beyond supporting roles in "let's pack in as many wrestlers as we can" pictures like *Los Campeones Justicieros* and *Leyendas Macabras de la Colonia*, Tinieblas became a fan favorite, though not on the level of El Santo or Blue Demon. Aside from being imposingly huge, he had a sleek-looking costume that made him look like a 70s era Marvel super hero. Definitely a step up from what he's rocking here.

THE WOLF-MAN! is just a hairy, kind of rough-looking middle-aged guy with a prosthetic nose slapped on him. No fake fur is employed for this wolfman; just the guy's natural, big scruffy beard and long unkempt-looking hair.

THE MUMMY! is an emaciated elderly man with stubble who has been wrapped from head to toe in surgical gauze, which makes him look more like a very old man who fell down a flight of stairs than a mummy. Being that he looks so fragile, the Mummy doesn't really present much of a threat, since it looks like the slightest amount of force would cause him to fall over and shatter his hip. Interestingly, it appears that the Mummy has a stunt double, because in the fight scenes there is a conspicuously more burly individual wearing the costume. This leads to the obvious question of why they didn't just have *that* guy play the Mummy.

THE VAMPIRE WOMEN! are just voluptuous young Latinas in lingerie with vampire teeth, which is pretty hard to mess up.

THE CYCLOPS! is an interesting case. His costume actually looks pretty cool. Or it did when it was first used, back in 1959, in *La Nave de los Monstruos*, an earlier Sotomayor production in which Lorena Velazquez and Ana Bertha Lepe played space women who were trying to mate with a singing cowboy. The costume is a perfectly respectable suit-mation effort, like something you'd see in a lesser *kaiju* movie or an episode of *Ultraman*. The only problem with it is that, in the ten years that lapsed between *La Nave de los Monstruos* and *Contra los Monstruos*, not much effort was taken to preserve it, so, as it appears in *Contra los Monstruos*, it's riddled with obvious tears, fraying, and areas where the stuffing is coming out of it. It actually looks like it may have served time as a *piñata* somewhere along the line. There's also a hand puppet Cyclops head used for the close-ups, which gets a real workout in *Contra los Monstruos* even though it's in just as pitiful shape as the costume.

There's also another costume from *La Nave de los Monstruos* on display in *Contra los Monstruos*, sort of a BONUS MONSTER! in the form of a troll-like creature with a giant, exposed brain. This monster just hangs out on the periphery of the laboratory scenes without anyone ever reacting or referring to him. One half expects someone else in th e film to notice this monster and have that awkward "I didn't invite him. I thought *you* invited him" conversation.

Though they might not be as fearsome as initially hoped, Dr. Halder sends this monster squad, along with evil Blue Demon and the green-faced zombies, out to do their worst, with the idea of drawing out El Santo. The Wolf-Man gets thing started by slaughtering an entire family. Frankenstein attacks a couple who are having a picnic and squashes the boy's head with his foot. The Cyclops comes up out of the swamp and attacks a guy who's camping. The first two of these scenes are actually quite bloody, and set *Contra los Monstruos* apart from the Santo films that preceded it, all of which, like most sixties Lucha films in general, were fairly family-friendly in their presentation of violence. There's even a severed head rolling onto the scene, which is a singular event in Santo's filmography.

After this initial orgy of monster mayhem, *Contra los Monstruos* unfolds as a rapid series of vignettes in which the monsters, the evil Blue Demon, and the green-faced zombies, in various combinations, though most frequently as one large and unruly group, attack Santo and try to kidnap Gloria, leading in most cases to a chaotic monster-on-wrestler free-for-all. Evil Blue ambushes Santo in a lovers' lane where he and Gloria are making out in Santo's car. Later, Santo takes on the Cyclops in a great scene in which Santo, after finding his usual hand-to-hand techniques ineffective, picks up a piece of wood and starts repeatedly clubbing the Cyclops on his big rubbery head. This is followed by an all-monster attack on Otto and Gloria's home, a scene that is impressive for how the negligee-clad Gloria, fending off The Vampire's attack, somehow manages in the course of her life-and-death struggle to put on underwear. This in turn is followed by a scene in which one of the Vampire Women hops uninvited into Santo's car and Santo makes a bee-line to the same lover's lane where he'd been with Gloria earlier for another make-out session. Again, all of the monsters attack.

One of the most memorable scenes in *Contra los Monstruos* is, depending on how charitably you choose to view it, either an homage to or a complete rip-off of

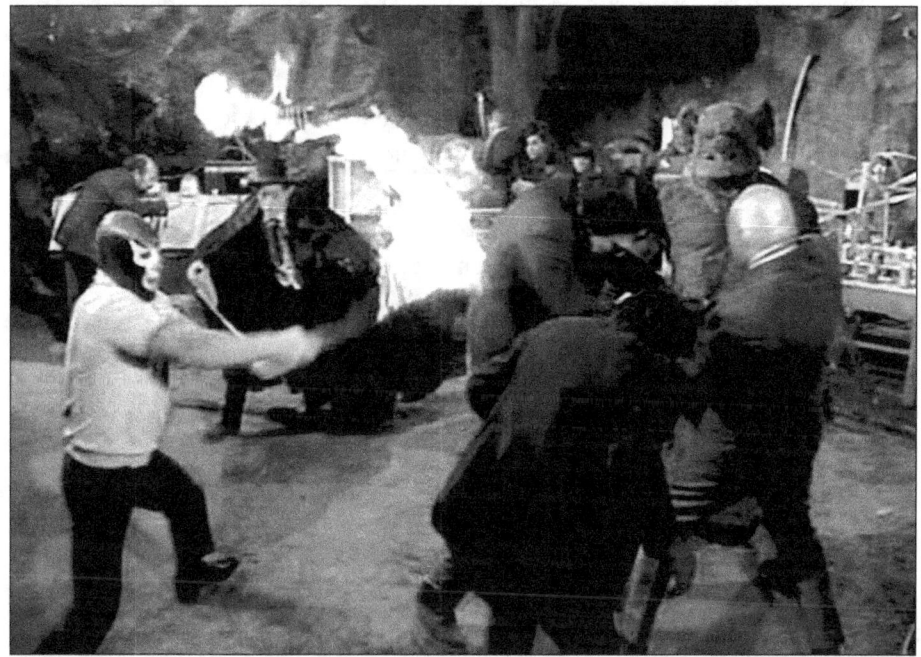

a famous scene in *Santo contra las Mujeres Vampiro*. That original scene had Santo unmasking an opponent in the ring, only to reveal a snarling werewolf, who then turned into a bat and flew out of the arena. In *Contra los Monstruos*, this scene is set up by The Vampire taking the guise of a masked wrestler called "The Vampire" and challenging Santo to a ring match. Santo, unable to see through this impenetrable ruse, accepts, and the fight is on. *Contra los Monstruos*, however, true to its overreaching nature, goes *Las Mujeres Vampiro* one better by having, at the moment that The Vampire is revealed and flies away, all of the monsters, including the Cyclops, jump up out of the audience and attack Santo in the ring.

So far, the monsters have been unsuccessful in their attempts to kidnap Gloria, but all of that will change at the conclusion of *Santo y Blue Demon contra los Monstruos*' unforgettable restaurant scene. Here, director Gilberto Martinez Solares does a masterful job of ratcheting up the tension as we watch Santo, Gloria and Gloria's father sitting in a cramped restaurant set, staring affectlessly into the middle distance beyond the camera's viewpoint. Interspersed with this is mismatched insert footage of a relatively lavish musical production number from a completely different movie made at least ten years previous to *Santo y Blue Demon contra los Monstruos*, which we watch in its entirety, punctuated by shots of Santo, Gloria and Gloria's father staring, the suggestion being that this large stage show is what they're actually supposed to be watching take place within the confines of the tiny restaurant even though its obvious that the actors have no idea what they're supposed to be looking at. Finally, the number stops, at which point *another* number begins, and we start the whole process over again. Finally, mercifully, the monsters attack.

The monsters, having successfully dragged Gloria from the restaurant, all pile into their monster mobile and, with Frankenstein at the wheel, speed off toward the castle. Fortunately, Santo has managed during the fight to place a tracking device on Frank's collar, and is able to follow them. Once at the castle, Santo takes on the evil Blue Demon and settles his hash once and for all, then revives the real Blue for a climactic battle royal with the whole motley crew.

To truly get a sense of where *Santo y Blue Demon contra los Monstruos* is coming from, keep in mind that a key element in Santo becoming the phenomenon he was, was that well before even the start of his movie career, he was the star of his own comic book. *Contra los Monstruos* is nothing if not a true comic book movie. No matter how shoddy and ridiculous the goings on, it always plays it straight. It staunchly resists the temptation to laugh at itself, and that is what really sells it. One wink, one moment of intentional camp, and it would have become unbearable, but, instead, every actor who looked upon those pitifully ridiculous monsters reacted to them as if they were the gravest threat ever faced by mankind. And bless them for it.

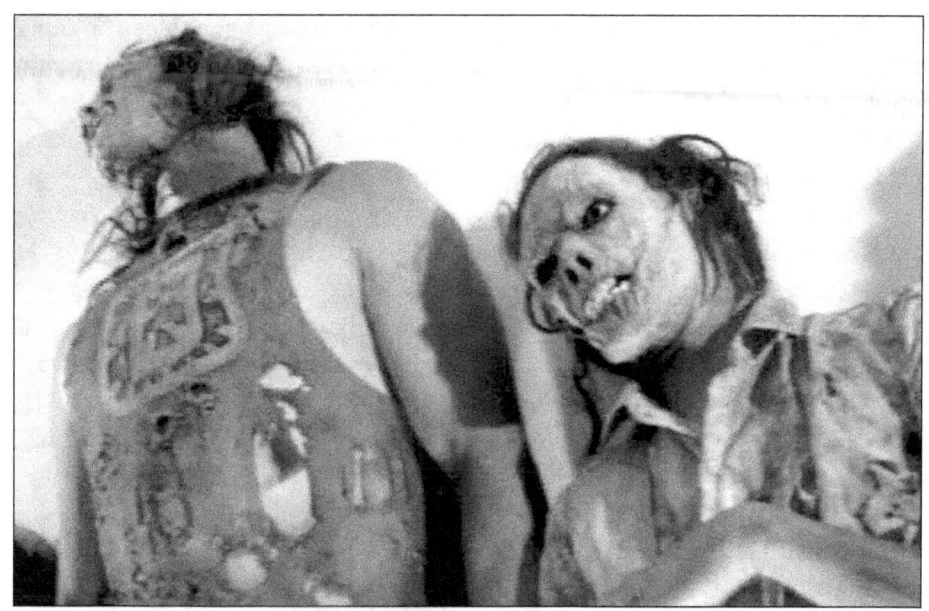

The Mummies and the Man of a Thousand Masks

One need only glance over the many titles in the lucha movie genre to see that there is a long history of enmity between Mexican wrestlers and mummies. This goes all the way back to 1964, when Elizabeth Campbell and Lorena Velazquez threw down against a pop-eyed, reconstituted Aztec warrior in their sophomore effort as The Wrestling Women, *Las Luchadoras contra la Momia*, and continued throughout the rest of the sixties, during which Santo would come up against shambling bandage jockeys in films like *Santo and Blue Demon vs. The Monsters* and *La Venganza de la Momia*. But the conflict didn't really kick into high gear until 1972, when the success of a little film called *The Mummies of Guanajuato* (aka *Las Momias de Guanajuato*) guaranteed that, for the next several years, Mexican movie screens would seldom see respite from the spectacle of colorfully-garbed, masked grapplers working their moves on a seemingly endless series of inexplicably muscular mummified adversaries.

The Mummies of Guanajuato was the brainchild of Mexican independent producer, distributor and writer Rogelio Agrasanchez. His films are emblematic of the type of haste and neglect that plagued lucha film during the 1970s, marked by sloppy storytelling rife with plot holes and continuity errors, lackadaisical pacing, hunger-strike production values, hit-or-miss technical execution, and a patience-testing reliance on padding, often in the form of footage lifted from other films, as well as poorly integrated musical numbers, beauty pageants, and anything else they could squeeze in. Of course, Agrasanchez was not the only Lucha filmmaker of the period who was guilty of these sins, and it should be kept in mind that this was a time during which, first of all, audience interest in the genre was waning and, second of all, government financial support for commercial Mexican films, which had been plentiful during the sixties, was at a temporary ebb due to a shift in priorities toward funding more "respectable" fare. As a result, the profitability of such films dictated a need for thrift and speed that Agrasanchez alone can't be held personally accountable for.

Still, the fact is that *lucha libre* films were never big budget items. What one sees occurring over the lifespan of the genre, from the dawn of the sixties to the end of the seventies, is not so much a reduction in the amount of money spent as a reduction in the amount of care put into insuring that the films were watchable. While an early film like *Santo contra las Mujeres Vampiro* seems to be the work of accomplished craftsmen determined to deliver an engaging and atmospheric B-movie to the fullest extent their means would allow, many of Agrasanchez's films seem to demonstrate a concern primarily with attaining acceptable feature-length by any means necessary while delivering the minimum number of bankable elements with minimal expenditure of time and resources.

While, again, these faults were not those of Rogelio Agrasanchez alone, that is not to say that he didn't, in other ways, put his personal stamp upon his work. There are several contributions to Mexican wrestling cinema that are indeed uniquely Agrasanchez's own. These are elements that you can not only count on from pretty much any one of his lucha films, but that also mark those film as being distinctly his. The first of these would have to be little people. There were little people in lucha movies before Rogelio Agrasanchez came upon the scene, such as Waldo, the hunchback in *Santo and Blue Demon vs. The Monsters*. Furthermore, *The Mummies of Guanajuato*, by Agrasanchez's standards, is fairly conservative in it use of little people, limiting itself to only one in the cast. But, generally, Agrasanchez's thinking seemed to be that, if you were going to have one little person, you might as well have a whole gang of them. It seems he felt there was something intrinsically thrilling about having a burly masked wrestler fighting several little people as opposed to just one normal-sized man. The result saw the employment of a troupe of Agrasanchez regulars. They wore matching superhero costumes with big "M"s emblazoned on their chests in *The Champions of Justice*, moonman suits in *Superzan el Invencible*, rat-person costumes fashioned from fuzzy footy pajamas in *The Champions of Justice Return*, and appeared as fanged mini-vampires in *The Vampires of Coyoacan*, which is probably one of the producer's most enjoyable films.

Another hallmark of Agrasanchez's films is its over-reliance on musical accompaniment that is inappropriate to the point of approaching ironic commentary. In the case of *The Mummies of Guanajuato*, this is perpetrated by frequent lucha movie scorer Gustavo Cesar Carrion in the form of sedately jaunty organ riffs that bring to mind nothing more than heavily medicated mental patients on furlough traversing endless dazed circles around an ice skating rink. Still, *Guanajuato* is far from the worst offender in this regard. The soundtrack to *The Champions of Justice* is more typical, seemingly comprised of the producer just letting a sub-par West Coast jazz album play out over all of the action, with the result that every bit of screen business, be it Mil Mascaras hurling a little person or Blue Demon staring blankly at a cue card, carries the same negligible dramatic weight.

The Champions of Justice also represents another one of the trends that ran through Agrasanchez's lucha work, and that was his tendency to stuff his films full of as many masked wrestlers as they could possibly hold. Of course, that he would do so is not all that surprising, given that *Champions*—which featured a total of six *luchador*s, including heavy-hitters Blue Demon and Mil Mascaras—was one of his early successes in the genre. Audiences had seen Santo and Blue paired onscreen before, but it was Agrasanchez who made the use of small armies comprised of three or more fighters his own.

The dependence of Agrasanchez on multiple wrestlers to make up his casts lead the producer to even invent new wrestlers of his own, which brings us to the last of the cinematic offenses he committed: Superzan. Superzan was a bodybuilder by the name of Alfonse Mora who Agrasanchez styled as a masked wrestler/superhero (the name was meant to suggest a combination of Superman and Tarzan) to both star in his own series of films and fill out the bill in some of the producer's multi-wrestler extravaganzas, such as the aforementioned *Vampires of Coyoacan* and the final entry in the *Champions of Justice* trilogy. Aside from a black hole-like lack of charisma, Superzan's biggest liability was probably his costume. While, by this time, other wrestling heroes were affecting a more casual look, wearing their street clothes, or at least a more basic wrestling ensemble, with their masks, Superzan in the field always wore a head-to-toe superhero outfit complete with cape, sparkly skin-tight body suit, and boots. When paired with a comparatively less flamboyant wrestler, this made him look kind of like the kid who insists on wearing his costume to the grocery store the day after Halloween. On top of this, it didn't help matters that the film meant to launch Superzan into stardom, *Superzan el Invencible*, is among the most lackluster and incomprehensible in Agrasanchez's body of work, so leaden with pointless filler that it stubbornly defies even the most masochistic viewer's efforts to view it to its conclusion.

The main reason *The Mummies of Guanajuato* had the success that it did is because it marked the first time the three biggest stars of lucha cinema appeared onscreen together: Santo, Blue Demon and Mil Mascaras. For those not well versed in the particulars of Mexican wrestling movies, Mil Mascaras will probably need some introduction. Like Santo and Blue Demon, Mil Mascaras enjoyed success in his own series of films prior to making *The Mummies of Guanajuato*, though, beyond that, he was separated from his costumed co-stars by some marked differences in terms of both his personal style and his career path. Born Aaron Rodríguez in 1942, he began his screen career in 1966 under the guidance of low-budget independent film producer Luis Enrique Vergara. Vergara had produced popular lucha film series for both Santo and Blue Demon, but, by the time of signing Mil, had found himself without a star as a result of Santo moving on to greener paychecks and Blue suffering a injury that would keep him off the boards for several months. Unlike Santo and Blue, who began their film careers later in life and thus made films that capitalized upon the stardom that they had already achieved in the ring, Mil at the time of his screen debut was a relatively unknown up-and-comer, a fact which made Vergara casting him something of a gamble. As a result, Mil Mascaras was unique among lucha cinema's top stars in that his public persona had in part been established as a result of him appearing in films, rather than the other way around. Of course, he would later go on to prove himself in the ring and, in that regard, achieve international fame that would in some ways even surpass Santo's, but that does not change the fact that, unlike his peers, he was, to some extent, a movie star first and a wrestler second.

Mil was also a dedicated bodybuilder and had a lean, chiseled physique that was a marked contrast to the stockier builds seen on many of the wrestling stars of the day. This not only made him stand out, but also fit in nicely with the superheroic persona that Vergara crafted for him. (*Mil Mascaras*, his scrupulously-titled debut film, even fitted him with a Captain America-like origin story, in which, left orphaned as an infant during the war, he is raised by a team of scientists to be an invincible super soldier.) Mil brought rockstar-like flamboyance to his style of dress that seemed exceptionally peacock-like even within the context of the colorful world of *lucha libre*. This may have been the result of his chosen gimmick, which was to wear numerous masks as opposed to one distinctive one, and which might have lead him to feel the need to visually distinguish himself by other means.

The reason for Mil's signature sartorial style was more likely that he was just a big, glammy ham. His clothes alone exponentially increase the entertainment value of any movie in which he appears. In *The Mummies of Guanajuato*, he spends much of his time wearing leopard-print hot pants on top of gold wrestling tights, topped off with a red velvet vest with gold trim. As fab as that may sound, it is a distant second in splendor to the outfit he wore in the loose *Mummies of Guanajuato* sequel, *The Mummies of San Angel*, which consisted of a silver, billowy-sleeved pirate shirt paired with a vest that had his face—in starburst—emblazoned on the back.

The Mummies of Guanajuato was intended to be a starring vehicle for Blue and Mil, but doubts on Agrasanchez's part that their names would carry the necessary clout lead him to make the eleventh hour addition of Santo. Mil Mascaras reacted to the resulting diminution of his role with pragmatic stoicism, but for Blue Demon this was just another insult in a long history of the rivalry. Agrasanchez and company were certainly less than sensitive to their top-billed stars' feelings in the ham-handed manner in which they inserted Santo into the action, essentially using him as a *deus ex machina* who shows up at the end to save the day with relatively little effort after Blue and Mil have proven ineffective for much of the time. While Santo was basically credited as a special guest star, with Blue and Mil's names above the title, the true nature of his participation can be gleaned from the title that the movie was given upon its release in Spain later the same year: *Santo vs. las Momias*.

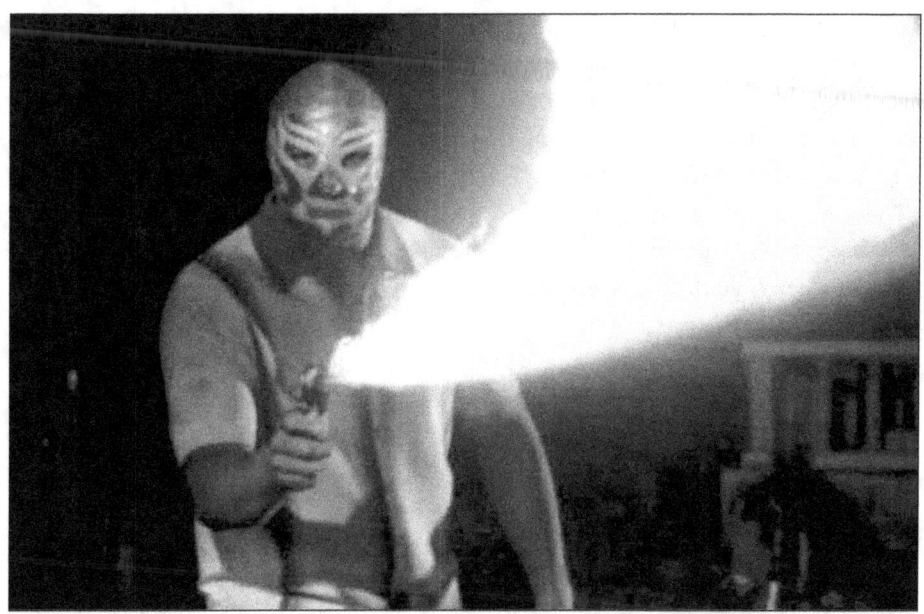

To fully understand and enjoy *The Mummies of Guanajuato*, one has to appreciate that the "mummies" of its title are not the kind of mummies that viewers of English-language horror films are normally accustomed to. Rather than being ancient mummies that are man-made in origin, they are naturally occurring mummies of much more recent vintage. The real mummies of Guanajuato were corpses, many of them casualties of a cholera epidemic that swept the city in 1933, that were disinterred from a cemetery in Guanajuato between the years of 1896 and 1958—said disinterment being the result of a law that required loved ones to pay an annual grave tax in order to keep their dearly departed safely ensconced underground. Inevitably, some of those loved ones were unable or unavailable to make payment, so up from the crypt old Aunt Paola and Uncle Gustavo came. Once those bodies were brought back into the cold light of day, it was found that many of them had undergone a natural process of mummification, the result, it has been conjectured, of soil and atmospheric conditions unique to the area.

As novel as that is in itself, the thing that ended up making the real-life mummies of Guanajuato the stuff of legend, as well as a popular tourist attraction, is the fact that many of their faces were contorted in what appeared to be horrified screams. While this has been explained away by some dull scientific types as a natural result of the skin constricting in the course of mummification, the creepier and thus much preferable explanation is that these particular mummies had been cholera victims who had been hastily buried before they were completely dead. As fascinating as we might like to pretend that the phenomenon of naturally occurring mummification is to us, it is, understandably, this tantalizing, spook show aspect of the mummies that has kept the coins of paying customers pouring into the till of the museum in Guanajuato where they are lovingly displayed.

The movie *Mummies of Guanajuato* indoctrinates us into its idiosyncratically meandering and lackadaisical way with storytelling in its opening moments, treating us to a startlingly ponderous sequence in which the camera appears to be following a tour bus in real time through the entire length of the city. The bus comes to a stop at the Mummies of Guanajuato Museum, at which point its party disembarks, lead by a miniature tour guide going by the name of Penguin (Jorge Pinguino, here the only little person in the cast, but otherwise a key member of the Agrasanchez revue). Soon thereafter, we are given a view of the actual mummies, which are every bit as creepy as advertised. After a few introductory words, Penguin leads the group into another room where a group of "special" mummies are housed. These seven mummies, he explains, are, for reasons unknown, markedly less decomposed than the others. He's not kidding. The muscle tone on these things is amazing. This, of course, is because they're portrayed by a group of professional wrestlers who have been mummied-up with tattered clothing and hash-faced zombie make-up.

At the center of this group of special mummies is a towering figure with a droopy-eyed make-up job that looks very similar to Gary Conway's in *I Was a Teenage Frankenstein*. This, Penguin tells the assembled vacationers, is a former wrestler called Satan. He is portrayed by Manuel Leal, who we last saw as the goatee'd Frankenstein's monster in *Santo and Blue Demon vs. The Monsters*, and who would also gain fame both in the ring and in a number of Agrasanchez's multi-starrer lucha movies as the masked wrestler Tinieblas. Satan, Penguin continues, lost his championship title to a masked ancestor of Santo a hundred years previous. At that time, having allegedly made a pact with the devil, Satan swore to return from the dead a hundred years hence to seek vengeance upon el Enmascarado de Plata's descendants and supporters. In response to this, one of the tourists innocently asks on which day Satan's curse would come due. "Exactly today," replies Penguin after a bit of mental calculation. Then, having neatly set up the entire plot of *The Mummies of Guanajuato*, he promptly moves on without a word of explanation as to the identities of the other six preternaturally-burly mummies on display.

The notion of the mantle of Santo being a legacy handed down from generation to generation is not unique to *The Mummies of Guanajuato*, and was in fact a plot element in a number of earlier Santo movies. Films like 1965's *Baron Brakola* and 1969's *El Mundo de los Muertos* even presented a Colonial-era version of Santo called the Caballero Enmascarado de Plata. This character was usually portrayed by Santo wearing a frilly collar along with his mask and required the wrestler to engage in some fancy rapier work in addition to his usual moves. The device was generally used as it is in *The Mummies of Guanajuato*: to justify the supernatural appearance of some vengeance-seeking foe of one of Santo's ancestors, a situation whose frequent re-occurrence throughout the series gives the clear impression that Santo's forebears were not very good at settling their scores in their own

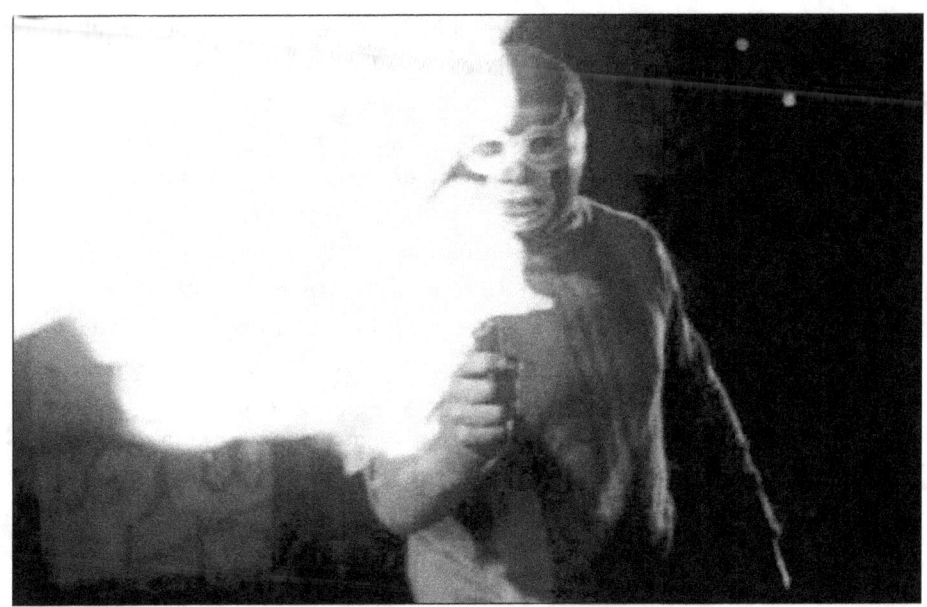

time. Soon after Penguin drops the bomb about Satan's fabled return, the guide catches a glimpse of the cadaver shuddering back to life. In response, he faints and lapses into druggy, fish-eye-lens-shot visions of the wrestler-mummies pawing at him, at which point the movie's action shifts to the nearby Santa Fe Inn. Here is where best friends Lina (played by lucha movie fixture Elsa Cardenaz) and Alicia (Patricia Ferrer) earn their daily bread, the former as a lounge singer and the latter as a cigarette girl. Lina is Mil Mascaras' girlfriend.

Because we have just had several uninterrupted minutes of fairly solid plot development, it is now time for to watch a musical number performed by an unidentified woman who plays absolutely no part in the rest of the film, despite the fact that we have just been introduced to a major character who is a singer. Once this is over, Penguin stumbles into the lounge in an agitated state, at which point we learn that, while we have been watching the lady sing, the plot of *The Mummies of Guanajuato* has moved on without us. Penguin tells the girls that, upon reviving from his faint, he found the body of Satan missing, and, upon follow-up, the three of them find footprints leading away from the pedestal on which it stood. Fortunately, Blue Demon and Mil Mascaras are in town, so the girls race with Penguin in tow to the arena where they are appearing, which affords the opportunity for a wrestling sequence in which Mil and Blue fight a couple of bearded goons.

After the match, Lina, Alicia and Penguin, find Blue and Mil in a much less heroic mood than they might have hoped for. It seems that both have had their memories wiped of all those encounters with vampires, werewolves, space aliens and mummies that have marked their cinematic careers up to this point, causing them to scoff at Penguin's story and offer all kinds of pragmatic-sounding explanations for why the mummy might be missing. Blue Demon will pay for his arrogance, as later that night, when he is leaving the deserted arena, the reanimated Satan comes up and clobbers him from behind. Satan then stands ringside and has a mummy flashback to his fateful match with Santo's ancestor all those years ago, providing another opportunity for a long wrestling sequence. Afterward, and perhaps with the intention of working his way up gradually to fighting within his own weight class, he kills the elderly caretaker at the arena and then an old drunk guy whom he encounters on the street outside.

The Guanajuato police speculate that the manner of death of these two victims suggests that a professional wrestler might be the culprit. Armed with clear evidence of sinister supernatural doings afoot, Blue, Mil and the girls hit the streets—Blue in his Alpha Romeo, and the rest in Mil's awesome green dune buggy—to do some mummy hunting. They are not so successful in this respect, but they do come across some kind of street fare where some people in Colonial era garb are performing a folk tune on traditional instruments, which enables us to take a much needed breather from what has been yet another several minutes of uninterrupted plot development. Penguin does his part to move things along by thoughtfully phoning Blue to let him know that he is being murdered by Satan at that very moment. The group rush to Penguin's apartment, only to find that Satan has had yet one more success in his campaign to practice his wrestling skills upon only the most impossibly over-matched opponents.

It is at this point, in the aftermath of Penguin's murder, that Blue Demon makes a couple of decisions that seriously put into question his leadership skills. First of all, he determines that the group shouldn't report Penguin's death to the authorities, for the reason that "they'd think it was us," despite the fact that there has been little reason established at this point why they would. Second of all, he fatefully rejects Mil Mascaras' suggestion that they get Santo involved, protesting that *that* would be exactly what the damn mummy wants. Of course, this is only a bad decision in light of how everything turns out, as it provides Blue with a mouthful of words that he will ultimately have to eat.

Finally, as they make their way out of Penguin's apartment, the gang is confronted by Satan himself and the other six wrestler-mummies. After a bit of grappling, Blue Demon bravely declares the mummies indestructible and orders a retreat, setting the tone for all of Mil and Blue's further encounters with the mummies over the remaining course of the movie. Compounding *The Mummies of Guanajuato*'s insult to Blue is the fact that it includes undoubtedly the most humiliating enactment of the time-tested "Evil Blue Demon" gimmick in his filmography. This trope born of the Blue-Santo team-ups achieved a life beyond its initial utility and began to turn up even in films in which Blue didn't have to fight Santo, as if audiences just grew to expect it.

In *The Mummies of Guanajuato*, the trick is accomplished by having Satan sneak up and clobber Blue from behind, then steal both his mask and the clothes off his back and give them to one of his hench-mummies to carry out the impersonation.

That hench-mummy then dresses up as Blue and goes out and kills some people, leading the police to suspect Blue is behind the recent string of murders. Soon, the TV is broadcasting reports that Blue Demon is wanted and "on the run," despite the fact that he's still just hanging out with Mil at Lina and Alicia's place like he was before all this happened.

Finally, someone behind the scenes decides that a suitable amount of running time has been achieved, and that it is time for a hastily contrived, entirely coincidence-dependent ending to be fashioned in order to wrap things up. To that end, Santo and his manager, while driving home from a match, happen to stop for the night in Guanajuato, pulling into the town square just as the mummies are attacking a group of townspeople. After a brief scuffle, Santo, echoing Blue's earlier sentiments, declares the mummies "undefeatable" and retreats. But he soon returns to the fray, joined in the fight by Mil and Blue. Things are looking grim until Santo, in a moment of sudden inspiration, asks Mil to go fetch some flamethrower pistols sitting on the seat of his car. Mil dutifully complies, and when he gets to Santo's car—what do you know?—there the pistols are, right on the seat where Carlos Suarez had been sitting only moments before. Mil returns and distributes the pistols to Santo and Blue, after which the three of them open fire, quickly reducing the previously-indestructible mummies to piles of smoking ash. Everyone laughs, and Lina turns to Blue and says, "You would have saved a lot of trouble if you had called Santo on time." Ouch.

In terms of box office success, *The Mummies of Guanajuato* was a sort of last hurrah for the once lucrative lucha genre, enjoying a run in Mexico City that, at nine weeks, was longer than that of any Santo movie previous or since. As a result, a slew of sequels was spawned, none of which were able to duplicate its impact, mainly due to the fact that they were unable to feature the same assemblage of talent (Superzan

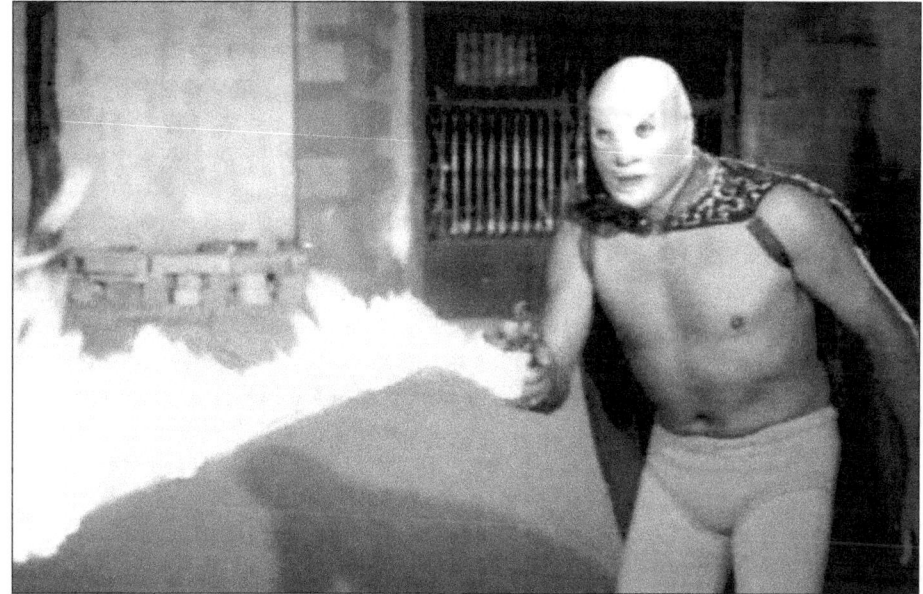

was even in one of them). The popularity of the film even had consequences for the actual mummies of Guanajuato, as the museum where they were housed saw a considerable rise in attendance as a result of the free publicity. That the film's impact was so profound is all the more impressive when you consider what an aimless, lazily-constructed mess *The Mummies of Guanajuato* is. You'd have to be kind of humorless, however, to also not find it to be a good bit of fun, and it is that, combined with the thrill of seeing its three heavy hitting stars sharing the screen for the first time, that I imagine accounted for its broad appeal.

In fact, it is by virtue of these very shortcomings that *The Mummies of Guanajuato* provides a perfect example of the lucha genre's beauty and magic. It is a film that, without the presence of Blue Demon, Mil Mascaras and Santo, would be completely unwatchable; but that somehow, by its inclusion of three grown men who conduct all of their affairs from behind constricting and colorfully-ornamented full head masks, attains an added dimension that renders it irresistibly compelling. You could call it "surrealism" or "absurdity", but the real key to these movie's allure is that, once you make the leap required to accept these improbable figures as your heroes, you have crossed a frontier in the suspension of disbelief that leaves you liberated in a state of unbounded, childlike credulity. Truly, to accept the notion that a masked wrestler in leopard print hot pants and gold lame tights is the world's best hope against a bunch of murderous mummies that all look like Hulk Hogan wearing a rubber fright mask from Walgreen's brings with it a joy of surrender paralleled by few other experiences on Earth.

The Mummies of Guanajuato is an important film in the history of lucha cinema, not to mention one that's a good time if you know what you're getting into. It generates enough goodwill by virtue of its sheer goofiness that it's an easy task to overlook most of its many flaws in the interest of just going along and enjoying the ride. Most of its flaws, that is, except one: the disrespect shown toward poor old Blue Demon. It's just a little painful to think that Blue went into this project thinking that it would be a star vehicle, only to have it turn into something of a prolonged joke at his expense. The man clearly deserved better.

Still, one can take heart in the fact that Blue Demon's film career was far from over at this point, with a number of its high points still ahead. One can also take solace in those few moments when *The Mummies of Guanajuato* takes a break from making him the butt of its jokes, actually manages to place Blue Demon in a suitably iconic context. Such is the movie's final sequence, in which he, Santo and Mil ride smiling off into the sunset, Blue and Santo in their respective sports cars, and Mil in his dune buggy. At that moment, all of those perhaps less-than-spectacular exploits we've witnessed on the parts of our heroes over the past ninety minutes are wiped away, and we see them only as their most perfect selves: three titans of lucha cinema heading off toward the vast unknown, heartily embracing the promise of greater dangers and grander adventures ahead. It's such an inspiring image that, even though we know that said promise will ultimately be realized by way of cheesy and unconvincing monster make-up and charity haunted house-level special effects (not to mention padded with lengthy wrestling matches and unwanted musical numbers) we cannot help but want to follow along.

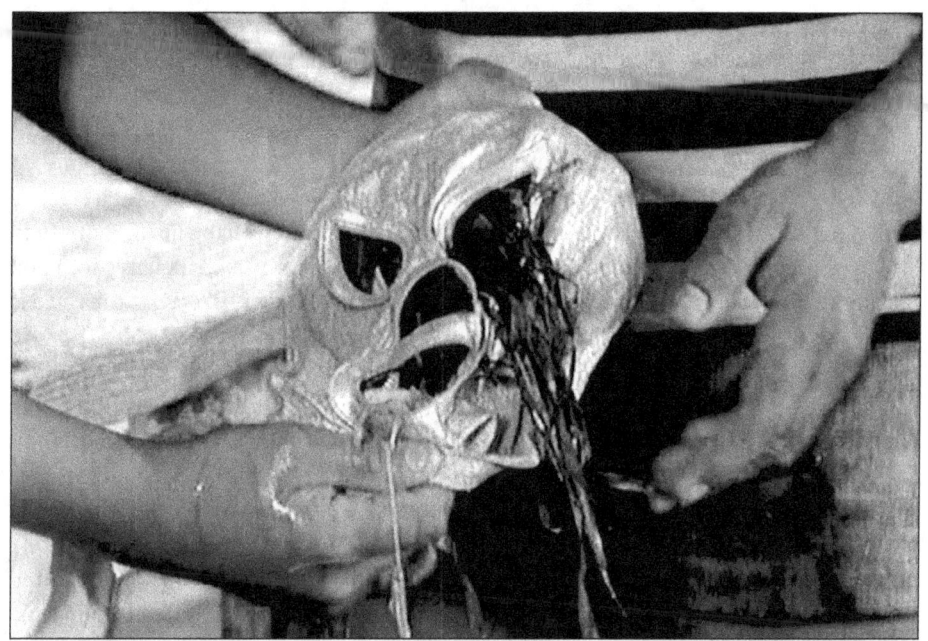

Down for the Count

Given that success of *The Mummies of Guanajuato*, one might think that producer Rogelio Agrasanchez would be anxious to repeat the formula as soon as possible. Agrasanchez did hope to include Santo, along with Blue Demon and Mil Mascaras, in the all-star lineup up of his Champions of Justice the following year. Santo's subsequent absence from that film is typically attributed to a scheduling conflict, though it's telling that, while both Blue Demon and Mil Mascaras would star in numerous Agrasanchez productions throughout the 1970s, Santo, with the exception of *The Mummies of Guanajuato*, would manage to avoid them for the better part of seven years. As a result, the three would not be reunited until 1977, in *Misterio en las Bermudas*, a film conceived and produced by Agrasanchez that would not see release in Mexico until the summer of 1979.

Of course, a lot had happened in the intervening years, not the least being that, by the time of *Misterio en las Bermudas*' release, *lucha* cinema had become a genre on life support. Waning audience interest in the films had seemingly come to be matched by a lack of interest in entertaining them on the part of filmmakers, with predictably diminishing results. Agrasanchez's films in particular could be seen as emblematic of this trend, though it's arguable whether or not they were a cause or victim of the public's apathy. Agrasanchez deserves credit for keeping the genre alive during this period, though in order to do so, he was apparently driven to resort to fly-by-night productions that were increasingly hasty, unfocused and tawdry.

Misterio en las Bermudas is not an exception to this tendency in Agrasanchez's work—though it's another aspect of its conception that makes it the doozy that it is. *Misterio* was the last *lucha* film produced by Agrasanchez, and at some point the decision seems to have been made by him or someone that it would also be the swan song of the genre *in toto*. Unfortunately, the dearth of members of the Mexican movie-going public who would see this as a loss effectively guaranteed that *Misterio* would usher off lucha cinema with, not a bang, but a whimper—albeit an odd and interesting whimper. And to be fair, there is—technically, at least—a bang.

Another thing that occurred between the releases of *The Mummies of Guanajuato* and *Misterio* was an increased public obsession with the Bermuda Triangle. The idea of the Triangle, that there was an area of the Atlantic that was hoovering up far more than its fair share of ships and planes, perhaps because of Atlantis, made its entry into pop culture in the early '60s. The tipping point, however, occurred in 1974, with the release of two bestselling books. One of these books was Richard Winer's *The Devil's Triangle*, which was accompanied by a feature documentary of the same name which Winer himself directed. The other was *The Bermuda Triangle*, written by Charles Berlitz. Berlitz's book also got the film treatment, though in that case the author's theories on the subject were dramatized by having John Huston, Hugo Stiglitz, and Claudine Auger terrorized by supernatural phenomena during an ill-fated summer cruise. Fittingly for our purposes, that 1978 film was directed by René Cardona Jr., a man who was no stranger to the lucha film genre, especially by way of his father and namesake, who had directed a number of its classics, including *Wrestling Women vs. the Aztec Mummy* and its sleazier counterpart *Night of the Bloody Apes*.

Of course, for every wild theory put forth, there was a corresponding, if not equal, effort at debunking them. Probably the most notable of these was Lawrence David Kusche's 1975 book *The Bermuda Triangle Mystery: Solved*, which countered many of their arguments by way of boring facts. No amount of facts, however, could change the fact that paranormal explanations for the phenomena in question were simply the sexier option, as would be borne out by the plethora of offshoots—including ancillary

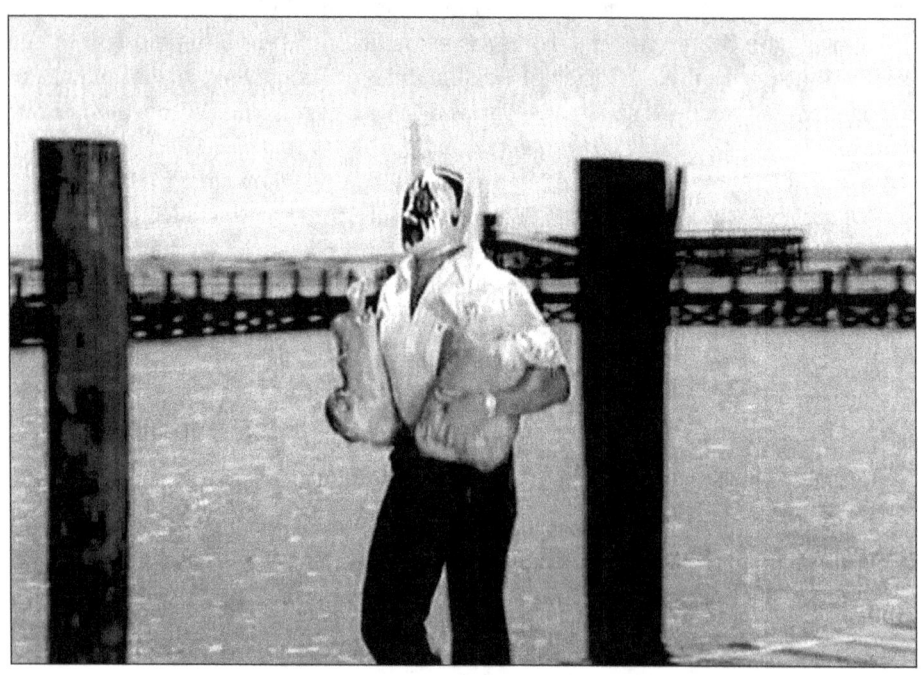

publications and a seeming multitude of American TV movies—that would continue to pop up throughout the remainder of the decade. This would likely also explain why the Triangle became the bogey of choice in *Misterio en las Bermudas*, replacing the usual vampires, werewolves, or space vixens seen in previous lucha outings.

The prologue to *Misterio en las Bermudas* is a tapestry of confusion, setting the stage, not only for the mystery to come, but for the mystery that is *Misterio en las Bermudas* itself. We first see some kind of sci-fi gizmo rise up out of the ocean, accompanied by the sound of a whistling tea kettle, after which the oceans roil and much stock footage of thunder and lightning is unleashed. A passenger airplane is shown disappearing from the sky. Next, we see a man and a young boy fishing off a pier. There is some loose talk about some missing English scientists, and then the boy catches something on his line. It is Santo's mask, waterlogged and draped in seaweed. This discovery sends the man, whose name is Anselmo, into a reverie. It all started, he tells the boy, "many years ago", when Santo, Blue Demon and Mil Mascaras arrived in town for a series of matches...

Where "town" is meant to be is unclear, but where *Misterio en las Bermudas* was filmed was Port Isabel, a Texas town just a few miles north of the border from Matamoros. Other exteriors were filmed on neighboring South Padre Island, a popular Spring Break spot that was home to the Bahia Mar Resort Hotel, which doubled as the movie's futuristic underwater city. That said, however attractive these locations might have been (not very), or inexpensive to shoot in (more likely), one thing is clear: neither was on the Bermuda Triangle.

For as formidable an assemblage of *luchador* might as Santo, Blue and Mil to descend upon one small town there has to be some kind of secret agenda. And, indeed, after the requisite tag team match we see the trio called to a hush-hush meeting with representatives from the fictional nation of Irania. The Princess Sobeida, daughter of the country's "Great Vizier," who is of course an old friend of Santo's, is coming through town to sign an important treaty, and there are sinister forces determined to stop her. Naturally, the Iranian-ian officials have adopted countermeasures to this plot, and they represent the sublime heights of absurd lucha movie plotting. An impostor will be substituted for the princess, while the real princess (Gaynor Kote) will pose as a karate expert visiting town for an exhibition. Yet, as foolproof as this plot may be, it is still felt that three lumbering masked wrestlers are needed on hand to provide protection for the girl.

No protection, of course, is deemed necessary for the impostor, so, once the terrorists, with little explication, hastily change their plot from one of kidnapping to assassination, she is brutally murdered in her bed with no one to hear her desperate cries. Princess Sobeida, on the other hand, proves to have some actual mastery of karate (it's suggested that Santo was one of her teachers) and is thus that much more fortified against attack. This makes it all the more laughable when it's revealed that, on the other side of this equation, is a gang of foreign thugs lead by Godard, who is played by Santo's frequent costar/manager Carlos Suarez.

All of this is of no matter, however, because Godard has a secret weapon: three treacherous bikini babes who shimmy their way into the good graces of the *luchadors*. Santo eagerly pairs off with Rina (Silvia Manriquez), who then somewhat inexplicably drugs him with a truth serum in order to find out the details of his mission. It turns out that Rina merely wants Santo's help in tracking down her missing scientist father, and that she is in fact a double agent working within Godard's gang in hopes of gaining some information.

Rina is herself being pursued by a pair of guys in chrome coveralls who have a habit of materializing out of thin air. Once they succeed in capturing her, it leads to a speedboat chase that ends when the shiny gizmo from the beginning of the movie rises from the sea and causes the captors' boat to disappear before the startled eyes of Santo, Blue Demon and Mil Mascaras. Rina finds herself in an underwater city that's pretty heavy on the wood grain, where she is greeted by her missing father. He tells her that this is a Utopian civilization whose inhabitants have made a long practice of taking the best and the brightest from the surface world in order that they may live in peace and harmony, away from the warlike stupidity of the warlike and stupid world. He also tells her he hopes she likes it there, because she will never be able to leave. This settled, we are now free to go back to the movie about the three masked wrestlers protecting a princess.

Misterio en las Bermudas was directed by Gilberto Martinez Solares, who proved himself capable of spinning out a pacey *luchador* adventure with the madcap *Santo and Blue Demon vs. The Monsters*. Yet the pacing of *Misterio* is at times perversely ponderous. Some of that is attributable to the filmmakers' apparent confusion over what story they were trying to tell, as if the film occasionally had to stop mid-run to ask, "Who am I?" The underwater civilization plot and the more straightforward international intrigue storyline never dovetail in any meaningful way, leaving the former to feel little more than a weird digression, and the latter to suffer from the impression that all involved felt it unworthy of full attention. On the other hand, *Misterio en las Bermudas'* plentiful longueurs can also be attributed to the fact that it was a late '70s lucha movie, and that's what late '70s lucha movies are like.

Late period lucha movies—and those produced by Rogelio Agrasanchez in particular—tended to eschew the Gothic trappings and atmosphere of their predecessors in favor of an almost stubborn adherence to the prosaic and homely. These movies implied that when they weren't punching vampires in the face, *luchadors* rode the bus just like us. There's a peculiar beauty in these "*luchadors* at home" moments, with *Misterio* containing one of the best: Mil Mascaras, wearing a polo shirt and slacks, walking back to his apartment with a brimming bag of groceries under each arm, without a care in the world.

Misterio's action is equitably divided between its stars, with each receiving showcase moments among numerous fights and action set pieces. While Santo, being the biggest draw, is the technical star of the film, it's a real treat to see just how much of their screen time the three wrestlers spend together, whether it's in a fight or simply lounging by the pool in their snazzy leisure wear. *Guanajuato* promised the thrill of seeing Santo, Blue Demon and Mil Mascaras on the screen together for the first time, but, ironically, it's *Misterio*, the inarguably weaker film, that actually delivers it.

Misterio en las Bermudas' climactic fight begins with Princess Sobeida cornered in her apartment by the razor-wielding Godard. Thanks to her karate skills, she's able to make good work of him before Santo, Blue and Mil show up to finish the job. It ends up taking a karate expert and three burly professional wrestlers to subdue an old man armed only with a straight razor. Such is the grandeur and sweep of this, the final film in the *luchadors* canon. Earlier, we have had a brief revisit with Rina and her father in the undersea city, during which she tells her father that she has fallen in love with Santo, and that she misses him. Thus, during a seemingly cheery *denouement* in which Santo, Blue Demon, and Mil Mascaras ride triumphantly into the sunset aboard the Princess's boat, do we abruptly cut back to the man and boy from the prologue.

"And they were never seen again", says the man. It is implied that Rina had the undersea people use their gizmo to bring Santo and his friends back to their undersea city so that she could be with Santo forever, ending things on a pleasingly romantic note, right? But then the man continues, saying something about the "predictions of revelations" being carried out, and then, finally: "The end of the world is near." Then we're shown stock footage of a nuclear blast, followed by an immense mushroom cloud. THE END.

El Santo foiled Agrasanchez's apocalyptic vision by appearing in several more lackluster features after *Misterio*, finally retiring with an especially woeful twofer of Florida-shot quickies in 1981. Blue Demon and Mil Mascaras, however, kept the faith and disappeared from the screen for the foreseeable future—in Blue's case, forever, and, in Mil's, until his who-would-have-seen-that-coming cinematic comeback in 2007. Thankfully, due to the survival and ready availability of so many of all three men's movie efforts, *Misterio en las Bermudas* need serve only as a footnote to, rather than the last word on, their esteemed careers. However, one wonders if that ending is an indication of just how catastrophic the loss of lucha cinema was to Rogelio Agrasanchez personally; if, for him, the only alternative to a world in which Santo, Blue Demon and Mil Mascaras no longer fought criminals and monsters on the big screen was no world at all? §

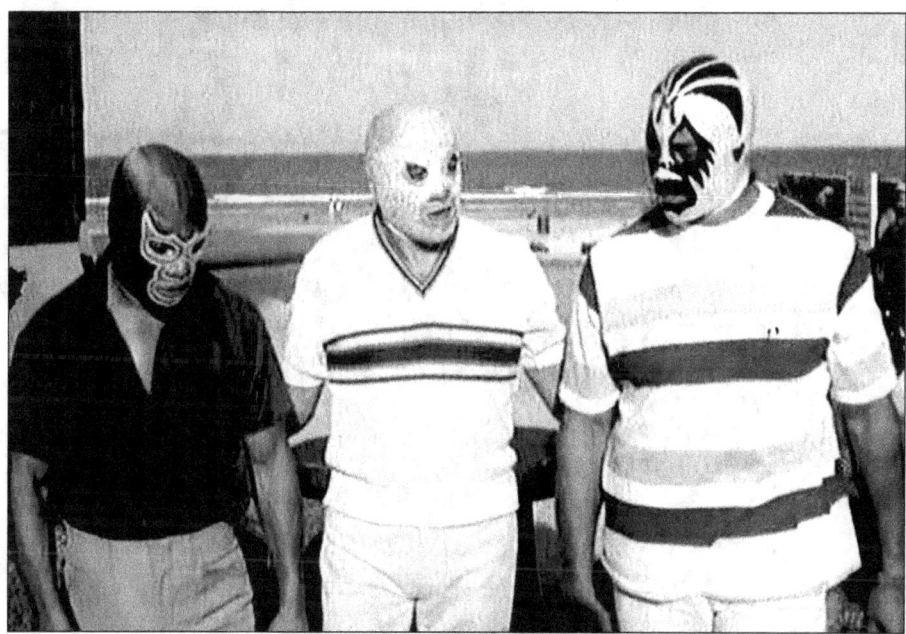

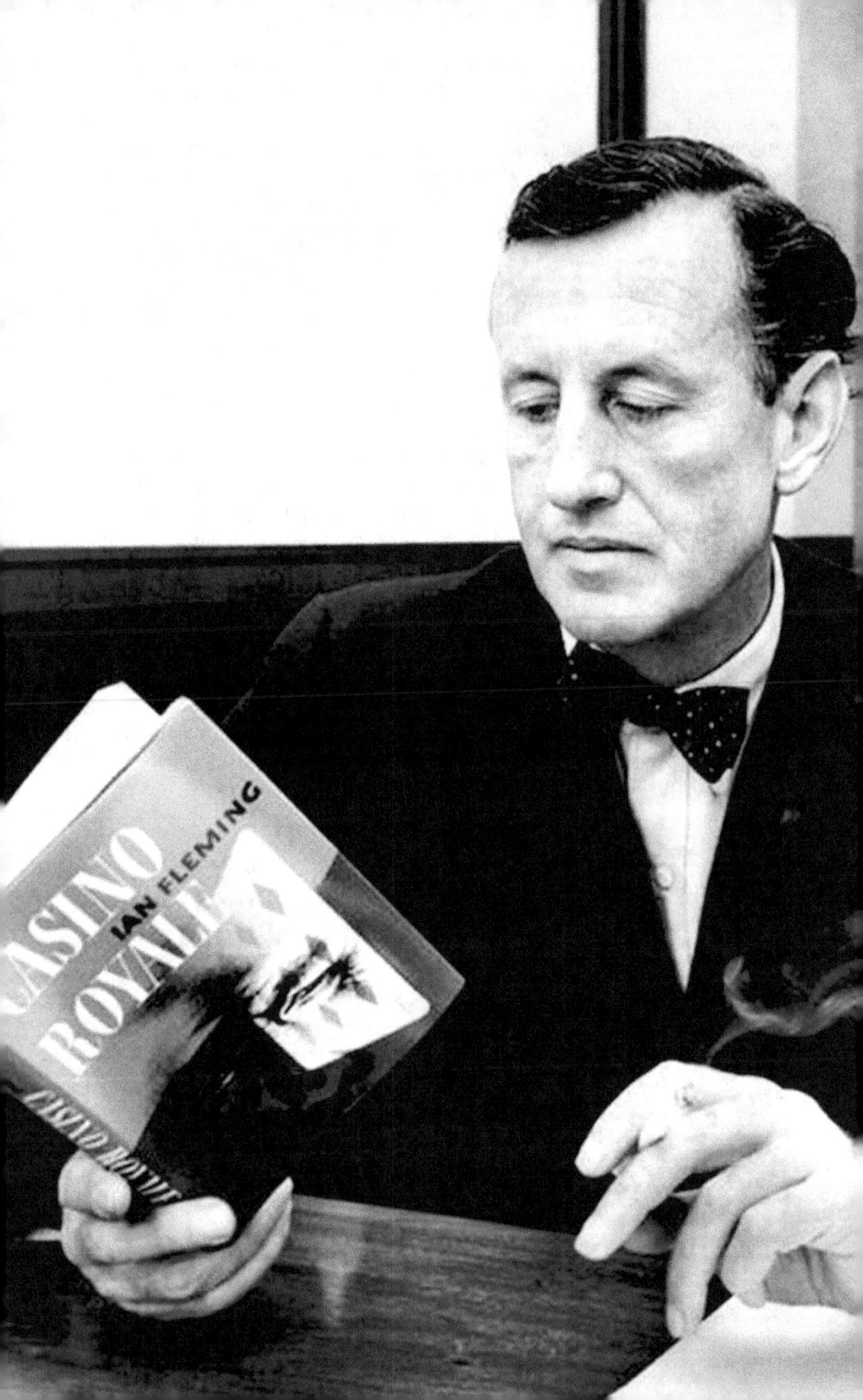

07 CASINO AMARO

Ian Fleming, Lucky Luciano, and the cocktail that kicked off a cultural phenomenon

The Americano is a fairly nondescript cocktail with which to kick off James Bond's illustrious drinking career. Of course, it's doubtful that, at the time he was writing his "dreadful oafish opus," Ian Fleming could have guessed that the Americano would be examined as the first drink of an international phenomenon. Fleming came of age during one of the great eras of imbibing. Many 19th century drinks were still around, and many 20th century drinks were being created. This was the time of hardboiled detective fiction and pulp anti-heroes, of bootleggers and rumrunners and Nick and Nora Charles. It was a time when people were having a weary drink after the end of one world war and hunkering down at the start of another. By the time Fleming sat down at the desk in his Jamaican villa to write *Casino Royale*, mid-century cocktail culture was in full swing.

In *Casino Royale*, Fleming's attitude toward the Americano is benign, even affectionate. "The room was sumptuous with those over-masculine trappings which, together with briar pipes and wire-haired terriers, spell luxury in France," he wrote. "Everything was brass-studded leather and polished mahogany. The curtains and carpets were in royal blue. The waiters wore striped waistcoats and green baize aprons. Bond ordered an Americano and examined the sprinkling of over-dressed customers, mostly from Paris he guessed, who sat talking with focus and vivacity, creating that theatrically clubbable atmosphere of *l'heure de l'aperitif*."

And why not? It's an enjoyable cocktail, perfectly harmless, difficult to screw up. Yet by the short story "From a View to a Kill" (published in the *Daily Express* in September, 1959), Bond's opinion of the Americano has changed dramatically. What he enjoyed about it in *Casino Royale* is exactly what irritates him in "From a View to a Kill." As Bond sits at Parisian street café Fouquet's (99 Avenue des Champs-Élysées), he orders an Americano, which he describes as "not a solid drink"—not because it was poorly made, but because it's a poor drink in general: "One cannot drink seriously in French cafés," Fleming writes. "Out of doors on pavement in the sun is no place for vodka or whisky or gin. A *fine a l'eau* is fairly serious, but it intoxicates without tasting very good. A *quart de champagne* or a *champagne a l'orange* is all right before luncheon, but in the evening one quart leads to another quart, and a bottle of indifferent champagne is a bad foundation for the night. Pernod is possible, but it should be drunk in company and anyway Bond had never liked the stuff because its licorice taste reminded him of his childhood. No, in cafés you have to drink the least offensive of the musical comedy drinks that go with them, and Bond always had the same thing—an Americano—bitter Campari, Cinzano, a large slice of lemon peel, and soda. For soda, he always stipulated Perrier, for in his opinion expensive soda water was the cheapest way to improve a poor drink." So much for the *joie de vivre* of *l'heure de l'aperitif.*

In this case, the Americano seems to be an innocent victim as Fleming takes aim at something he truly dislikes: Paris. In the late 1950s, *The Sunday Times* commissioned Fleming to write a series of travelogues about his impressions of some of the world's most famous cities. Collected in 1963 as *Thrilling Cities*, there is a fair bit of grousing, as one would expect from Fleming, as well as the sort of breathless enthusiasm for exotic locales that informed many of his Bond novels. Fleming's chapter on New York, for example, was regarded as a hatchet job, so much so that he issued an apology by way of a short story, "007 in New York," which went to great lengths to gush about how much James Bond loves New York. At least New York made it into the book. Paris is conspicuous by its exclusion.

Fleming makes clear his distaste with the city through Bond, most acidically in the short story "For Your Eyes Only," a good portion of which is dedicated to 007 dwelling on how much he hates Paris: "It was the heart that was gone," Bond grouses, "pawned to the tourists, pawned to the Russians and Roumanians and Bulgars, pawned to the scum of the world who had gradually taken the town over. And, of course, pawned to the Germans." That leads into a tirade about the sorry state of French architecture.

Even when he's in Venice, having an Americano at Florian on the Piazza San Marco in the story "Risico," Bond can't avoid tying the drink to France. His afternoon's reverie is interrupted by "a couple of French culture-snobs discussing the imbalance of the containing facade of St. Mark's Square." It's a shame the Americano gets swept up in 007's dislike of Paris. It's not even a French invention. The Americano traces its roots and its ingredients back to Italy, and more specifically to Gaspare Campari and Caffè Campari in Milan.

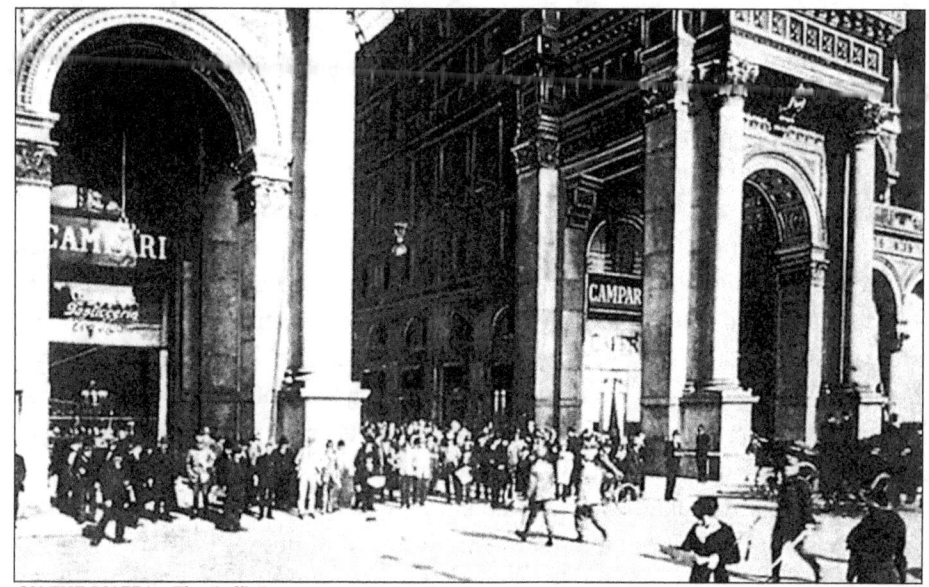

ON THE PIAZZA—The Caffè Capari.

The Italian Connection

Gaspare Campari was born in Cassolnovo, Lombardy, in 1828. As a boy, he held a job at the Bass Bar in Turin. By the time he was fourteen, he was considered a *maitre licoriste*—one part bartender, one part apothecary. Turin was a hub of *aperitif* and *digestif* production, and Gaspare Campari became adept at the art and science of blending a base liquor (usually a fortified wine or neutral grain spirit) with an assortment of herbs, spices, and other botanicals. These elixirs boast a wide variety of flavors, though most showcase a bitter quality.

By the 1840s, Gaspare Campari's concoctions were sold throughout what would become (but was not quite) Italy. By 1860, he had enough money and experience to found Gruppo Campari. Settling in Milan, he opened the first of his cafés in 1862. It was here that he took his signature Campari aperitif from Turin, mixed it with Cinzano Italian vermouth from Milan, added a splash of soda, and dubbed it the Milano-Torino in honor of the two cities from which its ingredients originated. During Prohibition, American citizens prowling the world for a decent drink settled into Gaspare's Caffè and became fans of the Milano-Torino, which was subsequently renamed the Americano in their honor, or so the legend goes.

Campari was a sharp businessman who, in partnership with his son Davide, expanded Campari beyond the confines of his own bar. Gaspare and Davide commissioned artists to paint exquisite advertisements. They made the popular *aperitivo* available to other cafés and bars on the condition that they displayed Campari advertising. This was no difficult pitch, since the Campari ads were gorgeous. Gaspare died in 1882, leaving Davide in charge of Gruppo Campari. He was the one who truly took Campari international, though to some degree this wasn't entirely motivated by business savvy. Davide, as legend has it, took Campari international in pursuit of Lina Cavalieri, a popular opera singer he met while working at Caffè Campari. Cavalieri was relocating to Nice, in the French Riviera, and Davide did not want to part with her. So he decided it was time to bring their popular bitter liqueur to the wider world beginning with, coincidentally, Nice.

In her time, Lina Cavalieri was regarded as one of the most beautiful women in the world. She was also considered rather a middling singer. Orphaned at the age of fifteen, she became a ward of the state but chafed under the strict stewardship of the nuns at the orphanage in which she was placed. When the opportunity arose to sneak out and join a traveling band of performers, she took it. Her travels brought her to Paris, where her looks and a passable singing voice got her jobs in cafés, music halls, and the popular Folies Bergère, famous as the home of Josephine Baker, who debuted her infamous banana skirt at the theater. It was also the subject of a painting by Edouard Manet, *A Bar at the Folies-Bergère*, in the early 1880s. The Folies still exists, at its original location of 32 rue Richer in Paris. James Bond may have been too busy being crabby about the French while drinking his Americano to swing by the actual location, but in the 1971 film *Diamonds are Forever* he does take in the Las Vegas re-creation of the Folies Bergère at the Tropicana—a hotel-casino opened by a man named Ben Jaffe, who also owned the Fontainebleau Miami Beach, where Bond stays during his Florida jaunt in *Goldfinger* and where, later, Frank Sinatra's Tony Rome (in the film of the same name) would luxuriate in full suit and tie beachside while awaiting the arrival of bikini-clad Jill St. John—the Bond Girl, coincidentally, in *Diamonds are Forever*.

Cavalieri's career began in 1900, at the Theatro San Carlos in Naples, where she appeared as Nedda in a production of *Pagliacci*. It was considered a disaster. Bad reviews followed her and the opera to Lisbon. There were serious doubts that this chanteuse from the cabarets had what it took to be a *diva*. Her singing was thin. She was confused by the choreography. She often changed her tempo, throwing off the conductor. Her acting was awkward and unfeeling. But she was beautiful, so people still came to see her, and she worked hard to improve, taking lessons with accomplished singer Mariani Masi.

If accounts of her performances are to be believed, it wasn't exactly money well spent, but what she lacked in talent she made up for with looks and bravado. Her star continued to rise in Europe and the United States, where she stayed on for two seasons at the Metropolitan Opera and was paid $1,000 a night—a sum substantially higher than that of the Met's most acclaimed diva, Geraldine Farrar. By this time, Cavalieri was being referred to as" the world's most photographed woman," not to mention the world's most beautiful. Writer Gabriele D'Annunzio called her "the personification of Venus on earth." Italian painter and designer Piero Fornasetti considered her his muse, using her likeness in over 350 creations. Not one to sit idly by, Lina capitalized on her popularity, opening a cosmetics store, writing beauty guides, and even parlaying her fame into a film career.

She attracted a long list of well-to-do suitors. The first, in 1900, was Prince Alexandre Bariatinsky of Russia. Her marriage to the prince didn't last. Neither did her marriage to her next husband, painter Robert Winthrop Chanler of New York's storied Astor family. They divorced on their honeymoon after his family discovered he had been convinced to sign a prenuptial agreement leaving Cavalieri the whole of his fortune. A court battle ensued. The family disowned Chanler, and the Met disowned Cavalieri. No one wanted to be on the bad side of the Astors. Her next marriage, to French tenor Lucien Muratore, didn't last, either. Much to his chagrin, at no point in her long list of lovers and husbands appears the name "Davide Campari."

Cavalieri was living in Italy with her fourth husband, Paolo d'Arvanni, when Italy joined World War II on the side of Germany. While trying to collect some of her valuables during an Allied air raid, both Lina and Paolo were killed during bombing on February 7, 1944. As fate would have it, one of her most famous roles was in Puccini's *Manon Lescaut*. The reviews of her performance were mixed, but Puccini himself loved her, exclaiming "Cavalieri was magnificent!" In Act II of the opera, Manon is arrested by a jealous military officer after she delays escape in order to gather up her jewels and clothing.

Enduring love may have never blossomed between Davide and Lina, but Gruppo Campari took off, so at least he had that. In 1904, Campari opened their first large-scale production facility, in Sesto San Giovanni, just north of Milan.

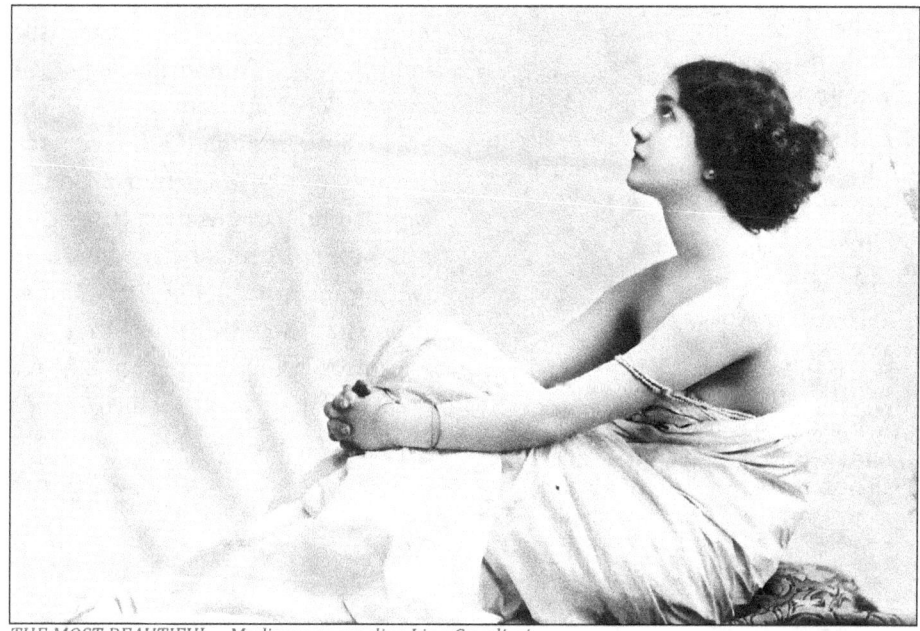

THE MOST BEAUTIFUL—Mediocre opera diva Lina Cavalieri.

MILANO-TORINO

- 2 oz Campari
- 2 oz Punt e Mes Sweet Vermouth

Add all ingredients to a rocks glass filled with ice. Stir well. Garnish with an orange slice.

AMERICANO

- 1 ½ oz Campari
- 1 ½ oz Punt e Mes Sweet Vermouth
- Club soda

Add the Campari and vermouth to a rocks glass filled with ice. Add a splash of club soda. Garnish with an orange twist.

APEROL SPRITZ

- 4 ½ oz Prosecco
- 2 ½ oz Aperol
- Lime Wheel
- 1 oz Club soda

Add the prosecco to a Collins glass filled with ice. Add the Aperol and lime wheel. Top with club soda.

GARIBALDI

- 1 oz Campari
- 3 oz Fresh Orange Juice

Add the Campari to a rocks glass filled with ice. Top it with orange juice. Stir. Garnish with half a slice of orange.

OLD PAL

- 1 ½ oz Rye Whiskey
- ¾ oz Dry Vermouth
- ¾ oz Campari

Add all ingredients to a mixing glass filled with ice. Stir well. Strain into chilled cocktail glass. Twist a piece of lemon peel over the drink and use as garnish.

In 1923, having weathered the Italian war of unification and the Great War, Davide focused the company on production of a single recipe. It is that recipe that is known today as Campari. Well, sort of. Originally, its distinctive red color came from the same source as much other red coloring: dye carmine, made from crushing cochineal insects. For decades, this was how large-scale red dye for food products was produced. In the Internet age, sensational stories about the beetles people were unwittingly consuming circulated, causing predictable panic. In 2006, Campari ceased using carmine. And because this is the modern age, the outrage that caused the dye to be reformulated itself caused an outrage among purists who did not want to see the time-tested Campari recipe altered.

Davide Campari died in 1936. The company he left behind, built on the bitter herbal liqueur his father mixed the century before, was a juggernaut. Today, Gruppo Campari is one of the largest beverage companies in the world, and though Campari itself remains one of only two products they produce themselves (the other is Campari bitter soda), they own companies producing all manner of spirits, including the other key ingredient in the Americano: Cinzano sweet Italian vermouth, which Gruppo Campari acquired in 1999.

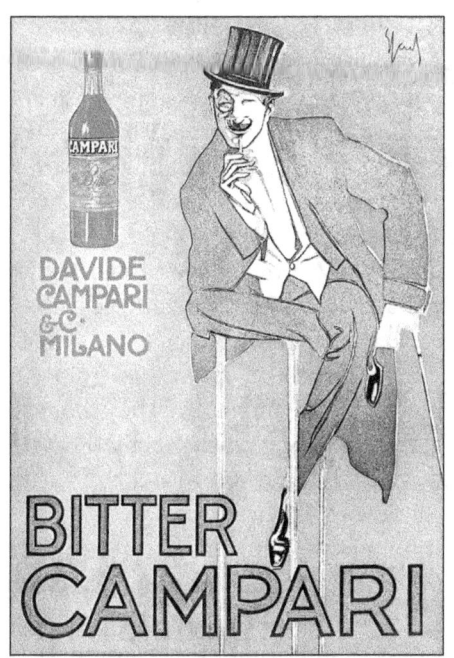
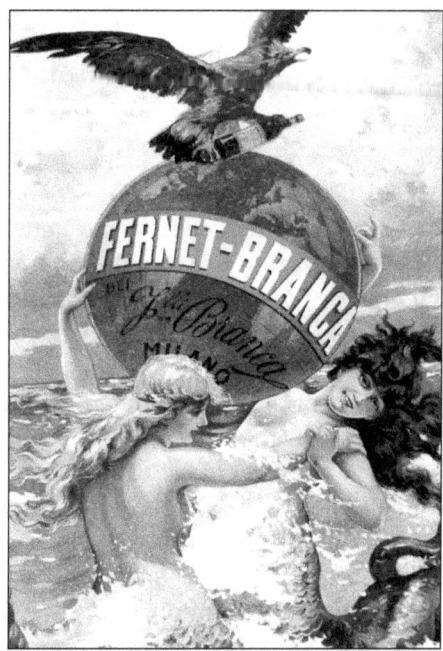

Why So Bitter?

Campari is a variation on bitter Italian liqueurs known collectively as *amaro*. The only notable difference is that Campari is used primarily as an ingredient in cocktails while amaro proper is meant to be consumed on its own ("neat") or perhaps with the addition of an ice cube. In many ways, amaro is to Italy what scotch is to Scotland—not just a national drink, but a national identity, a representative of cultural heritage. And just as it is with scotch whisky, pinpointing an exact when and where for amaro's creation is impossible. These things are not created whole and out of thin air, after all, but evolve over a period of decades, one thing becoming the next, until someone bothers to write a recipe down or gets caught making it and has to pay tax, thus codifying that particular beverage and entering it into the public record, giving people a date to which they can point. So while amaro, or something very much like it, existed before the 19th century, that's the easiest place to take up the story, because that's when people started writing the story down.

Amari is a diverse category of liqueur which comes in a variety of styles, proofs, and flavors, though as with whisky there is an underlying common character that binds them together. There are countless regional variations in France, Germany, and throughout the Alpine regions and Eastern Europe. It's one of those European alcohols that locals classify as a *digestif* (aiding in the process of digesting an exquisite meal), except when they are classified as *aperitifs* (aiding in the opening up of the appetite, in preparation for an exquisite meal). They are bitter drinks, except when they are sweet. Just about all of them claimed, at some point and like just about every type of booze, to possess medicinal properties, curing everything from heartburn to flatulence to high blood pressure. For the most part, they are made from an infusion of secret herbs, usually in a fortified Italian wine or a *grappa* (grappa being, more or less, "Italian brandy," usually distilled from the leftover skins of wine grapes), except when it isn't. It's a loose category that allows a lot of interpretation. For some, the flavors of amari can be a challenge. Bitter is not an unusual flavor, but its position as a pleasurable and even desirable taste is still relatively rare in the US. Amari categories are derived from strength and overall character, one of which seems to be "everything else that doesn't really fit into any of the above categories." A medium amaro is one with a moderate alcohol level, more than wine, less than whiskey—usually somewhere in the range of 32% alcohol by volume (ABV), which is around 64 proof; wine is typically 12-15% ABV, whiskey anywhere from 40-60%. Two of the most popular brands of medium style amaro are the Milanese brand Ramazzotti, which tastes like a bitter root beer, and the Sicilian brand Averna, named after its creator, Salvatore Averna, who came up with the recipe in 1868. Medium style amari balance between bitter, sweet, and citrus flavors.

Fernet style amari are the burly troublemakers. They have a more bitter flavor which dominates the other ingredients (some brands have as many 40, 50, even 60 or more ingredients as part of their herb and spice bundle). They also have a higher alcoholic content, roughly equivalent to that of whiskey. Fernet Branca is one of the most famous of this style, and perhaps the best known amaro in the world. Its name has been dropped everywhere from F. Scott Fitzgerald's *Tender is the Night* to the 2012 Batman movie *The Dark Knight Rises*, in which the character Alfred (Michael Caine) describes the perfect retirement: sitting at a café in Florence, drinking a Fernet Branca (which is exactly what he does, at the La Loggia Bar & Restaurant in Fiesole, just northeast of Florence).

Fernet Branca is also one of the few brands created by a woman—or so the story goes (that old qualifier again). Maria Scala purportedly finalized a fernet formula in 1845 and intended it to be used, like most herbal liqueurs, as a remedy for an upset stomach. She married into the Branca family shortly thereafter, and her potent concoction was dubbed Fernet Branca. Other sources claim that Fernet Branca was created by Bernardino Branca before Maria showed up. Muddying the origin further is the timeless tradition of making stuff up for marketing purposes. Early Fernet Branca ads touted it as an invention of Dr. Fernet Svedese, a Swedish doctor whose ingestion of his own potion helped him live to the ripe and healthy old age of 104—which made him a bit of an underachiever, since his mother and father, who also had a regular nip of Fernet Branca, lived to be 112 and 130 respectively. Or they would have, if they'd lived at all. Which they did not, at least not anywhere outside the mind of some advertising man who made them up.

Fernet Branca achieved a great deal of success despite the fiction behind its mythical creator. A Fernet Branca shop opened in 1845. Not too long after that, the use of Fernet Branca in hospitals became common when doctors at the Fatebenefratelli Hospital dosed patients with it during a cholera outbreak. In 1886, Branca launched a calendar campaign in which prominent artists were commissioned to create illustrations, not unlike what Campari would do. They were also one of the first companies to make use of photography in their promotions. The brand was managed primarily by Stefano Branca and Maria, until Stefano passed away in 1891, leaving control of the company to Maria. It broke into the US market in the 1870s. During Prohibition, it skirted the law when Dino, Maria's son and by then the head of the company, reverted to packaging as a medicine.

Traditionally, amaro is consumed by itself, either neat or on the rocks, perhaps with a twist of lemon or an orange peel, but some cocktails exist. One has achieved legendary status. It was created at the American Bar in London's Savoy Hotel. The main ingredient of the cocktail (even at only two dashes, it insists on being the main ingredient) is Fernet Branca, and while Branca's being invented by Maria Scala-Branca may be up for debate, the creator of the most famous Fernet Branca cocktail is not in dispute. She was Ada Coleman, the head bartender at the American Bar.

The staggering number of regional variations, the amazing number or local products, and the lack of any stringent codification of what comprises amari probably has its roots in the fact that, at the time amaro was emerging as a viable commercial enterprise, Italy as a unified country did not yet exist. In typically Italian fashion, the year in which "Italy" came to be is as vague as the definition of amaro, occurring more or less sometime after the dissolution of Napoleon's European empire in 1815 and the declaration of Rome as the capital city of the "Kingdom of Italy" in 1871. However, even then there were some stragglers, not joining the unified Italy until as late as 1918, after the close of the First World War.

The campaign of unification was waged primarily by four men: Camillo Cavour, Victor Emmanuel II, Giuseppe Mazzini, and towering above them all, Giuseppe Garibaldi, the only one who had a cocktail named after him. Which is a bit of a shame. Nothing against the legendary Garibaldi, but who wouldn't want to walk into a bar from time to time and order a Victor Emmanuel II? Once again, when it comes to any concept of rules, the recipe for a Garibaldi shows a distinctly Italian disregard for rigidity. At its simplest, it's a 50/50 mix of Campari and orange juice. Some recipes suggest substituting the San'pellegrino Aranciata sparkling Italian soda for the orange juice. Still other variations call for grapefruit juice instead of orange, or the addition of bourbon and honey. Invented by Antonio Micelotta, Bar Manager of the Hotel Excelsior in Rome (which is where James Bond checks into during "Risico"), the drink's red color is meant to pay homage to the "red shirts," the soldiers who followed the general. Garibaldi himself might not order one. He once dismissed alcohol by proclaiming "wine has drowned more men than Neptune."

Beyond *Risico*, James Bond's forays into Italy are often little more than passthroughs. Bond spends more time in Italy in the movies—most notably *Moonraker*, with the motorized amphibious gondola and the infamous pigeon double take, and the last big scene in 2006's *Casino Royale*. But Roger Moore usually stuck to champagne, and Daniel Craig was too busy punching people and chasing after Vesper Lynd to take much time out for drinking. In the later Bond novels, John Gardner takes 007 on an Italian road trip in 1986's *Nobody Lives*

Forever. It's a fun adventure that sees a price put on the head of James Bond by a resurgent SPECTRE, which had been revived in Gardner's earlier book, *For Special Services*, in 1982 under the leadership of Blofeld's daughter (and which involves a fantasy village straight out of *Diamonds are Forever* and a plot to take over NORAD using ice cream that is straight out of a much wackier series than James Bond is usually thought to be, even under the stewardship of Roger Moore). Bond spends most of the time in cars and on the run from a rogues gallery of hitmen and mercenaries, so there's little Italian flavor to the book.

That Bond spends so much of *Nobody Lives Forever* driving reflects Fleming's obsession with the horrible experience of driving in Italian cities, which occupies a substantial portion of his *Thrilling Cities* chapter on Rome and Naples. It is understandable. While driving through the Italian countryside is one of the most exquisite adventures than can be experienced, the cities were laid out for promenading Roman consuls and daydreaming Medici nobles.

In 1989's *Win, Lose, or Die*, in which Bond spends a brief holiday on an Italian island, John Gardner echoes Fleming's *Thrilling Cities* visit to Naples: "Naples was not James Bond's favorite city. Now, sitting in a bumper-to-bumper, horn-hooting, yelling traffic jam, cramming one of the narrow streets down to the harbor, he placed it almost at the bottom of his list." It's not the first time Gardner's Bond has been sour about a city to the point of refusing to partake of any local flavor (the only drink Bond has in Naples is "overpriced watery coffee" on the ferry to Ischia). In 1984's *Role of Honor*, Bond reflects on how package tourism and strip malls have scoured away the once-romantic atmosphere of Monte Carlo. It is a conscious undoing of the exotic globe-trotting mood of Fleming's book and a realistic, if cynical, reflection on how the world had changed since James Bond first sat down at the Casino Royale's baccarat table.

On the other hand, who can trust John Gardner? In his 1992 novel *Death is Forever*, Gardner has Bond reflect on how much he loves Paris, one of his favorite cities. He also had 007 enjoying tea in 1990's *Brokenclaw*. Now if there's two things Ian Fleming made it clear Bond doesn't care for, it's tea and Paris.

Fleming is quick to lose interest in Naples itself. Much of the Neapolitan chapter of *Thrilling Cities* is taken up by the extraordinary account of Fleming's audience with American gangster, Lucky Luciano—a man with whom Fleming had strange ties beyond that of a thriller author being fascinated by one of the most famous gangsters in history. It turns out both men played pivotal, if frequently disputed, roles in the Allied invasion of Sicily during World War II.

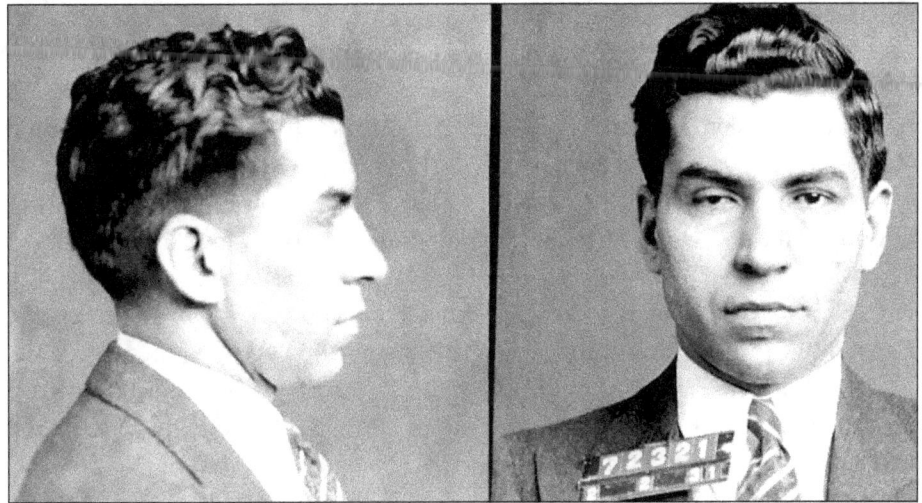

WHAT A MUG—Five Familes architect and Sicilian freedom fighter, Lucky Luciano.

New York to Sicily

On November 5, 1928, Arnold "the Brain" Rothstein was the most powerful men in New York. On November 6, 1928, he was gunned down while playing cards at the Park Central Hotel. The next day, after a night at the Stuyvesant Polyclinic Hospital, he was dead. Rothstein, an insatiable high-risk gambler famous for fixing the 1919 World Series and giving the United States the Chicago "Black Sox," was in the hole for $320,000 after a bad night at the table. He refused to pay, claiming the game was rigged. George "Hump" McManus was arrested for shooting Rothstein in the ensuing argument, but he was later acquitted. A number of other possible suspects have been named over the years, none conclusively. Rothstein himself refused to name names even as he was dying in his hospital bed, telling the police "You stick to your trade. I'll stick to mine."

Until that night, Rothstein was the mastermind (and the bankroll) behind one of the most powerful crime syndicates in the world. He is often considered the father of modern American organized crime, a brilliant strategist and a man of impeccable manners and style who often played the role of mediator when other New York gangs had disputes with one another. Even the infamous political machine Tammany Hall, by Rothstein's time already in a state of some decline, had to answer to Rothstein, who had successfully outmaneuvered Tammany and gained control of their most valuable asset: Immigrant street gangs. Among Rothstein's most valued operators were hungry up-and-coming gangsters Meyer Lansky, "Legs" Diamond, Dutch Schultz, and an ambitious young man named Charles "Lucky" Luciano. It was Luciano who, in the chaotic power vacuum that appeared after Rothstein's murder, stepped up and brought the city's criminal enterprises under his control. After Rothstein died, his various enterprises were divided among a number of different gangsters. Luciano allied himself with a man named Joe Masseria, a Lower East Side gang boss with whom Luciano had done business before becoming one of Arnold Rothstein's lieutenants. Masseria was embroiled in a territorial dispute with a rival named Salvatore Maranzano. The resulting Castellammarese War raged from 1928 to 1931. By the end of it, both Masseria and Maranzano were dead.

Masseria was killed on April 15, 1931, while dining at a restaurant in Coney Island. He was shot to death by four men: Benjamin "Bugsy" Siegel, Vito Genovese, Albert Anastasia, and Joe Adonis. Masseria had been dining with his trusted right-hand man, Lucky Luciano, who just happened to excuse himself to the bathroom right before the trigger men stepped into the room. Luciano inherited his former boss' rackets but still ranked below Salvatore Maranzano—until one day in September 10, 1931. That's when four men arrived at Maranzano's headquarters at 230 Park Avenue claiming to be federal agents. Under the aegis of their badges, two of the men disarmed Maranzano's bodyguards. The other two, stabbed and shot Maranzano to death. The killers were Jewish mobsters, unknowns to Maranzano, who was an old-school Sicilian mobster and refused to work with anyone not from Sicily. Luciano, by contrast, and the group of young gangsters with whom he surrounded himself (known collectively as The Young Turks, after the group of revolutionaries in Turkey who orchestrated the downfall of the creaking Ottoman Empire), was more than willing to work with anyone, as his long association with Arnold Rothstein proved. The men who assassinated Maranzano worked for Bugsy Siegel and Meyer Lansky, two ambitious Jewish gangsters who were close associates of Lucky Luciano. The hit was the first on what became known as the "Night of the Sicilian Vespers." By the end of this string of murders, Lucky Luciano found himself at the top of the heap.

Using lessons learned from Arnold Rothstein, Luciano maintained power through alliances. He devised the "five families" of the American Mafia, with himself as head of the powerful Genovese family, and the Commission, a governing body that drew up territories, established rules, and mediated internal disputes. Although the Five Families were Italian, Luciano remained willing to work with any criminal of any nationality. By the time of his conviction for 62 counts of "compulsory prostitution" in 1936, Luciano was the most powerful criminal in the history of the United States. Even while in prison, he controlled the Mafia and lived in relative comfort. In 1938, with his appeals exhausted, Luciano turned over control of the family to his trusted underling, Frank Costello—though most everyone knew Luciano was still the man calling the shots.

That same year, Gabriele D'Annunzio passed away, leaving fascist Italian dictator Benito Mussolini free to pursue an alliance with Adolf Hitler.

With his bald head, pointy Lenin beard and mustache, insecurity about his short stature, and tendency to lead his own private army in clandestine acts of conquest, Italian writer, poet, and political agitator Gabriele D'Annunzio

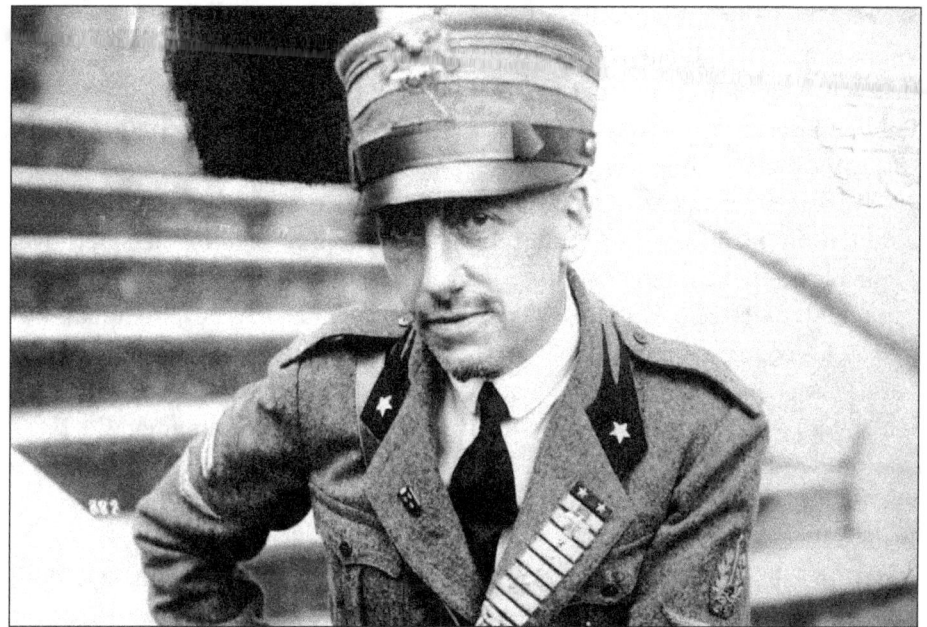
GENERAL GABE—Writer and revolutionary Gabriele D'Annunzio.

could have made a pretty good Bond villain. Born in 1836, D'Annunzio rose to prominence rapidly, publishing his first book of poetry when he was only sixteen years old. He became the face of Italy's Decadence movement, a literary movement that sought to banish Romanticism in favor of a more primal, sensual, and sexually-explicit approach. While he was a university student, he became an avid supporter of Italian irredentism, the belief that the sundry Italian-speaking territories and city-states should be united into a single nation, even if those territories, like Corsica, Nice, and Savoy happened to belong to other nations.

His first novel, *Child of Pleasure*, was published in 1889 and became a controversial sensation. When it was translated into English, it was substantially rearranged. Many of its more salacious passages were removed entirely by the translator, Georgina Harding, who thought the fiery novel's explicit nature simply would not meet with the high standards of proper Victorian morality. It was only recently that an uncensored English translation became available. Despite that, and thanks to an appetite for self-promotion that nearly matched his appetite for sexual indulgence, D'Annunzio became an international success—and an international scandal. He married in 1883 and had three sons, but by 1891 the marriage was over. In 1894, he began a high-profile relationship with actress Eleonora Duse, for whom D'Annunzio wrote a number of plays. He also carried on a turbulent affair with Marchesa Luisa Casati, a relationship that would continue on again, off again, until his death. He lived passionately and with great vigor, indulging his whims and, despite his success, bankrupting himself. He fled to France to avoid his debts, and there wrote a play, *The Martyrdom of*

St Sebastian, which earned him the ire of The Vatican. In 1914, at the onset of World War I, he returned to Italy, full of nationalistic fervor, and immediately threw himself into the effort to get Italy to enter the war on the side of the Entente Powers. He also found time to write the dialogue titles for one of the earliest and most stunning epic films, 1914's *Cabiria*.

D'Annunzio didn't limit his war effort to words. He entered the nascent Italian air force and made a name for himself as a combat pilot, leading the Flight Over Vienna in 1918, a mission to drop propaganda leaflets on the Austro-Hungarian capital. At the close of the war, D'Annunzio was furious that, despite Italian war efforts, his country was treated like a second-rate partner by the attendees of the Paris Peace Conference. In particular, the proposed secession of the city of Fiume, which had a large Italian population, infuriated him. On September 12, 1919, after raising his own army of some 2,000 men, D'Annunzio led a force into Fiume and took the city over, which up until then was occupied by a combined force of British, French, and Americans.

After failing to get Italy proper to annex the territory, D'Annunzio and his makeshift army declared it the independent Italian Regency of Carnaro. He even attempted to establish his own alternate League of Nations, including countries such as Ireland that he felt were being oppressed. In 1920, he even declared war on Italy itself, which got his insurrection more attention from the Italian military. In December, after sustained bombardment courtesy of the Italian Navy, D'Annunzio surrendered. Despite his little rebellion, he suffered few consequences for his actions. In fact, the Charter of Carnaro, the document drawn up to outline the governance of Fiume, became the blueprint for another ultra-nationalist faction quickly gaining notoriety: the Fascists. They took their name from the Latin *fasces*, which was a bundle of rods tied around an ax and served as a symbol of authority during the Roman era, as well as an instrument of punishment and, if need be, execution. The Fascists rose to prominence during the Great War, when the newly-unified Italian nation was deeply divided about joining the conflict. Ultranationalist in nature, and firmly believing that might makes right, the Fascist guilds, or *fasci*, were committed to pushing Italy to enter the war as well as to the opposition of Communism, Socialism, and liberalism. Among the most popular of the early *fasci* was the Fasci of Revolutionary Action, of which Benito Mussolini was a member. Although at one time a member of a socialist political party, Mussolini grew disillusioned with the philosophy. By the end of the war, there was no reconciling fascism and Marxism-Leninism, especially after the promises of the Russian Revolution gave way to the reality of the USSR.

Mussolini's forceful personality, dynamic manner of speaking, and unflinching devotion to standing with his arms akimbo while puffing out his lips, propelled him to the forefront of the fascist movement. In the years following the end of World War I, Italy was wracked by socialist uprisings, strikes, and worker unrest. Mussolini took advantage of the situation by allying his fascists with factory owners and captains of industry, helping to quell the strikes, often through shocking violence. Attempts to woo Italian conservatives saw many of fascism's original revolutionary ideas (especially as relates to equality, populism, and universal suffrage) stripped away. Mussolini and his "Black Shirts"—a clothing choice he'd adopted from D'Annunzio's rebels—soon expanded their campaign of violence from factory workers and socialists to entire towns. By 1922, Mussolini and the fascists were so powerful that the broken and divided Italian national government led by King Victor Emmanuel III, fearing the bloodshed that would come from opposing the Fascists, appointed Mussolini prime minister. On October 30, 1922, Il Duce assumed power.

Also that year, D'Annunzio fell out of a window. Exactly what happened on August 13, 1922, just two months before Mussolini was offered the prime ministership, remains unclear. What is clear is that on that day, D'Annunzio—reportedly high on cocaine and in the act of fondling his lover Luisa Baccara's sister while Luisa herself sat in the same room playing the piano—took a head-first tumble out of a window, fracturing his skull. The fall was attributed to many things: an ill-aimed lunge for the object of his affection, an overly forceful rebuke from the woman, or the simple fact that D'Annunzio was whacked out on drugs at the time. True to form, D'Annunzio made sure the accident became a major event and remained shrouded in mystery, only adding to his dangerous allure. And then there was the other theory: that it was attempted murder.

Although the poet's seizure of Fiume, his raising of his own private radical army, and the charter drawn up to govern their new territory, were a major influence on Mussolini and the Fascists, D'Annunzio himself did not care for Il Duce. By the same token, Mussolini regarded the wildly magnetic decadent as a

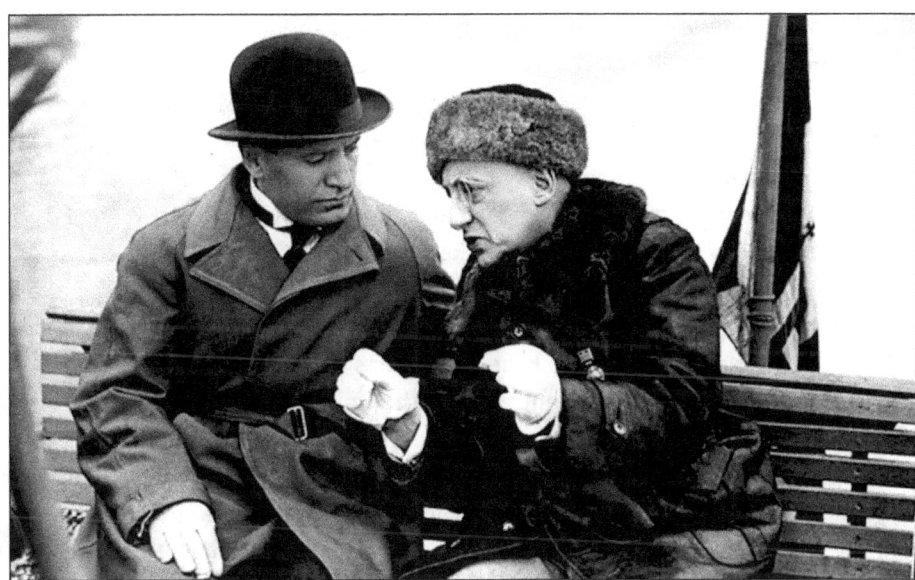

IL DUCE AND THE DECADENT—D'Annunzio chats up Mussolini. Photo by Henry Guttmann.

dangerous political opponent. On the day of D'Annunzio's accident, there was an additional guest at the writer's Lake Garda retreat: Aldo Finzi, one of Mussolini's most trusted lieutenants. Despite the appetite for scandal, there is little concrete proof that implicates Finzi in the accident or suggests that he was there to kill D'Annunzio. But the accident, whatever the cause may have been, effectively took D'Annunzio out of the game. He retired from politics, removing himself as the primary domestic threat to Mussolini's reign. Mussolini, for his part, wanted to make sure D'Annunzio stayed out of politics for good, indulging D'Annunzio's voracious appetites for sex and drugs and supplying him with a regular stipend. "When you have a rotten tooth you have two possibilities open to you," Mussolini said. "Either you pull the tooth or you fill it with gold. With D'Annunzio I have chosen for the latter treatment."

Among D'Annunzio's appetites was one for Amaro Montenegro, first produced in 1885 by Bolognese citizen Stanislao Cobianchi. While traveling through the territory of Montenegro, Cobianchi became obsessed with the restorative herbal elixir, Karik. Upon his return to Italy, Cobianchi set about reproducing the spirit, resulting in Amaro Montenegro. It's named after Princess Helen of Montenegro, who became the second queen of the new Italian state upon her marriage to King Victor Emmanuel III. Where many amari are known for the bitter, pungent flavor, Amaro Montenegro has a more balanced blend of some 40 different herbs and botanicals, resulting in a sweeter, more citrus, orange peel flavor. D'Annunzio wet his whistle with it frequently, calling it "*liquore delle Virtudi*"—the liquor of the virtues. Yet amazingly, sex, drugs, Amaro Montenegro, pratfalls, a fractured skull, and Mussolini weren't enough to keep D'Annunzio entirely out of the political spotlight. In the 1930s, D'Annunzio was critical of the alliance between Italy and Germany, campaigning against Italian entry into World War II and satirizing Hitler and the Nazis in his writing. Mussolini disregarded D'Annunzio's warnings, though in 1944, the dictator admitted that it had been a mistake. Less than a year later, Mussolini was dead, strung up by an Italian people who had had enough of fascism, Nazis, and Il Duce. D'Annunzio, alas, did not live to see Mussolini's downfall. He passed away in 1938 of heart failure, the same year Lucky Luciano symbolically turned over control of the New York mafia to Frank Costello.

But before the spectacular downfall of Mussolini, with the Italian socialists beat up, and with D'Annunzio sidelined (or dead), the one remaining force powerful enough to stand against the blackshirts and mobilize workers against the fascists was the Mafia, concentrated on the Italian island of Sicily. Mussolini declared war on them, rounding up its leaders, throwing them in jail, and making a bitter enemy of *la cosa nostra*. It's unlikely Mussolini ever imagined that Lucky Luciano would use this to his advantage, and to the advantage of the Allied Forces. All that was needed was to do some trout fishing with an unlikely ally from British Naval Intelligence.

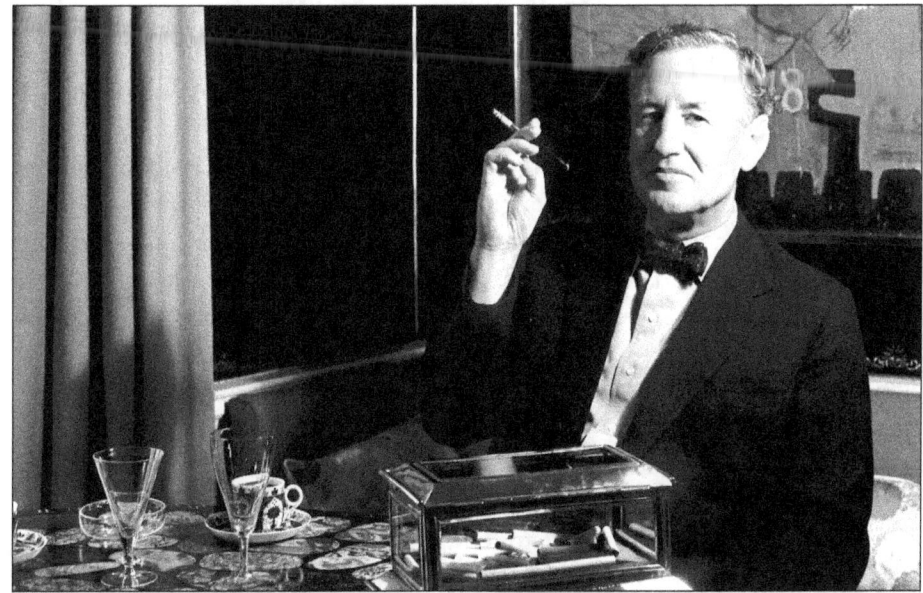

HEALTHY LUNCH—Ian Fleming contemplates his next novel and his next cigarette. Photo by Cecil Beaton.

Ungentlemanly Warfare

On September 29, 1939, Admiral John Godfrey, Britain's director of naval intelligence, issued a document comparing wartime deception of an enemy with fishing. "The Trout Fisher casts patiently all day. He frequently changes his venue and his lures. If he has frightened a fish he may 'give the water a rest for half-an-hour,' but his main endeavor, viz. to attract fish by something he sends out from his boat, is incessant." According to historian Ben McIntyre, the memo was signed by Admiral Godfrey but was written by Godfrey's assistant, Ian Fleming.

Fleming hadn't worked for Naval Intelligence very long at the time the memo was issued, having only joined in August of 1939, at which time he was given the codename 17F. He was not the sort of man who seemed fit for a promising military career. His position at Naval Intelligence was granted him as a favor to his mother, Evelyn Beatrice St. Croix Rose, who became Evelyn St. Croix Fleming—Eve for short—when she married Scotsman Valentine Fleming, the son of a successful banker. A graduate of Eton and Magdalen College, Oxford, Valentine quickly rose to prominence, becoming a member of Parliament in 1910. He was a popular politician, described by one of his fellow parliamentarians as "one of those younger Conservatives who easily and naturally combine loyalty to party ties with a broad liberal outlook upon affairs and a total absence of class prejudice... a man of thoughtful and tolerant opinions, which were not the less strongly or clearly held because they were not loudly or frequently asserted." The couple had four children, all boys: Richard, Michael, the black sheep Ian, and the star of the Fleming clan, Peter. At the outbreak of World War I—a war notable for the number of upper-class society members who enlisted to fight—Valentine joined the Queen's Own Oxfordshire Hussars. He was killed on May 20, 1917, by German bombardment in Picardy, France. His obituary was written by his close friend, the same man who had called him "a man of thoughtful and tolerant opinions"—Winston Churchill.

His will bequeathed Eve and their sons with a sizable fortune, provided she never remarry. Eve complied, though she didn't think much of the stipulation. She did, however, carry on a long-term affair with the painter Augustus John, with whom she had a daughter, Amaryllis Fleming. Amaryllis became a cellist of no small renown and even had an (admittedly awkward) compliment paid to her by her half-brother Ian in his short story "The Living Daylights," in which James Bond muses, "There was something almost indecent in the idea of that bulbous, ungainly instrument between her splayed thighs. Of course Suggia had managed to look elegant, and so did that girl Amaryllis somebody. But they should invent a way for women to play the damned thing side-saddle."

Young Ian was not a model student, though neither was he idle. With his friend Ivar Bryce, who became Ian's lifelong friend (not to mention the man responsible for the long passages about *guano* in *Dr. No*; the Bryce family money came from *guano*), Ian started a magazine called *The Wyvern*, which featured poems and artwork (including art from Augustus John, father of Ian's half-sister) as well as forays into political thought. Among his more controversial assertions was one in favor of the British Fascisti Party, which had been horrified by the events of the Russian Revolution and inspired by the uprisings of Gabriele D'Annunzio and Mussolini. Fleming never graduated from Eton. Nor did he graduate from his next school, the Sandhurst Royal Military College, which he departed under an air of scandal—something to do with a lady. He didn't graduate from his next two universities either, though his studies during that time took him to Austria, where he befriended a former British spy named Ernan Forbes Dennis and his wife, novelist Phyllis Bottome. His relationship with these two planted the seeds for both of Ian Fleming's future careers. Acquaintance with Bottome might have also taken the edge off Ian's early pro-fascist sentiments, as she herself was a committed anti-fascist and, later, an outspoken opponent of the Nazis. Her 1938 novel, *Mortal Storm*, was adapted into a movie in 1940 starring Jimmy Stewart as a German who refuses to join the Nazi Party. MGM was nervous about the movie. The United States was not yet in the war, after all, and Germany was still a viable and substantial market for movies. The studio did what it could to obscure the political message of the film, being vague about it being set in Germany and making sure never to overtly state that certain characters were persecuted because they were Jewish. The half-hearted concessions didn't pay off. The Nazis banned the movie, and in further reaction, banned all MGM movies.

Fleming tried becoming a diplomat but did not pass the requisite tests. All the while, his reputation as a womanizer and a bad egg grew. He carried on a string of affairs with an assortment of women, some married, others not. His mother finally used her connections to secure him a job in journalism, a trade for which he showed genuine talent. Ian's career as a journalist, however successful, was overshadowed by the writing career of his older brother, Peter. Unlike Ian, Peter had been a star pupil at Eton and was more amiable to marriage, to the actress Celia Johnson, in 1935. But he also possessed the same restless spirit as Ian. In 1932 an advertisement in *The Times* launched Peter's travel writing career: "Exploring and sporting expedition, under experienced guidance, leaving England June to explore rivers central Brazil, if possible ascertain fate Colonel Percy Fawcett; abundant game, big and small; exceptional fishing; room two more guns; highest references expected and given." Peter was in no way qualified for such an expedition in any way except one: he had some money. Peter was in.

Percy Harrison Fawcett was a famous explorer and British officer who disappeared in 1925 in Brazil while searching for a fabled lost city. Although an experienced explorer, Fawcett and his small expedition of two men (including his own son), never returned from the jungle. An account of the expedition, of Fawcett's life as a soldier and explorer, and of the speculation about what fate ultimately befell them, was recounted in the 2009 book *The Lost City of Z: A Tale of Deadly Obsession in the Amazon* by David Grann. A substantial amount of evidence and many subsequent expeditions had shed more light on the disappearance by the time of

JASMINE
- 1 ½ oz Dry Gin
- ¼ oz Campari
- ¼ oz Cointreau
- ¾ oz Fresh Lemon Juice

Add all of the ingredients to a shaker with ice. Shake well. Strain into a chilled cocktail glass. Garnish with a lemon twist.

JUNGLE BIRD
- 1 ½ oz Black Strap rum
- ¾ oz Campari
- ½ oz Simple syrup
- 1 ½ oz Fresh pineapple juice
- ½ oz Fresh lime juice

Add all of the ingredients to a shaker with ice. Shake well. Strain into a rocks glass with ice. Garnish with a pineapple wedge.

CARDINALE
- 2 oz Dry Gin
- ½ oz Dry Vermouth
- ½ oz Campari

Add all ingredients to a mixing glass with ice. Stir well. Strain into a rocks glass with ice. Rub a lemon twist over the top and discard. Garnish with a slice of lemon peel.

BIJOU
- 1 oz Dry Gin
- 1 oz Sweet Vermouth
- ¾ oz Green Chartreuse
- ¼ oz Campari

Add all ingredients to a mixing glass filled with ice. Stir well. Strain into a rocks glass over ice. Garnish with an orange twist.

Grann's book, but when Peter Fleming and his expedition set out in 1932 to uncover Fawcett's fate, it was still a mystery. If Peter was in no way qualified for the expedition, he needn't have worried. Neither was anyone else. The entire affair was a fiasco. Peter's self-deprecating, often hilarious account of the disastrous expedition, *Brazilian Adventure*, was published in 1933 and became a hit, cementing Fleming as a preeminent writer of non-fiction. He became a reporter for *The Times*, and in 1934 an account of his overland journey from Moscow to Peking was published as *One's Company*. Shortly thereafter, he completed a similar journey from China to India, which was published by Jonathan Cape—the same company that would publish Ian's James Bond novels—as *News from Tartary* in 1936. When the World War broke out, Peter enlisted, first with the Grenadier Guards infantry unit, and later as one of the organizers—along with his brother Ian—of the "Auxiliary Units," a secret organization that would become resistance fighters in the event of a German invasion of the British Isles.

As for Ian, his troubled continued. He entered the banking business, which he did not care for and at which he did not excel. Finally, in 1939 and at the behest of the Governor of the Bank of England, Ian joined Naval Intelligence as the assistant to Admiral Godfrey. Despite no real qualifications for the job, Fleming proved adept at devising new schemes and communicating them in a way that got them accepted, no matter that many of them seemed little more than the fanciful machinations of an overly-imaginative writer. Among them was the "Trout Memo." It opened the door for a number of "dirty tricks," including Operation Mincemeat. The idea for Operation Mincemeat (part of a larger campaign of deception called Operation Barclay) was credited to Captain Ewen Edward Samuel Montagu, but it is generally accepted that the idea began with Fleming, and that Montagu and Flight Lieutenant Charles Cholmondeley of the RAF took the idea and claimed it as his own.

Mincemeat, and the whole of Operation Barclay, was designed to trick the Axis powers into thinking an invasion of the European continent was going to come through Greece when, in fact, the plan was to attack through Italy, with the initial invasion landing in Sicily (codenamed Operation Husky). The deception included fabricating the existence of whole armies and transforming the body of a 34-year old Welshman named Glyndwr Michael into Captain William 'Bill' Martin of the Royal Marines. An entire back story for the fake soldier was devised, including snapshots of a non-existent girlfriend (in reality, photos of Nancy Jean Leslie, a staff member at MI5) and an impressive assemblage of pocket detritus—receipts, love letters, banknotes, and other such everyday pieces of personal ephemera. The makeshift marine also had on his corpse a letter from Lieutenant General Sir Archibald Nye, Vice Chief of the Imperial General Staff, mentioning plans for Operation Husky—an invasion of Europe through Greece and Sardinia—as well as a "fake" operation, Brimstone, meant to fool the Germans into thinking the Allies would invade through Sicily. The body of "Captain Bill Martin" was consigned to the sea, at a place where they could be certain it would wash up on the beach in Huelva, Spain, where authorities would doubtless report its discovery to the local German Abwehr (military intelligence) agent, a man by the name of Adolf Clauss. Eventually, it percolated all the way to the top of the German chain of command. Astoundingly, this is exactly how it played out. Nazi propaganda minister Joseph Goebbels didn't entirely buy it. Mussolini didn't buy it at all. He was convinced that the attack would come through Sicily. But Hitler bought it, and that was ultimately all that mattered. Substantial German forces, including Panzer tank divisions commanded by Erwin Rommel, were relocated to Greece and Sardinia. On July 9, 1943, Allied forces began Operation Husky, the invasion of Europe—by landing in Sicily. Even after weeks of fighting, Hitler was convinced that it was all a feint, that the true invasion would be through Greece. By August 17, it was too late. The Allies had taken Sicily.

For the Allies, a funny thing happened on the way to Italy. In advance of, and during the Allied landing, local Sicilian resistance fighters had been harrying the German and Italian troops. They greeted Allied soldiers and served as guides, local liaisons, and guerrilla fighters. It turned out they were members of the Sicilian Mafia, compliments of Lucky Luciano. Or so Luciano claimed.

The length to which Luciano's contacts helped facilitate Operation Husky is a topic of debate. According to Luciano himself, he single-handedly won the war for the Allies. According to others, he simply conned his way out of prison using lies about his contacts back in Sicily. As is usually the case with the history of espionage, the truth is probably some blend of these things. Luciano had already

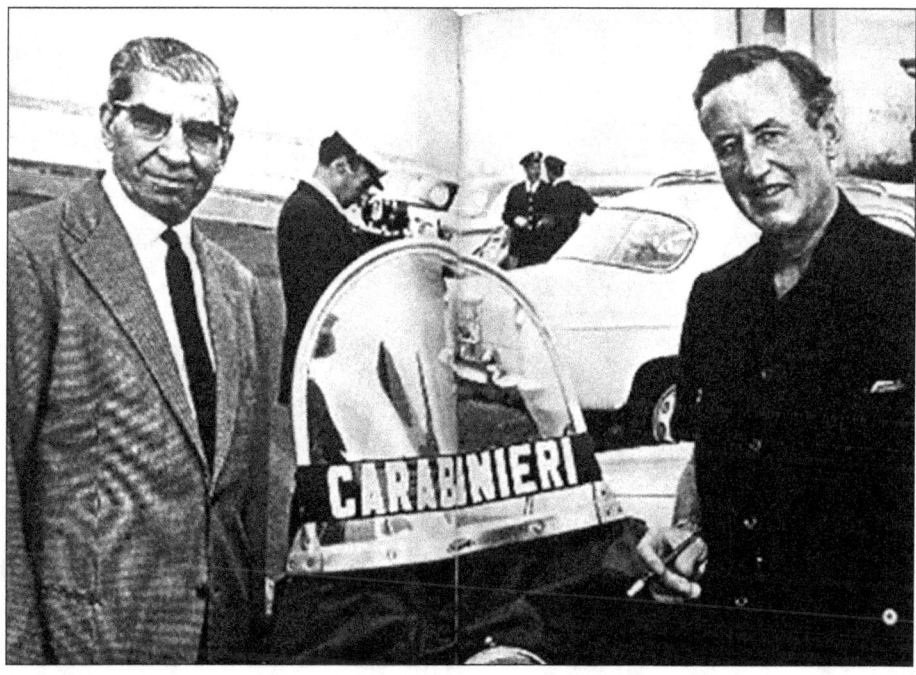

secured himself a transfer to a posher prison by agreeing to help the US Navy protect the strategic—and vulnerable—docks of New York from saboteurs and spies. The government had attempted to recruit the dockworkers to the cause of patriotism, but the docks belonged to the Mob, which meant they said nothing and cooperated with no one without the say-so from Luciano or Frank Costello. The government was hesitant to play ball with the notorious criminals, but when the burning and sinking of the ship SS Normandie was attributed to German agents, the United States decided to do business with Public Enemy Number One.

Once Luciano gave the OK, his associates Meyer Lansky and Alberto Anastasia (one of the founders of the Mafia's bloody hit squad, Murder, Inc.) worked the docks and the dock workers, ensuring no further incidents occurred and that no workers went on strike for the duration of the war. It was suspected that the burning of the Normandie had not been the work of German agents at all, but was in fact orchestrated by Anthony Anastasia (Alberto's brother) in order to help nudge the government toward working with Luciano. But whatever. War makes for really weird bedfellows. Right, Joe Stalin?

When planning commenced for Operation Husky, Luciano was again recruited to provide services to the Allies. Working with Luciano, Vito Genovese, and their associates in Sicily—who already had a chip on their shoulder thanks to Mussolini's crackdown—generated a large amount of intelligence for the Allies, including detailed maps and contacts. The Mafia had become freedom fighters. Once again, exactly how much of a contribution Luciano made remains a source of controversy, but it was enough that in January of 1946, Luciano's sentence was commuted. He was a free man, provided he left the country.

On February 10, 1946, Lucky Luciano set sail for Naples where, a little over ten years later, he would sit down for an interview with Ian Fleming, one of the architects of Operation Mincemeat. Sadly, by that time, Luciano's health was failing, so they did not share a Negroni. As to whether or not they reminisced about their shared roles in the invasion of Sicily...well, that remains within the realm of classified information. The sort of information, perhaps, than Fleming discussed over rounds of Pink Gin at a place in London called the American bar.

The Playlist: Themes for Secret Agents

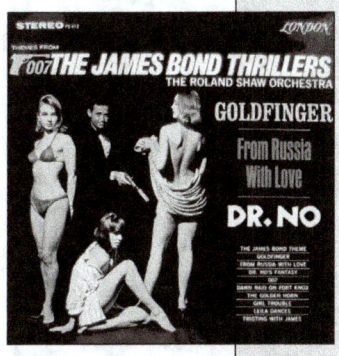

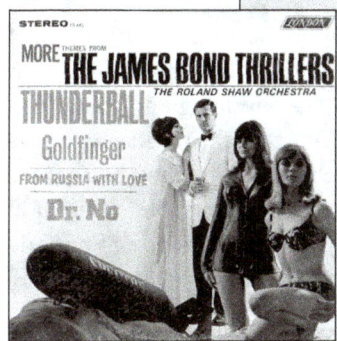

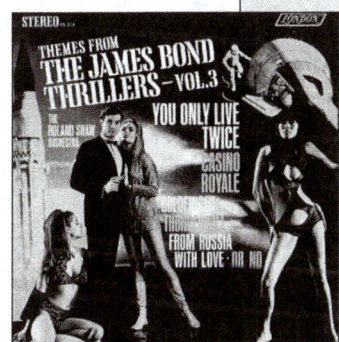

THE MAN WHO ALMOST COMPOSED BOND

There are plenty of elements that go into making and so have become defining factors of the Bond films. The clothes, the cars, the exotic locations, the women, the booze, and of course, the music. James Bond without John Barry and Monty Norman's instantly identifiable theme might as well be...well, *Never Say Never Again*. There was a huge cash-in industry of Bond-themed albums. Most were disposably enjoyable, offering up nondescript but professional covers of Bond themes ands music from espionage TV shows. Some mixed in original compositions. Towering above others was composer Roland Shaw, an accomplished musician who attended the Trinity College of Music and served in the Royal Air Force in World War II, where he lead the RAF No. 1 Band of the Middle East Forces. Shaw released a series of Bond cash-in records featuring arrangements of Bond themes and background music that were often just as good as the originals, and in some cases, even better. In fact, he came close to composing the theme for an actual Bond film. Well, sort of an actual James Bond theme. "Let the Love Come Through" was a contender to be the theme song for 1967's *Casino Royale*, until Burt Bacharach bumped him.

Shaw's willingness to delve into the library of background music is what set Shaw apart from his contemporaries, most of whom were happy to churn out a thousand different covers of the themes from *Goldfinger* and *Thunderball*. Recording for Decca between 1966 and 1971, Shaw released several Bond-themed albums, as well as one album of general spy themes. Keeping the albums straight can be a chore, as in the true spirit of cash-in albums, they were re-released multiple times, often with different names and covers. *Themes for Secret Agents, James Bond Thrillers, More Themes From James Bond Thrillers, Themes From The James Bond Thrillers Vol. 3*, and *The Return Of James Bond In Diamonds Are Forever...And Other Secret Agent Themes* are all great. The vocal version of *You Only Live Twice* is fantastic, and like much of his work, almost on par with the original film versions. The world of James Bond cash-in albums is fun to explore, and Roland Shaw is absolutely the place to begin.

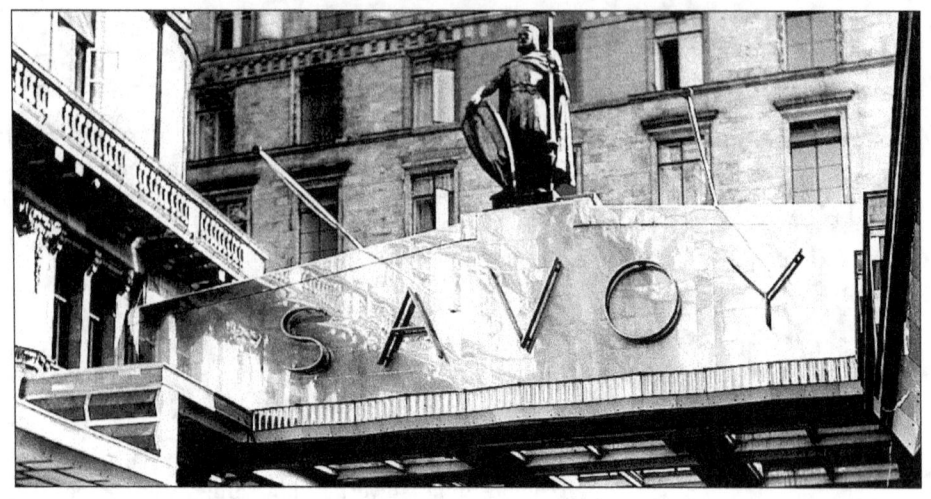

Spyin' at the Savoy

Nestled away on a cul-de-sac off the storied Strand in the City of Westminster, London, with a tight turn-around that allegedly determined the turning radius for London cabs, beneath a silver awning adorned with green neon, is the hotel that once played host to Winston Churchill's wartime briefings and served as a triage center during the Blitz. Established by theatre impresario Richard D'Oyly Carte, the doors to the regal Savoy Hotel opened in 1889. Carte financed the construction of the hotel with the fortune he made producing the operas of Gilbert and Sullivan, whose series of thirteen "Savoy Operas" included enduring hits such as *The Pirates of Penzance*.

With an astounding array of amenities for the late Victorian era—electric lights, a lift, and hot and cold running water—the Savoy became the preeminent hotel for London society and well-heeled travelers. For Great Britain's intelligence workers and leaders during World War II, including Winston Churchill and Ian Fleming, the Savoy was one of the most important spots in all of London, not just because of its historic and highly-regarded bar; but also because it had its own power supply. Even during power outages caused by bombing, the Savoy could continue to operate. It was also one of the first spots in the United Kingdom, and indeed, the whole of Europe, to import new American style "cocktails" and culture, courtesy of bartender Frank Wells, who ran the Savoy's bar from 1893 until 1902. Along with The Ritz in Paris, the Savoy was the beachfront for the "American bar" in Europe, which is why the bar at the Savoy is known as the American Bar.

The cocktail being an American invention is widely accepted and, of course, a more complicated claim than can be easily settled. Pretty much every culture in the world mixed together some manner of alcohol, juice, bitters, and whatever else they might have within arm's reach. British sailors and colonial governors were downing everything from grog to punch to gin and tonics. Americans (British at the time) were following suit. Between the United States and England, it starts to look a lot like the debate about whether punk was invented by the

Ramones or the Sex Pistols, which then of course has people citing Iggy and the Stooges or the MC5 and, well, before you know it people are fighting pitched battles in the street over the claim that Mozart was the first real punk rocker.

With cocktails, the argument is usually over when something stops being a punch or a "mixed drink" or an "elixir" and starts being this thing recognized today as a cocktail. Picking a point at which the cocktail was born is pointless. However, history has to start somewhere, and in the case of cocktails, the best that can be done is cite the first known mention of them in print. The first current known use of "cocktail" in reference to a beverage was turned up by historians Jared Brown and Anistatia Miller. It appears in the March of 1798, in an issue of London's *The Morning Post and Gazetteer*. In that paper was a story about the proprietor of the Axe & Gate tavern, on the corner of Downing and Whitehall, who had won a lottery and celebrated by forgiving the tabs of all his regulars. Four days after that story ran, a second, satirical story ran in which the make-believe tabs of British politicians were expounded upon. Among them was the imaginary tab of a man named Rose, who was charged for "gin and bitters." Another man, Mr. Pitt, was charged for: "two petit vers of L'huile de Venus. Ditto, one of perfeit amour. Ditto, cock-tail (vulgarly called ginger)."

Both Mr. Rose and Mr. Pitt enjoyed, or so the paper surmised, drinks close to what we think of as cocktails, including one actually called the "cock-tail," though in the case of Mr. Pitt's tipple, it is likely a specific drink rather than the category of drinks for which it would later come to stand. As the world continues to unearth, archive, and make available forgotten tomes, it's likely the origin of cocktails, both as a singular drink and as type of drink, will be pushed further back.

One can infer a few things from the list that suggest, even if the name had not yet been applied, people were enjoying cocktails in the 1700s. For the time being, let's skip the L'huile de Venus, which might have been a lovely drink at one point but is today a French brand of sexual lubricant (which I suppose the drink might have been, in its way, in 1798 as well). For starters, there is Mr. Rose's gin and bitters. Without knowing the specifics, the best that can be done is a guess, but gin with bitters sounds awfully close to Pink Gin—most definitely considered a cocktail today, albeit a simple one. Pink Gin originated, like so many things, in the British Navy. As far as cocktails go, it is even simpler than an Americano and yet emerges as something more than the sum of its scant two parts, those two parts being Plymouth Gin and a dash of Angostura bitters, which lend the drink its pink hue.

Bitters are a bit like concentrated blasts of amaro, similar in that they are a blend of herbs and botanicals often touted as possessing medicinal and digestive benefits. Most bitters are surprisingly potent. A dash or two into a glass filled with gin may not seem like much, but a little bitters goes a long way. Angostura is the best-known brand. The formula was devised by Dr. Johann Gottlieb Benjamin Siegert, Surgeon General for the army of Venezuelan leader Simón Bolívar. Dr. Siegert's mixture enjoyed substantial popularity, so much so that in 1824 he began to sell it commercially. In 1830, he opened a distillery in the town of Angostura. Naturally, he named it House of Angostura. In 1875, the operation was relocated to Port of Spain, Trinidad, where it remains still, though it always retained the Angostura name—which is more than can be said for the town of Angostura, which was renamed Ciudad Bolívar in 1846. Promoted as a cure for seasickness, Angostura Bitters became popular with the British Royal Navy. Officers would add a dash or two to their ration of gin, a habit that remained popularity among British Navy men well into the era of First Lord of the Admiralty Winston Churchill and Commander Ian Fleming, who counted Pink Gin among his favorite cocktails. It made it into *The Man with the Golden Gun*, in which Bond orders a Pink Gin—Beefeater and "plenty of bitters"—in the bar of the Thunderbird Hotel in Jamaica.

Fleming wasn't the only British writer of espionage thrillers to feature Pink Gin in one of his books. Graham Greene, a contemporary of Fleming and the premier writer of British thrillers while Fleming was busying himself with a journalism career, features the drink in his 1948 novel *The Heart of the Matter*. Greene was born in 1902, to a modestly successful family, comfortable but certainly not as rich or as highly-placed as the Flemings. He suffered bouts of depression early in life, even attempting suicide while at school and being sent for psychiatric evaluation. In 1922, he joined the Communist Party of Great Britain and attempted, unsuccessfully, to immigrate to the Soviet Union. Unwelcome by the Soviets, he attended Balliol College in Oxford, and in 1925 published his first work, a poorly received book of poetry. He also volunteered to spy on the French for the German secret service and write pro-German articles for the college periodical. Although his paths did not cross with Fleming's, he did attend Balliol and was acquainted with a man who would become one of Ian's dearest friends, Evelyn Waugh. Waugh, however, did not think much of the chronically depressed, politically dubious Greene, who he considered "childish and ostentatious. He certainly shared in none of our revelry." Greene and Fleming would not meet until some years later, though then to not much better a result.

After graduating, Greene converted to Catholicism and began more serious work as a writer, including stints as a tutor and journalist. In 1929, his first novel, *The Man Within*, was published to favorable reviews. His next two books, 1930's *The Name of Action* and 1932's *Rumour at Nightfall*, were less successful. Greene himself disowned them. In 1932, he published *Stamboul Train*, his first major success. Retitled *Orient Express* in the United States, it was adapted into a film of the same name in 1936. Shortly thereafter, Greene's sister, Elizabeth, recruited him into the British secret service, his affection for Germany having cooled since his college days. He was stationed in Sierra Leone during the Second World War. His acclaim as a writer grew during these war years. In 1939 he wrote *The Confidential Agent*, and a year later followed with *The Power and the Glory*, the book which cemented his reputation as one of the great writers of the 20th century. In 1943 he wrote another spy thriller, *The Ministry of Fear*, which was adapted into a highly-regarded film in 1944, directed by anti-Nazi German expatriate Fritz Lang. *The Power and the Glory*, controversial and under no small degree of scrutiny by the Vatican, was adapted into a movie as well, but not until 1947 and then under the title *The Fugitive*, directed by John Ford and starring Henry Fonda.

In 1941, while working for British intelligence, Greene was stationed in the espionage hotbed of Lisbon, where he became aware of Joan Pujol Garcia, codename Garbo, a double agent, working for the British while in the employ of German intelligence, to whom he would feed extravagant tales of the vast spy network he ran. None of these spies existed, though Garcia's German handlers believed every word and he himself collected tidy bonuses from the Abwehr. Greene was fascinated by Agent Garbo's elaborate web of non-existent operatives and by the spy's proficiency at convincing the Germans that these pretend spies were real and all this false information he was feeding them was true. So able a deceiver was Garcia that he played the key role in convincing Hitler that the Allied invasion of France would come through Calais, obscuring the fact that it was actually bound for Normandy. Greene, inspired by this high-stakes game of deception, used the concept as for his 1958 novel, *Our Man in Havana*.

Greene's experiences in Africa served as the inspiration for *The Heart of the Matter*, published in 1948. Not coincidentally, it is this book that 007 brings with him during his African adventure in William Boyd's 2013 James Bond novel, *Solo*. Bond's affection for thrillers about his chosen profession was entered into the franchise during the 1980s, when John Gardner was writing them and frequently portrayed Bond reading or talking about author Eric Ambler, who, like Graham Greene, was doubtless a major influence on Ian Fleming. Boyd, like Greene, spent time in Africa—

PINK GIN
- 2 oz Plymouth Gin
- 4-6 dashes Angostura bitters

Add the gin and bitters to a mixing glass filled with ice. Stir well. Strain into a chilled coupe glass.

WHITE LADY
- 2 oz Dry Gin
- 1/2 oz Cointreau
- 1/2 oz Fresh Lemon Juice
- 1 Fresh Egg White

Add all ingredients to a shaker. Shake without ice. Add ice and shake again. Strain into a chilled coupe glass. Garnish with a lemon peel.

PINK LADY
- 1 ½ oz Dry Gin
- ½ oz Applejack
- Juice of Half a Lemon
- 1 Fresh Egg White
- 2 dashes Grenadine

Add all of the ingredients to a shaker. Shake well. Strain into a chilled cocktail glass. Garnish with a cherry.

MINT JULEP
- 2 oz Bourbon
- ¼ oz Simple Syrup
- 8 Mint leaves

In a Julep cup or rocks glass, lightly muddle the mint and syrup. Add the bourbon and pack tightly with crushed ice. Stir until the cup is frosted. Top with more crushed ice. Garnish with a mint sprig.

Nigeria, specifically, during the Nigerian Civil War from July, 1967 until January, 1970. Much of *Solo*'s setting in the fictional African country of Zanzarim is drawn from Boyd's time in Biafra, just as Greene used a thinly-veiled version of Sierra Leone as the setting for *The Heart of the Matter*. Unlike Greene's Major Henry Scobie, however, Bond doesn't drink Pink Gin, preferring instead to tipple from his trusty bottle of Johnnie Walker blended scotch whisky. According to Bond, whisky is "best for the tropics. It doesn't need to be chilled. You're meant to drink it without ice, anyway. Tastes the same in Africa as it would in Scotland."

Ian Fleming considered Greene's thrillers among the most important influences of his own writing, "because each sentence he writes interests me, both as an individual and a writer." The two men, by then on parallel yet very different courses, finally met during a party thrown by Ian's wife, Ann, whose circle of literary friends held her husband's potboilers in low regard. In Greene, Fleming hoped to find a more empathetic reaction, not to mention savoring the chance to meet one of his writing heroes. Greene, however, had not grown any less haunted or socially difficult by this time. Ann Fleming described Greene attending her party as, "very anxious and quite impossible to engage in seductive conversation. He remained demoted from all, totally polite and holding the cocktail shaker as a kind of defensive weapon."

Fleming was nothing if not dogged, and he continued to pursue both friendship with and artistic praise from Greene. He offered him use of the Goldeneye home in Jamaica in exchange for Greene writing a dust jacket blurb for the omnibus *Gilt Edged Bonds*, a play on words referring to a type of financial bond issued by the British government. The omnibus edition included three 007 novels: *Casino Royale*, *From Russia with Love*, and *Dr. No*. Greene agreed to the vacation at Goldeneye but deflated Fleming by saying he preferred to simply pay rent for his use of the villa rather than write anything, even a dust jacket blurb, that was critically supportive of the James Bond novels. Greene further insulted Fleming by accusing the housekeeper at Goldeneye, a Jamaican woman named Violet who Fleming adored to the same degree Bond adored his housekeeper May, of stealing whisky from him.

It's not surprising that Greene would find little to enjoy in the friendship of Ian Fleming or the content of Fleming's books. Despite sharing careers as British agents and writers, the two men couldn't have been more unalike. Fleming, a passionate *bon vivant* who worked during the war in the office of one of Naval Intelligence's most respected admirals; Greene, a disillusioned, bipolar introvert who spent the war surrounded by the sort of double agents and dirty tricks Fleming was busy devising back in London, and on top of that mentored by a senior intelligence officer named Kim Philby, who was eventually discovered to himself be a double agent, spying on the British for the Soviet Union (he defected in 1963, then assuming a role with the KGB). Fleming and Greene took very different things away from their wartime service, and the two sets of experience were not particularly compatible. But at least they both liked Pink Gin.

The bar tabs of Mr. Pitt and Mr. Rose included another notable drink: Mr. Pitt's "cock-tail, vulgarly known as a ginger." It's possible that Mr. Pitt's mysterious cock-tail was gin and ginger, which in the parlance of modern cocktails, would be something perhaps not entirely unlike a Ginger Mule, though that cocktail wouldn't come about until the middle of the 20th century. As for why the drink was called a "cock-tail," that's another one shrouded in legend, one of which claims the word was British slang for a woman of easy virtue, while another claimed it was a reference to the American habit of ruining perfectly good gin by adding other ingredients to it. Another story claims the name came from French soldiers drinking in an American tavern in 1779, where proprietor Betsy Flanagan adorned her drinks with feathers plucked from a rooster's tail, resulting in the convivial soldiers shouting, "*Vive le cocktail!*" The only problem with this origin story is that Betsy Flanagan wasn't a real person; she was a character from James Fenimore Cooper's seminal work of espionage fiction, *The Spy*, published in 1821. Another tale is that the name was derived from colloquial American English, in which "cock" was a term referring to the tap on a barrel of spirits and "tail" a term referring to the dregs at the bottom of said barrel, which would be mixed together and sold at a reduced rate as a "cocktail."

The best-researched origin story comes from cocktail historian David Wondrich, who traced the etymology of "cocktail" when researching his book *Imbibe!* He discovered its use as relates to horses. And if you thought drinking Old Tom gin out of a wooden cat's butt was bad, well...according to Wondrich's research, "cocktail" was slang for a concoction, containing ginger, pepper, and other pick-me-ups, that was used to perk up listless horses in the morning. Mix it together, lift the horse's tail, and insert it up the...you get the picture. No word on whether it was shaken or stirred. The end result was a much friskier, alert-looking animal, tail held high and proud, which was known as a "cocked tail." As Wondrich details in an article for *Saveur*, sportsmen adding a little pepper or ginger (and later, bitters) to a drink referenced the practice, and before long a spirit with something added to it was a cocktail.

Whatever the etymology of the word, Mr. Pitt ordered himself one, and regardless of whether the phrase was born in England or the U.S, and regardless of how far back you want to trace the concept of mixed drinks being "cocktails," the concept of cocktails as we know them today, and of the culture surrounding them, begins in the United States, at a place called the City Hotel.

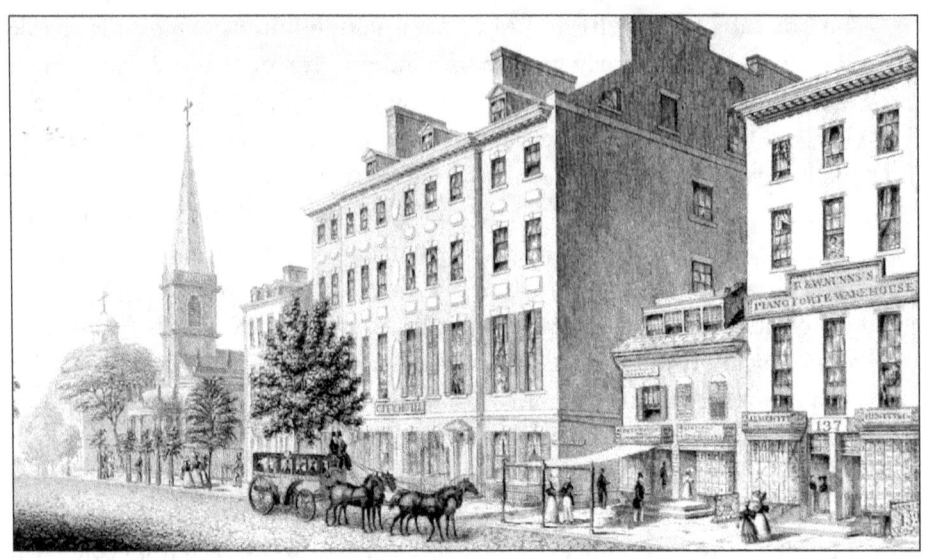

From New York, With Love

In 1790, New York was the capital of the fledgling United States. George Washington was sworn in as the country's first President in 1789, on the steps of Federal Hall, not far from Fraunces Tavern, a popular drinking spot where Washington met with his officers to raise a mug and bid them farewell at the end of the American Revolution. Further uptown, or at least what counted as uptown in the 1790s, the City Hotel opened at 115 Broadway, between Cedar and Thames streets. It was the first true hotel in the country, as opposed to the inns, taverns, and coach houses that served as colonial America's stop-offs for the night.

An opulent 70-room affair, it soon took its place among the best hotels of the world. In his 1864 novel, *Vigor*, author Joseph Alfred Scoville referred to the City Hotel as where "all the great balls and famous dinners came off, and it was at the City Hotel that strangers of any note stopped when they came to the city." Among the many amenities it could offer was a bar. At that bar, just a couple decades after the hotel first opened, worked a man named Orasmus Willard.

Willard was America's first celebrity bartender, a man renowned for his skill at mixing drinks. One of eight brothers, born in 1791 or 1792 in Massachusetts, Willard came to New York and started working at the hotel when he was nineteen. Before long, he had worked his way up, and hotel owner Chester Jennings—who scandalized the city when he introduced the opulent notion of room service in his hotel, an indulgence that was alternately described as a "dangerous blue-blood habits," "a menace to the foundations of the Republic," and "a threat to democracy"—made him a partner. Willard's deftness with a drink—he is credited with being the first man to think of shrinking the common punchbowl concoction down to an individually mixed drink—was second only to his acclaim as a man of incredible grace and consideration. In *Reminiscences of an*

Octogenarian of the City of New York (1816 to 1860) by Charles Haynes Haswell, Willard is mentioned with reverence for his "urbanity of manner and wonderful remembrance of persons."

Abram Dayton's memoir *Last Days of Knickerbocker Life in New York*, from 1882, also recalls Willard with fondness and recounts the tale of the sharp and witty barman's incredible ability to recall even the most casually-met of hotel patrons years after their first encounter. Dayton describes Willard as "of short, compact stature; had a well-moulded head, thickly covered with short cropped wiry grey hair, small quick twinkling eyes that seemed never at rest. Of an active, cheerful disposition, he had a ready reply to any question, and greeted each new arrival with an assuring smile of welcome. Between him and the traveling public there seemed to exist a bond of sympathetic freemasonry."

So tied to the City Hotel was Willard, according to Dayton, that upon the grand opening of the famed Niblo's Garden by impresario William Niblo, Willard was invited as a guest of honor. Willard, when finally confronted by the night he was to visit Niblo's Garden, immediately began searching for a reason to defer and stay at his post at the City Hotel. He settled on his lack of a hat as reason to stay in, though in this case his friends would have none of it. They spirited him across the street to the shop of hatter Charles St. John, who issued Willard a new hat on the spot and sent him along to his night at Niblo's. For his part, St. John had been shocked by the whole affair—not because Willard didn't own a hat, but because he was actually leaving the hotel for a bit.

Nearly as famous as Willard's memory for a patron and his dedication to customer service was his handiness behind the bar. Four of his mixed drinks in particular garnered international acclaim: the apple toddy, sling, peach punch, and a cocktail Bond himself would enjoy in *Goldfinger*, the mint julep. Throughout the 18th century, if there was one drink, one proto-cocktail, that could be said to define American drinking, it was the apple toddy. Proclaimed by some as the drink of the elegant and elite and others as the tipple of the unwashed masses, the apple toddy's contradiction makes it a particularly suitable drink for the United States. Willard would roll apples up in brown paper and pile on them glowing embers "till they were thoroughly roasted and quite soft; then a fourth part of apples, a fourth part of brandy, a fourth part of water, a lump of ice, and the whole to be rich with a fourth part of sugar," which made, according to Willard, an "agreeable compound."

Not too far away from the City Hotel, and not too long after Willard made a name for himself, a man named Jerry Thomas came up with his own version of the popular mixed drink. Shortly thereafter, Thomas would leave New York for San Francisco, where he would play a central role in the confusing history of the Martini. The primary difference between Willard's and Thomas' apple toddy is the base spirit. Willard used brandy, a spirit made from the distillation of grapes. Thomas suggested cider brandy or applejack, which is distilled, as you might guess, from apples or apple cider. Applejack was one of the most popular spirits during the American colonial period. In fact, the oldest continuously-licensed distillery in the United States was Laird's, an applejack maker established in New Jersey in 1780 and whose founder, Robert Laird, instructed no less than part-time distiller George Washington on the craft of making "cyder spirits." Laird's is still in the applejack business and makes two versions of the spirit: the common, inexpensive Laird's Applejack, which has been cut with neutral grain spirit; and a more expensive apple brandy, of which there are three expressions (Laird's Straight Apple Brandy, aged in charred oak barrels for three years; Laird's Old Apple Brandy, aged for 7 ½ years; and Laird's Rare Apple Brandy, aged for 12 years). For the purposes of Jerry Thomas' apple toddy, Laird's Applejack is not well suited to the task, though Laird's Straight Apple Brandy is perfect.

Like many drinks from the colonial and Gilded Age, applejack, as well as the apple toddy, was killed by Prohibition. In the case of the apple toddy, laborious processes like roasting apples over hot coals were simply too complicated for the sort of fast and dirty libations required by the times. And for applejack, it was simply the fact that so much cheap, poisonous rotgut was made under the name applejack that America abandoned the drink, forgetting the days when a good American applejack could have held its own against a fine French Calvados (the French version of apple brandy) and remember it only as "Jersey lightning." By the time Prohibition was over, Laird's had weathered the storm and returned to production, but they were alone. It wasn't until the 21st century that American distillers would rediscover the rich heritage of America's favorite spirit. The tragic fate of applejack was lamented by *bon vivant* Charles Baker, who in his 1931 book *The Gentleman's Companion*, wrote, "It is rather unfortunate that our prohibition era through its raw applejack and Jersey Lightning, managed completely to deflect American taste against this fine spirit. Decently aged-in-wood applejack is a fine thing." He then details his version of an apple toddy, dubbed the Jersey Lighthouse and which he first encountered while drinking with William Faulkner.

By the end of the 19th century, rich Americans visiting London were staying at the Savoy. The bartender in residence, Frank Wells, was inspired by men like Orasmus Willard and Jerry Thomas. He wanted to import the American cocktail to the Savoy. Wells turned the bar at the Savoy into one of the most acclaimed cocktail bars in the world. The proficiency with which he mixed these American-style drinks resulted in the Savoy naming Frank Wells' domain "the American Bar."

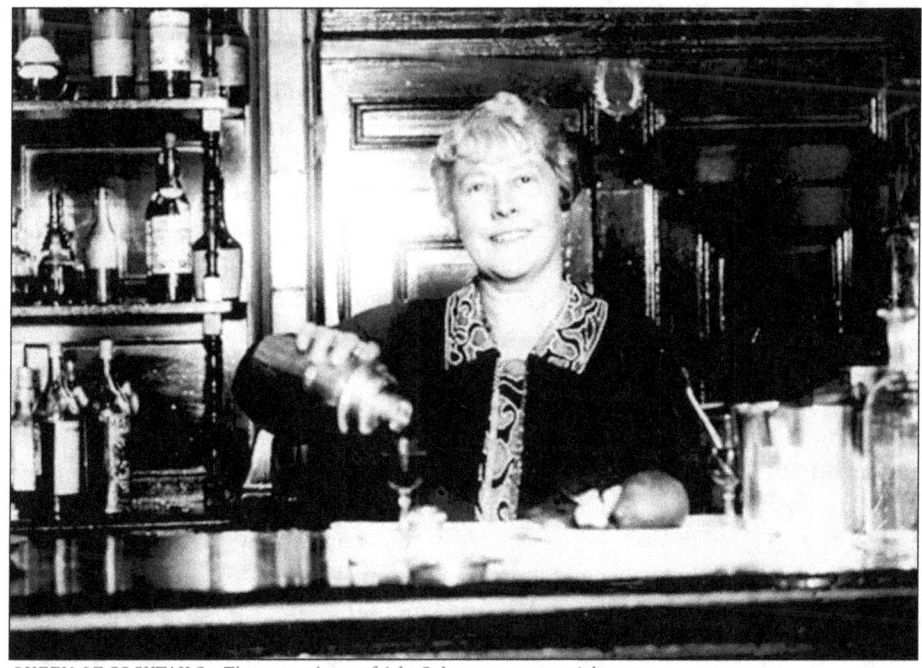

QUEEN OF COCKTAILS—That one photo of Ada Coleman every article uses.

A Little Hanky Panky

When Wells retired from the Savoy in 1902, he handed the American Bar over to Ada Coleman, the world's first female celebrity bartender and the world's first bartender to tame the powerful flavor of Fernet Branca and make it work in a cocktail: the Hanky Panky. Her career behind the bar began in 1899, after the death of her father. He had worked at a golf resort owned by Rupert D'Oyly Carte, son of the man who built the Savoy. Fond of the Colemans, Rupert offered Ada a job working the bar at Claridges. Under the stewardship of the bar's wine butler, Ada learned how to make cocktails, her first being a Manhattan. She proved so adept that the job of head bartender at the Savoy's American bar was offered to her upon Wells' retirement. While there, she became one of the icons of turn-of-the-century bartending, mixing drinks for everyone from Mark Twain to "Diamond" Jim Brady. Like Orasmus Willard before her, "Coley" focused not just on the technical aspects of bartending but also on the hospitality side of things. She was beloved by all. Except for one.

While Ada Coleman is known for the Hanky Panky, the fact that it is the only drink attributed to her in the famous *Savoy Cocktail Book* is almost certainly not a reflection of reality. It is, however a reflection of the prejudices of its author, Harry Craddock, a Brit turned American returned Brit who ran the American Bar upon Ada Coleman's retirement in 1924, and who compiled the legendary *Savoy Cocktail Book* in 1930. Born in Stroud in 1876, Craddock came of age in the United States, where he became a citizen and worked at New York's famed Knickerbocker Hotel. He made a name for himself as a bartender of exceptional talent, but Prohibition cut his career in the US short. By his own claim, he shook the last legal cocktail in the United States. The next day, the first day of Prohibition, he was on a ship bound for England, where he quickly found work at the Savoy's American Bar. And here is where some speculation kicks in.

It's possible that Craddock, already a seasoned veteran of the cocktail scene (and one with the added exotic appeal of being an American), chafed at the thought of working the cocktail-making assembly line. He certainly did not think he should be working under women, including Ada Coleman and her assistant behind the bar, Ruth Burgess. According to *The Deans of Drink*, a 2013 study of the lives and careers of Harry Craddock and fellow bartender Harry Johnson written by Jared Brown and Anistatia Renard Miller, shortly after his arrival at the American Bar, Craddock began a campaign to undermine Coley's position as head bartender. Not only did he think he shouldn't be subservient to a female bartender; he didn't think women belonged behind a bar at all. According to Craddock, citing his experience in America as an American, his fellow countrymen would be put off by the presence of a woman behind the bar— a silly claim, given the fact that, since the earliest days of taverns, women played key roles as both drink makers and tavern owners.

There is nothing in the career of Ada Coleman to back up Craddock's claim. She was, by all accounts, supremely popular and her skill as a bartender much praised by all for whom she mixed a drink, Americans included. But Craddock was a persuasive voice in the ear of the hotel's management, convincing them that they would be better off with an American—and a man—in charge. By 1924, he had successfully forced Coleman and Burgess out of the American Bar. Fearing that such foul treatment of a beloved icon of the Savoy in particular and London in general would result in blowback, the Savoy convinced Ada to frame it as a retirement. In 1925, Harry Craddock was promoted to the position of head bartender at the American Bar. Ada Coleman was transferred. To the hotel's flower shop.

Whatever he may have lacked in character as a human being, there's no denying that Harry Craddock was able to put his money where his mouth was when it came to being a bartender. He was also an exceptionally canny promoter, both of the bar and of himself. He would write articles for papers and challenge politicians tempted to throw their lot in with the temperance movement to taste one of his cocktails and see if they could honestly say it didn't enhance their enjoyment of a meal and of life. He claimed to have invented over 240 cocktails during his career—three in one day, for a willing journalist. With the publication of the *Savoy Cocktail Book*, he cemented his reputation as the world's most famous bartender. And indeed the book is a foundational text for anyone interested in the craft or history of cocktails, though one is rightfully incredulous at the book's implication by omission that, in two decades behind the bar as one of the Savoy's pioneering mixologists, Ada Coleman only created one drink worth writing down. Still, as Jerry Thomas' manual had done a century before, Craddock's book saved countless cocktail recipes from being forgotten. In fact, the book is considered so important to the art and business of cocktails that it is still in print and still regularly updated as new bartenders at the Savoy create new drinks.

Of the many cocktails Craddock mixed at the American Bar, none is more identified with him than the White Lady. A drink favored by the hapless spy Fred Leiser in John Le Carré's *Looking Glass War*. Enamored with British culture and self-conscious about his own Slav-ness, Leiser studiously attempts to mimic (with only moderate success) the affectations of what he thinks to be an upstanding, standard issue Englishman. Among those affectations is his fondness for the White Lady. Le Carré also paid tribute to Pink Gin, and once again, here was an author Ian Fleming admired but had nothing in common with beyond Pink Gin, the drink of choice of Jerry Westerby in Le Carré's *Tinker, Tailor, Soldier, Spy*. Where Fleming sought to excise real-world politics from his book in all but the vaguest of allusions ("the Soviets are the bad guys, and even that he abandoned in favor of SPECTRE), John Le Carré's thrillers were darker, more cynical, and more directly related to the realities of the Cold War.

In 1966, Le Carré trashed Fleming's creation, saying in an interview, "I dislike Bond. I'm not sure that Bond is a spy. I think that it's a great mistake if one's talking about espionage literature to include Bond in this category at all. It seems to me he's more some kind of international gangster with, as it is said, a licence to kill... he's a man entirely out of the political context. It's of no interest to Bond who, for instance, is president of the United States or of the Union of Soviet Republics."

Born David John Moore Cornwell in 1931, the man who would adopt the pen name John Le Carré had a rougher childhood than the pampered Fleming and the troubled Graham Greene. His mother abandoned the family when he was only five years old, and his father was a conman who spent time in prison for insurance fraud. He was an able student but chafed under the rigid, harsh academic environment. In 1948, he withdrew from the British school system and transferred to the University of Bern in Switzerland. In 1950 he joined the Intelligence Corps of the British Army in Austria, where his proficiency with German got him an assignment questioning political refugees fleeing East Germany.

He returned to England in 1952 but maintained his covert career, spying on far-left political groups at Lincoln College, Oxford, and looking for possible Soviet spies while freelancing for British Security Service. By 1958, Cornwell was a full-fledged MI5 officer, handling field agents and plotting operations. It was during this time that, encouraged by friend, fellow spy, and author of crime thrillers John Michael Ward Bingham, 7th Baron Clanmorris, to write a novel. Lord Clanmorris would become one of two models (the other being Vivian Hubert Howard Green, one of Le Carré's professors at Lincoln College) for the eventual novel's main character, semi-retired secret agent George Smiley. The book, which Cornwell published under the pseudonym John Le Carré (he was by then in the employ of the Foreign Office, and agents for the Foreign Office were forbidden from publishing anything under their real name), was titled *Call for the Dead*.

Although they share an affinity for whiskey and work for British intelligence, there is little similar between Fleming's Bond and Le Carré's Smiley. Smiley is chubby, bookish, unhappily separated from his wife, and possessed of considerably more empathy (and stolid British politeness) than

007. He appeared frequently throughout Le Carré's novels, sometimes as a main character, other times among the shadows in the background. He's been portrayed by actors as disparate in style and appearance as Rupert Davies, James Mason, Alec Guinness, and Gary Oldman. Le Carré's third novel, the bitter and bleak *The Spy Who Came in From the Cold*, is widely regarded as one of the best espionage stories ever written. Like Graham Greene before him, the game of deception and false intelligence so proficiently devised by Agent Garbo inspired Le Carré's 1996 novel, *The Tailor of Panama*, which was made into a film in 2001 starring then-James Bond Pierce Brosnan.

As different as their writing styles might have been from one another's, it's hard to think of a more quintessentially British circle of espionage novelists than Graham Greene, Ian Fleming, and John Le Carré. You could work John Buchan in somehow; he, at least, probably would have gotten along with Fleming and appreciated James Bond. One could easily imagine them sitting (uncomfortably) at a table together at The Savoy, ordering Pink Gins.

Craddock claimed the White Lady as his own creation, but David Wondrich credits the drink to Harry MacElhone, a celebrity bartender in his own right. MacElhone tended bar at the Plaza Hotel (where Arnold Rothstein was murdered) before Prohibition chased him, like Craddock, out of the United States. He found employment in London, at Ciro's Club, before opening his own bar in Paris: Harry's New York Bar, one of the most famous European cocktail bars of all time. According to Wondrich, MacElhone created the White Lady in 1919 while working at Ciro's. MacElhone's original version of the drink, which

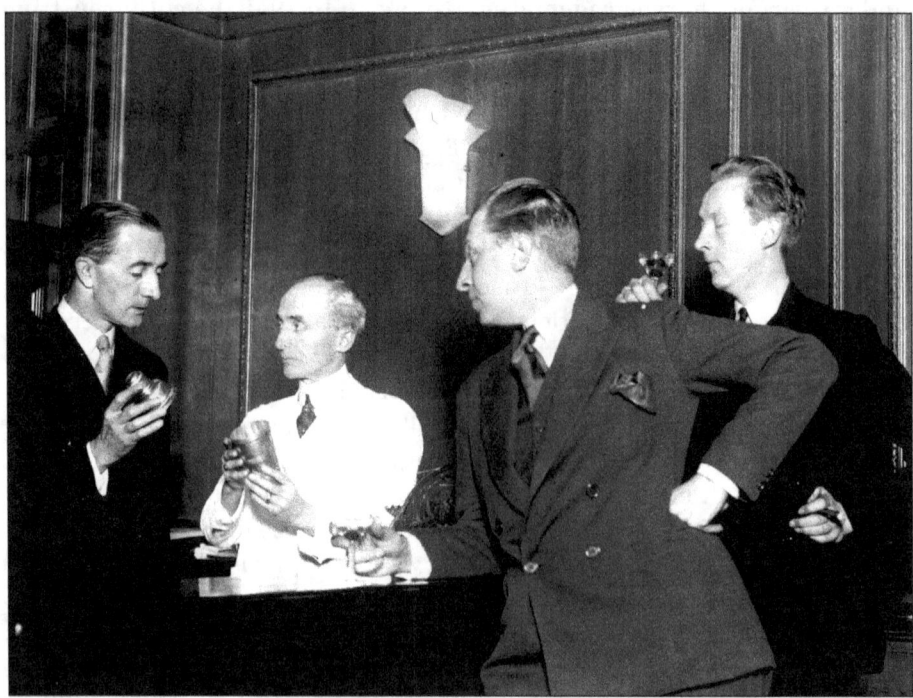

DEAN OF DRINKS—Harry Craddock, behind the bar.

Wondrich described in a column for *Esquire* as "the color of chlorine gas and unhealthily sweet, like the smell of orchids," has one notable difference from the recipe presented by Craddock in the *Savoy Cocktail Book*: Crème de menthe. This proved too much even for MacElhone, who by the time the drink was being made at his bar in Paris, had replaced the Crème de menthe with gin. It is this revision to the recipe that Craddock claimed as his own, and while there is no way to prove it one way or the other, it seems likely that a different bartender (Craddock) would make as dramatic a change as swapping out Crème de menthe for gin, rather than the man who came up with the Crème de menthe in the first place (MacElhone) suddenly having a change of heart.

Crème de menthe is a sweet liqueur made by soaking dried peppermint or Corsican mint leaves in grain alcohol for several weeks. The resultant flavored spirit is then filtered and dosed with sugar (and in some cases, green dye). In the Bond franchise, there is no bigger fan of Crème de menthe than SPECTRE's second-in-command in *Thunderball*, Emilio Largo. While he doesn't go for the Crème de menthe version of the White Lady (by the 1960s, that version would have been forgotten), Largo loves the Crème de menthe frappé, an silly, even childish drink for so macho a guy. This is not to imply that Crème de menthe is incapable of rendering a tasty cocktail. Its greatest triumph is the Stinger, an exceptional cocktail that Bond himself consumes in the book *Diamonds are Forever*. The Bond Girl of the story, Tiffany Case,

HANKY PANKY

- 1 ½ oz Dry Gin
- 1 ½ oz Sweet Vermouth
- 2 dashes Fernet Branca

Add all ingredients to a mixing glass with ice. Stir well. Strain into a chilled cocktail glass. Twist a sliver of orange peel over the surface of the drink then add as garnish

••••••••••••••••••••••

STINGER

- 2 oz Cognac
- 1 oz White Crème de Menthe

Add all ingredients to a shaker with ice. Shake well. Strain into a rocks glass over crushed ice.

••••••••••••••••••••••

ATTY

- 1 ½ oz Dry Gin
- ¾ oz Dry Vermouth
- ¼ tsp Absinthe
- ½ tsp Crème de Violette

Add gin, vermouth, absinthe, and crème de violette to a mixing glass filled with ice. Stir well. Strain into a chilled cocktail glass. Garnish with a lemon twist.

••••••••••••••••••••••

LEAP YEAR

- 2 oz Plymouth Gin
- ½ oz Grand Marnier
- ½ oz Sweet Vermouth
- 1 dash Fresh Lemon Juice

Add all ingredients to a shaker filled with ice. Shake well. Strain into a chilled cocktail glass. Twist a piece of lemon peel over the drink then add as garnish.

consumes several more throughout the slim volume. When it comes to taste in Crème de menthe cocktails, the advantage is definitely to Tiffany Case over Largo.

Ian Fleming joined the staff of Rear Admiral John Godfrey in May of 1939. That same year, Harry Craddock departed the Savoy, so it's unlikely the legendary barkeep ever made a cocktail for Fleming—at least at the Savoy. At Dukes, another of Fleming's favorite haunts and the bar Craddock joined after the Savoy, on the other hand...

Harry Craddock was replaced by a man named Eddie Clark, who was the Savoy's bartender throughout the Blitz, when the Savoy became the *de facto* headquarters of much of the British war effort, especially the covert and clandestine aspects of it. It would have been Eddie Clark making the drinks for everyone from Ian Fleming to Noel Coward to Winston Churchill. During his tenure behind the bar amid the tumult of the Blitz, Clark created a cocktail for each branch of the armed services: "Eight Bells" for the Navy (as if they weren't all just drinking Pink Gin), "New Contemptible" for the Army, and "Wings" for the R.A.F.

Clark enlisted in Britain's Mercantile Marine War Reserve. In 1942 he was called up and turned the bar over to his friend and coworker, Reginald "Johnnie" Johnson, who saw the American Bar through the rest of the war and clear into the dawn of mid-century cocktail culture, retiring in 1954. He created a cocktail, Wedding Bells, in honor of the wedding of Princess Elizabeth and Prince Philip. Today, the bar is under the stewardship of Erik Lorincz. They still serve a world-class Hanky Panky, including an antique version using vintage spirits (Gordon's gin and Cinzano Rosso from the 1950s and Fernet Branca from 1967) that will set you back a cool £120. The same price will get you a vintage White Lady made with non-vintage egg white—totally reasonable when measured against the bar's £5000 Sazerac made with 1858 Sazerac de Forage, Pernod absinthe from the 1950s, and bitters from 1900.

Those on a slightly tighter budget might elect for the non-vintage version of any of those drinks, or pick some of the more recent concoctions, like the Hackney Carriage (Diplomático Reserva Exclusiva rum, Umeshu fruit liqueur from Japan, dry vermouth, Laphroaig, simple syrup and Peychaud's bitters) or Napoleon's Wish (Chivas Regal 18, Boulard Calvados, Cocchi di Torino, pear eau de vie, simple syrup, and soda). And of course, one must order the Secret Agent (Woodford Reserve, Laphroaig, Cocchi Amaro, absinthe, lemon juice, simple syrup and egg white).

The Playlist: Boogie Woogie Bugle Boys

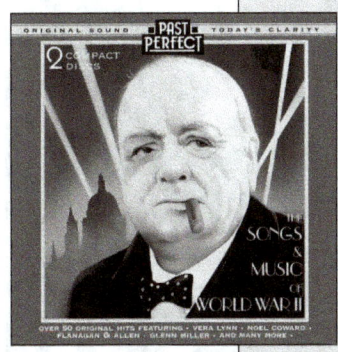

If television and film is to be believed, the only song that existed during World War II was Glenn Miller's "In the Mood." A damn fine song, but surprisingly, there were songs beyond that, and not just "Boogie Woogie Bugle Boy." There are a ton of "World War II music" compilations, both on CD and as digital downloads, usually for fairly cheap, sometimes of varying quality. If you're prepared to wade into the crowded waters, there are a few collections that stand out, either because they're so comprehensive, they're of exceptional quality, or they just have cool covers and knife-wielding women beating up Nazis. One word of warning: no matter what you do, you're going to end up with a fair number of songs repeated across various collections. Relax. No one ever suffered from having too many versions of "In the Mood."

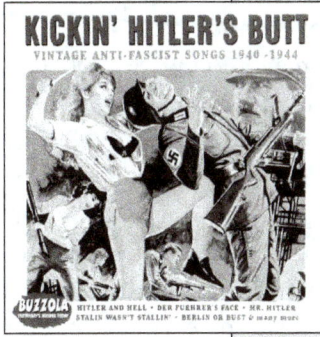

British label Past Perfect has a couple fantastic discs: *G.I. Jive*, which contains classic American songs from the War, and *The Songs & Music of World War 2*, a two-disc set containing wartime hits from both the U.S. and Britain, perfect for the Savoy Hotel ballroom. Plus, you really need at least one CD with Winston Churchill on the cover. Most of the songs are top hits from the 1930s and '40s, though you get more than a few songs expressly about the war. If you want something more direct and literal, *Kickin' Hitler's Butt*, from Buzzola, is a collection of wartime songs that don't beat around the bush. The theme is obvious, and you can never have too many songs about whuppin' the Nazis. Among other novel fightin' hits, there's Spike Jones' "Der Fuehrer's Face," written to accompany a short in which Donald Duck learns the errors of being a Nazi.

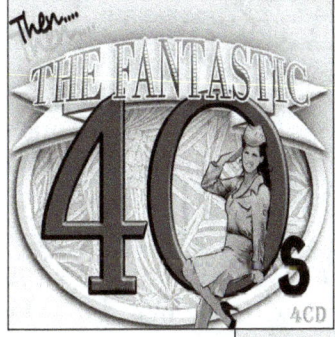

Perhaps the most comprehensive tour of wartime music, despite a somewhat slapdash "clipart for beginners" cover, is *Then...The Fantastic 40s*, a 4-disc library of classics including "In the Mood," "Boogie Woogie Bugle Boy," *and* "Der Fuehrer's Face." Also essential for any collection of music for dancing away the Blitz is at least one disc of British big bands. Past Perfect's *The Great British Dance Bands* will get Sir Winston up and dancing. If you want a taste of the music between the wars, there's Van Up Records' *British Dance Bands of the 1920s*.

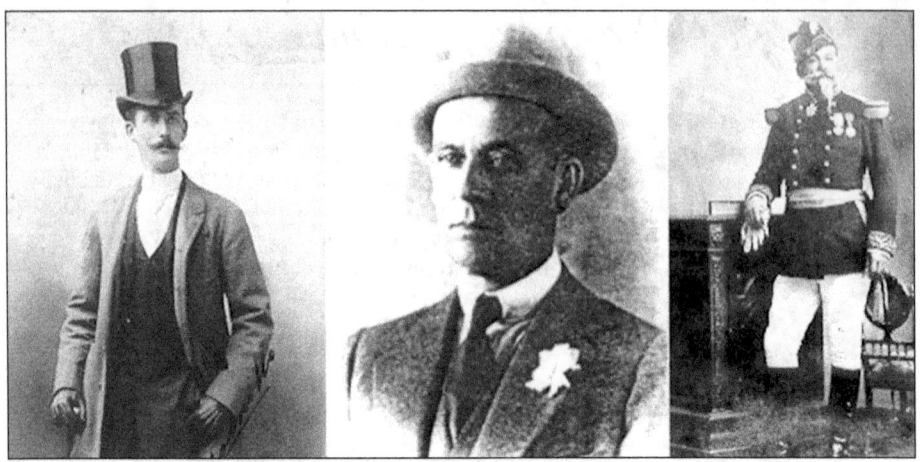

THREE OF COUNTS—One of these men maybe invented the Negroni, or not.

Dueling Counts

For a short story, Fleming packs quite a bit of detail and drinking into "Risico." Aside from the Hotel Excelsior in Rome (at Via Vittorio Veneto, 125 00187 Roma) and Caffè Florian in Venice, Bond drops in at Harry's Bar (Calle Vallaresso 1323, Venice). Harry's Bar should not be confused with Harry's New York Bar in that old villain of a city, Paris, where young James Bond spent a night drinking before losing his virginity. To confuse matters further, Harry's Bar in Venice is currently owned by restaurant company Cipriani S.A., which opened a Harry's Bar in New York—but not Harry's New York Bar. Caffè Florian and Harry's Bar have a storied list of clients and historical accomplishments. Aside from being one of Italy's oldest cafés, Florian is an opulent showcase for art and historic Venetian design, with a clientele that has included one of history's most famous womanizing spies, Casanova, and writers such as Lord Byron, Marcel Proust, and Charles Dickens. Harry's Bar in Venice was frequented by Ernest Hemingway (who also frequented Harry's New York Bar in Paris), Truman Capote, Orson Welles, Alfred Hitchcock, and Charlie Chaplin, though probably not all at the same time. It's the birthplace of the Bellini, so named because its pink hue reminded Giuseppe Cipriani of the toga of a saint in a painting by 15th-century Venetian artist Giovanni Bellini.

"Risico" does not state what James Bond drinks while at Harry's Bar in Venice. While it's safe to assume he probably stuck with the Americano, the bar is famous for its version of a cocktail near and dear to 007's heart: the Martini. They make them very dry indeed at Harry's Bar: 10 parts gin to one part vermouth and served in a glass with no stem. It's a variation on another variation of the Martini: the Montgomery, named after cautious British Field Marshal Bernard Montgomery and boasting even more contempt for vermouth. The Montgomery's 15 parts gin to one part dry vermouth are said to have been derived from always-cautious Monty's preferred ratio of "my troops to their troops." Bond completes his afternoon drinking tour of Venice at Quadri (Piazza San Marco 121, 30124 Venice). Again, "Risico" doesn't clue us in to what Bond ordered while visiting this caffè once visited by the likes of writer Alexander Dumas and former Soviet leader Mikhail Gorbachev (not to mention the world's second Jimmy Bond, Woody Allen). Perhaps he switched things up and moved on from the Americano to a Negroni, sometimes referred to as "an Americano with guts."

In his book *Everyday Drinking*, acclaimed British author Kingsley Amis described the Americano as "good at lunchtime and before Italian food." He then went on to write: "If you feel that, pleasant as it is, it still lacks something, throw in a shot of gin and the result is a Negroni. This is a really fine invention. It has the power, rare with drinks and indeed with anything else, of cheering you up." Among other literary accomplishments, Amis was hired to write the first official James Bond novel, *Colonel Sun*, after the death of Ian Fleming. The first drink Bond has in "Risico" is a Negroni "with Gordon's please." In the movie *For Your Eyes Only*, loosely adapted in part from "Risico," the drink is changed to the Greek *pastis* ouzo, which happens to play a major role in Amis' *Colonel Sun*. In the cinematic adaptation of *Thunderball*, Bond congratulates himself for disarming a henchman by mixing himself a Negroni.

The origin of the drink, like so many, is a mix of supposition, archaeology, and the acceptance of hearsay as fact because, "ehh, why not? That's been the story for a long time." As one story goes, the Negroni was invented at the Caffè Casoni (formerly Caffè Giacosa) in Florence when Italian Count Camillo Negroni explained to the resident bartender, Fosco Scarselli, that while the count did love himself an Americano, he wanted something similar but with a little more punch to it. Negroni suggested ditching the Americano's soda in favor of gin. Scarselli obliged, also substituting a garnish of orange peel for the Americano's lemon peel. And so was born the Negroni, according to the book *Sulle Tracce del Conte: La Vera Storia del Cocktail Negroni*, written in 2002 by Lucca Picchi. There is now also an English translation, *Negroni Cocktail: An Italian Legend*.

Count Camillo Negroni, according to the book, shared a peculiar trait with Seraffimo Spang, the head of the Spangled Mob in Fleming's *Diamonds Are Forever*: dressing up like a cowboy. Picchi's book claims Camillo was the grandson of English poet Walter Savage Landor. He spent a lot of time in America, first working as a cowboy (thus his affinity for dressing up like one) and later as a gambler in New York. Other than his existence, his presence in New York, and a photo that makes him look more like a humorless banker played by Lon Chaney than a professional adventurer, most of the claims about him remain difficult to independently substantiate.

This account of this Count seems reasonable but has been disputed hotly and with supporting documentation by Noel Negroni, who claims that it was *his* relative, a Corsican war hero named Pascal Olivier Count de Negroni, who led the first cavalry charge of the Franco-Prussian War, who invented the Negroni. According to Noel Negroni, there never was a Count Camillo Negroni; no such person shows up in the Negroni family histories. Instead, Pascal invented the cocktail while stationed in Senegal and dedicated it to his fiancée. This claim is supported by personal letters mentioning the drink, though it would have been a bit different back then since Campari was not yet in existence. However, there would have been any number of similar bitter liqueurs from which he could have chosen. He also probably wouldn't have called it a Negroni, though who knows with those aristocratic military types? More than likely, the thinking goes, people who liked it were asking for that "Count Negroni cocktail." The name stuck. And if it was Camillo who invented the drink? Well, same thing. "Give me an Americano the Negroni way" just becomes Negroni.

Of course, Noel's research doesn't preclude there being a different Negroni family than his own or of one man having multiple names. Which, it turns out, is exactly the case. The existence of Pascal Olivier Count de Negroni has never been in doubt, but like Noel Negroni, people began to think that this mysterious and flamboyant Count Camillo was just a myth—until confirmation of his immigration to New York was discovered by *Drinking Cup* writer Rusty Hawthorne and a phalanx of other researchers. Or at least, there was indeed a guy named Camillo Negroni who, it seems, was some manner of Count. As for the rest of his rather fanciful, biography...well, there is not any proof that Count Camillo was the swashbuckling cowboy cosplayer claimed by the legend.

The debate has escalated, as things inevitably do, to a battle for the honor of two competing families over a claim that it's unlikely could ever be definitively proven and which would, in the end, reap them no particular benefits other than points of pride. Still, the lengths to which the Corsican Negronis have gone to debunk the claims that Count Camillo Negroni invented the cocktail are as impressive as they are extreme and include hiring handwriting analysts and mounting an expedition to Senegal. That alone deserves a toast.

In any case, the almost universally accepted image of Count Negroni—a tall, mustachio'd man in a top hat, a cardboard cut-out of which accompanies almost every Negroni Week celebration and is widely circulated by writers and brands alike—isn't *any* Count Negroni, Camillo or Pascal. It's anthropologist and explorer Arnold Henry Savage Landor (incredibly, no relation to Walter Savage Landor). Count Camillo does have a possible tenuous link to the Landor family through his mother, but that link has yet to be proven as anything other than a coincidence of name, much like the one that confused the two Count Negronis. However, it might explain how a portrait of Arnold Henry Savage Landor ever came to be mistaken as a picture of Count Negroni. Whether or not you should affect a bad Sean Connery slur next time someone names Landor as Negroni and explain to them, "Actually, that'sh exshplorer Arnold Landor, a lover of catsh," depends entirely on you and whether or not you want any friends.

It seems like the true origin of the cocktail will remain disputed, but does it really matter? Look at those back stories! Both are great. While that may continue to be a bone of contention among the families vying for the claim of "inventor of the Negroni," the cocktail is better served by fanciful legend than truth. Negroni drinkers win either way. The thing was invented either by a fist-pumping 19th century war hero who led a dramatic charge, or it was invented by an eccentric count who dressed up like a cowboy and gambled with gangsters in New York. The important thing is, you can order one. If you happen to find yourself in Florence, drop by the Caffè Giacosa and toast both Counts. Cowboy attire is optional.

NEGRONI

- 1 oz London dry gin
- 1 oz Campari
- 1 oz Carpano Antica Vermouth

Add all ingredients to a shaker with ice. Shake well. Strain into a chilled cocktail glass. Garnish with a twist of orange peel. You can also strain it into a rocks glass over ice. And you can stir it if you want. This cocktail can do anything!

BELLINI

- 1 ½ oz Fresh White Peach Purée
- Chilled Prosecco

Add the peach purée to a Champagne flute and fill with prosecco. Garnish with a peach slice.

BRANDY ALEXANDER

- 2 oz Cognac
- 1 oz Dark Crème de Cacao
- 1 oz Cream

Add all ingredients to a shaker with ice. Shake well. Strain into a chilled cocktail glass. Garnish with freshly grated nutmeg.

PALOMA

- 2 oz Reposado Tequila
- ½ oz Fresh Lime Juice
- Grapefruit Soda

Add the tequila and lime juice to a highball glass filled with ice. Fill with grapefruit soda. Stir.

GIN AND DUBONNET

- 1 ½ oz Dubonnet Rouge
- 1 ½ oz Dry Gin
- 1 dash Angostura Bitters

Add all ingredients to a mixing glass. Fill with ice. Stir. Strain into a cocktail glass. Garnish with a lemon twist.

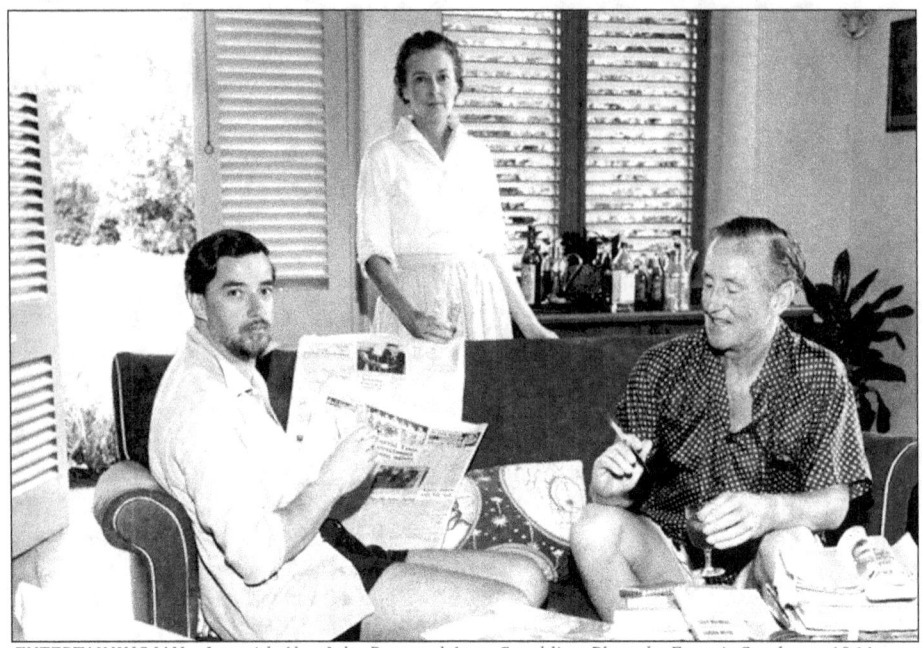

ENTERTAINING IAN—Ian with Alan John Ross and Anne Geraldine. Photo by Francis Goodman, 1964.

Goldeneye, No Time for Sweetness

"Risico" prominently features one more cocktail, if in a somewhat dismissive fashion. Kristatos identifies himself to Bond at the Excelsior's bar with a signal: an Alexander, which amuses 007. "Bond had been told to look for a man with a heavy moustache who would be by himself drinking an Alexandra. Bond had been amused by the secret recognition signal. The creamy, feminine drink was so much cleverer than the folded newspaper, the flower in the buttonhole, the yellow gloves that were the hoary, slipshod call-signs between agents."

There are several variations of the Alexander, the best known of which is the Brandy Alexander, but the original recipe is a mixture of gin, Crème de cacao, and sweet cream. It was rumored to have been invented at New York's Rector's restaurant in New York by bartender Troy Alexander, who wanted a drink to serve during a dinner celebrating the illustrated character Phoebe Snow (not to be confused with the singer-songwriter of the same name). Phoebe Snow was clad in white and used in promotions for "clean-burning" coal by the Delaware, Lackawanna and Western Railroad. Her likeness was co-opted in political cartoons skewering Chicago politician William Lorimer, who was accused of having special interests buy his way into the U.S. Senate.

Rector's was the bawdy toast of New York in its day, an opulent restaurant opened by Charles Rector in 1899 at Broadway and 44th Street. It was a "lobster palace" at a time when lobster was still considered blue collar grub for poor people and prisoners. Over-harvesting of lobster, however, was making it rare, so all of a sudden it went from trash to treasure, and Rector's became one of the most popular spots during the "Gay Nineties." It was particularly favored by actors, chorus girls from the nearby Ziegfeld Follies (which itself paid tribute to Rector's raucous reputation in the song "If the Tables at Rector's Could Talk"), and boisterous but well-heeled (but not necessarily sophisticated) theater goers—especially older men looking to flirt with the pretty girls from the Follies. The waiters were impeccably dressed in formal evening wear, and the table settings were exquisite. The food was beloved by no less voracious a gourmand than Gilded Age captain of industry "Diamond" Jim Brady. Felix Leiter would have loved the place.

Unfortunately, it wasn't around long enough for Leiter and Bond to enjoy a drink and grope a pretty girl. In 1911, Charles Rector expanded his empire into the hotel business, but the salacious reputation of his restaurant, coupled with a saucy play called *The Girl from Rector's*, meant that the hotel was assumed to be the sort of place one might go to take restaurant flirting and lap-sitting to the next level. Two years later, the hotel was out of business and Charles Rector, despondent over the failure and the unsavory reputation of the hotel, retired from the hospitality business altogether. His son Charles, who had been responsible for much of the success enjoyed by the kitchen, took over operations, but by then the nature of dining out was changing, and Rector's had lost it's opulent sheen. The restaurant closed permanently in 1914. Although James Bond never had a chance to drop by Rector's, he did visit New York's other most famous lobster palace. In the short story "007 in New York" (Fleming's apology for being so cranky about New York in *Thrilling Cities*), James Bond asserts that oyster stew with cream and crackers and a Miller High Life at the Oyster Bar in Grand Central Terminal is among the best meals he's ever had. Unlike Rector's, the Oyster Bar is still around.

The Alexander endured beyond the life of the bar where it was created. Exactly how it evolved into the Brandy Alexander is, as is usual for this shaky thing called cocktail history, a topic of debate. One story claims that brandy was substituted for gin in 1922 during the wedding of England's Princess Mary, daughter of King George V and Queen Mary, to Viscount Henry Charles George, Viscount Lascelles. But there doesn't seem anything particularly Brandy Alexander-esque about the event, which is remembered more these days (if it is remembered at all) as the first royal function attended by Elizabeth Angela Marguerite Bowes-Lyon, wife of King George VI, last Empress of India, and mother of the woman who would become Queen Elizabeth II. Both the Queen Mum and Queen Elizabeth were gin women, incidentally—specifically Gin and Dubonnet, a sweet herbal aperitif from France.

Czar Alexander II of Russia insisted that the Brandy Alexander was a creation wholly different from the Alexander and named in his honor. Literary critic Alexander Woollcott insisted the drink was named after him. While it's not likely this argument will ever be settled, it can be assumed with some certainty, even though it is not specified in "Risico," that Kristatos' drink was a Brandy Alexander, as it was more popular in Fleming's time than the largely forgotten Alexander with gin. Then again, Fleming liked messing with things, so who knows?

After the War, Fleming drifted back into journalism and, ultimately, into writing his first novel. When he retired to his modest Jamaican villa Goldeneye ("Goldeneye, nose and throat" quipped his neighbor, the entertainer Noel Coward, who was as unimpressed with Fleming's abode as he was with the fare served to him when he visited), he didn't expect the novel he produced to be much more than a passing trifle. It was an attempt to make good on a desire that boiled up during his wartime service to write a potboiler. It was also an attempt to keep himself occupied and his mind off his impending marriage to his on-again, off-again girlfriend of many years, Ann Charteris. So from February 17 to March 18, 1952—just one month—Fleming went about the task of creating "the spy story to end all spy stories," writing 2,000 words every morning. Titled *Casino Royale*, and drawing upon Fleming's experiences at Naval Intelligence, as well as those of others with whom he crossed paths during the war, the book was about the exploits of a British secret agent named James Bond, after an American ornithologist. As Fleming would later write in a letter to the *Manchester Guardian*, "One of the reasons why I chose the pseudonym of James Bond for my hero rather than, say, Peregrine Maltravers was that I wished him to be unobtrusive. Exotic things would happen to and around him, but he would be a neutral figure—an anonymous blunt instrument wielded by a Government Department."

Fleming referred to the manuscript as his "dreadful oafish opus." A friend advised him to never attempt to have it published, or if he insisted on pursuing it, then to at least publish it under a pen name (Robert Markham, perhaps?). Fleming was determined however, despite the self-deprecating assessment of his own work. In April of 1953, the first edition of *Casino Royale* was released by Peter Fleming's publisher, Jonathan Cape. It featured a cover designed by Fleming himself. In his goal to "write the spy story to end all spy stories," Fleming failed utterly. Rather than writing the spy story to end all spy stories, he wrote the spy story that began thousands more spy stories. And films. And comic books. And records. And an entire cottage industry revolving around documenting the phenomenon.

The introduction of Kingsley Amis' *James Bond Dossier*, one of the first serious critical looks at the James Bond novels, lays out Amis' failure to prevent a 5,000 word essay from becoming a full book, noting, "For every point I made I discovered two fresh ones that needed making, so that at times I wondered if I was ever going to get to the finish." "Part of my motive for writing about [James Bond]," wrote Amis, "was my conviction, vague at that stage but firm, that they were more than simple cloak-and-dagger stories with a bit of fashionable affluence and sex thrown in. I suspected that, on the contrary, I would find them to be just as complex and to have just as much in them as more ambitious kinds of fiction." Amis was correct. After all, would people still be watching James Bond movies, reading James Bond novels, making television specials about Ian Fleming, and devoting untold numbers of words to discussing, analyzing, celebrating, and vilifying 007 if Fleming's novels had really been nothing more than the "vulgar exercises in sex, sadism, and snobbery" they were often accused of being? James Bond transcended the ambitions of Ian Fleming and the accusations of critics, becoming a cultural icon known, celebrated, and in some cases reviled the world over. Every country, every culture, has their Bond, or their spoof of Bond, or their reaction to Bond.

One of the most interesting things Fleming's stories did, even if it was unintentional, was create a snapshot of a quasi-fantasy world that can actually be touched. Bond may be escapist, he may be wish fulfillment, but his world is not unobtainable. You can't go to Westeros from George RR Martin's *Game of Thrones* (and probably wouldn't want to), or to The Shire. Sure, you can visit the *locations* used for adaptations, but it's not quite the same as the fact that, even today, you can sit down at the King Cole Bar in New York's St. Regis Hotel and order a Martini, just like Bond and Felix Leiter.

Fleming's obsession with real locations and products may have seemed trite, indulgent, and even snobbish, but it resulted in a detailed world that bleeds into our own. Bond's travels and habits don't have to stay a vicarious thrill. Much of that world is still here. You can still go to the Oyster Bar at Grand Central Terminal. You can still pour yourself two fingers of Haig & Haig scotch whiskey, order an Americano at Florian's, or pop the cork on a bottle of Tattinger while staying at the Peninsula Hotel in Hong Kong. The world of James Bond is not one that exists purely on the page, only accessible through fiction, only understood through critical theory and analysis. You can be part of Bond's universe, something that is fairly unique among popular film and book series.

Fleming, the morally questionable son of an otherwise respectable British family, was a man who, like Bond, had a tremendous appetite for the finer things in life while, at the same time, never seemed fully compatible with the respectable

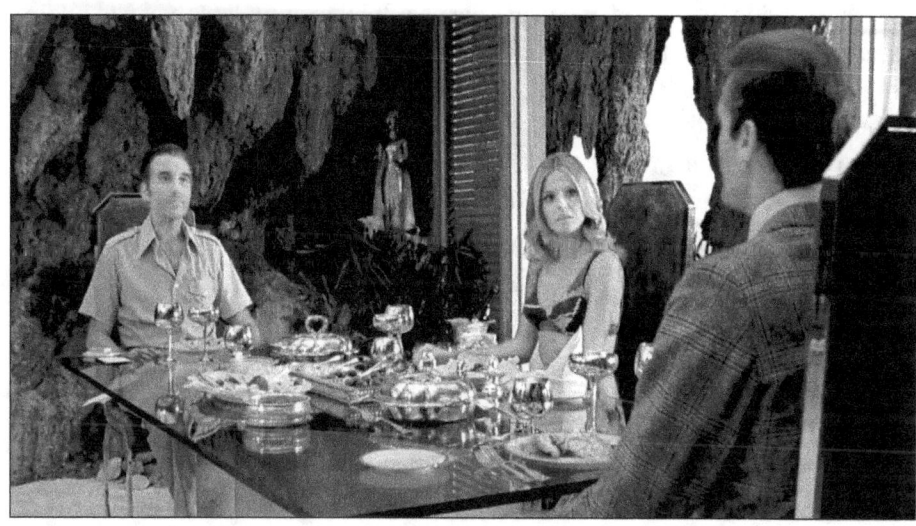

upper-crust who consumed such things. That wild Scottish heritage would keep him from being considered a true elite of British society. Similarly, Bond is not a "proper" Englishman. His heritage is even more disreputable than Fleming's, being half Scottish and half Swiss. He is both a pretender to upper class British society (of which, Bond's boss, M, is a much more credible example) and someone who disregards it with a sneer. Bond drifts easily from the world's rarest and most desirable champagnes to a bottle of Miller High Life, from the world's most exquisite hotels to threadbare roadside motels in the middle of nowhere.

Like Fleming at Goldeneye, where his meals were famously average (Noel Coward claimed he used to cross himself and ask for mercy before eating anything served to him at Fleming's home, spending most of the meal dreaming about all those delicious meals he read about in the Bond novels), 007 eats relatively simple fare at home. He is also adaptable, willing to sample the local fare and try the local specialty, rather than bring his Britishness with him like excess baggage. Raki with Darko Bey at a café in Istanbul, scotch with Felix Leiter in New York, vodka with M at the exclusive club Blades—but only then to annoy M.

Fleming referred to the Bond books as "fairytales for adults," and adults would appreciate the opportunity to occasionally experience such fairy tales in the real world. Bond was a blank slate upon which readers could project themselves, imagining that Bond's jet-set adventures, his opulent meals, and his indulgent expense account was their own. Such a vision would have been powerful indeed to a Britain still recovering from the brutality of the Second World War, still rebuilding the structures destroyed during the Blitz, still laboring under the austerity measures and rationing that England accepted as the price of victory. In 1953, the first of these austerity measures was lifted, and for the first time in years, Britain was able to consider the possibility that they might soon enjoy butter, bacon, eggs.

Casino Royale came out that same year. James Bond was more than just a mouth-watering bit of food and drink pornography to stimulate the taste buds of Brits who had long suffered under the meager, drab, rationed victuals of the war years. He was a promise of things to come, of better and tastier days ahead, even if the sun had finally set on the Empire. The lust with which James Bond tears into a plate of bacon and eggs is to food what Bond's globetrotting was to travel; it was wish fulfillment, but it was wish fulfillment with the bonus that the wishes could, even if only on occasion, be granted in exactly the manner they were described by Ian Fleming. And it all started with *Casino Royale*.

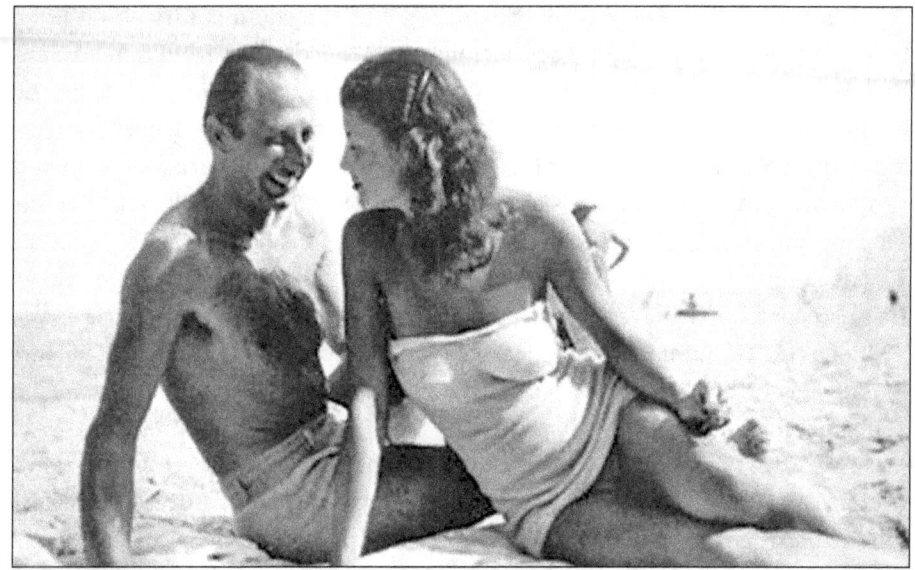
BETTER THAN BOND—*Secret agent Dusko Popov with his wife, Janine.*

The Spy Story to End All Spy Stories

Common knowledge holds that the character of James Bond is vastly different in the books than he is in the movies, that the literary Bond is more ruthless, cunning, and mean—a real bastard, if you will—while movie Bond, even as played by Sean Connery, is a bit more playful and whimsical. To investigate this claim, there is no better place to begin than with the first one, *Casino Royale*.

A Russian agent, Le Chiffre, with a penchant for the good life "borrowed" money earmarked for the French Communist party. Unfortunately, he invested it in a chain of high-class brothels on the eve of France outlawing prostitution (Communists just don't make good capitalists), and now all the money is gone. This is not, it turns out, his first transgression. The Russian agency SMERSH—the secret police who police the secret police and assassinate any Russian agents gone sour—is eying Le Chiffre. If he is found out, they will kill him, even though it means a crucial blow will be dealt to the cause of Communism in France. Le Chiffre's hope is to right his debt by winning the money back at the gambling table before SMERSH catches up with him and extracts deadly interest. News of this reaches London, and a scheme is hatched to beat Le Chiffre at his own game by sending an agent to out-gamble him. If they simply assassinated Le Chiffre, he would become a martyr. Instead, they have to insure that he dies at the hands of his own people, disgraced and humiliated. So the British agent must travel to France and beat Le Chiffre at the table, dashing any hope that he will recoup his losses and save himself from SMERSH. M, the head of British Intelligence, has just the man for the job: Bond. James Bond.

Based on *Casino Royale*, you should forget all the commentary about Bond being ruthless and calculating and vicious. He is these things from time to time, but the overreaching characteristics of the man in *Casino Royale* are doubt, emotionalism, a certain weepiness, definite crabbiness, and a tendency to wallow in self-pity. He's an ace gambler but in many ways a below-average spy. He fails to spot all but the most obvious of enemy agents, stumbles blindly into even the most obvious traps, and never really emerges victorious from any confrontation. He has moments of flash and cool, but for the most part, he's a bit of a bumbler. He's arrogant, but he never justifies that arrogance in action. He's humorless, and a bit of a prick—but not the fun prick he would become in later books. If you are looking for the cool-as-ice 007, you're not going to find him in *Casino Royale*. But you might find him in Portugal.

The list of men who have been named as "the real James Bond" is long. Most of them insist there is no way they were the inspiration for 007. One of them outright scoffed at the idea. As far as he himself was concerned, Dusan "Dusko" Popov was much cooler than James Bond. A better spy. A better *bon vivant*. A better playboy. Popov claimed, during a 1974 television interview on the *Mike Douglas Show* in support of his memoir, *Spy Counterspy*, that James Bond "wouldn't last 48 hours" in his world. If there was any spy to emerge from World War II who could boast of being "more James Bond than James Bond" and back it up, it was this brash, wild Serbian known as Agent Tricycle.

Popov was born in 1912, in Titel, a region of what was then the Austro-Hungarian Empire and later became Serbia. His was a wealthy, respected family and he received the very best education Europe could give him. He was an athlete, a wild child, and a polyglot, taking to new languages easily, including German. In 1936, he left home to pursue a PhD in law at the University of Freiburg in southern Germany. There, Popov met Johann "Johnny" Jebsen, a Dane whose parents—deceased by 1936—had become German citizens. Jebsen was born in Hamburg, though he never identified with his German citizenship, joking that it was nothing more than a "flag of convenience" when conducting business for the shipping empire he'd inherited.

Despite being a German-born Dane, his heart was with England, a country he'd fallen in love with during a visit in his youth. He and Popov became fast friends, cutting a wild path through university life. They were not particularly good students during this period. As Popov wrote, "We both had some intellectual pretensions, but [we were] addicted to sports cars and sporting girls and had enough money to keep them both running." The two playboys were also developing a belligerent view of the ascendant Nazi party. Popov was so vocal in his opposition that he was called in for interrogation and might have ended up in a concentration camp had not Jebsen contacted Popov's father, who pulled some strings and arranged for Dusko to go free so long as he left Germany. Under these circumstances, the two friends parted ways. Popov went to Yugoslavia, where he established his own import-export business. Jebsen announced he would be traveling to England, where he intended to continue his academic pursuits at Oxford. Jebsen, however, never made it to England, and Popov did not see his friend for the next three years. Europe was at war once again.

By 1940, Popov had abandoned his attempt at becoming an import-export magnate and opened his own law firm. One day, he received a letter from Jebsen which simply read, "Need to meet you urgently." The two rakehells reunited shortly thereafter in Belgrade, at the Hotel Royal, and immediately set about satiating their monstrous appetites for fun and vice, hitting every notable nightspot and picking up a chorus of girls to accompany them along the way. A couple of days later, after they'd recovered from their reunion, Jebsen confided a secret to his old friend: he had joined the Abwehr, the German military intelligence. Mostly, it had been to avoid being drafted into the infantry, but Popov could not believe his friend, who had been so opposed to the Nazis in college, had become part of the machine. Jebsen, who occupied the role of "talent scout" for the Abwehr, wanted to recruit Popov, to turn him into a Nazi spy in England. Dusko was shocked and confused—until Jebsen whispered one more thing to him: the best way to destroy a team is from within.

Understanding dawned quickly in Popov, and he agreed to meet with a representative from the Abwehr. The Germans, for their part, were happy to have a man like Popov, someone who spoke many languages, had a lot of money, and a lifestyle that had made him a familiar face across Europe and the United Kingdom. Abwehr head General Ernst Munzinger met with Popov and plied him with food, drink, and praise. Popov agreed to join. The next day, he

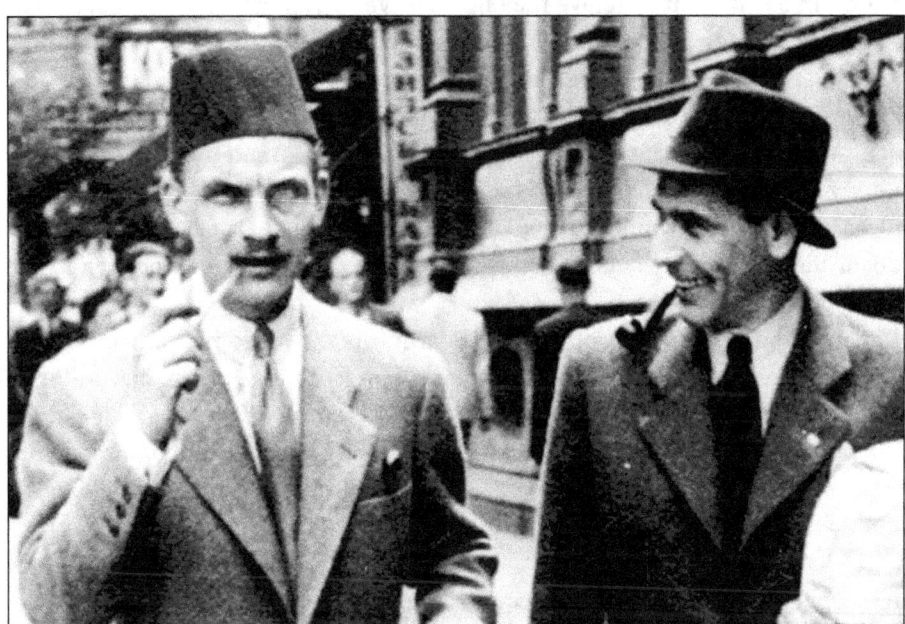

FATAL IN A FEZ—Johnny Jebsen, Popov's best friend and fellow double agent.

was officially working for the Abwehr. His first act as a German spy, completed without the knowledge of his new masters, was to visit the British embassy, explain the opportunity that had been handed to him, and offer his services to England as a double agent.

His career as Agent Tricycle was full of the incalculable risks, unbelievable nerve, incredible indulgence, and improbable luck that seems like the stuff of spy thrillers. And in at least one case, it was exactly that. Popov was in Portugal in 1941, gambling at the Casino Estoril just outside of Lisbon and connected to the Palacio Hotel, "the whispering hotel," as it was called due to its popularity with displaced European royalty and spies from both the Axis and Allied powers. Portugal's was a neutral country and one of the only open transit countries from Europe to the United Kingdom. Its capital city, Lisbon, was one of Europe's most infamous nests of spies. Irritated by a particularly pompous opponent at the baccarat table—baccarat being Popov's specialty—the daring double agent placed a bet for $38,000 (most of it British money earmarked for other purposes), forcing his opponent away from the table. In fact, Popov was known for his tendency to gamble against—and clean out—Nazi sympathizers and officers. That night at Casino Estoril, Popov was being watched from the shadows by a covert minder, a young Naval Intelligence officer by the name of Ian Fleming.

Like he did at the baccarat table, Popov played for higher and higher stakes in his espionage work. When he came into possession of a German checklist, Popov realized it was the rudimentary beginning of a plan for the Japanese to bomb the American Naval base at Pearl Harbor. He was sent to the United States by his German handlers, who knew him under the code name Ivan. While in the United States, Popov continued to live the high life, even striking up a scandalous affair with actress and *Cat People* star Simone Simon. He also tried to communicate a warning about Pearl Harbor to the United States, or so he claims, but FBI head J. Edgar Hoover despised Popov, who he regarded as a degenerate, a foreigner, and a sex maniac. Hoover not only dismissed Popov's information; he orchestrated Popov's deportation, using the Mann Act as an excuse. The Mann Act made it illegal to transport a woman across state lines for lascivious purposes. Popov had taken one of his many "Popov Girls" from New York to Florida, so Hoover had him busted and sent packing.

Years later, J. Edgar Hoover would administer the same dour judgment on another famous playboy British agent: James Bond. During the filming of *Goldfinger*, the FBI—still under the thumb of Director Hoover—grew concerned that the film might mention the FBI, and in doing so associate the Bureau with the stories of Ian Fleming, which, an internal FBI memo noted, "are generally filled with beautiful women presenting themselves to [Bond] in scanty attire" and "generally center around sex and bizarre situations, and certainly are not the type with which we would want to be associated." J. Edgar concurred—literally. At the bottom of another FBI memo that asserted "in the event the

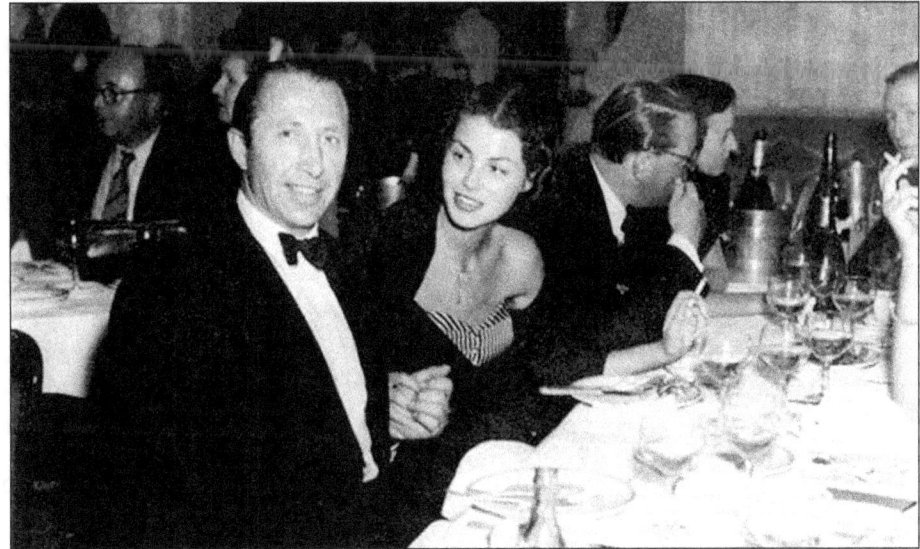

DINING WITH DUSKO—Popov and Janine enjoy a Bond-worthy dinner.

Bureau is contacted for permission to portray an FBI agent in the movie, it should be flatly denied," J. Edgar wrote, "I concur." Lucky for James Bond, the CIA were more than willing to help him out, eating Kentucky Fried Chicken and gunning down Goldfinger's terrorists in the gold vault at Fort Knox in Kentucky.

Johann Jebsen played a similarly dangerous game, one for which he eventually paid the ultimate price. On April 29, 1944, Jebsen ran afoul of German suspicions and was abducted from Lisbon and driven overnight to France. For the Allies, losing Jebsen was perhaps an even greater blow than it would have been to lose Popov. Jebsen not only knew Agent Tricycle;t he also had important information about another of England's most famous double agents, Joan Pujol Garcia, codename Agent Garbo. Garcia was the linchpin of Operation Fortitude, the Allied effort to fool the Germans into thinking the D-Day invasion would land in Calais. Despite constant interrogation and torture, Jebsen did not crack. In July 1944, he was transferred to a concentration camp. In February 1945, agents of the Gestapo arrived to take Jebsen away. He was never seen again. In one of those absurd twists so common during World War II, it was lated suspected that after his duplicitous nature was discovered, Jebsen was disappeared in order to protect the man the Abwehr considered among their most valuable spies: Dusko Popov, who the Germans feared Jebsen might expose as a German agent to the British.

After the war, Popov discovered the fate of his friend and accomplice, and he sought revenge against the man he held responsible for Jebsen's death. After tracking the man, a former commander of the Sachsenhausen concentration camp where Jebsen had been imprisoned, Popov beat the Nazi senseless but could not bring himself to kill someone he regarded as so pathetic. "How can you put a bullet in a bag of shit?" he wondered in his autobiography.

Popov's exploits at the Casino Estoril made an indelible impression on Commander Fleming. So impressed was he by Dusko's brash, cool demeanor that he decided to copy the double agent's style, seeking to bankrupt Nazis at the gambling table. Fleming, alas, proved rather less able a gambler than Popov. He lost spectacularly, and his boss, Admiral Godfrey, had to cover Fleming's debts. But the idea of beating an agent at the gambling table stuck with Fleming, and he had considerably more luck with it in fiction, when part of Dusan Popov became part of James Bond and the Casino Estoril became the Casino Royale.

Fleming didn't write *Casino Royale* intending it to be the start of a series or the origin story of one of the single most recognizable names in pop culture the world over, that's what it became. What *Casino Royale* functions best as is a window into Bond's soul, and the events that would turn him into the man popular culture recognizes. You won't be getting this level of soul-searching and self-evaluation in the other books, nor will you get the Bond present here, one so willing to throw himself into romance (though he does decide several times that he could marry this girl or that, though he never does—well, not until *On Her Majesty's Secret Service*). *Casino Royale* is as much a character study as it is a pulp action novel, and Bond is deeply flawed. It's a good story, and one that plants seeds Fleming would later grow and harvest as he realized he'd created a literary juggernaut.

In the final chapters of the book, we see a Bond who, emerging from a graphic torture session at the hands of Le Chiffre, begins to question the very nature of the spying game, of good and evil and the idea that one side is any more good or evil than the other. Bond decides to get out of the spy business, settle down with Vesper Lynd, and apply his energy to living. Of course, that doesn't happen, and as we watch Bond dragged through an emotionally-torturous final betrayal at a seaside bed-and-breakfast, we witness the emergence of a more recognizable character. The James Bond we've just read about—the emotional, easily-duped, self-pitying man—dies. With the final line in the book, we witness the birth of the man we know as James Bond. And this—not the baccarat game, not the final showdown with Le Chiffre—becomes the point of the story.

So raise a Martini to Fleming and Bond, two flawed men who created magic together. Raise a Haig & Haig and soda for Felix Leiter, a flute of champagne for Dusko Popov. But before any of those, mix yourself an Americano. It's where it all began. §

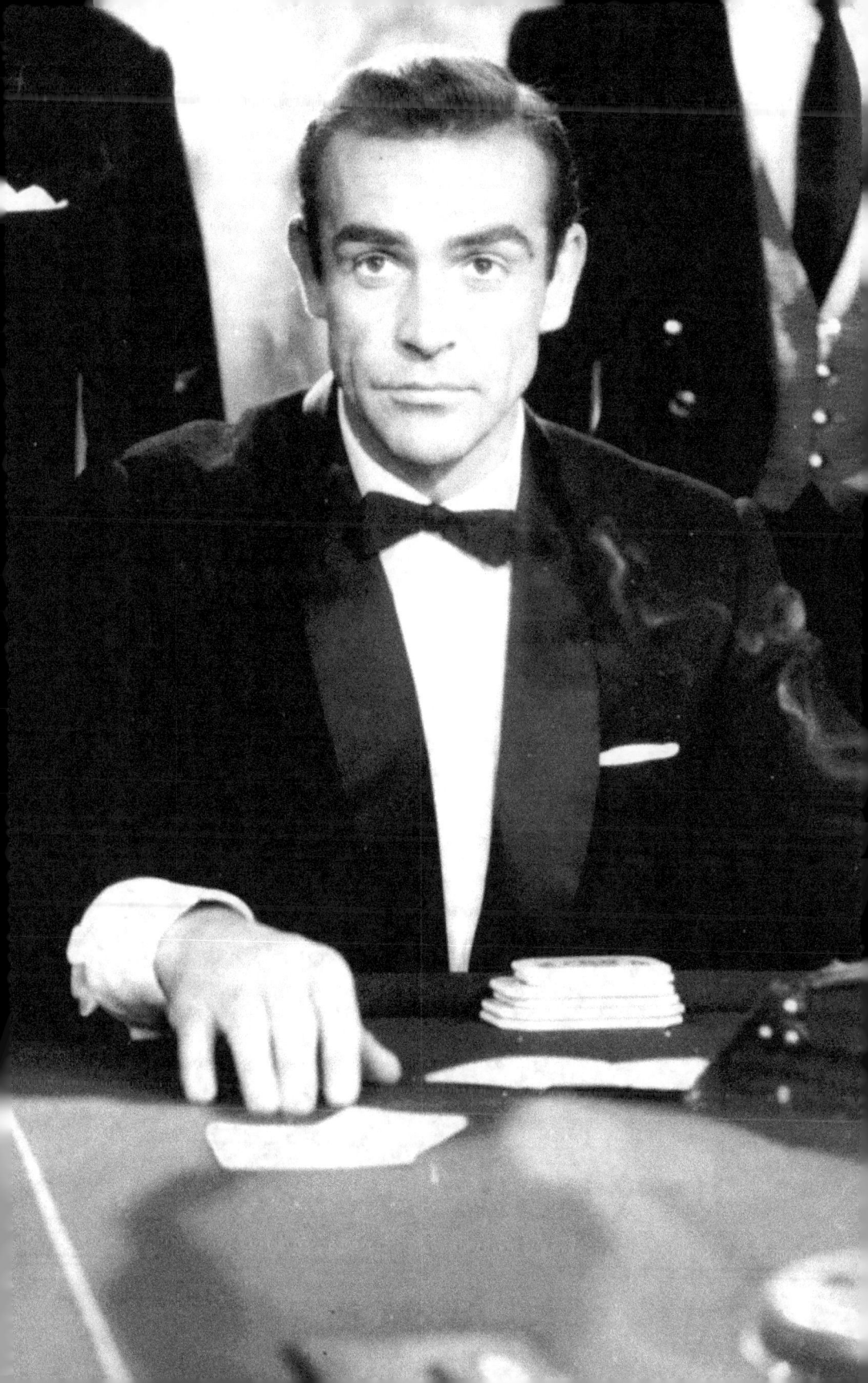

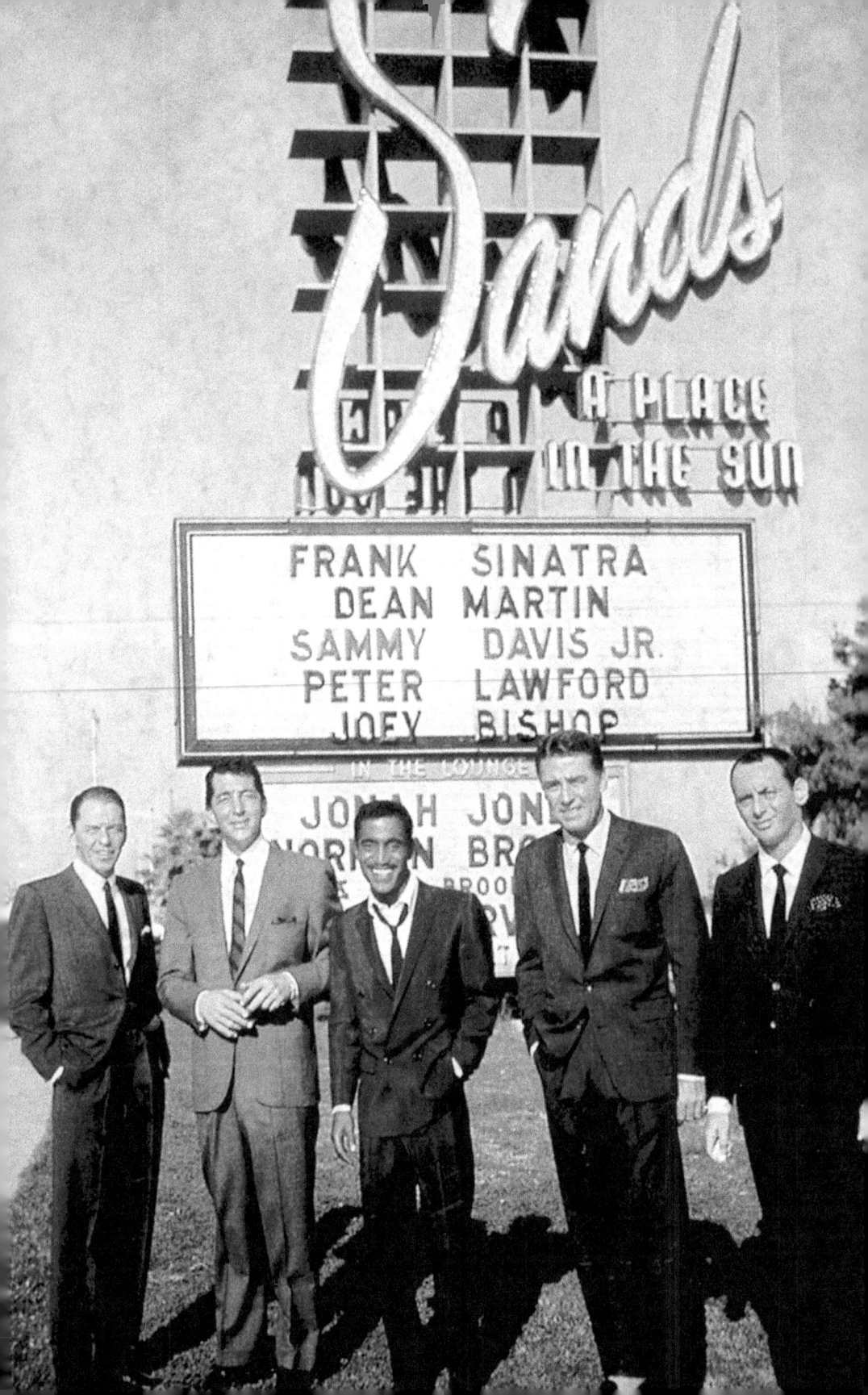

08 THEIR PLACE IN THE SUN

The Rat Pack, Ocean's 11, and the strange transformation of Matt Helm into Dean Martin

You can tell the story of Dean Martin's "Matt Helm" films—a quartet of goofy James Bond spoofs—without telling the story of the Rat Pack. But why would you? Why skip over the often hilarious, frequently sordid, at times triumphant, and occasionally tragic story of a group of show business friends who, for a brief period in the early 1960s, ruled the world—or at least Las Vegas and Palm Springs. Why gloss over a story too incredible to make a believable movie? It's a story that involves scheming CIA agents, bungled FBI wiretaps, tarnished Hollywood icons, plots to murder Fidel Castro, bellowing mobsters, presidential politics, civil rights, drug overdoses, assassination, tragedy, orgies, an ungodly amount of whiskey, and Frank Sinatra driving a golf cart through the front window of a casino.

The Rat Pack. The world remembers them by that name, but they never used it themselves. It was the media that called them the Rat Pack, a name originally applied to a group of friends gathered by Humphrey Bogart and Lauren Bacall. Among the members of this original Rat Pack were Judy Garland, Spencer Tracy, David Niven, Katharine Hepburn, and Cary Grant. Bacall, nicknamed "Den Mother," is rumored to have come up with the name when, upon seeing her husband and his cronies stumbling in after a trip to Vegas, remarked that they looked like "a god damned rat pack." Visiting dignitaries included Errol Flynn, Nat King Cole, Jerry Lewis (but not Dean Martin), and Cesar Romero. And, eventually, a kid named Frank Sinatra.

How did a skinny kid get in with this seasoned crew? Well Sinatra, who idolized Bogart and later pursued an awkward romance with the widowed Lauren Bacall, got in after Bogart challenged him one night. Bogart didn't care for dilettantes he thought were having the world handed to them without earning it. As the story goes, when the star of *Casablanca*, *The Maltese Falcon*, and *The Big Sleep* saw Sinatra at a restaurant, he walked up and said that he'd heard Sinatra was the kid with the voice that could make girls faint. But, Bogart wondered, could Sinatra make a *man*—a man like *Bogart*—faint? Sinatra shrugged. "Sorry. I'm taking the week off." Bogart was delighted. The kid had balls. Sinatra was in.

After Bogart's death in January, 1957, Sinatra kept the Rat Pack going. Like Bogart, Frank maintained it was a club only in that any group of people who enjoy hanging out together was a club. Some people left and others drifted in. Jerry Lewis was out, but his former partner, Dean Martin, was in. Joey Bishop was in, as was Sammy Davis Jr., and the "conduit to Camelot," Peter Lawford. This new squad never called themselves the Rat Pack, but Sinatra's ties to the original Rat Pack, to Bogart and Bacall, saw them, regardless of their wishes, branded with, as Sinatra referred to in the 1990s, "that stupid phrase."

They may have called themsleves the Summit. Probably not. More likely, they called themselves just a bunch of friends. But not everyone gets their wish. To everyone else they were, still are, and always will be the Rat Pack. Frank was the nucleus around which the others orbited. Most of them hungered for his company, his approval. They were willing to suffer the many abuses and indignities he inevitably visited upon them—as long as it meant they also received his occasional favor. And no one, with the possible exception of Joey Bishop, was allowed to dish out to Sinatra what he expected them to take. Frank could abuse just about anyone, and they'd smile. Except for Dean Martin. Dean made having a hard life seem easy and having an easy life seem like some sort of ridiculous lark about which he didn't really give a damn. And he didn't, which is why Frank couldn't bully him the way he could the others. The ambition that drove Frank wasn't something that motivated Dean. You got the feeling that if it all collapsed around him, Dean would smirk and just go back to his old job dealing blackjack and singing in small clubs. And he didn't crave Frank's company. Enjoyed it, sure, but he didn't *need* it the way others seemed to. Threaten Dean with exile from the inner circle, and he'd just make a quip and go his merry way, a part of it but above it, outside of himself looking in with amusement.

Which is why Dean Martin was, of all the people producers could have picked, such a bizarre choice to play Matt Helm, "America's answer to James Bond," in a series of films produced throughout the latter half of the 1960s. Matt Helm was ruthless, cynical, and haunted. Dean might have been cynical, but it was the cynicism of someone who knows it's all a big joke rather than the cynicism of someone plagued by bitterness and regret. Dean was a lover, and Matt Helm was a killer. But somehow, it happened.

You could follow the trail that led to Dean Martin assuming the role of Matt Helm from any number of starting points. But hell, this is Dean Martin. This is Frank Sinatra. This is the Rat Pack. This story starts in Las Vegas.

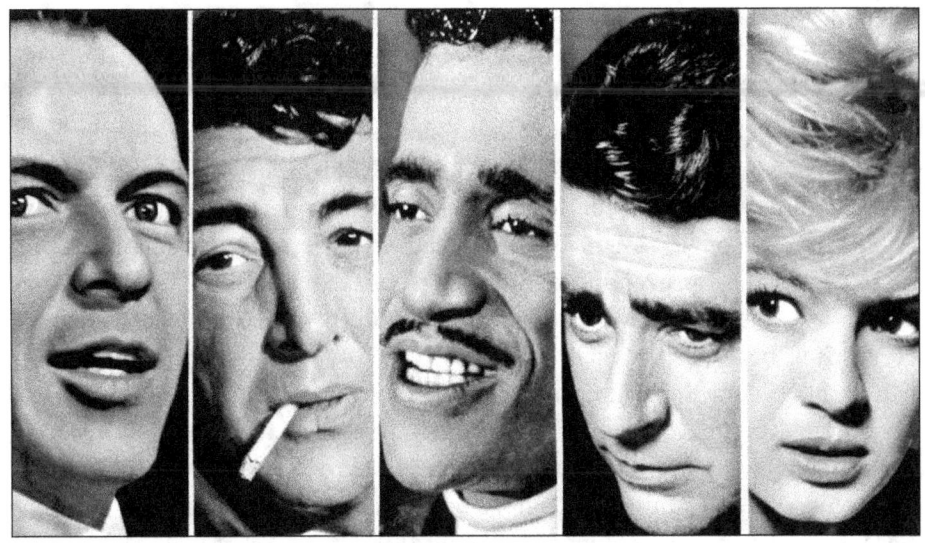

Ain't That a Kick in the Head

In the winter of 1960, or as winter as it gets in Las Vegas, they took to the stage at the Sands Hotel and Casino Copa Room for a series of freewheeling concerts. Frank Sinatra, Dean Martin, Sammy Davis Jr., Joey Bishop, and Peter Lawford. The concerts were known as the Summit at the Sands, but you wouldn't catch them using that name, any more than you'd catch them calling themselves the Rat Pack. To name it would be uncool. If you belonged, you didn't *need* to name it. And if you needed to name it...well then, you were *never* going to belong.

They were there to shoot a picture, a heist film titled *Ocean's 11*. Pete Lawford had the script, which he offered to Sinatra as thanks for letting him into the cabal. He didn't know he was only included because he provided access to his brother-in-law, John F. Kennedy. Somehow Peter, the playboy scion of a fractured family of British aristocrats in exile, fell in with the California beach bum scene. An injury to his arm when he was a kid precluded him from most sports—not that *that* kept the Kennedys from insisting he join in on games of football, mostly so they could knock the hell out of him. But he could surf. And Peter loved to surf.

It was while he was hanging out on the beach with director Gilbert Kay, who specialized in low-budget B westerns, that Peter heard the idea that would become *Ocean's 11*. Kay had heard a story about a group of soldiers who dabbled in a bit of Army-approved smuggling during World War II, and he thought a story about a reunion of such a group would make an excellent film, especially if they decided to pull a heist. Peter agreed, but what he didn't agree with was that Kay should direct. Unfortunately, Kay was only willing to offer a package deal. You didn't get the movie unless you also took Gilbert Kay. The thing is, Kay wasn't a very good director. His few credits were for television. His film work had been as an assistant editor on a lot of forgettable cowboy pictures. As much as Peter wanted the story, he wanted Kay less, and so in the end he passed on the offer. Luckily for Lawford, so did everyone else. In 1958, after failing to sell the film with himself attached as director, Kay came back to Peter and offered the story to him, this time without including himself in the bundle. Peter took the deal.

Lawford initially envisioned the film as a vehicle for William Holden, but by 1958 things had changed. He set about courting a new leading man—Frank Sinatra, with whom Peter had just reconciled after years of being snubbed by the mercurial superstar over some nonsense from 1953 involving Frank's eternal obsession, Ava Gardner. Not too long after she put the kibosh on the disastrous relationship between her and Frank, Ava was seen out on the town for drinks with this dashing young Englishman named Peter Lawford, a guy Sinatra ran into from time to time on the MGM lot. Frank reacted in typical Sinatra fashion, with lots of declarations of "you fucking asshole" and allusions to the shattering of leg bones.

Come 1958, Frank was still harboring an unhealthy obsession with Ava Gardner, but he was also looking for a way into the camp of Senator John F. Kennedy, from whom Sinatra predicted great things. Lawford was married to John's sister Pat, so Sinatra miraculously found it in his heart to forgive Peter. After all, that day Frank was more interested in hating Sammy Davis Jr. because Davis had dared suggest in an interview that, from time to time, Frank could treat those around him a tad shabbily. When Peter pitched *Ocean's 11* to Frank, he found Sinatra receptive to the idea, especially since it would give Frank and his pals, of whom Lawford was now one, a chance to screw around all day in Las Vegas. He even let Sammy in on the project, forgiving him for the uncomplimentary interview—but not without making Sammy do penance. When it came time to develop the characters for the movie (as much as any of the characters are developed) Sammy was told his guy would have to be a garbage man.

It was Sinatra's idea to film at the Sands, his go-to when he was in Vegas thanks to the generous line-of-credit extended to him by Meyer Lansky and Frank Costello, two legitimate businessmen from New York who owned shares in the casino. When the Sands opened in 1952, it aimed to be the place that put to shame all the other places in the rapidly modernizing cow town of Las Vegas, that desert mirage architected by Benjamin "Bugsy" Siegel. You know, back before someone shot him in the face a couple times with a .30 caliber M1 carbine. Sinatra himself would later buy into the casino as well.

Lansky and Costello's system was simple. Sinatra gambled at the Sands. If he won, he got his money. If he lost, the debt was overlooked. What the hell did the Sands care? No matter how much money Frank took from them or stuck them for, it was peanuts compared to the money he brought into the place just by being there. Whenever word got around—and they made sure it got around—that Sinatra was at the Sands, or even that he *might* be at the Sands, people came from across the country just to be at the same table or on the same floor, or just in the same building in hopes of catching a glimpse of the closest thing America had to royalty.

Sinatra had the run of the place, which made shooting the movie there a sensible thing. They could do whatever the hell they wanted. Disrupt it, shut it down, get drunk and go wild. Orgies, vandalism, picking on the staff. Dean Martin would commandeer the blackjack table, but at least he knew what he was doing back there. Dean cut his teeth in back-room "sneak joints" before he made it as a singer. Sure, he was giving out chips to people who hit 26, but only because it was funny. No matter what the Pack did, the Sands would chalk the mayhem up against the cash flooding in because Sinatra was there. Because Sinatra was shooting a movie there. Because on any given night, for three weeks starting on January 26, 1960, and wrapping February 16, you could see them all on stage at the Copa Room, in one combination or another. "Sinatra," they'd advertise, "And maybe Dean Martin. Or Sammy."

During the day, if any of the Pack showed up before late afternoon, it was all about the movie. Well, it was sort of about the movie, for some of them. For Joey Bishop it was about the movie. Even for Dean and Sammy, it was mostly about the movie. But for Frank? Well, Frank did what Frank wanted, and if that meant showing up for a 9:00 AM call time at 4:30 PM, well, what could you do? At least he showed up that day. On other days, most days in fact, he didn't bother.

If you were lucky, you might see one of them. Not just Sinatra, Martin, Davis, Bishop, or Lawford. OK, maybe no one was flocking to the lobby in hopes of catching a glimpse of Bishop or Lawford, but whatever. Angie Dickinson was in the cast, too, and Cesar Romero and Richard Conte and up-and-comers like young Henry Silva and never-young Norman Fell. And then there were the other celebrities, mobsters, and coattail riders who gravitated to the casino just to be associated by periphery. It was a circus, and who wouldn't want to be a spectator to such raucous pageantry?

After filming wrapped for the day, the principles retired to the steam room. Frank had it built special, just for him and his inner circle. A few hours later, they'd hit the stage. Two shows every night. The dinner show was relatively tame. Bring the kids. Bring grandma. Then there was the second show. The Late Show. The more ribald, more risqué, and certainly more inebriated show. You didn't know exactly who you'd get on any one night, but given the addiction Sinatra, Davis, and Martin had for screwing with one another, it was a decent bet that all three would be on stage at some point.

But see the show again and you might notice that it had the same "spontaneous" moments, the same surprises, the same "you never know what's going to happen next" anarchy. Whatever was happening on stage, like a well-honed magician's act, little of it was left to chance. Instead, it was left to Joey Bishop.

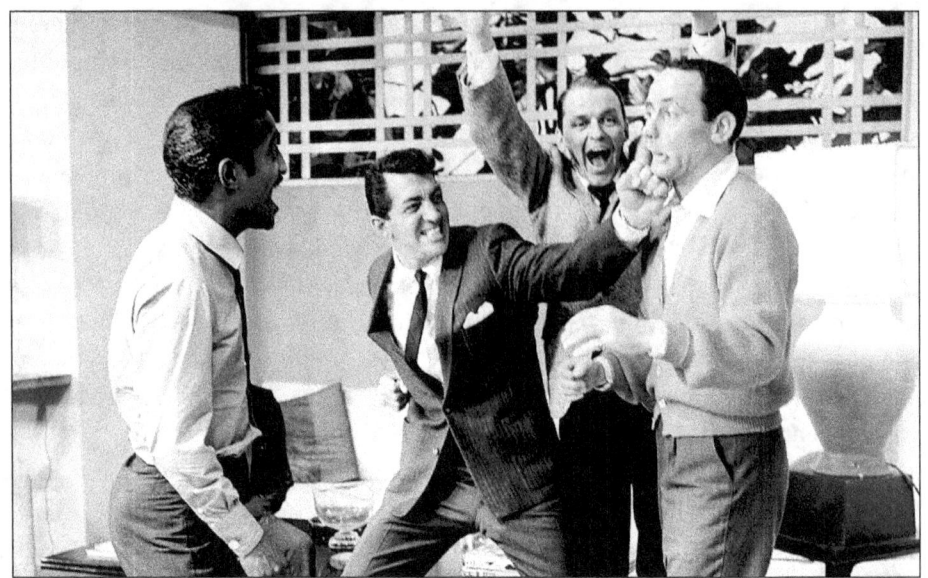

AIN'T THAT A PUNCH IN THE JAW—Dean discusses philosophy with Joey Bishop as Sammy and Frank solemnly attempt to discourage such antics. Photograph: Sid Avery/MPTV Images

The Frown Prince and the Brother-in-Lawford

Maybe Bishop was the least flamboyant member of the Summit, the one who skipped some of the parties, but he was also the one who held the shows together. Bishop was the straight man of the bunch, despite being the comedian. At times, he considered himself less of a full-fledged member of the crew and more of a mascot. "But even the mascot gets to carry the ball," he once joked. He was certainly carrying the ball, or at least coaching from the sidelines, during the Summit. As chaotic as it might have seemed, much of that apparent spontaneity was carefully crafted by Bishop, a hard-working kid born in The Bronx and raised in south Philly, the same place that fostered entertainers like Frankie Avallone, who went by Frankie Avalon, and Al Martino, the popular Italian-American crooner who appeared as a popular Italian-American crooner in Francis Ford Coppola's *The Godfather*.

1960 was a big year for Bishop, as it was for all of them. Not only was he scripting and performing in the Summit at the Sands and co-starring in *Ocean's 11*, he also served as master of ceremonies for JFK's Presidential inauguration gala. Lawford, who Sinatra sometimes called the Brother-in-Lawford, had stumped for the Pack to support JFK, and Bishop MC'ing the party that kicked off Kennedy's presidency was the first big payoff. The payoff before the kiss-off, as Sinatra would later discover. But that was years away yet, and no one was thinking about that during the Summit.

Bishop busted his chops working the nightclub circuit, sometimes alongside his brother, until one night when he was performing at a Manhattan joint called the Latin Quarter, at 1580 Broadway. That was when Sinatra first saw him. The

Latin Quarter was a prime spot, a competitor to the Copacabana, which would later become synonymous with people like Sinatra and Sammy Davis, Jr. (the two of whom were instrumental in forcing the club to integrate), as well as just about every big wig in the Mafia. A guy named Lou Walters opened the Latin Quarter in 1942, back when his daughter, Barbara, was just a kid. The location came with built-in prestige. It began life in the 1920s as the New York speakeasy Palais Royale, not that you had to speak very easy during Prohibition in New York, where the law was enforced with something less than diligence, especially if you were rich.

After that, the location was home to the Cotton Club, from 1936 through 1940, after the club was chased out of Harlem because of its policy of booking black entertainers but forbidding black customers. When Walters took over the space, he renamed it the Latin Quarter (he went on to open several more clubs of the same name in other cities). It quickly became one of the top spots in Manhattan, featuring acts as diverse as Ella Fitzgerald, Sophie Tucker, the Andrews Sisters, Mae West, and folk music trio the Carter Family. Who wouldn't want to see sexbomb Mae West followed by the earnest southern gospel of "Will the Circle Be Unbroken?" You name them, and they either played the stage or sat in the audience at the Latin Quarter, which was once sold as "more expensive than the Copa, but then the show's a bit bigger, nakeder, and longer."

Sinatra, a frequent performer at the Quarter, was in the audience the first time he saw Joey Bishop. Sinatra liked him. Enough, in fact, to hire Bishop to open for him at a nightclub called Bill Miller's Riviera in Ft. Lee, New Jersey. Before too long, Joey Bishop was known as "Sinatra's Comedian," and he opened for Frank all the time, from Vegas to the Copacabana, where he once spied Marilyn Monroe arriving and famously quipped at her from onstage, "I thought I told you to wait in the truck." Not bad for a kid who cut his teeth doing impressions of Edward G. Robinson and Jimmy Durante in clubs with names like El Dumpo, which boasted "Just 5 Minutes Ride from Loop to the House of Tough Steaks, Outrageous Prices, Insolent Waiters, Lousy Show, Raw Liquors."

But then, none of these guys, none of these Rat Packers, had it easy. Not even Peter Lawford. The Brother-in-Lawford. The guy with the keys to the Kennedys. The English aristocrat whose childhood was full of governesses and tennis lessons and ballet. Who became an actor when it was determined that he wasn't really going to be good at anything else. The blue blood who had a father named Lt. General Sir Sydney Turing Barlow Lawford. The honorable Lt. General Sir Sydney Turing Barlow Lawford might have been Peter's father, but he wasn't husband to Peter's mother, May Sommerville Bunny. When he got Bunny pregnant, Lt. General Sir Sydney was commanding officer of one Dr. Capt. Ernest Vaughn Aylen. He was also Bunny's husband, that Dr. Captain, while Lawford was married to a woman named Muriel Williams, the most sensibly-named of the bunch. A round of divorces and remarriages, but no challenges to a duel, sorted everything out to where Bunny and Lawford could wed.

Bunny was a piece of work, something bordering on genuine madness. Although she sought the benefits courtship and marriage bestowed upon her, she was repulsed by the idea of physical contact with her husband. Husbands. She had three. One she drove so mad that he committed suicide. The second, she refused to let touch her except in uncomfortable once-a-month sessions during which she would lie perfectly still and unresponsive, characterizing the act of lovemaking as grotesque and unhygienic. What caused this quirk is unknown. Still, she managed to do the deed with General Sir Sydney while the second husband was away, eventually leading to the general becoming her third husband and Peter becoming her first and only child.

Young Peter, the progeny of this illicit coupling, grew up mostly on the family estate in France. Bunny made it clear that she found children as ghastly as the act that created them. She foisted Peter off on a staff of caretakers and nannies and tutors who had little interest in educating the kid. Peter himself would often comment on how poorly-educated he was, though his British accent got him accepted as an intellectual when he immigrated to the United States. At least until he spent any amount of time with someone. Then the facade would fall apart, as it fell apart before the Kennedys. He was thrown into their ranks when he married Pat Kennedy, the sister of John and Bobby. Suddenly, Peter's con was in danger. Here he was among the power brokers. Among rich, brash, egotistical money that felt this Brit was looking down on them when he was, in fact, a moron from a family of nut jobs. So the Kennedys treated him like an outsider, and occasionally like a punching bag, at family get-togethers. He found solace in the ocean, on the waves, with the men who became his fellow surfers.

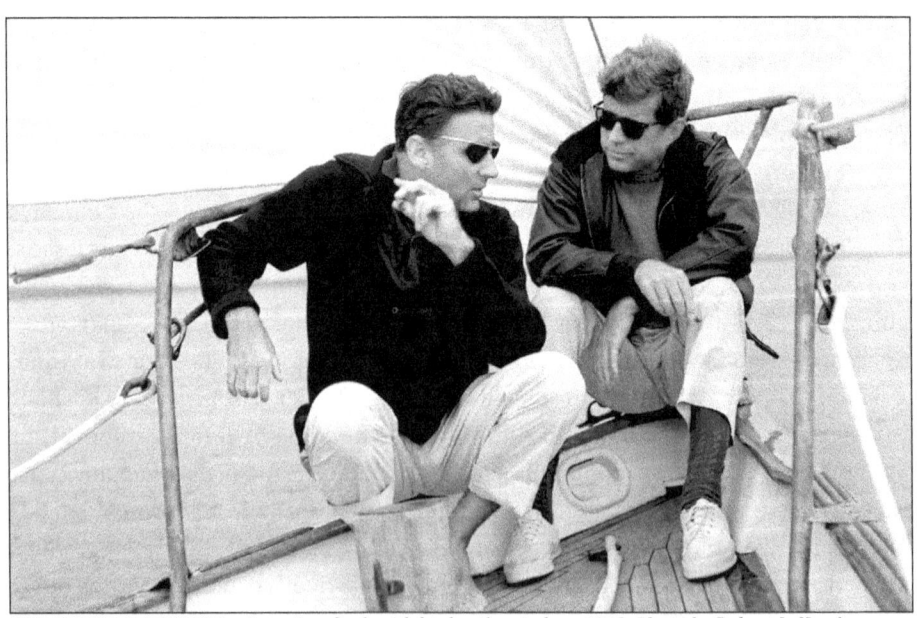

THE SUFFERING SURFER—Peter Lawford, with his brother-in-law, 1962. Photo by Robert L. Knudsen.

As much as the Kennedys might have dismissed Lawford as a buffoon, he was their connection to the entertainment world, just as he would be the entertainment world's connection to the Kennedys. Because the one thing Peter could do with at least some degree of proficiency was act. He wasn't Sir Laurence Olivier, but a British accent could take you a long way in Hollywood.

If Peter was an average actor, he was an excellent shmoozer. Before long, he had a circle of show biz luminaries as friends that his brother-in-law John coveted. JFK was a Hollywood fanboy. Younger brother Robert never saw what all the fuss was about. In time, he would come to regard his brother's infatuation with show folk as a serious detriment to both of their political careers. But for a while, Peter was able to stake his tenuous reputation within the Kennedy clan on the movie stars he could get to their parties. So Pete wasn't a kid from The Bronx or the son of a feminist in a blue collar Hoboken neighborhood. He wasn't a kid who grew up hustling on the showbiz circuit in Harlem or a former boxer turned crooner from the steel town of Steubenville, Ohio. But he did almost lose his arm in an accident when he was a teenager. Like Frank, like Sammy, he was an only child who was, deep down, desperate for someone to just hang out with. And he *did* know Jack Kennedy.

Kennedy had Camelot. Sinatra had the Sands. *Ocean's 11* was constructed on the assumption that you wanted to sit around for two hours watching Sinatra and his friends drink scotch, wear cardigans and turtlenecks, and eventually get around to pulling a heist. Sinatra and the Pack star as old Army buddies who figure they can use their skills, and the fact that they're non-existent in the world of high crime, to rob five casinos at the same time on New Year's Eve.

The main draw of the film, though, was always just going to be watching the Pack breaking each other's balls and filling time between scenes of Dean Martin on stage at the Copa Room singing "Ain't that a Kick in the Head" over and over. If you weren't down with that, you were better off seeing *Psycho* or *Spartacus*. *Breathless* if you were the arty type. *The Apartment* if you were daring. They all came out the same year as *Ocean's 11*, which ended up being one of the top ten grossing film of 1960, a year which also included *La Dolce Vita*, *The Magnificent Seven*, and a British film about a group of ex-Army buddies who decide to pull off a heist. Stop me if you've heard that one before.

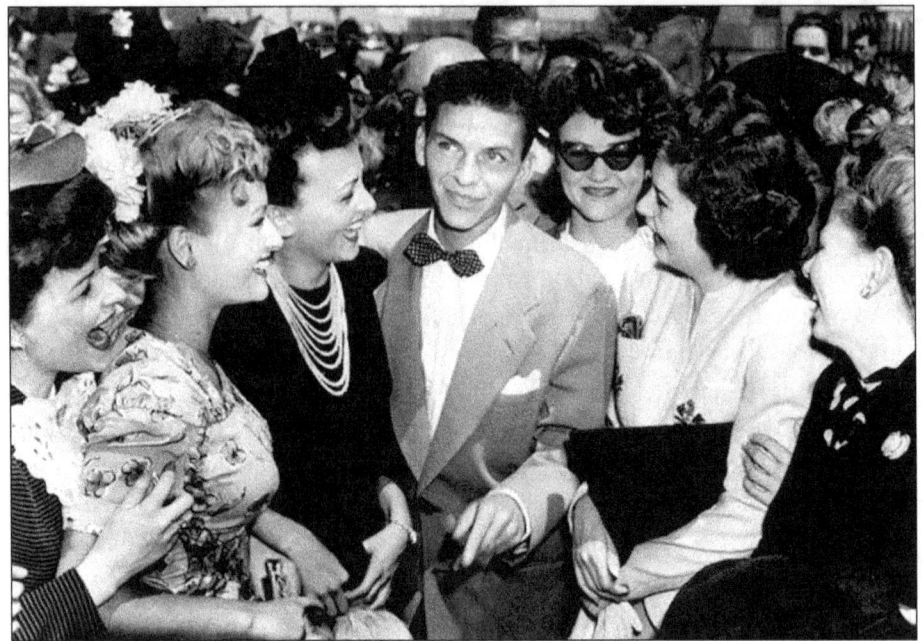

BLUE EYES AND THE BOBBYSOXERS—Young Frank Sinatra, in 1942, gets to know his fans.

Slacksey and the King of Cool

Basil Deardon's *League of Gentlemen* was one of the top grossing British films of 1960, just as *Ocean's 11* was in the United States. Plot similarities were not entirely coincidental, but neither was one film copying the other. Most of what became the finished *Ocean's 11* wasn't in the early version of the script. After Lawford handed the story to Sinatra, Frank hired a rotating cast of writers to help retool it. For starters, Frank decided from the get-go that whoever the studios had in mind for a cast didn't matter. He was casting his pals. By the time the script went through the Rat Pack meat grinder, there was hardly any script left. Director Lewis Milestone, who had directed the harrowing classic *All's Quiet on the Western Front* and the superb noir *The Strange Love of Martha Ivers* starring Barbara Stanwyck, was given the unenviable task of trying to organize the circus into some semblance of a production. Frank and the boys, however, mostly seemed interested in screwing around. Only Bishop seemed to handle the shoot with anything approaching professionalism, though Sammy did his share, mostly because Sammy was always excited to perform. During the twenty-five days they shot at the Sands and neighboring casinos, Sinatra was on hand for only nine of them, and then usually only for a couple hours. Only once during the Vegas shoot did Milestone get the entire Pack together at the same time, for the iconic final shot of the crew walking down the Vegas Strip with their names—their real names—prominently displayed on the marquee in front of the Sands.

How did any of it come to be, this bacchanal in the desert masquerading as a film shoot; a mad, impossible orgy that seemed to embody all that mid-century America wanted and much that it pretended to find morally disreputable. To answer that, you have to go back. Way back. Back before Frank was Sinatra, when he was just Slacksey O'Brien, a spoiled only child from a working-class Italian neighborhood in Hoboken, New Jersey. Just a scrawny, nattily-attired only child in a neighborhood where being an only child was unheard of. He was the son of a middling boxer turned speakeasy proprietor named Anthony Martin Sinatra (he fought under the name Marty O'Brien) and Natalie Della Garaventa, a neighborhood firebrand who found the limitations placed on women frustrating. She wanted more. More for herself. More for her gender. More for her son, who she lavished with gifts. They were a two-income home with a single child, which meant the Sinatras had more money than most of the families around them, and Natalie spent that money on little Frank.

His fancy clothing earned him the nickname Slacksey. But what Frank wanted was company. Brothers. Sisters. A *crew*. Voices and bodies that would keep the loneliness at bay. Things took the place of the brothers and sisters he did not have. Frank would eagerly trade these things out for human companionship. He took the money, the clothes, the gifts his parents gave him and bartered them to other kids in exchange for friendship, or at least for their temporary presence. It didn't matter if it was bought. Those neighborhood kids were his first Summit. His first Pack.

Frank followed that pattern for the rest of his life. A lonely boy, a lonely man, who was terrified of loneliness. Who surrounded himself with an entourage whenever he could. When Sinatra decided he wanted to be a singer, his mother was disappointed but willing to indulge her son. She publicized him, sold him, even bullied people when she had to, to get him in the front door. This wasn't an overprotective mother forcing an untalented child onto the neighborhood party, though. Even at a young age, it was obvious there was something special about Frank's voice. The Rustic Cabin in Englewood Cliffs sometimes broadcast their singing waiters, and that's how Frank's voice first got out there: as a singing waiter. Before long, he signed on with Harry James' Orchestra. They made some records, but they didn't sell. Sinatra's singing was getting more professional, but the gig with James wasn't going anywhere. In November of 1939, a frustrated Frank Sinatra parted ways with James and joined up with band leader Tommy Dorsey. That's when Frank became Sinatra.

Singing with Dorsey's orchestra, Sinatra achieved a startling amount of fame in a short time. Much of that fame came from a segment of the population that had never been thought of as having much consumer or pop culture value: teenage girls. These "bobbysoxers," the daughters of flappers who had outgrown their own youthful indiscretions, went nuts for Sinatra. An they did it with a passion hitherto unseen in pop music. Screaming, crying, fainting, even rioting.

Yet, no matter how much fame he achieved, Sinatra felt trapped. Forty-three percent of what Sinatra earned went to Dorsey. Sinatra thought Dorsey was holding him back, so as not to be overshadowed himself. Frank wanted to go head-to-head with his icon and greatest rival: Bing Crosby. But he would not get that chance laboring in Dorsey's orchestra. In 1942, the two parted ways. Not amicably. Rumor had it the split was facilitated by Sinatra's godfather, Willie Moretti, while Dorsey was choking on the business end of a gun that had been rammed into his mouth. That negotiating tactic did the trick. Dorsey let Sinatra break his contract for the penalty fee of a single dollar. Natalie Sinatra knew Moretti through her paternal cousin, John Barbato, also known as Johnny Sausage, also also known as Johnny Pistachio. He later worked for a cat named Benny Eggs, making them the most delicious crew in Mob history. Less delicious was Moretti's ultimate fate. In 1950, he was one of a few alleged Mafiosos who agreed to testify in front of the U.S. Senate Select Committee on Organized Crime. Most took the 5th, but Moretti took the stage, answering every question with a zinger or a joke (a circus that later showed up as a scene in *The Godfather, Part II*). Joking aside, Moretti had violated the Code. He was one of the first members to confirm on record the existence of the Mafia. *Omerta* had been betrayed, and Moretti had to pay. On October 4, 1951, while having lunch at Joe's Elbow Room in Cliffside Park, New Jersey, Willie Moretti was shot multiple times in the face and head.

Before that unfortunate turn, Moretti was one of the men Natalie asked to get young Frank booked at local clubs. Moretti, an early member of the Genovese crime family and cousin of Frank Costello (who ran the family while Mafia kingpin Charlie "Lucky "Luciano was doing time), also happened to be a fan of a comedy duo he'd seen performing at a nightclub called Bill Miller's Riviera. In fact, his guests for lunch on October 4, 1951, were supposed to be that very comedy duo. But one of them, a guy named Jerry Lewis, got the mumps and couldn't make the appointment—or so he claimed. When Sinatra launched his solo career at New York's Riobamba nightclub, one of the acts that followed him went on to become the other member of that comedy duo of which Willie Moretti was so fond and which had almost been sitting at the table when he was gunned down. That kid, hailing from blue collar Steubenville, Ohio, bombed at the Riobamba. But Dean Martin's road to the Rat Pack didn't end or begin that night when he performed after Sinatra.

Dean Martin was born in 1917 to an Italian-American mother and Italian father who had migrated to Steubenville, just west of Pittsburgh, where he worked as a barber. Young Dino Paul Crocetti—he wouldn't be rechristened Dean Martin until the 1940s—was raised Italian despite being in the heartland of America. He didn't even learn to speak English until elementary school. By high school, he decided he'd had enough school and dropped out. From there, his string of professions is the stuff of "life experience" dreams. He worked as a bootlegger, and later as a croupier in a speakeasy casino. He dealt blackjack, worked in a steel mill, and eventually started boxing. His boxing career earned him a broken nose and little else. Martin himself once remarked on his boxing prowess by saying that of the twelve professional bouts he fought, he only lost eleven.

After being pounded in the ring, he returned to working back room gambling parlors. It was around then that he also started moonlighting as a singer, having discovered that he was a pretty decent crooner. He took the stage name Dino Martini, a play on famed opera singer Nino Martini. He performed as part of the Ernie McKay Orchestra and later joined Sammy Watkins and His Orchestra, where his name was further simplified to the less "ethnic" Dean Martin. He took work with any band that would hire him. That's how he ended up on stage one night in 1943 at a New York nightclub called Riobamba, a "glitzy jewel box of a joint" meant to compete with the Copa and owned by Louis "Lepke" Buchalter, who was branching out a little from his previous profession—boss of the infamous Mafia hit squad Murder, Inc.

Buchalter's killers operated out of a Lower East Side bodega and had no ties to any of the Five Families. This meant that Murder, Inc. couldn't rat on anyone if one of the hits went wrong. Buchalter had been under indictment and on the run, on and off, since 1936 for everything from tax evasion to trafficking in rabbit pelts to murder. His position as a fugitive didn't stop him from opening a nightclub in 1942, probably because despite reports that he was hiding in places as far-flung as Jerusalem and Poland, he actually spent most of his time "on the run" at home in New York. That plan didn't work out too well, because eventually he was caught. In fact, for most of the Riobamba's brief lifespan (it closed in 1944), it's infamous owner was awaiting execution on Death Row. He was the only major Mafia figure of the era to get the death penalty, a sentence that was carried out on March 4, 1944. Later that spring, the nightclub was shuttered for nonpayment of taxes.

Dean Martin took the Riobamba's stage in 1943. It was terrible. He was the closer for the club's star attraction, that kid from Hoboken who just a few weeks earlier had nervously launched a solo career. Dorsey had reportedly bid Sinatra farewell by saying, "I hope you fall on your ass." Sinatra wanted to start his solo career at the Copa, but they weren't interested in booking him despite his popularity. The Copa was for adults with style. Sinatra was a teenybopper pop star who only appealed to squealing bobbysoxers. He settled on the Riobamba, where for his debut performance he was billed as an "extra added attraction" on a show already crowded with performers. By the end of the week, those performers were forgotten, and Sinatra was doing "standing room only" shows. Even in the wee small hours of the morning, people packed the club to hear him sing.

It must have seemed like one hell of a break for the crooner from Ohio to take the stage following the man who quickly became the biggest ticket in New York. But it didn't work out. Sinatra was a powerhouse, and no one was that interested in the guy who came on after him. It was back to the small club circuit for Martin, where he enjoyed success but nothing on the scale of the guy he met for the first time at the Riobamba in 1943. However, it was at one of those smaller clubs, the Glass Hat Club in New York, that Martin found himself on a bill with young comedian Jerry Lewis. The two became friends and started appearing in one another's acts. On July 24, 1946, the partnership became official when they debuted as Martin and Lewis on stage at Atlantic City's 500 Club. They bombed and were told they had to come up with a new act for their later show or they could kiss their engagement at the club goodbye. So they figured, what the hell. "What the hell" was always Dino's way, after all. Lewis dressed up as a busboy and continuously interrupted Martin's otherwise straight singing show as the duo ad-libbed their way through anarchy that including singing, vaudeville shtick, goofball nonsense, pratfalls, and Martin running around and beating Lewis with breadsticks. This time, it worked. The act started drawing bigger crowds, culminating in a show at the Copa during which

Lewis played the part of a heckler while Martin gamely tried to sing. As always, the show ended with a slapstick chase around the club as an "enraged" Martin attempted to assault the braying man-child that had heckled him all night. From there it was on to Ed Sullivan, then a radio show, and in 1949 their first appearance as a team in the movies. They made a series of films together for Paramount producer Hal B. Wallis, but by the middle of the 1950s, it was starting to fray at the edges. Lewis was a difficult person to get along with, and critics were getting tired of the formulaic nature of the films. Martin was also itching to prove himself something more than the straight man in a slapstick duo. On July 24, 1956—ten years to the day they debuted—Martin and Lewis parted ways.

Neither man was sure what the future held. Did anyone want to see Jerry Lewis without Martin balancing out his manic flailing? Did anyone want to watch smooth, steady Dean Martin without Lewis flopping about? Martin's first solo film, 1957's *Ten Thousand Bedrooms*, performed poorly, but he had his singing to fall back on. He took a stab at serious acting alongside Marlon Brando and Montgomery Clift in the war drama *The Young Lions*, replacing Tony Randall. The film was a success. Martin was lauded for his role as a Broadway star who spends most of the war on a safe assignment, filled with guilt as he watches the men with whom he went through basic training get sent to the front lines. That same year, Dean Martin was reunited with Frank Sinatra when they starred together in *Some Came Running*, directed by Vincent Minnelli and co-starring Shirley McClaine, a member of the extended Summit.

It wasn't just the ground beneath Dean Martin's feet that had grown shaky. Sinatra, perhaps the most popular entertainer in the world during the 1940s, saw it all come tumbling down at the start of the 1950s. His concerts were no longer sell-

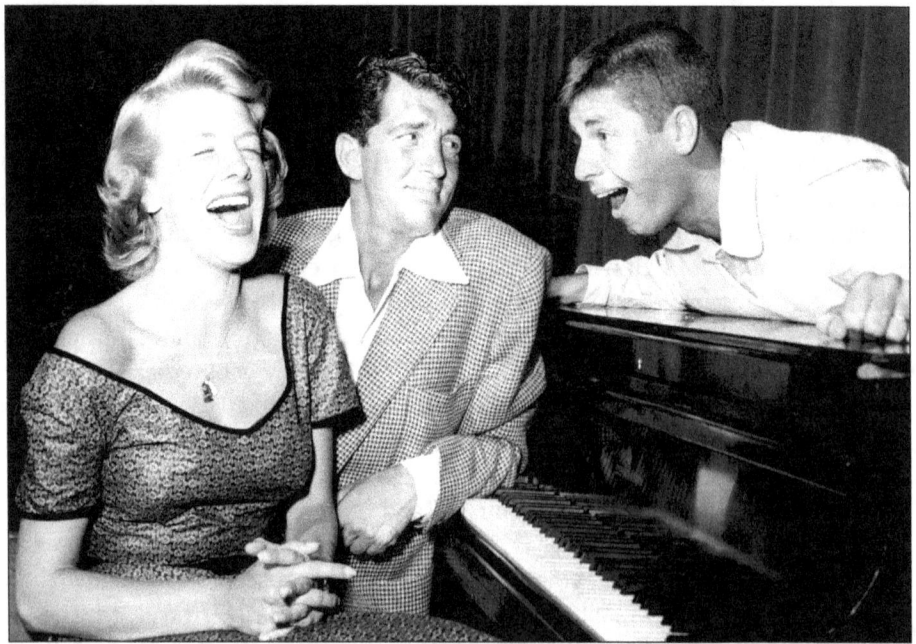

HEY LADY—*Dean Martin and Jerry Lewis assist Rosemary Clooney on NBC's Colgate Comedy Hour, 1952.*

outs. His records weren't what they used to be. His film career, a natural outgrowth of his success on stage, wasn't going much of anywhere. And then he started dating actress Ava Gardner. Up until then, his image had been carefully crafted along lines that would become the template for all the teen idols that would follow his example.

First and foremost, he was a good guy. A guy who married his childhood sweetheart, Nancy, and had two kids, a son and a daughter, each named after one of the parents. Behind the scenes, he'd been a tomcat, but he'd always had a publicist chasing around behind him to cover up any scandals and affairs and to smooth things over with the press. Frank himself didn't give a damn. He was from a take-no-shit neighborhood, and what's more, he was ingrained with the petulance of a spoiled only child. He got what he wanted, and like so many teen idols after him, he could be a monster without ever even realizing this wasn't how people were supposed to behave.

When he became infatuated with Gardner, that carefully-constructed facade collapsed. Gardner openly courted controversy. She was a hellraiser, a drinker, a philanderer. It was more than Nancy could bear. She and Frank divorced, and Frank became obsessed with Ava, so much so that the press, realizing it was finally open season on Frank Sinatra, tore him apart. He was emasculated by his wild *femme fatale*, they said. Her plaything. A teenybopper who wandered into the adult world and was getting batted around by a woman much crazier and more sophisticated than he. A woman who had already destroyed, they said, one of the richest men in the world—a man who, incidentally, classified Sinatra as a lifelong enemy.

Sinatra's mental stability also became fodder for the press now that the gloves were off, the masks discarded, and no one was protecting Frank. He didn't qualify for service during WWII. The official reason was that he was 4F (perforated eardrum), but now people were saying it was because he failed the psychological review. During his stormy relationship with Gardner, he twice attempted suicide, once with pills, a second time with a razor. In 1952, his label dropped him. You couldn't give away tickets to a Sinatra concert. By the time it all went to hell with Ava, Frank was on the road to has-been.

And he might have stayed on that course. He might have gone back to being nobody, just like Dean might have gone back to dealing blackjack after he and Jerry Lewis split. But that didn't happen. Instead, Sinatra pushed hard for a role in *From Here to Eternity*, a role he eventually won thanks to lobbying by a guy named Johnny Roselli, a legitimate businessman with a lot of sway at Columbia Studios. Instead of fading away, Sinatra won an Academy Award and revived his moribund recording career, now working alongside composer Nelson Riddle. Those who counted Sinatra out had to eat their shoe. After *From Here to Eternity*, he went on to star in a string of hit films and sell more records. The one-time teen idol was a man now, and his art was reflecting a new maturity, even if he was still a lonely, spoiled little kid inside.

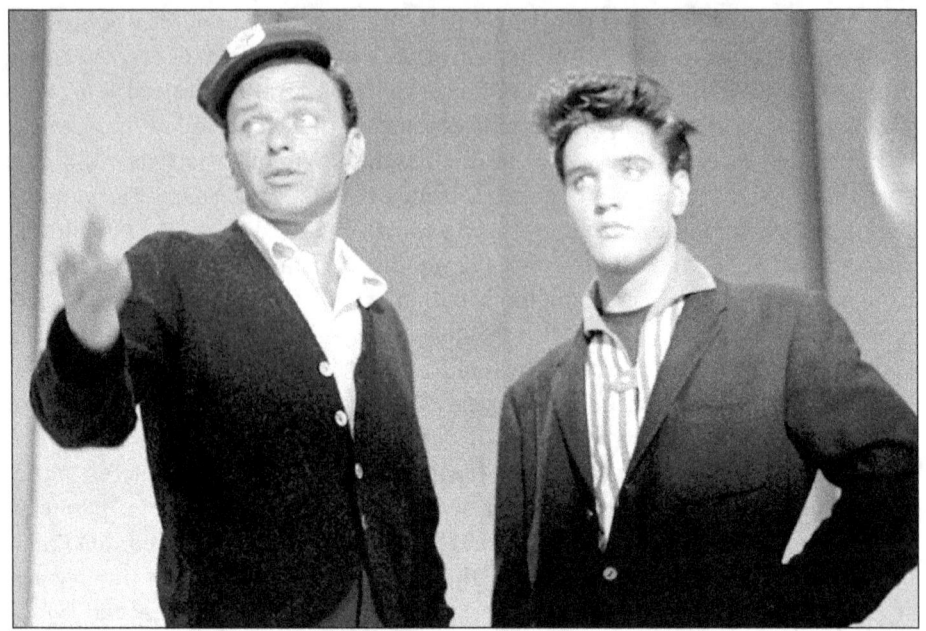

WISE MEN SAY—Sinatra gets over his hatred of rock 'n' roll and welcomes Elvis back from the Army.

The Men Who Would Be King

Two years after *Some Came Running*, Sinatra and Martin were on stage together, along with the rest of the Pack, for the Summit at the Sands, and on screen together in *Ocean's 11*. The movie was a nightmare for director Lew Milestone. After production in Vegas wrapped, the shoot moved to a sound stage in California. Milestone hoped things would settle down and he'd be able to squeeze a movie out of the madness. To no one's surprise except Milestone's, the Pack just brought the party with them. Fireworks and squirt guns ruled the set. Most of the principles would disappear, sometimes for days. No one bothered to learn their lines. Frank wouldn't do more than one take, and if he was ready to leave, he'd just rip out pages of the script and proclaim they were no longer happening. Somehow though, he finished the picture and brought it in under budget. But it very nearly destroyed him. He only directed one more movie before his retirement: 1962's *The Mutiny on the Bounty*, with a leading man that proved more difficult than the entire Rat Pack combined: Marlon Brando.

As awful an experience as *Ocean's 11* had been for Milestone, it was a dream for the Sands. February was a dead time for Vegas, and suddenly here they were with every room in town filled with celebrities and gawkers. Even the Kennedys showed up. Frank lauded the senator, now running for president, from the stage. Then Dean came on, looked at the future leader of the free world, and slurred, "What was your name again?" Dean's lackadaisical attitude might have rubbed Sinatra the wrong way, but Dean wasn't Sammy or Peter. Sure, he loved the Rat Pack life, but he'd proven he didn't need Frank Sinatra to achieve it. He didn't care about Jack Kennedy. He didn't care about politics. He barely cared about his own career. Dean's entire life had been handled with something between hard work and not giving a shit. Peter and Sammy craved Frank's approval. Like him, they were only children and wanted to belong. But Dean came from a big family. He lacked that empty space inside that bound Sinatra, Davis, and Lawford into a dysfunctional, abusive family.

1960 was a big year for Frank, even if Dean couldn't be bothered to show interest. Sinatra wrapped himself in politics. In Jack Kennedy. He started his own record company. And weirdly, it was the year Sinatra became the man to welcome Elvis Presley home after the King of Rock 'n' Roll's stint in the Army. That one was surreal. Sinatra, the teen idol of the '30s and '40s, was outspoken in his disdain for the next generation of teen idols. Ensconced in the decadence of the Summit, Sinatra described rock 'n' roll as a "brutal, ugly, degenerate, vicious form of expression." But he was only just getting started. "It is sung, played and written for the most part by cretinous goons and by means of its almost imbecilic reiterations and sly, lewd—in plain fact dirty—lyrics, and as I said before, it manages to be the martial music of every sideburned delinquent on the face of the earth." *This* was the guy who was going to welcome Elvis back from the Army on national television?

Presley, arguably the man who dethroned Sinatra as America's most beloved (and reviled) performer, responded with the self-deprecating sense of humor that was his trademark, explaining about rock 'n' roll, "I like it, and I'm sure many other persons feel the same way. I also admit it's the only thing I can do." Elvis also proved he might know more about Sinatra's career than Sinatra knew about his when he continued, "He has a right to his opinion, but I can't see him knocking my music for no good reason. I admire him as a performer and an actor, but I think he's badly mistaken about this. If I remember correctly he was also part of a trend. I don't see how he can call the youth of today immoral and delinquent."

Sinatra had good reason to be wary of rock 'n' roll, though given the profound decadence of the Rat pack at the height of their power (not to mention the associated violence and corruption), one has to take his moral stance against it with a pretty massive grain of salt. Sinatra was lifted into super-stardom on the shoulders of adoring teenage girls. But teenagers don't stay teenagers forever, and the next wave of teenagers generally rebel against what the last, now adults and parents, cherished. The daughters of the girls who loved Sinatra weren't going to scream for their mom's pop idol. Then Elvis showed up. *Their* Frank Sinatra. The girls adored him. The boys wanted to emulate him. Frank wasn't cool anymore, not with the kids who, in post-war America, were the arbiters of cool. What could he do against Elvis Presley? Or this guy named James Brown, who was also starting to make a name for himself?

Frank also wasn't good on television. That didn't stop him from trying. Dean could ad lib, riff, and banter like nobody's business. Sammy could get by. Joey was a stage comedian, so that sort of thing was in his blood. But Frank always struggled. His greatest talent was delivering the songs, leading people into a state of awe or, in his darker moments, tear-streaked melancholy. When he needed to ad lib or crack wise, he usually floundered. Variety shows of the time were built on that sort of off-the-cuff wisecracking, and Frank couldn't do it. His television show, as a result, was a bomb despite the fact that the rest of the Rat Pack showed up to lend a hand. Not since his torrid go-round with Ava Gardner had Sinatra seemed so weak. There wasn't much that was going to save the show, but at least it could go out on a high note. That high note was Elvis.

No matter what Frank thought of him, he knew the audacious young rocker would bring massive numbers. Elvis' manager, cartoon villain Colonel Tom Parker, also happened to be worried that Elvis' two years in the Army might have resulted in America moving on without the King. Parker was plotting ways to make the rebel more palatable to older, mainstream audiences. So Sinatra put aside his disdain (and jealousy) and approached Colonel Tom about hosting Elvis' first televised appearance since his discharge. Parker was willing to deal, and what a deal he made. It was so transparently in Presley's favor (and thus, in Colonel Parker's) that it even became a joke on the show itself. Frank was losing money on the deal, but for Frank it was about getting the numbers. Elvis, meanwhile, made a bundle for a few minutes work. He showed up in his Army uniform, bantered briefly with

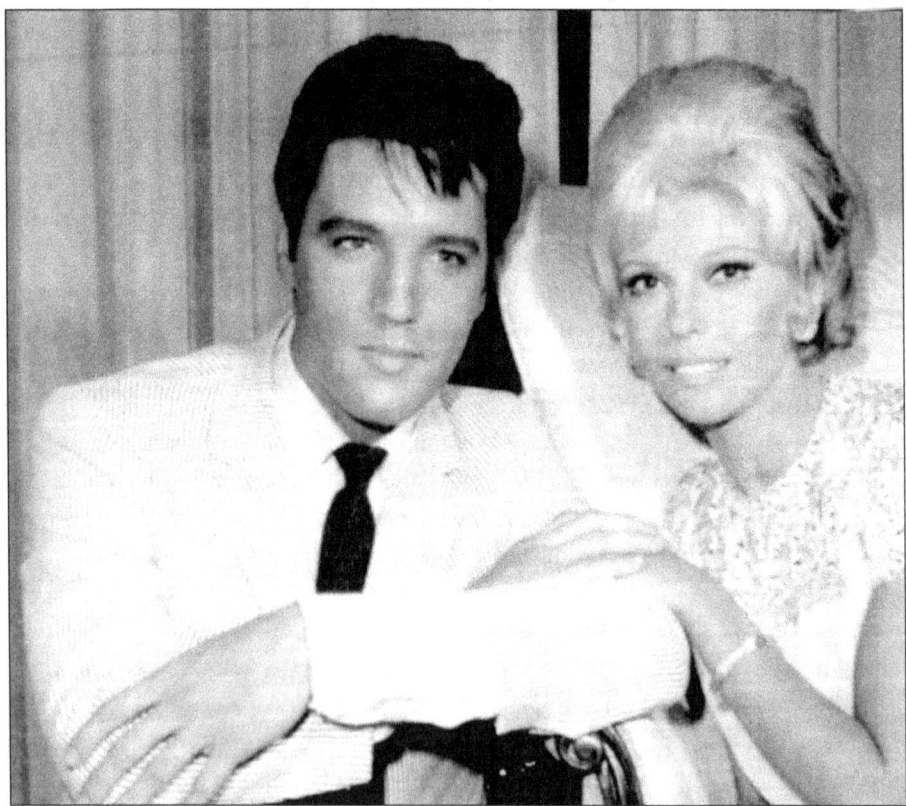

HIS LATEST FLAME—Elvis with Nancy Sinatra, who would be his co-star in the film Speedway.

Frank and Frank's 20-year-old daughter Nancy (who was probably a lot more excited than her father), then disappeared for most of the program, leaving the bulk of the proceedings to Sinatra, Joey Bishop, and Sammy. Frank was more than willing to take his lumps, most of them delivered by Joey Bishop and revolving around the fact that Frank was old and a bit of a has-been who was being forced to hold court for the usurper to the throne. There's even a poignant moment when Frank performs with Nancy, who happened at the time to be engaged to Tommy Sands (a teen idol who heavily aped Elvis' style, right down to enlisting in the Army). Nancy, it's obvious, is very happy to be kidding around with Elvis (they'd do it again years later, when she co-starred with him in *Speedway*), the guy her dad just doesn't get. Frank sings one of his hits, switching it up slightly to turn it into "You Make Me Feel So Old."

Eventually, Elvis saunters back out, clad in a slim-cut evening tux, to sing a few songs and do a duet with Sinatra. As uncomfortable as it might have been, and as bad as most of the show was (the banter between Bishop and Sinatra is awful), there is indeed something magical in the meeting of these two men. Their physical presence couldn't be more unalike, with Elvis towering over Frank and barely containing his trademark bump and grind. But those two voices together? That worked. That worked really well.

Whatever friction might have existed between the generations, Elvis was no enemy to the Rat Pack, at least in his own mind. He idolized Dean Martin and adored Sammy Davis., Jr. He considered Frank the ideal model for how a teen heartthrob could transition into an adult performer and studied Frank's every career move—and made many of Frank's career mistakes. The trajectory of Sinatra and Presley would be eerily similar. Like Sinatra, Elvis soon found himself considerably less cool when the new kings, in this case the Beatles, showed up on the scene and made him seem like yesterday's news. Like Frank, Elvis surrounded himself with a pack. His Rat Pack, his Summit, was the Memphis Mafia, a gang of fellow performers, friends, sycophants, sexual conquests, and gangsters. And like Frank, Elvis' name would become synonymous with Las Vegas.

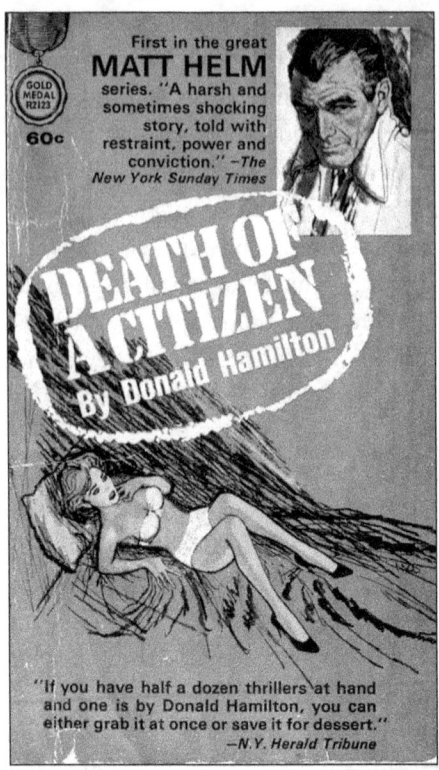

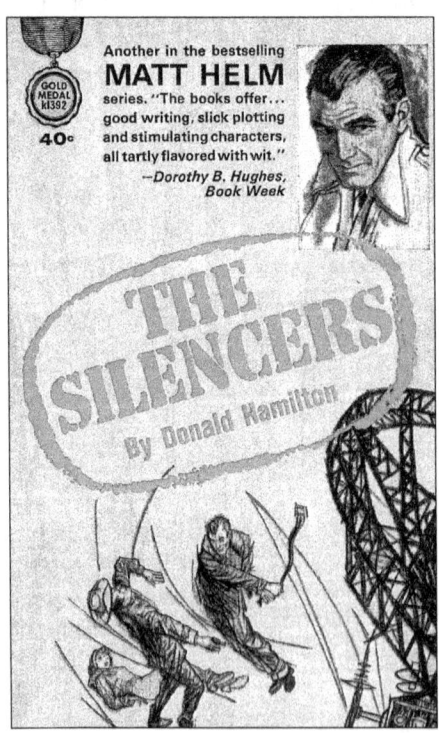

An American James Bond

The same year as the Summit at the Sands, author Donald Hamilton published *Death of a Citizen*, the first of what would become many Matt Helm espionage adventures. It's not fair to compare every spy character to James Bond, but it also still probably has to be done given the long shadow Bond casts. Despite being dumped into the big pile of James Bond-inspired espionage novels that flooded the '60s and '70s, Helm and Bond are as different—and as similar—as Hamilton and Fleming. Like Ian Fleming did with Bond, Donald Hamilton put a lot of himself into the character of Matt Helm. Hamilton was born in Sweden and immigrated to the United States on the eve of the Great Depression. As a kid he was an avid teller of ghost stories. As a young man he assumed he would follow in his father's footsteps and become a doctor. He earned a degree in chemistry, and then served as a chemist for the Navy during World War II. It was during the war that Hamilton began writing regularly. After the war, it became something less than a profession but more than a hobby. He and his family settled in Santa Fe, New Mexico. He became an avid outdoorsman and photographer. He wrote everything from magazine features to books (mostly westerns) with many of those books being optioned and made into films or television series.

Hamilton made the jump from westerns to spy novels after the success of Ian Fleming inspired him. His most enduring character, Matt Helm, incorporates most of the same traits one would find in Hamilton himself.

Helm is a World War II veteran, an outdoorsman, a photographer, and in his spare time a writer of westerns. Bond was also an avid outdoorsman in his youth, an accomplished skier and mountaineer, and a WWII veteran. Both men are sinister, ruthless when they need to be, and haunted by loss. However, the worlds they inhabit are very different. Fleming's Bond is not quite the playboy of the movies, but he still lives a jet-set lifestyle. The best champagne, the finest hotels, the most elegant women, and of course always showering with "Pinaud Elixir, that prince among shampoos." Helm probably has to shampoo with a bottle of Suave from the drug store. When he stays in a hotel, it's usually some anonymous roadside motel. Or even more likely, Helm is in a sleeping bag in the back of what passes for an Aston Martin in the world of Matt Helm: a junky old pick-up truck.

Death of a Citizen sets the mood carried throughout the series. Bond may have been the inspiration, but the real influences of *Death of a Citizen* and Matt Helm were the same ones Fleming had: John Buchan's Richard Hannay adventures and Raymond Chandler's Philip Marlowe. Helm, a retired secret agent who specialized in assassinating Nazis, has built a new life for himself in Santa Fe, complete with a wife and kids, normal friends, and a new career. That lasts for all of a few pages, until a former partner, Tina, corners Matt at a party and, through manipulation and blackmail, presses the retired killer back into the cloak and dagger game. Matt and Tina must protect a scientist targeted for assassination. Helm discovers, to his chagrin, that the old ways he thought behind him were never as far behind as he had hoped. *Death of a Citizen* is a lean, ruthless thriller. Coming before that army of smirking, wisecracking, playboy spies that typified Bond copycats means Matt Helm does not contain many of the things often thought of as defining the genre. No jokes, no gadgets, not a lot of glamor, not much in the way of sex (at least not at first). The first-person voice allows the reader greater access to Helm's inner demons and moral conundrums. The citizen facing death is ostensibly the scientist, but in reality it's Helm's identity as a regular guy. His home, his wife and children, this entire new life he'd so painstakingly constructed for himself proves hopelessly fragile, leaving him bitter, resentful, and faced with the reality that his past will never allow him to have a future.

The final chapter of *Death of a Citizen* finds Helm forced to lay bare to his wife that he has been lying to her their entire relationship. Furthermore, to save her, he must reveal his gruesome skills and willingness to commit unspeakable acts. He saves her life and kills their relationship. He turns into a monster in her mind, someone at which she will never be able to look, let alone share a life. It's a heart-wrenching scene, not least of all because we are inside Matt's head and privy to the thought process that is gutting him from the inside.

Death of a Citizen was a big success, both with critics and readers. After that, Donald Hamilton was pretty much full-time on Matt Helm books. Each one proved successful, and by 1966, he'd written eight. That year he got a call from a film producer named Irving Allen. Allen was a former partner of Cubby Broccoli, one of the producers of the James Bond movies, and he was looking to salvage a somewhat flailing career by jumping on the Bond bandwagon. Having run across one of Hamilton's Matt Helm books at an airport, Allen was keen on turning the grim-faced killer into America's answer to the James Bond movies. Hamilton was happy to see the character brought to the big screen and happier still to cash the check that came with it.

Allen has been charitably referred to as gruff; rough around the edges. Less charitably, a bully. Even less charitably, an asshole. Working his way from junior editor up through the ranks, he carved out a successful career as producer and director on a number of shorts, including the Academy Award-winning *Climbing the Matterhorn*. Wanting more from his career, he partnered with struggling British producer Albert "Cubby" Broccoli to form Warwick Films. Based out of England so they could take advantage of lucrative tax breaks, Warwick made "boy's own adventure" style films that allowed Allen to indulge his taste for costumed epics and gave Broccoli a chance to get his name out there. Allen and Cubby sometimes collaborated on projects, but more times than not, they trusted each other to work independently.

One day, Broccoli set up an interview with Ian Fleming, who was interested in seeing James Bond brought to life on screen but had so far been unsuccessful in convincing anyone to make it happen. So far, the only adaptation of 007 was for the American television series *Climax!* in which the character was rechristened Jimmy Bond and had his nationality switched to American. Fleming collaborated on a script for a movie that, at the time, also went nowhere, though he later adapted it into the book *Thunderball*. That became a decades-long legal nightmare for Fleming when his collaborators on the script, Kevin McClory and Jack Whittingham, took umbrage to Fleming using it for the book without their permission and without giving them any credit.

Cubby Broccoli was enthusiastic about getting a Bond film made. Tragically, Broccoli's wife fell ill, and in an effort to secure better care for her, he traveled to New York and stayed by her side through treatment and her eventual final days. In Cubby's absence, Irving Allen handled the meeting with Ian Fleming. There was just one problem: Allen hated the James Bond books. In his typically "candid" way, he told Fleming the books were rubbish, not even fit to be adapted for television. Unsurprisingly, no deal was struck. Broccoli was upset with Allen's rude dismissal of Fleming. Broccoli sought to patch things up while Allen pursued a personal passion project: a lavish period biopic titled *The Trials of Oscar Wilde*. Cubby Broccoli eventually entered into a separate partnership with producer Harry Saltzman, founding Eon Studios for the express purpose of making a James Bond movie without Allen's involvement. Allen, meanwhile, faced disappointment when his Oscar Wilde movie tanked at the box office. By the time *Dr. No* was released in 1962, Warwick Films was dead and Bondmania had been born.

Allen produced a few more historical epics, including 1964's Viking epic *The Long Ships* starring Richard Widmark, Sidney Poitier, and Russ Tamblyn. The massive failure a year later of another historical epic, *Genghis Khan*, put Allen in a precarious financial position. By that time, his former partner had become quite possibly the most successful film producer in the world, thanks entirely to the James Bond movies Allen had so obnoxiously chased out his own front door. Broccoli had produced four James Bond films by the time *Genghis Khan* was released: *Dr. No*,

From Russia with Love, *Goldfinger*, and the legally-problematic *Thunderball*. Most film studios were doing their best to copy Bond's formula. Allen, defeated but not bowed, shrugged and decided to follow the leader like everyone else. The question was, what would he use as his source material?

Allen didn't want to start from scratch. While it was unlikely he would develop a juggernaut on the level of James Bond, he still wanted a success. The easiest way to do that was to hit the ground with material that already had an audience. Allen was perusing the paperbacks at an airport and picked up one of Donald Hamilton's Matt Helm novels—*Death of a Citizen* or *The Silencers*, "I don't remember which" he later said, though it's possible it was both given the structure of the movie he produced. Whatever the case, he liked what he read and thought Helm would be a good counter to Bond. Hamilton, having already sold many stories to be adapted into movies, was happy to sign a deal with Allen, giving the producer rights to all of the existing Matt Helm novels. He formed a new company and convinced Columbia Pictures—like Allen, they had turned their nose up at Ian Fleming and James Bond and were now looking to play catch-up—to make the movies, though Allen himself had to front a sizable portion of the money.

The plan was to stick close to the tone of Hamilton's books. Allen hired screenwriter Oscar Saul (*A Streetcar Named Desire*) to pen the script and noir veteran Phil Karlson (*Kansas City Confidential*, *Phenix City Story*) to direct. Like Allen and Columbia Pictures, Karlson had his own brush with Bond when he was approached by Broccoli and Saltzman to direct *Dr. No*. That fell through when Eon balked at the price tag. They went with Terence Young instead, perhaps for the best. Young, himself known as something of a daredevil playboy, ended up being a perfect fit for *Dr. No*. Allen's line-up for the Helm film, if not all-star, was an impressive assembly of talent. Karlson and Saul were respected and had shown the ability to work well in the hardboiled world Matt Helm inhabited. Irving Allen may have had a short-fuse and a number of flops, but he also had a number of successes—and his flops had at least been ambitious. All that was left was to find the right actor to play the part.

Allen's first choice was Tony Curtis, but Curtis was involved with his own project and turned the part down. Hugh O'Brian was next, but that didn't pan out either. Donald Hamilton wanted Richard Boone, star of the hit television show *Have Gun, Will Travel*, but again, no dice (it's unclear whether he was ever even considered by Allen). As the first day of filming was approaching, Allen was throwing the role at the feet of a number of actors, but no one wanted to be the guy competing with Sean Connery. Sensing that they would never find the right actor, Allen called in new writers to retool the script. If he couldn't compete with Bond, Allen reasoned, he'd spoof Bond. And so the Matt Helm project went from a hard-hitting, serious noir spin on the spy movie to a comedy.

Once they changed the tone of the film, they changed the tone of the star. After seeing him out on the town one night, charming everyone, Irving Allen knew who he wanted for this new version of Matt Helm: Dean Martin.

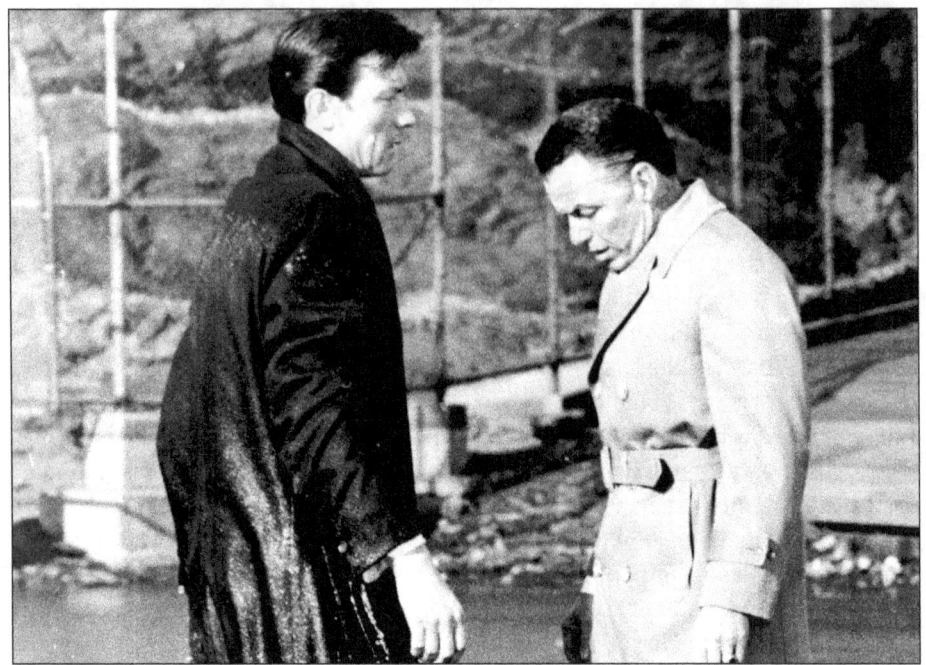

AUTUMN IN NEW YORK— Laurence Harvey and Sinatra meet in The Manchurian Candidate.

El Dorado 5-9970

The 1960s were the best of times and worst of time for the Rat Pack. They were among the most popular performers in the country, but they were being muscled out of the limelight, first by Elvis Presley and then by the Beatles. Sinatra, the skinny heartthrob who "only appealed to bobbysoxers, not adults" was the music your parents listened to. In early 1962, Pete found himself kicked out of the crew once again, scapegoat for Sinatra's wrath, this time over an incident involving John Kennedy. Lawford had been instrumental in arranging many of the hangout sessions between Sinatra and Kennedy, and in 1960 convinced the Pack to throw their support behind JFK by appearing at the Democratic National Convention. It was a reasonable fit. Frank and Sammy ended up being an unlikely force for civil rights. When Frank discovered that the Sands would let Nat King Cole perform but not allow him on the casino floor or into the dining room, Sinatra was furious. He threatened to boycott the Sands if they didn't change their tune. They changed. When Sammy performed at the Copa in New York and discovered he was welcome as an entertainer but not a customer, Sinatra threatened to shut the whole show down and never again set foot in the Copa if the club didn't integrate. It integrated. On the surface, JFK's crusade for civil rights was the perfect fit for Sinatra and Davis. The rest of the Pack would, of course, do what Frank wanted. So they showed up at the DNC in Los Angeles in July of 1960.

In 1962, Lawford asked if Frank would be willing to host the Kennedys at his Palm Springs home. Sinatra readily agreed and then set about making a number of expensive modifications to his property. He even installed a helipad so the President and First Lady could arrive by air. But President Kennedy's younger brother, US Attorney General Robert Kennedy, was attempting to build a legacy for himself by taking on organized crime. Specifically, the Mafia. Robert asked his brother not to associate with Sinatra, a man with Mafia ties both known and rumored. Despite the money Sinatra spent getting his place ready, the President no-showed, opting instead to stay with Sinatra's rival, Bing Crosby.

Sinatra was not known for dealing well with not getting his way. He was furious over the snub, especially after Kennedy had been more than happy to use the whole Rat Pack during the campaign. Rumor had it that Sinatra even did favors for Kennedy by allowing the CIA to use Frank's private plane to smuggle persons-of-interest back and forth across borders, though the only source for this claim is Frank's daughter Tina, who mentioned it in her memoirs. It isn't an outrageous claim. Many intelligence agencies asked touring performers to do them small favors. Carry a message here, take a passenger there. Who was going to search Frank Sinatra's plane? So all that, and then to stay with Bing Crosby? *Bing fucking Crosby*? Sinatra couldn't lash out directly at either John or Robert Kennedy, so he focused his fury on the one man he *could* punish: Pete Lawford, who'd set the whole thing up. Lawford became *persona non grata*, exiled from the Pack's shows and written out of their films. Sinatra even replaced him in the film *Robin and the Seven Hoods*. With Bing Crosby.

The tangle involving Sinatra, the Kennedys, Monroe, the Mob, and Fidel Castro yields an almost limitless amount of speculation and conspiracy theory. One claims JFK wanted Sinatra on the campaign trail because Kennedy needed vote guarantees from blocks controlled by the Mafia...by Joseph Colombo, the man who later prevented Johnny Carson's assassination. In exchange for the votes, Kennedy would, by hook or by crook (or by stolen beard and exploding cigar), orchestrate the overthrow of Fidel Castro and the return Havana's casinos to Mob control. If Lawford was Sinatra's connection to JFK, then JFK's connection to the Five Families was Frank Sinatra, or so the theory sometimes goes. Not that the Kennedys were without their own criminal roots. Joe Kennedy, John and Bobby's father, was a successful bootleggers during Prohibition, a trade that almost certainly connected him directly to men like Lucky Luciano. Among Luciano's closest business associates were Frank Costello and Meyer Lansky—the very men who had a stake in the Sands casino and offered Sinatra that generous line of credit. When JFK won the Presidency and appointed his little brother Attorney General, the legitimate businessmen who felt they'd delivered the election to JFK suddenly found themselves on the outs. Robert Kennedy went after the Mafia with a vengeance. JFK was behaving like a mobster who pulls off a big heist then cuts the ties to his associates by murdering them.

On top of that, attempts to retake Cuba from Castro were botched. The Mafia didn't get back the Havana casinos. And so, as some of the impossible-to-substantiate rumors claim, the Mob began plotting the downfall of the brothers Kennedy. And that downfall involved Marilyn Monroe, romantically linked (at least in scandal sheets) to Sinatra and both Bobby and Jack Kennedy. Monroe was in rough shape then, and it's alleged that she became even worse as the Mob strung her out on drugs to make her more willing to participate in the plan. She'd already slept with both the Kennedy brothers, they figured. What was one more time? Only this time, it would be filmed.

John, Robert, it didn't really matter as long as they got one of them on film having an illicit encounter. But however strung out she might have been, however at the end of her rope emotionally, she wouldn't do it. In another impossible-to-verify claim, it was a few days after her final refusal that she was found dead. August 5, 1962. The last person she ever spoke to was Peter Lawford, the one guy among the Pack and the Kennedys who didn't use and abuse her. "Say goodbye to Pat," she said to him over the phone. "Say goodbye to the President, and say goodbye to yourself because you're such a nice guy."

On November 22, 1963, John Kennedy was assassinated in Texas by Lee Harvey Oswald. Bobby Kennedy was killed in June 6, 1968, in the midst of what looked to be a successful presidential campaign of his own. 1962, the same year Sinatra was snubbed by Ian Fleming fan John Kennedy, the same year Marilyn died, was also the year *Dr. No* was released. Once again, cool realigned itself, this time defined by Sean Connery. *Dr. No* wasn't just a film. It was a revolution. Fleming had been writing James Bond novels for a decade by then. *Dr. No*, published in 1958, was his sixth. Despite being dismissed as violent, lurid trash, the books were hugely popular. Bing Crosby's house guest John Kennedy loved them, naming *From Russia with Love* one of his top ten favorite books. That opened the door for one of the weirder footnotes in the very weird story of the CIA and Cuba.

If Kennedy asking Sinatra to ferry CIA operatives across borders seems weird, it's nothing compared to the time Ian Fleming sat down with JFK at a party in 1960 and advised the President on how to deal with Fidel. The key to Castro's charisma, Fleming said, was the beard. Remove the beard and you would remove the man from power. So, Ian continued, what you needed to do was circulate a false scientific report finding that beards retain greater amounts of radioactivity, causing disease and sterility. In a panic, Castro would shave off his beard, and then...well, who would follow a revolutionary without a beard?

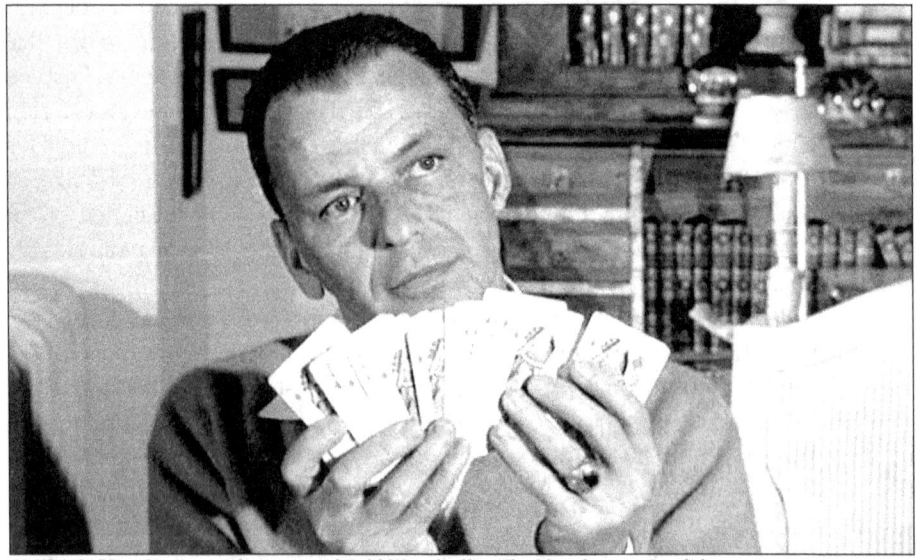

PICK A CARD—*Sinatra in the paranoid Cold War thriller, The Manchurian Candidate.*

In 1961, Kennedy's administration launched the Bay of Pigs invasion. It was a disaster, most likely because Fidel Castro still had his beard. Subsequent plans to assassinate Castro by way of exploding cigars were devised by the CIA and a bizarre assemblage of Cuban exiles and Mafiosos and were no less silly—and no more successful. And yet, that was just the tip of the iceberg. While *Dr. No* was lighting up screens and Kennedy's botched invasion was lighting up a Cuban beach, Frank Sinatra became the first Rat Packer to star in a spy film. *The Manchurian Candidate* is a more somber affair than James Bond. Directed by John Frankenheimer and based on a novel by Richard Condon, *The Manchurian Candidate* is about a group of soldiers trapped behind enemy lines during the Korean War. Most of them show up on the US side of the lines after an escape orchestrated by their fellow captive, Staff Sergeant Raymond Shaw (Laurence Harvey). Two of the soldiers, however, remain MIA. Repatriated after the war, one of the men, Captain Bennett Marco (Sinatra) starts having nightmares. And slowly a plot begins to unravel that involves paranoia, psychosis, brain washing, and sleeper assassins.

None of the glamor of *Dr. No* is in *The Manchurian Candidate*. It's the spy film as noir: bleak, haunted, serious. It was an excellent thriller, released during the height of the Cuban Missile Crisis and more attuned to the real politics of the Cold War than *Dr. No*, which by Fleming's own admission was largely apolitical fantasy. Sinatra was great as a soldier slowly realizing that something horrible has been done to him. Unfortunately, it wasn't enough to get him included in the round of Oscar nominations handed out to the film, which included Angela Lansbury for Best Supporting Actress. The editor, Ferris Webster, was also nominated for an Oscar. His work is the reason *The Manchurian Candidate* looks unlike any film that had come before it. It is regarded as one of the classics of American cinema.

But then there was *Dr. No*—silly colorful, violent, sexy *Dr. No*. It had more in common with *Ocean's 11* than with *The Manchurian Candidate*. Both *Dr. No* and *The Manchurian Candidate* were among the five highest-grossing films of 1962, but only *Dr. No* became a cultural touchstone. With nuclear war between the US and the Soviet Union seeming all but a done deal, *Dr. No* allowed audiences to dip a toe into the world of espionage and come away with no consequences. *The Manchurian Candidate* did not afford them the same innocence. Once *Dr. No* was released, the Bond formula of exotic locations, thrilling violence, leering sex, and a dash of knowing camp made them the template for an entire genre of film.

Sinatra may have harvested accolades for *The Manchurian Candidate*, but it was Dean Martin who found himself goofing around in the spy-fantasy universe created by James Bond.

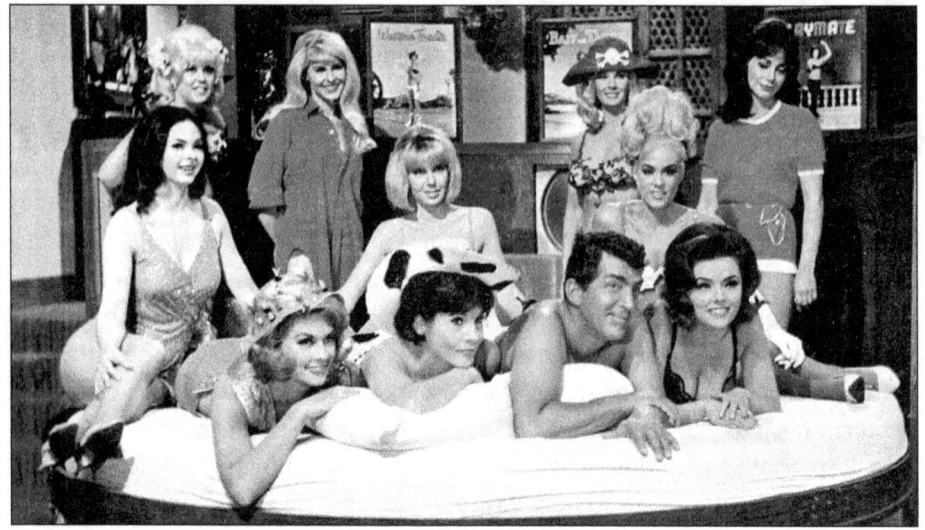

THAT'S AMORE!—Matt Helm, surrounded by his Slay Girls in The Silencers.

You're Nobody 'til Somebody Loves You

Sinatra's stormy personality provided a dramatic tumult for the Rat Pack, but during it all Dean Martin was the calm at the eye of the hurricane. Although he received complimentary reviews for his dramatic roles in *The Young Lions* and as an alcoholic deputy in *Rio Lobo*, it was the persona he crafted for stage and television that America adored: the lovable boozer who didn't take anything seriously, at least until he belted out "You Belong to Me" or "Innamorata." He wasn't a master of melancholy the way Sinatra was, but it was damn hard not to pull your loved one close when Dean started singing. There wasn't much of the cynical anti-hero Matt Helm in Dean Martin. No one could believe Allen was serious about casting him, least of all Dean Martin himself. He was also hesitant to commit to a potential series, so he jokingly made a number of outrageous demands, including 10% of the profits on top of his salary, figuring that they would turn him down and he could go on his merry way. When Irving Allen accepted the deal, Martin shrugged and became Matt Helm.

It's possible that Martin could have handled a serious script, but everyone, including Dean, figured no one wanted to see a dark, violent performance from the King of Cool. They wanted *Ocean's 11* Dean Martin. They wanted Rat Pack Dean Martin. They wanted fun, drunk Uncle Dino. And boy did they get him. The script was tweaked by Martin's writing buddies to better reflect his stage persona. They added a bunch of musical asides and sexy daydreams, and they scrapped Matt Helm's wife and kids, transforming him into a Bondian bachelor. He now had a space-age pad that included a nubile young assistant named Lovey Kravezit (Beverly Adams) and a rotating bed that slid forward and tilted to dump Helm into his indoor pool/hot tub, complete with a wet bar that dropped from the ceiling (he has a similar bar in his car, because it was the 1960s).

It was a disappointing turn of events for fans of Donald Hamilton, who had been hoping to see the cruel, violent, unglamorous world of the literary Matt Helm brought to the big screen. Hamilton was disappointed as well and thought taking the comedic route to be a cop-out. But he was also a professional who had sold many stories, so he knew the drill and didn't take it personally. Hamilton continued writing Matt Helm novels in his usual style while, as he stated in an interview, taking the money from Irving Allen and crying all the way to the bank.

The Silencers novel is grim and straight-forward, with no jet-setting unless you count Juarez, Mexico. Although it was the first of the movies, *The Silencers* is the fourth of the books, so certain things have been established in previous stories. It begins with Helm heading toward El Paso, where he is to extract an agent working undercover in a seedy Juarez strip club. Things don't go according to plan, and before too long Matt is traveling north toward the small mountain town of Carrizozo, New Mexico with a mysterious woman who hates him and is most likely trying to set him up. He is also trying to track down an enemy agent and stop the bad guys from hijacking a missile and redirecting it to blow up a bunch of important scientists and politicians.

In keeping with Matt Helm's down-home style, most of the villains he faces are similarly low-key. There are the occasional megalomaniacs with dreams of conquest, but most of the time, he's just facing off against other assassins, thugs, agents, and flunkies. There are no Nehru jacket-wearing masterminds with sprawling secret lairs beneath the ocean. The antagonists in *The Silencers* are camped out in a cold, dilapidated church outside a small New Mexico town. Likewise, Helm's allies are rarely slick playboys and captains of industry. They are, instead, cab drivers and grumpy fellow agents. He frequently butts heads with Washington not over the

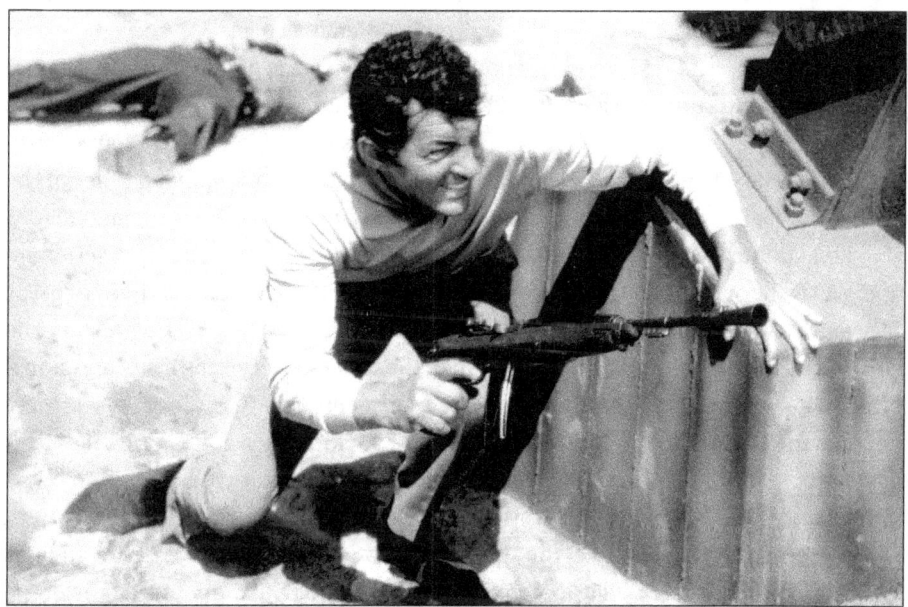

classic "your methods are too extreme" argument—they pay him to be extreme, after all—but over the simple and all too real frustration of investigative and secret agencies refusing to share information with one another, resulting in lots of mishaps and misunderstandings.

Leading up to the release of the film *The Silencers*, there was a barrage of publicity, most of it focused on the bevy of semi-clad beauties populating the film (Dean Martin was too busy with the launch of his new TV variety show to participate). In 1966, in the wake of *Thunderball* and alongside another high-profile Bond spoof, *Our Man Flint* starring James Coburn, Irving Allen, Dean Martin, and *The Silencers* staggered drunkenly onto American screens. It opens with a pointless prologue (the first of many jokes aimed at Bond) in which four assassins who will never appear in the movie are given golden bullets etched with the name Matt Helm. These, also, play no role in the movie. We then move on to a colorful burlesque of an opening credit sequence anchored by legendary dancer-actress Cyd Charisse, performing a risqué (by 1960s American movie standards; not by seedy Juarez strip club standards) striptease. So not exactly the book, but it's not entirely out of left field.

The movie then promptly jettisons the plot of *The Silencers* in favor of *Death of a Citizen*, with all the seriousness abandoned in favor of juvenile sex jokes and Dean Martin cracking wise. If Bond films were the epitome of jet-set cool, *The Silencers* was a leering, middle-aged lounge lizard. The image of Ursula Andress emerging from the ocean in a white bikini in *Dr. No* became an iconic image of sophisticated sex appeal. By contrast, *The Silencers* is a drawing of naked ladies on the wall of a public bathroom. Everything is cheaper and cruder. It's somehow both threadbare and lavish at the same time, with great scenery and costumes. But then there are things like the villain's lair, which looks like someone crinkled up brown trash bags, glued it to the wall, and called it a cave.

As an adaptation of Hamilton's novels, *The Silencers* is a failure. But as a spoof of spy and Bond films—well, *The Silencers* is indeed dumb and juvenile, but it's also colorful, entertaining, and as charming as its tipsy lead actor. Dean Martin brings easy charisma to the role. His Matt Helm isn't the cold-blooded killer of the books, but he *is* a fan of judo fights and women in lingerie, so there's that.

The supporting cast, including James Gregory as Matt's superior McDonald and Victor Buono as the foppish, eyeliner-etched criminal mastermind Tung-Tze (rather than being another in a long line of Caucasians poorly imitating Asians, the role seems to be intentionally making fun of the practice), is giving it a professional effort. Most of the jokes are dumb, but a few are genuinely funny, or at least funny enough to inspire a combination groan and chuckle. It manages to be a decent spy spoof and, if it isn't exactly thrill-a-minute, it's good-natured enough that you don't mind hanging around. Critics were, predictably, split on the movie, with some seeing it as the affable spoof it tries to be and others seeing it as a lazy, vulgar cash-in on the Bond craze, which it also is. Minus disappointed fans of the

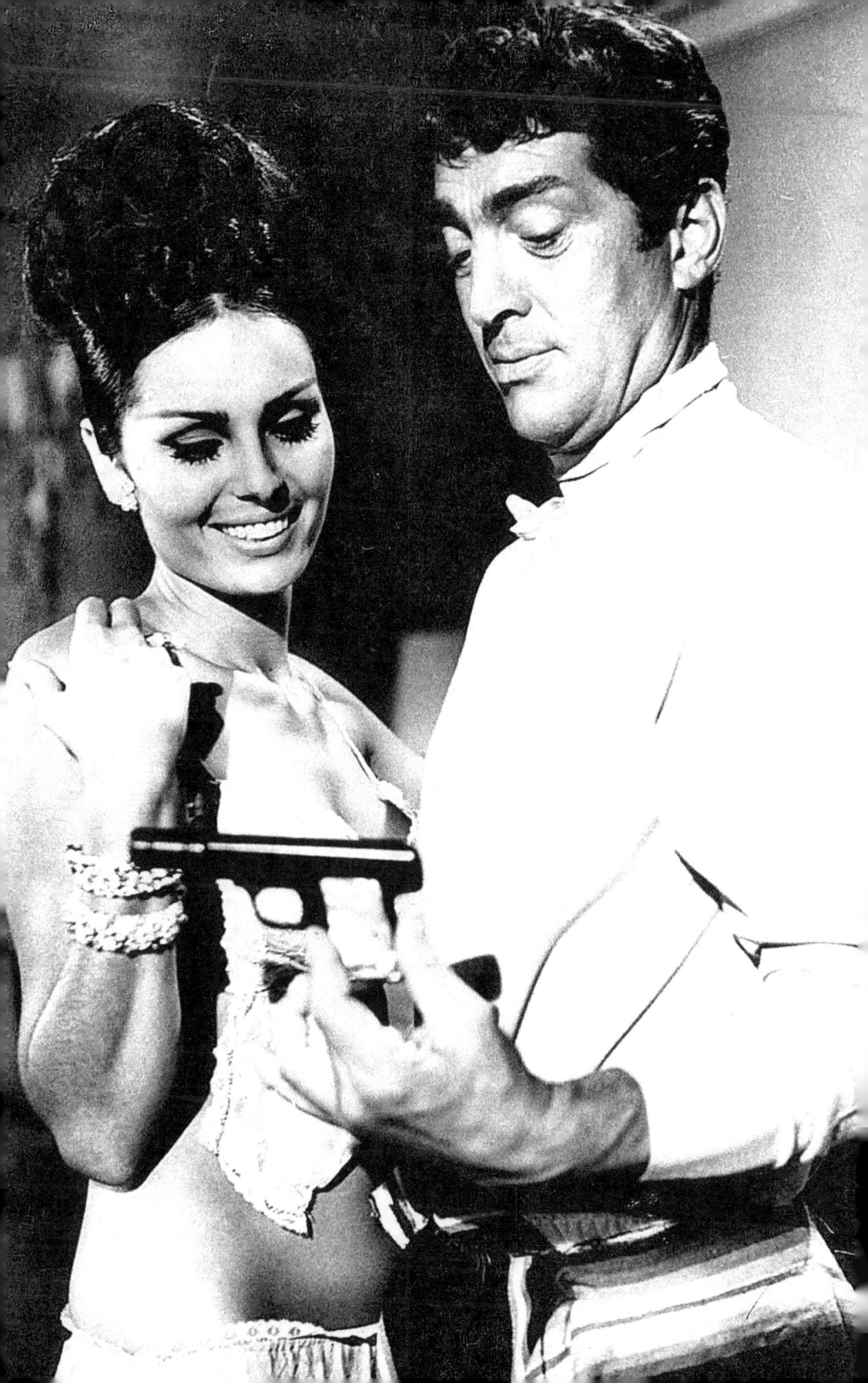

Matt Helm novels, audiences were a bit more unified than critics in their support of the film. Irving Allen planned to make more Helm movies even before the numbers were in, but the success of *The Silencers* guaranteed another.

Thanks to his demand for a portion of the film's box office, Dean Martin suddenly found himself one of the highest-paid actors in Hollywood. Although the profits of *The Silencers* paled in comparison to those of *Thunderball*, Dean Martin ended up making more money than Sean Connery. Connery, perhaps looking at Martin's pay-day, thought that maybe as the iconic star of the most popular movie franchise in the world, he should be making something a little closer to the bank made by the drunken star of a jokey Bond knock-off.

So James Bond walked into the office of producer Cubby Broccoli, pointed to the high paycheck being cashed by the star of the film made by Broccoli's old partner, and suggested that maybe ol' Sean ought to have himself a similar profit-sharing plan. Broccoli rejected the idea, claiming that it was James Bond, not Sean Connery that people wanted to see. Bond made Connery, so Bond could just as easily make another guy. Maybe some unknown male model from Australia who had never acted before. Connery was furious. In the wake of *The Silencers*, he announced that the next Bond film, 1967's *You Only Live Twice* (theme song by Nancy Sinatra) would be his last.

If the success of Dean Martin and *The Silencers* caused waves at Eon Productions even while never really challenging the Bond films at the box office, it was nothing but sunshine and roses for Irving Allen, Dean Martin, and Donald Hamilton. Between the movie and his TV show, Martin was one of the most popular, highest-paid entertainers in America. Even though the film bore only the scantest resemblance to Donald Hamilton's source material, interest in his books spiked. In 1966, he released the tenth book in the series, *The Betrayers*, and enjoyed a greater level of critical and mass appeal than he'd ever had.

Irving Allen announced that the next Matt Helm movie was already in production, with Martin reprising his role and the ante being upped in terms of gorgeous locations, action, and beautiful women. Based on one of the darkest and most violent of Hamilton's novels, the new movie, *Murderers' Row*, promised to be very much the opposite of its source material.

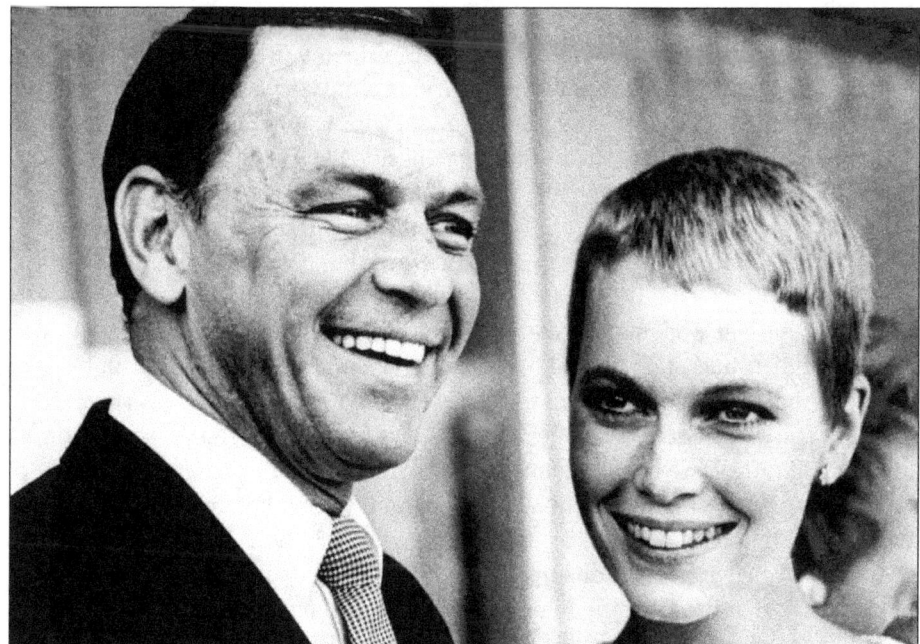

YOU MAKE ME FEEL SO OLD—*Frank Sinatra and Mia Farrow.*

The Old Man and the Hippie

Things may have been pretty swell for Dean Martin, but that wasn't the case for his pal, Frank Sinatra. Manic-depressive Sinatra was in one of his depressive stages. He was settling poorly into middle age—into being thought of as an icon of the previous generation, the old man singing show tunes and standards when pop had moved on to the Stones, the Beatles, the Who, the Doors, and Pink Floyd. Sinatra still drew big numbers, but they were big numbers from an aging fanbase. In 1966, as Martin was working on *Murderers' Row*, Sinatra began a romance with young actress Mia Farrow, famous then for her role in the trashy soap opera *Peyton Place*.

A slip of a young woman who looked more like someone in her mid-teens than twenty, Mia was shooting *Peyton Place* on the old Fox lots, which had fallen into disuse after the massively over-budget epic *Cleopatra* pretty much bankrupted Fox Studios. *Peyton Place* was one of the first shoots to return to the lot, but other productions soon followed, including a World War II adventure called *Von Ryan's Express*, starring Frank Sinatra. One of Mia's friends, actor John Leyton, was also in the film, so she decided to visit him on the set. It was there that she first met Frank, or rather, that she met Frank for the second time; it turned out she'd met him once before, as a young girl, when he'd been an acquaintance of her father.

Mia *might* have noticed Sinatra on set, but Sinatra *definitely* noticed Mia. The next day, she was visited by one of his associates who was charged with finding out one thing: was she legal? When Farrow assured him that she was nineteen, the associate asked if she'd like to meet Frank Sinatra. Up until then, Frank's love life was playing out like one of his forlorn songs, partly because relationships between entertainers are usually difficult, and partly because Frank wasn't the easiest of boyfriends. Exceptional at the art of wooing, he had difficulty following through once the woo proved successful. Sinatra was a deeply insecure man. The list of demands he placed upon any potential girlfriend almost always proved too much to bear. He pursued dancer-actress Juliet Prowse, with whom he'd co-starred in *Can-Can* in 1960 (the same year she appeared alongside Elvis in his first since returning from the Army, *G.I. Blues*, and the same year Sinatra welcomed Elvis home on national TV). But he demanded she give up her career so she could devote herself to being Mrs. Frank Sinatra. Prowse was uninterested in giving everything up for the privilege of standing alongside Sinatra, so she rejected his advances.

From there, it was on to a relationship with Marilyn Monroe. Her health was failing, her drug addiction was taking its toll, and she was in constant disputes over what she thought—with good reason—were awful contracts. She was rumored to be having an affair with President Kennedy at the same time she was romantically linked to Sinatra (one can imagine a sit-com in which Peter Lawford is trying to juggle Marilyn meeting with both Sinatra and Kennedy without one knowing about the other). That all came to a crashing halt on August 5, 1962.

Sinatra's previous relationships had been no less complicated, often as a result of his own behavior. His creepy pursuit of Lauren Bacall, so soon after Bogart's death, was something he wanted to keep secret. His relationship before that, perhaps the one that defined his difficult attitudes toward women and romance for the rest of his life, was the one with Ava Gardner. By the time he spied young, moddish Mia Farrow, Sinatra was well past the point of being damaged goods. But he was still Frank Sinatra, and even pushing fifty, he was in decent shape, good-looking, and possessed a worldliness that made him seem a man among boys—at least until his next tantrum.

Farrow was hesitant to meet him one on one. She'd never listened to any of his music or seen any of his films. Different generations, after all. Plus, she was young, inexperienced, and had never had a serious romance. Eventually, though, he convinced her to go on a date—to see one of his own movies (*None but the Brave*, which he also directed). After the film, Sinatra invited her to fly on his private jet to his home in Palm Springs. Farrow, terrified of the prospect since she had no experience with anything like this, stammered out an excuse having to do with taking care of her cat. The next day, he extended the offer again, telling her it was cool; she could bring the cat.

Something clicked. Terror turned to exhilaration as she packed the cat and flew off to Frank's home. The first thing she saw was Yul Brynner sunning himself by the pool. Brynner, in fact, became something of a confidant. He was the only other person who knew Sinatra and Farrow were together. Frank labored to keep the relationship a secret, anxious over what his friends and the press might think of this middle-aged man dating a teenager. It's also possible he just didn't want her cramping his style. Most nights he spent with some configuration of his entourage while Mia stayed at home. Frank's home. A home still filled with photos of Ava Gardner. The night of his 50th birthday party, their relationship was finally outed. Sinatra didn't invite her to the bash itself, but when some of his friends showed up at the Palm Springs house with a plotzed Sinatra propped between them, they found Mia quietly sitting on the couch. It was hard to keep it under wraps then, so Frank decided to let the cat out of the bag. Their official "coming out" party as a couple famously boasted a toast to Farrow from Dean Martin: "I've got a bottle of scotch older than you." Mia quickly discovered she enjoyed being a secret girlfriend more than a public spectacle. Before they were a confirmed couple, she and Frank spent most of their time alone (except, presumably, for a perpetually-sunbathing Yul Brynner out back). It was time she felt was meaningful. Once the relationship was in the open, those quiet moments disappeared. Her life became a whirlwind of paparazzi, Vegas glam, sycophants, and a social circle that had more in common with Mia's parents than with Mia. She was particularly unhappy in Vegas, where she was expected to be well-trained arm candy surrounded by prostitutes, girlfriends, and wives twice her age.

Even Frank's daughter, Nancy, was five years Mia's senior. What was *she* going to do? Invite Mia to go out with her? Introduce a woman barely out of her teens as her new mom? Nancy was hanging out with the Fonda kids, starring in biker movies, recording with pop-country iconoclast Lee Hazlewood, and singing the theme for *You Only Live Twice*. Poor Mia was relegated to a table at some stale-smelling Vegas nightclub, listening to catty conversations and tired Henny Youngman jokes, sometimes dozing off out of sheer boredom. Her only relief came when childhood friend Liza Minnelli was in town. Frank might have sung "You Make Me Feel So Young," but he made Mia feel like an old woman.

In 1965, Mia and Frank took a long vacation, sailing up the coast from Cape Cod to Manhattan. If Mia thought this was going to be a return to quiet time, she was mistaken. Frank brought along actresses Claudette Colbert and Rosalind Russell.

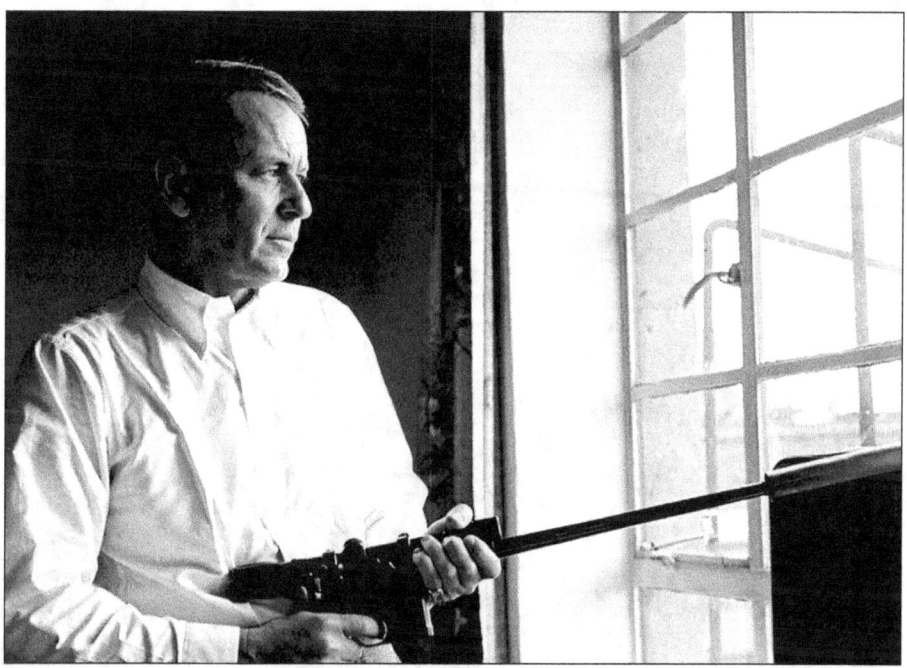

NAKED AND AFRAID—Sinatra in the disastrous The Naked Runner.

They were surrounded from the very beginning by boats and helicopters full of paparazzi. The quartet was forced to spend most of the cruise in the cabin. When a member of the crew fell overboard and disappeared, the whole disaster was called off.

Mia returned to work on the next season of *Peyton Place*. When she was told her character was going to have a nervous breakdown, she chopped her hair, almost into a crew cut. Her short, androgynous cut and slim build might have been cool among the kids of Mia's generation, but for the press, it only illustrated the gulf between her and Frank, though Frank reportedly thought the cut was fine, leading Ava Gardner to accuse him of having been a homosexual all long. Those two really were made for each other.

Despite the age difference, the generation gap, despite drunken furies that sometimes horrified Mia, and despite a brief break up, the two married in July of 1966. It barely lasted a year. Sinatra was dissatisfied that Mia maintained a career and that she wasn't willing to make sure her work timed perfectly with whatever mood he was in. She paid attention to him, traveling to be on set with him, but he rarely returned the favor. The only time he showed interest in her work was when it impacted him by messing up whatever schedule he made for the two of them. One of these conflicts arose while she was in London and Berlin filming the spy movie *A Dandy in Aspic*. Production was delayed when the film's director, Anthony Mann passed away during filming and a new director had to pick up the film in mid-production. Sinatra failed to see much in the way of tragedy or extenuating circumstances. He was just angry that Mia was going to be away longer than she originally said.

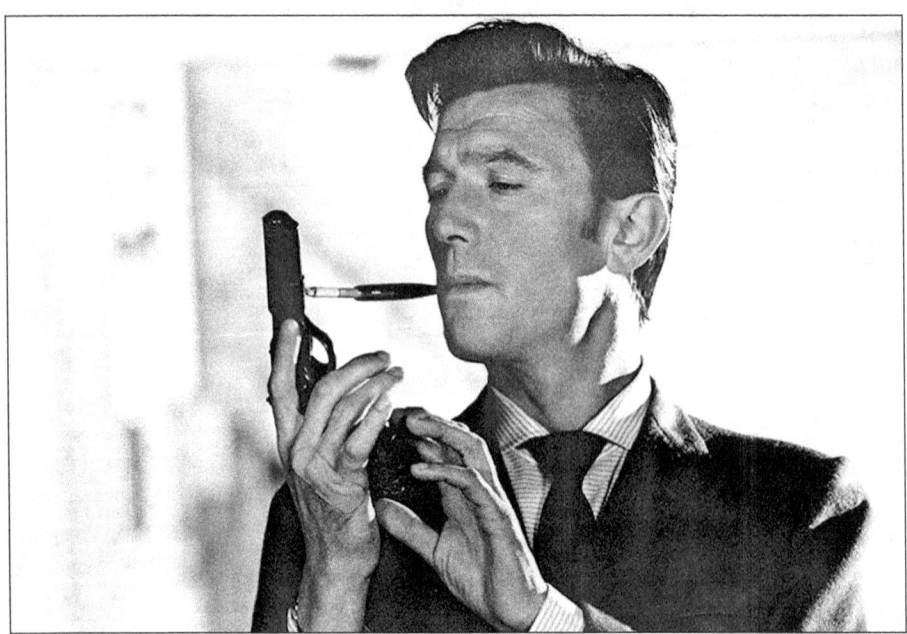

THE DISMAL DANDY—Lawrence Harvey in A Dandy in Aspic.

After Mann's death, lead actor Lawrence Harvey (Sinatra's co-star in *The Manchurian Candidate*) stepped in to direct and try to pull everything together. Lawrence doesn't make much of an effort to match Mann's style, but these shifts in direction are minimally invasive except in a few instances. The larger problems with the movie already existed before Mann's untimely demise, and his passing only served to conflate them. Derek Marlowe's script contains a good movie, but it was still a couple drafts away from being realized. The premise, at least, is intriguing. Lawrence Harvey stars as Eberlin, an MI5 operative who is, like James Bond, fussy about his clothing but, unlike Bond, is also asexual. When he walks into a room, everyone admires his sartorial taste then whispers about what a frigid, boring guy he is. Eberlin is also a Soviet double agent named Krasnevin. He's at the end of his rope, suspecting that his years as a double with a cold, remote personality have left him a man without a home who has truly become the cold, remote thing he pretends to be. He longs to retire to the socialist paradises awaiting him on the other side of the Berlin Wall. Unfortunately, the Soviets find him too effective an operative to allow him to retire. The British also have a high opinion of him, because when it comes time to assassinate the Soviet's number-one killer, Eberlin gets the job. Which is funny, since Krasnevin is the Soviet's number-one killer. Eberlin meets free-spirited young Caroline (Farrow), a rich girl who travels the world, working (barely) as a wannabe photographer. Caroline represents the vivacious, fun life Eberlin has denied himself, but the character is so slight and so flighty that she never comes across as anything more than a well-meaning but spoiled kid. It's hard to believe someone so insubstantial could affect a man as hard as Eberlin.

Farrow was between *Peyton Place* and the iconic status she would achieve in *Rosemary's Baby*. She's the embodiment of the willowy look of the swinging sixties, but for all the talent she had beneath her gamine beauty, none of it surfaces in *A Dandy in Aspic*. She disappears for much of the movie. When she is on screen, she has little to do beyond lounge about and look cute in fashionable clothing. It's hinted that, since she tends to appear in whichever country Eberlin has traveled to, she might herself be a spy. Nothing ever comes of that, though. Her character is perfunctory. It hardly seems worth the stress it put on her marriage—but that's assuming she did it for the movie and not just to get out from under Sinatra's thumb. No worries. 1967 had greater things in store for Mia Farrow.

Frank, in the meantime, kept busy making his own spy film, *The Naked Runner*, and the closest thing since *Ocean's 11* that he ever made to a James Bond film, the sun-drenched private eye film *Tony Rome*, set in Miami (including locations used in *Goldfinger* and a leading lady later to appear in *Diamonds Are Forever*) and based on the book *Miami Mayhem* by Marvin H. Albert. Sinatra needed a hit. His last couple movies hadn't done much at the box office. Between that and the increasingly difficult-to-ignore generation gap between he and Farrow, Frank was starting to panic. He was pushing for the lead in *Harper*, co-starring Lauren Bacall, but the role went to Paul Newman. Sinatra settled on *The Naked Runner*.

Like *The Manchurian Candidate*, it was a solemn Cold War thriller. Sinatra took the part because he admired *The IPCRESS File*, a film that combined the realism of John Le Carré with the stylized look of Bond. Its director, Sydney J. Furie, was slated to direct *The Naked Runner*. Production began in 1966 and was instantly derailed by Sinatra's mercurial temperament.

The plot sounds a bit like it could have passed muster as a Matt Helm story (the Donald Hamilton kind, not the Dean Martin ones). Sinatra plays a retired OSS operative recruited back into the service for one last mission while on a business trip in Leipzig. Or rather, Sinatra *mostly* stars. Near the end of filming, Sinatra refused to return from California to Europe, demanding that the production be moved and finished on a soundstage. Instead, Furie hired a stand-in and finished the film without the star. For Furie, it was the final insult in a series of outrageous demands placed on the production by its star. Early on, Sinatra halted production for two weeks to fly to Vegas, where he married Mia. Anxious to get things up and running again, Furie was further frustrated when Sinatra, upon his return, declared that he was now on his honeymoon, planning to balance his shooting schedule with jaunts to France. When fog caused Sinatra's helicopter to get lost, Sinatra made his demand that shooting move to California. Furie threatened to walk off the picture, and it took a substantial amount of negotiation to get the two men to continue working with one another. It hardly seems to have been worth it. Shortly after shooting in Europe resumed, Sinatra took off for California, this time for a political rally, and refused to return. That was it. Furie told Sinatra he could piss off and hired a guy named James Payne to take Sinatra's place, stitching together the finale using existing footage, look-alikes, and outtakes.

The resulting product is, not surprisingly, a schizophrenic, disjointed affair. Furie brought a considerable amount of directorial flair to *The IPCRESS File*, and while there are flashes of that in *The Naked Runner*, the production made it impossible to come up with anything approaching the caliber of Furie's previous film. It's awkwardly edited, full of unsettling close-ups and people staring directly into the camera while listlessly reciting dialogue. The tricks Furie used in *The IPCRESS File* to give it a surreal atmosphere despite being set in drab London flats and offices are employed in *The Naked Runner* in a way that illustrates how good *The IPCRESS File* was. Here, those stylistic indulgences are purposeless. It's also full of repetitive conversations that go on longer than they need to, contained in scenes that go on longer than they need to, punctuated by pauses that go on longer than they need to. It's like everyone is continuously missing their cues.

Despite mostly negative reviews, *The Naked Runner* managed to ride the coattails of the spy craze and become a minor hit. Maybe not what Sinatra wanted, but at least what he needed. Because *A Dandy in Aspic* experienced substantial delays after Allen's death, *The Naked Runner* beat it to the theaters, coming out in July of 1967, situated comfortably between the release of Dean Martin's *Murderer's Row* and its follow-up, *The Ambushers*.

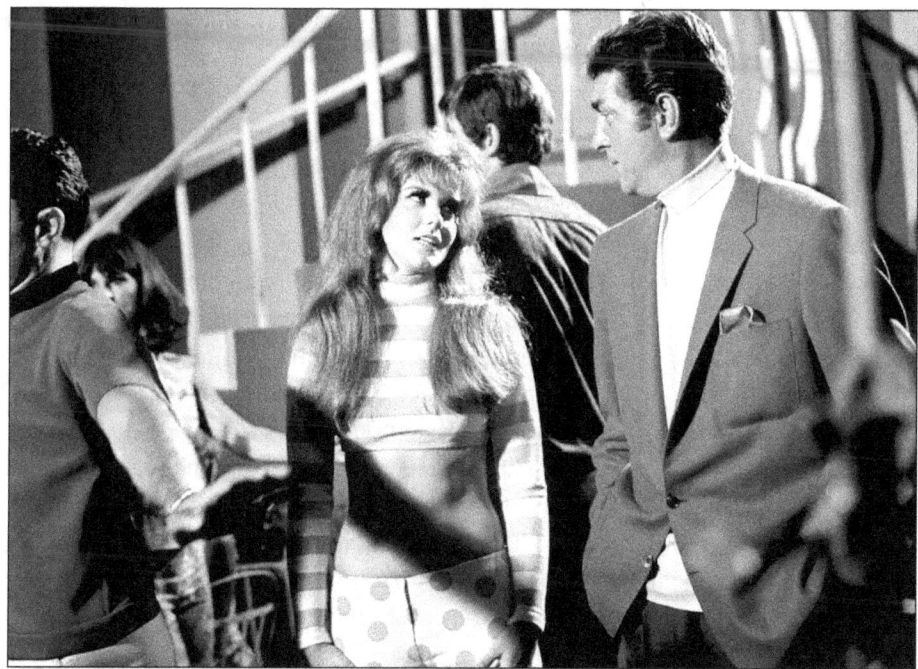

DRUNK UNCLE—Dean hits the go-go clubs with Ann-Margret in Murderers' Row.

Ann-Margaret and a Hovercraft

Sinatra was squeaking by, but Dean Martin was riding high. For whatever reason, despite announcing his next film would be *The Ambushers*, Allen moved things around. *Murderers' Row* became the second Matt Helm movie, not that the order really mattered. Although one can't imagine any fan of Donald Hamilton's books holding out hope that the movies would be anything like the novels after the drunken hijinks of *The Silencers*, it still must have given readers pause to hear that *Murderers' Row* was the next to get the swingin' cocktail treatment. The fifth book in the series, published in 1962 immediately after *The Silencers*, is among the bleakest and angriest of the Helm stories. Matt is preparing for some long overdue time off. Of course, no spy in the history of spy stories has been able to take his leave without having it interrupted.

When a scientist disappears, either kidnapped or defected, Helm is given a distasteful mission. A female agent has been working her way into the enemy organization, convincing them that she is a disillusioned agent with a drinking problem, on the verge of a nervous breakdown, and ready to defect. Her real assignment is to get in, find out if the scientist is dead or alive, and either rescue him or kill him. Matt's job is to make her cover story seem more plausible, primarily by beating her within an inch of her life in order to make the opposition believe the US is genuinely concerned she might betray them. Despite careful planning, the female agent dies during the roughing up. Making things worse, a group of drunken college kids witness Matt leaving her room. To complicate matters even further since this is a spy novel, another agent who happens to be in love with the female agent attacks Matt. Helm, of course, is better than the novice agent and leaves him lying with a belly full of knife, though nothing fatal. The whole affair makes Helm's superiors wonder if he's gone over the edge, become so callous and bitter that he can kill his own people without so much as a tinge of guilt. They decide to bring him in.

Helm's certain of his own sanity, though, and goes rogue in order to pick up the trail. He assumes the identity of a brutish hustler, and he's immediately picked up by the cops for murder. The drunks from the motel are on hand, and although one, Robin Rosten, is certain he's the man they saw leaving the room of the dead woman, another young woman, Teddy, vehemently denies it, taking the heat off Matt. When Helm asks her why she lied, he discovers she wants to hire him to kill someone: Robin Rosten. Turns out the missing scientist is the young girl's father, and she's convinced Robin had him killed as part of some convoluted tangle of love affairs. Teddy, assuming Matt is just a thug, hopes he can get a little revenge on her behalf. No sooner is Matt hired to kill Robin than Robin in turn hires him to kill her husband, who in turn hires Matt to kill his wife. Set among the East Coast aristocracy of America, *Murderers' Row*, more than any other Helm novel, could have been one of Raymond Chandler's Philip Marlowe story. It has that same sense of something foul and oily beneath the wealthy veneer, the same sense of world-weariness, the same sense of anger tinged with sadness. It might have also made a pretty good story arc for *Peyton Place*.

The movie version of *Murderers' Row* has Ann-Margaret go-go dancing furiously and Dean Martin tearing around Monaco in a hovercraft. So...not exactly the same, though vague elements of the book do show up in the movie. Helm is briefly undercover as a Chicago thug, and Ann-Margaret is the daughter of a kidnapped scientist. Beyond that, though, there's not much to tie the movie to the book. Released Christmas 1966, less than a year after *The Silencers*, *Murderers' Row* feels less like a Bond spoof and more like a Frankie and Annette beach party movie. Directed by Henry Levin (*Where the Boys Are, Journey to the Center of the Earth*), it's actually an improvement in almost every way over fun-but-sloppy *The Silencers*. The jokes are not as cornball, and there are fewer dumb double entendres. The action is more frequent and better filmed. Karl Malden is a better villain. The scenery and sets don't look as cheap. There is some serious hovercraft action. And best of all, there's Ann-Margaret (who would have made an excellent Teddy in a more straight-forward adaptation of the book as well), who brings a ridiculous amount of energy to her role. With her in the mix, the movie doesn't try to play Dean Martin off as a cool killer. Instead, he's portrayed as out of step, unable to hang with these crazy go-go dancing kids (who have a mural of Frank Sinatra in their dance club; these films crack a lot of wise at the expense of Frank Sinatra).

The Monaco location work is also gorgeous—even though most of it wasn't Monaco. Martin, busy with the rest of his film career and his popular television show, had no interest in going abroad. A second unit crew got the plum job of jetting off to Monaco for exteriors and establishing shots while the bulk of the film was made in the studio. It was a foregone conclusion that *Murderers' Row* would be a success (it was) and that a third film would get produced (it did). Allen might have missed the James Bond boat, but he had learned from his mistakes and was damn well going to strike while the iron was still hot. And strike. And strike. For the next go-round, it was finally *The Ambushers*' turn. And that's when everything started to fall apart.

Speaking of falling apart, after a busy year apart that frayed their relationship, Sinatra and Farrow both agreed to take a little time off, relax, then make a movie together during the coming year. Frank decided on a project called *The Detective*, but no sooner had he made this decision than Mia got an offer to be in a film by hot new director Roman Polanski. Against Frank's wishes, Farrow accepted the offer, figuring she could wrap the film, *Rosemary's Baby*, before shooting was scheduled to start for *The Detective*. Sinatra, meanwhile, spent 1967 working on *Tony Rome*, which filled a goodly portion of its run time with bikini-clad beauties and lots of scenes of Sinatra lounging in shirt and tie around the pool of the Fontainebleau Hotel.

It doesn't, however, entirely ape the tone of James Bond or Matt Helm. It belongs among the crop of neo-noir films released around the same time—John Boorman's *Point Blank* starring Lee Marvin, and Peter Yates' *Bullitt*, starring Steve McQueen. *Tony Rome* was, perhaps, Sinatra's way of making it up to himself for missing out on *Harper*. It doesn't carry the same artistic weight as *Point Blank* or have the same iconic cool as *Bullitt*, but it was still a good role and a good film for Sinatra, who seemed comfortable as the wry private eye. It's only real misstep is the inability to commit to its neo-noir mood. Too often, it falls back on letting Sinatra be Sinatra. The Rat Pack Sinatra, a guy who just doesn't belong in the hardboiled world of Tony Rome. It was directed by Gordon Douglas, who directed Sinatra and the Pack (except for Peter Lawford, who was in Sinatra's doghouse) in 1961's *Robin and the Seven Hoods*, and the second, more outrageous of James Coburn's Flint movies, *In Like Flint*.

With *Tony Rome* in the can, Frank expected to get to work on *The Detective*, but Mia was still working on *Rosemary's Baby*. Sinatra grew increasingly irritable as her shoot dragged on. He was famous for getting it right in one take, or if not right, at least refusing to do a second. Polanski was infamous for demanding forty, fifty, even sixty takes. As the filming of *Rosemary's Baby* crept along, Sinatra realized that it was going to conflict with the start date for *The Detective*. He demanded Mia abandon *Rosemary's Baby*. She almost did, but the threat of being sued and blacklisted for breach of contract dissuaded her. Then she saw a rough cut of the film and was certain she'd made the right call. *The Detective* might turn out to be a good movie, but it would be Frank Sinatra's good movie. But *Rosemary's Baby* was *hers*. It would, producer Robert Evans promised, win her an Oscar. Coincidentally, Evans was also the producer for *The Detective*, the film he would later say launched his career. Yet there he was, encouraging Mia to blow it off.

In November 1967, the same month *Tony Rome* was released, Mia received a visitor on the set of *Rosemary's Baby*. It was one of Frank's lawyers, serving her with divorce papers. Sinatra hadn't even bothered to divorce her in person. 1967 continued to be a very bad year for Sinatra. He unexpectedly found himself exiled from the Sands. It was purchased that year by eccentric billionaire, inventor, and moviemaker Howard Hughes, who hated Sinatra. *Really* hated him. Before Ava Gardner married Frank Sinatra, Sinatra had to steal her...from Howard Hughes.

It's difficult to say whether Hughes ever actually loved anyone, but he certainly became obsessed with them—and Ava Gardner was one of his great obsessions. When Sinatra swooped in and, as Hughes saw it, stole her (as if she had no say in the matter), there was no forgiving that. One of the first things Hughes did upon taking ownership of the Sands—and for all anyone knows, he bought the hotel *specifically* to do this—was revoke Sinatra's liberal line of credit. He set Frank's new line of credit at $3,000. Frank flew off the handle in a tirade that ended when he smashed a golf cart through one of the hotel's windows and assaulted the casino manager, Carl Cohen. Wrong guy to pick a fight with, apparently. Cohen socked Sinatra in the jaw, knocking out two of his teeth.

You could call it disrespect. Or you could look at it as Sinatra reaping what he'd sown. Sinatra could be a good guy, but Sinatra wasn't a *good* guy. He could be cruel, selfish, mean, unpredictable, abusive. A bully. He could turn on a friend at the drop of a pork pie hat, enacting the pettiest and most vindictive of revenges for even the slightest of perceived offense. He could also be warm, loving, sad, generous. Give you everything. Take it all away. In short, he was complicated. Like everyone is complicated. Only he lived a life where the nastier extremes of being complicated didn't need to be kept in check the way they do for most people. He could do whatever he wanted, and when you can do whatever you want, you tend to do everything you want. And then you tend to demand everything you want, or might want, or wanted at one time. Or just can't have. And if you're surrounded by people who say "Yes, Mr. Sinatra" to everything? Well, eventually Howard Hughes' casino manager knocks out a couple of your teeth.

While the Rat Pack had been at the height of their popularity, and while the Mob had been in control of the casino, Sinatra and his cronies could and often did terrorize the staff at the Sands. A guy who socked Sinatra in the jaw back then would have been out on his ass or in a shallow grave. Those days were over. The Rat Pack was yesterday's news. For the first time in a long time, Frank Sinatra pushed someone and found someone willing to push back.

Sinatra started playing Caesar's Palace instead of the Sands. He divorced Mia Farrow and cast Jacqueline Bissett in *The Detective*. I guess Bing Crosby wasn't available. Mia Farrow didn't win an Oscar, but she did win a Golden Globe and a BAFTA. *Rosemary's Baby*, released the same weekend as *The Detective*, trounced Sinatra at the box office. Robert Evans claimed that Farrow herself orchestrated the release of *Rosemary's Baby* at the same time as revenge, and that she wanted to take out a full page ad after the fact listing the box office take of *Rosemary's Baby* next to that of *The Detective* (by no means a failure; it just wasn't a game changer). Roberts also characterized her sticking with *Rosemary's Baby* instead of Sinatra as a case of an uppity broad choosing fame over love—even though he'd been the one encouraging her. But then, Robert Evans *was* often full of shit.

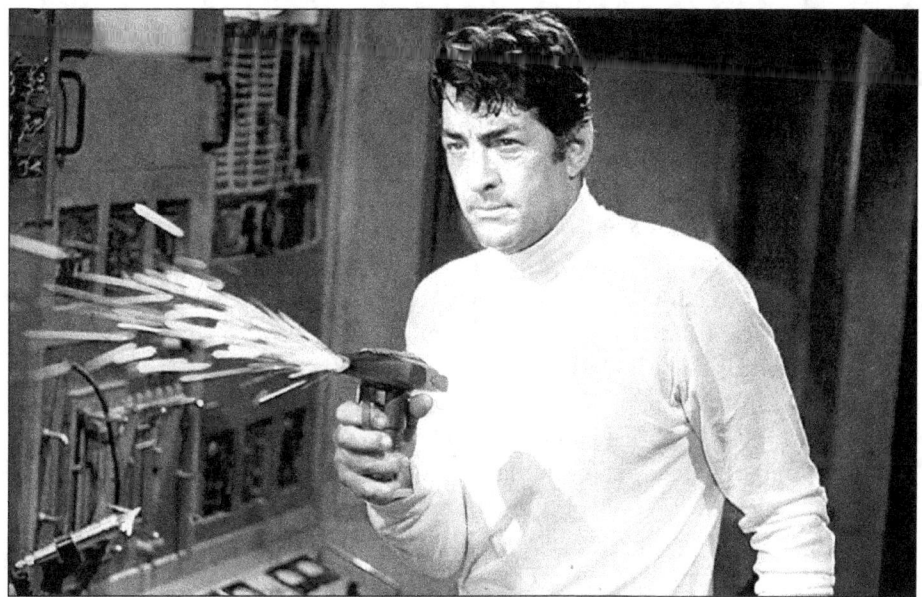

SPARKS FLY—Dean returns to the role of Matt Helm, this time with a ray gun!

Little Ole Wine Drinker, Me

While Sinatra was busy divorcing Mia Farrow by delivery boy, Dino was heading down to Mexico. The third Matt Helm movie retains the beach party feel of *Murderers' Row*, complete with go-go dancing bikini girls during the title sequence, and seems to be built entirely around the single high concept of, "What if Dean Martin fell into a vat of beer?" Not much effort was put into anything beyond that. Where *Murderers' Row* went abroad but was mostly filmed on sets, for *The Ambushers* the entire production was on location in Mexico. Almost nothing went right. Dean Martin was unhappy being away. He had always been a drinker on set, but it was worse in Mexico and with crankier results. The group of women hired to be the film's requisite Slay Girls were also unhappy. Many of them had been misinformed as to the nature of their role. They thought they were going to have substantial parts rather than being extras with no lines. Most of the women were professional models. They'd left jobs that paid upwards of $1,000 a week for what turned out to be a couple hundred bucks a week and a few seconds of screen time. One of the young women was even assaulted when her boyfriend surprised her by showing up on set only to discover she was shacked up with a member of the film's crew.

Still, they managed to squeeze a movie out of the troubled production. It's a pretty lazy film, especially after the more professional-looking *Murderers' Row*. Martin is still sleazily charming as Matt Helm, but cracks were starting to show. There are times you can see the actor behind the…well…there was no actor behind anything. It was just Dean Martin playing Dean Martin. But you can see the places where he is visibly bored or irritated. Once again, he has a good cast around him, with the fantastic Senta Berger as the female lead and a plot custom-made for Dean's version of Matt Helm. It involves a Mexican beer baron stealing an experimental UFO.

Any vestige of reality is tossed out the window once you see Dean Martin sliding down a mountain railway whilst waving an anti-gravity gun over his head (and if you think he isn't going to use that gun to levitate a woman's bra off, you obviously haven't been paying attention). As has been the pattern, bits and pieces of Donald Hamilton's original 1963 novel, the sixth in the series, make it into the movie. But the plot pulls the same trick as *The Silencers*, combining parts of *The Ambushers* novel with a plot from the most recent Matt Helm novel, 1968's *The Menacers*. The idea of Matt Helm being in a refresher course and meeting a damaged young agent named Sheila is from the *The Ambushers*. The ridiculousness about Mexico and the stolen UFO comes from *The Menacers*. It's not quite as silly in the book as it is in the movie, though critics—usually fans of Hamilton's writing—noted that *The Menacers* perhaps does indeed wander too far into the realm of the silly.

Although *The Ambushers* movie is pretty fun, about on par with *The Silencers*, audiences didn't think the same. It made money and was a nominal hit, but it was a step down both in terms of quality and box office. Released in 1968, with the world amidst incredible social upheaval, with Vietnam on the front page, and with a new era of terrorism ripping through Europe, moviegoers just weren't as forgiving of colorful, out-of-touch spy fantasy. As pre-production started for another entry in the series, regular cast members started abandoning ship. Dean Martin was still on board, remarking that as long as they kept making them, he guessed he would keep starring in them. His personal assistant of three films, Bev Adams' Lovey Kravezit, departed the series after she met a real-life Matt Helm while on a press junket for *The Ambushers*: former Israeli commando turned international playboy and world-

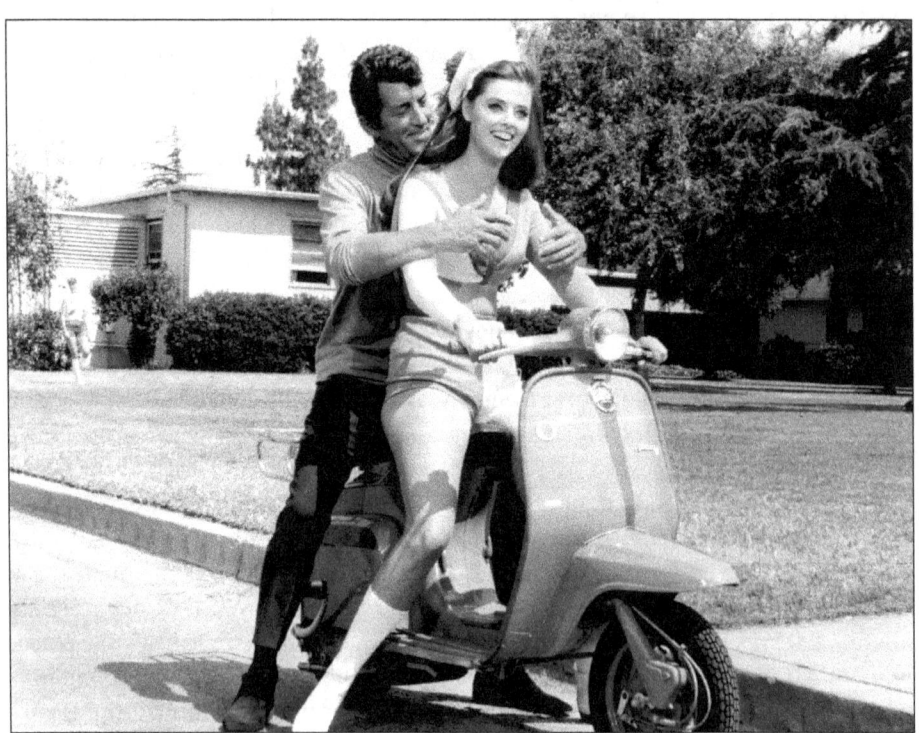

HANDS-ON TRAINING—Dean Martin's Matt Helm takes an interest in his newest recruit.

famous hair stylist Vidal Sassoon. James Gregory also decided he wouldn't reprise the role of Helm's boss. While neither Adams nor Gregory played major roles in the films, it's not a good sign when series regulars start leaving. Still, Irving Allen made enough money with *The Ambushers*—and had already committed himself anyway—that a fourth film was rushed into production. In 1968, cameras starting rolling on *The Wrecking Crew*.

Cameras also started rolling on *Dead Run*, a European spy movie featuring an appearance by the exiled Peter Lawford, who also teamed up with Sammy Davis, Jr. for their own little series of goofball spy films, the thoroughly fun *Salt and Pepper* and its thoroughly unfun sequel, *One More Time*. The only members of the Rat Pack who really embraced the counterculture with enthusiasm were Sammy (especially the free love part of it) and Pete (being the old surf bum that he was). While Sinatra was grousing and Martin was just stumbling happily along, Davis was hitting New York swingers' club Plato's Retreat, flashing the peace sign, and having his picture taken with Church of Satan founder Anton Lavey, who, one assumes, imbued Sammy with the arcane powers of a warlock. He even starred in a TV movie called *Poor Devil* alongside *The Odd Couple*'s Jack Klugman, *Batman*'s Adam West, and venerated horror film icon Christopher Lee as Satan. Sammy plays a recruiter for the devil trying to convince sad sack accountant Jack Klugman to sell his soul. The movie, a pilot for a TV show that never got made, is decidedly pro-Hell.

Born in Harlem on December 8, 1925, Sammy started working in showbiz almost immediately. His father, Sammy Sr., and mother, Elvera Sanchez, were dancers on the vaudeville circuit. They met and married in 1923. In 1925, Sammy Jr. was born. He grew up around the theater. His parents split when he was three, and his father retained sole custody, taking young Sammy on tour. On the road, Sammy Sr. taught his son how to dance, and before too long they were performing together alongside singer-dancer Will Mastin as the Will Mastin Trio.

When World War II broke out, Sammy joined the Army and discovered something about the world he'd not known: racism. As a performer, Sammy had spent most of his time around other showfolk in nightclubs and theaters. When they encountered a racist policy or reaction, his father and Will Mastin shielded him from it. When Sammy joined the Army, though, the racism from which he'd been insulated most his life hit him square in the face. Because of his slight stature as much as his talent, he was assigned to an entertainment unit. It was while on stage there that he realized his talent could go a long way in changing the minds of racist white enlisted men. He was athletically built, thanks to a life in dance, but topped out at 5'5" and 120 pounds. He wasn't a match for some racist bruiser. But Davis could *perform*. He could win people over with his talent. At first, white soldiers forced him to dance, to perform for them as they belittled him. But then...he was good. Really good. And he wasn't some celebrity on a stage—he was a soldier, same as everyone else. They knew him; bunked with him; ate with him. It got harder for people to hate him. It's a lot harder to hate a person when you know them as a person, not as a race.

Once Sammy had his awakening, he vowed to become a force for racial equality. After the war, Sammy began to use his fame as a song and dance man to try and

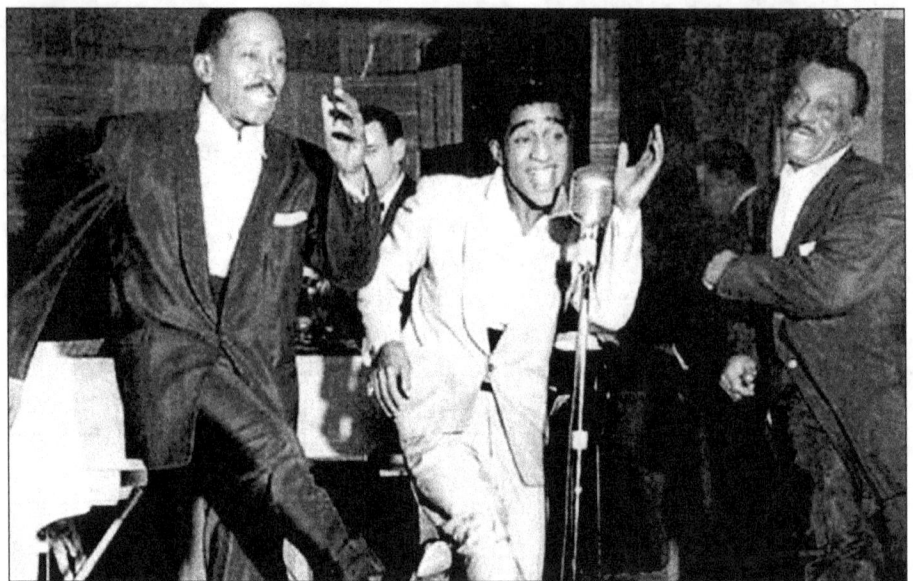
THE WILL MASTIN TRIO—Sammy performs with his dad and their long-time partner, Will Mastin.

enact change at the venues where he performed. Most clubs still followed the racist example of the Cotton Club and booked black entertainers while refusing black customers. Davis discovered firsthand that black performers, despite their star power, were banned from the hotels, something his father had obscured from him when he was younger. Blacks were banned from the audience, from the dining room, from the front door. They were forced to use service entrances and remain out of sight—except when they were on stage. They didn't even have dressing rooms and were expected to change in closets or alleys and to spend their time between numbers waiting outside. Davis started boycotting clubs with such policies, but it was tough going. Tough, that is, until he found an unexpected ally in the fight against discrimination.

Sammy met Frank Sinatra in 1947. He was back singing and dancing with the Will Mastin Trio. Their rising acclaim got them a spot opening for Sinatra during a run at the Capitol Theater in New York. Sinatra, who had grown up admiring the musicians of the Harlem Renaissance and who named his contemporary Billie Holiday as the most important voice in the history of American music, did not harbor the same prejudices against black Americans. He and Davis struck up a friendship. They performed together many times throughout their career, and any time Sinatra discovered a club was discriminating against Davis, Frank threw the full weight of his celebrity behind combating the slight. Together, they forced the integration of both the Copa and the Sands, among others.

In 1954, with his star still rising quickly, Davis was involved in a car accident which robbed him of his eye and nearly robbed him of his life. The wreck took place on the one night Davis had forgotten the good luck charm he always wore around his neck: a *mezuzah*, which had been given to him by one of the legendary performers of the 1920s, Eddie Cantor, who Davis had befriended in 1953. During his convalescence, Davis and Cantor met frequently and talked about religion and history. In the long plight of Jews, Davis saw the same discrimination and suffering endured by blacks. Davis felt so strongly about the bond between blacks and Jews that, in 1961, he converted to Judaism.

After he recovered, Davis recorded and released his debut album, *Starring Sammy Davis Jr.*, the cover of which features him wearing an eye patch. He was later fitted with a glass eye, something that, like the nose that had been broken frequently when he was attacked in the Army, he parlayed into a signature look—though honestly, that eye patch worked remarkably well for him, too.

Whatever obstacles he overcame, whatever battles he won or survived, something was always waiting on the horizon. In 1957, a time when mixed race relationships were discouraged, if not outright illegal, in parts of the U.S., Davis struck up a romance with actress Kim Novak, then on the verge of her star-making appearance in Alfred Hitchcock's *Vertigo*. Columbia studio head Harry Cohn was terrified that news of a mixed-race relationship would destroy Novak's career (not to mention his own). He contacted a man named "Handsome" Johnny Roselli to see that the romance between Davis and Novak ended.

Roselli was a Chicago mobster who came up as part of Al Capone's Chicago Outfit before being transferred to the west coast. There, he fell in with bootlegger and Mob boss Jack Dragna, "The Capone of Los Angeles." While in California, he became friends with film producer Bryan Foy. Many historians point to Roselli as the man who launched the Mafia's involvement in Hollywood, which mostly involved extorting money but also involved the occasional foray into talent scouting. It was Roselli who, in 1947, met with Harry Cohn to strongly suggest that it would be in Cohn's best interest to sign an unknown aspiring actress to a multi-year deal. Cohn, realizing exactly who and what he was dealing with, agreed. Coincidentally, the actress' mother, Gladys Pearl Monroe, had worked at Columbia as a negative cutter. Gladys' daughter, Norma Jeane Mortenson, had adopted a new stage name only a few months before Roselli came calling on Cohn: Marilyn Monroe. Roselli helped Sinatra get the role in *From Here to Eternity*. He moved to Las Vegas to serve as the Chicago Outfit's heavy in the desert oasis. He also maintained a position as a producer at Monogram Pictures. Then things got weird.

After the Cuban Revolution in January of 1959, the Mafia was kicked out of the country. The CIA reckoned a good many mobsters might be amenable to assassinating Fidel Castro. Roselli was in Vegas, running the Flamingo hotel and casino just a few buildings down from the Sands. The Agency sent former FBI recruiter Robert Maheu (who later worked for Howard Hughes) to meet with Handsome Johnny. Roselli, in turn, introduced the agent to legitimate businessmen "Sam Gold" and a guy known only as "Joe." Maheu pitched a plot to poison Castro. They accepted. Sam Gold and Joe had a grudge against Castro, because Sam Gold and Joe were really Chicago Mob boss Sam Giancana and Tampa boss Santo Trafficante, who before the revolution had been one of the most powerful gangsters in Cuba.

Roselli helped set up a base in the Florida Keys where CIA-contracted hit teams could hone their skills, none of which, sadly, involved beard shaving. Castro, however, wasn't so easy to kill. None of Roselli's would-be poisoners got close enough to dose Fidel's food with the pills they'd been issued. After the Bay of Pigs, Roselli and his associates bowed out of the cloak and dagger game, turning the Keys base over to the new man in charge of killing Fidel Castro: William "Wild Bill" Harvey, a disgraced FBI agent who found great success at the CIA—but never at killing Fidel Castro.

Before Handsome Johnny Roselli was neck-deep in international espionage, he was the guy Harry Cohn called to take care of the Sammy-Kim problem. Cohn figured Roselli could put the fear of God into Sammy; or if not of God, then certainly of a grave somewhere outside Las Vegas. Roselli approached the assignment in subtle fashion, promising to dig out Sammy's one good eye. Roselli didn't just demand Sammy end the romance with Novak; he expected Sammy to repent by getting married—*not* to a white woman—within 48 hours. Shortly thereafter, Davis married a dancer named, ironically, Loray White. The marriage lasted less than a year. Novak went on to cause Harry Cohn some well-deserved stress by going on strike until he gave her a better contract. Sammy avoided death and continued to soar, becoming a member of the Summit shortly thereafter.

In 1960, the year of *Ocean's 11* and the Summit at the Sands, Davis married Swedish actress May Britt—a white woman—who had appeared in *The Young Lions* alongside Dean Martin and would, in 1960, appear in *Murder, Inc.*, a film based on the bloody exploits of the hit squad fostered by killers such as Albert Anastasia and, yes, Louis "Lepke" Buchalter, one-time owner of the Riobamba, where Sinatra kicked off his solo career. As for Roselli, he had a number of brushes with the law and was eventually deported to Sicily.

Turns out Italy didn't want him either, so he got to stay in the United States, which, in retrospect, maybe wasn't the best thing for him. On August 9, 1976, a 55-gallon drum was found floating off the coast of Miami. Inside was the corpse of Handsome Johnny Roselli. No one did time for the hit. No one even knew who did it, but there were theories. Roselli had been testifying before a committee on the conspiracy to assassinate Castro, and he was scheduled to testify in a hearing about a conspiracy to assassinate John Kennedy. It turns out that maybe some of the people Roselli sent to kill Castro had in turn been sent back by Castro to kill Kennedy. Then there was the theory that the Mob had Kennedy killed. Mafioso Bill Bonanno went so far as to name Johnny Roselli as the trigger man, or at least *a* trigger man, who took shots at JFK on that tragic day in 1963. Others said the Roselli hit was nothing more than payback after he'd been caught skimming profits in Vegas. The CIA. The Chicago Outfit. The Five Families. Fidel Castro. If Roselli could find any silver lining in his own murder, it's that at least a lot of interesting people were potentially responsible for it.

While Roselli was decomposing in a barrel off the coast of Florida, you could hear Sammy Davis, Jr. every week singing the theme song for the hit television show, *Baretta*.

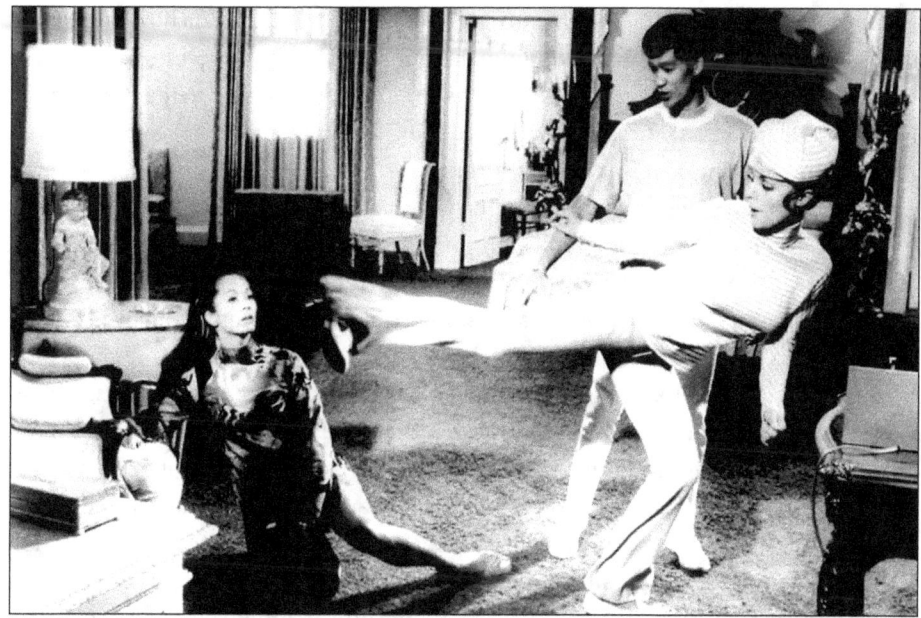
ENTER THE DRAGON—Fight choreographer Bruce Lee coaches Sharon Tate and Nancy Kwan.

Train Wreck

As always, things were less dire for Dean Martin. What did he care if some nutcase billionaire with Kleenex boxes on his feet kicked the Rat Pack out of the Sands over some decades-old feud between he and Sinatra over some dame neither of them were even with anymore? Dino was becoming a bit of a homebody anyway. Business was good. The TV show was doing well. Even if he knew the films were junk, Matt Helm was making a tidy sum for all involved. Plus, word came down that the next Helm film would pair Dean with a woman many regarded as the most beautiful in Hollywood, even though her career had yet to take off. Sharon Tate was the 25-year-old girlfriend (soon to be wife) of *Rosemary's Baby* director Roman Polanski. After a series of setbacks that included appearing in the infamous camp disaster *The Valley of the Dolls*, Tate was determined to prove that she was more than a pretty face, more than Roman Polanski's girlfriend. Although no prestige picture, working alongside Dean Martin in the goofy spy series would give her a chance to do action and comedy. But by 1969, the year *The Wrecking Crew* was released, not only were Frank and Mia well past over; the Matt Helm film series was canceled. Dean Martin began his retreat from the public eye. And Sharon Tate? Sharon Tate was dead.

1968's *The Wrecking Crew* had even less to do with the Donald Hamilton book of the same name than the previous movies. It's one of the best Matt Helm novels. It's also one of the few stories where Matt gets to go to another country and spend at least a little bit of time in a nice hotel. Usually he had to stay at some Econo-Lodge in a Southwestern American backwater. In *The Wrecking Crew*, he actually got to go to Stockholm, Sweden, and stay in a nice place...up until he's dragged out into the muddy, frosty Swedish north country to get shot at. But hey, at least he got to see some sights first. Matt ends up in Sweden—an obvious choice for his first international foray, as it was Donald Hamilton's place of birth (as well as his home during the final years of his life)—in the hopes of tracking down and killing an elusive espionage mastermind named Caselius whom no one has lived to describe. He's helped and hindered on his mission by a Swedish agent named Sarah Lundgren. The problem with her is that she considers Sweden a peaceful, nonviolent nation and wants no part of helping Matt Helm assassinate another man, an act she considers barbaric. Matt, surprisingly, is not especially sympathetic to her beliefs, which makes for some interesting philosophical debate, though Sarah herself doesn't stay in the picture for long.

The primary woman here is Louise Taylor. Her husband, a globe-trotting journalist of somewhat questionable morals, had recently been gunned down at an East German checkpoint, presumably because he'd learned and revealed too much about Caselius. The death, however, was suspicious for other reasons. No body was ever identified, and Louise herself disappeared for a long time before turning up on the free and righteous side of the Iron Curtain, leading to speculation that her husband faked his death, or that Lou was somehow responsible for it since she survived the attack. Helm's cover is as a photographer aiding Lou on her own first job as a journalist, writing about the Swedish mining business. He has to find out what she knows about Caselius and, with any luck, find a way for her to lead him to his target.

The Wrecking Crew was the second Helm novel, published in 1960. Fresh off the life-changing events of *Death of a Citizen*, Helm's in a particularly bad mood. The ink on his divorce was still drying, and seeing no alternative, he admits to himself that he's not cut out for a normal life and returns to his old job. The exact nature of his job is given a lot of thought here. Although most readers put Matt Helm under the general banner of "spy," the point is made that he's not a spy; he's an assassin. His job is not to collect information, identify leaks, or anything of that nature. His job is to go in and kill someone. This is the book's central philosophical debate. Helm knows it's a nasty business, but he also regards it as a necessary and not altogether honorless business. He ruminates about why people make heroes of men who drop bombs that kill thousands, many of them innocent civilians, yet are repulsed by one man with a knife or a gun being assigned to track down one other man. There is something in that relationship that is too personal, too close, for people to deal with. They prefer death to come in great waves and from a great distance.

It is a foregone conclusion that the fourth in the Matt Helm movie series won't be long on rumination about the nature of war and violence. It will, however, be long—very long indeed—on shots of a slumbering Dean Martin dreaming about scantily-clad women while he sing-narrates everything we see on screen. Both the dream sequences and the singing narration were part of *The Silencers*, but there they were used in moderation and with some degree of wit. Here, Dean spends a good ten minutes dreaming about models, and the songs have very little in the way of cleverness, rhyming, or structure. Any time Matt enters a new hotel room, we have to watch him wander around inspecting the pillows and bar. This, too, goes on for a while. And if you thought his double entendres and goofy sex jokes were getting stretched thin in *The Ambushers* and often became so nonsensical that they qualified as non-sequiturs more than sex jokes, well apparently so did the people writing *The Wrecking Crew*. Rather than make lewd comments this time around, anything that calls for one is filled by Dean Martin staring bleary-eyed at something off camera for about ten second and then stammering, "Yep."

In fact, roughly 90% of Dean Martin's dialogue is either some such half-hearted utterance or, more annoyingly, him repeating whatever Sharon Tate just said to him, only in the form of a question. Sometimes, his lines are slurred and mumbled so bad they you couldn't understand what he was saying if Sharon hadn't just said the same thing. He's barely able to spit out even the simplest lines, and he always seems just about ready to fall over every time he lumbers into action. Thus, the first hour of the film moves slowly, with much of it consisting of Dean walking in and out of hotel rooms accompanied by little snippets of himself crooning about whatever is happening to him on screen, as if the classical Greek Chorus had just been Dean stating facts in his warm, musical voice. "If your sweetheart... hides a pistol...under her pillow..." Things pick up for the final third of the film, but by then plenty of viewers will have been lost to the tedium. But even with Dean oblivious to everything going on around him, and even though he's looking particularly worn-out and has way too much greasy stuff in his hair (and his skin looks like Arby's roast beef), he's still Dino. Charm comes easy to him. He can't help but be likable, even when he obviously doesn't give a damn. Maybe *because* he doesn't give a damn.

There are other things about this film that keep it from ending up in the trash bin. Chief among the film's assets is, once again, the supporting cast. As his bumbling assistant, Sharon Tate brings the same energy to her role as Ann-Margaret did in *Murderers' Row*. She shows a knack for comedy and pretty good timing despite the fact that Dean sometimes seems to fall asleep in between lines.

Of course, when one mentions Sharon Tate, there is the gloomy specter of her death to deal with. On August 9, 1969, she was at a party with some friends, taking time off in anticipation of giving birth to her first child, when members of the Manson Family murdered her and several other guests. It's a melancholy ending to a life that was only just beginning. She turns in an energetic performance in *The Wrecking Crew*. Like everyone else, she seems to enjoy getting paid to goof off. Her character retains the basic story of Sarah Lundgren from the book, and some of Sarah's naivety, but if you were waiting for earnest debates over the nature of espionage and the morality of killing, well, need you be reminded that it's Dean Martin up there on the screen?

Tina Louise, the bombshell best known for her role as Ginger on *Gilligan's Island*, has a brief but memorable role as a female informant who ends up on the wrong end of a an exploding bottle of scotch. There was, incidentally, a trick bottle of scotch in Donald Hamilton's *The Devastators*, though not an exploding one, meaning that this movie actually has more in common with that book than with the one from which it draws its name. She's great for the few minutes she is on screen, especially when she does her wild gypsy dance.

On the evil end of the spectrum are the delightful duo of Nancy Kwan and Elke Sommer. Both are hitwomen working for the villainous Count Massimo Contini, played by Nigel Green. It's not the first time Green has employed Elke Sommer as a hitwoman. He was in much the same position when the two starred together in the spectacular *Deadlier than the Male*. She, like him, is in pretty much the same role here. Nancy Kwan, best known for her role in the notorious *World of Suzie Wong* and less-notorious *Flower Drum Song*, gets to spend this movie in a slinky mini-dress, do kung fu (fights were choreographed by none other than Bruce Lee), and spend a lot of time in the back seat of cars chasing Matt Helm—which is the aspect of her character that makes her similar to Madame Ling in *The Devastators*. Nigel Green is, naturally, as reliable a stuffy criminal mastermind as he always is.

Most of the rest of the cast are hired goons, many of them karate and judo experts, including a young Chuck Norris in a "blink and you'll miss him" part as a karate-kicking guard who gets beat up by Dean Martin a couple of times. Bruce Lee had been working as a fight instructor to a lot of people who ended up making spy movies, including Steve McQueen and James Coburn. He worked on *The Wrecking Crew* as a fight advisor and choreographer and would have been, at the time, extremely green when it came to such a job. Plus Dean was really getting on in years, as opposed to someone like Coburn who was still quite fit in the late 1960s. Thus most of the fights wouldn't wow a modern martial arts fans, but it's cool to see so many of them in an American film of this vintage. With Bruce trucking in so many other fighting masters, it means that there is *some* good action to be had, even when it's obviously being performed by someone in a cheap Dean Martin wig.

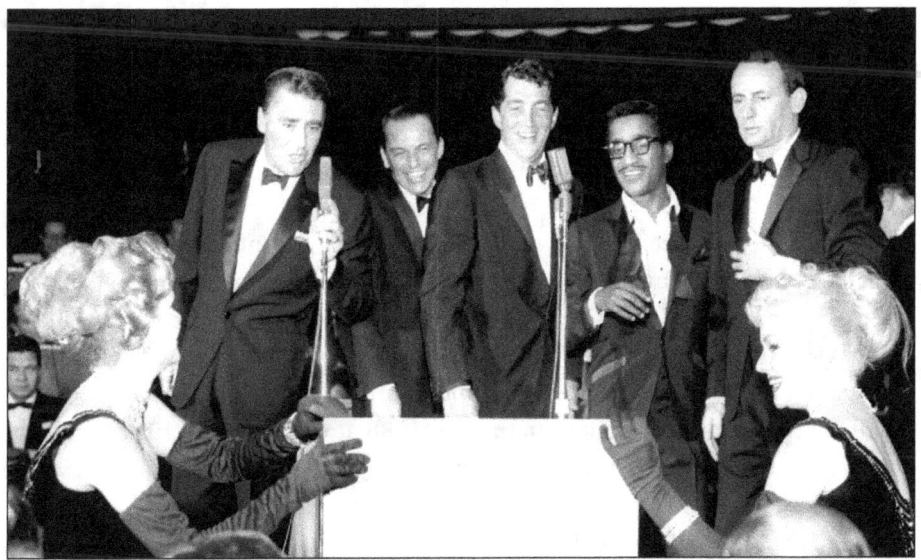

THE SUMMIT—Lawford, Sinatra, Martin, Davis, and Bishop at the Sands. Image, Las Vegas News Bureau.

G'night, Folks

The Wrecking Crew is a pretty shoddy movie. Dean looks like a formerly smart suit that has seen better days and needs to be retired, which is sort of what happened. *The Wrecking Crew* was his last cinematic hurrah. He appeared only sporadically on screen after that, usually as a favor to a friend. *The Wrecking Crew* isn't exactly an artistic high point on which to start winding down your acting career, but it is an oddly fitting beginning to the end. It's not very good, but once you get over the initial portion that coughs and sputters like someone trying to learn to drive stick for the first time, it manages to be just fun enough. Behind the scenes, everything was coming apart. Dean Martin's mother was sick, and he wanted to be with her. Sharon Tate impressed both Martin and Irving Allen, and the intention was to have her return for the next film. The murder cast a ghastly darkness over everything. Allen himself, perhaps picking up on some subconscious warning, was starting to concentrate on other projects. When *The Wrecking Crew* proved unimpressive at the box office, the writing was on the wall. Amid the Tate-LaBianca murders, Vietnam, the assassination of Robert Kennedy and Martin Luther King Jr.—well, there just wasn't room for dumb, harmless little fantasies like the Helm movies. The world had suddenly started looking much more like that of the Matt Helm novels. The series was scrapped. Dean Martin remained largely out of sight until his death on Christmas day, 1995. The lights along the Vegas strip were dimmed in his honor. The epitaph he chose for his grave marker: "Everybody Loves Somebody Sometime."

Still holding the rights to the series, Irving Allen tried to revive Matt Helm in the 1970s. By then, the spy film had changed a lot. James Bond was still hanging around, but the order of the day was less Dean Martin, more *Three Days of the Condor—*

serious, paranoid, anti-authoritarian takes on the genre. Irving Allen ended up bringing Matt Helm to television, in a series starring Tony Franciosa. Franciosa would have made a pretty good Matt Helm as written by Donald Hamilton, but once again the formula was tweaked by Allen, rewriting Helm into a private eye and sticking pretty close to the cop show trend. The series didn't last long. It was Allen's final credit as a producer.

Donald Hamilton continued writing Matt Helm novels into the 1990s, and they remained popular, though never at quite the level they had been before and during the movies. When his health began to fail, he and his wife moved back to Sweden. Late in life, he began work on a new Matt Helm book. Although he finished it before his death in 2006, it remains as yet unpublished.

Peter Lawford died of a heart attack in 1988 at the age of 61. His ashes were scattered into the Pacific Ocean, that great body of water in which he'd found solace during life.

Sammy took the twilight of the Summit better than anyone except maybe Dean. He continued to be a popular performer on variety shows and a frequent guest star on sitcoms. Throughout the 1970s, he seemed perfectly comfortable being the goofy old dude in the Nehru jacket and love beads. In 1989, he was diagnosed with throat cancer. He was told surgery might save his life, but it would definitely cost him his voice. He chose his voice, but he could only put off career-ending surgery for so long. He passed away in May of 1990. As had been done for Dean, the lights on the Vegas strip were dimmed in his honor.

Joey Bishop outlived them all, passing away in 2007. That stubborn son of a bitch always *was* a hard worker.

Frank lived to the age of 82, passing away in 1998. In the 1990s, he made up with Mia Farrow—in his own way. After the scandalous behavior of her soon-to-be ex Woody Allen became public, Frank reached out to Mia and asked, in earnest, if she wanted Allen's legs broken. He outlived the Sands—it was demolished in 1996—and outlived his own obscurity, sticking around the party long enough to see his music and lifestyle rediscovered by a new generation. The night after Sinatra's death, the lights on the Empire State Building were blue. Naturally, the Vegas Strip, no longer what it had been in Frank's time, dimmed its lights. Sadly, no one took advantage of the darkness to rob the casinos. Eee-o-eleven. §

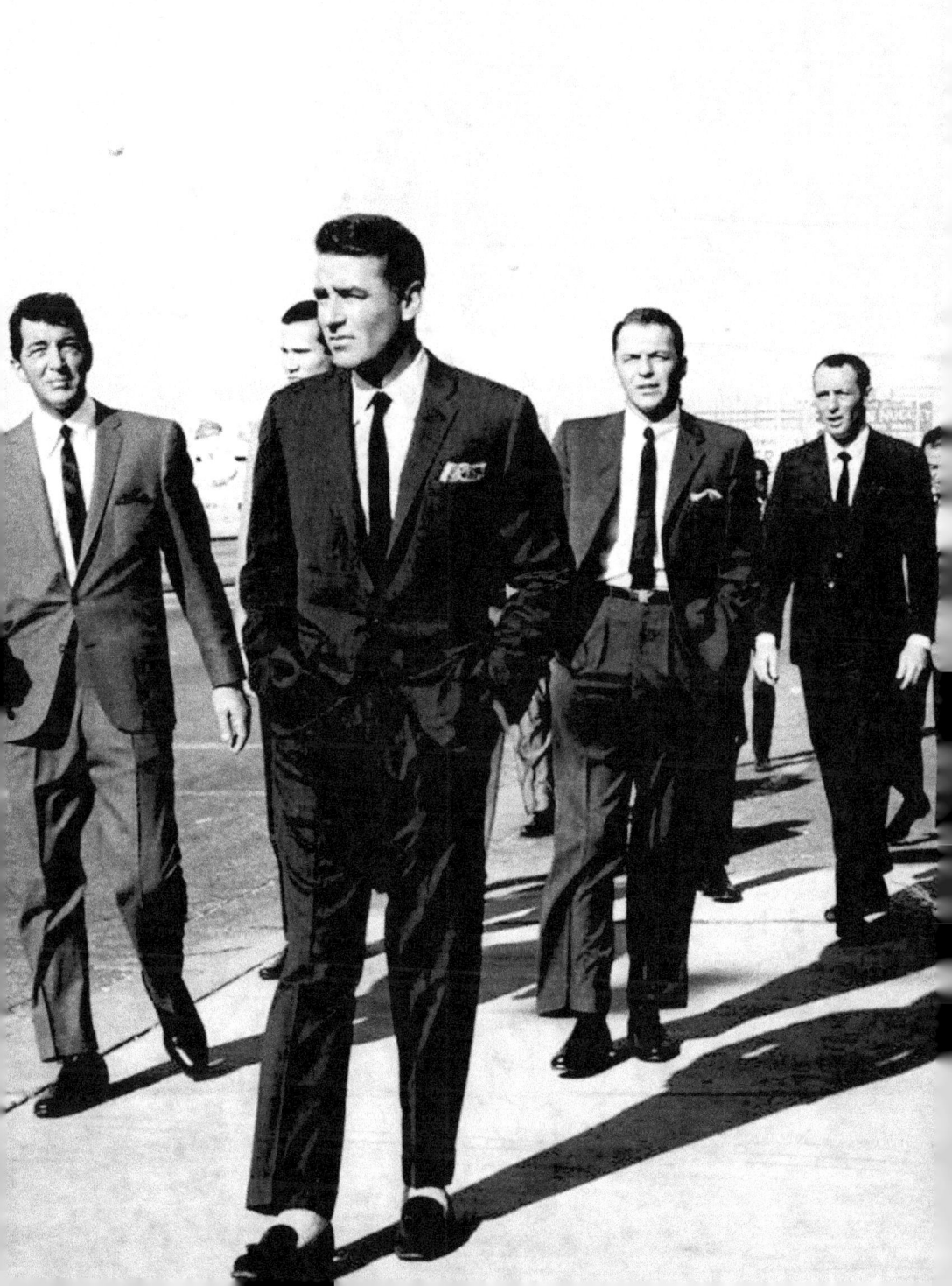

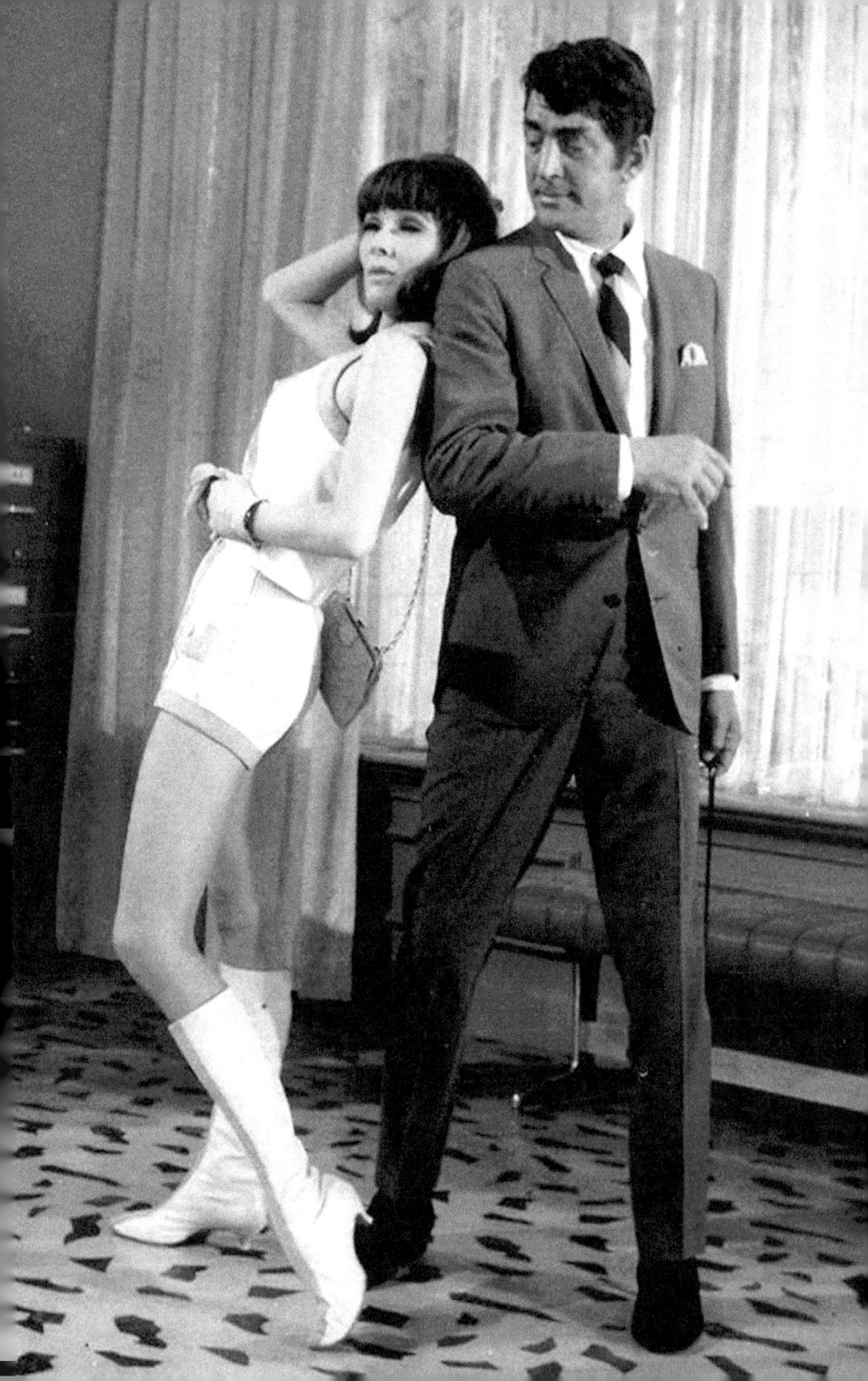

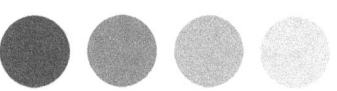

BIBLIOGRAPHY & FURTHER READING

Chapter 1

- Apmann, Sarah Bean. "Cafe Society, The Wrong Place for the Right People." *Off the Grid*, Greenwich Village Society for Historical Preservation, 23 Dec. 2015, gvshp.org/blog/2015/12/30/cafe-society-the-wrong-place-for-the-right-people/.

- Blair, Elizabeth. "The Strange Story Of The Man Behind 'Strange Fruit'." *NPR*, National Public Radio, 5 Sept. 2012, www.npr.org/2012/09/05/158933012/the-strange-story-of-the-man-behind-strange-fruit.

- Caiafa, Frank, et al. *The Waldorf Astoria Bar Book*. Penguin, 2016.

- Chandler, Raymond. *The Long Goodbye*. Penguin, 2005.

- Craddock, Harry, and Gilbert Rumbold. *The Savoy Cocktail Book*. Martino Publishing, 2015.

- Delvecchio, Tony, and Rich Herschlag. *Sinatra, Gotti and Me: the Rise and Fall of Jilly's Nightclub*. Arche Books, 2011.

- "Frank Sinatra and Billie Holiday: They Did It Their Way." *The New York Times*, The New York Times, 21 Dec. 2017, www.nytimes.com/2015/10/19/t-magazine/frank-sinatra-and-billie-holiday-bond.html.

- Fredericks, Bob. "Mob Wanted Johnny Carson Dead for Flirting." **New York Post**, New York Post, 10 Oct. 2013, nypost.com/2013/10/09/mob-wanted-johnny-carson-dead-after-drunken-flirtation/.

- Gaffney, Dennis. "Bernard 'Toots' Shor." *PBS*, Public Broadcasting Service, www.pbs.org/wgbh/americanexperience/features/dimaggio-bernard-toots-shor/.

- Jacobson, Kristi, director. *Toots*. IndiePix, 2009.

- "Jilly Rizzo, Close Aide To Sinatra, Killed at 75." *The New York Times*, The New York Times, 7 May 1992, www.nytimes.com/1992/05/07/us/jilly-rizzo-close-aide-to-sinatra-killed-at-75.html.

- Jorgensen, Jillian. "How to Dine and Drink like Frank Sinatra." *am New York*, am New York, 11 Dec. 2016, www.amny.com/eat-and-drink/frank-sinatra-s-nyc-restaurant-haunts-patsy-s-p-j-clarke-s-and-more-1.12730733.

- Josephson, Barney, and Terry Trilling-Josephson. *Cafe Society: the Wrong Place for the Right People*. University of Illinois Press, 2016.

- Kaplan, James. *Frank: The Voice*. Sphere, 2012.

- "Leon Enken, 67, Of Leon & Eddie's; Nightclub Proprietor Dies-Ran Business Side." *The New York Times*, The New York Times, 21 Feb. 1964, www.nytimes.com/1964/02/21/archives/leon-enken-67-of-leon-eddies-nightclub-proprietor-diesran-business.html.

- Moss, Jeremiah. "Leon & Eddie's." *Jeremiah's Vanishing New York*, 24 Jan. 2011, vanishingnewyork.blogspot.com/2011/01/leon-eddies.html.

- Shteir, Rachel. *Striptease: the Untold History of the Girlie Show*. Oxford University Press, 2006.

- O'Brien, Timothy L. "Borscht and Small Talk; Restaurant Serves as a Russian Island in Manhattan." *The New York Times*, The New York Times, 15 Apr. 2000, www.nytimes.com/2000/04/15/nyregion/borscht-and-small-talk-restaurant-serves-as-a-russian-island-in-manhattan.html.

- Riedel, Michael. "Why Sinatra Loved to Eat in His Car, and More on His Secret NYC Life." *New York Post*, New York Post, 7 Mar. 2015, nypost.com/2015/03/07/why-frank-sinatra-loved-to-eat-in-his-car-and-more-on-his-secret-nyc-life/.

- "Toots Shor's Closes Its Doors -And It May Be for Last Time." *The New York Times*, 2 Apr. 1971, www.nytimes.com/1971/04/02/archives/toots-shors-closes-its-doors-and-it-may-be-for-last-time.html.

- Wilson, John S. "Barney Josephson, Owner of Cafe Society Jazz Club, Is Dead at 86." *The New York Times*, The New York Times, 30 Sept. 1988, www.nytimes.com/1988/09/30/obituaries/barney-josephson-owner-of-cafe-society-jazz-club-is-dead-at-86.html.

- Young, Greg, and Tom Meyers. "Billie Holiday's New York: Here's to Swing Street, Harlem's 133rd Street and Other Landmarks of Jazz." *The Bowery Boys: New York City History*, 23 Jan. 2015, www.boweryboyshistory.com/2015/01/billie-holidays-new-york-heres-swing-street-harlems-133rd-street-landmarks-jazz.html.

- Young, Greg and Tom Meyers. "Toots Shor's and the Art of Celebrity Male Bonding." *The Bowery Boys: New York City History*, 12 Jun. 2009, www.boweryboyshistory.com/2009/06/toots-shors-and-art-of-celebrity-male.html.

Chapter 2

- Baatz, Simon. *The Girl on the Velvet Swing: Sex, Murder, and Madness at the Dawn of the Twentieth Century*. Little Brown & Co, 2018.

- Backer, Ron. *Mystery Movie Series of 1930s Hollywood*. McFarland, 2012.

- Bleiler, Richard. "Raffles: The Gentleman Thief." *Strand Magazine*, strandmag.com/the-magazine/articles/raffles-the-gentleman-thief/.

- Evers, Stuart. "It's Time for AJ Raffles to Emerge from the Shadow of Sherlock Holmes." *The Guardian*, Guardian News and Media, 28 Apr. 2009, www.theguardian.com/books/booksblog/2009/apr/27/aj-raffles-sherlock-holmes.

- Fowler, Gene. *Good Night, Sweet Prince: the Life and Times of John Barrymore*. Mercury House, 1989.

- Hornung, Ernest William, and Clive Bloom. *The Collected Raffles Stories*. Oxford University Press, 1996.
- Hornung, E. W. *Raffles: The Amateur Cracksman*. Dover Publications, 2018.
- Kobler, John. *Damned in Paradise: the Life of John Barrymore*. Atheneum, 1977.
- Luperi, Kim. "Jewel Robbery." *The Pre-Code Companion*, Issue 6, 28 Aug. 2016.
- Orwell, George. "Raffles and Miss Blandish." *Horizon Magazine*, Oct. 1944.
- Peters, Margot. *The House of Barrymore*. Knopf, 1991.
- Roberts, Sarah. "The Gilded Age Starlet Whose Sexual Assault Prompted the 'Trial of the Century'." *Broadly*, Broadly, 13 Oct. 2017, broadly.vice.com/en_us/article/9k3pez/evelyn-nesbit-gilded-age-starlet-sexual-assault-trial-century.
- Rowland, Peter. *Raffles and His Creator: the Life and Works of E.W. Hornung*. Nekta, 1999.
- Schaefer, Eric. *"Bold! Daring! Shocking! True!": A History of Exploitation Films*, 1919-1959. Duke University Press, 2001.
- Uruburu, Paula M. *American Eve: Evelyn Nesbit, Stanford White, the Birth of the "It" Girl, and the Crime of the Century*. Riverhead Books, 2009.

Chapter 3

- Fleming, Ian. *Live and Let Die*. Macmillan, 1954.
- Haigh, Ted. *Vintage Spirits and Forgotten Cocktails: from the Alamagoozlum to the Zombie and bBeyond: 100 Rediscovered Recipes and the Stories behind Them*. Quarry Books, 2009.
- Leigh, David. *Complete Guide to the Drinks of James Bond*, Second Edition. Lulu, 2012.
- Lycett, Andrew. *Ian Fleming*. St. Martins Press, 2013.
- McCammon, Ross, and David Wondrich. *Drink Like a Man: the Only Cocktail Guide Anyone Really Needs*. Chronicle Books, 2016.
- Pearson, John. *The Life of Ian Fleming*. Bloomsbury Reader, 2013.
- Thomas, Jerry. *The Bar-Tenders Guide, or, How to Mix All Kinds of Plain and Fancy Drinks*. Fitzgerald Publishing, 1887.
- Wondrich, David. *Imbibe!: from Absinthe Cocktail to Whiskey Smash, a Salute in Stories and Drinks to "Professor" Jerry Thomas, Pioneer of the American Bar*. Perigee, 2015.

Chapter 4

- Abel, Richard. *The Ciné Goes to Town: French Cinema, 1896-1914*. University of California Press, 1998.
- Bean, Jennifer M. *Flickers of Desire: Movie Stars of the 1910s*. Rutgers University Press, 2011.

- Callahan, Vicki. *Zones of Anxiety: Movement, Musidora, and the Crime Serials of Louis Feuillade*. Wayne State University Press, 2005.
- Feuillade, Louis, director. *Fantômas* Collection. Kino International, 2010.
- Feuillade, Louis, director. *Les Vampires*. Kino International, 2012.
- Fussell, Paul, and Jay Murray Winter. *The Great War and Modern Memory*. Oxford University Press, 2013.
- Golden, Eve. *Vamp: the Rise and Fall of Theda Bara*. Emprise, 1998.
- Haberman, Steve. *Silent Screams: the History of the Silent Horror Film*. Midnight Marquee Press, 2010.
- Howarth, Troy, and Christopher Workman. *Tome of Terror: Horror Films of the Silent Era*. Midnight Marquee Press, 2016.
- Hulse, Ed. *Distressed Damsels and Masked Marauders: Cliffhanger Serials of the Silent-Movie Era*. Murania Press, 2014.
- McMahan, Alison. *Alice Guy Blache: Lost Visionary of the Cinema*. Continuum, 2003.
- Souvestre, Pierre, and Marcel Allain. *Fantômas*. Penguin, 2006.
- Wiebel, Frederick C. *Edisons Frankenstein*. Bear Manor Media, 2010.

Chapter 5

- Curti, Roberto. *Diabolika: Supercriminals, Superheroes and the Comic Book Universe in Italian Cinema*. Midnight Marquee Press, 2016.
- Curti, Roberto. *Italian Crime Filmography, 1968-1980*. McFarland, 2013.
- Howarth, Troy. *The Haunted World of Mario Bava*. Midnight Marquee Press, 2014.
- Lucas, Tim, et al. *Mario Bava: All the Colors of the Dark*. Video Watchdog, 2007.

Chapter 6

- Cotter, Robert Michael. *The Mexican Masked Wrestler and Monster Filmography*. McFarland, 2005.
- Greene, Doyle. *Mexploitation Cinema: a Critical History of Mexican Vampire, Wrestler, Ape-Man and Similar Films, 1957-1977*. McFarland, 2005.
- Grobet, Lourdes, et al. *Lucha Libre: Masked Superstars of Mexican Wrestling*. Distributed Art Publishers, 2005.
- Levi, Heather. *The World of Lucha Libre: Secrets, Revelations, and Mexican National Identity*. Duke University Press, 2009.
- Madigan, Dan. *Mondo Lucha a Go-Go: the Bizarre and Honorable World of Wild Mexican Wrestling*. Harper Collins, 2007.

Chapter 7

- Amis, Kingsley. *The James Bond Dossier*. New American Library, 1965.
- Baker, Charles H. *Jigger, Beaker, & Glass: Drinking around the World*. Derrydale Press, 2001.
- Benson, Raymond. *The James Bond Bedside Companion*. Galahad Books, 1986.
- Brown, Jared M., and Anistatia R. Miller. *The Mixellany Guide to Vermouth & Other Aperitifs*. Mixellany, 2011.
- Brown, Jared M., and Anistatia R. Miller. *Spirituous Journey: Travels through the History of Drinks & Drinking*. Mixellany, 2009.
- Caiafa, Frank, et al. *The Waldorf Astoria Bar Book*. Penguin, 2016.
- Chancellor, Henry. *James Bond: the Man and His World: the Official Companion to Ian Flemings Creation*. John Murray, 2005.
- Cohen, Rich. *Tough Jews*. Vintage, 1999.
- Conant, Jennet. *The Irregulars: Roald Dahl and the British Spy Ring in Wartime Washington*. Simon & Schuster, 2010.
- Craddock, Harry, and Gilbert Rumbold. *The Savoy Cocktail Book*. Martino Publishing, 2015.
- Dayton, Abram. *Last Days of Knickerbocker Life in New York*.
- English, T. J. *Havana Nocturne: How the Mob Owned Cuba-- and Then Lost It to the Revolution*. Harper, 2009.
- Fleming, Ian. *Casino Royale*. Penguin, 2002.
- Fleming, Ian. *For Your Eyes Only*. Penguin, 2002.
- Fleming, Peter. *Brazilian Adventure*. Marlboro Press/Northwestern, 1999.
- Grann, David. *The Lost City of Z: a Tale of Deadly Obsession in the Amazon*. Vintage Books, 2017.
- Haigh, Ted. *Vintage Spirits and Forgotten Cocktails: from the Alamagoozlum to the Zombie and Beyond: 100 Rediscovered Recipes and the Stories behind Them*. Quarry Books, 2009.
- Haswell, Charles H. *Reminiscences of an Octogenarian of the City of New York (1816 to 1860)*.
- Hortis, C. Alexander. *The Mob and the City: the Hidden History of How the Mafia Captured New York*. Prometheus Books, 2014.
- Huff, Marisa. *Aperitivo: the Cocktail Culture of Ituly*. Rizzoli, 2016.
- Johnson, Nelson, and Terence Winter. *Boardwalk Empire: the Birth, High Times, and Corruption of Atlantic City*. Medford Press, 2013.
- Leigh, David. *Complete Guide to the Drinks of James Bond, Second Edition*. Lulu, 2012.
- Lycett, Andrew. *Ian Fleming*. St. Martins Press, 2013.
- Macintyre, Ben. *For Your Eyes Only: Ian Fleming James Bond*. Bloomsbury, 2009.

- Macintyre, Ben. *Operation Mincemeat: How a Dead Man and a Bizarre Plan Fooled the Nazis and Assured an Allied Victory*. Broadway Paperbacks, 2011.

- Miller, Anistatia R., and Jared M. Brown. *The Deans of Drink: the Amazing Lives & Turbulent Times of Harry Johnson & Harry Craddock as Seen in a New Light*. Mixellany, 2013.

- Miller, Russell. *Codename Tricycle: the True Story of the Second World Wars Most Extraordinary Double Agent*. Pimlico, 2005.

- Parsons, Brad Thomas. *Amaro: the Spirited World of Bittersweet, Herbal Liqueurs with Cocktails, Recipes & Formulas*. Ten Speed Press, 2016.

- Parsons, Brad Thomas. *Bitters: A Spirited History of a Classic Cure-All, with Cocktails, Recipes, and Formulas*. Ten Speed Press, 2011.

- Pearson, John. *The Life of Ian Fleming*. Bloomsbury Reader, 2013.

- Pietrusza, David. *Rothstein: the Life, Times, and Murder of the Criminal Genius Who Fixed the 1919 World Series*. Basic Books, 2010.

- Popov, Dusko. *Spy/Counterspy: The Autobiography of Dusko Popov*. Fawcett, 1975.

- Raab, Selwyn. *Five Families: the Rise, Decline, and Resurgence of America's Most Powerful Mafia Empires*. St. Martins Griffin, 2016.

- Regan, Gary. *The Negroni: Drinking to La Dolce Vita, with Recipes and Lore*. Ten Speed Press, 2015.

- Sismondo, Christine. *America Walks into a Bar: A Spirited History of Taverns and Saloons, Speakeasies and Grog Shops*. Oxford University Press, 2014.

- Sweet, Matthew. "Ballroom Blitz: Sex and Spying in London's Wartime Hotels." *The Guardian*, Guardian News and Media, 29 Oct. 2011, www.theguardian.com/travel/2011/oct/30/sex-politics-spying-londons-wartime-hotels.

- Thomas, Jerry. *The Bar-Tenders Guide, or, How to Mix All Kinds of Plain and Fancy Drinks*. Fitzgerald Publishing Corporation, 1887.

- Turkus, Burton B. *Murder Inc.: The Story of the Syndicate Killing Machine*. Tenacity Media Books, 2012.

- Wilson, Jason. *Boozehound: on the Trail of the Rare, the Obscure, and the Overrated in Spirits*. Ten Speed Press, 2010.

- Wondrich, David. *Imbibe!: from Absinthe Cocktail to Whiskey Smash, a Salute in Stories and Drinks to "Professor" Jerry Thomas, Pioneer of the American Bar*. Perigee, 2015.

- Wondrich, David. *Punch: the Delights (and Dangers) of the Flowing Bowl*. Perigee, 2010.

Chapter 8

- Birkbeck, Matt. *Deconstructing Sammy: Music, Money, and Madness*. Amistad, 2009.

- Casillo, Charles. *Marilyn Monroe: the Private Life of a Public Icon*. St. Martins Press, 2018.

- Buntin, John. *L.A. Noir: the Struggle for the Soul of America's Most Seductive City*. Broadway Books, 2009.

- Davis, Sammy, et al. *Yes I Can: the Story of Sammy Davis, Jr.* Farrar, Straus & Giroux, 1990.
- Delvecchio, Tony, and Rich Herschlag. *Sinatra, Gotti and Me: The Rise and Fall of Jilly's Nightclub.* ArcheBooks Publishing, 2011.
- Denton, Sally, and Roger Morris. *The Money and the Power: the Making of Las Vegas and Its Hold on America.* Vintage Books, 2002.
- English, T. J. *Havana Nocturne: How the Mob Owned Cuba-- and Then Lost It to the Revolution.* Harper Paperbacks, 2009.
- Evans, Robert. *The Kid Stays in the Picture: A Notorious Life.* It Books, 2013.
- Fischer, Steve. *When the Mob Ran Vegas Stories of Murder, Mayhem, and Money.* Berkline Press, 2007.
- Griffin, Dennis N. *The Battle for Las Vegas: the Law vs. the Mob.* Huntington Press, 2006.
- Hersh, Seymour M. *The Dark Side of Camelot.* Back Bay Books, 1998.
- Jacobs, George, and William Stadiem. *Mr. S: My Life with Frank Sinatra.* Harper Entertainment, 2004.
- Kaplan, James. *Frank: the Voice.* Anchor, 2011.
- Kaplan, James. *Sinatra: the Chairman.* Anchor Books, 2016.
- Kelley, Kitty. *His Way: the Unauthorized Biography of Frank Sinatra.* Bantam Books, 2015.
- Levy, Shawn. *Rat Pack Confidential: Frank, Dean, Sammy, Peter, Joey & the Last Great Showbiz Party.* Broadway Books, 2001.
- Martin, Deana, and Wendy Holden. *Memories Are Made of This: Dean Martin through His Daughter's Eyes.* Three Rivers Press, 2004.
- Munn, Michael. *The Hollywood Connection: the True Story of Organized Crime in Hollywood.* Robson, 1999.
- Oliphant, Thomas. *Road To Camelot: Inside JFK's Five-Year Campaign.* Simon & Schuster, 2018.
- Petersen, Anne Helen. *Scandals of Classic Hollywood: Sex, Deviance, and Drama from the Golden Age of American Cinema.* Plume, 2014.
- Polisi, Salvatore, and Steve Dougherty. *The Sinatra Club: My Life inside the New York Mafia.* Gallery Books, 2012.
- Scivally, Bruce. *Booze, Bullets & Broads: The Story of Matt Helm, Spy of the Mad Men Era.* Amazon Digital Services, 2013.
- Spada, James. *Peter Lawford: the Man Who Kept the Secrets.* Doubleday, 1991.
- Talbot, David. *Brothers: the Hidden History of the Kennedy Years.* Free Press, 2008.
- Taraborrelli, J. Randy. *The Secret Life of Marilyn Monroe.* Grand Central Pub., 2010.
- Thompson, Douglas. *The Dark Heart of Hollywood.* Transworld, 2013.
- Wolfe, Donald H. *The Last Days of Marilyn Monroe.* William Morrow, 2012.

www.ingramcontent.com/pod-product-compliance
Lightning Source LLC
Chambersburg PA
CBHW071017240526
45469CB00006BD/1954